P9-BIU-509

The Loan Calculator

CONTEMPORARY
BOOKS, INC.
CHICAGO

Copyright © 1979 by Delphi Information Sciences Corporation
All rights reserved
Published by Contemporary Books, Inc.
180 North Michigan Avenue, Chicago, Illinois 60601
Manufactured in the United States of America
International Standard Book Number: 0-8092-5708-4

Published simultaneously in Canada by
Beaverbooks, Ltd.
150 Lesmill Road
Don Mills, Ontario M3B 2T5
Canada

This edition published by arrangement
with Delphi Information Sciences Corporation

TABLE OF CONTENTS

SCOPE

9% to 16¾% every 1/8 percent
17% to 18% every 1/4 percent

LOAN TO APPRAISED VALUE
CONVENTIONAL LOANS

APPRAISED VALUE	RATIOS 50%	60%	65%	70%	75%	80%
10000	5000	6000	6500	7000	7500	8000
11000	5500	6600	7150	7700	8250	8800
12000	6000	7200	7800	8400	9000	9600
13000	6500	7800	8450	9100	9750	10400
14000	7000	8400	9100	9800	10500	11200
15000	7500	9000	9750	10500	11250	12000
16000	8000	9600	10400	11200	12000	12800
17000	8500	10200	11050	11900	12750	13600
18000	9000	10800	11700	12600	13500	14400
19000	9500	11400	12350	13300	14250	15200
20000	10000	12000	13000	14000	15000	16000
21000	10500	12600	13650	14700	15750	16800
22000	11000	13200	14300	15400	16500	17600
23000	11500	13800	14950	16100	17250	18400
24000	12000	14400	15600	16800	18000	19200
25000	12500	15000	16250	17500	18750	20000
26000	13000	15600	16900	18200	19500	20800
27000	13500	16200	17550	18900	20250	21600
28000	14000	16800	18200	19600	21000	22400
29000	14500	17400	18850	20300	21750	23200
30000	15000	18000	19500	21000	22500	24000
31000	15500	18600	20150	21700	23250	24800
32000	16000	19200	20800	22400	24000	25600
33000	16500	19800	21450	23100	24750	26400
34000	17000	20400	22100	23800	25500	27200
35000	17500	21000	22750	24500	26250	28000
36000	18000	21600	23400	25200	27000	28800
37000	18500	22200	24050	25900	27750	29600
38000	19000	22800	24700	26600	28500	30400
39000	19500	23400	25350	27300	29250	31200
40000	20000	24000	26000	28000	30000	32000
41000	20500	24600	26650	28700	30750	32800
42000	21000	25200	27300	29400	31500	33600
43000	21500	25800	27950	30100	32250	34400
44000	22000	26400	28600	30800	33000	35200
45000	22500	27000	29250	31500	33750	36000
46000	23000	27600	29900	32200	34500	36800
47000	23500	28200	30550	32900	35250	37600
48000	24000	28800	31200	33600	36000	38400
49000	24500	29400	31850	34300	36750	39200
50000	25000	30000	32500	35000	37500	40000
51000	25500	30600	33150	35700	38250	40800
52000	26000	31200	33800	36400	39000	41600
53000	26500	31800	34450	37100	39750	42400
54000	27000	32400	35100	37800	40500	43200
55000	27500	33000	35750	38500	41250	44000
56000	28000	33600	36400	39200	42000	44800
57000	28500	34200	37050	39900	42750	45600
58000	29000	34800	37700	40600	43500	46400
59000	29500	35400	38350	41300	44250	47200
60000	30000	36000	39000	42000	45000	48000
61000	30500	36600	39650	42700	45750	48800
62000	31000	37200	40300	43400	46500	49600
63000	31500	37800	40950	44100	47250	50400
64000	32000	38400	41600	44800	48000	51200
65000	32500	39000	42250	45500	48750	52000
66000	33000	39600	42900	46200	49500	52800
67000	33500	40200	43550	46900	50250	53600
68000	34000	40800	44200	47600	51000	54400
69000	34500	41400	44850	48300	51750	55200

LOAN TO APPRAISED VALUE

CONVENTIONAL LOANS

APPRAISED VALUE	RATIOS 50%	60%	65%	70%	75%	80%
70000	35000	42000	45500	49000	52500	56000
71000	35500	42600	46150	49700	53250	56800
72000	36000	43200	46800	50400	54000	57600
73000	36500	43800	47450	51100	54750	58400
74000	37000	44400	48100	51800	55500	59200
75000	37500	45000	48750	52500	56250	60000
76000	38000	45600	49400	53200	57000	60800
77000	38500	46200	50050	53900	57750	61600
78000	39000	46800	50700	54600	58500	62400
79000	39500	47400	51350	55300	59250	63200
80000	40000	48000	52000	56000	60000	64000
81000	40500	48600	52650	56700	60750	64800
82000	41000	49200	53300	57400	61500	65600
83000	41500	49800	53950	58100	62250	66400
84000	42000	50400	54600	58800	63000	67200
85000	42500	51000	55250	59500	63750	68000
86000	43000	51600	55900	60200	64500	68800
87000	43500	52200	56550	60900	65250	69600
88000	44000	52800	57200	61600	66000	70400
89000	44500	53400	57850	62300	66750	71200
90000	45000	54000	58500	63000	67500	72000
91000	45500	54600	59150	63700	68250	72800
92000	46000	55200	59800	64400	69000	73600
93000	46500	55800	60450	65100	69750	74400
94000	47000	56400	61100	65800	70500	75200
95000	47500	57000	61750	66500	71250	76000
96000	48000	57600	62400	67200	72000	76800
97000	48500	58200	63050	67900	72750	77600
98000	49000	58800	63700	68600	73500	78400
99000	49500	59400	64350	69300	74250	79200
100000	50000	60000	65000	70000	75000	80000
101000	50500	60600	65650	70700	75750	80800
102000	51000	61200	66300	71400	76500	81600
103000	51500	61800	66950	72100	77250	82400
104000	52000	62400	67600	72800	78000	83200
105000	52500	63000	68250	73500	78750	84000
106000	53000	63600	68900	74200	79500	84800
107000	53500	64200	69550	74900	80250	85600
108000	54000	64800	70200	75600	81000	86400
109000	54500	65400	70850	76300	81750	87200
110000	55000	66000	71500	77000	82500	88000
111000	55500	66600	72150	77700	83250	88800
112000	56000	67200	72800	78400	84000	89600
113000	56500	67800	73450	79100	84750	90400
114000	57000	68400	74100	79800	85500	91200
115000	57500	69000	74750	80500	86250	92000
116000	58000	69600	75400	81200	87000	92800
117000	58500	70200	76050	81900	87750	93600
118000	59000	70800	76700	82600	88500	94400
119000	59500	71400	77350	83300	89250	95200
120000	60000	72000	78000	84000	90000	96000
121000	60500	72600	78650	84700	90750	96800
122000	61000	73200	79300	85400	91500	97600
123000	61500	73800	79950	86100	92250	98400
124000	62000	74400	80600	86800	93000	99200
125000	62500	75000	81250	87500	93750	100000
126000	63000	75600	81900	88200	94500	100800
127000	63500	76200	82550	88900	95250	101600
128000	64000	76800	83200	89600	96000	102400
129000	64500	77400	83850	90300	96750	103200

9%

MONTHLY AMORTIZING PAYMENTS

AMOUNT OF LOAN	NUMBER OF YEARS IN TERM 1	1-1/2	2	3	4	5	6	7
$ 50	4.38	2.98	2.29	1.59	1.25	1.04	.91	.81
100	8.75	5.96	4.57	3.18	2.49	2.08	1.81	1.61
200	17.50	11.92	9.14	6.36	4.98	4.16	3.61	3.22
300	26.24	17.88	13.71	9.54	7.47	6.23	5.41	4.83
400	34.99	23.84	18.28	12.72	9.96	8.31	7.22	6.44
500	43.73	29.80	22.85	15.90	12.45	10.38	9.02	8.05
600	52.48	35.76	27.42	19.08	14.94	12.46	10.82	9.66
700	61.22	41.72	31.98	22.26	17.42	14.54	12.62	11.27
800	69.97	47.68	36.55	25.44	19.91	16.61	14.43	12.88
900	78.71	53.64	41.12	28.62	22.40	18.69	16.23	14.49
1000	87.46	59.60	45.69	31.80	24.89	20.76	18.03	16.09
2000	174.91	119.20	91.37	63.60	49.78	41.52	36.06	32.18
3000	262.36	178.80	137.06	95.40	74.66	62.28	54.08	48.27
4000	349.81	238.40	182.74	127.20	99.55	83.04	72.11	64.36
5000	437.26	297.99	228.43	159.00	124.43	103.80	90.13	80.45
6000	524.71	357.59	274.11	190.80	149.32	124.56	108.16	96.54
7000	612.17	417.19	319.80	222.60	174.20	145.31	126.18	112.63
8000	699.62	476.79	365.48	254.40	199.09	166.07	144.21	128.72
9000	787.07	536.38	411.17	286.20	223.97	186.83	162.23	144.81
10000	874.52	595.98	456.85	318.00	248.86	207.59	180.26	160.90
11000	961.97	655.58	502.54	349.80	273.74	228.35	198.29	176.98
12000	1049.42	715.18	548.22	381.60	298.63	249.11	216.31	193.07
13000	1136.87	774.77	593.91	413.40	323.51	269.86	234.34	209.16
14000	1224.33	834.37	639.59	445.20	348.40	290.62	252.36	225.25
15000	1311.78	893.97	685.28	477.00	373.28	311.38	270.39	241.34
16000	1399.23	953.57	730.96	508.80	398.17	332.14	288.41	257.43
17000	1486.68	1013.17	776.65	540.60	423.05	352.90	306.44	273.52
18000	1574.13	1072.76	822.33	572.40	447.94	373.66	324.46	289.61
19000	1661.58	1132.36	868.02	604.20	472.82	394.41	342.49	305.70
20000	1749.03	1191.96	913.70	636.00	497.71	415.17	360.52	321.79
21000	1836.49	1251.56	959.38	667.80	522.59	435.93	378.54	337.88
22000	1923.94	1311.15	1005.07	699.60	547.48	456.69	396.57	353.96
23000	2011.39	1370.75	1050.75	731.40	572.36	477.45	414.59	370.05
24000	2098.84	1430.35	1096.44	763.20	597.25	498.21	432.62	386.14
25000	2186.29	1489.95	1142.12	795.00	622.13	518.96	450.64	402.23
26000	2273.74	1549.54	1187.81	826.80	647.02	539.72	468.67	418.32
27000	2361.19	1609.14	1233.49	858.60	671.90	560.48	486.69	434.41
28000	2448.65	1668.74	1279.18	890.40	696.79	581.24	504.72	450.50
29000	2536.10	1728.34	1324.86	922.20	721.67	602.00	522.75	466.59
30000	2623.55	1787.93	1370.55	954.00	746.56	622.76	540.77	482.68
31000	2711.00	1847.53	1416.23	985.80	771.44	643.51	558.80	498.77
32000	2798.45	1907.13	1461.92	1017.60	796.33	664.27	576.82	514.86
33000	2885.90	1966.73	1507.60	1049.40	821.21	685.03	594.85	530.94
34000	2973.36	2026.33	1553.29	1081.20	846.10	705.79	612.87	547.03
35000	3060.81	2085.92	1598.97	1113.00	870.98	726.55	630.90	563.12
40000	3498.06	2383.91	1827.39	1271.99	995.41	830.34	721.03	643.57
45000	3935.32	2681.90	2055.82	1430.99	1119.83	934.13	811.15	724.01
50000	4372.58	2979.89	2284.24	1589.99	1244.26	1037.92	901.28	804.46
55000	4809.84	3277.88	2512.67	1748.99	1368.68	1141.71	991.41	884.90
60000	5247.09	3575.86	2741.09	1907.99	1493.11	1245.51	1081.54	965.35
65000	5684.35	3873.85	2969.51	2066.99	1617.53	1349.30	1171.66	1045.80
70000	6121.61	4171.84	3197.94	2225.99	1741.96	1453.09	1261.79	1126.24
75000	6558.87	4469.83	3426.36	2384.98	1866.38	1556.88	1351.92	1206.69
80000	6996.12	4767.82	3654.78	2543.98	1990.81	1660.67	1442.05	1287.13
85000	7433.38	5065.81	3883.21	2702.98	2115.23	1764.47	1532.18	1367.58
90000	7870.64	5363.79	4111.63	2861.98	2239.66	1868.26	1622.30	1448.02
95000	8307.90	5661.78	4340.06	3020.98	2364.08	1972.05	1712.43	1528.47
100000	8745.15	5959.77	4568.48	3179.98	2488.51	2075.84	1802.56	1608.91
105000	9182.41	6257.76	4796.90	3338.98	2612.93	2179.63	1892.69	1689.36
110000	9619.67	6555.75	5025.33	3497.98	2737.36	2283.42	1982.81	1769.80
115000	10056.92	6853.74	5253.75	3656.97	2861.78	2387.22	2072.94	1850.25
120000	10494.18	7151.72	5482.17	3815.97	2986.21	2491.01	2163.07	1930.69
125000	10931.44	7449.71	5710.60	3974.97	3110.64	2594.80	2253.20	2011.14
130000	11368.70	7747.70	5939.02	4133.97	3235.06	2698.59	2343.32	2091.59
135000	11805.95	8045.69	6167.45	4292.97	3359.49	2802.38	2433.45	2172.03
140000	12243.21	8343.68	6395.87	4451.97	3483.91	2906.17	2523.58	2252.48
145000	12680.47	8641.67	6624.29	4610.97	3608.34	3009.97	2613.71	2332.92
150000	13117.73	8939.65	6852.72	4769.96	3732.76	3113.76	2703.84	2413.37
155000	13554.98	9237.64	7081.14	4928.96	3857.19	3217.55	2793.96	2493.81
160000	13992.24	9535.63	7309.56	5087.96	3981.61	3321.34	2884.09	2574.26

AMOUNT OF LOAN	NUMBER OF YEARS IN TERM							
	8	9	10	11	12	14	15	16
$ 50	.74	.68	.64	.60	.57	.53	.51	.50
100	1.47	1.36	1.27	1.20	1.14	1.05	1.02	.99
200	2.94	2.71	2.54	2.40	2.28	2.10	2.03	1.97
300	4.40	4.07	3.81	3.59	3.42	3.15	3.05	2.96
400	5.87	5.42	5.07	4.79	4.56	4.20	4.06	3.94
500	7.33	6.78	6.34	5.99	5.70	5.25	5.08	4.93
600	8.80	8.13	7.61	7.18	6.83	6.30	6.09	5.91
700	10.26	9.49	8.87	8.38	7.97	7.35	7.10	6.90
800	11.73	10.84	10.14	9.57	9.11	8.40	8.12	7.88
900	13.19	12.19	11.41	10.77	10.25	9.45	9.13	8.87
1000	14.66	13.55	12.67	11.97	11.39	10.49	10.15	9.85
2000	29.31	27.09	25.34	23.93	22.77	20.98	20.29	19.70
3000	43.96	40.63	38.01	35.89	34.15	31.47	30.43	29.54
4000	58.61	54.18	50.68	47.85	45.53	41.96	40.58	39.39
5000	73.26	67.72	63.34	59.81	56.91	52.45	50.72	49.23
6000	87.91	81.26	76.01	71.77	68.29	62.94	60.86	59.08
7000	102.56	94.81	88.68	83.73	79.67	73.43	71.00	68.92
8000	117.21	108.35	101.35	95.69	91.05	83.92	81.15	78.77
9000	131.86	121.89	114.01	107.65	102.43	94.41	91.29	88.61
10000	146.51	135.43	126.68	119.61	113.81	104.90	101.43	98.46
11000	161.16	148.98	139.35	131.57	125.19	115.39	111.57	108.30
12000	175.81	162.52	152.02	143.53	136.57	125.88	121.72	118.15
13000	190.46	176.06	164.68	155.50	147.95	136.37	131.86	127.99
14000	205.11	189.61	177.35	167.46	159.33	146.86	142.00	137.84
15000	219.76	203.15	190.02	179.42	170.71	157.35	152.14	147.68
16000	234.41	216.69	202.69	191.38	182.09	167.83	162.29	157.53
17000	249.06	230.23	215.35	203.34	193.47	178.32	172.43	167.37
18000	263.71	243.78	228.02	215.30	204.85	188.81	182.57	177.22
19000	278.36	257.32	240.69	227.26	216.23	199.30	192.72	187.06
20000	293.01	270.86	253.36	239.22	227.61	209.79	202.86	196.91
21000	307.66	284.41	266.02	251.18	238.99	220.28	213.00	206.75
22000	322.31	297.95	278.69	263.14	250.37	230.77	223.14	216.60
23000	336.96	311.49	291.36	275.10	261.75	241.26	233.29	226.44
24000	351.61	325.03	304.03	287.06	273.13	251.75	243.43	236.29
25000	366.26	338.58	316.69	299.03	284.51	262.24	253.57	246.13
26000	380.91	352.12	329.36	310.99	295.89	272.73	263.71	255.98
27000	395.56	365.66	342.03	322.95	307.27	283.22	273.86	265.82
28000	410.21	379.21	354.70	334.91	318.65	293.71	284.00	275.67
29000	424.86	392.75	367.36	346.87	330.03	304.20	294.14	285.51
30000	439.51	406.29	380.03	358.83	341.41	314.69	304.28	295.36
31000	454.16	419.84	392.70	370.79	352.79	325.18	314.43	305.20
32000	468.81	433.38	405.37	382.75	364.17	335.67	324.57	315.05
33000	483.46	446.92	418.04	394.71	375.56	346.15	334.71	324.90
34000	498.11	460.46	430.70	406.67	386.94	356.64	344.86	334.74
35000	512.76	474.01	443.37	418.63	398.32	367.13	355.00	344.59
40000	586.01	541.72	506.71	478.44	455.22	419.58	405.71	393.81
45000	659.26	609.44	570.05	538.24	512.12	472.03	456.42	443.04
50000	732.52	677.15	633.38	598.05	569.02	524.47	507.14	492.26
55000	805.77	744.86	696.72	657.85	625.92	576.92	557.85	541.49
60000	879.02	812.58	760.06	717.65	682.82	629.37	608.56	590.71
65000	952.27	880.29	823.40	777.46	739.72	681.81	659.28	639.94
70000	1025.52	948.01	886.74	837.26	796.63	734.26	709.99	689.17
75000	1098.77	1015.72	950.07	897.07	853.53	786.71	760.70	738.39
80000	1172.02	1083.44	1013.41	956.87	910.43	839.16	811.42	787.62
85000	1245.27	1151.15	1076.75	1016.67	967.33	891.60	862.13	836.84
90000	1318.52	1218.87	1140.09	1076.48	1024.23	944.05	912.84	886.07
95000	1391.77	1286.58	1203.42	1136.28	1081.13	996.50	963.56	935.30
100000	1465.03	1354.30	1266.76	1196.09	1138.04	1048.94	1014.27	984.52
105000	1538.28	1422.01	1330.10	1255.89	1194.94	1101.39	1064.98	1033.75
110000	1611.53	1489.72	1393.44	1315.69	1251.84	1153.84	1115.70	1082.97
115000	1684.78	1557.44	1456.78	1375.50	1308.74	1206.28	1166.41	1132.20
120000	1758.03	1625.15	1520.11	1435.30	1365.64	1258.73	1217.12	1181.42
125000	1831.28	1692.87	1583.45	1495.11	1422.54	1311.18	1267.84	1230.65
130000	1904.53	1760.58	1646.79	1554.91	1479.44	1363.62	1318.55	1279.88
135000	1977.78	1828.30	1710.13	1614.71	1536.35	1416.07	1369.26	1329.10
140000	2051.03	1896.01	1773.47	1674.52	1593.25	1468.52	1419.98	1378.33
145000	2124.28	1963.73	1836.80	1734.32	1650.15	1520.96	1470.69	1427.55
150000	2197.54	2031.44	1900.14	1794.13	1707.05	1573.41	1521.40	1476.78
155000	2270.79	2099.16	1963.48	1853.93	1763.95	1625.86	1572.12	1526.00
160000	2344.04	2166.87	2026.82	1913.73	1820.85	1678.31	1622.83	1575.23

MONTHLY AMORTIZING PAYMENTS

AMOUNT OF LOAN	NUMBER OF YEARS IN TERM							
	17	18	19	20	21	22	23	24
$ 50	.48	.47	.46	.45	.45	.44	.43	.43
100	.96	.94	.92	.90	.89	.88	.86	.85
200	1.92	1.88	1.84	1.80	1.77	1.75	1.72	1.70
300	2.88	2.81	2.76	2.70	2.66	2.62	2.58	2.55
400	3.84	3.75	3.67	3.60	3.54	3.49	3.44	3.40
500	4.80	4.69	4.59	4.50	4.43	4.36	4.30	4.25
600	5.76	5.62	5.51	5.40	5.31	5.23	5.16	5.10
700	6.72	6.56	6.42	6.30	6.20	6.10	6.02	5.95
800	7.68	7.50	7.34	7.20	7.08	6.97	6.88	6.79
900	8.63	8.43	8.26	8.10	7.97	7.85	7.74	7.64
1000	9.59	9.37	9.17	9.00	8.85	8.72	8.60	8.49
2000	19.18	18.73	18.34	18.00	17.70	17.43	17.19	16.98
3000	28.77	28.10	27.51	27.00	26.54	26.14	25.78	25.46
4000	38.36	37.46	36.68	35.99	35.39	34.85	34.38	33.95
5000	47.95	46.83	45.85	44.99	44.23	43.56	42.97	42.44
6000	57.53	56.19	55.02	53.99	53.08	52.28	51.56	50.92
7000	67.12	65.56	64.19	62.99	61.93	60.99	60.15	59.41
8000	76.71	74.92	73.36	71.98	70.77	69.70	68.75	67.90
9000	86.30	84.29	82.53	80.98	79.62	78.41	77.34	76.38
10000	95.89	93.65	91.69	89.98	88.46	87.12	85.93	84.87
11000	105.47	103.01	100.86	98.97	97.31	95.83	94.52	93.36
12000	115.06	112.38	110.03	107.97	106.15	104.55	103.12	101.84
13000	124.65	121.74	119.20	116.97	115.00	113.26	111.71	110.33
14000	134.24	131.11	128.37	125.97	123.85	121.97	120.30	118.82
15000	143.83	140.47	137.54	134.96	132.69	130.68	128.90	127.30
16000	153.41	149.84	146.71	143.96	141.54	139.39	137.49	135.79
17000	163.00	159.20	155.88	152.96	150.38	148.10	146.08	144.28
18000	172.59	168.57	165.05	161.96	159.23	156.82	154.67	152.76
19000	182.18	177.93	174.22	170.95	168.08	165.53	163.27	161.25
20000	191.77	187.29	183.38	179.95	176.92	174.24	171.86	169.74
21000	201.35	196.66	192.55	188.95	185.77	182.95	180.45	178.22
22000	210.94	206.02	201.72	197.94	194.61	191.66	189.04	186.71
23000	220.53	215.39	210.89	206.94	203.46	200.38	197.64	195.20
24000	230.12	224.75	220.06	215.94	212.30	209.09	206.23	203.68
25000	239.71	234.12	229.23	224.94	221.15	217.80	214.82	212.17
26000	249.29	243.48	238.40	233.93	230.00	226.51	223.41	220.66
27000	258.88	252.85	247.57	242.93	238.84	235.22	232.01	229.14
28000	268.47	262.21	256.74	251.93	247.69	243.93	240.60	237.63
29000	278.06	271.57	265.91	260.93	256.53	252.65	249.19	246.12
30000	287.65	280.94	275.07	269.92	265.38	261.36	257.79	254.60
31000	297.23	290.30	284.24	278.92	274.23	270.07	266.38	263.09
32000	306.82	299.67	293.41	287.92	283.07	278.78	274.97	271.58
33000	316.41	309.03	302.58	296.91	291.92	287.49	283.56	280.06
34000	326.00	318.40	311.75	305.91	300.76	296.20	292.16	288.55
35000	335.59	327.76	320.92	314.91	309.61	304.92	300.75	297.04
40000	383.53	374.58	366.76	359.90	353.84	348.47	343.71	339.47
45000	431.47	421.41	412.61	404.88	398.07	392.03	386.68	381.90
50000	479.41	468.23	458.45	449.87	442.30	435.59	429.64	424.34
55000	527.35	515.05	504.30	494.85	486.52	479.15	472.60	466.77
60000	575.29	561.87	550.14	539.84	530.75	522.71	515.57	509.20
65000	623.23	608.69	595.99	584.83	574.98	566.27	558.53	551.64
70000	671.17	655.52	641.83	629.81	619.21	609.83	601.49	594.07
75000	719.11	702.34	687.68	674.80	663.44	653.39	644.46	636.50
80000	767.05	749.16	733.52	719.79	707.67	696.94	687.42	678.94
85000	814.99	795.98	779.37	764.77	751.90	740.50	730.38	721.37
90000	862.93	842.81	825.21	809.76	796.13	784.06	773.35	763.80
95000	910.87	889.63	871.06	854.74	840.36	827.62	816.31	806.24
100000	958.81	936.45	916.90	899.73	884.59	871.18	859.27	848.67
105000	1006.75	983.27	962.75	944.72	928.82	914.74	902.24	891.10
110000	1054.69	1030.09	1008.59	989.70	973.04	958.30	945.20	933.54
115000	1102.63	1076.92	1054.44	1034.69	1017.27	1001.86	988.16	975.97
120000	1150.57	1123.74	1100.28	1079.68	1061.50	1045.41	1031.13	1018.40
125000	1198.51	1170.56	1146.13	1124.66	1105.73	1088.97	1074.09	1060.84
130000	1246.45	1217.38	1191.97	1169.65	1149.96	1132.53	1117.05	1103.27
135000	1294.39	1264.21	1237.82	1214.64	1194.19	1176.09	1160.02	1145.70
140000	1342.33	1311.03	1283.66	1259.62	1238.42	1219.65	1202.98	1188.14
145000	1390.27	1357.85	1329.51	1304.61	1282.65	1263.21	1245.94	1230.57
150000	1438.21	1404.67	1375.35	1349.59	1326.88	1306.77	1288.91	1273.00
155000	1486.15	1451.49	1421.20	1394.58	1371.11	1350.33	1331.87	1315.43
160000	1534.09	1498.32	1467.04	1439.57	1415.33	1393.88	1374.83	1357.87

AMOUNT OF LOAN	NUMBER OF YEARS IN TERM							
	25	26	27	28	29	30	35	40
$ 50	.42	.42	.42	.41	.41	.41	.40	.39
100	.84	.84	.83	.82	.82	.81	.79	.78
200	1.68	1.67	1.65	1.64	1.63	1.61	1.57	1.55
300	2.52	2.50	2.47	2.45	2.44	2.42	2.36	2.32
400	3.36	3.33	3.30	3.27	3.25	3.22	3.14	3.09
500	4.20	4.16	4.12	4.09	4.06	4.03	3.92	3.86
600	5.04	4.99	4.94	4.90	4.87	4.83	4.71	4.63
700	5.88	5.82	5.77	5.72	5.68	5.64	5.49	5.40
800	6.72	6.65	6.59	6.54	6.49	6.44	6.28	6.18
900	7.56	7.48	7.41	7.35	7.30	7.25	7.06	6.95
1000	8.40	8.31	8.24	8.17	8.11	8.05	7.84	7.72
2000	16.79	16.62	16.47	16.33	16.21	16.10	15.68	15.43
3000	25.18	24.93	24.70	24.49	24.31	24.14	23.52	23.15
4000	33.57	33.23	32.93	32.66	32.41	32.19	31.36	30.86
5000	41.96	41.54	41.16	40.82	40.51	40.24	39.20	38.57
6000	50.36	49.85	49.39	48.98	48.61	48.28	47.04	46.29
7000	58.75	58.16	57.62	57.15	56.72	56.33	54.88	54.00
8000	67.14	66.46	65.86	65.31	64.82	64.37	62.72	61.71
9000	75.53	74.77	74.09	73.47	72.92	72.42	70.56	69.43
10000	83.92	83.08	82.32	81.63	81.02	80.47	78.40	77.14
11000	92.32	91.38	90.55	89.80	89.12	88.51	86.24	84.85
12000	100.71	99.69	98.78	97.96	97.22	96.56	94.08	92.57
13000	109.10	108.00	107.01	106.12	105.33	104.61	101.92	100.28
14000	117.49	116.31	115.24	114.29	113.43	112.65	109.76	108.00
15000	125.88	124.61	123.47	122.45	121.53	120.70	117.60	115.71
16000	134.28	132.92	131.71	130.61	129.63	128.74	125.44	123.42
17000	142.67	141.23	139.94	138.78	137.73	136.79	133.28	131.14
18000	151.06	149.54	148.17	146.94	145.83	144.84	141.12	138.85
19000	159.45	157.84	156.40	155.10	153.93	152.88	148.96	146.56
20000	167.84	166.15	164.63	163.26	162.04	160.93	156.80	154.28
21000	176.24	174.46	172.86	171.43	170.14	168.98	164.64	161.99
22000	184.63	182.76	181.09	179.59	178.24	177.02	172.48	169.70
23000	193.02	191.07	189.32	187.75	186.34	185.07	180.32	177.42
24000	201.41	199.38	197.56	195.92	194.44	193.11	188.16	185.13
25000	209.80	207.69	205.79	204.08	202.54	201.16	196.00	192.85
26000	218.20	215.99	214.02	212.24	210.65	209.21	203.84	200.56
27000	226.59	224.30	222.25	220.41	218.75	217.25	211.68	208.27
28000	234.98	232.61	230.48	228.57	226.85	225.30	219.52	215.99
29000	243.37	240.91	238.71	236.73	234.95	233.35	227.36	223.70
30000	251.76	249.22	246.94	244.89	243.05	241.39	235.20	231.41
31000	260.16	257.53	255.17	253.06	251.15	249.44	243.04	239.13
32000	268.55	265.84	263.41	261.22	259.26	257.48	250.88	246.84
33000	276.94	274.14	271.64	269.38	267.36	265.53	258.72	254.55
34000	285.33	282.45	279.87	277.55	275.46	273.58	266.56	262.27
35000	293.72	290.76	288.10	285.71	283.56	281.62	274.40	269.98
40000	335.68	332.29	329.26	326.52	324.07	321.85	313.60	308.55
45000	377.64	373.83	370.41	367.34	364.58	362.09	352.80	347.12
50000	419.60	415.37	411.57	408.15	405.08	402.32	392.00	385.69
55000	461.56	456.90	452.72	448.97	445.59	442.55	431.20	424.25
60000	503.52	498.44	493.88	489.78	486.10	482.78	470.40	462.82
65000	545.48	539.98	535.04	530.60	526.61	523.01	509.60	501.39
70000	587.44	581.51	576.19	571.41	567.12	563.24	548.80	539.96
75000	629.40	623.05	617.35	612.23	607.62	603.47	588.00	578.53
80000	671.36	664.58	658.51	653.04	648.13	643.70	627.20	617.09
85000	713.32	706.12	699.66	693.86	688.64	683.93	666.40	655.66
90000	755.28	747.66	740.82	734.67	729.15	724.17	705.60	694.23
95000	797.24	789.19	781.97	775.49	769.65	764.40	744.80	732.80
100000	839.20	830.73	823.13	816.30	810.16	804.63	784.00	771.37
105000	881.16	872.26	864.29	857.12	850.67	844.86	823.20	809.93
110000	923.12	913.80	905.44	897.93	891.18	885.09	862.40	848.50
115000	965.08	955.34	946.60	938.75	931.69	925.32	901.60	887.07
120000	1007.04	996.87	987.76	979.56	972.19	965.55	940.80	925.64
125000	1049.00	1038.41	1028.91	1020.38	1012.70	1005.78	980.00	964.21
130000	1090.96	1079.95	1070.07	1061.19	1053.21	1046.01	1019.20	1002.77
135000	1132.92	1121.48	1111.22	1102.01	1093.72	1086.25	1058.40	1041.34
140000	1174.88	1163.02	1152 38	1142.82	1134.23	1126.48	1097.60	1079.91
145000	1216.84	1204.55	1193.54	1183.64	1174.73	1166.71	1136.79	1118.48
150000	1258.80	1246.09	1234.69	1224.45	1215.24	1206.94	1175.99	1157.05
155000	1300.76	1287.63	1275.85	1265.27	1255.75	1247.17	1215.19	1195.62
160000	1342.72	1329.16	1317.01	1306.08	1296.26	1287.40	1254.39	1234.18

MONTHLY AMORTIZING PAYMENTS

AMOUNT OF LOAN	NUMBER OF YEARS IN TERM							
	1	1-1/2	2	3	4	5	6	7
$ 50	4.38	2.99	2.29	1.60	1.25	1.05	.91	.81
100	8.76	5.97	4.58	3.19	2.50	2.09	1.81	1.62
200	17.51	11.94	9.15	6.38	4.99	4.17	3.62	3.24
300	26.26	17.90	13.73	9.56	7.49	6.25	5.43	4.85
400	35.01	23.87	18.30	12.75	9.98	8.33	7.24	6.47
500	43.76	29.83	22.88	15.93	12.48	10.41	9.05	8.08
600	52.51	35.80	27.45	19.12	14.97	12.50	10.86	9.70
700	61.26	41.76	32.02	22.31	17.47	14.58	12.67	11.31
800	70.01	47.73	36.60	25.49	19.96	16.66	14.48	12.93
900	78.76	53.69	41.17	28.68	22.45	18.74	16.28	14.54
1000	87.51	59.66	45.75	31.86	24.95	20.82	18.09	16.16
2000	175.02	119.31	91.49	63.72	49.89	41.64	36.18	32.31
3000	262.53	178.97	137.23	95.58	74.84	62.46	54.27	48.46
4000	350.04	238.62	182.97	127.44	99.78	83.28	72.36	64.62
5000	437.55	298.28	228.72	159.29	124.73	104.10	90.44	80.77
6000	525.06	357.93	274.46	191.15	149.67	124.92	108.53	96.92
7000	612.57	417.59	320.20	223.01	174.62	145.74	126.62	113.07
8000	700.08	477.24	365.94	254.87	199.56	166.56	144.71	129.23
9000	787.59	536.90	411.68	286.73	224.50	187.38	162.79	145.38
10000	875.10	596.55	457.43	318.58	249.45	208.20	180.88	161.53
11000	962.61	656.21	503.17	350.44	274.39	229.01	198.97	177.68
12000	1050.12	715.86	548.91	382.30	299.34	249.83	217.06	193.84
13000	1137.63	775.52	594.65	414.16	324.28	270.65	235.14	209.99
14000	1225.14	835.17	640.39	446.02	349.23	291.47	253.23	226.14
15000	1312.65	894.83	686.14	477.87	374.17	312.29	271.32	242.29
16000	1400.16	954.48	731.88	509.73	399.12	333.11	289.41	258.45
17000	1487.67	1014.14	777.62	541.59	424.06	353.93	307.49	274.60
18000	1575.18	1073.79	823.36	573.45	449.00	374.75	325.58	290.75
19000	1662.68	1133.45	869.11	605.31	473.95	395.57	343.67	306.90
20000	1750.19	1193.10	914.85	637.16	498.89	416.39	361.76	323.06
21000	1837.70	1252.76	960.59	669.02	523.84	437.21	379.85	339.21
22000	1925.21	1312.41	1006.33	700.88	548.78	458.02	397.93	355.36
23000	2012.72	1372.07	1052.07	732.74	573.73	478.84	416.02	371.51
24000	2100.23	1431.72	1097.82	764.60	598.67	499.66	434.11	387.67
25000	2187.74	1491.38	1143.56	796.45	623.62	520.48	452.20	403.82
26000	2275.25	1551.03	1189.30	828.31	648.56	541.30	470.28	419.97
27000	2362.76	1610.69	1235.04	860.17	673.50	562.12	488.37	436.12
28000	2450.27	1670.34	1280.78	892.03	698.45	582.94	506.46	452.28
29000	2537.78	1730.00	1326.53	923.89	723.39	603.76	524.55	468.43
30000	2625.29	1789.65	1372.27	955.74	748.34	624.58	542.63	484.58
31000	2712.80	1849.31	1418.01	987.60	773.28	645.40	560.72	500.74
32000	2800.31	1908.96	1463.75	1019.46	798.23	666.22	578.81	516.89
33000	2887.82	1968.62	1509.49	1051.32	823.17	687.03	596.90	533.04
34000	2975.33	2028.27	1555.24	1083.17	848.12	707.85	614.98	549.19
35000	3062.84	2087.93	1600.98	1115.03	873.06	728.67	633.07	565.35
40000	3500.38	2386.20	1829.69	1274.32	997.78	832.77	723.51	646.11
45000	3937.93	2684.48	2058.40	1433.61	1122.50	936.86	813.95	726.87
50000	4375.48	2982.75	2287.11	1592.90	1247.23	1040.96	904.39	807.63
55000	4813.02	3281.03	2515.82	1752.19	1371.95	1145.05	994.83	888.40
60000	5250.57	3579.30	2744.53	1911.48	1496.67	1249.15	1085.26	969.16
65000	5688.12	3877.58	2973.24	2070.77	1621.39	1353.24	1175.70	1049.92
70000	6125.67	4175.85	3201.95	2230.06	1746.12	1457.34	1266.14	1130.69
75000	6563.21	4474.13	3430.66	2389.35	1870.84	1561.44	1356.58	1211.45
80000	7000.76	4772.40	3659.37	2548.64	1995.56	1665.53	1447.02	1292.21
85000	7438.31	5070.68	3888.08	2707.93	2120.28	1769.63	1537.45	1372.97
90000	7875.86	5368.95	4116.80	2867.22	2245.00	1873.72	1627.89	1453.74
95000	8313.40	5667.23	4345.51	3026.51	2369.73	1977.82	1718.33	1534.50
100000	8750.95	5965.50	4574.22	3185.80	2494.45	2081.91	1808.77	1615.26
105000	9188.50	6263.78	4802.93	3345.09	2619.17	2186.01	1899.21	1696.03
110000	9626.04	6562.05	5031.64	3504.38	2743.89	2290.10	1989.65	1776.79
115000	10063.59	6860.33	5260.35	3663.67	2868.62	2394.20	2080.08	1857.55
120000	10501.14	7158.60	5489.06	3822.96	2993.34	2498.29	2170.52	1938.32
125000	10938.69	7456.88	5717.77	3982.25	3118.06	2602.39	2260.96	2019.08
130000	11376.23	7755.15	5946.48	4141.54	3242.78	2706.48	2351.40	2099.84
135000	11813.78	8053.43	6175.19	4300.83	3367.50	2810.58	2441.84	2180.60
140000	12251.33	8351.70	6403.90	4460.12	3492.23	2914.68	2532.27	2261.37
145000	12688.88	8649.98	6632.61	4619.41	3616.95	3018.77	2622.71	2342.13
150000	13126.42	8948.25	6861.32	4778.70	3741.67	3122.87	2713.15	2422.89
155000	13563.97	9246.53	7090.03	4937.99	3866.39	3226.96	2803.59	2503.66
160000	14001.52	9544.80	7318.74	5097.28	3991.12	3331.06	2894.03	2584.42

AMOUNT OF LOAN	NUMBER OF YEARS IN TERM							
	8	9	10	11	12	14	15	16
$ 50	.74	.69	.64	.61	.58	.53	.52	.50
100	1.48	1.37	1.28	1.21	1.15	1.06	1.03	1.00
200	2.95	2.73	2.55	2.41	2.30	2.12	2.05	1.99
300	4.42	4.09	3.83	3.61	3.44	3.17	3.07	2.98
400	5.89	5.45	5.10	4.82	4.59	4.23	4.09	3.97
500	7.36	6.81	6.37	6.02	5.73	5.29	5.11	4.97
600	8.83	8.17	7.65	7.22	6.88	6.34	6.14	5.96
700	10.31	9.53	8.92	8.43	8.02	7.40	7.16	6.95
800	11.78	10.89	10.19	9.63	9.17	8.46	8.18	7.94
900	13.25	12.25	11.47	10.83	10.31	9.51	9.20	8.93
1000	14.72	13.61	12.74	12.03	11.46	10.57	10.22	9.93
2000	29.44	27.22	25.48	24.06	22.91	21.13	20.44	19.85
3000	44.15	40.83	38.21	36.09	34.36	31.69	30.66	29.77
4000	58.87	54.44	50.95	48.12	45.81	42.26	40.87	39.69
5000	73.58	68.05	63.68	60.15	57.26	52.82	51.09	49.61
6000	88.30	81.66	76.42	72.18	68.71	63.38	61.31	59.53
7000	103.01	95.27	89.15	84.21	80.16	73.94	71.53	69.45
8000	117.73	108.88	101.89	96.24	91.61	84.51	81.74	79.37
9000	132.44	122.49	114.62	108.27	103.06	95.07	91.96	89.29
10000	147.16	136.10	127.36	120.30	114.51	105.63	102.18	99.21
11000	161.87	149.71	140.09	132.33	125.96	116.19	112.39	109.14
12000	176.59	163.32	152.83	144.36	137.41	126.76	122.61	119.06
13000	191.30	176.93	165.56	156.39	148.87	137.32	132.83	128.98
14000	206.02	190.53	178.30	168.42	160.32	147.88	143.05	138.90
15000	220.73	204.14	191.03	180.45	171.77	158.44	153.26	148.82
16000	235.45	217.75	203.77	192.48	183.22	169.01	163.48	158.74
17000	250.16	231.36	216.51	204.51	194.67	179.57	173.70	168.66
18000	264.88	244.97	229.24	216.54	206.12	190.13	183.91	178.58
19000	279.59	258.58	241.98	228.57	217.57	200.69	194.13	188.50
20000	294.31	272.19	254.71	240.60	229.02	211.26	204.35	198.42
21000	309.02	285.80	267.45	252.63	240.47	221.82	214.57	208.34
22000	323.74	299.41	280.18	264.66	251.92	232.38	224.78	218.27
23000	338.45	313.02	292.92	276.69	263.37	242.94	235.00	228.19
24000	353.17	326.63	305.65	288.72	274.82	253.51	245.22	238.11
25000	367.88	340.24	318.39	300.75	286.28	264.07	255.43	248.03
26000	382.60	353.85	331.12	312.78	297.73	274.63	265.65	257.95
27000	397.31	367.45	343.86	324.81	309.18	285.19	275.87	267.87
28000	412.03	381.06	356.59	336.84	320.63	295.76	286.09	277.79
29000	426.74	394.67	369.33	348.87	332.08	306.32	296.30	287.71
30000	441.46	408.28	382.06	360.90	343.53	316.88	306.52	297.63
31000	456.17	421.89	394.80	372.93	354.98	327.44	316.74	307.55
32000	470.89	435.50	407.54	384.96	366.43	338.01	326.95	317.47
33000	485.60	449.11	420.27	396.99	377.88	348.57	337.17	327.40
34000	500.32	462.72	433.01	409.02	389.33	359.13	347.39	337.32
35000	515.03	476.33	445.74	421.05	400.78	369.69	357.61	347.24
40000	588.61	544.38	509.42	481.20	458.04	422.51	408.69	396.84
45000	662.19	612.42	573.09	541.35	515.29	475.32	459.78	446.45
50000	735.76	680.47	636.77	601.50	572.55	528.13	510.86	496.05
55000	809.34	748.51	700.45	661.65	629.80	580.95	561.95	545.66
60000	882.91	816.56	764.12	721.80	687.05	633.76	613.03	595.26
65000	956.49	884.61	827.80	781.95	744.31	686.57	664.12	644.87
70000	1030.06	952.65	891.48	842.10	801.56	739.38	715.21	694.47
75000	1103.64	1020.70	955.15	902.25	858.82	792.20	766.29	744.07
80000	1177.22	1088.75	1018.83	962.40	916.07	845.01	817.38	793.68
85000	1250.79	1156.79	1082.51	1022.55	973.32	897.82	868.46	843.28
90000	1324.37	1224.84	1146.18	1082.70	1030.58	950.64	919.55	892.89
95000	1397.94	1292.88	1209.86	1142.85	1087.83	1003.45	970.64	942.49
100000	1471.52	1360.93	1273.54	1203.00	1145.09	1056.26	1021.72	992.10
105000	1545.09	1428.98	1337.21	1263.15	1202.34	1109.07	1072.81	1041.70
110000	1618.67	1497.02	1400.89	1323.30	1259.60	1161.89	1123.89	1091.31
115000	1692.24	1565.07	1464.57	1383.45	1316.85	1214.70	1174.98	1140.91
120000	1765.82	1633.12	1528.24	1443.60	1374.10	1267.51	1226.06	1190.52
125000	1839.40	1701.16	1591.92	1503.75	1431.36	1320.33	1277.15	1240.12
130000	1912.97	1769.21	1655.60	1563.90	1488.61	1373.14	1328.24	1289.73
135000	1986.55	1837.25	1719.27	1624.05	1545.87	1425.95	1379.32	1339.33
140000	2060.12	1905.30	1782.95	1684.20	1603.12	1478.76	1430.41	1388.93
145000	2133.70	1973.35	1846.63	1744.35	1660.37	1531.58	1481.49	1438.54
150000	2207.27	2041.39	1910.30	1804.50	1717.63	1584.39	1532.58	1488.14
155000	2280.85	2109.44	1973.98	1864.65	1774.88	1637.20	1583.66	1537.75
160000	2354.43	2177.49	2037.66	1924.80	1832.14	1690.02	1634.75	1587.35

MONTHLY AMORTIZING PAYMENTS

AMOUNT OF LOAN	NUMBER OF YEARS IN TERM							
	17	18	19	20	21	22	23	24
$ 50	.49	.48	.47	.46	.45	.44	.44	.43
100	.97	.95	.93	.91	.90	.88	.87	.86
200	1.94	1.89	1.85	1.82	1.79	1.76	1.74	1.72
300	2.90	2.84	2.78	2.73	2.68	2.64	2.61	2.58
400	3.87	3.78	3.70	3.64	3.58	3.52	3.48	3.43
500	4.84	4.73	4.63	4.54	4.47	4.40	4.34	4.29
600	5.80	5.67	5.55	5.45	5.36	5.28	5.21	5.15
700	6.77	6.61	6.48	6.36	6.25	6.16	6.08	6.01
800	7.74	7.56	7.40	7.27	7.15	7.04	6.95	6.86
900	8.70	8.50	8.33	8.18	8.04	7.92	7.81	7.72
1000	9.67	9.45	9.25	9.08	8.93	8.80	8.68	8.58
2000	19.34	18.89	18.50	18.16	17.86	17.59	17.36	17.15
3000	29.00	28.33	27.75	27.24	26.79	26.39	26.03	25.72
4000	38.67	37.78	37.00	36.32	35.71	35.18	34.71	34.29
5000	48.33	47.22	46.25	45.39	44.64	43.98	43.39	42.86
6000	58.00	56.66	55.50	54.47	53.57	52.77	52.06	51.43
7000	67.66	66.10	64.74	63.55	62.50	61.57	60.74	60.01
8000	77.33	75.55	73.99	72.63	71.42	70.36	69.42	68.58
9000	86.99	84.99	83.24	81.71	80.35	79.16	78.09	77.15
10000	96.66	94.43	92.49	90.78	89.28	87.95	86.77	85.72
11000	106.32	103.87	101.74	99.86	98.21	96.74	95.45	94.29
12000	115.99	113.32	110.99	108.94	107.13	105.54	104.12	102.86
13000	125.65	122.76	120.23	118.02	116.06	114.33	112.80	111.43
14000	135.32	132.20	129.48	127.09	124.99	123.13	121.48	120.01
15000	144.98	141.65	138.73	136.17	133.92	131.92	130.15	128.58
16000	154.65	151.09	147.98	145.25	142.84	140.72	138.83	137.15
17000	164.31	160.53	157.23	154.33	151.77	149.51	147.50	145.72
18000	173.98	169.97	166.48	163.41	160.70	158.31	156.18	154.29
19000	183.64	179.42	175.72	172.48	169.63	167.10	164.86	162.86
20000	193.31	188.86	184.97	181.56	178.55	175.89	173.53	171.43
21000	202.97	198.30	194.22	190.64	187.48	184.69	182.21	180.01
22000	212.64	207.74	203.47	199.72	196.41	193.48	190.89	188.58
23000	222.30	217.19	212.72	208.79	205.34	202.28	199.56	197.15
24000	231.97	226.63	221.97	217.87	214.26	211.07	208.24	205.72
25000	241.63	236.07	231.21	226.95	223.19	219.87	216.92	214.29
26000	251.30	245.51	240.46	236.03	232.12	228.66	225.59	222.86
27000	260.96	254.96	249.71	245.11	241.05	237.46	234.27	231.43
28000	270.63	264.40	258.96	254.18	249.97	246.25	242.95	240.01
29000	280.29	273.84	268.21	263.26	258.90	255.04	251.62	248.58
30000	289.96	283.29	277.46	272.34	267.83	263.84	260.30	257.15
31000	299.62	292.73	286.70	281.42	276.76	272.63	268.98	265.72
32000	309.29	302.17	295.95	290.49	285.68	281.43	277.65	274.29
33000	318.95	311.61	305.20	299.57	294.61	290.22	286.33	282.86
34000	328.62	321.06	314.45	308.65	303.54	299.02	295.00	291.43
35000	338.28	330.50	323.70	317.73	312.47	307.81	303.68	300.01
40000	386.61	377.71	369.94	363.12	357.10	351.78	347.06	342.86
45000	434.93	424.93	416.18	408.51	401.74	395.76	390.45	385.72
50000	483.26	472.14	462.42	453.90	446.38	439.73	433.83	428.58
55000	531.58	519.35	508.67	499.28	491.02	483.70	477.21	471.43
60000	579.91	566.57	554.91	544.67	535.65	527.67	520.59	514.29
65000	628.23	613.78	601.15	590.06	580.29	571.65	563.98	557.15
70000	676.56	660.99	647.39	635.45	624.93	615.62	607.36	600.01
75000	724.88	708.21	693.63	680.84	669.57	659.59	650.74	642.86
80000	773.21	755.42	739.87	726.23	714.20	703.56	694.12	685.72
85000	821.53	802.63	786.12	771.62	758.84	747.54	737.50	728.58
90000	869.86	849.85	832.36	817.01	803.48	791.51	780.89	771.43
95000	918.18	897.06	878.60	862.40	848.11	835.48	824.27	814.29
100000	966.51	944.27	924.84	907.79	892.75	879.45	867.65	857.15
105000	1014.84	991.49	971.08	953.17	937.39	923.43	911.03	900.01
110000	1063.16	1038.70	1017.33	998.56	982.03	967.40	954.42	942.86
115000	1111.49	1085.91	1063.57	1043.95	1026.66	1011.37	997.80	985.72
120000	1159.81	1133.13	1109.81	1089.34	1071.30	1055.34	1041.18	1028.58
125000	1208.14	1180.34	1156.05	1134.73	1115.94	1099.32	1084.56	1071.43
130000	1256.46	1227.55	1202.29	1180.12	1160.58	1143.29	1127.95	1114.29
135000	1304.79	1274.77	1248.53	1225.51	1205.21	1187.26	1171.33	1157.15
140000	1353.11	1321.98	1294.78	1270.90	1249.85	1231.23	1214.71	1200.01
145000	1401.44	1369.19	1341.02	1316.29	1294.49	1275.20	1258.09	1242.86
150000	1449.76	1416.41	1387.26	1361.68	1339.13	1319.18	1301.47	1285.72
155000	1498.09	1463.62	1433.50	1407.07	1383.76	1363.15	1344.86	1328.58
160000	1546.41	1510.83	1479.74	1452.45	1428.40	1407.12	1388.24	1371.43

AMOUNT OF LOAN	NUMBER OF YEARS IN TERM 25	26	27	28	29	30	35	40
$ 50	.43	.42	.42	.42	.41	.41	.40	.40
100	.85	.84	.84	.83	.82	.82	.80	.79
200	1.70	1.68	1.67	1.66	1.64	1.63	1.59	1.57
300	2.55	2.52	2.50	2.48	2.46	2.45	2.39	2.35
400	3.40	3.36	3.33	3.31	3.28	3.26	3.18	3.13
500	4.24	4.20	4.16	4.13	4.10	4.07	3.97	3.91
600	5.09	5.04	5.00	4.96	4.92	4.89	4.77	4.69
700	5.94	5.88	5.83	5.78	5.74	5.70	5.56	5.47
800	6.79	6.72	6.66	6.61	6.56	6.51	6.35	6.25
900	7.63	7.56	7.49	7.43	7.38	7.33	7.15	7.03
1000	8.48	8.40	8.32	8.26	8.20	8.14	7.94	7.81
2000	16.96	16.79	16.64	16.51	16.39	16.28	15.87	15.62
3000	25.44	25.19	24.96	24.76	24.58	24.41	23.81	23.43
4000	33.92	33.58	33.28	33.01	32.77	32.55	31.74	31.24
5000	42.39	41.97	41.60	41.26	40.96	40.69	39.67	39.05
6000	50.87	50.37	49.92	49.51	49.15	48.82	47.61	46.86
7000	59.35	58.76	58.24	57.77	57.34	56.96	55.54	54.67
8000	67.83	67.16	66.56	66.02	65.53	65.10	63.47	62.48
9000	76.30	75.55	74.87	74.27	73.72	73.23	71.41	70.29
10000	84.78	83.94	83.19	82.52	81.91	81.37	79.34	78.10
11000	93.26	92.34	91.51	90.77	90.10	89.50	87.27	85.91
12000	101.74	100.73	99.83	99.02	98.30	97.64	95.21	93.72
13000	110.22	109.13	108.15	107.27	106.49	105.78	103.14	101.53
14000	118.69	117.52	116.47	115.53	114.68	113.91	111.07	109.34
15000	127.17	125.91	124.79	123.78	122.87	122.05	119.01	117.15
16000	135.65	134.31	133.11	132.03	131.06	130.19	126.94	124.96
17000	144.13	142.70	141.43	140.28	139.25	138.32	134.88	132.77
18000	152.60	151.10	149.74	148.53	147.44	146.46	142.81	140.58
19000	161.08	159.49	158.06	156.78	155.63	154.60	150.74	148.39
20000	169.56	167.88	166.38	165.03	163.82	162.73	158.68	156.20
21000	178.04	176.28	174.70	173.29	172.01	170.87	166.61	164.01
22000	186.51	184.67	183.02	181.54	180.20	179.00	174.54	171.82
23000	194.99	193.07	191.34	189.79	188.40	187.14	182.48	179.63
24000	203.47	201.46	199.66	198.04	196.59	195.28	190.41	187.44
25000	211.95	209.85	207.98	206.29	204.78	203.41	198.34	195.25
26000	220.43	218.25	216.30	214.54	212.97	211.55	206.28	203.06
27000	228.90	226.64	224.61	222.79	221.16	219.69	214.21	210.87
28000	237.38	235.04	232.93	231.05	229.35	227.82	222.14	218.68
29000	245.86	243.43	241.25	239.30	237.54	235.96	230.08	226.49
30000	254.34	251.82	249.57	247.55	245.73	244.09	238.01	234.30
31000	262.81	260.22	257.89	255.80	253.92	252.23	245.94	242.11
32000	271.29	268.61	266.21	264.05	262.11	260.37	253.88	249.92
33000	279.77	277.00	274.53	272.30	270.30	268.50	261.81	257.73
34000	288.25	285.40	282.85	280.55	278.49	276.64	269.75	265.54
35000	296.73	293.79	291.17	288.81	286.69	284.78	277.68	273.35
40000	339.11	335.76	332.76	330.06	327.64	325.46	317.35	312.40
45000	381.50	377.73	374.35	371.32	368.59	366.14	357.01	351.45
50000	423.89	419.70	415.95	412.58	409.55	406.82	396.68	390.50
55000	466.28	461.67	457.54	453.84	450.50	447.50	436.35	429.55
60000	508.67	503.64	499.14	495.09	491.46	488.18	476.02	468.60
65000	551.06	545.61	540.73	536.35	532.41	528.87	515.68	507.65
70000	593.45	587.58	582.33	577.61	573.37	569.55	555.35	546.70
75000	635.83	629.55	623.92	618.87	614.32	610.23	595.02	585.75
80000	678.22	671.52	665.51	660.12	655.28	650.91	634.69	624.80
85000	720.61	713.49	707.11	701.38	696.23	691.59	674.36	663.85
90000	763.00	755.46	748.70	742.64	737.18	732.27	714.02	702.90
95000	805.39	797.43	790.30	783.89	778.14	772.96	753.69	741.95
100000	847.78	839.40	831.89	825.15	819.09	813.64	793.36	781.00
105000	890.17	881.37	873.49	866.41	860.05	854.32	833.03	820.05
110000	932.55	923.34	915.08	907.67	901.00	895.00	872.69	859.10
115000	974.94	965.31	956.67	948.92	941.96	935.68	912.36	898.15
120000	1017.33	1007.28	998.27	990.18	982.91	976.36	952.03	937.20
125000	1059.72	1049.25	1039.86	1031.44	1023.87	1017.05	991.70	976.25
130000	1102.11	1091.22	1081.46	1072.70	1064.82	1057.73	1031.36	1015.30
135000	1144.50	1133.19	1123.05	1113.95	1105.77	1098.41	1071.03	1054.35
140000	1186.89	1175.16	1164.65	1155.21	1146.73	1139.09	1110.70	1093.40
145000	1229.28	1217.13	1206.24	1196.47	1187.68	1179.77	1150.37	1132.45
150000	1271.66	1259.10	1247.83	1237.73	1228.64	1220.45	1190.04	1171.50
155000	1314.05	1301.06	1289.43	1278.98	1269.59	1261.14	1229.70	1210.55
160000	1356.44	1343.03	1331.02	1320.24	1310.55	1301.82	1269.37	1249.60

MONTHLY AMORTIZING PAYMENTS

AMOUNT OF LOAN	NUMBER OF YEARS IN TERM							
	1	1-1/2	2	3	4	5	6	7
$ 50	4.38	2.99	2.29	1.60	1.26	1.05	.91	.82
100	8.76	5.98	4.58	3.20	2.51	2.09	1.82	1.63
200	17.52	11.95	9.16	6.39	5.01	4.18	3.63	3.25
300	26.28	17.92	13.74	9.58	7.51	6.27	5.45	4.87
400	35.03	23.89	18.32	12.77	10.01	8.36	7.26	6.49
500	43.79	29.86	22.90	15.96	12.51	10.44	9.08	8.11
600	52.55	35.83	27.48	19.15	15.01	12.53	10.89	9.73
700	61.30	41.80	32.06	22.35	17.51	14.62	12.71	11.36
800	70.06	47.77	36.64	25.54	20.01	16.71	14.52	12.98
900	78.82	53.75	41.22	28.73	22.51	18.80	16.34	14.60
1000	87.57	59.72	45.80	31.92	25.01	20.88	18.15	16.22
2000	175.14	119.43	91.60	63.84	50.01	41.76	36.30	32.44
3000	262.71	179.14	137.40	95.75	75.02	62.64	54.45	48.65
4000	350.27	238.85	183.20	127.67	100.02	83.52	72.60	64.87
5000	437.84	298.57	229.00	159.59	125.02	104.40	90.75	81.09
6000	525.41	358.28	274.80	191.50	150.03	125.28	108.90	97.30
7000	612.98	417.99	320.60	223.42	175.03	146.16	127.05	113.52
8000	700.54	477.70	366.40	255.33	200.04	167.04	145.20	129.73
9000	788.11	537.42	412.20	287.25	225.04	187.92	163.35	145.95
10000	875.68	597.13	458.00	319.17	250.04	208.80	181.50	162.17
11000	963.25	656.84	503.80	351.08	275.05	229.68	199.65	178.38
12000	1050.81	716.55	549.60	383.00	300.05	250.56	217.80	194.60
13000	1138.38	776.27	595.40	414.92	325.06	271.44	235.95	210.82
14000	1225.95	835.98	641.20	446.83	350.06	292.32	254.10	227.03
15000	1313.52	895.69	687.00	478.75	375.06	313.20	272.25	243.25
16000	1401.08	955.40	732.80	510.66	400.07	334.08	290.40	259.46
17000	1488.65	1015.11	778.60	542.58	425.07	354.96	308.55	275.68
18000	1576.22	1074.83	824.40	574.50	450.08	375.84	326.70	291.90
19000	1663.79	1134.54	870.20	606.41	475.08	396.72	344.85	308.11
20000	1751.35	1194.25	916.00	638.33	500.08	417.60	363.00	324.33
21000	1838.92	1253.96	961.80	670.25	525.09	438.48	381.15	340.55
22000	1926.49	1313.68	1007.59	702.16	550.09	459.36	399.30	356.76
23000	2014.06	1373.39	1053.39	734.08	575.10	480.24	417.45	372.98
24000	2101.62	1433.10	1099.19	765.99	600.10	501.12	435.60	389.19
25000	2189.19	1492.81	1144.99	797.91	625.10	522.00	453.75	405.41
26000	2276.76	1552.53	1190.79	829.83	650.11	542.88	471.90	421.63
27000	2364.33	1612.24	1236.59	861.74	675.11	563.76	490.05	437.84
28000	2451.89	1671.95	1282.39	893.66	700.11	584.64	508.20	454.06
29000	2539.46	1731.66	1328.19	925.58	725.12	605.52	526.35	470.28
30000	2627.03	1791.37	1373.99	957.49	750.12	626.40	544.50	486.49
31000	2714.60	1851.09	1419.79	989.41	775.13	647.28	562.65	502.71
32000	2802.16	1910.80	1465.59	1021.32	800.13	668.16	580.80	518.92
33000	2889.73	1970.51	1511.39	1053.24	825.13	689.04	598.95	535.14
34000	2977.30	2030.22	1557.19	1085.16	850.14	709.92	617.10	551.36
35000	3064.87	2089.94	1602.99	1117.07	875.14	730.80	635.25	567.57
40000	3502.70	2388.50	1831.99	1276.65	1000.16	835.20	726.00	648.65
45000	3940.54	2687.06	2060.98	1436.23	1125.18	939.60	816.75	729.74
50000	4378.38	2985.62	2289.98	1595.82	1250.20	1044.00	907.50	810.82
55000	4816.21	3284.18	2518.98	1755.40	1375.22	1148.40	998.25	891.90
60000	5254.05	3582.74	2747.98	1914.98	1500.24	1252.80	1089.00	972.98
65000	5691.89	3881.31	2976.97	2074.56	1625.26	1357.20	1179.75	1054.06
70000	6129.73	4179.87	3205.97	2234.14	1750.28	1461.60	1270.50	1135.14
75000	6567.56	4478.43	3434.97	2393.72	1875.30	1566.00	1361.24	1216.22
80000	7005.40	4776.99	3663.97	2553.30	2000.32	1670.40	1451.99	1297.30
85000	7443.24	5075.55	3892.97	2712.88	2125.34	1774.80	1542.74	1378.39
90000	7881.08	5374.11	4121.96	2872.46	2250.36	1879.20	1633.49	1459.47
95000	8318.91	5672.68	4350.96	3032.05	2375.38	1983.60	1724.24	1540.55
100000	8756.75	5971.24	4579.96	3191.63	2500.40	2087.99	1814.99	1621.63
105000	9194.59	6269.80	4808.96	3351.21	2625.42	2192.39	1905.74	1702.71
110000	9632.42	6568.36	5037.95	3510.79	2750.44	2296.79	1996.49	1783.79
115000	10070.26	6866.92	5266.95	3670.37	2875.46	2401.19	2087.24	1864.87
120000	10508.10	7165.48	5495.95	3829.95	3000.48	2505.59	2177.99	1945.95
125000	10945.94	7464.05	5724.95	3989.53	3125.50	2609.99	2268.74	2027.04
130000	11383.77	7762.61	5953.94	4149.11	3250.51	2714.39	2359.49	2108.12
135000	11821.61	8061.17	6182.94	4308.69	3375.53	2818.79	2450.24	2189.20
140000	12259.45	8359.73	6411.94	4468.27	3500.55	2923.19	2540.99	2270.28
145000	12697.29	8658.29	6640.94	4627.86	3625.57	3027.59	2631.74	2351.36
150000	13135.12	8956.85	6869.93	4787.44	3750.59	3131.99	2722.48	2432.44
155000	13572.96	9255.42	7098.93	4947.02	3875.61	3236.39	2813.23	2513.52
160000	14010.80	9553.98	7327.93	5106.60	4000.63	3340.79	2903.98	2594.60

AMOUNT OF LOAN	NUMBER OF YEARS IN TERM							
	8	9	10	11	12	14	15	16
$ 50	.74	.69	.65	.61	.58	.54	.52	.50
100	1.48	1.37	1.29	1.21	1.16	1.07	1.03	1.00
200	2.96	2.74	2.57	2.42	2.31	2.13	2.06	2.00
300	4.44	4.11	3.85	3.63	3.46	3.20	3.09	3.00
400	5.92	5.48	5.13	4.84	4.61	4.26	4.12	4.00
500	7.40	6.84	6.41	6.05	5.77	5.32	5.15	5.00
600	8.87	8.21	7.69	7.26	6.92	6.39	6.18	6.00
700	10.35	9.58	8.97	8.47	8.07	7.45	7.21	7.00
800	11.83	10.95	10.25	9.68	9.22	8.51	8.24	8.00
900	13.31	12.31	11.53	10.89	10.37	9.58	9.27	9.00
1000	14.79	13.68	12.81	12.10	11.53	10.64	10.30	10.00
2000	29.57	27.36	25.61	24.20	23.05	21.28	20.59	20.00
3000	44.35	41.03	38.41	36.30	34.57	31.91	30.88	30.00
4000	59.13	54.71	51.22	48.40	46.09	42.55	41.17	39.99
5000	73.91	68.38	64.02	60.50	57.61	53.19	51.46	49.99
6000	88.69	82.06	76.82	72.60	69.13	63.82	61.76	59.99
7000	103.47	95.74	89.63	84.70	80.66	74.46	72.05	69.98
8000	118.25	109.41	102.43	96.80	92.18	85.09	82.34	79.98
9000	133.03	123.09	115.23	108.90	103.70	95.73	92.63	89.98
10000	147.81	136.76	128.04	121.00	115.22	106.37	102.92	99.97
11000	162.59	150.44	140.84	133.10	126.74	117.00	113.22	109.97
12000	177.37	164.11	153.64	145.20	138.26	127.64	123.51	119.97
13000	192.15	177.79	166.45	157.30	149.79	138.27	133.80	129.97
14000	206.93	191.47	179.25	169.40	161.31	148.91	144.09	139.96
15000	221.71	205.14	192.05	181.49	172.83	159.55	154.38	149.96
16000	236.49	218.82	204.86	193.59	184.35	170.18	164.68	159.96
17000	251.27	232.49	217.66	205.69	195.87	180.82	174.97	169.95
18000	266.05	246.17	230.46	217.79	207.39	191.45	185.26	179.95
19000	280.83	259.84	243.27	229.89	218.91	202.09	195.55	189.95
20000	295.61	273.52	256.07	241.99	230.44	212.73	205.84	199.94
21000	310.39	287.20	268.87	254.09	241.96	223.36	216.14	209.94
22000	325.17	300.87	281.68	266.19	253.48	234.00	226.43	219.94
23000	339.95	314.55	294.48	278.29	265.00	244.63	236.72	229.94
24000	354.73	328.22	307.28	290.39	276.52	255.27	247.01	239.93
25000	369.51	341.90	320.09	302.49	288.04	265.91	257.30	249.93
26000	384.29	355.58	332.89	314.59	299.57	276.54	267.59	259.93
27000	399.07	369.25	345.69	326.69	311.09	287.18	277.89	269.92
28000	413.85	382.93	358.50	338.79	322.61	297.81	288.18	279.92
29000	428.63	396.60	371.30	350.88	334.13	308.45	298.47	289.92
30000	443.41	410.28	384.10	362.98	345.65	319.09	308.76	299.91
31000	458.19	423.95	396.91	375.08	357.17	329.72	319.05	309.91
32000	472.97	437.63	409.71	387.18	368.70	340.36	329.35	319.91
33000	487.75	451.31	422.51	399.28	380.22	350.99	339.64	329.91
34000	502.53	464.98	435.32	411.38	391.74	361.63	349.93	339.90
35000	517.31	478.66	448.12	423.48	403.26	372.27	360.22	349.90
40000	591.21	547.04	512.14	483.98	460.87	425.45	411.68	399.88
45000	665.11	615.41	576.15	544.47	518.48	478.63	463.14	449.87
50000	739.02	683.79	640.17	604.97	576.08	531.81	514.60	499.85
55000	812.92	752.17	704.18	665.47	633.69	584.99	566.06	549.84
60000	886.82	820.55	768.20	725.96	691.30	638.17	617.52	599.82
65000	960.72	888.93	832.22	786.46	748.91	691.35	668.98	649.81
70000	1034.62	957.31	896.23	846.96	806.51	744.53	720.44	699.79
75000	1108.52	1025.69	960.25	907.45	864.12	797.71	771.90	749.78
80000	1182.42	1094.07	1024.27	967.95	921.73	850.89	823.36	799.76
85000	1256.32	1162.45	1088.28	1028.45	979.34	904.07	874.82	849.75
90000	1330.22	1230.82	1152.30	1088.94	1036.95	957.25	926.28	899.73
95000	1404.13	1299.20	1216.32	1149.44	1094.55	1010.43	977.74	949.72
100000	1478.03	1367.58	1280.33	1209.93	1152.16	1063.61	1029.20	999.70
105000	1551.93	1435.96	1344.35	1270.43	1209.77	1116.79	1080.66	1049.69
110000	1625.83	1504.34	1408.36	1330.93	1267.38	1169.97	1132.12	1099.67
115000	1699.73	1572.72	1472.38	1391.42	1324.98	1223.15	1183.58	1149.66
120000	1773.63	1641.10	1536.40	1451.92	1382.59	1276.33	1235.04	1199.64
125000	1847.53	1709.48	1600.41	1512.42	1440.20	1329.51	1286.50	1249.63
130000	1921.43	1777.86	1664.43	1572.91	1497.81	1382.69	1337.95	1299.61
135000	1995.33	1846.23	1728.45	1633.41	1555.42	1435.87	1389.41	1349.60
140000	2069.24	1914.61	1792.46	1693.91	1613.02	1489.05	1440.87	1399.58
145000	2143.14	1982.99	1856.48	1754.40	1670.63	1542.23	1492.33	1449.57
150000	2217.04	2051.37	1920.50	1814.90	1728.24	1595.41	1543.79	1499.55
155000	2290.94	2119.75	1984.51	1875.40	1785.85	1648.59	1595.25	1549.54
160000	2364.84	2188.13	2048.53	1935.89	1843.46	1701.77	1646.71	1599.52

MONTHLY AMORTIZING PAYMENTS

AMOUNT OF LOAN	NUMBER OF YEARS IN TERM							
	17	18	19	20	21	22	23	24
$ 50	.49	.48	.47	.46	.46	.45	.44	.44
100	.98	.96	.94	.92	.91	.89	.88	.87
200	1.95	1.91	1.87	1.84	1.81	1.78	1.76	1.74
300	2.93	2.86	2.80	2.75	2.71	2.67	2.63	2.60
400	3.90	3.81	3.74	3.67	3.61	3.56	3.51	3.47
500	4.88	4.77	4.67	4.58	4.51	4.44	4.39	4.33
600	5.85	5.72	5.60	5.50	5.41	5.33	5.26	5.20
700	6.82	6.67	6.53	6.42	6.31	6.22	6.14	6.06
800	7.80	7.62	7.47	7.33	7.21	7.11	7.01	6.93
900	8.77	8.57	8.40	8.25	8.11	7.99	7.89	7.80
1000	9.75	9.53	9.33	9.16	9.01	8.88	8.77	8.66
2000	19.49	19.05	18.66	18.32	18.02	17.76	17.53	17.32
3000	29.23	28.57	27.99	27.48	27.03	26.64	26.29	25.97
4000	38.97	38.09	37.32	36.64	36.04	35.52	35.05	34.63
5000	48.72	47.61	46.65	45.80	45.05	44.39	43.81	43.29
6000	58.46	57.13	55.97	54.96	54.06	53.27	52.57	51.94
7000	68.20	66.65	65.30	64.12	63.07	62.15	61.33	60.60
8000	77.94	76.17	74.63	73.27	72.08	71.03	70.09	69.26
9000	87.69	85.70	83.96	82.43	81.09	79.90	78.85	77.91
10000	97.43	95.22	93.29	91.59	90.10	88.78	87.61	86.57
11000	107.17	104.74	102.61	100.75	99.11	97.66	96.37	95.23
12000	116.91	114.26	111.94	109.91	108.12	106.54	105.13	103.88
13000	126.66	123.78	121.27	119.07	117.13	115.41	113.89	112.54
14000	136.40	133.30	130.60	128.23	126.14	124.29	122.65	121.20
15000	146.14	142.82	139.93	137.39	135.15	133.17	131.41	129.85
16000	155.88	152.34	149.25	146.54	144.16	142.05	140.17	138.51
17000	165.62	161.87	158.58	155.70	153.17	150.92	148.93	147.17
18000	175.37	171.39	167.91	164.86	162.18	159.80	157.70	155.82
19000	185.11	180.91	177.24	174.02	171.18	168.68	166.46	164.48
20000	194.85	190.43	186.57	183.18	180.19	177.56	175.22	173.14
21000	204.59	199.95	195.89	192.34	189.20	186.43	183.98	181.79
22000	214.34	209.47	205.22	201.50	198.21	195.31	192.74	190.45
23000	224.08	218.99	214.55	210.65	207.22	204.19	201.50	199.11
24000	233.82	228.51	223.88	219.81	216.23	213.07	210.26	207.76
25000	243.56	238.03	233.21	228.97	225.24	221.94	219.02	216.42
26000	253.31	247.56	242.54	238.13	234.25	230.82	227.78	225.08
27000	263.05	257.08	251.86	247.29	243.26	239.70	236.54	233.73
28000	272.79	266.60	261.19	256.45	252.27	248.58	245.30	242.39
29000	282.53	276.12	270.52	265.61	261.28	257.45	254.06	251.04
30000	292.28	285.64	279.85	274.77	270.29	266.33	262.82	259.70
31000	302.02	295.16	289.18	283.92	279.30	275.21	271.58	268.36
32000	311.76	304.68	298.50	293.08	288.31	284.09	280.34	277.01
33000	321.50	314.20	307.83	302.24	297.32	292.96	289.10	285.67
34000	331.24	323.73	317.16	311.40	306.33	301.84	297.86	294.33
35000	340.99	333.25	326.49	320.56	315.34	310.72	306.62	302.98
40000	389.70	380.85	373.13	366.35	360.38	355.11	350.43	346.27
45000	438.41	428.46	419.77	412.15	405.43	399.49	394.23	389.55
50000	487.12	476.06	466.41	457.94	450.48	443.88	438.03	432.83
55000	535.83	523.67	513.05	503.73	495.52	488.27	481.84	476.12
60000	584.55	571.28	559.69	549.53	540.57	532.66	525.64	519.40
65000	633.26	618.88	606.33	595.32	585.62	577.05	569.44	562.68
70000	681.97	666.49	652.97	641.11	630.67	621.43	613.24	605.96
75000	730.68	714.09	699.61	686.91	675.71	665.82	657.05	649.25
80000	779.39	761.70	746.25	732.70	720.76	710.21	700.85	692.53
85000	828.10	809.31	792.89	778.49	765.81	754.60	744.65	735.81
90000	876.82	856.91	839.53	824.29	810.86	798.98	788.46	779.09
95000	925.53	904.52	886.17	870.08	855.90	843.37	832.26	822.38
100000	974.24	952.12	932.81	915.87	900.95	887.76	876.06	865.66
105000	1022.95	999.73	979.45	961.67	946.00	932.15	919.86	908.94
110000	1071.66	1047.34	1026.09	1007.46	991.04	976.53	963.67	952.23
115000	1120.38	1094.94	1072.73	1053.25	1036.09	1020.92	1007.47	995.51
120000	1169.09	1142.55	1119.37	1099.05	1081.14	1065.31	1051.27	1038.79
125000	1217.80	1190.15	1166.01	1144.84	1126.19	1109.70	1095.08	1082.07
130000	1266.51	1237.76	1212.66	1190.63	1171.23	1154.09	1138.88	1125.36
135000	1315.22	1285.37	1259.30	1236.43	1216.28	1198.47	1182.68	1168.64
140000	1363.93	1332.97	1305.94	1282.22	1261.33	1242.86	1226.48	1211.92
145000	1412.65	1380.58	1352.58	1328.01	1306.38	1287.25	1270.29	1255.20
150000	1461.36	1428.18	1399.22	1373.81	1351.42	1331.64	1314.09	1298.49
155000	1510.07	1475.79	1445.86	1419.60	1396.47	1376.02	1357.89	1341.77
160000	1558.78	1523.40	1492.50	1465.39	1441.52	1420.41	1401.70	1385.05

MONTHLY AMORTIZING PAYMENTS 9¼%

AMOUNT OF LOAN	NUMBER OF YEARS IN TERM							
	25	26	27	28	29	30	35	40
$ 50	.43	.43	.43	.42	.42	.42	.41	.40
100	.86	.85	.85	.84	.83	.83	.81	.80
200	1.72	1.70	1.69	1.67	1.66	1.65	1.61	1.59
300	2.57	2.55	2.53	2.51	2.49	2.47	2.41	2.38
400	3.43	3.40	3.37	3.34	3.32	3.30	3.22	3.17
500	4.29	4.25	4.21	4.18	4.15	4.12	4.02	3.96
600	5.14	5.09	5.05	5.01	4.97	4.94	4.82	4.75
700	6.00	5.94	5.89	5.84	5.80	5.76	5.62	5.54
800	6.86	6.79	6.73	6.68	6.63	6.59	6.43	6.33
900	7.71	7.64	7.57	7.51	7.46	7.41	7.23	7.12
1000	8.57	8.49	8.41	8.35	8.29	8.23	8.03	7.91
2000	17.13	16.97	16.82	16.69	16.57	16.46	16.06	15.82
3000	25.70	25.45	25.23	25.03	24.85	24.69	24.09	23.72
4000	34.26	33.93	33.63	33.37	33.13	32.91	32.11	31.63
5000	42.82	42.41	42.04	41.71	41.41	41.14	40.14	39.54
6000	51.39	50.89	50.45	50.05	49.69	49.37	48.17	47.44
7000	59.95	59.37	58.85	58.39	57.97	57.59	56.20	55.35
8000	68.52	67.85	67.26	66.73	66.25	65.82	64.22	63.26
9000	77.08	76.33	75.67	75.07	74.53	74.05	72.25	71.16
10000	85.64	84.81	84.07	83.41	82.81	82.27	80.28	79.07
11000	94.21	93.30	92.48	91.75	91.09	90.50	88.31	86.98
12000	102.77	101.78	100.89	100.09	99.37	98.73	96.33	94.88
13000	111.33	110.26	109.29	108.43	107.65	106.95	104.36	102.79
14000	119.90	118.74	117.70	116.77	115.93	115.18	112.39	110.70
15000	128.46	127.22	126.11	125.11	124.21	123.41	120.42	118.60
16000	137.03	135.70	134.51	133.45	132.49	131.63	128.44	126.51
17000	145.59	144.18	142.92	141.79	140.77	139.86	136.47	134.42
18000	154.15	152.66	151.33	150.13	149.05	148.09	144.50	142.32
19000	162.72	161.14	159.73	158.47	157.33	156.31	152.53	150.23
20000	171.28	169.62	168.14	166.81	165.62	164.54	160.55	158.14
21000	179.85	178.11	176.55	175.15	173.90	172.77	168.58	166.04
22000	188.41	186.59	184.95	183.49	182.18	180.99	176.61	173.95
23000	196.97	195.07	193.36	191.83	190.46	189.22	184.64	181.86
24000	205.54	203.55	201.77	200.17	198.74	197.45	192.66	189.76
25000	214.10	212.03	210.17	208.51	207.02	205.67	200.69	197.67
26000	222.66	220.51	218.58	216.85	215.30	213.90	208.72	205.58
27000	231.23	228.99	226.99	225.19	223.58	222.13	216.75	213.48
28000	239.79	237.47	235.40	233.53	231.86	230.35	224.77	221.39
29000	248.36	245.95	243.80	241.87	240.14	238.58	232.80	229.30
30000	256.92	254.43	252.21	250.21	248.42	246.81	240.83	237.20
31000	265.48	262.91	260.62	258.55	256.70	255.03	248.86	245.11
32000	274.05	271.40	269.02	266.89	264.98	263.26	256.88	253.02
33000	282.61	279.88	277.43	275.23	273.26	271.49	264.91	260.92
34000	291.17	288.36	285.84	283.57	281.54	279.71	272.94	268.83
35000	299.74	296.84	294.24	291.91	289.82	287.94	280.97	276.74
40000	342.56	339.24	336.28	333.62	331.23	329.08	321.10	316.27
45000	385.38	381.65	378.31	375.32	372.63	370.21	361.24	355.80
50000	428.20	424.05	420.34	417.02	414.03	411.34	401.38	395.34
55000	471.02	466.46	462.38	458.72	455.43	452.48	441.51	434.87
60000	513.83	508.86	504.41	500.42	496.84	493.61	481.65	474.40
65000	556.65	551.27	546.45	542.12	538.24	534.74	521.79	513.93
70000	599.47	593.67	588.48	583.82	579.64	575.88	561.93	553.47
75000	642.29	636.08	630.51	625.52	621.04	617.01	602.06	593.00
80000	685.11	678.48	672.55	667.23	662.45	658.15	642.20	632.53
85000	727.93	720.89	714.58	708.93	703.85	699.28	682.34	672.07
90000	770.75	763.29	756.62	750.63	745.25	740.41	722.47	711.60
95000	813.57	805.70	798.65	792.33	786.65	781.55	762.61	751.13
100000	856.39	848.10	840.68	834.03	828.06	822.68	802.75	790.67
105000	899.21	890.51	882.72	875.73	869.46	863.81	842.89	830.20
110000	942.03	932.91	924.75	917.43	910.86	904.95	883.02	869.73
115000	984.84	975.32	966.79	959.14	952.26	946.08	923.16	909.26
120000	1027.66	1017.72	1008.82	1000.84	993.67	987.22	963.30	948.80
125000	1070.48	1060.13	1050.85	1042.54	1035.07	1028.35	1003.44	988.33
130000	1113.30	1102.53	1092.89	1084.24	1076.47	1069.48	1043.57	1027.86
135000	1156.12	1144.94	1134.92	1125.94	1117.87	1110.62	1083.71	1067.40
140000	1198.94	1187.34	1176.96	1167.64	1159.28	1151.75	1123.85	1106.93
145000	1241.76	1229.74	1218.99	1209.34	1200.68	1192.88	1163.98	1146.46
150000	1284.58	1272.15	1261.02	1251.04	1242.08	1234.02	1204.12	1186.00
155000	1327.40	1314.55	1303.06	1292.75	1283.48	1275.15	1244.26	1225.53
160000	1370.22	1356.96	1345.09	1334.45	1324.89	1316.29	1284.40	1265.06

MONTHLY AMORTIZING PAYMENTS

AMOUNT OF LOAN	NUMBER OF YEARS IN TERM							
	1	1-1/2	2	3	4	5	6	7
$ 50	4.39	2.99	2.30	1.60	1.26	1.05	.92	.82
100	8.77	5.98	4.59	3.20	2.51	2.10	1.83	1.63
200	17.53	11.96	9.18	6.40	5.02	4.19	3.65	3.26
300	26.29	17.94	13.76	9.60	7.52	6.29	5.47	4.89
400	35.06	23.91	18.35	12.79	10.03	8.38	7.29	6.52
500	43.82	29.89	22.93	15.99	12.54	10.48	9.11	8.15
600	52.58	35.87	27.52	19.19	15.04	12.57	10.93	9.77
700	61.34	41.84	32.10	22.39	17.55	14.66	12.75	11.40
800	70.11	47.82	36.69	25.58	20.06	16.76	14.57	13.03
900	78.87	53.80	41.28	28.78	22.56	18.85	16.40	14.66
1000	87.63	59.77	45.86	31.98	25.07	20.95	18.22	16.29
2000	175.26	119.54	91.72	63.95	50.13	41.89	36.43	32.57
3000	262.88	179.31	137.58	95.93	75.20	62.83	54.64	48.85
4000	350.51	239.08	183.43	127.90	100.26	83.77	72.85	65.13
5000	438.13	298.85	229.29	159.88	125.32	104.71	91.07	81.41
6000	525.76	358.62	275.15	191.85	150.39	125.65	109.28	97.69
7000	613.38	418.39	321.00	223.83	175.45	146.59	127.49	113.97
8000	701.01	478.16	366.86	255.80	200.51	167.53	145.70	130.25
9000	788.63	537.93	412.72	287.78	225.58	188.47	163.91	146.53
10000	876.26	597.70	458.57	319.75	250.64	209.41	182.13	162.81
11000	963.89	657.47	504.43	351.73	275.70	230.35	200.34	179.09
12000	1051.51	717.24	550.29	383.70	300.77	251.29	218.55	195.37
13000	1139.14	777.01	596.15	415.67	325.83	272.24	236.76	211.65
14000	1226.76	836.78	642.00	447.65	350.89	293.18	254.98	227.93
15000	1314.39	896.55	687.86	479.62	375.96	314.12	273.19	244.21
16000	1402.01	956.32	733.72	511.60	401.02	335.06	291.40	260.49
17000	1489.64	1016.09	779.57	543.57	426.08	356.00	309.61	276.77
18000	1577.26	1075.86	825.43	575.55	451.15	376.94	327.82	293.05
19000	1664.89	1135.63	871.29	607.52	476.21	397.88	346.04	309.33
20000	1752.51	1195.40	917.14	639.50	501.27	418.82	364.25	325.61
21000	1840.14	1255.17	963.00	671.47	526.34	439.76	382.46	341.89
22000	1927.77	1314.94	1008.86	703.45	551.40	460.70	400.67	358.17
23000	2015.39	1374.71	1054.72	735.42	576.47	481.64	418.89	374.45
24000	2103.02	1434.48	1100.57	767.39	601.53	502.58	437.10	390.73
25000	2190.64	1494.25	1146.43	799.37	626.59	523.53	455.31	407.01
26000	2278.27	1554.02	1192.29	831.34	651.66	544.47	473.52	423.29
27000	2365.89	1613.79	1238.14	863.32	676.72	565.41	491.73	439.57
28000	2453.52	1673.56	1284.00	895.29	701.78	586.35	509.95	455.85
29000	2541.14	1733.33	1329.86	927.27	726.85	607.29	528.16	472.13
30000	2628.77	1793.10	1375.71	959.24	751.91	628.23	546.37	488.41
31000	2716.39	1852.87	1421.57	991.22	776.97	649.17	564.58	504.69
32000	2804.02	1912.64	1467.43	1023.19	802.04	670.11	582.80	520.97
33000	2891.65	1972.41	1513.29	1055.17	827.10	691.05	601.01	537.25
34000	2979.27	2032.17	1559.14	1087.14	852.16	711.99	619.22	553.53
35000	3066.90	2091.94	1605.00	1119.11	877.23	732.93	637.43	569.81
40000	3505.02	2390.79	1834.28	1278.99	1002.54	837.64	728.49	651.21
45000	3943.15	2689.64	2063.57	1438.86	1127.86	942.34	819.55	732.61
50000	4381.28	2988.49	2292.85	1598.73	1253.18	1047.05	910.62	814.01
55000	4819.41	3287.34	2522.14	1758.61	1378.50	1151.75	1001.68	895.41
60000	5257.53	3586.19	2751.42	1918.48	1503.81	1256.45	1092.74	976.81
65000	5695.66	3885.04	2980.71	2078.35	1629.13	1361.16	1183.80	1058.21
70000	6133.79	4183.88	3209.99	2238.22	1754.45	1465.86	1274.86	1139.61
75000	6571.92	4482.73	3439.28	2398.10	1879.77	1570.57	1365.92	1221.01
80000	7010.04	4781.58	3668.56	2557.97	2005.08	1675.27	1456.98	1302.41
85000	7448.17	5080.43	3897.85	2717.84	2130.40	1779.98	1548.04	1383.81
90000	7886.30	5379.28	4127.13	2877.71	2255.72	1884.68	1639.10	1465.21
95000	8324.42	5678.13	4356.42	3037.59	2381.04	1989.38	1730.17	1546.61
100000	8762.55	5976.98	4585.70	3197.46	2506.35	2094.09	1821.23	1628.01
105000	9200.68	6275.82	4814.99	3357.33	2631.67	2198.79	1912.29	1709.41
110000	9638.81	6574.67	5044.27	3517.21	2756.99	2303.50	2003.35	1790.81
115000	10076.93	6873.52	5273.56	3677.08	2882.31	2408.20	2094.41	1872.21
120000	10515.06	7172.37	5502.84	3836.95	3007.62	2512.90	2185.47	1953.61
125000	10953.19	7471.22	5732.13	3996.82	3132.94	2617.61	2276.53	2035.01
130000	11391.32	7770.07	5961.41	4156.70	3258.26	2722.31	2367.59	2116.41
135000	11829.44	8068.92	6190.70	4316.57	3383.58	2827.02	2458.65	2197.81
140000	12267.57	8367.76	6419.98	4476.44	3508.89	2931.72	2549.72	2279.21
145000	12705.70	8666.61	6649.27	4636.31	3634.21	3036.42	2640.78	2360.61
150000	13143.83	8965.46	6878.55	4796.19	3759.53	3141.13	2731.84	2442.01
155000	13581.95	9264.31	7107.84	4956.06	3884.85	3245.83	2822.90	2523.41
160000	14020.08	9563.16	7337.12	5115.93	4010.16	3350.54	2913.96	2604.81

MONTHLY AMORTIZING PAYMENTS 9⅜%

AMOUNT OF LOAN	NUMBER OF YEARS IN TERM 8	9	10	11	12	14	15	16
$ 50	.75	.69	.65	.61	.58	.54	.52	.51
100	1.49	1.38	1.29	1.22	1.16	1.08	1.04	1.01
200	2.97	2.75	2.58	2.44	2.32	2.15	2.08	2.02
300	4.46	4.13	3.87	3.66	3.48	3.22	3.12	3.03
400	5.94	5.50	5.15	4.87	4.64	4.29	4.15	4.03
500	7.43	6.88	6.44	6.09	5.80	5.36	5.19	5.04
600	8.91	8.25	7.73	7.31	6.96	6.43	6.23	6.05
700	10.40	9.62	9.01	8.52	8.12	7.50	7.26	7.06
800	11.88	11.00	10.30	9.74	9.28	8.57	8.30	8.06
900	13.37	12.37	11.59	10.96	10.44	9.64	9.34	9.07
1000	14.85	13.75	12.88	12.17	11.60	10.71	10.37	10.08
2000	29.70	27.49	25.75	24.34	23.19	21.42	20.74	20.15
3000	44.54	41.23	38.62	36.51	34.78	32.13	31.11	30.22
4000	59.39	54.97	51.49	48.68	46.38	42.84	41.47	40.30
5000	74.23	68.72	64.36	60.85	57.97	53.55	51.84	50.37
6000	89.08	82.46	77.23	73.02	69.56	64.26	62.21	60.44
7000	103.92	96.20	90.10	85.19	81.15	74.97	72.57	70.52
8000	118.77	109.94	102.98	97.36	92.75	85.68	82.94	80.59
9000	133.61	123.69	115.85	109.52	104.34	96.39	93.31	90.66
10000	148.46	137.43	128.72	121.69	115.93	107.10	103.67	100.74
11000	163.31	151.17	141.59	133.86	127.52	117.81	114.04	110.81
12000	178.15	164.91	154.46	146.03	139.12	128.52	124.41	120.88
13000	193.00	178.66	167.33	158.20	150.71	139.23	134.78	130.96
14000	207.84	192.40	180.20	170.37	162.30	149.94	145.14	141.03
15000	222.69	206.14	193.08	182.54	173.89	160.65	155.51	151.10
16000	237.53	219.88	205.95	194.71	185.49	171.36	165.88	161.18
17000	252.38	233.63	218.82	206.88	197.08	182.07	176.24	171.25
18000	267.22	247.37	231.69	219.04	208.67	192.78	186.61	181.32
19000	282.07	261.11	244.56	231.21	220.26	203.49	196.98	191.40
20000	296.91	274.85	257.43	243.38	231.86	214.20	207.34	201.47
21000	311.76	288.60	270.30	255.55	243.45	224.91	217.71	211.54
22000	326.61	302.34	283.18	267.72	255.04	235.62	228.08	221.62
23000	341.45	316.08	296.05	279.89	266.63	246.33	238.44	231.69
24000	356.30	329.82	308.92	292.06	278.23	257.04	248.81	241.76
25000	371.14	343.57	321.79	304.23	289.82	267.75	259.18	251.84
26000	385.99	357.31	334.66	316.40	301.41	278.46	269.55	261.91
27000	400.83	371.05	347.53	328.56	313.00	289.17	279.91	271.98
28000	415.68	384.79	360.40	340.73	324.60	299.88	290.28	282.06
29000	430.52	398.54	373.28	352.90	336.19	310.59	300.65	292.13
30000	445.37	412.28	386.15	365.07	347.78	321.30	311.01	302.20
31000	460.21	426.02	399.02	377.24	359.37	332.01	321.38	312.28
32000	475.06	439.76	411.89	389.41	370.97	342.72	331.75	322.35
33000	489.91	453.51	424.76	401.58	382.56	353.43	342.11	332.42
34000	504.75	467.25	437.63	413.75	394.15	364.14	352.48	342.50
35000	519.60	480.99	450.50	425.92	405.74	374.85	362.85	352.57
40000	593.82	549.70	514.86	486.76	463.71	428.39	414.68	402.94
45000	668.05	618.42	579.22	547.60	521.67	481.94	466.52	453.30
50000	742.28	687.13	643.58	608.45	579.63	535.49	518.35	503.67
55000	816.51	755.84	707.93	669.29	637.59	589.04	570.19	554.04
60000	890.73	824.55	772.29	730.14	695.56	642.59	622.02	604.40
65000	964.96	893.27	836.65	790.98	753.52	696.14	673.86	654.77
70000	1039.19	961.98	901.00	851.83	811.48	749.69	725.69	705.14
75000	1113.42	1030.69	965.36	912.67	869.45	803.23	777.53	755.50
80000	1187.64	1099.40	1029.72	973.51	927.41	856.78	829.36	805.87
85000	1261.87	1168.12	1094.08	1034.36	985.37	910.33	881.20	856.24
90000	1336.10	1236.83	1158.43	1095.20	1043.33	963.88	933.03	906.60
95000	1410.32	1305.54	1222.79	1156.05	1101.30	1017.43	984.87	956.97
100000	1484.55	1374.25	1287.15	1216.89	1159.26	1070.98	1036.70	1007.33
105000	1558.78	1442.97	1351.50	1277.74	1217.22	1124.53	1088.53	1057.70
110000	1633.01	1511.68	1415.86	1338.58	1275.18	1178.07	1140.37	1108.07
115000	1707.23	1580.39	1480.22	1399.42	1333.15	1231.62	1192.20	1158.43
120000	1781.46	1649.10	1544.57	1460.27	1391.11	1285.17	1244.04	1208.80
125000	1855.69	1717.81	1608.93	1521.11	1449.07	1338.72	1295.87	1259.17
130000	1929.92	1786.53	1673.29	1581.96	1507.03	1392.27	1347.71	1309.53
135000	2004.14	1855.24	1737.65	1642.80	1565.00	1445.82	1399.54	1359.90
140000	2078.37	1923.95	1802.00	1703.65	1622.96	1499.37	1451.38	1410.27
145000	2152.60	1992.66	1866.36	1764.49	1680.92	1552.91	1503.21	1460.63
150000	2226.83	2061.38	1930.72	1825.33	1738.89	1606.46	1555.05	1511.00
155000	2301.05	2130.09	1995.07	1886.18	1796.85	1660.01	1606.88	1561.37
160000	2375.28	2198.80	2059.43	1947.02	1854.81	1713.56	1658.72	1611.73

MONTHLY AMORTIZING PAYMENTS

AMOUNT OF LOAN	NUMBER OF YEARS IN TERM							
	17	18	19	20	21	22	23	24
$ 50	.50	.48	.48	.47	.46	.45	.45	.44
100	.99	.96	.95	.93	.91	.90	.89	.88
200	1.97	1.93	1.89	1.85	1.82	1.80	1.77	1.75
300	2.95	2.89	2.83	2.78	2.73	2.69	2.66	2.63
400	3.93	3.85	3.77	3.70	3.64	3.59	3.54	3.50
500	4.91	4.81	4.71	4.62	4.55	4.49	4.43	4.38
600	5.90	5.77	5.65	5.55	5.46	5.38	5.31	5.25
700	6.88	6.73	6.59	6.47	6.37	6.28	6.20	6.12
800	7.86	7.69	7.53	7.40	7.28	7.17	7.08	7.00
900	8.84	8.65	8.47	8.32	8.19	8.07	7.97	7.87
1000	9.82	9.61	9.41	9.24	9.10	8.97	8.85	8.75
2000	19.64	19.21	18.82	18.48	18.19	17.93	17.69	17.49
3000	29.46	28.81	28.23	27.72	27.28	26.89	26.54	26.23
4000	39.28	38.41	37.64	36.96	36.37	35.85	35.38	34.97
5000	49.10	48.01	47.05	46.20	45.46	44.81	44.23	43.71
6000	58.92	57.61	56.45	55.44	54.56	53.77	53.07	52.46
7000	68.74	67.21	65.86	64.68	63.65	62.73	61.92	61.20
8000	78.56	76.81	75.27	73.92	72.74	71.69	70.76	69.94
9000	88.38	86.41	84.68	83.16	81.83	80.65	79.61	78.68
10000	98.20	96.01	94.09	92.40	90.92	89.61	88.45	87.42
11000	108.02	105.61	103.49	101.64	100.01	98.58	97.30	96.17
12000	117.84	115.21	112.90	110.88	109.11	107.54	106.14	104.91
13000	127.66	124.81	122.31	120.12	118.20	116.50	114.99	113.65
14000	137.48	134.41	131.72	129.36	127.29	125.46	123.83	122.39
15000	147.30	144.01	141.13	138.60	136.38	134.42	132.68	131.13
16000	157.12	153.61	150.53	147.84	145.47	143.38	141.52	139.88
17000	166.94	163.21	159.94	157.08	154.56	152.34	150.37	148.62
18000	176.76	172.81	169.35	166.32	163.66	161.30	159.21	157.36
19000	186.58	182.41	178.76	175.56	172.75	170.26	168.06	166.10
20000	196.40	192.01	188.17	184.80	181.84	179.22	176.90	174.84
21000	206.22	201.61	197.57	194.04	190.93	188.18	185.75	183.59
22000	216.04	211.21	206.98	203.28	200.02	197.15	194.59	192.33
23000	225.86	220.81	216.39	212.52	209.12	206.11	203.44	201.07
24000	235.68	230.41	225.80	221.76	218.21	215.07	212.28	209.81
25000	245.50	240.01	235.21	231.00	227.30	224.03	221.13	218.55
26000	255.32	249.61	244.62	240.24	236.39	232.99	229.97	227.30
27000	265.14	259.21	254.02	249.48	245.48	241.95	238.82	236.04
28000	274.96	268.81	263.43	258.72	254.57	250.91	247.66	244.78
29000	284.78	278.41	272.84	267.96	263.67	259.87	256.51	253.52
30000	294.60	288.01	282.25	277.20	272.76	268.83	265.35	262.26
31000	304.42	297.61	291.66	286.44	281.85	277.79	274.20	271.01
32000	314.24	307.21	301.06	295.68	290.94	286.75	283.04	279.75
33000	324.06	316.81	310.47	304.92	300.03	295.72	291.89	288.49
34000	333.88	326.41	319.88	314.16	309.12	304.68	300.73	297.23
35000	343.70	336.01	329.29	323.40	318.22	313.64	309.58	305.97
40000	392.80	384.01	376.33	369.60	363.67	358.44	353.80	349.68
45000	441.90	432.01	423.37	415.80	409.13	403.25	398.03	393.39
50000	491.00	480.01	470.41	462.00	454.59	448.05	442.25	437.10
55000	540.10	528.01	517.45	508.20	500.05	492.86	486.48	480.81
60000	589.20	576.01	564.49	554.40	545.51	537.66	530.70	524.52
65000	638.30	624.01	611.53	600.59	590.97	582.46	574.93	568.23
70000	687.40	672.01	658.57	646.79	636.43	627.27	619.15	611.94
75000	736.50	720.01	705.61	692.99	681.89	672.07	663.38	655.65
80000	785.60	768.01	752.65	739.19	727.34	716.88	707.60	699.36
85000	834.70	816.01	799.69	785.39	772.80	761.68	751.83	743.07
90000	883.80	864.01	846.73	831.59	818.26	806.49	796.05	786.78
95000	932.90	912.01	893.77	877.79	863.72	851.29	840.28	830.49
100000	982.00	960.01	940.81	923.99	909.18	896.10	884.50	874.20
105000	1031.10	1008.01	987.85	970.19	954.64	940.90	928.73	917.91
110000	1080.20	1056.01	1034.89	1016.39	1000.10	985.71	972.95	961.62
115000	1129.30	1104.01	1081.93	1062.59	1045.56	1030.51	1017.18	1005.33
120000	1178.40	1152.01	1128.98	1108.79	1091.01	1075.32	1061.40	1049.04
125000	1227.50	1200.01	1176.02	1154.98	1136.47	1120.12	1105.63	1092.75
130000	1276.60	1248.01	1223.06	1201.18	1181.93	1164.92	1149.85	1136.46
135000	1325.70	1296.01	1270.10	1247.38	1227.39	1209.73	1194.08	1180.17
140000	1374.80	1344.01	1317.14	1293.58	1272.85	1254.53	1238.30	1223.88
145000	1423.90	1392.01	1364.18	1339.78	1318.31	1299.34	1282.53	1267.59
150000	1473.00	1440.01	1411.22	1385.98	1363.77	1344.14	1326.75	1311.30
155000	1522.09	1488.01	1458.26	1432.18	1409.22	1388.95	1370.98	1355.01
160000	1571.19	1536.01	1505.30	1478.38	1454.68	1433.75	1415.20	1398.72

AMOUNT OF LOAN	25	26	27	28	29	30	35	40
	NUMBER OF YEARS IN TERM							
$ 50	.44	.43	.43	.43	.42	.42	.41	.41
100	.87	.86	.85	.85	.84	.84	.82	.81
200	1.74	1.72	1.70	1.69	1.68	1.67	1.63	1.61
300	2.60	2.58	2.55	2.53	2.52	2.50	2.44	2.41
400	3.47	3.43	3.40	3.38	3.35	3.33	3.25	3.21
500	4.33	4.29	4.25	4.22	4.19	4.16	4.07	4.01
600	5.20	5.15	5.10	5.06	5.03	5.00	4.88	4.81
700	6.06	6.00	5.95	5.91	5.86	5.83	5.69	5.61
800	6.93	6.86	6.80	6.75	6.70	6.66	6.50	6.41
900	7.79	7.72	7.65	7.59	7.54	7.49	7.31	7.21
1000	8.66	8.57	8.50	8.43	8.38	8.32	8.13	8.01
2000	17.31	17.14	17.00	16.86	16.75	16.64	16.25	16.01
3000	25.96	25.71	25.49	25.29	25.12	24.96	24.37	24.02
4000	34.61	34.28	33.99	33.72	33.49	33.27	32.49	32.02
5000	43.26	42.85	42.48	42.15	41.86	41.59	40.61	40.02
6000	51.91	51.41	50.98	50.58	50.23	49.91	48.73	48.03
7000	60.56	59.98	59.47	59.01	58.60	58.23	56.86	56.03
8000	69.21	68.55	67.97	67.44	66.97	66.54	64.98	64.03
9000	77.86	77.12	76.46	75.87	75.34	74.86	73.10	72.04
10000	86.51	85.69	84.96	84.30	83.71	83.18	81.22	80.04
11000	95.16	94.26	93.45	92.73	92.08	91.50	89.34	88.04
12000	103.81	102.82	101.95	101.16	100.45	99.81	97.46	96.05
13000	112.46	111.39	110.44	109.59	108.82	108.13	105.59	104.05
14000	121.11	119.96	118.94	118.02	117.19	116.45	113.71	112.05
15000	129.76	128.53	127.43	126.45	125.56	124.77	121.83	120.06
16000	138.41	137.10	135.93	134.88	133.93	133.08	129.95	128.06
17000	147.06	145.67	144.42	143.30	142.30	141.40	138.07	136.06
18000	155.71	154.23	152.92	151.73	150.67	149.72	146.19	144.07
19000	164.36	162.80	161.41	160.16	159.04	158.04	154.32	152.07
20000	173.01	171.37	169.91	168.59	167.41	166.35	162.44	160.07
21000	181.66	179.94	178.40	177.02	175.78	174.67	170.56	168.08
22000	190.31	188.51	186.90	185.45	184.16	182.99	178.68	176.08
23000	198.96	197.08	195.39	193.88	192.53	191.31	186.80	184.09
24000	207.61	205.64	203.89	202.31	200.90	199.62	194.92	192.09
25000	216.26	214.21	212.38	210.74	209.27	207.94	203.05	200.09
26000	224.91	222.78	220.88	219.17	217.64	216.26	211.17	208.10
27000	233.56	231.35	229.37	227.60	226.01	224.58	219.29	216.10
28000	242.21	239.92	237.87	236.03	234.38	232.89	227.41	224.10
29000	250.86	248.49	246.36	244.46	242.75	241.21	235.53	232.11
30000	259.51	257.05	254.86	252.89	251.12	249.53	243.65	240.11
31000	268.16	265.62	263.35	261.32	259.49	257.85	251.78	248.11
32000	276.81	274.19	271.85	269.75	267.86	266.16	259.90	256.12
33000	285.46	282.76	280.34	278.17	276.23	274.48	268.02	264.12
34000	294.11	291.33	288.84	286.60	284.60	282.80	276.14	272.12
35000	302.76	299.90	297.33	295.03	292.97	291.12	284.26	280.13
40000	346.01	342.74	339.81	337.18	334.82	332.70	324.87	320.14
45000	389.27	385.58	382.28	379.33	376.68	374.29	365.48	360.16
50000	432.52	428.42	424.76	421.47	418.53	415.88	406.09	400.18
55000	475.77	471.26	467.23	463.62	460.38	457.47	446.70	440.20
60000	519.02	514.10	509.71	505.77	502.23	499.05	487.30	480.21
65000	562.27	556.95	552.18	547.91	544.08	540.64	527.91	520.23
70000	605.52	599.79	594.66	590.06	585.94	582.23	568.52	560.25
75000	648.77	642.63	637.13	632.21	627.79	623.82	609.13	600.27
80000	692.02	685.47	679.61	674.36	669.64	665.40	649.74	640.28
85000	735.27	728.31	722.08	716.50	711.49	706.99	690.34	680.30
90000	778.53	771.15	764.56	758.65	753.35	748.58	730.95	720.32
95000	821.78	814.00	807.03	800.80	795.20	790.17	771.56	760.34
100000	865.03	856.84	849.51	842.94	837.05	831.75	812.17	800.35
105000	908.28	899.68	891.98	885.09	878.90	873.34	852.78	840.37
110000	951.53	942.52	934.46	927.24	920.76	914.93	893.39	880.39
115000	994.78	985.36	976.93	969.38	962.61	956.52	933.99	920.41
120000	1038.03	1028.20	1019.41	1011.53	1004.46	998.10	974.60	960.42
125000	1081.28	1071.04	1061.89	1053.68	1046.31	1039.69	1015.21	1000.44
130000	1124.54	1113.89	1104.36	1095.82	1088.16	1081.28	1055.82	1040.46
135000	1167.79	1156.73	1146.84	1137.97	1130.02	1122.87	1096.43	1080.48
140000	1211.04	1199.57	1189.31	1180.12	1171.87	1164.45	1137.03	1120.49
145000	1254.29	1242.41	1231.79	1222.27	1213.72	1206.04	1177.64	1160.51
150000	1297.54	1285.25	1274.26	1264.41	1255.57	1247.63	1218.25	1200.53
155000	1340.79	1328.09	1316.74	1306.56	1297.43	1289.22	1258.86	1240.55
160000	1384.04	1370.94	1359.21	1348.71	1339.28	1330.80	1299.47	1280.56

MONTHLY AMORTIZING PAYMENTS

AMOUNT OF LOAN	NUMBER OF YEARS IN TERM							
	1	1-1/2	2	3	4	5	6	7
$ 50	4.39	3.00	2.30	1.61	1.26	1.06	.92	.82
100	8.77	5.99	4.60	3.21	2.52	2.11	1.83	1.64
200	17.54	11.97	9.19	6.41	5.03	4.21	3.66	3.27
300	26.31	17.95	13.78	9.61	7.54	6.31	5.49	4.91
400	35.08	23.94	18.37	12.82	10.05	8.41	7.31	6.54
500	43.85	29.92	22.96	16.02	12.57	10.51	9.14	8.18
600	52.62	35.90	27.55	19.22	15.08	12.61	10.97	9.81
700	61.38	41.88	32.15	22.43	17.59	14.71	12.80	11.45
800	70.15	47.87	36.74	25.63	20.10	16.81	14.62	13.08
900	78.92	53.85	41.33	28.83	22.62	18.91	16.45	14.71
1000	87.69	59.83	45.92	32.04	25.13	21.01	18.28	16.35
2000	175.37	119.66	91.83	64.07	50.25	42.01	36.55	32.69
3000	263.06	179.49	137.75	96.10	75.37	63.01	54.83	49.04
4000	350.74	239.31	183.66	128.14	100.50	84.01	73.10	65.38
5000	438.42	299.14	229.58	160.17	125.62	105.01	91.38	81.72
6000	526.11	358.97	275.49	192.20	150.74	126.02	109.65	98.07
7000	613.79	418.79	321.41	224.24	175.87	147.02	127.93	114.41
8000	701.47	478.62	367.32	256.27	200.99	168.02	146.20	130.76
9000	789.16	538.45	413.24	288.30	226.11	189.02	164.48	147.10
10000	876.84	598.28	459.15	320.33	251.24	210.02	182.75	163.44
11000	964.52	658.10	505.06	352.37	276.36	231.03	201.03	179.79
12000	1052.21	717.93	550.98	384.40	301.48	252.03	219.30	196.13
13000	1139.89	777.76	596.89	416.43	326.61	273.03	237.58	212.48
14000	1227.57	837.58	642.81	448.47	351.73	294.03	255.85	228.82
15000	1315.26	897.41	688.72	480.50	376.85	315.03	274.13	245.16
16000	1402.94	957.24	734.64	512.53	401.98	336.03	292.40	261.51
17000	1490.62	1017.07	780.55	544.57	427.10	357.04	310.67	277.85
18000	1578.31	1076.89	826.47	576.60	452.22	378.04	328.95	294.20
19000	1665.99	1136.72	872.38	608.63	477.34	399.04	347.22	310.54
20000	1753.68	1196.55	918.29	640.66	502.47	420.04	365.50	326.88
21000	1841.36	1256.37	964.21	672.70	527.59	441.04	383.77	343.23
22000	1929.04	1316.20	1010.12	704.73	552.71	462.05	402.05	359.57
23000	2016.73	1376.03	1056.04	736.76	577.84	483.05	420.32	375.92
24000	2104.41	1435.86	1101.95	768.80	602.96	504.05	438.60	392.26
25000	2192.09	1495.68	1147.87	800.83	628.08	525.05	456.87	408.60
26000	2279.78	1555.51	1193.78	832.86	653.21	546.05	475.15	424.95
27000	2367.46	1615.34	1239.70	864.89	678.33	567.06	493.42	441.29
28000	2455.14	1675.16	1285.61	896.93	703.45	588.06	511.70	457.64
29000	2542.83	1734.99	1331.53	928.96	728.58	609.06	529.97	473.98
30000	2630.51	1794.82	1377.44	960.99	753.70	630.06	548.25	490.32
31000	2718.19	1854.65	1423.35	993.03	778.82	651.06	566.52	506.67
32000	2805.88	1914.47	1469.27	1025.06	803.95	672.06	584.80	523.01
33000	2893.56	1974.30	1515.18	1057.09	829.07	693.07	603.07	539.36
34000	2981.24	2034.13	1561.10	1089.13	854.19	714.07	621.34	555.70
35000	3068.93	2093.95	1607.01	1121.16	879.31	735.07	639.62	572.04
40000	3507.35	2393.09	1836.58	1281.32	1004.93	840.08	730.99	653.76
45000	3945.76	2692.23	2066.16	1441.49	1130.55	945.09	822.37	735.48
50000	4384.18	2991.36	2295.73	1601.65	1256.16	1050.10	913.74	817.20
55000	4822.60	3290.50	2525.30	1761.82	1381.78	1155.11	1005.11	898.92
60000	5261.02	3589.63	2754.87	1921.98	1507.39	1260.12	1096.49	980.64
65000	5699.43	3888.77	2984.45	2082.15	1633.01	1365.13	1187.86	1062.36
70000	6137.85	4187.90	3214.02	2242.31	1758.62	1470.14	1279.23	1144.08
75000	6576.27	4487.04	3443.59	2402.48	1884.24	1575.14	1370.61	1225.80
80000	7014.69	4786.17	3673.16	2562.64	2009.86	1680.15	1461.98	1307.52
85000	7453.10	5085.31	3902.74	2722.81	2135.47	1785.16	1553.35	1389.24
90000	7891.52	5384.45	4132.31	2882.97	2261.09	1890.17	1644.73	1470.96
95000	8329.94	5683.58	4361.88	3043.14	2386.70	1995.18	1736.10	1552.68
100000	8768.36	5982.72	4591.45	3203.30	2512.32	2100.19	1827.47	1634.40
105000	9206.77	6281.85	4821.03	3363.46	2637.93	2205.20	1918.85	1716.12
110000	9645.19	6580.99	5050.60	3523.63	2763.55	2310.21	2010.22	1797.84
115000	10083.61	6880.12	5280.17	3683.79	2889.17	2415.22	2101.59	1879.56
120000	10522.03	7179.26	5509.74	3843.96	3014.78	2520.23	2192.97	1961.28
125000	10960.44	7478.39	5739.32	4004.12	3140.40	2625.24	2284.34	2043.00
130000	11398.86	7777.53	5968.89	4164.29	3266.01	2730.25	2375.71	2124.72
135000	11837.28	8076.67	6198.46	4324.45	3391.63	2835.26	2467.09	2206.44
140000	12275.70	8375.80	6428.03	4484.62	3517.24	2940.27	2558.46	2288.16
145000	12714.11	8674.94	6657.61	4644.78	3642.86	3045.27	2649.84	2369.88
150000	13152.53	8974.07	6887.18	4804.95	3768.48	3150.28	2741.21	2451.60
155000	13590.95	9273.21	7116.75	4965.11	3894.09	3255.29	2832.58	2533.32
160000	14029.37	9572.34	7346.32	5125.28	4019.71	3360.30	2923.96	2615.04

AMOUNT OF LOAN	NUMBER OF YEARS IN TERM 8	9	10	11	12	14	15	16
$ 50	.75	.70	.65	.62	.59	.54	.53	.51
100	1.50	1.39	1.30	1.23	1.17	1.08	1.05	1.02
200	2.99	2.77	2.59	2.45	2.34	2.16	2.09	2.03
300	4.48	4.15	3.89	3.68	3.50	3.24	3.14	3.05
400	5.97	5.53	5.18	4.90	4.67	4.32	4.18	4.06
500	7.46	6.91	6.47	6.12	5.84	5.40	5.23	5.08
600	8.95	8.29	7.77	7.35	7.00	6.48	6.27	6.09
700	10.44	9.67	9.06	8.57	8.17	7.55	7.31	7.11
800	11.93	11.05	10.36	9.80	9.34	8.63	8.36	8.12
900	13.42	12.43	11.65	11.02	10.50	9.71	9.40	9.14
1000	14.92	13.81	12.94	12.24	11.67	10.79	10.45	10.15
2000	29.83	27.62	25.88	24.48	23.33	21.57	20.89	20.30
3000	44.74	41.43	38.82	36.72	35.00	32.36	31.33	30.45
4000	59.65	55.24	51.76	48.96	46.66	43.14	41.77	40.60
5000	74.56	69.05	64.70	61.20	58.32	53.92	52.22	50.75
6000	89.47	82.86	77.64	73.44	69.99	64.71	62.66	60.90
7000	104.38	96.67	90.58	85.68	81.65	75.49	73.10	71.05
8000	119.29	110.48	103.52	97.91	93.31	86.27	83.54	81.20
9000	134.20	124.29	116.46	110.15	104.98	97.06	93.99	91.35
10000	149.11	138.10	129.40	122.39	116.64	107.84	104.43	101.50
11000	164.02	151.91	142.34	134.63	128.31	118.63	114.87	111.65
12000	178.94	165.72	155.28	146.87	139.97	129.41	125.31	121.80
13000	193.85	179.53	168.22	159.11	151.63	140.19	135.75	131.95
14000	208.76	193.34	181.16	171.35	163.30	150.98	146.20	142.10
15000	223.67	207.15	194.10	183.58	174.96	161.76	156.64	152.25
16000	238.58	220.95	207.04	195.82	186.62	172.54	167.08	162.40
17000	253.49	234.76	219.98	208.06	198.29	183.33	177.52	172.55
18000	268.40	248.57	232.92	220.30	209.95	194.11	187.97	182.70
19000	283.31	262.38	245.86	232.54	221.62	204.89	198.41	192.85
20000	298.22	276.19	258.80	244.78	233.28	215.68	208.85	203.00
21000	313.13	290.00	271.74	257.02	244.94	226.46	219.29	213.15
22000	328.04	303.81	284.68	269.26	256.61	237.25	229.73	223.30
23000	342.96	317.62	297.62	281.49	268.27	248.03	240.18	233.45
24000	357.87	331.43	310.56	293.73	279.93	258.81	250.62	243.60
25000	372.78	345.24	323.50	305.97	291.60	269.60	261.06	253.75
26000	387.69	359.05	336.44	318.21	303.26	280.38	271.50	263.90
27000	402.60	372.86	349.38	330.45	314.93	291.16	281.95	274.05
28000	417.51	386.67	362.32	342.69	326.59	301.95	292.39	284.20
29000	432.42	400.48	375.26	354.93	338.25	312.73	302.83	294.35
30000	447.33	414.29	388.20	367.16	349.92	323.52	313.27	304.50
31000	462.24	428.10	401.14	379.40	361.58	334.30	323.71	314.65
32000	477.15	441.90	414.08	391.64	373.24	345.08	334.16	324.80
33000	492.06	455.71	427.02	403.88	384.91	355.87	344.60	334.95
34000	506.98	469.52	439.96	416.12	396.57	366.65	355.04	345.10
35000	521.89	483.33	452.90	428.36	408.24	377.43	365.48	355.25
40000	596.44	552.38	517.60	489.55	466.55	431.35	417.69	406.00
45000	670.99	621.43	582.29	550.74	524.87	485.27	469.91	456.75
50000	745.55	690.47	646.99	611.94	583.19	539.19	522.12	507.50
55000	820.10	759.52	711.69	673.13	641.51	593.11	574.33	558.25
60000	894.66	828.57	776.39	734.32	699.83	647.03	626.54	609.00
65000	969.21	897.61	841.09	795.52	758.15	700.94	678.75	659.75
70000	1043.77	966.66	905.79	856.71	816.47	754.86	730.96	710.50
75000	1118.32	1035.71	970.49	917.90	874.78	808.78	783.17	761.25
80000	1192.88	1104.75	1035.19	979.10	933.10	862.70	835.38	812.00
85000	1267.43	1173.80	1099.88	1040.29	991.42	916.62	887.60	862.75
90000	1341.98	1242.85	1164.58	1101.48	1049.74	970.54	939.81	913.50
95000	1416.54	1311.89	1229.28	1162.68	1108.06	1024.45	992.02	964.25
100000	1491.09	1380.94	1293.98	1223.87	1166.38	1078.37	1044.23	1014.99
105000	1565.65	1449.99	1358.68	1285.06	1224.70	1132.29	1096.44	1065.74
110000	1640.20	1519.03	1423.38	1346.26	1283.02	1186.21	1148.65	1116.49
115000	1714.76	1588.08	1488.08	1407.45	1341.33	1240.13	1200.86	1167.24
120000	1789.31	1657.13	1552.78	1468.64	1399.65	1294.05	1253.07	1217.99
125000	1863.87	1726.18	1617.47	1529.84	1457.97	1347.97	1305.29	1268.74
130000	1938.42	1795.22	1682.17	1591.03	1516.29	1401.88	1357.50	1319.49
135000	2012.97	1864.27	1746.87	1652.22	1574.61	1455.80	1409.71	1370.24
140000	2087.53	1933.32	1811.57	1713.42	1632.93	1509.72	1461.92	1420.99
145000	2162.08	2002.36	1876.27	1774.61	1691.25	1563.64	1514.13	1471.74
150000	2236.64	2071.41	1940.97	1835.80	1749.56	1617.56	1566.34	1522.49
155000	2311.19	2140.46	2005.67	1897.00	1807.88	1671.48	1618.55	1573.24
160000	2385.75	2209.50	2070.37	1958.19	1866.20	1725.39	1670.76	1623.99

MONTHLY AMORTIZING PAYMENTS

AMOUNT OF LOAN	NUMBER OF YEARS IN TERM							
	17	18	19	20	21	22	23	24
$ 50	.50	.49	.48	.47	.46	.46	.45	.45
100	.99	.97	.95	.94	.92	.91	.90	.89
200	1.98	1.94	1.90	1.87	1.84	1.81	1.79	1.77
300	2.97	2.91	2.85	2.80	2.76	2.72	2.68	2.65
400	3.96	3.88	3.80	3.73	3.67	3.62	3.58	3.54
500	4.95	4.84	4.75	4.67	4.59	4.53	4.47	4.42
600	5.94	5.81	5.70	5.60	5.51	5.43	5.36	5.30
700	6.93	6.78	6.65	6.53	6.43	6.34	6.26	6.18
800	7.92	7.75	7.60	7.46	7.34	7.24	7.15	7.07
900	8.91	8.72	8.54	8.39	8.26	8.15	8.04	7.95
1000	9.90	9.68	9.49	9.33	9.18	9.05	8.93	8.83
2000	19.80	19.36	18.98	18.65	18.35	18.09	17.86	17.66
3000	29.70	29.04	28.47	27.97	27.53	27.14	26.79	26.49
4000	39.60	38.72	37.96	37.29	36.70	36.18	35.72	35.32
5000	49.49	48.40	47.45	46.61	45.88	45.23	44.65	44.14
6000	59.39	58.08	56.94	55.93	55.05	54.27	53.58	52.97
7000	69.29	67.76	66.42	65.25	64.23	63.32	62.51	61.80
8000	79.19	77.44	75.91	74.58	73.40	72.36	71.44	70.63
9000	89.09	87.12	85.40	83.90	82.57	81.41	80.37	79.45
10000	98.98	96.80	94.89	93.22	91.75	90.45	89.30	88.28
11000	108.88	106.48	104.38	102.54	100.92	99.50	98.23	97.11
12000	118.78	116.15	113.87	111.86	110.10	108.54	107.16	105.94
13000	128.68	125.83	123.35	121.18	119.27	117.58	116.09	114.77
14000	138.57	135.51	132.84	130.50	128.45	126.63	125.02	123.59
15000	148.47	145.19	142.33	139.82	137.62	135.67	133.95	132.42
16000	158.37	154.87	151.82	149.15	146.79	144.72	142.88	141.25
17000	168.27	164.55	161.31	158.47	155.97	153.76	151.81	150.08
18000	178.17	174.23	170.80	167.79	165.14	162.81	160.74	158.90
19000	188.06	183.91	180.28	177.11	174.32	171.85	169.67	167.73
20000	197.96	193.59	189.77	186.43	183.49	180.90	178.60	176.56
21000	207.86	203.27	199.26	195.75	192.67	189.94	187.53	185.39
22000	217.76	212.95	208.75	205.07	201.84	198.99	196.46	194.22
23000	227.65	222.62	218.24	214.40	211.01	208.03	205.39	203.04
24000	237.55	232.30	227.73	223.72	220.19	217.08	214.32	211.87
25000	247.45	241.98	237.21	233.04	229.36	226.12	223.25	220.70
26000	257.35	251.66	246.70	242.36	238.54	235.16	232.18	229.53
27000	267.25	261.34	256.19	251.68	247.71	244.21	241.11	238.35
28000	277.14	271.02	265.68	261.00	256.89	253.25	250.04	247.18
29000	287.04	280.70	275.17	270.32	266.06	262.30	258.97	256.01
30000	296.94	290.38	284.66	279.64	275.24	271.34	267.90	264.84
31000	306.84	300.06	294.15	288.97	284.41	280.39	276.83	273.67
32000	316.73	309.74	303.63	298.29	293.58	289.43	285.76	282.49
33000	326.63	319.42	313.12	307.61	302.76	298.48	294.69	291.32
34000	336.53	329.09	322.61	316.93	311.93	307.52	303.62	300.15
35000	346.43	338.77	332.10	326.25	321.11	316.57	312.55	308.98
40000	395.92	387.17	379.54	372.86	366.98	361.79	357.19	353.11
45000	445.41	435.57	426.98	419.46	412.85	407.01	401.84	397.25
50000	494.90	483.96	474.42	466.07	458.72	452.24	446.49	441.39
55000	544.38	532.36	521.87	512.68	504.59	497.46	491.14	485.53
60000	593.87	580.75	569.31	559.28	550.47	542.68	535.79	529.67
65000	643.36	629.15	616.75	605.89	596.34	587.90	580.44	573.81
70000	692.85	677.54	664.19	652.50	642.21	633.13	625.09	617.95
75000	742.34	725.94	711.63	699.10	688.08	678.35	669.74	662.09
80000	791.83	774.33	759.08	745.71	733.95	723.57	714.38	706.22
85000	841.32	822.73	806.52	792.32	779.82	768.80	759.03	750.36
90000	890.81	871.13	853.96	838.92	825.70	814.02	803.68	794.50
95000	940.30	919.52	901.40	885.53	871.57	859.24	848.33	838.64
100000	989.79	967.92	948.84	932.14	917.44	904.47	892.98	882.78
105000	1039.27	1016.31	996.29	978.74	963.31	949.69	937.63	926.92
110000	1088.76	1064.71	1043.73	1025.35	1009.18	994.91	982.28	971.06
115000	1138.25	1113.10	1091.17	1071.96	1055.05	1040.14	1026.93	1015.20
120000	1187.74	1161.50	1138.61	1118.56	1100.93	1085.36	1071.57	1059.33
125000	1237.23	1209.89	1186.05	1165.17	1146.80	1130.58	1116.22	1103.47
130000	1286.72	1258.29	1233.50	1211.78	1192.67	1175.80	1160.87	1147.61
135000	1336.21	1306.69	1280.94	1258.38	1238.54	1221.03	1205.52	1191.75
140000	1385.70	1355.08	1328.38	1304.99	1284.41	1266.25	1250.17	1235.89
145000	1435.19	1403.48	1375.82	1351.60	1330.28	1311.47	1294.82	1280.03
150000	1484.68	1451.87	1423.26	1398.20	1376.16	1356.70	1339.47	1324.17
155000	1534.16	1500.27	1470.71	1444.81	1422.03	1401.92	1384.12	1368.31
160000	1583.65	1548.66	1518.15	1491.41	1467.90	1447.14	1428.76	1412.44

AMOUNT OF LOAN	NUMBER OF YEARS IN TERM 25	26	27	28	29	30	35	40
$ 50	.44	.44	.43	.43	.43	.43	.42	.41
100	.88	.87	.86	.86	.85	.85	.83	.82
200	1.75	1.74	1.72	1.71	1.70	1.69	1.65	1.63
300	2.63	2.60	2.58	2.56	2.54	2.53	2.47	2.44
400	3.50	3.47	3.44	3.41	3.39	3.37	3.29	3.25
500	4.37	4.33	4.30	4.26	4.24	4.21	4.11	4.06
600	5.25	5.20	5.16	5.12	5.08	5.05	4.93	4.87
700	6.12	6.06	6.01	5.97	5.93	5.89	5.76	5.68
800	6.99	6.93	6.87	6.82	6.77	6.73	6.58	6.49
900	7.87	7.80	7.73	7.67	7.62	7.57	7.40	7.30
1000	8.74	8.66	8.59	8.52	8.47	8.41	8.22	8.11
2000	17.48	17.32	17.17	17.04	16.93	16.82	16.44	16.21
3000	26.22	25.97	25.76	25.56	25.39	25.23	24.65	24.31
4000	34.95	34.63	34.34	34.08	33.85	33.64	32.87	32.41
5000	43.69	43.28	42.92	42.60	42.31	42.05	41.09	40.51
6000	52.43	51.94	51.51	51.12	50.77	50.46	49.30	48.61
7000	61.16	60.60	60.09	59.64	59.23	58.86	57.52	56.71
8000	69.90	69.25	68.67	68.16	67.69	67.27	65.73	64.81
9000	78.64	77.91	77.26	76.67	76.15	75.68	73.95	72.91
10000	87.37	86.56	85.84	85.19	84.61	84.09	82.17	81.01
11000	96.11	95.22	94.42	93.71	93.07	92.50	90.38	89.11
12000	104.85	103.88	103.01	102.23	101.53	100.91	98.60	97.21
13000	113.59	112.53	111.59	110.75	109.99	109.32	106.81	105.31
14000	122.32	121.19	120.18	119.27	118.45	117.72	115.03	113.41
15000	131.06	129.84	128.76	127.79	126.92	126.13	123.25	121.51
16000	139.80	138.50	137.34	136.31	135.38	134.54	131.46	129.61
17000	148.53	147.16	145.93	144.82	143.84	142.95	139.68	137.72
18000	157.27	155.81	154.51	153.34	152.30	151.36	147.90	145.82
19000	166.01	164.47	163.09	161.86	160.76	159.77	156.11	153.92
20000	174.74	173.12	171.68	170.38	169.22	168.18	164.33	162.02
21000	183.48	181.78	180.26	178.90	177.68	176.58	172.54	170.12
22000	192.22	190.44	188.84	187.42	186.14	184.99	180.76	178.22
23000	200.96	199.09	197.43	195.94	194.60	193.40	188.98	186.32
24000	209.69	207.75	206.01	204.46	203.06	201.81	197.19	194.42
25000	218.43	216.40	214.60	212.98	211.52	210.22	205.41	202.52
26000	227.17	225.06	223.18	221.49	219.98	218.63	213.62	210.62
27000	235.90	233.72	231.76	230.01	228.44	227.04	221.84	218.72
28000	244.64	242.37	240.35	238.53	236.91	235.44	230.06	226.82
29000	253.38	251.03	248.93	247.05	245.37	243.85	238.27	234.92
30000	262.11	259.68	257.51	255.57	253.83	252.26	246.49	243.02
31000	270.85	268.34	266.10	264.09	262.29	260.67	254.70	251.12
32000	279.59	277.00	274.68	272.61	270.75	269.08	262.92	259.22
33000	288.32	285.65	283.26	281.13	279.21	277.49	271.14	267.33
34000	297.06	294.31	291.85	289.64	287.67	285.90	279.35	275.43
35000	305.80	302.96	300.43	298.16	296.13	294.30	287.57	283.53
40000	349.48	346.24	343.35	340.76	338.43	336.35	328.65	324.03
45000	393.17	389.52	386.27	383.35	380.74	378.39	369.73	364.53
50000	436.85	432.80	429.19	425.95	423.04	420.43	410.81	405.04
55000	480.54	476.08	472.10	468.54	465.34	462.47	451.89	445.54
60000	524.22	519.36	515.02	511.13	507.65	504.52	492.97	486.04
65000	567.91	562.64	557.94	553.73	549.95	546.56	534.05	526.55
70000	611.59	605.92	600.86	596.32	592.26	588.60	575.13	567.05
75000	655.28	649.20	643.78	638.92	634.56	630.65	616.21	607.55
80000	698.96	692.48	686.69	681.51	676.86	672.69	657.29	648.05
85000	742.65	735.76	729.61	724.10	719.17	714.73	698.37	688.56
90000	786.33	779.04	772.53	766.70	761.47	756.77	739.46	729.06
95000	830.02	822.32	815.45	809.29	803.77	798.82	780.54	769.56
100000	873.70	865.60	858.37	851.89	846.08	840.86	821.62	810.07
105000	917.39	908.88	901.28	894.48	888.38	882.90	862.70	850.57
110000	961.07	952.16	944.20	937.07	930.68	924.94	903.78	891.07
115000	1004.76	995.44	987.12	979.67	972.99	966.99	944.86	931.58
120000	1048.44	1038.72	1030.04	1022.26	1015.29	1009.03	985.94	972.08
125000	1092.13	1082.00	1072.96	1064.86	1057.59	1051.07	1027.02	1012.58
130000	1135.81	1125.28	1115.87	1107.45	1099.90	1093.12	1068.10	1053.09
135000	1179.50	1168.56	1158.79	1150.05	1142.20	1135.16	1109.18	1093.59
140000	1223.18	1211.84	1201.71	1192.64	1184.51	1177.20	1150.26	1134.09
145000	1266.87	1255.12	1244.63	1235.23	1226.81	1219.24	1191.34	1174.59
150000	1310.55	1298.40	1287.55	1277.83	1269.11	1261.29	1232.42	1215.10
155000	1354.23	1341.68	1330.47	1320.42	1311.42	1303.33	1273.50	1255.60
160000	1397.92	1384.96	1373.38	1363.02	1353.72	1345.37	1314.58	1296.10

9⅝% MONTHLY AMORTIZING PAYMENTS

AMOUNT OF LOAN	NUMBER OF YEARS IN TERM							
	1	1-1/2	2	3	4	5	6	7
$ 50	4.39	3.00	2.30	1.61	1.26	1.06	.92	.83
100	8.78	5.99	4.60	3.21	2.52	2.11	1.84	1.65
200	17.55	11.98	9.20	6.42	5.04	4.22	3.67	3.29
300	26.33	17.97	13.80	9.63	7.56	6.32	5.51	4.93
400	35.10	23.96	18.39	12.84	10.08	8.43	7.34	6.57
500	43.88	29.95	22.99	16.05	12.60	10.54	9.17	8.21
600	52.65	35.94	27.59	19.26	15.11	12.64	11.01	9.85
700	61.42	41.92	32.19	22.47	17.63	14.75	12.84	11.49
800	70.20	47.91	36.78	25.68	20.15	16.86	14.67	13.13
900	78.97	53.90	41.38	28.89	22.67	18.96	16.51	14.77
1000	87.75	59.89	45.98	32.10	25.19	21.07	18.34	16.41
2000	175.49	119.77	91.95	64.19	50.37	42.13	36.68	32.82
3000	263.23	179.66	137.92	96.28	75.55	63.19	55.02	49.23
4000	350.97	239.54	183.89	128.37	100.74	84.26	73.35	65.64
5000	438.71	299.43	229.87	160.46	125.92	105.32	91.69	82.05
6000	526.45	359.31	275.84	192.55	151.10	126.38	110.03	98.45
7000	614.20	419.20	321.81	224.64	176.29	147.45	128.37	114.86
8000	701.94	479.08	367.78	256.74	201.47	168.51	146.70	131.27
9000	789.68	538.97	413.75	288.83	226.65	189.57	165.04	147.68
10000	877.42	598.85	459.73	320.92	251.83	210.64	183.38	164.09
11000	965.16	658.74	505.70	353.01	277.02	231.70	201.72	180.49
12000	1052.90	718.62	551.67	385.10	302.20	252.76	220.05	196.90
13000	1140.65	778.50	597.64	417.19	327.38	273.82	238.39	213.31
14000	1228.39	838.39	643.61	449.28	352.57	294.89	256.73	229.72
15000	1316.13	898.27	689.59	481.38	377.75	315.95	275.06	246.13
16000	1403.87	958.16	735.56	513.47	402.93	337.01	293.40	262.53
17000	1491.61	1018.04	781.53	545.56	428.11	358.08	311.74	278.94
18000	1579.35	1077.93	827.50	577.65	453.30	379.14	330.08	295.35
19000	1667.09	1137.81	873.47	609.74	478.48	400.20	348.41	311.76
20000	1754.84	1197.70	919.45	641.83	503.66	421.27	366.75	328.17
21000	1842.58	1257.58	965.42	673.92	528.85	442.33	385.09	344.57
22000	1930.32	1317.47	1011.39	706.02	554.03	463.39	403.43	360.98
23000	2018.06	1377.35	1057.36	738.11	579.21	484.45	421.76	377.39
24000	2105.80	1437.23	1103.33	770.20	604.39	505.52	440.10	393.80
25000	2193.54	1497.12	1149.31	802.29	629.58	526.58	458.44	410.21
26000	2281.29	1557.00	1195.28	834.38	654.76	547.64	476.77	426.61
27000	2369.03	1616.89	1241.25	866.47	679.94	568.71	495.11	443.02
28000	2456.77	1676.77	1287.22	898.56	705.13	589.77	513.45	459.43
29000	2544.51	1736.66	1333.19	930.66	730.31	610.83	531.79	475.84
30000	2632.25	1796.54	1379.17	962.75	755.49	631.90	550.12	492.25
31000	2719.99	1856.43	1425.14	994.84	780.67	652.96	568.46	508.66
32000	2807.74	1916.31	1471.11	1026.93	805.86	674.02	586.80	525.06
33000	2895.48	1976.20	1517.08	1059.02	831.04	695.08	605.14	541.47
34000	2983.22	2036.08	1563.05	1091.11	856.22	716.15	623.47	557.88
35000	3070.96	2095.96	1609.03	1123.20	881.41	737.21	641.81	574.29
40000	3509.67	2395.39	1838.89	1283.66	1007.32	842.53	733.50	656.33
45000	3948.38	2694.81	2068.75	1444.12	1133.23	947.84	825.18	738.37
50000	4387.08	2994.23	2298.61	1604.58	1259.15	1053.16	916.87	820.41
55000	4825.79	3293.66	2528.47	1765.03	1385.06	1158.47	1008.56	902.45
60000	5264.50	3593.08	2758.33	1925.49	1510.98	1263.79	1100.24	984.49
65000	5703.21	3892.50	2988.19	2085.95	1636.89	1369.10	1191.93	1066.53
70000	6141.92	4191.92	3218.05	2246.40	1762.81	1474.42	1283.62	1148.57
75000	6580.62	4491.35	3447.91	2406.86	1888.72	1579.73	1375.30	1230.61
80000	7019.33	4790.77	3677.77	2567.32	2014.63	1685.05	1466.99	1312.65
85000	7458.04	5090.19	3907.63	2727.78	2140.55	1790.36	1558.67	1394.69
90000	7896.75	5389.62	4137.49	2888.23	2266.46	1895.68	1650.36	1476.73
95000	8335.45	5689.04	4367.35	3048.69	2392.38	2000.99	1742.05	1558.77
100000	8774.16	5988.46	4597.21	3209.15	2518.29	2106.31	1833.73	1640.81
105000	9212.87	6287.88	4827.07	3369.60	2644.21	2211.62	1925.42	1722.85
110000	9651.58	6587.31	5056.93	3530.06	2770.12	2316.94	2017.11	1804.89
115000	10090.29	6886.73	5286.79	3690.52	2896.04	2422.25	2108.79	1886.93
120000	10528.99	7186.15	5516.65	3850.97	3021.95	2527.57	2200.48	1968.97
125000	10967.70	7485.57	5746.51	4011.43	3147.86	2632.88	2292.17	2051.01
130000	11406.41	7785.00	5976.37	4171.89	3273.78	2738.20	2383.85	2133.05
135000	11845.12	8084.42	6206.23	4332.35	3399.69	2843.51	2475.54	2215.09
140000	12283.83	8383.84	6436.09	4492.80	3525.61	2948.83	2567.23	2297.13
145000	12722.53	8683.27	6665.95	4653.26	3651.52	3054.14	2658.91	2379.17
150000	13161.24	8982.69	6895.81	4813.72	3777.44	3159.46	2750.60	2461.22
155000	13599.95	9282.11	7125.67	4974.17	3903.35	3264.77	2842.29	2543.26
160000	14038.66	9581.53	7355.53	5134.63	4029.26	3370.09	2933.97	2625.30

MONTHLY AMORTIZING PAYMENTS 9⅝%

AMOUNT OF LOAN	NUMBER OF YEARS IN TERM							
	8	9	10	11	12	14	15	16
$ 50	.75	.70	.66	.62	.59	.55	.53	.52
100	1.50	1.39	1.31	1.24	1.18	1.09	1.06	1.03
200	3.00	2.78	2.61	2.47	2.35	2.18	2.11	2.05
300	4.50	4.17	3.91	3.70	3.53	3.26	3.16	3.07
400	6.00	5.56	5.21	4.93	4.70	4.35	4.21	4.10
500	7.49	6.94	6.51	6.16	5.87	5.43	5.26	5.12
600	8.99	8.33	7.81	7.39	7.05	6.52	6.32	6.14
700	10.49	9.72	9.11	8.62	8.22	7.61	7.37	7.16
800	11.99	11.11	10.41	9.85	9.39	8.69	8.42	8.19
900	13.48	12.49	11.71	11.08	10.57	9.78	9.47	9.21
1000	14.98	13.88	13.01	12.31	11.74	10.86	10.52	10.23
2000	29.96	27.76	26.02	24.62	23.48	21.72	21.04	20.46
3000	44.93	41.63	39.03	36.93	35.21	32.58	31.56	30.69
4000	59.91	55.51	52.04	49.24	46.95	43.44	42.08	40.91
5000	74.89	69.39	65.05	61.55	58.68	54.29	52.59	51.14
6000	89.86	83.26	78.05	73.86	70.42	65.15	63.11	61.37
7000	104.84	97.14	91.06	86.17	82.15	76.01	73.63	71.59
8000	119.82	111.02	104.07	98.47	93.89	86.87	84.15	81.82
9000	134.79	124.89	117.08	110.78	105.62	97.73	94.67	92.05
10000	149.77	138.77	130.09	123.09	117.36	108.58	105.18	102.27
11000	164.75	152.65	143.10	135.40	129.09	119.44	115.70	112.50
12000	179.72	166.52	156.10	147.71	140.83	130.30	126.22	122.73
13000	194.70	180.40	169.11	160.02	152.56	141.16	136.74	132.95
14000	209.68	194.27	182.12	172.33	164.30	152.02	147.25	143.18
15000	224.65	208.15	195.13	184.63	176.03	162.87	157.77	153.41
16000	239.63	222.03	208.14	196.94	187.77	173.73	168.29	163.63
17000	254.60	235.90	221.15	209.25	199.50	184.59	178.81	173.86
18000	269.58	249.78	234.15	221.56	211.24	195.45	189.33	184.09
19000	284.56	263.66	247.16	233.87	222.97	206.30	199.84	194.31
20000	299.53	277.53	260.17	246.18	234.71	217.16	210.36	204.54
21000	314.51	291.41	273.18	258.49	246.44	228.02	220.88	214.77
22000	329.49	305.29	286.19	270.80	258.18	238.88	231.40	224.99
23000	344.46	319.16	299.20	283.10	269.91	249.74	241.91	235.22
24000	359.44	333.04	312.20	295.41	281.65	260.59	252.43	245.45
25000	374.42	346.92	325.21	307.72	293.38	271.45	262.95	255.67
26000	389.39	360.79	338.22	320.03	305.12	282.31	273.47	265.90
27000	404.37	374.67	351.23	332.34	316.85	293.17	283.99	276.13
28000	419.35	388.54	364.24	344.65	328.59	304.03	294.50	286.35
29000	434.32	402.42	377.25	356.96	340.32	314.88	305.02	296.58
30000	449.30	416.30	390.25	369.26	352.06	325.74	315.54	306.81
31000	464.28	430.17	403.26	381.57	363.79	336.60	326.06	317.03
32000	479.25	444.05	416.27	393.88	375.53	347.46	336.57	327.26
33000	494.23	457.93	429.28	406.19	387.27	358.32	347.09	337.49
34000	509.20	471.80	442.29	418.50	399.00	369.17	357.61	347.72
35000	524.18	485.68	455.30	430.81	410.74	380.03	368.13	357.94
40000	599.06	555.06	520.34	492.35	469.41	434.32	420.72	409.08
45000	673.95	624.44	585.38	553.89	528.09	488.61	473.31	460.21
50000	748.83	693.83	650.42	615.44	586.76	542.90	525.90	511.34
55000	823.71	763.21	715.46	676.98	645.44	597.19	578.48	562.48
60000	898.59	832.59	780.50	738.52	704.11	651.48	631.07	613.61
65000	973.48	901.97	845.54	800.07	762.79	705.77	683.66	664.75
70000	1048.36	971.35	910.59	861.61	821.47	760.06	736.25	715.88
75000	1123.24	1040.74	975.63	923.15	880.14	814.35	788.84	767.01
80000	1198.12	1110.12	1040.67	984.70	938.82	868.64	841.43	818.15
85000	1273.00	1179.50	1105.71	1046.24	997.49	922.93	894.02	869.28
90000	1347.89	1248.88	1170.75	1107.78	1056.17	977.22	946.61	920.41
95000	1422.77	1318.27	1235.79	1169.33	1114.84	1031.50	999.20	971.55
100000	1497.65	1387.65	1300.83	1230.87	1173.52	1085.79	1051.79	1022.68
105000	1572.53	1457.03	1365.88	1292.41	1232.20	1140.08	1104.37	1073.82
110000	1647.42	1526.41	1430.92	1353.96	1290.87	1194.37	1156.96	1124.95
115000	1722.30	1595.79	1495.96	1415.50	1349.55	1248.66	1209.55	1176.08
120000	1797.18	1665.18	1561.00	1477.04	1408.22	1302.95	1262.14	1227.22
125000	1872.06	1734.56	1626.04	1538.58	1466.90	1357.24	1314.73	1278.35
130000	1946.95	1803.94	1691.08	1600.13	1525.58	1411.53	1367.32	1329.49
135000	2021.83	1873.32	1756.12	1661.67	1584.25	1465.82	1419.91	1380.62
140000	2096.71	1942.70	1821.17	1723.21	1642.93	1520.11	1472.50	1431.75
145000	2171.59	2012.09	1886.21	1784.76	1701.60	1574.40	1525.09	1482.89
150000	2246.47	2081.47	1951.25	1846.30	1760.28	1628.69	1577.68	1534.02
155000	2321.36	2150.85	2016.29	1907.84	1818.95	1682.98	1630.26	1585.15
160000	2396.24	2220.23	2081.33	1969.39	1877.63	1737.27	1682.85	1636.29

MONTHLY AMORTIZING PAYMENTS

AMOUNT OF LOAN	NUMBER OF YEARS IN TERM							
	17	18	19	20	21	22	23	24
$ 50	.50	.49	.48	.48	.47	.46	.46	.45
100	1.00	.98	.96	.95	.93	.92	.91	.90
200	2.00	1.96	1.92	1.89	1.86	1.83	1.81	1.79
300	3.00	2.93	2.88	2.83	2.78	2.74	2.71	2.68
400	4.00	3.91	3.83	3.77	3.71	3.66	3.61	3.57
500	4.99	4.88	4.79	4.71	4.63	4.57	4.51	4.46
600	5.99	5.86	5.75	5.65	5.56	5.48	5.41	5.35
700	6.99	6.84	6.70	6.59	6.49	6.40	6.32	6.24
800	7.99	7.81	7.66	7.53	7.41	7.31	7.22	7.14
900	8.98	8.79	8.62	8.47	8.34	8.22	8.12	8.03
1000	9.98	9.76	9.57	9.41	9.26	9.13	9.02	8.92
2000	19.96	19.52	19.14	18.81	18.52	18.26	18.03	17.83
3000	29.93	29.28	28.71	28.21	27.78	27.39	27.05	26.75
4000	39.91	39.04	38.28	37.62	37.03	36.52	36.06	35.66
5000	49.88	48.80	47.85	47.02	46.29	45.65	45.08	44.57
6000	59.86	58.56	57.42	56.42	55.55	54.78	54.09	53.49
7000	69.84	68.31	66.99	65.83	64.81	63.91	63.11	62.40
8000	79.81	78.07	76.56	75.23	74.06	73.03	72.12	71.32
9000	89.79	87.83	86.13	84.63	83.32	82.16	81.14	80.23
10000	99.76	97.59	95.70	94.04	92.58	91.29	90.15	89.14
11000	109.74	107.35	105.26	103.44	101.83	100.42	99.17	98.06
12000	119.72	117.11	114.83	112.84	111.09	109.55	108.18	106.97
13000	129.69	126.87	124.40	122.25	120.35	118.68	117.20	115.88
14000	139.67	136.62	133.97	131.65	129.61	127.81	126.21	124.80
15000	149.64	146.38	143.54	141.05	138.86	136.93	135.23	133.71
16000	159.62	156.14	153.11	150.45	148.12	146.06	144.24	142.63
17000	169.60	165.90	162.68	159.86	157.38	155.19	153.26	151.54
18000	179.57	175.66	172.25	169.26	166.64	164.32	162.27	160.45
19000	189.55	185.42	181.82	178.66	175.89	173.45	171.29	169.37
20000	199.52	195.18	191.39	188.07	185.15	182.58	180.30	178.28
21000	209.50	204.93	200.95	197.47	194.41	191.71	189.32	187.20
22000	219.48	214.69	210.52	206.87	203.66	200.83	198.33	196.11
23000	229.45	224.45	220.09	216.28	212.92	209.96	207.35	205.02
24000	239.43	234.21	229.66	225.68	222.18	219.09	216.36	213.94
25000	249.40	243.97	239.23	235.08	231.44	228.22	225.38	222.85
26000	259.38	253.73	248.80	244.49	240.69	237.35	234.39	231.76
27000	269.36	263.48	258.37	253.89	249.95	246.48	243.40	240.68
28000	279.33	273.24	267.94	263.29	259.21	255.61	252.42	249.59
29000	289.31	283.00	277.51	272.69	268.47	264.73	261.43	258.51
30000	299.28	292.76	287.08	282.10	277.72	273.86	270.45	267.42
31000	309.26	302.52	296.64	291.50	286.98	282.99	279.46	276.33
32000	319.24	312.28	306.21	300.90	296.24	292.12	288.48	285.25
33000	329.21	322.04	315.78	310.31	305.49	301.25	297.49	294.16
34000	339.19	331.79	325.35	319.71	314.75	310.38	306.51	303.07
35000	349.16	341.55	334.92	329.11	324.01	319.51	315.52	311.99
40000	399.04	390.35	382.77	376.13	370.30	365.15	360.60	356.56
45000	448.92	439.14	430.61	423.14	416.58	410.79	405.67	401.13
50000	498.80	487.93	478.46	470.16	462.87	456.44	450.75	445.70
55000	548.68	536.72	526.30	517.17	509.15	502.08	495.82	490.27
60000	598.56	585.52	574.15	564.19	555.44	547.72	540.89	534.83
65000	648.44	634.31	621.99	611.21	601.73	593.37	585.97	579.40
70000	698.32	683.10	669.84	658.22	648.01	639.01	631.04	623.97
75000	748.20	731.89	717.68	705.24	694.30	684.65	676.12	668.54
80000	798.08	780.69	765.53	752.25	740.59	730.29	721.19	713.11
85000	847.96	829.48	813.37	799.27	786.87	775.94	766.26	757.68
90000	897.84	878.27	861.22	846.28	833.16	821.58	811.34	802.25
95000	947.72	927.06	909.06	893.30	879.44	867.22	856.41	846.82
100000	997.60	975.86	956.91	940.31	925.73	912.87	901.49	891.39
105000	1047.48	1024.65	1004.75	987.33	972.02	958.51	946.56	935.96
110000	1097.36	1073.44	1052.60	1034.34	1018.30	1004.15	991.63	980.53
115000	1147.24	1122.23	1100.44	1081.36	1064.59	1049.80	1036.71	1025.09
120000	1197.12	1171.03	1148.29	1128.38	1110.88	1095.44	1081.78	1069.66
125000	1247.00	1219.82	1196.13	1175.39	1157.16	1141.08	1126.86	1114.23
130000	1296.88	1268.61	1243.98	1222.41	1203.45	1186.73	1171.93	1158.80
135000	1346.76	1317.40	1291.82	1269.42	1249.73	1232.37	1217.00	1203.37
140000	1396.64	1366.20	1339.67	1316.44	1296.02	1278.01	1262.08	1247.94
145000	1446.52	1414.99	1387.51	1363.45	1342.31	1323.65	1307.15	1292.51
150000	1496.40	1463.78	1435.36	1410.47	1388.59	1369.30	1352.23	1337.08
155000	1546.28	1512.57	1483.20	1457.48	1434.88	1414.94	1397.30	1381.65
160000	1596.16	1561.37	1531.05	1504.50	1481.17	1460.58	1442.37	1426.22

AMOUNT OF LOAN	25	26	27	28	29	30	35	40
	NUMBER OF YEARS IN TERM							
$ 50	.45	.44	.44	.44	.43	.43	.42	.41
100	.89	.88	.87	.87	.86	.85	.84	.82
200	1.77	1.75	1.74	1.73	1.72	1.70	1.67	1.64
300	2.65	2.63	2.61	2.59	2.57	2.55	2.50	2.46
400	3.53	3.50	3.47	3.45	3.43	3.40	3.33	3.28
500	4.42	4.38	4.34	4.31	4.28	4.25	4.16	4.10
600	5.30	5.25	5.21	5.17	5.14	5.10	4.99	4.92
700	6.18	6.13	6.08	6.03	5.99	5.95	5.82	5.74
800	7.06	7.00	6.94	6.89	6.85	6.80	6.65	6.56
900	7.95	7.87	7.81	7.75	7.70	7.65	7.48	7.38
1000	8.83	8.75	8.68	8.61	8.56	8.50	8.32	8.20
2000	17.65	17.49	17.35	17.22	17.11	17.00	16.63	16.40
3000	26.48	26.24	26.02	25.83	25.66	25.50	24.94	24.60
4000	35.30	34.98	34.69	34.44	34.21	34.00	33.25	32.80
5000	44.13	43.72	43.37	43.05	42.76	42.50	41.56	40.99
6000	52.95	52.47	52.04	51.66	51.31	51.00	49.87	49.19
7000	61.77	61.21	60.71	60.26	59.86	59.50	58.18	57.39
8000	70.60	69.96	69.38	68.87	68.42	68.00	66.49	65.59
9000	79.42	78.70	78.06	77.48	76.97	76.50	74.80	73.79
10000	88.25	87.44	86.73	86.09	85.52	85.00	83.11	81.98
11000	97.07	96.19	95.40	94.70	94.07	93.50	91.42	90.18
12000	105.89	104.93	104.07	103.31	102.62	102.00	99.74	98.38
13000	114.72	113.68	112.75	111.92	111.17	110.50	108.05	106.58
14000	123.54	122.42	121.42	120.52	119.72	119.00	116.36	114.78
15000	132.37	131.16	130.09	129.13	128.27	127.50	124.67	122.97
16000	141.19	139.91	138.76	137.74	136.83	136.00	132.98	131.17
17000	150.01	148.65	147.44	146.35	145.38	144.50	141.29	139.37
18000	158.84	157.40	156.11	154.96	153.93	153.00	149.60	147.57
19000	167.66	166.14	164.78	163.57	162.48	161.50	157.91	155.77
20000	176.49	174.88	173.45	172.18	171.03	170.00	166.22	163.96
21000	185.31	183.63	182.13	180.78	179.58	178.50	174.53	172.16
22000	194.13	192.37	190.80	189.39	188.13	187.00	182.84	180.36
23000	202.96	201.12	199.47	198.00	196.68	195.50	191.16	188.56
24000	211.78	209.86	208.14	206.61	205.24	204.00	199.47	196.76
25000	220.61	218.60	216.82	215.22	213.79	212.50	207.78	204.95
26000	229.43	227.35	225.49	223.83	222.34	221.00	216.09	213.15
27000	238.25	236.09	234.16	232.44	230.89	229.50	224.40	221.35
28000	247.08	244.84	242.83	241.04	239.44	238.00	232.71	229.55
29000	255.90	253.58	251.51	249.65	247.99	246.50	241.02	237.75
30000	264.73	262.32	260.18	258.26	256.54	255.00	249.33	245.94
31000	273.55	271.07	268.85	266.87	265.09	263.50	257.64	254.14
32000	282.37	279.81	277.52	275.48	273.65	272.00	265.95	262.34
33000	291.20	288.56	286.20	284.09	282.20	280.50	274.26	270.54
34000	300.02	297.30	294.87	292.70	290.75	289.00	282.57	278.74
35000	308.85	306.04	303.54	301.30	299.30	297.50	290.89	286.93
40000	352.97	349.76	346.90	344.35	342.06	340.00	332.44	327.92
45000	397.09	393.48	390.27	387.39	384.81	382.50	373.99	368.91
50000	441.21	437.20	433.63	430.43	427.57	425.00	415.55	409.90
55000	485.33	480.92	476.99	473.48	470.33	467.50	457.10	450.89
60000	529.45	524.64	520.35	516.52	513.08	510.00	498.66	491.88
65000	573.57	568.36	563.72	559.56	555.84	552.50	540.21	532.87
70000	617.69	612.08	607.08	602.60	598.59	595.00	581.77	573.86
75000	661.81	655.80	650.44	645.65	641.35	637.50	623.32	614.85
80000	705.93	699.52	693.80	688.69	684.11	680.00	664.87	655.84
85000	750.05	743.24	737.17	731.73	726.86	722.50	706.43	696.83
90000	794.17	786.96	780.53	774.78	769.62	765.00	747.98	737.82
95000	838.29	830.68	823.89	817.82	812.38	807.49	789.54	778.81
100000	882.41	874.40	867.25	860.86	855.13	849.99	831.09	819.80
105000	926.53	918.12	910.62	903.90	897.89	892.49	872.65	860.79
110000	970.65	961.84	953.98	946.95	940.65	934.99	914.20	901.78
115000	1014.77	1005.56	997.34	989.99	983.40	977.49	955.76	942.77
120000	1058.89	1049.28	1040.70	1033.03	1026.16	1019.99	997.31	983.76
125000	1103.01	1093.00	1084.07	1076.08	1068.92	1062.49	1038.86	1024.75
130000	1147.13	1136.72	1127.43	1119.12	1111.67	1104.99	1080.42	1065.74
135000	1191.25	1180.44	1170.79	1162.16	1154.43	1147.49	1121.97	1106.73
140000	1235.37	1224.16	1214.15	1205.20	1197.18	1189.99	1163.53	1147.72
145000	1279.49	1267.88	1257.52	1248.25	1239.94	1232.49	1205.08	1188.71
150000	1323.61	1311.60	1300.88	1291.29	1282.70	1274.99	1246.64	1229.70
155000	1367.73	1355.32	1344.24	1334.33	1325.45	1317.49	1288.19	1270.69
160000	1411.85	1399.04	1387.60	1377.37	1368.21	1359.99	1329.74	1311.68

MONTHLY AMORTIZING PAYMENTS

AMOUNT OF LOAN	NUMBER OF YEARS IN TERM							
	1	1-1/2	2	3	4	5	6	7
$ 50	4.39	3.00	2.31	1.61	1.27	1.06	.92	.83
100	8.78	6.00	4.61	3.22	2.53	2.12	1.85	1.65
200	17.56	11.99	9.21	6.43	5.05	4.23	3.69	3.30
300	26.34	17.99	13.81	9.65	7.58	6.34	5.53	4.95
400	35.12	23.98	18.42	12.86	10.10	8.45	7.37	6.59
500	43.90	29.98	23.02	16.08	12.63	10.57	9.21	8.24
600	52.68	35.97	27.62	19.29	15.15	12.68	11.05	9.89
700	61.46	41.96	32.23	22.51	17.67	14.79	12.89	11.54
800	70.24	47.96	36.83	25.72	20.20	16.90	14.73	13.18
900	79.02	53.95	41.43	28.94	22.72	19.02	16.57	14.83
1000	87.80	59.95	46.03	32.15	25.25	21.13	18.41	16.48
2000	175.60	119.89	92.06	64.30	50.49	42.25	36.81	32.95
3000	263.40	179.83	138.09	96.45	75.73	63.38	55.21	49.42
4000	351.20	239.77	184.12	128.60	100.98	84.50	73.61	65.89
5000	439.00	299.72	230.15	160.75	126.22	105.63	92.01	82.37
6000	526.80	359.66	276.18	192.90	151.46	126.75	110.41	98.84
7000	614.60	419.60	322.21	225.05	176.70	147.87	128.81	115.31
8000	702.40	479.54	368.24	257.20	201.95	169.00	147.21	131.78
9000	790.20	539.48	414.27	289.35	227.19	190.12	165.61	148.26
10000	878.00	599.43	460.30	321.50	252.43	211.25	184.01	164.73
11000	965.80	659.37	506.33	353.65	277.67	232.37	202.41	181.20
12000	1053.60	719.31	552.36	385.80	302.92	253.50	220.81	197.67
13000	1141.40	779.25	598.39	417.95	328.16	274.62	239.21	214.14
14000	1229.20	839.19	644.42	450.10	353.40	295.74	257.61	230.62
15000	1317.00	899.14	690.45	482.25	378.65	316.87	276.01	247.09
16000	1404.80	959.08	736.48	514.40	403.89	337.99	294.41	263.56
17000	1492.60	1019.02	782.51	546.55	429.13	359.12	312.81	280.03
18000	1580.40	1078.96	828.54	578.70	454.37	380.24	331.21	296.51
19000	1668.20	1138.90	874.57	610.85	479.62	401.37	349.61	312.98
20000	1756.00	1198.85	920.60	643.00	504.86	422.49	368.01	329.45
21000	1843.80	1258.79	966.63	675.15	530.10	443.61	386.41	345.92
22000	1931.60	1318.73	1012.66	707.30	555.34	464.74	404.81	362.40
23000	2019.40	1378.67	1058.69	739.45	580.59	485.86	423.21	378.87
24000	2107.20	1438.61	1104.72	771.60	605.83	506.99	441.61	395.34
25000	2195.00	1498.56	1150.75	803.75	631.07	528.11	460.01	411.81
26000	2282.80	1558.50	1196.78	835.90	656.31	549.24	478.41	428.28
27000	2370.60	1618.44	1242.80	868.05	681.56	570.36	496.81	444.76
28000	2458.40	1678.38	1288.83	900.20	706.80	591.48	515.21	461.23
29000	2546.20	1738.32	1334.86	932.35	732.04	612.61	533.61	477.70
30000	2633.99	1798.27	1380.89	964.50	757.29	633.73	552.01	494.17
31000	2721.79	1858.21	1426.92	996.65	782.53	654.86	570.41	510.65
32000	2809.59	1918.15	1472.95	1028.80	807.77	675.98	588.81	527.12
33000	2897.39	1978.09	1518.98	1060.95	833.01	697.11	607.21	543.59
34000	2985.19	2038.03	1565.01	1093.10	858.26	718.23	625.61	560.06
35000	3072.99	2097.98	1611.04	1125.25	883.50	739.35	644.01	576.54
40000	3511.99	2397.69	1841.19	1286.00	1009.71	844.97	736.01	658.90
45000	3950.99	2697.40	2071.34	1446.75	1135.93	950.60	828.01	741.26
50000	4389.99	2997.11	2301.49	1607.50	1262.14	1056.22	920.01	823.62
55000	4828.99	3296.82	2531.63	1768.25	1388.35	1161.84	1012.01	905.98
60000	5267.98	3596.53	2761.78	1929.00	1514.57	1267.46	1104.01	988.34
65000	5706.98	3896.24	2991.93	2089.75	1640.78	1373.08	1196.01	1070.70
70000	6145.98	4195.95	3222.08	2250.50	1766.99	1478.70	1288.01	1153.07
75000	6584.98	4495.66	3452.23	2411.25	1893.21	1584.32	1380.01	1235.43
80000	7023.98	4795.37	3682.37	2572.00	2019.42	1689.94	1472.01	1317.79
85000	7462.98	5095.08	3912.52	2732.75	2145.63	1795.57	1564.01	1400.15
90000	7901.97	5394.79	4142.67	2893.50	2271.85	1901.19	1656.01	1482.51
95000	8340.97	5694.50	4372.82	3054.25	2398.06	2006.81	1748.01	1564.87
100000	8779.97	5994.21	4602.97	3215.00	2524.27	2112.43	1840.01	1647.23
105000	9218.97	6293.92	4833.12	3375.75	2650.49	2218.05	1932.01	1729.60
110000	9657.97	6593.63	5063.26	3536.50	2776.70	2323.67	2024.01	1811.96
115000	10096.97	6893.34	5293.41	3697.25	2902.91	2429.29	2116.01	1894.32
120000	10535.96	7193.05	5523.56	3858.00	3029.13	2534.91	2208.01	1976.68
125000	10974.96	7492.76	5753.71	4018.75	3155.34	2640.54	2300.01	2059.04
130000	11413.96	7792.47	5983.86	4179.50	3281.55	2746.16	2392.01	2141.40
135000	11852.96	8092.18	6214.00	4340.25	3407.77	2851.78	2484.01	2223.76
140000	12291.96	8391.89	6444.15	4501.00	3533.98	2957.40	2576.01	2306.13
145000	12730.96	8691.60	6674.30	4661.75	3660.20	3063.02	2668.01	2388.49
150000	13169.95	8991.31	6904.45	4822.50	3786.41	3168.64	2760.01	2470.85
155000	13608.95	9291.02	7134.60	4983.25	3912.62	3274.26	2852.01	2553.21
160000	14047.95	9590.73	7364.74	5144.00	4038.84	3379.88	2944.01	2635.57

MONTHLY AMORTIZING PAYMENTS 9¾%

AMOUNT OF LOAN	NUMBER OF YEARS IN TERM							
	8	9	10	11	12	14	15	16
$ 50	.76	.70	.66	.62	.60	.55	.53	.52
100	1.51	1.40	1.31	1.24	1.19	1.10	1.06	1.04
200	3.01	2.79	2.62	2.48	2.37	2.19	2.12	2.07
300	4.52	4.19	3.93	3.72	3.55	3.28	3.18	3.10
400	6.02	5.58	5.24	4.96	4.73	4.38	4.24	4.13
500	7.53	6.98	6.54	6.19	5.91	5.47	5.30	5.16
600	9.03	8.37	7.85	7.43	7.09	6.56	6.36	6.19
700	10.53	9.77	9.16	8.67	8.27	7.66	7.42	7.22
800	12.04	11.16	10.47	9.91	9.45	8.75	8.48	8.25
900	13.54	12.55	11.77	11.15	10.63	9.84	9.54	9.28
1000	15.05	13.95	13.08	12.38	11.81	10.94	10.60	10.31
2000	30.09	27.89	26.16	24.76	23.62	21.87	21.19	20.61
3000	45.13	41.84	39.24	37.14	35.43	32.80	31.79	30.92
4000	60.17	55.78	52.31	49.52	47.23	43.73	42.38	41.22
5000	75.22	69.72	65.39	61.90	59.04	54.67	52.97	51.52
6000	90.26	83.67	78.47	74.28	70.85	65.60	63.57	61.83
7000	105.30	97.61	91.54	86.66	82.65	76.53	74.16	72.13
8000	120.34	111.55	104.62	99.04	94.46	87.46	84.75	82.44
9000	135.38	125.50	117.70	111.41	106.27	98.40	95.35	92.74
10000	150.43	139.44	130.78	123.79	118.07	109.33	105.94	103.04
11000	165.47	153.39	143.85	136.17	129.88	120.26	116.53	113.35
12000	180.51	167.33	156.93	148.55	141.69	131.19	127.13	123.65
13000	195.55	181.27	170.01	160.93	153.49	142.13	137.72	133.96
14000	210.60	195.22	183.08	173.31	165.30	153.06	148.32	144.26
15000	225.64	209.16	196.16	185.69	177.11	163.99	158.91	154.56
16000	240.68	223.10	209.24	198.07	188.91	174.92	169.50	164.87
17000	255.72	237.05	222.31	210.45	200.72	185.85	180.10	175.17
18000	270.76	250.99	235.39	222.82	212.53	196.79	190.69	185.48
19000	285.81	264.93	248.47	235.20	224.33	207.72	201.28	195.78
20000	300.85	278.88	261.55	247.58	236.14	218.65	211.88	206.08
21000	315.89	292.82	274.62	259.96	247.95	229.58	222.47	216.39
22000	330.93	306.77	287.70	272.34	259.75	240.52	233.06	226.69
23000	345.98	320.71	300.78	284.72	271.56	251.45	243.66	237.00
24000	361.02	334.65	313.85	297.10	283.37	262.38	254.25	247.30
25000	376.06	348.60	326.93	309.48	295.18	273.31	264.85	257.60
26000	391.10	362.54	340.01	321.85	306.98	284.25	275.44	267.91
27000	406.14	376.48	353.08	334.23	318.79	295.18	286.03	278.21
28000	421.19	390.43	366.16	346.61	330.60	306.11	296.63	288.51
29000	436.23	404.37	379.24	358.99	342.40	317.04	307.22	298.82
30000	451.27	418.31	392.32	371.37	354.21	327.98	317.81	309.12
31000	466.31	432.26	405.39	383.75	366.02	338.91	328.41	319.43
32000	481.36	446.20	418.47	396.13	377.82	349.84	339.00	329.73
33000	496.40	460.15	431.55	408.51	389.63	360.77	349.59	340.03
34000	511.44	474.09	444.62	420.89	401.44	371.70	360.19	350.34
35000	526.48	488.03	457.70	433.26	413.24	382.64	370.78	360.64
40000	601.69	557.75	523.09	495.16	472.28	437.30	423.75	412.16
45000	676.90	627.47	588.47	557.05	531.31	491.96	476.72	463.68
50000	752.12	697.19	653.86	618.95	590.35	546.62	529.69	515.20
55000	827.33	766.91	719.24	680.84	649.38	601.28	582.65	566.72
60000	902.54	836.62	784.63	742.74	708.41	655.95	635.62	618.24
65000	977.75	906.34	850.01	804.63	767.45	710.61	688.59	669.76
70000	1052.96	976.06	915.40	866.52	826.48	765.27	741.56	721.28
75000	1128.17	1045.78	980.78	928.42	885.52	819.93	794.53	772.80
80000	1203.38	1115.50	1046.17	990.31	944.55	874.59	847.50	824.32
85000	1278.59	1185.22	1111.55	1052.21	1003.58	929.25	900.46	875.84
90000	1353.80	1254.93	1176.94	1114.10	1062.62	983.92	953.43	927.36
95000	1429.01	1324.65	1242.32	1175.99	1121.65	1038.58	1006.40	978.88
100000	1504.23	1394.37	1307.71	1237.89	1180.69	1093.24	1059.37	1030.40
105000	1579.44	1464.09	1373.09	1299.78	1239.72	1147.90	1112.34	1081.92
110000	1654.65	1533.81	1438.48	1361.68	1298.75	1202.56	1165.30	1133.44
115000	1729.86	1603.53	1503.86	1423.57	1357.79	1257.23	1218.27	1184.96
120000	1805.07	1673.24	1569.25	1485.47	1416.82	1311.89	1271.24	1236.47
125000	1880.28	1742.96	1634.63	1547.36	1475.86	1366.55	1324.21	1287.99
130000	1955.49	1812.68	1700.02	1609.25	1534.89	1421.21	1377.18	1339.51
135000	2030.70	1882.40	1765.40	1671.15	1593.92	1475.87	1430.14	1391.03
140000	2105.91	1952.12	1830.79	1733.04	1652.96	1530.53	1483.11	1442.55
145000	2181.12	2021.84	1896.17	1794.94	1711.99	1585.20	1536.08	1494.07
150000	2256.34	2091.55	1961.56	1856.83	1771.03	1639.86	1589.05	1545.59
155000	2331.55	2161.27	2026.94	1918.73	1830.06	1694.52	1642.02	1597.11
160000	2406.76	2230.99	2092.33	1980.62	1889.09	1749.18	1694.99	1648.63

MONTHLY AMORTIZING PAYMENTS

AMOUNT OF LOAN	NUMBER OF YEARS IN TERM							
	17	18	19	20	21	22	23	24
$ 50	.51	.50	.49	.48	.47	.47	.46	.46
100	1.01	.99	.97	.95	.94	.93	.92	.91
200	2.02	1.97	1.93	1.90	1.87	1.85	1.83	1.81
300	3.02	2.96	2.90	2.85	2.81	2.77	2.74	2.71
400	4.03	3.94	3.86	3.80	3.74	3.69	3.65	3.61
500	5.03	4.92	4.83	4.75	4.68	4.61	4.56	4.51
600	6.04	5.91	5.79	5.70	5.61	5.53	5.47	5.41
700	7.04	6.89	6.76	6.64	6.54	6.45	6.38	6.31
800	8.05	7.88	7.72	7.59	7.48	7.38	7.29	7.21
900	9.05	8.86	8.69	8.54	8.41	8.30	8.20	8.11
1000	10.06	9.84	9.65	9.49	9.35	9.22	9.11	9.01
2000	20.11	19.68	19.30	18.98	18.69	18.43	18.21	18.01
3000	30.17	29.52	28.95	28.46	28.03	27.64	27.31	27.01
4000	40.22	39.36	38.60	37.95	37.37	36.86	36.41	36.01
5000	50.28	49.20	48.25	47.43	46.71	46.07	45.51	45.01
6000	60.33	59.03	57.90	56.92	56.05	55.28	54.61	54.01
7000	70.39	68.87	67.55	66.40	65.39	64.50	63.71	63.01
8000	80.44	78.71	77.20	75.89	74.73	73.71	72.81	72.01
9000	90.49	88.55	86.85	85.37	84.07	82.92	81.91	81.01
10000	100.55	98.39	96.50	94.86	93.41	92.13	91.01	90.01
11000	110.60	108.23	106.15	104.34	102.75	101.35	100.11	99.01
12000	120.66	118.06	115.80	113.83	112.09	110.56	109.21	108.01
13000	130.71	127.90	125.45	123.31	121.43	119.77	118.31	117.01
14000	140.77	137.74	135.10	132.80	130.77	128.99	127.41	126.01
15000	150.82	147.58	144.75	142.28	140.11	138.20	136.51	135.01
16000	160.88	157.42	154.40	151.77	149.45	147.41	145.61	144.01
17000	170.93	167.25	164.05	161.25	158.79	156.62	154.71	153.01
18000	180.98	177.09	173.70	170.74	168.13	165.84	163.81	162.01
19000	191.04	186.93	183.35	180.22	177.47	175.05	172.91	171.01
20000	201.09	196.77	193.00	189.71	186.81	184.26	182.01	180.01
21000	211.15	206.61	202.65	199.19	196.15	193.48	191.11	189.01
22000	221.20	216.45	212.30	208.68	205.50	202.69	200.21	198.01
23000	231.26	226.28	221.95	218.16	214.84	211.90	209.31	207.01
24000	241.31	236.12	231.60	227.65	224.18	221.12	218.41	216.01
25000	251.36	245.96	241.25	237.13	233.52	230.33	227.51	225.01
26000	261.42	255.80	250.90	246.62	242.86	239.54	236.61	234.01
27000	271.47	265.64	260.55	256.10	252.20	248.75	245.71	243.01
28000	281.53	275.47	270.20	265.59	261.54	257.97	254.81	252.01
29000	291.58	285.31	279.85	275.07	270.88	267.18	263.91	261.01
30000	301.64	295.15	289.50	284.56	280.22	276.39	273.01	270.01
31000	311.69	304.99	299.15	294.05	289.56	285.61	282.11	279.01
32000	321.75	314.83	308.80	303.53	298.90	294.82	291.21	288.01
33000	331.80	324.67	318.45	313.02	308.24	304.03	300.31	297.01
34000	341.85	334.50	328.10	322.50	317.58	313.24	309.41	306.01
35000	351.91	344.34	337.75	331.99	326.92	322.46	318.51	315.01
40000	402.18	393.53	386.00	379.41	373.62	368.52	364.01	360.01
45000	452.45	442.72	434.25	426.84	420.33	414.59	409.51	405.01
50000	502.72	491.92	482.50	474.26	467.03	460.65	455.01	450.02
55000	553.00	541.11	530.75	521.69	513.73	506.72	500.51	495.02
60000	603.27	590.30	579.00	569.12	560.43	552.78	546.02	540.02
65000	653.54	639.49	627.25	616.54	607.14	598.85	591.52	585.02
70000	703.81	688.68	675.50	663.97	653.84	644.91	637.02	630.02
75000	754.08	737.87	723.75	711.39	700.54	690.97	682.52	675.02
80000	804.36	787.06	772.00	758.82	747.24	737.04	728.02	720.02
85000	854.63	836.25	820.25	806.24	793.94	783.10	773.52	765.02
90000	904.90	885.44	868.50	853.67	840.65	829.17	819.02	810.02
95000	955.17	934.63	916.75	901.10	887.35	875.23	864.52	855.02
100000	1005.44	983.83	965.00	948.52	934.05	921.30	910.02	900.03
105000	1055.72	1033.02	1013.25	995.95	980.75	967.36	955.52	945.03
110000	1105.99	1082.21	1061.49	1043.37	1027.46	1013.43	1001.02	990.03
115000	1156.26	1131.40	1109.74	1090.80	1074.16	1059.49	1046.52	1035.03
120000	1206.53	1180.59	1157.99	1138.23	1120.86	1105.56	1092.03	1080.03
125000	1256.80	1229.78	1206.24	1185.65	1167.56	1151.62	1137.53	1125.03
130000	1307.08	1278.97	1254.49	1233.08	1214.27	1197.69	1183.03	1170.03
135000	1357.35	1328.16	1302.74	1280.50	1260.97	1243.75	1228.53	1215.03
140000	1407.62	1377.35	1350.99	1327.93	1307.67	1289.81	1274.03	1260.03
145000	1457.89	1426.54	1399.24	1375.35	1354.37	1335.88	1319.53	1305.03
150000	1508.16	1475.74	1447.49	1422.78	1401.08	1381.94	1365.03	1350.04
155000	1558.44	1524.93	1495.74	1470.21	1447.78	1428.01	1410.53	1395.04
160000	1608.71	1574.12	1543.99	1517.63	1494.48	1474.07	1456.03	1440.04

AMOUNT OF LOAN	NUMBER OF YEARS IN TERM							
	25	26	27	28	29	30	35	40
$ 50	.45	.45	.44	.44	.44	.43	.43	.42
100	.90	.89	.88	.87	.87	.86	.85	.83
200	1.79	1.77	1.76	1.74	1.73	1.72	1.69	1.66
300	2.68	2.65	2.63	2.61	2.60	2.58	2.53	2.49
400	3.57	3.54	3.51	3.48	3.46	3.44	3.37	3.32
500	4.46	4.42	4.39	4.35	4.33	4.30	4.21	4.15
600	5.35	5.30	5.26	5.22	5.19	5.16	5.05	4.98
700	6.24	6.19	6.14	6.09	6.05	6.02	5.89	5.81
800	7.13	7.07	7.01	6.96	6.92	6.88	6.73	6.64
900	8.03	7.95	7.89	7.83	7.78	7.74	7.57	7.47
1000	8.92	8.84	8.77	8.70	8.65	8.60	8.41	8.30
2000	17.83	17.67	17.53	17.40	17.29	17.19	16.82	16.60
3000	26.74	26.50	26.29	26.10	25.93	25.78	25.22	24.89
4000	35.65	35.33	35.05	34.80	34.57	34.37	33.63	33.19
5000	44.56	44.17	43.81	43.50	43.22	42.96	42.03	41.48
6000	53.47	53.00	52.58	52.20	51.86	51.55	50.44	49.78
7000	62.38	61.83	61.34	60.90	60.50	60.15	58.85	58.07
8000	71.30	70.66	70.10	69.59	69.14	68.74	67.25	66.37
9000	80.21	79.50	78.86	78.29	77.78	77.33	75.66	74.67
10000	89.12	88.33	87.62	86.99	86.43	85.92	84.06	82.96
11000	98.03	97.16	96.38	95.69	95.07	94.51	92.47	91.26
12000	106.94	105.99	105.15	104.39	103.71	103.10	100.88	99.55
13000	115.85	114.82	113.91	113.09	112.35	111.70	109.28	107.85
14000	124.76	123.66	122.67	121.79	121.00	120.29	117.69	116.14
15000	133.68	132.49	131.43	130.48	129.64	128.88	126.09	124.44
16000	142.59	141.32	140.19	139.18	138.28	137.47	134.50	132.73
17000	151.50	150.15	148.95	147.88	146.92	146.06	142.91	141.03
18000	160.41	158.99	157.72	156.58	155.56	154.65	151.31	149.33
19000	169.32	167.82	166.48	165.28	164.21	163.24	159.72	157.62
20000	178.23	176.65	175.24	173.98	172.85	171.84	168.12	165.92
21000	187.14	185.48	184.00	182.68	181.49	180.43	176.53	174.21
22000	196.06	194.31	192.76	191.37	190.13	189.02	184.93	182.51
23000	204.97	203.15	201.52	200.07	198.77	197.61	193.34	190.80
24000	213.88	211.98	210.29	208.77	207.42	206.20	201.75	199.10
25000	222.79	220.81	219.05	217.47	216.06	214.79	210.15	207.39
26000	231.70	229.64	227.81	226.17	224.70	223.39	218.56	215.69
27000	240.61	238.48	236.57	234.87	233.34	231.98	226.96	223.99
28000	249.52	247.31	245.33	243.57	241.99	240.57	235.37	232.28
29000	258.43	256.14	254.09	252.26	250.63	249.16	243.78	240.58
30000	267.35	264.97	262.86	260.96	259.27	257.75	252.18	248.87
31000	276.26	273.81	271.62	269.66	267.91	266.34	260.59	257.17
32000	285.17	282.64	280.38	278.36	276.55	274.93	268.99	265.46
33000	294.08	291.47	289.14	287.06	285.20	283.53	277.40	273.76
34000	302.99	300.30	297.90	295.76	293.84	292.12	285.81	282.05
35000	311.90	309.13	306.66	304.46	302.48	300.71	294.21	290.35
40000	356.46	353.30	350.47	347.95	345.69	343.67	336.24	331.83
45000	401.02	397.46	394.28	391.44	388.90	386.62	378.27	373.31
50000	445.57	441.62	438.09	434.94	432.11	429.58	420.30	414.78
55000	490.13	485.78	481.90	478.43	475.32	472.54	462.33	456.26
60000	534.69	529.94	525.71	521.92	518.53	515.50	504.36	497.74
65000	579.24	574.10	569.51	565.41	561.74	558.46	546.39	539.22
70000	623.80	618.26	613.32	608.91	604.96	601.41	588.42	580.70
75000	668.36	662.43	657.13	652.40	648.17	644.37	630.45	622.17
80000	712.91	706.59	700.94	695.89	691.38	687.33	672.48	663.65
85000	757.47	750.75	744.75	739.39	734.59	730.29	714.51	705.13
90000	802.03	794.91	788.56	782.88	777.80	773.24	756.54	746.61
95000	846.59	839.07	832.37	826.37	821.01	816.20	798.56	788.09
100000	891.14	883.23	876.17	869.87	864.22	859.16	840.59	829.56
105000	935.70	927.39	919.98	913.36	907.43	902.12	882.62	871.04
110000	980.26	971.55	963.79	956.85	950.64	945.07	924.65	912.52
115000	1024.81	1015.72	1007.60	1000.35	993.85	988.03	966.68	954.00
120000	1069.37	1059.88	1051.41	1043.84	1037.06	1030.99	1008.71	995.48
125000	1113.93	1104.04	1095.22	1087.33	1080.27	1073.95	1050.74	1036.95
130000	1158.48	1148.20	1139.02	1130.82	1123.48	1116.91	1092.77	1078.43
135000	1203.04	1192.36	1182.83	1174.32	1166.70	1159.86	1134.80	1119.91
140000	1247.60	1236.52	1226.64	1217.81	1209.91	1202.82	1176.83	1161.39
145000	1292.15	1280.68	1270.45	1261.30	1253.12	1245.78	1218.86	1202.86
150000	1336.71	1324.85	1314.26	1304.80	1296.33	1288.74	1260.89	1244.34
155000	1381.27	1369.01	1358.07	1348.29	1339.54	1331.69	1302.92	1285.82
160000	1425.82	1413.17	1401.88	1391.78	1382.75	1374.65	1344.95	1327.30

MONTHLY AMORTIZING PAYMENTS

AMOUNT OF LOAN	NUMBER OF YEARS IN TERM							
	1	1-1/2	2	3	4	5	6	7
$ 50	4.40	3.00	2.31	1.62	1.27	1.06	.93	.83
100	8.79	6.00	4.61	3.23	2.54	2.12	1.85	1.66
200	17.58	12.00	9.22	6.45	5.07	4.24	3.70	3.31
300	26.36	18.00	13.83	9.67	7.60	6.36	5.54	4.97
400	35.15	24.00	18.44	12.89	10.13	8.48	7.39	6.62
500	43.93	30.00	23.05	16.11	12.66	10.60	9.24	8.27
600	52.72	36.00	27.66	19.33	15.19	12.72	11.08	9.93
700	61.51	42.00	32.27	22.55	17.72	14.83	12.93	11.58
800	70.29	48.00	36.87	25.77	20.25	16.95	14.78	13.23
900	79.08	54.00	41.48	28.99	22.78	19.07	16.62	14.89
1000	87.86	60.00	46.09	32.21	25.31	21.19	18.47	16.54
2000	175.72	120.00	92.18	64.42	50.61	42.38	36.93	33.08
3000	263.58	180.00	138.27	96.63	75.91	63.56	55.39	49.62
4000	351.44	240.00	184.35	128.84	101.22	84.75	73.86	66.15
5000	439.29	300.00	230.44	161.05	126.52	105.93	92.32	82.69
6000	527.15	360.00	276.53	193.26	151.82	127.12	110.78	99.23
7000	615.01	420.00	322.62	225.46	177.12	148.30	129.25	115.76
8000	702.87	480.00	368.70	257.67	202.43	169.49	147.71	132.30
9000	790.72	540.00	414.79	289.88	227.73	190.68	166.17	148.84
10000	878.58	600.00	460.88	322.09	253.03	211.86	184.63	165.37
11000	966.44	660.00	506.96	354.30	278.33	233.05	203.10	181.91
12000	1054.30	720.00	553.05	386.51	303.64	254.23	221.56	198.45
13000	1142.16	780.00	599.14	418.72	328.94	275.42	240.02	214.98
14000	1230.01	840.00	645.23	450.92	354.24	296.60	258.49	231.52
15000	1317.87	900.00	691.31	483.13	379.54	317.79	276.95	248.06
16000	1405.73	960.00	737.40	515.34	404.85	338.97	295.41	264.59
17000	1493.59	1020.00	783.49	547.55	430.15	360.16	313.87	281.13
18000	1581.44	1080.00	829.58	579.76	455.45	381.35	332.34	297.67
19000	1669.30	1140.00	875.66	611.97	480.75	402.53	350.80	314.20
20000	1757.16	1200.00	921.75	644.18	506.06	423.72	369.26	330.74
21000	1845.02	1260.00	967.84	676.38	531.36	444.90	387.73	347.28
22000	1932.88	1319.99	1013.92	708.59	556.66	466.09	406.19	363.81
23000	2020.73	1379.99	1060.01	740.80	581.96	487.27	424.65	380.35
24000	2108.59	1439.99	1106.10	773.01	607.27	508.46	443.11	396.89
25000	2196.45	1499.99	1152.19	805.22	632.57	529.64	461.58	413.42
26000	2284.31	1559.99	1198.27	837.43	657.87	550.83	480.04	429.96
27000	2372.16	1619.99	1244.36	869.64	683.18	572.02	498.50	446.50
28000	2460.02	1679.99	1290.45	901.84	708.48	593.20	516.97	463.03
29000	2547.88	1739.99	1336.54	934.05	733.78	614.39	535.43	479.57
30000	2635.74	1799.99	1382.62	966.26	759.08	635.57	553.89	496.11
31000	2723.60	1859.99	1428.71	998.47	784.39	656.76	572.35	512.64
32000	2811.45	1919.99	1474.80	1030.68	809.69	677.94	590.82	529.18
33000	2899.31	1979.99	1520.88	1062.89	834.99	699.13	609.28	545.72
34000	2987.17	2039.99	1566.97	1095.10	860.29	720.32	627.74	562.25
35000	3075.03	2099.99	1613.06	1127.30	885.60	741.50	646.21	578.79
40000	3514.32	2399.99	1843.50	1288.35	1012.11	847.43	738.52	661.47
45000	3953.60	2699.98	2073.93	1449.39	1138.62	953.36	830.83	744.16
50000	4392.89	2999.98	2304.37	1610.43	1265.13	1059.28	923.15	826.84
55000	4832.18	3299.98	2534.80	1771.47	1391.65	1165.21	1015.46	909.52
60000	5271.47	3599.98	2765.24	1932.52	1518.16	1271.14	1107.78	992.21
65000	5710.76	3899.98	2995.68	2093.56	1644.67	1377.07	1200.09	1074.89
70000	6150.05	4199.97	3226.11	2254.60	1771.19	1483.00	1292.41	1157.57
75000	6589.34	4499.97	3456.55	2415.64	1897.70	1588.92	1384.72	1240.26
80000	7028.63	4799.97	3686.99	2576.69	2024.21	1694.85	1477.03	1322.94
85000	7467.91	5099.97	3917.42	2737.73	2150.73	1800.78	1569.35	1405.62
90000	7907.20	5399.96	4147.86	2898.77	2277.24	1906.71	1661.66	1488.31
95000	8346.49	5699.96	4378.29	3059.82	2403.75	2012.64	1753.98	1570.99
100000	8785.78	5999.96	4608.73	3220.86	2530.26	2118.56	1846.29	1653.67
105000	9225.07	6299.96	4839.17	3381.90	2656.78	2224.49	1938.61	1736.36
110000	9664.36	6599.95	5069.60	3542.94	2783.29	2330.42	2030.92	1819.04
115000	10103.65	6899.95	5300.04	3703.99	2909.80	2436.35	2123.23	1901.72
120000	10542.94	7199.95	5530.48	3865.03	3036.32	2542.28	2215.55	1984.41
125000	10982.23	7499.95	5760.91	4026.07	3162.83	2648.20	2307.86	2067.09
130000	11421.51	7799.95	5991.35	4187.11	3289.34	2754.13	2400.18	2149.77
135000	11860.80	8099.94	6221.78	4348.16	3415.86	2860.06	2492.49	2232.46
140000	12300.09	8399.94	6452.22	4509.20	3542.37	2965.99	2584.81	2315.14
145000	12739.38	8699.94	6682.66	4670.24	3668.88	3071.92	2677.12	2397.82
150000	13178.67	8999.94	6913.09	4831.28	3795.39	3177.84	2769.43	2480.51
155000	13617.96	9299.93	7143.53	4992.33	3921.91	3283.77	2861.75	2563.19
160000	14057.25	9599.93	7373.97	5153.37	4048.42	3389.70	2954.06	2645.87

MONTHLY AMORTIZING PAYMENTS 9⅞%

AMOUNT OF LOAN	NUMBER OF YEARS IN TERM							
	8	9	10	11	12	14	15	16
$ 50	.76	.71	.66	.63	.60	.56	.54	.52
100	1.52	1.41	1.32	1.25	1.19	1.11	1.07	1.04
200	3.03	2.81	2.63	2.49	2.38	2.21	2.14	2.08
300	4.54	4.21	3.95	3.74	3.57	3.31	3.21	3.12
400	6.05	5.61	5.26	4.98	4.76	4.41	4.27	4.16
500	7.56	7.01	6.58	6.23	5.94	5.51	5.34	5.20
600	9.07	8.41	7.89	7.47	7.13	6.61	6.41	6.23
700	10.58	9.81	9.21	8.72	8.32	7.71	7.47	7.27
800	12.09	11.21	10.52	9.96	9.51	8.81	8.54	8.31
900	13.60	12.61	11.84	11.21	10.70	9.91	9.61	9.35
1000	15.11	14.02	13.15	12.45	11.88	11.01	10.67	10.39
2000	30.22	28.03	26.30	24.90	23.76	22.02	21.34	20.77
3000	45.33	42.04	39.44	37.35	35.64	33.03	32.01	31.15
4000	60.44	56.05	52.59	49.80	47.52	44.03	42.68	41.53
5000	75.55	70.06	65.73	62.25	59.40	55.04	53.35	51.91
6000	90.65	84.07	78.88	74.70	71.28	66.05	64.02	62.29
7000	105.76	98.08	92.03	87.15	83.16	77.05	74.69	72.67
8000	120.87	112.09	105.17	99.60	95.03	88.06	85.36	83.06
9000	135.98	126.10	118.32	112.05	106.91	99.07	96.03	93.44
10000	151.09	140.12	131.46	124.50	118.79	110.08	106.70	103.82
11000	166.19	154.13	144.61	136.95	130.67	121.08	117.37	114.20
12000	181.30	168.14	157.76	149.40	142.55	132.09	128.04	124.58
13000	196.41	182.15	170.90	161.85	154.43	143.10	138.71	134.96
14000	211.52	196.16	184.05	174.29	166.31	154.10	149.38	145.34
15000	226.63	210.17	197.19	186.74	178.19	165.11	160.05	155.72
16000	241.73	224.18	210.34	199.19	190.06	176.12	170.72	166.11
17000	256.84	238.19	223.49	211.64	201.94	187.13	181.39	176.49
18000	271.95	252.20	236.63	224.09	213.82	198.13	192.06	186.87
19000	287.06	266.22	249.78	236.54	225.70	209.14	202.73	197.25
20000	302.17	280.23	262.92	248.99	237.58	220.15	213.40	207.63
21000	317.28	294.24	276.07	261.44	249.46	231.15	224.07	218.01
22000	332.38	308.25	289.22	273.89	261.34	242.16	234.74	228.39
23000	347.49	322.26	302.36	286.34	273.21	253.17	245.41	238.78
24000	362.60	336.27	315.51	298.79	285.09	264.17	256.08	249.16
25000	377.71	350.28	328.65	311.24	296.97	275.18	266.75	259.54
26000	392.82	364.29	341.80	323.69	308.85	286.19	277.42	269.92
27000	407.92	378.30	354.95	336.13	320.73	297.20	288.09	280.30
28000	423.03	392.32	368.09	348.58	332.61	308.20	298.76	290.68
29000	438.14	406.33	381.24	361.03	344.49	319.21	309.43	301.06
30000	453.25	420.34	394.38	373.48	356.37	330.22	320.10	311.44
31000	468.36	434.35	407.53	385.93	368.24	341.22	330.77	321.83
32000	483.46	448.36	420.68	398.38	380.12	352.23	341.44	332.21
33000	498.57	462.37	433.82	410.83	392.00	363.24	352.11	342.59
34000	513.68	476.38	446.97	423.28	403.88	374.25	362.78	352.97
35000	528.79	490.39	460.11	435.73	415.76	385.25	373.44	363.35
40000	604.33	560.45	525.84	497.98	475.15	440.29	426.79	415.26
45000	679.87	630.50	591.57	560.22	534.55	495.32	480.14	467.16
50000	755.41	700.56	657.30	622.47	593.94	550.36	533.49	519.07
55000	830.95	770.61	723.03	684.71	653.33	605.39	586.84	570.98
60000	906.49	840.67	788.76	746.96	712.73	660.43	640.19	622.88
65000	982.03	910.73	854.49	809.21	772.12	715.46	693.54	674.79
70000	1057.57	980.78	920.22	871.45	831.51	770.50	746.88	726.70
75000	1133.11	1050.84	985.95	933.70	890.91	825.53	800.23	778.60
80000	1208.65	1120.89	1051.68	995.95	950.30	880.57	853.58	830.51
85000	1284.19	1190.95	1117.41	1058.19	1009.69	935.61	906.93	882.42
90000	1359.73	1261.00	1183.14	1120.44	1069.09	990.64	960.28	934.32
95000	1435.27	1331.06	1248.87	1182.68	1128.48	1045.68	1013.63	986.23
100000	1510.82	1401.11	1314.60	1244.93	1187.87	1100.71	1066.98	1038.14
105000	1586.36	1471.17	1380.33	1307.18	1247.27	1155.75	1120.32	1090.04
110000	1661.90	1541.22	1446.06	1369.42	1306.66	1210.78	1173.67	1141.95
115000	1737.44	1611.28	1511.79	1431.67	1366.05	1265.82	1227.02	1193.86
120000	1812.98	1681.34	1577.52	1493.92	1425.45	1320.85	1280.37	1245.76
125000	1888.52	1751.39	1643.25	1556.16	1484.84	1375.89	1333.72	1297.67
130000	1964.06	1821.45	1708.98	1618.41	1544.23	1430.92	1387.07	1349.58
135000	2039.60	1891.50	1774.71	1680.65	1603.63	1485.96	1440.42	1401.48
140000	2115.14	1961.56	1840.44	1742.90	1663.02	1540.99	1493.76	1453.39
145000	2190.68	2031.61	1906.17	1805.15	1722.41	1596.03	1547.11	1505.30
150000	2266.22	2101.67	1971.90	1867.39	1781.81	1651.06	1600.46	1557.20
155000	2341.76	2171.72	2037.63	1929.64	1841.20	1706.10	1653.81	1609.11
160000	2417.30	2241.78	2103.36	1991.89	1900.59	1761.14	1707.16	1661.02

MONTHLY AMORTIZING PAYMENTS

AMOUNT OF LOAN	NUMBER OF YEARS IN TERM							
	17	18	19	20	21	22	23	24
$ 50	.51	.50	.49	.48	.48	.47	.46	.46
100	1.02	1.00	.98	.96	.95	.93	.92	.91
200	2.03	1.99	1.95	1.92	1.89	1.86	1.84	1.82
300	3.04	2.98	2.92	2.88	2.83	2.79	2.76	2.73
400	4.06	3.97	3.90	3.83	3.77	3.72	3.68	3.64
500	5.07	4.96	4.87	4.79	4.72	4.65	4.60	4.55
600	6.08	5.96	5.84	5.75	5.66	5.58	5.52	5.46
700	7.10	6.95	6.82	6.70	6.60	6.51	6.44	6.37
800	8.11	7.94	7.79	7.66	7.54	7.44	7.35	7.27
900	9.12	8.93	8.76	8.62	8.49	8.37	8.27	8.18
1000	10.14	9.92	9.74	9.57	9.43	9.30	9.19	9.09
2000	20.27	19.84	19.47	19.14	18.85	18.60	18.38	18.18
3000	30.40	29.76	29.20	28.71	28.28	27.90	27.56	27.27
4000	40.54	39.68	38.93	38.28	37.70	37.20	36.75	36.35
5000	50.67	49.60	48.66	47.84	47.12	46.49	45.93	45.44
6000	60.80	59.51	58.39	57.41	56.55	55.79	55.12	54.53
7000	70.94	69.43	68.12	66.98	65.97	65.09	64.31	63.61
8000	81.07	79.35	77.85	76.55	75.40	74.39	73.49	72.70
9000	91.20	89.27	87.58	86.11	84.82	83.68	82.68	81.79
10000	101.34	99.19	97.32	95.68	94.24	92.98	91.86	90.87
11000	111.47	109.10	107.05	105.25	103.67	102.28	101.05	99.96
12000	121.60	119.02	116.78	114.82	113.09	111.58	110.24	109.05
13000	131.74	128.94	126.51	124.38	122.52	120.87	119.42	118.13
14000	141.87	138.86	136.24	133.95	131.94	130.17	128.61	127.22
15000	152.00	148.78	145.97	143.52	141.36	139.47	137.79	136.31
16000	162.13	158.70	155.70	153.09	150.79	148.77	146.98	145.40
17000	172.27	168.61	165.43	162.65	160.21	158.06	156.16	154.48
18000	182.40	178.53	175.16	172.22	169.64	167.36	165.35	163.57
19000	192.53	188.45	184.90	181.79	179.06	176.66	174.54	172.66
20000	202.67	198.37	194.63	191.36	188.48	185.96	183.72	181.74
21000	212.80	208.29	204.36	200.92	197.91	195.25	192.91	190.83
22000	222.93	218.20	214.09	210.49	207.33	204.55	202.09	199.92
23000	233.07	228.12	223.82	220.06	216.76	213.85	211.28	209.00
24000	243.20	238.04	233.55	229.63	226.18	223.15	220.47	218.09
25000	253.33	247.96	243.28	239.19	235.60	232.44	229.65	227.18
26000	263.47	257.88	253.01	248.76	245.03	241.74	238.84	236.26
27000	273.60	267.80	262.74	258.33	254.45	251.04	248.02	245.35
28000	283.73	277.71	272.48	267.90	263.88	260.34	257.21	254.44
29000	293.87	287.63	282.21	277.46	273.30	269.63	266.39	263.52
30000	304.00	297.55	291.94	287.03	282.72	278.93	275.58	272.61
31000	314.13	307.47	301.67	296.60	292.15	288.23	284.77	281.70
32000	324.26	317.39	311.40	306.17	301.57	297.53	293.95	290.79
33000	334.40	327.30	321.13	315.73	311.00	306.82	303.14	299.87
34000	344.53	337.22	330.86	325.30	320.42	316.12	312.32	308.96
35000	354.66	347.14	340.59	334.87	329.84	325.42	321.51	318.05
40000	405.33	396.73	389.25	382.71	376.96	371.91	367.44	363.48
45000	456.00	446.32	437.90	430.54	424.08	418.39	413.37	408.92
50000	506.66	495.91	486.56	478.38	471.20	464.88	459.30	454.35
55000	557.33	545.50	535.22	526.22	518.32	511.37	505.23	499.78
60000	607.99	595.10	583.87	574.06	565.44	557.86	551.16	545.22
65000	658.66	644.69	632.53	621.90	612.56	604.35	597.08	590.65
70000	709.32	694.28	681.18	669.73	659.68	650.83	643.01	636.09
75000	759.99	743.87	729.84	717.57	706.80	697.32	688.94	681.52
80000	810.65	793.46	778.49	765.41	753.92	743.81	734.87	726.96
85000	861.32	843.05	827.15	813.25	801.04	790.30	780.80	772.39
90000	911.99	892.64	875.80	861.08	848.16	836.78	826.73	817.83
95000	962.65	942.23	924.46	908.92	895.28	883.27	872.66	863.26
100000	1013.32	991.82	973.12	956.76	942.40	929.76	918.59	908.69
105000	1063.98	1041.41	1021.77	1004.60	989.52	976.25	964.52	954.13
110000	1114.65	1091.00	1070.43	1052.43	1036.64	1022.73	1010.45	999.56
115000	1165.31	1140.60	1119.08	1100.27	1083.76	1069.22	1056.38	1045.00
120000	1215.98	1190.19	1167.74	1148.11	1130.88	1115.71	1102.31	1090.43
125000	1266.64	1239.78	1216.39	1195.95	1178.00	1162.20	1148.24	1135.87
130000	1317.31	1289.37	1265.05	1243.79	1225.12	1208.69	1194.16	1181.30
135000	1367.98	1338.96	1313.70	1291.62	1272.24	1255.17	1240.09	1226.74
140000	1418.64	1388.55	1362.36	1339.46	1319.36	1301.66	1286.02	1272.17
145000	1469.31	1438.14	1411.01	1387.30	1366.48	1348.15	1331.95	1317.60
150000	1519.97	1487.73	1459.67	1435.14	1413.60	1394.64	1377.88	1363.04
155000	1570.64	1537.32	1508.33	1482.97	1460.72	1441.12	1423.81	1408.47
160000	1621.30	1586.91	1556.98	1530.81	1507.84	1487.61	1469.74	1453.91

AMOUNT OF LOAN	NUMBER OF YEARS IN TERM							
	25	26	27	28	29	30	35	40
$ 50	.45	.45	.45	.44	.44	.44	.43	.42
100	.90	.90	.89	.88	.88	.87	.86	.84
200	1.80	1.79	1.78	1.76	1.75	1.74	1.71	1.68
300	2.70	2.68	2.66	2.64	2.62	2.61	2.56	2.52
400	3.60	3.57	3.55	3.52	3.50	3.48	3.41	3.36
500	4.50	4.47	4.43	4.40	4.37	4.35	4.26	4.20
600	5.40	5.36	5.32	5.28	5.24	5.22	5.11	5.04
700	6.30	6.25	6.20	6.16	6.12	6.08	5.96	5.88
800	7.20	7.14	7.09	7.04	6.99	6.95	6.81	6.72
900	8.10	8.03	7.97	7.92	7.86	7.82	7.66	7.56
1000	9.00	8.93	8.86	8.79	8.74	8.69	8.51	8.40
2000	18.00	17.85	17.71	17.58	17.47	17.37	17.01	16.79
3000	27.00	26.77	26.56	26.37	26.20	26.06	25.51	25.19
4000	36.00	35.69	35.41	35.16	34.94	34.74	34.01	33.58
5000	45.00	44.61	44.26	43.95	43.67	43.42	42.51	41.97
6000	54.00	53.53	53.11	52.74	52.40	52.11	51.01	50.37
7000	63.00	62.45	61.96	61.53	61.14	60.79	59.51	58.76
8000	72.00	71.37	70.81	70.32	69.87	69.47	68.01	67.15
9000	81.00	80.29	79.67	79.11	78.60	78.16	76.52	75.55
10000	90.00	89.21	88.52	87.89	87.34	86.84	85.02	83.94
11000	98.99	98.13	97.37	96.68	96.07	95.52	93.52	92.33
12000	107.99	107.06	106.22	105.47	104.80	104.21	102.02	100.73
13000	116.99	115.98	115.07	114.26	113.54	112.89	110.52	109.12
14000	125.99	124.90	123.92	123.05	122.27	121.57	119.02	117.51
15000	134.99	133.82	132.77	131.84	131.00	130.26	127.52	125.91
16000	143.99	142.74	141.62	140.63	139.74	138.94	136.02	134.30
17000	152.99	151.66	150.48	149.42	148.47	147.62	144.53	142.69
18000	161.99	160.58	159.33	158.21	157.20	156.31	153.03	151.09
19000	170.99	169.50	168.18	167.00	165.94	164.99	161.53	159.48
20000	179.99	178.42	177.03	175.78	174.67	173.67	170.03	167.87
21000	188.98	187.34	185.88	184.57	183.40	182.36	178.53	176.27
22000	197.98	196.26	194.73	193.36	192.14	191.04	187.03	184.66
23000	206.98	205.18	203.58	202.15	200.87	199.73	195.53	193.05
24000	215.98	214.11	212.43	210.94	209.60	208.41	204.03	201.45
25000	224.98	223.03	221.28	219.73	218.34	217.09	212.53	209.84
26000	233.98	231.95	230.14	228.52	227.07	225.78	221.04	218.23
27000	242.98	240.87	238.99	237.31	235.80	234.46	229.54	226.63
28000	251.98	249.79	247.84	246.10	244.54	243.14	238.04	235.02
29000	260.98	258.71	256.69	254.88	253.27	251.83	246.54	243.41
30000	269.98	267.63	265.54	263.67	262.00	260.51	255.04	251.81
31000	278.98	276.55	274.39	272.46	270.74	269.19	263.54	260.20
32000	287.97	285.47	283.24	281.25	279.47	277.88	272.04	268.59
33000	296.97	294.39	292.09	290.04	288.20	286.56	280.54	276.99
34000	305.97	303.31	300.95	298.83	296.94	295.24	289.05	285.38
35000	314.97	312.24	309.80	307.62	305.67	303.93	297.55	293.77
40000	359.97	356.84	354.05	351.56	349.34	347.34	340.05	335.74
45000	404.96	401.44	398.31	395.51	393.00	390.76	382.56	377.71
50000	449.96	446.05	442.56	439.45	436.67	434.18	425.06	419.68
55000	494.95	490.65	486.82	483.40	480.34	477.60	467.57	461.64
60000	539.95	535.26	531.08	527.34	524.00	521.01	510.08	503.61
65000	584.94	579.86	575.33	571.29	567.67	564.43	552.58	545.58
70000	629.94	624.47	619.59	615.23	611.34	607.85	595.09	587.54
75000	674.93	669.07	663.84	659.18	655.00	651.27	637.59	629.51
80000	719.93	713.67	708.10	703.12	698.67	694.68	680.10	671.48
85000	764.92	758.28	752.36	747.07	742.34	738.10	722.61	713.45
90000	809.92	802.88	796.61	791.01	786.00	781.52	765.11	755.41
95000	854.91	847.49	840.87	834.96	829.67	824.94	807.62	797.38
100000	899.91	892.09	885.12	878.90	873.34	868.35	850.12	839.35
105000	944.90	936.70	929.38	922.85	917.00	911.77	892.63	881.31
110000	989.90	981.30	973.64	966.79	960.67	955.19	935.13	923.28
115000	1034.89	1025.90	1017.89	1010.74	1004.34	998.61	977.64	965.25
120000	1079.89	1070.51	1062.15	1054.68	1048.00	1042.02	1020.15	1007.21
125000	1124.88	1115.11	1106.40	1098.62	1091.67	1085.44	1062.65	1049.18
130000	1169.88	1159.72	1150.66	1142.57	1135.34	1128.86	1105.16	1091.15
135000	1214.88	1204.32	1194.91	1186.51	1179.00	1172.28	1147.66	1133.12
140000	1259.87	1248.93	1239.17	1230.46	1222.67	1215.69	1190.17	1175.08
145000	1304.87	1293.53	1283.43	1274.40	1266.34	1259.11	1232.68	1217.05
150000	1349.86	1338.14	1327.68	1318.35	1310.00	1302.53	1275.18	1259.02
155000	1394.86	1382.74	1371.94	1362.29	1353.67	1345.95	1317.69	1300.98
160000	1439.85	1427.34	1416.19	1406.24	1397.34	1389.36	1360.19	1342.95

10%

MONTHLY AMORTIZING PAYMENTS

AMOUNT OF LOAN	NUMBER OF YEARS IN TERM							
	1	1-1/2	2	3	4	5	6	7
$ 50	4.40	3.01	2.31	1.62	1.27	1.07	.93	.84
100	8.80	6.01	4.62	3.23	2.54	2.13	1.86	1.67
200	17.59	12.02	9.23	6.46	5.08	4.25	3.71	3.33
300	26.38	18.02	13.85	9.69	7.61	6.38	5.56	4.99
400	35.17	24.03	18.46	12.91	10.15	8.50	7.42	6.65
500	43.96	30.03	23.08	16.14	12.69	10.63	9.27	8.31
600	52.75	36.04	27.69	19.37	15.22	12.75	11.12	9.97
700	61.55	42.04	32.31	22.59	17.76	14.88	12.97	11.63
800	70.34	48.05	36.92	25.82	20.30	17.00	14.83	13.29
900	79.13	54.06	41.54	29.05	22.83	19.13	16.68	14.95
1000	87.92	60.06	46.15	32.27	25.37	21.25	18.53	16.61
2000	175.84	120.12	92.29	64.54	50.73	42.50	37.06	33.21
3000	263.75	180.18	138.44	96.81	76.09	63.75	55.58	49.81
4000	351.67	240.23	184.58	129.07	101.46	84.99	74.11	66.41
5000	439.58	300.29	230.73	161.34	126.82	106.24	92.63	83.01
6000	527.50	360.35	276.87	193.61	152.18	127.49	111.16	99.61
7000	615.42	420.40	323.02	225.88	177.54	148.73	129.69	116.21
8000	703.33	480.46	369.16	258.14	202.91	169.98	148.21	132.81
9000	791.25	540.52	415.31	290.41	228.27	191.23	166.74	149.42
10000	879.16	600.58	461.45	322.68	253.63	212.48	185.26	166.02
11000	967.08	660.63	507.60	354.94	278.99	233.72	203.79	182.62
12000	1055.00	720.69	553.74	387.21	304.36	254.97	222.32	199.22
13000	1142.91	780.75	599.89	419.48	329.72	276.22	240.84	215.82
14000	1230.83	840.80	646.03	451.75	355.08	297.46	259.37	232.42
15000	1318.74	900.86	692.18	484.01	380.44	318.71	277.89	249.02
16000	1406.66	960.92	738.32	516.28	405.81	339.96	296.42	265.62
17000	1494.58	1020.98	784.47	548.55	431.17	361.20	314.94	282.23
18000	1582.49	1081.03	830.61	580.81	456.53	382.45	333.47	298.83
19000	1670.41	1141.09	876.76	613.08	481.89	403.70	352.00	315.43
20000	1758.32	1201.15	922.90	645.35	507.26	424.95	370.52	332.03
21000	1846.24	1261.20	969.05	677.62	532.62	446.19	389.05	348.63
22000	1934.15	1321.26	1015.19	709.88	557.98	467.44	407.57	365.23
23000	2022.07	1381.32	1061.34	742.15	583.34	488.69	426.10	381.83
24000	2109.99	1441.37	1107.48	774.42	608.71	509.93	444.63	398.43
25000	2197.90	1501.43	1153.63	806.68	634.07	531.18	463.15	415.03
26000	2285.82	1561.49	1199.77	838.95	659.43	552.43	481.68	431.64
27000	2373.73	1621.55	1245.92	871.22	684.79	573.68	500.20	448.24
28000	2461.65	1681.60	1292.06	903.49	710.16	594.92	518.73	464.84
29000	2549.57	1741.66	1338.21	935.75	735.52	616.17	537.25	481.44
30000	2637.48	1801.72	1384.35	968.02	760.88	637.42	555.78	498.04
31000	2725.40	1861.77	1430.50	1000.29	786.25	658.66	574.31	514.64
32000	2813.31	1921.83	1476.64	1032.55	811.61	679.91	592.83	531.24
33000	2901.23	1981.89	1522.79	1064.82	836.97	701.16	611.36	547.84
34000	2989.15	2041.95	1568.93	1097.09	862.33	722.40	629.88	564.45
35000	3077.06	2102.00	1615.08	1129.36	887.70	743.65	648.41	581.05
40000	3516.64	2402.29	1845.80	1290.69	1014.51	849.89	741.04	664.05
45000	3956.22	2702.57	2076.53	1452.03	1141.32	956.12	833.67	747.06
50000	4395.80	3002.86	2307.25	1613.36	1268.13	1062.36	926.30	830.06
55000	4835.38	3303.14	2537.98	1774.70	1394.95	1168.59	1018.93	913.07
60000	5274.96	3603.43	2768.70	1936.04	1521.76	1274.83	1111.56	996.08
65000	5714.54	3903.72	2999.43	2097.37	1648.57	1381.06	1204.18	1079.08
70000	6154.12	4204.00	3230.15	2258.71	1775.39	1487.30	1296.81	1162.09
75000	6593.70	4504.29	3460.87	2420.04	1902.20	1593.53	1389.44	1245.09
80000	7033.28	4804.57	3691.60	2581.38	2029.01	1699.77	1482.07	1328.10
85000	7472.86	5104.86	3922.32	2742.72	2155.82	1806.00	1574.70	1411.11
90000	7912.43	5405.14	4153.05	2904.05	2282.64	1912.24	1667.33	1494.11
95000	8352.01	5705.43	4383.77	3065.39	2409.45	2018.47	1759.96	1577.12
100000	8791.59	6005.71	4614.50	3226.72	2536.26	2124.71	1852.59	1660.12
105000	9231.17	6306.00	4845.22	3388.06	2663.08	2230.94	1945.22	1743.13
110000	9670.75	6606.28	5075.95	3549.40	2789.89	2337.18	2037.85	1826.14
115000	10110.33	6906.57	5306.67	3710.73	2916.70	2443.42	2130.48	1909.14
120000	10549.91	7206.85	5537.40	3872.07	3043.52	2549.65	2223.11	1992.15
125000	10989.49	7507.14	5768.12	4033.40	3170.33	2655.89	2315.73	2075.15
130000	11429.07	7807.43	5998.85	4194.74	3297.14	2762.12	2408.36	2158.16
135000	11868.65	8107.71	6229.57	4356.08	3423.95	2868.36	2500.99	2241.16
140000	12308.23	8408.00	6460.29	4517.41	3550.77	2974.59	2593.62	2324.17
145000	12747.81	8708.28	6691.02	4678.75	3677.58	3080.83	2686.25	2407.18
150000	13187.39	9008.57	6921.74	4840.08	3804.39	3187.06	2778.88	2490.18
155000	13626.97	9308.85	7152.47	5001.42	3931.21	3293.30	2871.51	2573.19
160000	14066.55	9609.14	7383.19	5162.75	4058.02	3399.53	2964.14	2656.19

AMOUNT OF LOAN	NUMBER OF YEARS IN TERM							
	8	9	10	11	12	14	15	16
$ 50	.76	.71	.67	.63	.60	.56	.54	.53
100	1.52	1.41	1.33	1.26	1.20	1.11	1.08	1.05
200	3.04	2.82	2.65	2.51	2.40	2.22	2.15	2.10
300	4.56	4.23	3.97	3.76	3.59	3.33	3.23	3.14
400	6.07	5.64	5.29	5.01	4.79	4.44	4.30	4.19
500	7.59	7.04	6.61	6.26	5.98	5.55	5.38	5.23
600	9.11	8.45	7.93	7.52	7.18	6.65	6.45	6.28
700	10.63	9.86	9.26	8.77	8.37	7.76	7.53	7.33
800	12.14	11.27	10.58	10.02	9.57	8.87	8.60	8.37
900	13.66	12.68	11.90	11.27	10.76	9.98	9.68	9.42
1000	15.18	14.08	13.22	12.52	11.96	11.09	10.75	10.46
2000	30.35	28.16	26.44	25.04	23.91	22.17	21.50	20.92
3000	45.53	42.24	39.65	37.56	35.86	33.25	32.24	31.38
4000	60.70	56.32	52.87	50.08	47.81	44.33	42.99	41.84
5000	75.88	70.40	66.08	62.60	59.76	55.42	53.74	52.30
6000	91.05	84.48	79.30	75.12	71.71	66.50	64.48	62.76
7000	106.22	98.56	92.51	87.64	83.66	77.58	75.23	73.22
8000	121.40	112.63	105.73	100.16	95.61	88.66	85.97	83.68
9000	136.57	126.71	118.94	112.68	107.56	99.74	96.72	94.14
10000	151.75	140.79	132.16	125.20	119.51	110.83	107.47	104.60
11000	166.92	154.87	145.37	137.72	131.46	121.91	118.21	115.05
12000	182.09	168.95	158.59	150.24	143.41	132.99	128.96	125.51
13000	197.27	183.03	171.80	162.76	155.37	144.07	139.70	135.97
14000	212.44	197.11	185.02	175.28	167.32	155.15	150.45	146.43
15000	227.62	211.19	198.23	187.80	179.27	166.24	161.20	156.89
16000	242.79	225.26	211.45	200.32	191.22	177.32	171.94	167.35
17000	257.97	239.34	224.66	212.84	203.17	188.40	182.69	177.81
18000	273.14	253.42	237.88	225.36	215.12	199.48	193.43	188.27
19000	288.31	267.50	251.09	237.88	227.07	210.56	204.18	198.73
20000	303.49	281.58	264.31	250.40	239.02	221.65	214.93	209.19
21000	318.66	295.66	277.52	262.92	250.97	232.73	225.67	219.64
22000	333.84	309.74	290.74	275.44	262.92	243.81	236.42	230.10
23000	349.01	323.81	303.95	287.96	274.87	254.89	247.16	240.56
24000	364.18	337.89	317.17	300.48	286.82	265.97	257.91	251.02
25000	379.36	351.97	330.38	313.00	298.77	277.06	268.66	261.48
26000	394.53	366.05	343.60	325.52	310.73	288.14	279.40	271.94
27000	409.71	380.13	356.81	338.04	322.68	299.22	290.15	282.40
28000	424.88	394.21	370.03	350.56	334.63	310.30	300.89	292.86
29000	440.06	408.29	383.24	363.08	346.58	321.38	311.64	303.32
30000	455.23	422.37	396.46	375.60	358.53	332.47	322.39	313.78
31000	470.40	436.44	409.67	388.12	370.48	343.55	333.13	324.23
32000	485.58	450.52	422.89	400.64	382.43	354.63	343.88	334.69
33000	500.75	464.60	436.10	413.16	394.38	365.71	354.62	345.15
34000	515.93	478.68	449.32	425.68	406.33	376.79	365.37	355.61
35000	531.10	492.76	462.53	438.20	418.28	387.88	376.12	366.07
40000	606.97	563.15	528.61	500.80	478.04	443.29	429.85	418.37
45000	682.84	633.55	594.68	563.40	537.79	498.70	483.58	470.66
50000	758.71	703.94	660.76	626.00	597.54	554.11	537.31	522.96
55000	834.58	774.33	726.83	688.60	657.30	609.52	591.04	575.25
60000	910.45	844.73	792.91	751.20	717.05	664.93	644.77	627.55
65000	986.33	915.12	858.98	813.80	776.81	720.34	698.50	679.84
70000	1062.20	985.51	925.06	876.40	836.56	775.75	752.23	732.14
75000	1138.07	1055.91	991.14	939.00	896.31	831.16	805.96	784.43
80000	1213.94	1126.30	1057.21	1001.60	956.07	886.57	859.69	836.73
85000	1289.81	1196.69	1123.29	1064.19	1015.82	941.98	913.42	889.02
90000	1365.68	1267.09	1189.36	1126.79	1075.58	997.39	967.15	941.32
95000	1441.55	1337.48	1255.44	1189.39	1135.33	1052.80	1020.88	993.61
100000	1517.42	1407.87	1321.51	1251.99	1195.08	1108.21	1074.61	1045.91
105000	1593.29	1478.27	1387.59	1314.59	1254.84	1163.62	1128.34	1098.20
110000	1669.16	1548.66	1453.66	1377.19	1314.59	1219.03	1182.07	1150.50
115000	1745.03	1619.05	1519.74	1439.79	1374.35	1274.44	1235.80	1202.79
120000	1820.90	1689.45	1585.81	1502.39	1434.10	1329.85	1289.53	1255.09
125000	1896.78	1759.84	1651.89	1564.99	1493.85	1385.26	1343.26	1307.38
130000	1972.65	1830.23	1717.96	1627.59	1553.61	1440.67	1396.99	1359.68
135000	2048.52	1900.63	1784.04	1690.19	1613.36	1496.08	1450.72	1411.97
140000	2124.39	1971.02	1850.12	1752.79	1673.11	1551.49	1504.45	1464.27
145000	2200.26	2041.41	1916.19	1815.39	1732.87	1606.90	1558.18	1516.56
150000	2276.13	2111.81	1982.27	1877.99	1792.62	1662.31	1611.91	1568.86
155000	2352.00	2182.20	2048.34	1940.59	1852.38	1717.72	1665.64	1621.15
160000	2427.87	2252.59	2114.42	2003.19	1912.13	1773.13	1719.37	1673.45

MONTHLY AMORTIZING PAYMENTS

AMOUNT OF LOAN	NUMBER OF YEARS IN TERM							
	17	18	19	20	21	22	23	24
$ 50	.52	.50	.50	.49	.48	.47	.47	.46
100	1.03	1.00	.99	.97	.96	.94	.93	.92
200	2.05	2.00	1.97	1.94	1.91	1.88	1.86	1.84
300	3.07	3.00	2.95	2.90	2.86	2.82	2.79	2.76
400	4.09	4.00	3.93	3.87	3.81	3.76	3.71	3.67
500	5.11	5.00	4.91	4.83	4.76	4.70	4.64	4.59
600	6.13	6.00	5.89	5.80	5.71	5.63	5.57	5.51
700	7.15	7.00	6.87	6.76	6.66	6.57	6.50	6.43
800	8.17	8.00	7.86	7.73	7.61	7.51	7.42	7.34
900	9.20	9.00	8.84	8.69	8.56	8.45	8.35	8.26
1000	10.22	10.00	9.82	9.66	9.51	9.39	9.28	9.18
2000	20.43	20.00	19.63	19.31	19.02	18.77	18.55	18.35
3000	30.64	30.00	29.44	28.96	28.53	28.15	27.82	27.53
4000	40.85	40.00	39.26	38.61	38.04	37.53	37.09	36.70
5000	51.07	50.00	49.07	48.26	47.54	46.92	46.36	45.87
6000	61.28	60.00	58.88	57.91	57.05	56.30	55.64	55.05
7000	71.49	69.99	68.69	67.56	66.56	65.68	64.91	64.22
8000	81.70	79.99	78.51	77.21	76.07	75.06	74.18	73.40
9000	91.91	89.99	88.32	86.86	85.58	84.45	83.45	82.57
10000	102.13	99.99	98.13	96.51	95.08	93.83	92.72	91.74
11000	112.34	109.99	107.94	106.16	104.59	103.21	101.99	100.92
12000	122.55	119.99	117.76	115.81	114.10	112.59	111.27	110.09
13000	132.76	129.98	127.57	125.46	123.61	121.98	120.54	119.27
14000	142.97	139.98	137.38	135.11	133.11	131.36	129.81	128.44
15000	153.19	149.98	147.19	144.76	142.62	140.74	139.08	137.61
16000	163.40	159.98	157.01	154.41	152.13	150.12	148.35	146.79
17000	173.61	169.98	166.82	164.06	161.64	159.51	157.63	155.96
18000	183.82	179.98	176.63	173.71	171.15	168.89	166.90	165.13
19000	194.03	189.98	186.44	183.36	180.65	178.27	176.17	174.31
20000	204.25	199.97	196.26	193.01	190.16	187.65	185.44	183.48
21000	214.46	209.97	206.07	202.66	199.67	197.04	194.71	192.66
22000	224.67	219.97	215.88	212.31	209.18	206.42	203.98	201.83
23000	234.88	229.97	225.69	221.96	218.68	215.80	213.26	211.00
24000	245.10	239.97	235.51	231.61	228.19	225.18	222.53	220.18
25000	255.31	249.97	245.32	241.26	237.70	234.57	231.80	229.35
26000	265.52	259.96	255.13	250.91	247.21	243.95	241.07	238.53
27000	275.73	269.96	264.94	260.56	256.72	253.33	250.34	247.70
28000	285.94	279.96	274.76	270.21	266.22	262.71	259.62	256.87
29000	296.16	289.96	284.57	279.86	275.73	272.10	268.89	266.05
30000	306.37	299.96	294.38	289.51	285.24	281.48	278.16	275.22
31000	316.58	309.96	304.20	299.16	294.75	290.86	287.43	284.40
32000	326.79	319.95	314.01	308.81	304.25	300.24	296.70	293.57
33000	337.00	329.95	323.82	318.46	313.76	309.63	305.97	302.74
34000	347.22	339.95	333.63	328.11	323.27	319.01	315.25	311.92
35000	357.43	349.95	343.45	337.76	332.78	328.39	324.52	321.09
40000	408.49	399.94	392.51	386.01	380.32	375.30	370.88	366.96
45000	459.55	449.93	441.57	434.26	427.86	422.22	417.24	412.83
50000	510.61	499.93	490.63	482.52	475.40	469.13	463.60	458.70
55000	561.67	549.92	539.70	530.77	522.93	516.04	509.95	504.57
60000	612.73	599.91	588.76	579.02	570.47	562.95	556.31	550.44
65000	663.79	649.90	637.82	627.27	618.01	609.86	602.67	596.31
70000	714.85	699.90	686.89	675.52	665.55	656.78	649.03	642.18
75000	765.91	749.89	735.95	723.77	713.09	703.69	695.39	688.05
80000	816.97	799.88	785.01	772.02	760.63	750.60	741.75	733.92
85000	868.03	849.87	834.08	820.27	808.17	797.51	788.11	779.79
90000	919.09	899.86	883.14	868.52	855.71	844.43	834.47	825.65
95000	970.15	949.86	932.20	916.78	903.25	891.34	880.83	871.52
100000	1021.22	999.85	981.26	965.03	950.79	938.25	927.19	917.39
105000	1072.28	1049.84	1030.33	1013.28	998.32	985.16	973.55	963.26
110000	1123.34	1099.83	1079.39	1061.53	1045.86	1032.08	1019.90	1009.13
115000	1174.40	1149.83	1128.45	1109.78	1093.40	1078.99	1066.26	1055.00
120000	1225.46	1199.82	1177.52	1158.03	1140.94	1125.90	1112.62	1100.87
125000	1276.52	1249.81	1226.58	1206.28	1188.48	1172.81	1158.98	1146.74
130000	1327.58	1299.80	1275.64	1254.53	1236.02	1219.72	1205.34	1192.61
135000	1378.64	1349.79	1324.70	1302.78	1283.56	1266.64	1251.70	1238.48
140000	1429.70	1399.79	1373.77	1351.04	1331.10	1313.55	1298.06	1284.35
145000	1480.76	1449.78	1422.83	1399.29	1378.64	1360.46	1344.42	1330.22
150000	1531.82	1499.77	1471.89	1447.54	1426.18	1407.37	1390.78	1376.09
155000	1582.88	1549.76	1520.96	1495.79	1473.71	1454.29	1437.14	1421.96
160000	1633.94	1599.75	1570.02	1544.04	1521.25	1501.20	1483.50	1467.83

AMOUNT OF LOAN	NUMBER OF YEARS IN TERM							
	25	26	27	28	29	30	35	40
$ 50	.46	.46	.45	.45	.45	.44	.43	.43
100	.91	.91	.90	.89	.89	.88	.86	.85
200	1.82	1.81	1.79	1.78	1.77	1.76	1.72	1.70
300	2.73	2.71	2.69	2.67	2.65	2.64	2.58	2.55
400	3.64	3.61	3.58	3.56	3.53	3.52	3.44	3.40
500	4.55	4.51	4.48	4.44	4.42	4.39	4.30	4.25
600	5.46	5.41	5.37	5.33	5.30	5.27	5.16	5.10
700	6.37	6.31	6.26	6.22	6.18	6.15	6.02	5.95
800	7.27	7.21	7.16	7.11	7.06	7.03	6.88	6.80
900	8.18	8.11	8.05	8.00	7.95	7.90	7.74	7.65
1000	9.09	9.01	8.95	8.88	8.83	8.78	8.60	8.50
2000	18.18	18.02	17.89	17.76	17.65	17.56	17.20	16.99
3000	27.27	27.03	26.83	26.64	26.48	26.33	25.80	25.48
4000	36.35	36.04	35.77	35.52	35.30	35.11	34.39	33.97
5000	45.44	45.05	44.71	44.40	44.13	43.88	42.99	42.46
6000	54.53	54.06	53.65	53.28	52.95	52.66	51.59	50.95
7000	63.61	63.07	62.59	62.16	61.78	61.44	60.18	59.45
8000	72.70	72.08	71.53	71.04	70.60	70.21	68.78	67.94
9000	81.79	81.09	80.47	79.92	79.43	78.99	77.38	76.43
10000	90.88	90.10	89.41	88.80	88.25	87.76	85.97	84.92
11000	99.96	99.11	98.36	97.68	97.08	96.54	94.57	93.41
12000	109.05	108.12	107.30	106.56	105.90	105.31	103.17	101.90
13000	118.14	117.13	116.24	115.44	114.73	114.09	111.76	110.39
14000	127.22	126.14	125.18	124.32	123.55	122.87	120.36	118.89
15000	136.31	135.15	134.12	133.20	132.38	131.64	128.96	127.38
16000	145.40	144.16	143.06	142.08	141.20	140.42	137.55	135.87
17000	154.48	153.17	152.00	150.96	150.03	149.19	146.15	144.36
18000	163.57	162.18	160.94	159.84	158.85	157.97	154.75	152.85
19000	172.66	171.19	169.88	168.72	167.68	166.74	163.34	161.34
20000	181.75	180.20	178.82	177.60	176.50	175.52	171.94	169.83
21000	190.83	189.21	187.77	186.48	185.33	184.30	180.54	178.33
22000	199.92	198.22	196.71	195.36	194.15	193.07	189.13	186.82
23000	209.01	207.23	205.65	204.24	202.97	201.85	197.73	195.31
24000	218.09	216.24	214.59	213.12	211.80	210.62	206.33	203.80
25000	227.18	225.25	223.53	222.00	220.62	219.40	214.92	212.29
26000	236.27	234.26	232.47	230.87	229.45	228.17	223.52	220.78
27000	245.35	243.27	241.41	239.75	238.27	236.95	232.12	229.27
28000	254.44	252.28	250.35	248.63	247.10	245.73	240.71	237.77
29000	263.53	261.29	259.29	257.51	255.92	254.50	249.31	246.26
30000	272.62	270.30	268.23	266.39	264.75	263.28	257.91	254.75
31000	281.70	279.31	277.18	275.27	273.57	272.05	266.50	263.24
32000	290.79	288.32	286.12	284.15	282.40	280.83	275.10	271.73
33000	299.88	297.33	295.06	293.03	291.22	289.60	283.70	280.22
34000	308.96	306.34	304.00	301.91	300.05	298.38	292.29	288.71
35000	318.05	315.35	312.94	310.79	308.87	307.16	300.89	297.21
40000	363.49	360.40	357.64	355.19	353.00	351.03	343.87	339.66
45000	408.92	405.44	402.35	399.59	397.12	394.91	386.86	382.12
50000	454.36	450.49	447.05	443.99	441.24	438.79	429.84	424.58
55000	499.79	495.54	491.76	488.38	485.37	482.67	472.82	467.04
60000	545.23	540.59	536.46	532.78	529.49	526.55	515.81	509.49
65000	590.66	585.64	581.17	577.18	573.62	570.43	558.79	551.95
70000	636.10	630.69	625.87	621.58	617.74	614.31	601.78	594.41
75000	681.53	675.74	670.58	665.98	661.86	658.18	644.76	636.86
80000	726.97	720.79	715.28	710.37	705.99	702.06	687.74	679.32
85000	772.40	765.84	759.99	754.77	750.11	745.94	730.73	721.78
90000	817.84	810.88	804.69	799.17	794.23	789.82	773.71	764.24
95000	863.27	855.93	849.40	843.57	838.36	833.70	816.69	806.69
100000	908.71	900.98	894.10	887.97	882.48	877.58	859.68	849.15
105000	954.14	946.03	938.81	932.36	926.61	921.46	902.66	891.61
110000	999.58	991.08	983.51	976.76	970.73	965.33	945.64	934.07
115000	1045.01	1036.13	1028.22	1021.16	1014.85	1009.21	988.63	976.52
120000	1090.45	1081.18	1072.92	1065.56	1058.98	1053.09	1031.61	1018.98
125000	1135.88	1126.23	1117.63	1109.96	1103.10	1096.97	1074.60	1061.44
130000	1181.32	1171.28	1162.33	1154.35	1147.23	1140.85	1117.58	1103.89
135000	1226.75	1216.32	1207.04	1198.75	1191.35	1184.73	1160.56	1146.35
140000	1272.19	1261.37	1251.74	1243.15	1235.47	1228.61	1203.55	1188.81
145000	1317.62	1306.42	1296.45	1287.55	1279.60	1272.48	1246.53	1231.27
150000	1363.06	1351.47	1341.15	1331.95	1323.72	1316.36	1289.51	1273.72
155000	1408.49	1396.52	1385.86	1376.34	1367.84	1360.24	1332.50	1316.18
160000	1453.93	1441.57	1430.56	1420.74	1411.97	1404.12	1375.48	1358.64

MONTHLY AMORTIZING PAYMENTS

AMOUNT OF LOAN	NUMBER OF YEARS IN TERM							
	1	1-1/2	2	3	4	5	6	7
$ 50	4.40	3.01	2.32	1.62	1.28	1.07	.93	.84
100	8.80	6.02	4.63	3.24	2.55	2.14	1.86	1.67
200	17.60	12.03	9.25	6.47	5.09	4.27	3.72	3.34
300	26.40	18.04	13.87	9.70	7.63	6.40	5.58	5.00
400	35.19	24.05	18.49	12.94	10.17	8.53	7.44	6.67
500	43.99	30.06	23.11	16.17	12.72	10.66	9.30	8.34
600	52.79	36.07	27.73	19.40	15.26	12.79	11.16	10.00
700	61.59	42.09	32.35	22.63	17.80	14.92	13.02	11.67
800	70.38	48.10	36.97	25.87	20.34	17.05	14.88	13.34
900	79.18	54.11	41.59	29.10	22.89	19.18	16.74	15.00
1000	87.98	60.12	46.21	32.33	25.43	21.31	18.59	16.67
2000	175.95	120.23	92.41	64.66	50.85	42.62	37.18	33.34
3000	263.93	180.35	138.61	96.98	76.27	63.93	55.77	50.00
4000	351.90	240.46	184.82	129.31	101.70	85.24	74.36	66.67
5000	439.88	300.58	231.02	161.63	127.12	106.55	92.95	83.33
6000	527.85	360.69	277.22	193.96	152.54	127.86	111.54	100.00
7000	615.82	420.81	323.42	226.29	177.96	149.17	130.13	116.67
8000	703.80	480.92	369.63	258.61	203.39	170.47	148.72	133.33
9000	791.77	541.04	415.83	290.94	228.81	191.78	167.31	150.00
10000	879.75	601.15	462.03	323.26	254.23	213.09	185.89	166.66
11000	967.72	661.27	508.23	355.59	279.65	234.40	204.48	183.33
12000	1055.69	721.38	554.44	387.92	305.08	255.71	223.07	200.00
13000	1143.67	781.50	600.64	420.24	330.50	277.02	241.66	216.66
14000	1231.64	841.61	646.84	452.57	355.92	298.33	260.25	233.33
15000	1319.62	901.72	693.04	484.89	381.34	319.63	278.84	249.99
16000	1407.59	961.84	739.25	517.22	406.77	340.94	297.43	266.66
17000	1495.56	1021.95	785.45	549.55	432.19	362.25	316.02	283.32
18000	1583.54	1082.07	831.65	581.87	457.61	383.56	334.61	299.99
19000	1671.51	1142.18	877.86	614.20	483.04	404.87	353.19	316.66
20000	1759.49	1202.30	924.06	646.52	508.46	426.18	371.78	333.32
21000	1847.46	1262.41	970.26	678.85	533.88	447.49	390.37	349.99
22000	1935.43	1322.53	1016.46	711.17	559.30	468.79	408.96	366.65
23000	2023.41	1382.64	1062.67	743.50	584.73	490.10	427.55	383.32
24000	2111.38	1442.76	1108.87	775.83	610.15	511.41	446.14	399.99
25000	2199.36	1502.87	1155.07	808.15	635.57	532.72	464.73	416.65
26000	2287.33	1562.99	1201.27	840.48	660.99	554.03	483.32	433.32
27000	2375.30	1623.10	1247.48	872.80	686.42	575.34	501.91	449.98
28000	2463.28	1683.22	1293.68	905.13	711.84	596.65	520.50	466.65
29000	2551.25	1743.33	1339.88	937.46	737.26	617.95	539.08	483.31
30000	2639.23	1803.44	1386.08	969.78	762.68	639.26	557.67	499.98
31000	2727.20	1863.56	1432.29	1002.11	788.11	660.57	576.26	516.65
32000	2815.17	1923.67	1478.49	1034.43	813.53	681.88	594.85	533.31
33000	2903.15	1983.79	1524.69	1066.76	838.95	703.19	613.44	549.98
34000	2991.12	2043.90	1570.89	1099.09	864.38	724.50	632.03	566.64
35000	3079.10	2104.02	1617.10	1131.41	889.80	745.81	650.62	583.31
40000	3518.97	2404.59	1848.11	1293.04	1016.91	852.35	743.56	666.64
45000	3958.84	2705.16	2079.12	1454.67	1144.02	958.89	836.51	749.97
50000	4398.71	3005.74	2310.14	1616.30	1271.14	1065.44	929.45	833.30
55000	4838.58	3306.31	2541.15	1777.93	1398.25	1171.98	1022.40	916.63
60000	5278.45	3606.88	2772.16	1939.56	1525.36	1278.52	1115.34	999.96
65000	5718.32	3907.46	3003.18	2101.19	1652.48	1385.06	1208.29	1083.28
70000	6158.19	4208.03	3234.19	2262.82	1779.59	1491.61	1301.23	1166.61
75000	6598.06	4508.60	3465.20	2424.45	1906.70	1598.15	1394.18	1249.94
80000	7037.93	4809.18	3696.22	2586.08	2033.82	1704.69	1487.12	1333.27
85000	7477.80	5109.75	3927.23	2747.71	2160.93	1811.24	1580.06	1416.60
90000	7917.67	5410.32	4158.24	2909.34	2288.04	1917.78	1673.01	1499.93
95000	8357.54	5710.90	4389.26	3070.97	2415.16	2024.32	1765.95	1583.26
100000	8797.41	6011.47	4620.27	3232.60	2542.27	2130.87	1858.90	1666.59
105000	9237.28	6312.04	4851.28	3394.23	2669.38	2237.41	1951.84	1749.92
110000	9677.15	6612.62	5082.30	3555.85	2796.50	2343.95	2044.79	1833.25
115000	10117.02	6913.19	5313.31	3717.48	2923.61	2450.49	2137.73	1916.58
120000	10556.89	7213.76	5544.32	3879.11	3050.72	2557.04	2230.68	1999.91
125000	10996.76	7514.34	5775.34	4040.74	3177.84	2663.58	2323.62	2083.24
130000	11436.63	7814.91	6006.35	4202.37	3304.95	2770.12	2416.57	2166.56
135000	11876.50	8115.48	6237.36	4364.00	3432.06	2876.67	2509.51	2249.89
140000	12316.37	8416.06	6468.37	4525.63	3559.18	2983.21	2602.46	2333.22
145000	12756.24	8716.63	6699.39	4687.26	3686.29	3089.75	2695.40	2416.55
150000	13196.11	9017.20	6930.40	4848.89	3813.40	3196.30	2788.35	2499.88
155000	13635.98	9317.78	7161.41	5010.52	3940.52	3302.84	2881.29	2583.21
160000	14075.85	9618.35	7392.43	5172.15	4067.63	3409.38	2974.23	2666.54

AMOUNT OF LOAN	NUMBER OF YEARS IN TERM							
	8	9	10	11	12	14	15	16
$ 50	.77	.71	.67	.63	.61	.56	.55	.53
100	1.53	1.42	1.33	1.26	1.21	1.12	1.09	1.06
200	3.05	2.83	2.66	2.52	2.41	2.24	2.17	2.11
300	4.58	4.25	3.99	3.78	3.61	3.35	3.25	3.17
400	6.10	5.66	5.32	5.04	4.81	4.47	4.33	4.22
500	7.63	7.08	6.65	6.30	6.02	5.58	5.42	5.27
600	9.15	8.49	7.98	7.56	7.22	6.70	6.50	6.33
700	10.67	9.91	9.30	8.82	8.42	7.82	7.58	7.38
800	12.20	11.32	10.63	10.08	9.62	8.93	8.66	8.43
900	13.72	12.74	11.96	11.34	10.83	10.05	9.75	9.49
1000	15.25	14.15	13.29	12.60	12.03	11.16	10.83	10.54
2000	30.49	28.30	26.57	25.19	24.05	22.32	21.65	21.08
3000	45.73	42.44	39.86	37.78	36.07	33.48	32.47	31.62
4000	60.97	56.59	53.14	50.37	48.10	44.63	43.30	42.15
5000	76.21	70.74	66.43	62.96	60.12	55.79	54.12	52.69
6000	91.45	84.88	79.71	75.55	72.14	66.95	64.94	63.23
7000	106.69	99.03	93.00	88.14	84.17	78.11	75.76	73.76
8000	121.93	113.18	106.28	100.73	96.19	89.26	86.59	84.30
9000	137.17	127.32	119.56	113.32	108.21	100.42	97.41	94.84
10000	152.41	141.47	132.85	125.91	120.24	111.58	108.23	105.37
11000	167.65	155.62	146.13	138.50	132.26	122.73	119.05	115.91
12000	182.89	169.76	159.42	151.09	144.28	133.89	129.88	126.45
13000	198.13	183.91	172.70	163.68	156.31	145.05	140.70	136.99
14000	213.37	198.06	185.99	176.27	168.33	156.21	151.52	147.52
15000	228.61	212.20	199.27	188.87	180.35	167.36	162.34	158.06
16000	243.85	226.35	212.56	201.46	192.37	178.52	173.17	168.60
17000	259.09	240.49	225.84	214.05	204.40	189.68	183.99	179.13
18000	274.33	254.64	239.12	226.64	216.42	200.84	194.81	189.67
19000	289.57	268.79	252.41	239.23	228.44	211.99	205.64	200.21
20000	304.81	282.93	265.69	251.82	240.47	223.15	216.46	210.74
21000	320.05	297.08	278.98	264.41	252.49	234.31	227.28	221.28
22000	335.29	311.23	292.26	277.00	264.51	245.46	238.10	231.82
23000	350.53	325.37	305.55	289.59	276.54	256.62	248.93	242.36
24000	365.77	339.52	318.83	302.18	288.56	267.78	259.75	252.89
25000	381.01	353.67	332.11	314.77	300.58	278.94	270.57	263.43
26000	396.26	367.81	345.40	327.36	312.61	290.09	281.39	273.97
27000	411.50	381.96	358.68	339.95	324.63	301.25	292.22	284.50
28000	426.74	396.11	371.97	352.54	336.65	312.41	303.04	295.04
29000	441.98	410.25	385.25	365.14	348.68	323.56	313.86	305.58
30000	457.22	424.40	398.54	377.73	360.70	334.72	324.68	316.11
31000	472.46	438.55	411.82	390.32	372.72	345.88	335.51	326.65
32000	487.70	452.69	425.11	402.91	384.74	357.04	346.33	337.19
33000	502.94	466.84	438.39	415.50	396.77	368.19	357.15	347.73
34000	518.18	480.98	451.67	428.09	408.79	379.35	367.98	358.26
35000	533.42	495.13	464.96	440.68	420.81	390.51	378.80	368.80
40000	609.62	565.86	531.38	503.63	480.93	446.29	432.91	421.48
45000	685.82	636.60	597.80	566.59	541.04	502.08	487.02	474.17
50000	762.02	707.33	664.22	629.54	601.16	557.87	541.14	526.85
55000	838.23	778.06	730.65	692.49	661.28	613.65	595.25	579.54
60000	914.43	848.79	797.07	755.45	721.39	669.44	649.36	632.22
65000	990.63	919.53	863.49	818.40	781.51	725.23	703.48	684.91
70000	1066.83	990.26	929.91	881.35	841.62	781.01	757.59	737.59
75000	1143.03	1060.99	996.33	944.31	901.74	836.80	811.70	790.28
80000	1219.24	1131.72	1062.76	1007.26	961.85	892.58	865.82	842.96
85000	1295.44	1202.45	1129.18	1070.22	1021.97	948.37	919.93	895.65
90000	1371.64	1273.19	1195.60	1133.17	1082.08	1004.16	974.04	948.33
95000	1447.84	1343.92	1262.02	1196.12	1142.20	1059.94	1028.16	1001.02
100000	1524.04	1414.65	1328.44	1259.08	1202.32	1115.73	1082.27	1053.70
105000	1600.25	1485.38	1394.87	1322.03	1262.43	1171.51	1136.38	1106.39
110000	1676.45	1556.12	1461.29	1384.98	1322.55	1227.30	1190.50	1159.07
115000	1752.65	1626.85	1527.71	1447.94	1382.66	1283.09	1244.61	1211.76
120000	1828.85	1697.58	1594.13	1510.89	1442.78	1338.87	1298.72	1264.44
125000	1905.05	1768.31	1660.55	1573.84	1502.89	1394.66	1352.84	1317.13
130000	1981.26	1839.05	1726.98	1636.80	1563.01	1450.45	1406.95	1369.81
135000	2057.46	1909.78	1793.40	1699.75	1623.12	1506.23	1461.06	1422.50
140000	2133.66	1980.51	1859.82	1762.70	1683.24	1562.02	1515.18	1475.18
145000	2209.86	2051.24	1926.24	1825.66	1743.36	1617.80	1569.29	1527.87
150000	2286.06	2121.97	1992.66	1888.61	1803.47	1673.59	1623.40	1580.55
155000	2362.26	2192.71	2059.09	1951.57	1863.59	1729.38	1677.52	1633.24
160000	2438.47	2263.44	2125.51	2014.52	1923.70	1785.16	1731.63	1685.92

MONTHLY AMORTIZING PAYMENTS

AMOUNT OF LOAN	NUMBER OF YEARS IN TERM							
	17	18	19	20	21	22	23	24
$ 50	.52	.51	.50	.49	.48	.48	.47	.47
100	1.03	1.01	.99	.98	.96	.95	.94	.93
200	2.06	2.02	1.98	1.95	1.92	1.90	1.88	1.86
300	3.09	3.03	2.97	2.92	2.88	2.85	2.81	2.78
400	4.12	4.04	3.96	3.90	3.84	3.79	3.75	3.71
500	5.15	5.04	4.95	4.87	4.80	4.74	4.68	4.64
600	6.18	6.05	5.94	5.84	5.76	5.69	5.62	5.56
700	7.21	7.06	6.93	6.82	6.72	6.63	6.56	6.49
800	8.24	8.07	7.92	7.79	7.68	7.58	7.49	7.41
900	9.27	9.08	8.91	8.76	8.64	8.53	8.43	8.34
1000	10.30	10.08	9.90	9.74	9.60	9.47	9.36	9.27
2000	20.59	20.16	19.79	19.47	19.19	18.94	18.72	18.53
3000	30.88	30.24	29.69	29.20	28.78	28.41	28.08	27.79
4000	41.17	40.32	39.58	38.94	38.37	37.88	37.44	37.05
5000	51.46	50.40	49.48	48.67	47.96	47.34	46.80	46.31
6000	61.75	60.48	59.37	58.40	57.56	56.81	56.15	55.57
7000	72.04	70.56	69.27	68.14	67.15	66.28	65.51	64.83
8000	82.34	80.64	79.16	77.87	76.74	75.75	74.87	74.09
9000	92.63	90.72	89.05	87.60	86.33	85.21	84.23	83.36
10000	102.92	100.79	98.95	97.34	95.92	94.68	93.59	92.62
11000	113.21	110.87	108.84	107.07	105.52	104.15	102.94	101.88
12000	123.50	120.95	118.74	116.80	115.11	113.62	112.30	111.14
13000	133.79	131.03	128.63	126.54	124.70	123.08	121.66	120.40
14000	144.08	141.11	138.53	136.27	134.29	132.55	131.02	129.66
15000	154.38	151.19	148.42	146.00	143.88	142.02	140.38	138.92
16000	164.67	161.27	158.31	155.74	153.48	151.49	149.73	148.18
17000	174.96	171.35	168.21	165.47	163.07	160.96	159.09	157.45
18000	185.25	181.43	178.10	175.20	172.66	170.42	168.45	166.71
19000	195.54	191.51	188.00	184.94	182.25	179.89	177.81	175.97
20000	205.83	201.58	197.89	194.67	191.84	189.36	187.17	185.23
21000	216.12	211.66	207.79	204.40	201.44	198.83	196.52	194.49
22000	226.42	221.74	217.68	214.13	211.03	208.29	205.88	203.75
23000	236.71	231.82	227.58	223.87	220.62	217.76	215.24	213.01
24000	247.00	241.90	237.47	233.60	230.21	227.23	224.60	222.27
25000	257.29	251.98	247.36	243.33	239.80	236.70	233.96	231.53
26000	267.58	262.06	257.26	253.07	249.39	246.16	243.32	240.80
27000	277.87	272.14	267.15	262.80	258.99	255.63	252.67	250.06
28000	288.16	282.22	277.05	272.53	268.58	265.10	262.03	259.32
29000	298.45	292.30	286.94	282.27	278.17	274.57	271.39	268.58
30000	308.75	302.37	296.84	292.00	287.76	284.04	280.75	277.84
31000	319.04	312.45	306.73	301.73	297.35	293.50	290.11	287.10
32000	329.33	322.53	316.62	311.47	306.95	302.97	299.46	296.36
33000	339.62	332.61	326.52	321.20	316.54	312.44	308.82	305.62
34000	349.91	342.69	336.41	330.93	326.13	321.91	318.18	314.89
35000	360.20	352.77	346.31	340.67	335.72	331.37	327.54	324.15
40000	411.66	403.16	395.78	389.33	383.68	378.71	374.33	370.45
45000	463.12	453.56	445.25	438.00	431.64	426.05	421.12	416.76
50000	514.57	503.95	494.72	486.66	479.60	473.39	467.91	463.06
55000	566.03	554.35	544.19	535.33	527.56	520.73	514.70	509.37
60000	617.49	604.74	593.67	584.00	575.52	568.07	561.49	555.68
65000	668.94	655.14	643.14	632.66	623.48	615.40	608.28	601.98
70000	720.40	705.53	692.61	681.33	671.44	662.74	655.07	648.29
75000	771.86	755.93	742.08	729.99	719.40	710.08	701.86	694.59
80000	823.31	806.32	791.55	778.66	767.36	757.42	748.65	740.90
85000	874.77	856.72	841.03	827.33	815.32	804.76	795.44	787.21
90000	926.23	907.11	890.50	875.99	863.28	852.10	842.23	833.51
95000	977.69	957.51	939.97	924.66	911.24	899.43	889.02	879.82
100000	1029.14	1007.90	989.44	973.32	959.20	946.77	935.81	926.12
105000	1080.60	1058.30	1038.91	1021.99	1007.16	994.11	982.60	972.43
110000	1132.06	1108.69	1088.38	1070.65	1055.12	1041.45	1029.40	1018.73
115000	1183.51	1159.09	1137.86	1119.32	1103.07	1088.79	1076.19	1065.04
120000	1234.97	1209.48	1187.33	1167.99	1151.03	1136.13	1122.98	1111.35
125000	1286.43	1259.88	1236.80	1216.65	1198.99	1183.46	1169.77	1157.65
130000	1337.88	1310.27	1286.27	1265.32	1246.95	1230.80	1216.56	1203.96
135000	1389.34	1360.67	1335.74	1313.98	1294.91	1278.14	1263.35	1250.26
140000	1440.80	1411.06	1385.22	1362.65	1342.87	1325.48	1310.14	1296.57
145000	1492.25	1461.46	1434.69	1411.32	1390.83	1372.82	1356.93	1342.88
150000	1543.71	1511.85	1484.16	1459.98	1438.79	1420.16	1403.72	1389.18
135000	1595.17	1562.25	1533.63	1508.65	1486.75	1467.49	1450.51	1435.49
160000	1646.62	1612.64	1583.10	1557.31	1534.71	1514.83	1497.30	1481.79

AMOUNT OF LOAN	NUMBER OF YEARS IN TERM							
	25	26	27	28	29	30	35	40
$ 50	.46	.46	.46	.45	.45	.45	.44	.43
100	.92	.91	.91	.90	.90	.89	.87	.86
200	1.84	1.82	1.81	1.80	1.79	1.78	1.74	1.72
300	2.76	2.73	2.71	2.70	2.68	2.67	2.61	2.58
400	3.68	3.64	3.62	3.59	3.57	3.55	3.48	3.44
500	4.59	4.55	4.52	4.49	4.46	4.44	4.35	4.30
600	5.51	5.46	5.42	5.39	5.35	5.33	5.22	5.16
700	6.43	6.37	6.33	6.28	6.25	6.21	6.09	6.02
800	7.35	7.28	7.23	7.18	7.14	7.10	6.96	6.88
900	8.26	8.19	8.13	8.08	8.03	7.99	7.83	7.74
1000	9.18	9.10	9.04	8.98	8.92	8.87	8.70	8.59
2000	18.36	18.20	18.07	17.95	17.84	17.74	17.39	17.18
3000	27.53	27.30	27.10	26.92	26.75	26.61	26.08	25.77
4000	36.71	36.40	36.13	35.89	35.67	35.48	34.78	34.36
5000	45.88	45.50	45.16	44.86	44.59	44.35	43.47	42.95
6000	55.06	54.60	54.19	53.83	53.50	53.21	52.16	51.54
7000	64.23	63.70	63.22	62.80	62.42	62.08	60.85	60.13
8000	73.41	72.80	72.25	71.77	71.34	70.95	69.55	68.72
9000	82.58	81.90	81.28	80.74	80.25	79.82	78.24	77.31
10000	91.76	90.99	90.32	89.71	89.17	88.69	86.93	85.90
11000	100.93	100.09	99.35	98.68	98.09	97.56	95.62	94.49
12000	110.11	109.19	108.38	107.65	107.00	106.42	104.32	103.08
13000	119.28	118.29	117.41	116.62	115.92	115.29	113.01	111.67
14000	128.46	127.39	126.44	125.59	124.84	124.16	121.70	120.26
15000	137.63	136.49	135.47	134.56	133.75	133.03	130.39	128.85
16000	146.81	145.59	144.50	143.53	142.67	141.90	139.09	137.44
17000	155.98	154.69	153.53	152.50	151.59	150.76	147.78	146.03
18000	165.16	163.79	162.56	161.47	160.50	159.63	156.47	154.62
19000	174.34	172.89	171.60	170.45	169.42	168.50	165.16	163.21
20000	183.51	181.98	180.63	179.42	178.34	177.37	173.86	171.80
21000	192.69	191.08	189.66	188.39	187.25	186.24	182.55	180.39
22000	201.86	200.18	198.69	197.36	196.17	195.11	191.24	188.98
23000	211.04	209.28	207.72	206.33	205.08	203.97	199.93	197.57
24000	220.21	218.38	216.75	215.30	214.00	212.84	208.63	206.16
25000	229.39	227.48	225.78	224.27	222.92	221.71	217.32	214.75
26000	238.56	236.58	234.81	233.24	231.83	230.58	226.01	223.34
27000	247.74	245.68	243.84	242.21	240.75	239.45	234.70	231.93
28000	256.91	254.78	252.87	251.18	249.67	248.32	243.40	240.52
29000	266.09	263.88	261.91	260.15	258.58	257.18	252.09	249.11
30000	275.26	272.97	270.94	269.12	267.50	266.05	260.78	257.70
31000	284.44	282.07	279.97	278.09	276.42	274.92	269.47	266.29
32000	293.61	291.17	289.00	287.06	285.33	283.79	278.17	274.88
33000	302.79	300.27	298.03	296.03	294.25	292.66	286.86	283.47
34000	311.96	309.37	307.06	305.00	303.17	301.52	295.55	292.06
35000	321.14	318.47	316.09	313.97	312.08	310.39	304.24	300.65
40000	367.02	363.96	361.25	358.83	356.67	354.73	347.71	343.59
45000	412.89	409.46	406.40	403.68	401.25	399.08	391.17	386.54
50000	458.77	454.95	451.56	448.53	445.83	443.42	434.63	429.49
55000	504.65	500.45	496.71	493.38	490.41	487.76	478.09	472.44
60000	550.52	545.94	541.87	538.24	535.00	532.10	521.56	515.39
65000	596.40	591.44	587.02	583.09	579.58	576.44	565.02	558.34
70000	642.27	636.93	632.18	627.94	624.16	620.78	608.48	601.29
75000	688.15	682.43	677.33	672.80	668.74	665.12	651.94	644.23
80000	734.03	727.92	722.49	717.65	713.33	709.46	695.41	687.18
85000	779.90	773.42	767.65	762.50	757.91	753.80	738.87	730.13
90000	825.78	818.91	812.80	807.35	802.49	798.15	782.33	773.08
95000	871.66	864.41	857.96	852.21	847.07	842.49	825.79	816.03
100000	917.53	909.90	903.11	897.06	891.66	886.83	869.26	858.98
105000	963.41	955.40	948.27	941.91	936.24	931.17	912.72	901.93
110000	1009.29	1000.89	993.42	986.76	980.82	975.51	956.18	944.87
115000	1055.16	1046.39	1038.58	1031.62	1025.40	1019.85	999.64	987.82
120000	1101.04	1091.88	1083.73	1076.47	1069.99	1064.19	1043.11	1030.77
125000	1146.91	1137.38	1128.89	1121.32	1114.57	1108.53	1086.57	1073.72
130000	1192.79	1182.87	1174.04	1166.18	1159.15	1152.87	1130.03	1116.67
135000	1238.67	1228.37	1219.20	1211.03	1203.73	1197.22	1173.49	1159.62
140000	1284.54	1273.86	1264.35	1255.88	1248.32	1241.56	1216.96	1202.57
145000	1330.42	1319.36	1309.51	1300.73	1292.90	1285.90	1260.42	1245.51
150000	1376.30	1364.85	1354.66	1345.59	1337.48	1330.24	1303.88	1288.46
155000	1422.17	1410.34	1399.82	1390.44	1382.06	1374.58	1347.35	1331.41
160000	1468.05	1455.84	1444.98	1435.29	1426.65	1418.92	1390.81	1374.36

MONTHLY AMORTIZING PAYMENTS

AMOUNT OF LOAN	NUMBER OF YEARS IN TERM							
	1	1-1/2	2	3	4	5	6	7
$ 50	4.41	3.01	2.32	1.62	1.28	1.07	.94	.84
100	8.81	6.02	4.63	3.24	2.55	2.14	1.87	1.68
200	17.61	12.04	9.26	6.48	5.10	4.28	3.74	3.35
300	26.41	18.06	13.88	9.72	7.65	6.42	5.60	5.02
400	35.22	24.07	18.51	12.96	10.20	8.55	7.47	6.70
500	44.02	30.09	23.14	16.20	12.75	10.69	9.33	8.37
600	52.82	36.11	27.76	19.44	15.29	12.83	11.20	10.04
700	61.63	42.13	32.39	22.67	17.84	14.96	13.06	11.72
800	70.43	48.14	37.01	25.91	20.39	17.10	14.93	13.39
900	79.23	54.16	41.64	29.15	22.94	19.24	16.79	15.06
1000	88.04	60.18	46.27	32.39	25.49	21.38	18.66	16.74
2000	176.07	120.35	92.53	64.77	50.97	42.75	37.31	33.47
3000	264.10	180.52	138.79	97.16	76.45	64.12	55.96	50.20
4000	352.13	240.69	185.05	129.54	101.94	85.49	74.61	66.93
5000	440.17	300.87	231.31	161.93	127.42	106.86	93.27	83.66
6000	528.20	361.04	277.57	194.31	152.90	128.23	111.92	100.39
7000	616.23	421.21	323.83	226.70	178.38	149.60	130.57	117.12
8000	704.26	481.38	370.09	259.08	203.87	170.97	149.22	133.85
9000	792.29	541.56	416.35	291.47	229.35	192.34	167.87	150.58
10000	880.33	601.73	462.61	323.85	254.83	213.71	186.53	167.31
11000	968.36	661.90	508.87	356.24	280.32	235.08	205.18	184.04
12000	1056.39	722.07	555.13	388.62	305.80	256.45	223.83	200.77
13000	1144.42	782.24	601.39	421.01	331.28	277.82	242.48	217.50
14000	1232.46	842.42	647.65	453.39	356.76	299.19	261.14	234.23
15000	1320.49	902.59	693.91	485.78	382.25	320.56	279.79	250.96
16000	1408.52	962.76	740.17	518.16	407.73	341.93	298.44	267.70
17000	1496.55	1022.93	786.43	550.54	433.21	363.30	317.09	284.43
18000	1584.58	1083.11	832.69	582.93	458.70	384.67	335.74	301.16
19000	1672.62	1143.28	878.95	615.31	484.18	406.04	354.40	317.89
20000	1760.65	1203.45	925.21	647.70	509.66	427.41	373.05	334.62
21000	1848.68	1263.62	971.47	680.08	535.14	448.78	391.70	351.35
22000	1936.71	1323.79	1017.73	712.47	560.63	470.15	410.35	368.08
23000	2024.75	1383.97	1063.99	744.85	586.11	491.52	429.00	384.81
24000	2112.78	1444.14	1110.25	777.24	611.59	512.89	447.66	401.54
25000	2200.81	1504.31	1156.51	809.62	637.08	534.26	466.31	418.27
26000	2288.84	1564.48	1202.78	842.01	662.56	555.63	484.96	435.00
27000	2376.87	1624.66	1249.04	874.39	688.04	577.00	503.61	451.73
28000	2464.91	1684.83	1295.30	906.78	713.52	598.37	522.27	468.46
29000	2552.94	1745.00	1341.56	939.16	739.01	619.74	540.92	485.19
30000	2640.97	1805.17	1387.82	971.55	764.49	641.11	559.57	501.92
31000	2729.00	1865.34	1434.08	1003.93	789.97	662.48	578.22	518.65
32000	2817.04	1925.52	1480.34	1036.32	815.46	683.85	596.87	535.39
33000	2905.07	1985.69	1526.60	1068.70	840.94	705.22	615.53	552.12
34000	2993.10	2045.86	1572.86	1101.08	866.42	726.59	634.18	568.85
35000	3081.13	2106.03	1619.12	1133.47	891.90	747.96	652.83	585.58
40000	3521.29	2406.90	1850.42	1295.39	1019.32	854.82	746.09	669.23
45000	3961.45	2707.76	2081.72	1457.32	1146.73	961.67	839.35	752.88
50000	4401.62	3008.62	2313.02	1619.24	1274.15	1068.52	932.61	836.54
55000	4841.78	3309.48	2544.33	1781.16	1401.56	1175.37	1025.87	920.19
60000	5281.94	3610.34	2775.63	1943.09	1528.97	1282.22	1119.13	1003.84
65000	5722.10	3911.20	3006.93	2105.01	1656.39	1389.07	1212.40	1087.50
70000	6162.26	4212.06	3238.23	2266.93	1783.80	1495.92	1305.66	1171.15
75000	6602.42	4512.92	3469.53	2428.86	1911.22	1602.77	1398.92	1254.80
80000	7042.58	4813.79	3700.84	2590.78	2038.63	1709.63	1492.18	1338.46
85000	7482.74	5114.65	3932.14	2752.70	2166.04	1816.48	1585.44	1422.11
90000	7922.90	5415.51	4163.44	2914.63	2293.46	1923.33	1678.70	1505.76
95000	8363.06	5716.37	4394.74	3076.55	2420.87	2030.18	1771.96	1589.42
100000	8803.23	6017.23	4626.04	3238.47	2548.29	2137.03	1865.22	1673.07
105000	9243.39	6318.09	4857.35	3400.40	2675.70	2243.88	1958.48	1756.72
110000	9683.55	6618.95	5088.65	3562.32	2803.11	2350.73	2051.74	1840.38
115000	10123.71	6919.81	5319.95	3724.24	2930.53	2457.59	2145.00	1924.03
120000	10563.87	7220.68	5551.25	3886.17	3057.94	2564.44	2238.26	2007.68
125000	11004.03	7521.54	5782.55	4048.09	3185.36	2671.29	2331.52	2091.34
130000	11444.19	7822.40	6013.86	4210.01	3312.77	2778.14	2424.79	2174.99
135000	11884.35	8123.26	6245.16	4371.94	3440.18	2884.99	2518.05	2258.64
140000	12324.51	8424.12	6476.46	4533.86	3567.60	2991.84	2611.31	2342.30
145000	12764.67	8724.98	6707.76	4695.78	3695.01	3098.69	2704.57	2425.95
150000	13204.84	9025.84	6939.06	4857.71	3822.43	3205.54	2797.83	2509.60
155000	13645.00	9326.70	7170.37	5019.63	3949.84	3312.40	2891.09	2593.25
160000	14085.16	9627.57	7401.67	5181.56	4077.26	3419.25	2984.35	2676.91

MONTHLY AMORTIZING PAYMENTS 10¼%

AMOUNT OF LOAN	NUMBER OF YEARS IN TERM							
	8	9	10	11	12	14	15	16
$ 50	.77	.72	.67	.64	.61	.57	.55	.54
100	1.54	1.43	1.34	1.27	1.21	1.13	1.09	1.07
200	3.07	2.85	2.68	2.54	2.42	2.25	2.18	2.13
300	4.60	4.27	4.01	3.80	3.63	3.37	3.27	3.19
400	6.13	5.69	5.35	5.07	4.84	4.50	4.36	4.25
500	7.66	7.11	6.68	6.34	6.05	5.62	5.45	5.31
600	9.19	8.53	8.02	7.60	7.26	6.74	6.54	6.37
700	10.72	9.96	9.35	8.87	8.47	7.87	7.63	7.44
800	12.25	11.38	10.69	10.13	9.68	8.99	8.72	8.50
900	13.78	12.80	12.02	11.40	10.89	10.11	9.81	9.56
1000	15.31	14.22	13.36	12.67	12.10	11.24	10.90	10.62
2000	30.62	28.43	26.71	25.33	24.20	22.47	21.80	21.24
3000	45.93	42.65	40.07	37.99	36.29	33.70	32.70	31.85
4000	61.23	56.86	53.42	50.65	48.39	44.94	43.60	42.47
5000	76.54	71.08	66.77	63.31	60.48	56.17	54.50	53.08
6000	91.85	85.29	80.13	75.98	72.58	67.40	65.40	63.70
7000	107.15	99.51	93.48	88.64	84.67	78.63	76.30	74.31
8000	122.46	113.72	106.84	101.30	96.77	89.87	87.20	84.93
9000	137.77	127.93	120.19	113.96	108.87	101.10	98.10	95.54
10000	153.07	142.15	133.54	126.62	120.96	112.33	109.00	106.16
11000	168.38	156.36	146.90	139.28	133.06	123.56	119.90	116.77
12000	183.69	170.58	160.25	151.95	145.15	134.80	130.80	127.39
13000	198.99	184.79	173.61	164.61	157.25	146.03	141.70	138.00
14000	214.30	199.01	186.96	177.27	169.34	157.26	152.60	148.62
15000	229.61	213.22	200.31	189.93	181.44	168.50	163.50	159.23
16000	244.91	227.44	213.67	202.59	193.54	179.73	174.40	169.85
17000	260.22	241.65	227.02	215.25	205.63	190.96	185.30	180.46
18000	275.53	255.86	240.38	227.92	217.73	202.19	196.20	191.08
19000	290.83	270.08	253.73	240.58	229.82	213.43	207.10	201.69
20000	306.14	284.29	267.08	253.24	241.92	224.66	218.00	212.31
21000	321.45	298.51	280.44	265.90	254.01	235.89	228.89	222.92
22000	336.75	312.72	293.79	278.56	266.11	247.12	239.79	233.54
23000	352.06	326.94	307.14	291.23	278.20	258.36	250.69	244.15
24000	367.37	341.15	320.50	303.89	290.30	269.59	261.59	254.77
25000	382.67	355.37	333.85	316.55	302.40	280.82	272.49	265.38
26000	397.98	369.58	347.21	329.21	314.49	292.06	283.39	276.00
27000	413.29	383.79	360.56	341.87	326.59	303.29	294.29	286.62
28000	428.59	398.01	373.91	354.53	338.68	314.52	305.19	297.23
29000	443.90	412.22	387.27	367.20	350.78	325.75	316.09	307.85
30000	459.21	426.44	400.62	379.86	362.87	336.99	326.99	318.46
31000	474.51	440.65	413.98	392.52	374.97	348.22	337.89	329.08
32000	489.82	454.87	427.33	405.18	387.07	359.45	348.79	339.69
33000	505.13	469.08	440.68	417.84	399.16	370.68	359.69	350.31
34000	520.44	483.30	454.04	430.50	411.26	381.92	370.59	360.92
35000	535.74	497.51	467.39	443.17	423.35	393.15	381.49	371.54
40000	612.28	568.58	534.16	506.48	483.83	449.31	435.99	424.61
45000	688.81	639.65	600.93	569.78	544.31	505.48	490.48	477.69
50000	765.34	710.73	667.70	633.09	604.79	561.64	544.98	530.76
55000	841.88	781.80	734.47	696.40	665.27	617.80	599.48	583.84
60000	918.41	852.87	801.24	759.71	725.74	673.97	653.98	636.92
65000	994.95	923.94	868.01	823.02	786.22	730.13	708.47	689.99
70000	1071.48	995.01	934.78	886.33	846.70	786.29	762.97	743.07
75000	1148.01	1066.09	1001.55	949.64	907.18	842.46	817.47	796.14
80000	1224.55	1137.16	1068.32	1012.95	967.66	898.62	871.97	849.22
85000	1301.08	1208.23	1135.09	1076.25	1028.14	954.78	926.46	902.30
90000	1377.61	1279.30	1201.86	1139.56	1088.61	1010.95	980.96	955.37
95000	1454.15	1350.37	1268.63	1202.87	1149.09	1067.11	1035.46	1008.45
100000	1530.68	1421.45	1335.40	1266.18	1209.57	1123.27	1089.96	1061.52
105000	1607.22	1492.52	1402.16	1329.49	1270.05	1179.44	1144.45	1114.60
110000	1683.75	1563.59	1468.93	1392.80	1330.53	1235.60	1198.95	1167.68
115000	1760.28	1634.66	1535.70	1456.11	1391.00	1291.76	1253.45	1220.75
120000	1836.82	1705.74	1602.47	1519.42	1451.48	1347.93	1307.95	1273.83
125000	1913.35	1776.81	1669.24	1582.72	1511.96	1404.09	1362.44	1326.90
130000	1989.89	1847.88	1736.01	1646.03	1572.44	1460.26	1416.94	1379.98
135000	2066.42	1918.95	1802.78	1709.34	1632.92	1516.42	1471.44	1433.06
140000	2142.95	1990.02	1869.55	1772.65	1693.40	1572.58	1525.94	1486.13
145000	2219.49	2061.10	1936.32	1835.96	1753.87	1628.75	1580.43	1539.21
150000	2296.02	2132.17	2003.09	1899.27	1814.35	1684.91	1634.93	1592.28
155000	2372.55	2203.24	2069.86	1962.58	1874.83	1741.07	1689.43	1645.36
160000	2449.09	2274.31	2136.63	2025.89	1935.31	1797.24	1743.93	1698.44

MONTHLY AMORTIZING PAYMENTS

AMOUNT OF LOAN	NUMBER OF YEARS IN TERM							
	17	18	19	20	21	22	23	24
$ 50	.52	.51	.50	.50	.49	.48	.48	.47
100	1.04	1.02	1.00	.99	.97	.96	.95	.94
200	2.08	2.04	2.00	1.97	1.94	1.92	1.89	1.87
300	3.12	3.05	3.00	2.95	2.91	2.87	2.84	2.81
400	4.15	4.07	4.00	3.93	3.88	3.83	3.78	3.74
500	5.19	5.08	4.99	4.91	4.84	4.78	4.73	4.68
600	6.23	6.10	5.99	5.89	5.81	5.74	5.67	5.61
700	7.26	7.12	6.99	6.88	6.78	6.69	6.62	6.55
800	8.30	8.13	7.99	7.86	7.75	7.65	7.56	7.48
900	9.34	9.15	8.98	8.84	8.71	8.60	8.51	8.42
1000	10.38	10.16	9.98	9.82	9.68	9.56	9.45	9.35
2000	20.75	20.32	19.96	19.64	19.36	19.11	18.89	18.70
3000	31.12	30.48	29.93	29.45	29.03	28.66	28.34	28.05
4000	41.49	40.64	39.91	39.27	38.71	38.22	37.78	37.40
5000	51.86	50.80	49.89	49.09	48.39	47.77	47.23	46.75
6000	62.23	60.96	59.86	58.90	58.06	57.32	56.67	56.10
7000	72.60	71.12	69.84	68.72	67.74	66.88	66.12	65.45
8000	82.97	81.28	79.82	78.54	77.42	76.43	75.56	74.80
9000	93.34	91.44	89.79	88.35	87.09	85.98	85.01	84.14
10000	103.71	101.60	99.77	98.17	96.77	95.54	94.45	93.49
11000	114.09	111.76	109.75	107.99	106.44	105.09	103.90	102.84
12000	124.46	121.92	119.72	117.80	116.12	114.64	113.34	112.19
13000	134.83	132.08	129.70	127.62	125.80	124.20	122.79	121.54
14000	145.20	142.24	139.67	137.44	135.47	133.75	132.23	130.89
15000	155.57	152.40	149.65	147.25	145.15	143.30	141.67	140.24
16000	165.94	162.56	159.63	157.07	154.83	152.86	151.12	149.59
17000	176.31	172.72	169.60	166.88	164.50	162.41	160.56	158.93
18000	186.68	182.88	179.58	176.70	174.18	171.96	170.01	168.28
19000	197.05	193.04	189.56	186.52	183.85	181.52	179.45	177.63
20000	207.42	203.20	199.53	196.33	193.53	191.07	188.90	186.98
21000	217.79	213.36	209.51	206.15	203.21	200.62	198.34	196.33
22000	228.17	223.52	219.49	215.97	212.88	210.18	207.79	205.68
23000	238.54	233.68	229.46	225.78	222.56	219.73	217.23	215.03
24000	248.91	243.84	239.44	235.60	232.24	229.28	226.68	224.38
25000	259.28	254.00	249.42	245.42	241.91	238.83	236.12	233.72
26000	269.65	264.16	259.39	255.23	251.59	248.39	245.57	243.07
27000	280.02	274.32	269.37	265.05	261.27	257.94	255.01	252.42
28000	290.39	284.48	279.34	274.87	270.94	267.49	264.46	261.77
29000	300.76	294.64	289.32	284.68	280.62	277.05	273.90	271.12
30000	311.13	304.80	299.30	294.50	290.29	286.60	283.34	280.47
31000	321.50	314.96	309.27	304.31	299.97	296.15	292.79	289.82
32000	331.87	325.12	319.25	314.13	309.65	305.71	302.23	299.17
33000	342.25	335.28	329.23	323.95	319.32	315.26	311.68	308.51
34000	352.62	345.44	339.20	333.76	329.00	324.81	321.12	317.86
35000	362.99	355.60	349.18	343.58	338.68	334.37	330.57	327.21
40000	414.84	406.40	399.06	392.66	387.06	382.13	377.79	373.96
45000	466.70	457.20	448.94	441.74	435.44	429.90	425.01	420.70
50000	518.55	508.00	498.83	490.83	483.82	477.66	472.24	467.44
55000	570.41	558.79	548.71	539.91	532.20	525.43	519.46	514.19
60000	622.26	609.59	598.59	588.99	580.58	573.20	566.68	560.93
65000	674.11	660.39	648.47	638.07	628.97	620.96	613.91	607.67
70000	725.97	711.19	698.35	687.16	677.35	668.73	661.13	654.42
75000	777.82	761.99	748.24	736.24	725.73	716.49	708.35	701.16
80000	829.68	812.79	798.12	785.32	774.11	764.26	755.58	747.91
85000	881.53	863.59	848.00	834.40	822.49	812.03	802.80	794.65
90000	933.39	914.39	897.88	883.48	870.87	859.79	850.02	841.39
95000	985.24	965.19	947.77	932.57	919.25	907.56	897.25	888.14
100000	1037.10	1015.99	997.65	981.65	967.64	955.32	944.47	934.88
105000	1088.95	1066.78	1047.53	1030.73	1016.02	1003.09	991.69	981.63
110000	1140.81	1117.58	1097.41	1079.81	1064.40	1050.86	1038.92	1028.37
115000	1192.66	1168.38	1147.29	1128.89	1112.78	1098.62	1086.14	1075.11
120000	1244.51	1219.18	1197.18	1177.98	1161.16	1146.39	1133.36	1121.86
125000	1296.37	1269.98	1247.06	1227.06	1209.54	1194.15	1180.59	1168.60
130000	1348.22	1320.78	1296.94	1276.14	1257.93	1241.92	1227.81	1215.34
135000	1400.08	1371.58	1346.82	1325.22	1306.31	1289.68	1275.03	1262.09
140000	1451.93	1422.38	1396.70	1374.31	1354.69	1337.45	1322.26	1308.83
145000	1503.79	1473.18	1446.59	1423.39	1403.07	1385.22	1369.48	1355.58
150000	1555.64	1523.98	1496.47	1472.47	1451.45	1432.98	1416.70	1402.32
155000	1607.50	1574.77	1546.35	1521.55	1499.83	1480.75	1463.93	1449.06
160000	1659.35	1625.57	1596.23	1570.63	1548.22	1528.51	1511.15	1495.81

MONTHLY AMORTIZING PAYMENTS 10¼%

AMOUNT OF LOAN	NUMBER OF YEARS IN TERM							
	25	26	27	28	29	30	35	40
$ 50	.47	.46	.46	.46	.46	.45	.44	.44
100	.93	.92	.92	.91	.91	.90	.88	.87
200	1.86	1.84	1.83	1.82	1.81	1.80	1.76	1.74
300	2.78	2.76	2.74	2.72	2.71	2.69	2.64	2.61
400	3.71	3.68	3.65	3.63	3.61	3.59	3.52	3.48
500	4.64	4.60	4.57	4.54	4.51	4.49	4.40	4.35
600	5.56	5.52	5.48	5.44	5.41	5.38	5.28	5.22
700	6.49	6.44	6.39	6.35	6.31	6.28	6.16	6.09
800	7.42	7.36	7.30	7.25	7.21	7.17	7.04	6.96
900	8.34	8.27	8.21	8.16	8.11	8.07	7.91	7.82
1000	9.27	9.19	9.13	9.07	9.01	8.97	8.79	8.69
2000	18.53	18.38	18.25	18.13	18.02	17.93	17.58	17.38
3000	27.80	27.57	27.37	27.19	27.03	26.89	26.37	26.07
4000	37.06	36.76	36.49	36.25	36.04	35.85	35.16	34.76
5000	46.32	45.95	45.61	45.31	45.05	44.81	43.95	43.45
6000	55.59	55.14	54.73	54.38	54.06	53.77	52.74	52.13
7000	64.85	64.32	63.86	63.44	63.06	62.73	61.52	60.82
8000	74.12	73.51	72.98	72.50	72.07	71.69	70.31	69.51
9000	83.38	82.70	82.10	81.56	81.08	80.65	79.10	78.20
10000	92.64	91.89	91.22	90.62	90.09	89.62	87.89	86.89
11000	101.91	101.08	100.34	99.68	99.10	98.58	96.68	95.58
12000	111.17	110.27	109.46	108.75	108.11	107.54	105.47	104.26
13000	120.43	119.45	118.58	117.81	117.12	116.50	114.26	112.95
14000	129.70	128.64	127.71	126.87	126.12	125.46	123.04	121.64
15000	138.96	137.83	136.83	135.93	135.13	134.42	131.83	130.33
16000	148.23	147.02	145.95	144.99	144.14	143.38	140.62	139.02
17000	157.49	156.21	155.07	154.05	153.15	152.34	149.41	147.70
18000	166.75	165.40	164.19	163.12	162.16	161.30	158.20	156.39
19000	176.02	174.59	173.31	172.18	171.17	170.26	166.99	165.08
20000	185.28	183.77	182.43	181.24	180.18	179.23	175.78	173.77
21000	194.55	192.96	191.56	190.30	189.18	188.19	184.56	182.46
22000	203.81	202.15	200.68	199.36	198.19	197.15	193.35	191.15
23000	213.07	211.34	209.80	208.43	207.20	206.11	202.14	199.83
24000	222.34	220.53	218.92	217.49	216.21	215.07	210.93	208.52
25000	231.60	229.72	228.04	226.55	225.22	224.03	219.72	217.21
26000	240.86	238.90	237.16	235.61	234.23	232.99	228.51	225.90
27000	250.13	248.09	246.28	244.67	243.24	241.95	237.30	234.59
28000	259.39	257.28	255.41	253.73	252.24	250.91	246.08	243.27
29000	268.66	266.47	264.53	262.80	261.25	259.87	254.87	251.96
30000	277.92	275.66	273.65	271.86	270.26	268.84	263.66	260.65
31000	287.18	284.85	282.77	280.92	279.27	277.80	272.45	269.34
32000	296.45	294.04	291.89	289.98	288.28	286.76	281.24	278.03
33000	305.71	303.22	301.01	299.04	297.29	295.72	290.03	286.72
34000	314.98	312.41	310.13	308.10	306.30	304.68	298.82	295.40
35000	324.24	321.60	319.26	317.17	315.30	313.64	307.60	304.09
40000	370.56	367.54	364.86	362.48	360.35	358.45	351.55	347.53
45000	416.88	413.49	410.47	407.78	405.39	403.25	395.49	390.97
50000	463.20	459.43	456.08	453.09	450.43	448.06	439.43	434.41
55000	509.52	505.37	501.68	498.40	495.47	492.86	483.38	477.86
60000	555.83	551.31	547.29	543.71	540.52	537.67	527.32	521.30
65000	602.15	597.25	592.90	589.02	585.56	582.47	571.26	564.74
70000	648.47	643.20	638.51	634.33	630.60	627.28	615.20	608.18
75000	694.79	689.14	684.11	679.64	675.65	672.08	659.15	651.62
80000	741.11	735.08	729.72	724.95	720.69	716.89	703.09	695.06
85000	787.43	781.02	775.33	770.25	765.73	761.69	747.03	738.50
90000	833.75	826.97	820.93	815.56	810.77	806.50	790.98	781.94
95000	880.07	872.91	866.54	860.87	855.82	851.30	834.92	825.38
100000	926.39	918.85	912.15	906.18	900.86	896.11	878.86	868.82
105000	972.71	964.79	957.76	951.49	945.90	940.91	922.80	912.26
110000	1019.03	1010.74	1003.36	996.80	990.94	985.72	966.75	955.71
115000	1065.35	1056.68	1048.97	1042.11	1035.99	1030.52	1010.69	999.15
120000	1111.66	1102.62	1094.58	1087.42	1081.03	1075.33	1054.63	1042.59
125000	1157.98	1148.56	1140.18	1132.72	1126.07	1120.13	1098.57	1086.03
130000	1204.30	1194.50	1185.79	1178.03	1171.11	1164.94	1142.52	1129.47
135000	1250.62	1240.45	1231.40	1223.34	1216.16	1209.74	1186.46	1172.91
140000	1296.94	1286.39	1277.01	1268.65	1261.20	1254.55	1230.40	1216.35
145000	1343.26	1332.33	1322.61	1313.96	1306.24	1299.35	1274.35	1259.79
150000	1389.58	1378.27	1368.22	1359.27	1351.29	1344.16	1318.29	1303.23
155000	1435.90	1424.22	1413.83	1404.58	1396.33	1388.96	1362.23	1346.67
160000	1482.22	1470.16	1459.44	1449.89	1441.37	1433.77	1406.17	1390.11

MONTHLY AMORTIZING PAYMENTS

AMOUNT OF LOAN	NUMBER OF YEARS IN TERM							
	1	1-1/2	2	3	4	5	6	7
$ 50	4.41	3.02	2.32	1.63	1.28	1.08	.94	.84
100	8.81	6.03	4.64	3.25	2.56	2.15	1.88	1.68
200	17.62	12.05	9.27	6.49	5.11	4.29	3.75	3.36
300	26.43	18.07	13.90	9.74	7.67	6.43	5.62	5.04
400	35.24	24.10	18.53	12.98	10.22	8.58	7.49	6.72
500	44.05	30.12	23.16	16.23	12.78	10.72	9.36	8.40
600	52.86	36.14	27.80	19.47	15.33	12.86	11.23	10.08
700	61.67	42.17	32.43	22.72	17.89	15.01	13.11	11.76
800	70.48	48.19	37.06	25.96	20.44	17.15	14.98	13.44
900	79.29	54.21	41.69	29.20	22.99	19.29	16.85	15.12
1000	88.10	60.23	46.32	32.45	25.55	21.44	18.72	16.80
2000	176.19	120.46	92.64	64.89	51.09	42.87	37.44	33.60
3000	264.28	180.69	138.96	97.34	76.63	64.30	56.15	50.39
4000	352.37	240.92	185.28	129.78	102.18	85.73	74.87	67.19
5000	440.46	301.15	231.60	162.22	127.72	107.17	93.58	83.98
6000	528.55	361.38	277.91	194.67	153.26	128.60	112.30	100.78
7000	616.64	421.61	324.23	227.11	178.81	150.03	131.01	117.57
8000	704.73	481.84	370.55	259.55	204.35	171.46	149.73	134.37
9000	792.82	542.07	416.87	292.00	229.89	192.89	168.44	151.17
10000	880.91	602.30	463.19	324.44	255.44	214.33	187.16	167.96
11000	969.00	662.53	509.51	356.88	280.98	235.76	205.88	184.76
12000	1057.09	722.76	555.82	389.33	306.52	257.19	224.59	201.55
13000	1145.18	782.99	602.14	421.77	332.06	278.62	243.31	218.35
14000	1233.27	843.22	648.46	454.21	357.61	300.05	262.02	235.14
15000	1321.36	903.45	694.78	486.66	383.15	321.49	280.74	251.94
16000	1409.45	963.68	741.10	519.10	408.69	342.92	299.45	268.73
17000	1497.54	1023.91	787.41	551.55	434.24	364.35	318.17	285.53
18000	1585.63	1084.14	833.73	583.99	459.78	385.78	336.88	302.33
19000	1673.72	1144.37	880.05	616.43	485.32	407.21	355.60	319.12
20000	1761.81	1204.60	926.37	648.88	510.87	428.65	374.32	335.92
21000	1849.90	1264.83	972.69	681.32	536.41	450.08	393.03	352.71
22000	1937.99	1325.06	1019.01	713.76	561.95	471.51	411.75	369.51
23000	2026.08	1385.29	1065.32	746.21	587.50	492.94	430.46	386.30
24000	2114.17	1445.52	1111.64	778.65	613.04	514.37	449.18	403.10
25000	2202.26	1505.75	1157.96	811.09	638.58	535.81	467.89	419.89
26000	2290.36	1565.98	1204.28	843.54	664.12	557.24	486.61	436.69
27000	2378.45	1626.21	1250.60	875.98	689.67	578.67	505.32	453.49
28000	2466.54	1686.44	1296.91	908.42	715.21	600.10	524.04	470.28
29000	2554.63	1746.67	1343.23	940.87	740.75	621.53	542.75	487.08
30000	2642.72	1806.90	1389.55	973.31	766.30	642.97	561.47	503.87
31000	2730.81	1867.13	1435.87	1005.75	791.84	664.40	580.19	520.67
32000	2818.90	1927.36	1482.19	1038.20	817.38	685.83	598.90	537.46
33000	2906.99	1987.59	1528.51	1070.64	842.93	707.26	617.62	554.26
34000	2995.08	2047.82	1574.82	1103.09	868.47	728.69	636.33	571.05
35000	3083.17	2108.05	1621.14	1135.53	894.01	750.13	655.05	587.85
40000	3523.62	2409.20	1852.73	1297.75	1021.73	857.29	748.63	671.83
45000	3964.07	2710.35	2084.32	1459.96	1149.44	964.45	842.20	755.81
50000	4404.52	3011.50	2315.91	1622.18	1277.16	1071.61	935.78	839.78
55000	4844.98	3312.65	2547.51	1784.40	1404.87	1178.77	1029.36	923.76
60000	5285.43	3613.80	2779.10	1946.62	1532.59	1285.93	1122.94	1007.74
65000	5725.88	3914.95	3010.69	2108.83	1660.30	1393.09	1216.51	1091.72
70000	6166.33	4216.10	3242.28	2271.05	1788.02	1500.25	1310.09	1175.70
75000	6606.78	4517.25	3473.87	2433.27	1915.73	1607.41	1403.67	1259.67
80000	7047.24	4818.40	3705.46	2595.49	2043.45	1714.57	1497.25	1343.65
85000	7487.69	5119.55	3937.05	2757.71	2171.16	1821.73	1590.82	1427.63
90000	7928.14	5420.69	4168.64	2919.92	2298.88	1928.89	1684.40	1511.61
95000	8368.59	5721.84	4400.23	3082.14	2426.60	2036.05	1777.98	1595.59
100000	8809.04	6022.99	4631.82	3244.36	2554.31	2143.21	1871.56	1679.56
105000	9249.50	6324.14	4863.42	3406.58	2682.03	2250.37	1965.13	1763.54
110000	9689.95	6625.29	5095.01	3568.79	2809.74	2357.53	2058.71	1847.52
115000	10130.40	6926.44	5326.60	3731.01	2937.46	2464.69	2152.29	1931.50
120000	10570.85	7227.59	5558.19	3893.23	3065.17	2571.85	2245.87	2015.48
125000	11011.30	7528.74	5789.78	4055.45	3192.89	2679.01	2339.44	2099.45
130000	11451.76	7829.89	6021.37	4217.66	3320.60	2786.17	2433.02	2183.43
135000	11892.21	8131.04	6252.96	4379.88	3448.32	2893.33	2526.60	2267.41
140000	12332.66	8432.19	6484.55	4542.10	3576.03	3000.49	2620.18	2351.39
145000	12773.11	8733.34	6716.14	4704.32	3703.75	3107.65	2713.75	2435.37
150000	13213.56	9034.49	6947.73	4866.54	3831.46	3214.81	2807.33	2519.34
155000	13654.02	9335.64	7179.33	5028.75	3959.18	3321.97	2900.91	2603.32
160000	14094.47	9636.79	7410.92	5190.97	4086.89	3429.13	2994.49	2687.30

AMOUNT OF LOAN	NUMBER OF YEARS IN TERM							
	8	9	10	11	12	14	15	16
$ 50	.77	.72	.68	.64	.61	.57	.55	.54
100	1.54	1.43	1.35	1.28	1.22	1.14	1.10	1.07
200	3.08	2.86	2.69	2.55	2.44	2.27	2.20	2.14
300	4.62	4.29	4.03	3.82	3.66	3.40	3.30	3.21
400	6.15	5.72	5.37	5.10	4.87	4.53	4.40	4.28
500	7.69	7.15	6.72	6.37	6.09	5.66	5.49	5.35
600	9.23	8.57	8.06	7.64	7.31	6.79	6.59	6.42
700	10.77	10.00	9.40	8.92	8.52	7.92	7.69	7.49
800	12.30	11.43	10.74	10.19	9.74	9.05	8.79	8.56
900	13.84	12.86	12.09	11.46	10.96	10.18	9.88	9.63
1000	15.38	14.29	13.43	12.74	12.17	11.31	10.98	10.70
2000	30.75	28.57	26.85	25.47	24.34	22.62	21.96	21.39
3000	46.12	42.85	40.28	38.20	36.51	33.93	32.93	32.09
4000	61.50	57.14	53.70	50.94	48.68	45.24	43.91	42.78
5000	76.87	71.42	67.12	63.67	60.85	56.55	54.89	53.47
6000	92.24	85.70	80.55	76.40	73.02	67.86	65.86	64.17
7000	107.62	99.98	93.97	89.14	85.18	79.16	76.84	74.86
8000	122.99	114.27	107.39	101.87	97.35	90.47	87.82	85.55
9000	138.36	128.55	120.82	114.60	109.52	101.78	98.79	96.25
10000	153.74	142.83	134.24	127.34	121.69	113.09	109.77	106.94
11000	169.11	157.11	147.66	140.07	133.86	124.40	120.75	117.64
12000	184.48	171.40	161.09	152.80	146.03	135.71	131.72	128.33
13000	199.86	185.68	174.51	165.53	158.19	147.01	142.70	139.02
14000	215.23	199.96	187.94	178.27	170.36	158.32	153.68	149.72
15000	230.60	214.24	201.36	191.00	182.53	169.63	164.65	160.41
16000	245.98	228.53	214.78	203.73	194.70	180.94	175.63	171.10
17000	261.35	242.81	228.21	216.47	206.87	192.25	186.61	181.80
18000	276.72	257.09	241.63	229.20	219.04	203.56	197.58	192.49
19000	292.10	271.37	255.05	241.93	231.20	214.86	208.56	203.18
20000	307.47	285.66	268.48	254.67	243.37	226.17	219.54	213.88
21000	322.84	299.94	281.90	267.40	255.54	237.48	230.51	224.57
22000	338.22	314.22	295.32	280.13	267.71	248.79	241.49	235.27
23000	353.59	328.50	308.75	292.86	279.88	260.10	252.47	245.96
24000	368.96	342.79	322.17	305.60	292.05	271.41	263.44	256.65
25000	384.34	357.07	335.60	318.33	304.22	282.71	274.42	267.35
26000	399.71	371.35	349.02	331.06	316.38	294.02	285.40	278.04
27000	415.08	385.63	362.44	343.80	328.55	305.33	296.37	288.73
28000	430.46	399.92	375.87	356.53	340.72	316.64	307.35	299.43
29000	445.83	414.20	389.29	369.26	352.89	327.95	318.33	310.12
30000	461.20	428.48	402.71	382.00	365.06	339.26	329.30	320.82
31000	476.58	442.76	416.14	394.73	377.23	350.57	340.28	331.51
32000	491.95	457.05	429.56	407.46	389.39	361.87	351.26	342.20
33000	507.32	471.33	442.98	420.19	401.56	373.18	362.23	352.90
34000	522.70	485.61	456.41	432.93	413.73	384.49	373.21	363.59
35000	538.07	499.89	469.83	445.66	425.90	395.80	384.19	374.28
40000	614.94	571.31	536.95	509.33	486.74	452.34	439.07	427.75
45000	691.80	642.72	604.07	572.99	547.58	508.88	493.95	481.22
50000	768.67	714.13	671.19	636.66	608.43	565.42	548.84	534.69
55000	845.54	785.55	738.30	700.32	669.27	621.97	603.72	588.16
60000	922.40	856.96	805.42	763.99	730.11	678.51	658.60	641.63
65000	999.27	928.37	872.54	827.65	790.95	735.05	713.49	695.09
70000	1076.14	999.78	939.66	891.32	851.79	791.59	768.37	748.56
75000	1153.00	1071.20	1006.78	954.98	912.64	848.13	823.25	802.03
80000	1229.87	1142.61	1073.89	1018.65	973.48	904.68	878.13	855.50
85000	1306.74	1214.02	1141.01	1082.31	1034.32	961.22	933.02	908.97
90000	1383.60	1285.43	1208.13	1145.98	1095.16	1017.76	987.90	962.44
95000	1460.47	1356.85	1275.25	1209.64	1156.00	1074.30	1042.78	1015.90
100000	1537.34	1428.26	1342.37	1273.31	1216.85	1130.84	1097.67	1069.37
105000	1614.20	1499.67	1409.48	1336.97	1277.69	1187.39	1152.55	1122.84
110000	1691.07	1571.09	1476.60	1400.64	1338.53	1243.93	1207.43	1176.31
115000	1767.94	1642.50	1543.72	1464.30	1399.37	1300.47	1262.32	1229.78
120000	1844.80	1713.91	1610.84	1527.97	1460.22	1357.01	1317.20	1283.25
125000	1921.67	1785.32	1677.96	1591.63	1521.06	1413.55	1372.08	1336.71
130000	1998.54	1856.74	1745.07	1655.30	1581.90	1470.10	1426.97	1390.18
135000	2075.40	1928.15	1812.19	1718.96	1642.74	1526.64	1481.85	1443.65
140000	2152.27	1999.56	1879.31	1782.63	1703.58	1583.18	1536.73	1497.12
145000	2229.14	2070.97	1946.43	1846.29	1764.43	1639.72	1591.62	1550.59
150000	2306.00	2142.39	2013.55	1909.96	1825.27	1696.26	1646.50	1604.06
155000	2382.87	2213.80	2080.66	1973.62	1886.11	1752.81	1701.38	1657.53
160000	2459.74	2285.21	2147.78	2037.29	1946.95	1809.35	1756.26	1710.99

10⅜% MONTHLY AMORTIZING PAYMENTS

AMOUNT OF LOAN	NUMBER OF YEARS IN TERM							
	17	18	19	20	21	22	23	24
$ 50	.53	.52	.51	.50	.49	.49	.48	.48
100	1.05	1.03	1.01	.99	.98	.97	.96	.95
200	2.10	2.05	2.02	1.98	1.96	1.93	1.91	1.89
300	3.14	3.08	3.02	2.97	2.93	2.90	2.86	2.84
400	4.19	4.10	4.03	3.96	3.91	3.86	3.82	3.78
500	5.23	5.13	5.03	4.95	4.89	4.82	4.77	4.72
600	6.28	6.15	6.04	5.94	5.86	5.79	5.72	5.67
700	7.32	7.17	7.05	6.93	6.84	6.75	6.68	6.61
800	8.37	8.20	8.05	7.92	7.81	7.72	7.63	7.55
900	9.41	9.22	9.06	8.91	8.79	8.68	8.58	8.50
1000	10.46	10.25	10.06	9.90	9.77	9.64	9.54	9.44
2000	20.91	20.49	20.12	19.80	19.53	19.28	19.07	18.88
3000	31.36	30.73	30.18	29.70	29.29	28.92	28.60	28.31
4000	41.81	40.97	40.24	39.60	39.05	38.56	38.13	37.75
5000	52.26	51.21	50.30	49.50	48.81	48.20	47.66	47.19
6000	62.71	61.45	60.36	59.40	58.57	57.84	57.19	56.62
7000	73.16	71.69	70.42	69.30	68.33	67.48	66.73	66.06
8000	83.61	81.93	80.48	79.20	78.09	77.12	76.26	75.50
9000	94.06	92.17	90.53	89.10	87.85	86.76	85.79	84.93
10000	104.51	102.41	100.59	99.00	97.62	96.39	95.32	94.37
11000	114.96	112.65	110.65	108.90	107.38	106.03	104.85	103.81
12000	125.41	122.90	120.71	118.80	117.14	115.67	114.38	113.24
13000	135.86	133.14	130.77	128.70	126.90	125.31	123.91	122.68
14000	146.32	143.38	140.83	138.60	136.66	134.95	133.45	132.12
15000	156.77	153.62	150.89	148.50	146.42	144.59	142.98	141.55
16000	167.22	163.86	160.95	158.40	156.18	154.23	152.51	150.99
17000	177.67	174.10	171.00	168.30	165.94	163.87	162.04	160.43
18000	188.12	184.34	181.06	178.20	175.70	173.51	171.57	169.86
19000	198.57	194.58	191.12	188.10	185.46	183.15	181.10	179.30
20000	209.02	204.82	201.18	198.00	195.23	192.78	190.64	188.74
21000	219.47	215.06	211.24	207.90	204.99	202.42	200.17	198.17
22000	229.92	225.30	221.30	217.80	214.75	212.06	209.70	207.61
23000	240.37	235.55	231.36	227.70	224.51	221.70	219.23	217.05
24000	250.82	245.79	241.42	237.60	234.27	231.34	228.76	226.48
25000	261.27	256.03	251.47	247.50	244.03	240.98	238.29	235.92
26000	271.72	266.27	261.53	257.40	253.79	250.62	247.82	245.36
27000	282.17	276.51	271.59	267.30	263.55	260.26	257.36	254.79
28000	292.63	286.75	281.65	277.20	273.31	269.90	266.89	264.23
29000	303.08	296.99	291.71	287.10	283.07	279.54	276.42	273.67
30000	313.53	307.23	301.77	297.00	292.84	289.17	285.95	283.10
31000	323.98	317.47	311.83	306.90	302.60	298.81	295.48	292.54
32000	334.43	327.71	321.89	316.80	312.36	308.45	305.01	301.98
33000	344.88	337.95	331.94	326.70	322.12	318.09	314.55	311.41
34000	355.33	348.20	342.00	336.60	331.88	327.73	324.08	320.85
35000	365.78	358.44	352.06	346.50	341.64	337.37	333.61	330.29
40000	418.03	409.64	402.36	396.00	390.45	385.56	381.27	377.47
45000	470.29	460.85	452.65	445.50	439.25	433.76	428.92	424.65
50000	522.54	512.05	502.94	495.00	488.06	481.95	476.58	471.84
55000	574.80	563.25	553.24	544.50	536.86	530.15	524.24	519.02
60000	627.05	614.46	603.53	594.00	585.67	578.34	571.90	566.20
65000	679.30	665.66	653.82	643.50	634.47	626.54	619.55	613.39
70000	731.56	716.87	704.12	693.00	683.28	674.73	667.21	660.57
75000	783.81	768.07	754.41	742.50	732.08	722.93	714.87	707.75
80000	836.06	819.28	804.71	792.00	780.89	771.12	762.53	754.94
85000	888.32	870.48	855.00	841.50	829.69	819.32	810.18	802.12
90000	940.57	921.69	905.29	891.00	878.50	867.51	857.84	849.30
95000	992.82	972.89	955.59	940.50	927.30	915.71	905.50	896.49
100000	1045.08	1024.10	1005.88	990.00	976.11	963.90	953.16	943.67
105000	1097.33	1075.30	1056.18	1039.50	1024.91	1012.10	1000.81	990.85
110000	1149.59	1126.50	1106.47	1089.00	1073.72	1060.29	1048.47	1038.04
115000	1201.84	1177.71	1156.76	1138.50	1122.52	1108.49	1096.13	1085.22
120000	1254.09	1228.91	1207.06	1188.00	1171.33	1156.68	1143.79	1132.40
125000	1306.35	1280.12	1257.35	1237.50	1220.13	1204.88	1191.45	1179.59
130000	1358.60	1331.32	1307.64	1287.00	1268.94	1253.07	1239.10	1226.77
135000	1410.85	1382.53	1357.94	1336.50	1317.74	1301.27	1286.76	1273.95
140000	1463.11	1433.73	1408.23	1386.00	1366.55	1349.46	1334.42	1321.14
145000	1515.36	1484.94	1458.53	1435.50	1415.35	1397.66	1382.08	1368.32
150000	1567.61	1536.14	1508.82	1485.00	1464.16	1445.85	1429.73	1415.50
155000	1619.87	1587.34	1559.11	1534.50	1512.96	1494.05	1477.39	1462.68
160000	1672.12	1638.55	1609.41	1584.00	1561.77	1542.24	1525.05	1509.87

AMOUNT OF LOAN	NUMBER OF YEARS IN TERM							
	25	26	27	28	29	30	35	40
$ 50	.47	.47	.47	.46	.46	.46	.45	.44
100	.94	.93	.93	.92	.92	.91	.89	.88
200	1.88	1.86	1.85	1.84	1.83	1.82	1.78	1.76
300	2.81	2.79	2.77	2.75	2.74	2.72	2.67	2.64
400	3.75	3.72	3.69	3.67	3.65	3.63	3.56	3.52
500	4.68	4.64	4.61	4.58	4.56	4.53	4.45	4.40
600	5.62	5.57	5.53	5.50	5.47	5.44	5.34	5.28
700	6.55	6.50	6.45	6.41	6.38	6.34	6.22	6.16
800	7.49	7.43	7.37	7.33	7.29	7.25	7.11	7.03
900	8.42	8.36	8.30	8.24	8.20	8.15	8.00	7.91
1000	9.36	9.28	9.22	9.16	9.11	9.06	8.89	8.79
2000	18.71	18.56	18.43	18.31	18.21	18.11	17.77	17.58
3000	28.06	27.84	27.64	27.46	27.31	27.17	26.66	26.37
4000	37.42	37.12	36.85	36.62	36.41	36.22	35.54	35.15
5000	46.77	46.40	46.07	45.77	45.51	45.28	44.43	43.94
6000	56.12	55.67	55.28	54.92	54.61	54.33	53.31	52.73
7000	65.47	64.95	64.49	64.08	63.71	63.38	62.20	61.51
8000	74.83	74.23	73.70	73.23	72.81	72.44	71.08	70.30
9000	84.18	83.51	82.91	82.38	81.91	81.49	79.97	79.09
10000	93.53	92.79	92.13	91.54	91.01	90.55	88.85	87.87
11000	102.88	102.07	101.34	100.69	100.11	99.60	97.74	96.66
12000	112.24	111.34	110.55	109.84	109.22	108.65	106.62	105.45
13000	121.59	120.62	119.76	119.00	118.32	117.71	115.51	114.23
14000	130.94	129.90	128.97	128.15	127.42	126.76	124.39	123.02
15000	140.30	139.18	138.19	137.30	136.52	135.82	133.28	131.81
16000	149.65	148.46	147.40	146.46	145.62	144.87	142.16	140.59
17000	159.00	157.73	156.61	155.61	154.72	153.92	151.05	149.38
18000	168.35	167.01	165.82	164.76	163.82	162.98	159.93	158.17
19000	177.71	176.29	175.03	173.92	172.92	172.03	168.82	166.96
20000	187.06	185.57	184.25	183.07	182.02	181.09	177.70	175.74
21000	196.41	194.85	193.46	192.22	191.12	190.14	186.59	184.53
22000	205.76	204.13	202.67	201.38	200.22	199.19	195.47	193.32
23000	215.12	213.40	211.88	210.53	209.32	208.25	204.36	202.10
24000	224.47	222.68	221.10	219.68	218.43	217.30	213.24	210.89
25000	233.82	231.96	230.31	228.84	227.53	226.36	222.13	219.68
26000	243.17	241.24	239.52	237.99	236.63	235.41	231.01	228.46
27000	252.53	250.52	248.73	247.14	245.73	244.46	239.90	237.25
28000	261.88	259.80	257.94	256.30	254.83	253.52	248.78	246.04
29000	271.23	269.07	267.16	265.45	263.93	262.57	257.67	254.82
30000	280.59	278.35	276.37	274.60	273.03	271.63	266.55	263.61
31000	289.94	287.63	285.58	283.76	282.13	280.68	275.43	272.40
32000	299.29	296.91	294.79	292.91	291.23	289.74	284.32	281.18
33000	308.64	306.19	304.00	302.06	300.33	298.79	293.20	289.97
34000	318.00	315.46	313.22	311.22	309.43	307.84	302.09	298.76
35000	327.35	324.74	322.43	320.37	318.53	316.90	310.97	307.54
40000	374.11	371.13	368.49	366.14	364.04	362.17	355.40	351.48
45000	420.88	417.53	414.55	411.90	409.54	407.44	399.82	395.41
50000	467.64	463.92	460.61	457.67	455.05	452.71	444.25	439.35
55000	514.40	510.31	506.67	503.43	500.55	497.98	488.67	483.28
60000	561.17	556.70	552.73	549.20	546.06	543.25	533.09	527.22
65000	607.93	603.09	598.79	594.97	591.56	588.52	577.52	571.15
70000	654.69	649.48	644.85	640.73	637.06	633.79	621.94	615.08
75000	701.46	695.87	690.91	686.50	682.57	679.06	666.37	659.02
80000	748.22	742.26	736.97	732.27	728.07	724.33	710.79	702.95
85000	794.98	788.65	783.03	778.03	773.58	769.60	755.22	746.89
90000	841.75	835.05	829.09	823.80	819.08	814.87	799.64	790.82
95000	888.51	881.44	875.15	869.56	864.58	860.14	844.06	834.76
100000	935.27	927.83	921.21	915.33	910.09	905.41	888.49	878.69
105000	982.04	974.22	967.28	961.10	955.59	950.68	932.91	922.62
110000	1028.80	1020.61	1013.34	1006.86	1001.10	995.95	977.34	966.56
115000	1075.56	1067.00	1059.40	1052.63	1046.60	1041.22	1021.76	1010.49
120000	1122.33	1113.39	1105.46	1098.40	1092.11	1086.49	1066.18	1054.43
125000	1169.09	1159.78	1151.52	1144.16	1137.61	1131.76	1110.61	1098.36
130000	1215.85	1206.18	1197.58	1189.93	1183.11	1177.03	1155.03	1142.29
135000	1262.62	1252.57	1243.64	1235.70	1228.62	1222.30	1199.46	1186.23
140000	1309.38	1298.96	1289.70	1281.46	1274.12	1267.57	1243.88	1230.16
145000	1356.14	1345.35	1335.76	1327.23	1319.63	1312.85	1288.31	1274.10
150000	1402.91	1391.74	1381.82	1372.99	1365.13	1358.12	1332.73	1318.03
155000	1449.67	1438.13	1427.88	1418.76	1410.63	1403.39	1377.15	1361.97
160000	1496.43	1484.52	1473.94	1464.53	1456.14	1448.66	1421.58	1405.90

MONTHLY AMORTIZING PAYMENTS

AMOUNT OF LOAN	NUMBER OF YEARS IN TERM							
	1	1-1/2	2	3	4	5	6	7
$ 50	4.41	3.02	2.32	1.63	1.29	1.08	.94	.85
100	8.82	6.03	4.64	3.26	2.57	2.15	1.88	1.69
200	17.63	12.06	9.28	6.51	5.13	4.30	3.76	3.38
300	26.45	18.09	13.92	9.76	7.69	6.45	5.64	5.06
400	35.26	24.12	18.56	13.01	10.25	8.60	7.52	6.75
500	44.08	30.15	23.19	16.26	12.81	10.75	9.39	8.44
600	52.89	36.18	27.83	19.51	15.37	12.90	11.27	10.12
700	61.71	42.21	32.47	22.76	17.93	15.05	13.15	11.81
800	70.52	48.24	37.11	26.01	20.49	17.20	15.03	13.49
900	79.34	54.26	41.74	29.26	23.05	19.35	16.91	15.18
1000	88.15	60.29	46.38	32.51	25.61	21.50	18.78	16.87
2000	176.30	120.58	92.76	65.01	51.21	42.99	37.56	33.73
3000	264.45	180.87	139.13	97.51	76.82	64.49	56.34	50.59
4000	352.60	241.16	185.51	130.01	102.42	85.98	75.12	67.45
5000	440.75	301.44	231.89	162.52	128.02	107.47	93.90	84.31
6000	528.90	361.73	278.26	195.02	153.63	128.97	112.68	101.17
7000	617.05	422.02	324.64	227.52	179.23	150.46	131.46	118.03
8000	705.19	482.31	371.01	260.02	204.83	171.96	150.24	134.89
9000	793.34	542.59	417.39	292.53	230.44	193.45	169.02	151.75
10000	881.49	602.88	463.77	325.03	256.04	214.94	187.79	168.61
11000	969.64	663.17	510.14	357.53	281.64	236.44	206.57	185.47
12000	1057.79	723.46	556.52	390.03	307.25	257.93	225.35	202.33
13000	1145.94	783.74	602.89	422.54	332.85	279.43	244.13	219.19
14000	1234.09	844.03	649.27	455.04	358.45	300.92	262.91	236.05
15000	1322.23	904.32	695.65	487.54	384.06	322.41	281.69	252.92
16000	1410.38	964.61	742.02	520.04	409.66	343.91	300.47	269.78
17000	1498.53	1024.89	788.40	552.55	435.26	365.40	319.25	286.64
18000	1586.68	1085.18	834.77	585.05	460.87	386.90	338.03	303.50
19000	1674.83	1145.47	881.15	617.55	486.47	408.39	356.81	320.36
20000	1762.98	1205.76	927.53	650.05	512.07	429.88	375.58	337.22
21000	1851.13	1266.04	973.90	682.56	537.68	451.38	394.36	354.08
22000	1939.27	1326.33	1020.28	715.06	563.28	472.87	413.14	370.94
23000	2027.42	1386.62	1066.65	747.56	588.88	494.36	431.92	387.80
24000	2115.57	1446.91	1113.03	780.06	614.49	515.86	450.70	404.66
25000	2203.72	1507.19	1159.41	812.57	640.09	537.35	469.48	421.52
26000	2291.87	1567.48	1205.78	845.07	665.69	558.85	488.26	438.38
27000	2380.02	1627.77	1252.16	877.57	691.30	580.34	507.04	455.24
28000	2468.17	1688.06	1298.53	910.07	716.90	601.83	525.82	472.10
29000	2556.31	1748.34	1344.91	942.58	742.50	623.33	544.60	488.96
30000	2644.46	1808.63	1391.29	975.08	768.11	644.82	563.37	505.83
31000	2732.61	1868.92	1437.66	1007.58	793.71	666.32	582.15	522.69
32000	2820.76	1929.21	1484.04	1040.08	819.31	687.81	600.93	539.55
33000	2908.91	1989.49	1530.41	1072.59	844.92	709.30	619.71	556.41
34000	2997.06	2049.78	1576.79	1105.09	870.52	730.80	638.49	573.27
35000	3085.21	2110.07	1623.17	1137.59	896.12	752.29	657.27	590.13
40000	3525.95	2411.51	1855.05	1300.10	1024.14	859.76	751.16	674.43
45000	3966.69	2712.95	2086.93	1462.61	1152.16	967.23	845.06	758.74
50000	4407.44	3014.38	2318.81	1625.13	1280.17	1074.70	938.95	843.04
55000	4848.18	3315.82	2550.69	1787.64	1408.19	1182.17	1032.85	927.34
60000	5288.92	3617.26	2782.57	1950.15	1536.21	1289.64	1126.74	1011.65
65000	5729.66	3918.70	3014.45	2112.66	1664.22	1397.11	1220.64	1095.95
70000	6170.41	4220.13	3246.33	2275.18	1792.24	1504.58	1314.53	1180.25
75000	6611.15	4521.57	3478.21	2437.69	1920.26	1612.05	1408.43	1264.56
80000	7051.89	4823.01	3710.09	2600.20	2048.28	1719.52	1502.32	1348.86
85000	7492.64	5124.45	3941.97	2762.71	2176.29	1826.99	1596.22	1433.16
90000	7933.38	5425.89	4173.85	2925.22	2304.31	1934.46	1690.11	1517.47
95000	8374.12	5727.32	4405.73	3087.74	2432.33	2041.93	1784.01	1601.77
100000	8814.87	6028.76	4637.61	3250.25	2560.34	2149.40	1877.90	1686.07
105000	9255.61	6330.20	4869.49	3412.76	2688.36	2256.86	1971.80	1770.38
110000	9696.35	6631.64	5101.37	3575.27	2816.38	2364.33	2065.69	1854.68
115000	10137.09	6933.07	5333.25	3737.79	2944.39	2471.80	2159.59	1938.98
120000	10577.84	7234.51	5565.13	3900.30	3072.41	2579.27	2253.48	2023.29
125000	11018.58	7535.95	5797.01	4062.81	3200.43	2686.74	2347.38	2107.59
130000	11459.32	7837.39	6028.89	4225.32	3328.44	2794.21	2441.27	2191.89
135000	11900.07	8138.83	6260.77	4387.83	3456.46	2901.68	2535.17	2276.20
140000	12340.81	8440.26	6492.65	4550.35	3584.48	3009.15	2629.06	2360.50
145000	12781.55	8741.70	6724.53	4712.86	3712.50	3116.62	2722.96	2444.80
150000	13222.30	9043.14	6956.41	4875.37	3840.51	3224.09	2816.85	2529.11
155000	13663.04	9344.58	7188.29	5037.88	3968.53	3331.56	2910.75	2613.41
160000	14103.78	9646.01	7420.17	5200.40	4096.55	3439.03	3004.64	2697.71

AMOUNT OF LOAN	NUMBER OF YEARS IN TERM							
	8	9	10	11	12	14	15	16
$ 50	.78	.72	.68	.65	.62	.57	.56	.54
100	1.55	1.44	1.35	1.29	1.23	1.14	1.11	1.08
200	3.09	2.88	2.70	2.57	2.45	2.28	2.22	2.16
300	4.64	4.31	4.05	3.85	3.68	3.42	3.32	3.24
400	6.18	5.75	5.40	5.13	4.90	4.56	4.43	4.31
500	7.73	7.18	6.75	6.41	6.13	5.70	5.53	5.39
600	9.27	8.62	8.10	7.69	7.35	6.84	6.64	6.47
700	10.81	10.05	9.45	8.97	8.57	7.97	7.74	7.55
800	12.36	11.49	10.80	10.25	9.80	9.11	8.85	8.62
900	13.90	12.92	12.15	11.53	11.02	10.25	9.95	9.70
1000	15.45	14.36	13.50	12.81	12.25	11.39	11.06	10.78
2000	30.89	28.71	26.99	25.61	24.49	22.77	22.11	21.55
3000	46.33	43.06	40.49	38.42	36.73	34.16	33.17	32.32
4000	61.77	57.41	53.98	51.22	48.97	45.54	44.22	43.09
5000	77.21	71.76	67.47	64.03	61.21	56.93	55.27	53.87
6000	92.65	86.11	80.97	76.83	73.45	68.31	66.33	64.64
7000	108.09	100.46	94.46	89.64	85.69	79.70	77.38	75.41
8000	123.53	114.81	107.95	102.44	97.94	91.08	88.44	86.18
9000	138.97	129.16	121.45	115.25	110.18	102.46	99.49	96.96
10000	154.41	143.51	134.94	128.05	122.42	113.85	110.54	107.73
11000	169.85	157.86	148.43	140.85	134.66	125.23	121.60	118.50
12000	185.29	172.22	161.93	153.66	146.90	136.62	132.65	129.27
13000	200.73	186.57	175.42	166.46	159.14	148.00	143.71	140.05
14000	216.17	200.92	188.91	179.27	171.38	159.39	154.76	150.82
15000	231.61	215.27	202.41	192.07	183.63	170.77	165.81	161.59
16000	247.05	229.62	215.90	204.88	195.87	182.15	176.87	172.36
17000	262.49	243.97	229.39	217.68	208.11	193.54	187.92	183.14
18000	277.93	258.32	242.89	230.49	220.35	204.92	198.98	193.91
19000	293.37	272.67	256.38	243.29	232.59	216.31	210.03	204.68
20000	308.81	287.02	269.87	256.09	244.83	227.69	221.08	215.45
21000	324.25	301.37	283.37	268.90	257.07	239.08	232.14	226.23
22000	339.69	315.72	296.86	281.70	269.32	250.46	243.19	237.00
23000	355.13	330.07	310.36	294.51	281.56	261.84	254.25	247.77
24000	370.57	344.43	323.85	307.31	293.80	273.23	265.30	258.54
25000	386.01	358.78	337.34	320.12	306.04	284.61	276.35	269.32
26000	401.45	373.13	350.84	332.92	318.28	296.00	287.41	280.09
27000	416.89	387.48	364.33	345.73	330.52	307.38	298.46	290.86
28000	432.33	401.83	377.82	358.53	342.76	318.77	309.52	301.63
29000	447.77	416.18	391.32	371.33	355.01	330.15	320.57	312.41
30000	463.21	430.53	404.81	384.14	367.25	341.54	331.62	323.18
31000	478.65	444.88	418.30	396.94	379.49	352.92	342.68	333.95
32000	494.09	459.23	431.80	409.75	391.73	364.30	353.73	344.72
33000	509.53	473.58	445.29	422.55	403.97	375.69	364.79	355.50
34000	524.97	487.93	458.78	435.36	416.21	387.07	375.84	366.27
35000	540.41	502.29	472.28	448.16	428.45	398.46	386.89	377.04
40000	617.61	574.04	539.74	512.18	489.66	455.38	442.16	430.90
45000	694.81	645.79	607.21	576.21	550.87	512.30	497.43	484.76
50000	772.01	717.55	674.68	640.23	612.08	569.22	552.70	538.63
55000	849.21	789.30	742.15	704.25	673.28	626.14	607.97	592.49
60000	926.41	861.06	809.61	768.27	734.49	683.07	663.24	646.35
65000	1003.61	932.81	877.08	832.29	795.70	739.99	718.51	700.21
70000	1080.81	1004.57	944.55	896.32	856.90	796.91	773.78	754.07
75000	1158.01	1076.32	1012.02	960.34	918.11	853.83	829.05	807.94
80000	1235.21	1148.07	1079.48	1024.36	979.32	910.75	884.32	861.80
85000	1312.41	1219.83	1146.95	1088.38	1040.52	967.67	939.59	915.66
90000	1389.61	1291.58	1214.42	1152.41	1101.73	1024.60	994.86	969.52
95000	1466.81	1363.34	1281.89	1216.43	1162.94	1081.52	1050.13	1023.39
100000	1544.01	1435.09	1349.35	1280.45	1224.15	1138.44	1105.40	1077.25
105000	1621.21	1506.85	1416.82	1344.47	1285.35	1195.36	1160.67	1131.11
110000	1698.41	1578.60	1484.29	1408.50	1346.56	1252.28	1215.94	1184.97
115000	1775.61	1650.35	1551.76	1472.52	1407.77	1309.20	1271.21	1238.83
120000	1852.81	1722.11	1619.22	1536.54	1468.97	1366.13	1326.48	1292.70
125000	1930.01	1793.86	1686.69	1600.56	1530.18	1423.05	1381.75	1346.56
130000	2007.21	1865.62	1754.16	1664.58	1591.39	1479.97	1437.02	1400.42
135000	2084.41	1937.37	1821.63	1728.61	1652.59	1536.89	1492.29	1454.28
140000	2161.61	2009.13	1889.09	1792.63	1713.80	1593.81	1547.56	1508.14
145000	2238.81	2080.88	1956.56	1856.65	1775.01	1650.73	1602.83	1562.01
150000	2316.01	2152.63	2024.03	1920.67	1836.22	1707.66	1658.10	1615.87
155000	2393.21	2224.39	2091.50	1984.70	1897.42	1764.58	1713.37	1669.73
160000	2470.41	2296.14	2158.96	2048.72	1958.63	1821.50	1768.64	1723.59

MONTHLY AMORTIZING PAYMENTS

AMOUNT OF LOAN	NUMBER OF YEARS IN TERM							
	17	18	19	20	21	22	23	24
$ 50	.53	.52	.51	.50	.50	.49	.49	.48
100	1.06	1.04	1.02	1.00	.99	.98	.97	.96
200	2.11	2.07	2.03	2.00	1.97	1.95	1.93	1.91
300	3.16	3.10	3.05	3.00	2.96	2.92	2.89	2.86
400	4.22	4.13	4.06	4.00	3.94	3.90	3.85	3.81
500	5.27	5.17	5.08	5.00	4.93	4.87	4.81	4.77
600	6.32	6.20	6.09	6.00	5.91	5.84	5.78	5.72
700	7.38	7.23	7.10	6.99	6.90	6.81	6.74	6.67
800	8.43	8.26	8.12	7.99	7.88	7.79	7.70	7.62
900	9.48	9.30	9.13	8.99	8.87	8.76	8.66	8.58
1000	10.54	10.33	10.15	9.99	9.85	9.73	9.62	9.53
2000	21.07	20.65	20.29	19.97	19.70	19.46	19.24	19.05
3000	31.60	30.97	30.43	29.96	29.54	29.18	28.86	28.58
4000	42.13	41.29	40.57	39.94	39.39	38.91	38.48	38.10
5000	52.66	51.62	50.71	49.92	49.23	48.63	48.10	47.63
6000	63.19	61.94	60.85	59.91	59.08	58.36	57.72	57.15
7000	73.72	72.26	70.99	69.89	68.93	68.08	67.34	66.68
8000	84.25	82.58	81.14	79.88	78.77	77.81	76.95	76.20
9000	94.78	92.91	91.28	89.86	88.62	87.53	86.57	85.73
10000	105.31	103.23	101.42	99.84	98.46	97.26	96.19	95.25
11000	115.84	113.55	111.56	109.83	108.31	106.98	105.81	104.78
12000	126.37	123.87	121.70	119.81	118.16	116.71	115.43	114.30
13000	136.91	134.19	131.84	129.79	128.00	126.43	125.05	123.83
14000	147.44	144.52	141.98	139.78	137.85	136.16	134.67	133.35
15000	157.97	154.84	152.13	149.76	147.69	145.88	144.29	142.88
16000	168.50	165.16	162.27	159.75	157.54	155.61	153.90	152.40
17000	179.03	175.48	172.41	169.73	167.39	165.33	163.52	161.93
18000	189.56	185.81	182.55	179.71	177.23	175.06	173.14	171.45
19000	200.09	196.13	192.69	189.70	187.08	184.78	182.76	180.98
20000	210.62	206.45	202.83	199.68	196.92	194.51	192.38	190.50
21000	221.15	216.77	212.97	209.66	206.77	204.23	202.00	200.03
22000	231.68	227.10	223.12	219.65	216.62	213.96	211.62	209.55
23000	242.21	237.42	233.26	229.63	226.46	223.68	221.23	219.08
24000	252.74	247.74	243.40	239.62	236.31	233.41	230.85	228.60
25000	263.28	258.06	253.54	249.60	246.15	243.13	240.47	238.13
26000	273.81	268.38	263.68	259.58	256.00	252.86	250.09	247.65
27000	284.34	278.71	273.82	269.57	265.85	262.58	259.71	257.17
28000	294.87	289.03	283.96	279.55	275.69	272.31	269.33	266.70
29000	305.40	299.35	294.11	289.54	285.54	282.03	278.95	276.22
30000	315.93	309.67	304.25	299.52	295.38	291.76	288.57	285.75
31000	326.46	320.00	314.39	309.50	305.23	301.48	298.18	295.27
32000	336.99	330.32	324.53	319.49	315.08	311.21	307.80	304.80
33000	347.52	340.64	334.67	329.47	324.92	320.93	317.42	314.32
34000	358.05	350.96	344.81	339.45	334.77	330.66	327.04	323.85
35000	368.58	361.28	354.95	349.44	344.61	340.38	336.66	333.37
40000	421.24	412.90	405.66	399.36	393.84	389.01	384.75	381.00
45000	473.89	464.51	456.37	449.28	443.07	437.63	432.85	428.62
50000	526.55	516.12	507.07	499.19	492.30	486.26	480.94	476.25
55000	579.20	567.73	557.78	549.11	541.53	534.88	529.03	523.87
60000	631.85	619.34	608.49	599.03	590.76	583.51	577.13	571.49
65000	684.51	670.95	659.20	648.95	639.99	632.13	625.22	619.12
70000	737.16	722.56	709.90	698.87	689.22	680.76	673.31	666.74
75000	789.82	774.18	760.61	748.79	738.45	729.39	721.41	714.37
80000	842.47	825.79	811.32	798.71	787.68	778.01	769.50	761.99
85000	895.12	877.40	862.02	848.63	836.91	826.64	817.59	809.61
90000	947.78	929.01	912.73	898.55	886.14	875.26	865.69	857.24
95000	1000.43	980.62	963.44	948.47	935.37	923.89	913.78	904.86
100000	1053.09	1032.23	1014.14	998.38	984.60	972.51	961.87	952.49
105000	1105.74	1083.84	1064.85	1048.30	1033.83	1021.14	1009.97	1000.11
110000	1158.39	1135.46	1115.56	1098.22	1083.06	1069.76	1058.06	1047.73
115000	1211.05	1187.07	1166.26	1148.14	1132.29	1118.39	1106.15	1095.36
120000	1263.70	1238.68	1216.97	1198.06	1181.52	1167.01	1154.25	1142.98
125000	1316.36	1290.29	1267.68	1247.98	1230.75	1215.64	1202.34	1190.61
130000	1369.01	1341.90	1318.39	1297.90	1279.98	1264.26	1250.43	1238.23
135000	1421.66	1393.51	1369.09	1347.82	1329.21	1312.89	1298.53	1285.85
140000	1474.32	1445.12	1419.80	1397.74	1378.44	1361.51	1346.62	1333.48
145000	1526.97	1496.74	1470.51	1447.66	1427.67	1410.14	1394.71	1381.10
150000	1579.63	1548.35	1521.21	1497.57	1476.90	1458.77	1442.81	1428.73
155000	1632.28	1599.96	1571.92	1547.49	1526.13	1507.39	1490.90	1476.35
160000	1684.93	1651.57	1622.63	1597.41	1575.36	1556.02	1538.99	1523.97

AMOUNT OF LOAN	NUMBER OF YEARS IN TERM							
	25	26	27	28	29	30	35	40
$ 50	.48	.47	.47	.47	.46	.46	.45	.45
100	.95	.94	.94	.93	.92	.92	.90	.89
200	1.89	1.88	1.87	1.85	1.84	1.83	1.80	1.78
300	2.84	2.82	2.80	2.78	2.76	2.75	2.70	2.67
400	3.78	3.75	3.73	3.70	3.68	3.66	3.60	3.56
500	4.73	4.69	4.66	4.63	4.60	4.58	4.50	4.45
600	5.67	5.63	5.59	5.55	5.52	5.49	5.39	5.34
700	6.61	6.56	6.52	6.48	6.44	6.41	6.29	6.22
800	7.56	7.50	7.45	7.40	7.36	7.32	7.19	7.11
900	8.50	8.44	8.38	8.33	8.28	8.24	8.09	8.00
1000	9.45	9.37	9.31	9.25	9.20	9.15	8.99	8.89
2000	18.89	18.74	18.61	18.50	18.39	18.30	17.97	17.78
3000	28.33	28.11	27.91	27.74	27.59	27.45	26.95	26.66
4000	37.77	37.48	37.22	36.99	36.78	36.59	35.93	35.55
5000	47.21	46.85	46.52	46.23	45.97	45.74	44.91	44.43
6000	56.66	56.21	55.82	55.48	55.17	54.89	53.89	53.32
7000	66.10	65.58	65.13	64.72	64.36	64.04	62.87	62.20
8000	75.54	74.95	74.43	73.97	73.55	73.18	71.86	71.09
9000	84.98	84.32	83.73	83.21	82.75	82.33	80.84	79.98
10000	94.42	93.69	93.04	92.46	91.94	91.48	89.82	88.86
11000	103.86	103.06	102.34	101.70	101.13	100.63	98.80	97.75
12000	113.31	112.42	111.64	110.95	110.33	109.77	107.78	106.63
13000	122.75	121.79	120.94	120.19	119.52	118.92	116.76	115.52
14000	132.19	131.16	130.25	129.44	128.71	128.07	125.74	124.40
15000	141.63	140.53	139.55	138.68	137.91	137.22	134.73	133.29
16000	151.07	149.90	148.85	147.93	147.10	146.36	143.71	142.18
17000	160.52	159.27	158.16	157.17	156.29	155.51	152.69	151.06
18000	169.96	168.63	167.46	166.42	165.49	164.66	161.67	159.95
19000	179.40	178.00	176.76	175.66	174.68	173.81	170.65	168.83
20000	188.84	187.37	186.07	184.91	183.87	182.95	179.63	177.72
21000	198.28	196.74	195.37	194.15	193.07	192.10	188.61	186.60
22000	207.72	206.11	204.67	203.40	202.26	201.25	197.59	195.49
23000	217.17	215.48	213.97	212.64	211.45	210.40	206.58	204.38
24000	226.61	224.84	223.28	221.89	220.65	219.54	215.56	213.26
25000	236.05	234.21	232.58	231.13	229.84	228.69	224.54	222.15
26000	245.49	243.58	241.88	240.38	239.03	237.84	233.52	231.03
27000	254.93	252.95	251.19	249.62	248.23	246.98	242.50	239.92
28000	264.38	262.32	260.49	258.87	257.42	256.13	251.48	248.80
29000	273.82	271.69	269.79	268.11	266.61	265.28	260.46	257.69
30000	283.26	281.05	279.10	277.36	275.81	274.43	269.45	266.58
31000	292.70	290.42	288.40	286.60	285.00	283.57	278.43	275.46
32000	302.14	299.79	297.70	295.85	294.19	292.72	287.41	284.35
33000	311.58	309.16	307.01	305.09	303.39	301.87	296.39	293.23
34000	321.03	318.53	316.31	314.34	312.58	311.02	305.37	302.12
35000	330.47	327.90	325.61	323.58	321.77	320.16	314.35	311.00
40000	377.68	374.74	372.13	369.81	367.74	365.90	359.26	355.43
45000	424.89	421.58	418.64	416.03	413.71	411.64	404.17	399.86
50000	472.10	468.42	465.16	462.26	459.68	457.37	449.07	444.29
55000	519.30	515.26	511.67	508.48	505.64	503.11	493.98	488.72
60000	566.51	562.10	558.19	554.71	551.61	548.85	538.89	533.15
65000	613.72	608.94	604.70	600.93	597.58	594.59	583.79	577.58
70000	660.93	655.79	651.22	647.16	643.54	640.32	628.70	622.00
75000	708.14	702.63	697.73	693.38	689.51	686.06	673.61	666.43
80000	755.35	749.47	744.25	739.61	735.48	731.80	718.51	710.86
85000	802.56	796.31	790.76	785.83	781.44	777.53	763.42	755.29
90000	849.77	843.15	837.28	832.06	827.41	823.27	808.33	799.72
95000	896.98	889.99	883.79	878.28	873.38	869.01	853.23	844.15
100000	944.19	936.83	930.31	924.51	919.35	914.74	898.14	888.58
105000	991.40	983.68	976.82	970.73	965.31	960.48	943.05	933.00
110000	1038.60	1030.52	1023.34	1016.96	1011.28	1006.22	987.95	977.43
115000	1085.81	1077.36	1069.85	1063.18	1057.25	1051.96	1032.86	1021.86
120000	1133.02	1124.20	1116.37	1109.41	1103.21	1097.69	1077.77	1066.29
125000	1180.23	1171.04	1162.88	1155.63	1149.18	1143.43	1122.67	1110.72
130000	1227.44	1217.88	1209.40	1201.86	1195.15	1189.17	1167.58	1155.15
135000	1274.65	1264.72	1255.92	1248.08	1241.11	1234.90	1212.49	1199.57
140000	1321.86	1311.57	1302.43	1294.31	1287.08	1280.64	1257.39	1244.00
145000	1369.07	1358.41	1348.95	1340.54	1333.05	1326.38	1302.30	1288.43
150000	1416.28	1405.25	1395.46	1386.76	1379.02	1372.11	1347.21	1332.86
155000	1463.49	1452.09	1441.98	1432.99	1424.98	1417.85	1392.11	1377.29
160000	1510.70	1498.93	1488.49	1479.21	1470.95	1463.59	1437.02	1421.72

10⅝%

MONTHLY AMORTIZING PAYMENTS

AMOUNT OF LOAN	NUMBER OF YEARS IN TERM							
	1	1-1/2	2	3	4	5	6	7
$ 50	4.42	3.02	2.33	1.63	1.29	1.08	.95	.85
100	8.83	6.04	4.65	3.26	2.57	2.16	1.89	1.70
200	17.65	12.07	9.29	6.52	5.14	4.32	3.77	3.39
300	26.47	18.11	13.94	9.77	7.70	6.47	5.66	5.08
400	35.29	24.14	18.58	13.03	10.27	8.63	7.54	6.78
500	44.11	30.18	23.22	16.29	12.84	10.78	9.43	8.47
600	52.93	36.21	27.87	19.54	15.40	12.94	11.31	10.16
700	61.75	42.25	32.51	22.80	17.97	15.09	13.19	11.85
800	70.57	48.28	37.15	26.05	20.54	17.25	15.08	13.55
900	79.39	54.32	41.80	29.31	23.10	19.41	16.96	15.24
1000	88.21	60.35	46.44	32.57	25.67	21.56	18.85	16.93
2000	176.42	120.70	92.87	65.13	51.33	43.12	37.69	33.86
3000	264.63	181.04	139.31	97.69	77.00	64.67	56.53	50.78
4000	352.83	241.39	185.74	130.25	102.66	86.23	75.38	67.71
5000	441.04	301.73	232.17	162.81	128.32	107.78	94.22	84.63
6000	529.25	362.08	278.61	195.37	153.99	129.34	113.06	101.56
7000	617.45	422.42	325.04	227.93	179.65	150.90	131.90	118.49
8000	705.66	482.77	371.48	260.50	205.32	172.45	150.75	135.41
9000	793.87	543.11	417.91	293.06	230.98	194.01	169.59	152.34
10000	882.07	603.46	464.34	325.62	256.64	215.56	188.43	169.26
11000	970.28	663.80	510.78	358.18	282.31	237.12	207.27	186.19
12000	1058.49	724.15	557.21	390.74	307.97	258.68	226.12	203.12
13000	1146.69	784.49	603.65	423.30	333.63	280.23	244.96	220.04
14000	1234.90	844.84	650.08	455.86	359.30	301.79	263.80	236.97
15000	1323.11	905.18	696.51	488.43	384.96	323.34	282.64	253.89
16000	1411.31	965.53	742.95	520.99	410.63	344.90	301.49	270.82
17000	1499.52	1025.87	789.38	553.55	436.29	366.45	320.33	287.75
18000	1587.73	1086.22	835.82	586.11	461.95	388.01	339.17	304.67
19000	1675.93	1146.56	882.25	618.67	487.62	409.57	358.01	321.60
20000	1764.14	1206.91	928.68	651.23	513.28	431.12	376.86	338.52
21000	1852.35	1267.26	975.12	683.79	538.94	452.68	395.70	355.45
22000	1940.56	1327.60	1021.55	716.36	564.61	474.23	414.54	372.37
23000	2028.76	1387.95	1067.99	748.92	590.27	495.79	433.38	389.30
24000	2116.97	1448.29	1114.42	781.48	615.94	517.35	452.23	406.23
25000	2205.18	1508.64	1160.85	814.04	641.60	538.90	471.07	423.15
26000	2293.38	1568.98	1207.29	846.60	667.26	560.46	489.91	440.08
27000	2381.59	1629.33	1253.72	879.16	692.93	582.01	508.75	457.00
28000	2469.80	1689.67	1300.15	911.72	718.59	603.57	527.60	473.93
29000	2558.00	1750.02	1346.59	944.29	744.25	625.13	546.44	490.86
30000	2646.21	1810.36	1393.02	976.85	769.92	646.68	565.28	507.78
31000	2734.42	1870.71	1439.46	1009.41	795.58	668.24	584.12	524.71
32000	2822.62	1931.05	1485.89	1041.97	821.25	689.79	602.97	541.63
33000	2910.83	1991.40	1532.32	1074.53	846.91	711.35	621.81	558.56
34000	2999.04	2051.74	1578.76	1107.09	872.57	732.90	640.65	575.49
35000	3087.24	2112.09	1625.19	1139.65	898.24	754.46	659.49	592.41
40000	3528.28	2413.82	1857.36	1302.46	1026.56	862.24	753.71	677.04
45000	3969.31	2715.54	2089.53	1465.27	1154.88	970.02	847.92	761.67
50000	4410.35	3017.27	2321.70	1628.08	1283.19	1077.80	942.13	846.30
55000	4851.38	3318.99	2553.87	1790.88	1411.51	1185.58	1036.35	930.93
60000	5292.42	3620.72	2786.04	1953.69	1539.83	1293.36	1130.56	1015.56
65000	5733.45	3922.45	3018.21	2116.50	1668.15	1401.14	1224.77	1100.19
70000	6174.48	4224.17	3250.38	2279.30	1796.47	1508.92	1318.98	1184.82
75000	6615.52	4525.90	3482.55	2442.11	1924.79	1616.70	1413.20	1269.45
80000	7056.55	4827.63	3714.72	2604.92	2053.11	1724.47	1507.41	1354.08
85000	7497.59	5129.35	3946.89	2767.73	2181.43	1832.25	1601.62	1438.71
90000	7938.62	5431.08	4179.06	2930.53	2309.75	1940.03	1695.84	1523.34
95000	8379.65	5732.80	4411.23	3093.34	2438.06	2047.81	1790.05	1607.97
100000	8820.69	6034.53	4643.40	3256.15	2566.38	2155.59	1884.26	1692.60
105000	9261.72	6336.26	4875.57	3418.95	2694.70	2263.37	1978.47	1777.22
110000	9702.76	6637.98	5107.74	3581.76	2823.02	2371.15	2072.69	1861.85
115000	10143.79	6939.71	5339.91	3744.57	2951.34	2478.93	2166.90	1946.48
120000	10584.83	7241.44	5572.08	3907.37	3079.66	2586.71	2261.11	2031.11
125000	11025.86	7543.16	5804.25	4070.18	3207.98	2694.49	2355.33	2115.74
130000	11466.89	7844.89	6036.42	4232.99	3336.30	2802.27	2449.54	2200.37
135000	11907.93	8146.61	6268.59	4395.80	3464.62	2910.05	2543.75	2285.00
140000	12348.96	8448.34	6500.75	4558.60	3592.94	3017.83	2637.96	2369.63
145000	12790.00	8750.07	6732.92	4721.41	3721.25	3125.61	2732.18	2454.26
150000	13231.03	9051.79	6965.09	4884.22	3849.57	3233.39	2826.39	2538.89
155000	13672.06	9353.52	7197.26	5047.02	3977.89	3341.17	2920.60	2623.52
160000	14113.10	9655.25	7429.43	5209.83	4106.21	3448.94	3014.81	2708.15

AMOUNT OF LOAN	NUMBER OF YEARS IN TERM							
	8	9	10	11	12	14	15	16
$ 50	.78	.73	.68	.65	.62	.58	.56	.55
100	1.56	1.45	1.36	1.29	1.24	1.15	1.12	1.09
200	3.11	2.89	2.72	2.58	2.47	2.30	2.23	2.18
300	4.66	4.33	4.07	3.87	3.70	3.44	3.34	3.26
400	6.21	5.77	5.43	5.16	4.93	4.59	4.46	4.35
500	7.76	7.21	6.79	6.44	6.16	5.74	5.57	5.43
600	9.31	8.66	8.14	7.73	7.39	6.88	6.68	6.52
700	10.86	10.10	9.50	9.02	8.63	8.03	7.80	7.60
800	12.41	11.54	10.86	10.31	9.86	9.17	8.91	8.69
900	13.96	12.98	12.21	11.59	11.09	10.32	10.02	9.77
1000	15.51	14.42	13.57	12.88	12.32	11.47	11.14	10.86
2000	31.02	28.84	27.13	25.76	24.63	22.93	22.27	21.71
3000	46.53	43.26	40.70	38.63	36.95	34.39	33.40	32.56
4000	62.03	57.68	54.26	51.51	49.26	45.85	44.53	43.41
5000	77.54	72.10	67.82	64.39	61.58	57.31	55.66	54.26
6000	93.05	86.52	81.39	77.26	73.89	68.77	66.79	65.11
7000	108.55	100.94	94.95	90.14	86.21	80.23	77.93	75.97
8000	124.06	115.36	108.51	103.01	98.52	91.69	89.06	86.82
9000	139.57	129.78	122.08	115.89	110.84	103.15	100.19	97.67
10000	155.07	144.20	135.64	128.77	123.15	114.61	111.32	108.52
11000	170.58	158.62	149.20	141.64	135.47	126.07	122.45	119.37
12000	186.09	173.04	162.77	154.52	147.78	137.53	133.58	130.22
13000	201.59	187.46	176.33	167.39	160.09	148.99	144.72	141.07
14000	217.10	201.88	189.90	180.27	172.41	160.45	155.85	151.93
15000	232.61	216.30	203.46	193.15	184.72	171.91	166.98	162.78
16000	248.12	230.71	217.02	206.02	197.04	183.37	178.11	173.63
17000	263.62	245.13	230.59	218.90	209.35	194.83	189.24	184.48
18000	279.13	259.55	244.15	231.78	221.67	206.29	200.37	195.33
19000	294.64	273.97	257.71	244.65	233.98	217.76	211.51	206.18
20000	310.14	288.39	271.28	257.53	246.30	229.22	222.64	217.03
21000	325.65	302.81	284.84	270.40	258.61	240.68	233.77	227.89
22000	341.16	317.23	298.40	283.28	270.93	252.14	244.90	238.74
23000	356.66	331.65	311.97	296.16	283.24	263.60	256.03	249.59
24000	372.17	346.07	325.53	309.03	295.56	275.06	267.16	260.44
25000	387.68	360.49	339.09	321.91	307.87	286.52	278.30	271.29
26000	403.18	374.91	352.66	334.78	320.18	297.98	289.43	282.14
27000	418.69	389.33	366.22	347.66	332.50	309.44	300.56	292.99
28000	434.20	403.75	379.79	360.54	344.81	320.90	311.69	303.85
29000	449.70	418.17	393.35	373.41	357.13	332.36	322.82	314.70
30000	465.21	432.59	406.91	386.29	369.44	343.82	333.95	325.55
31000	480.72	447.00	420.48	399.16	381.76	355.28	345.08	336.40
32000	496.23	461.42	434.04	412.04	394.07	366.74	356.22	347.25
33000	511.73	475.84	447.60	424.92	406.39	378.20	367.35	358.10
34000	527.24	490.26	461.17	437.79	418.70	389.66	378.48	368.95
35000	542.75	504.68	474.73	450.67	431.02	401.12	389.61	379.81
40000	620.28	576.78	542.55	515.05	492.59	458.43	445.27	434.06
45000	697.81	648.88	610.37	579.43	554.16	515.73	500.93	488.32
50000	775.35	720.97	678.18	643.81	615.74	573.03	556.59	542.58
55000	852.88	793.07	746.00	708.19	677.31	630.33	612.24	596.83
60000	930.42	865.17	813.82	772.57	738.88	687.64	667.90	651.09
65000	1007.95	937.26	881.64	836.95	800.45	744.94	723.56	705.35
70000	1085.49	1009.36	949.46	901.33	862.03	802.24	779.22	759.61
75000	1163.02	1081.46	1017.27	965.71	923.60	859.54	834.88	813.86
80000	1240.56	1153.55	1085.09	1030.09	985.17	916.85	890.53	868.12
85000	1318.09	1225.65	1152.91	1094.48	1046.75	974.15	946.19	922.38
90000	1395.62	1297.75	1220.73	1158.86	1108.32	1031.45	1001.85	976.63
95000	1473.16	1369.84	1288.55	1223.24	1169.89	1088.76	1057.51	1030.89
100000	1550.69	1441.94	1356.36	1287.62	1231.47	1146.06	1113.17	1085.15
105000	1628.23	1514.04	1424.18	1352.00	1293.04	1203.36	1168.82	1139.41
110000	1705.76	1586.13	1492.00	1416.38	1354.61	1260.66	1224.48	1193.66
115000	1783.30	1658.23	1559.82	1480.76	1416.19	1317.97	1280.14	1247.92
120000	1860.83	1730.33	1627.64	1545.14	1477.76	1375.27	1335.80	1302.18
125000	1938.36	1802.42	1695.45	1609.52	1539.33	1432.57	1391.46	1356.43
130000	2015.90	1874.52	1763.27	1673.90	1600.90	1489.87	1447.11	1410.69
135000	2093.43	1946.62	1831.09	1738.28	1662.48	1547.18	1502.77	1464.95
140000	2170.97	2018.71	1898.91	1802.66	1724.05	1604.48	1558.43	1519.21
145000	2248.50	2090.81	1966.73	1867.04	1785.62	1661.78	1614.09	1573.46
150000	2326.04	2162.91	2034.54	1931.42	1847.20	1719.08	1669.75	1627.72
155000	2403.57	2235.00	2102.36	1995.80	1908.77	1776.39	1725.40	1681.98
160000	2481.11	2307.10	2170.18	2060.18	1970.34	1833.69	1781.06	1736.23

MONTHLY AMORTIZING PAYMENTS

AMOUNT OF LOAN	NUMBER OF YEARS IN TERM							
	17	18	19	20	21	22	23	24
$ 50	.54	.53	.52	.51	.50	.50	.49	.49
100	1.07	1.05	1.03	1.01	1.00	.99	.98	.97
200	2.13	2.09	2.05	2.02	1.99	1.97	1.95	1.93
300	3.19	3.13	3.07	3.03	2.98	2.95	2.92	2.89
400	4.25	4.17	4.09	4.03	3.98	3.93	3.89	3.85
500	5.31	5.21	5.12	5.04	4.97	4.91	4.86	4.81
600	6.37	6.25	6.14	6.05	5.96	5.89	5.83	5.77
700	7.43	7.29	7.16	7.05	6.96	6.87	6.80	6.73
800	8.49	8.33	8.18	8.06	7.95	7.85	7.77	7.70
900	9.56	9.37	9.21	9.07	8.94	8.84	8.74	8.66
1000	10.62	10.41	10.23	10.07	9.94	9.82	9.71	9.62
2000	21.23	20.81	20.45	20.14	19.87	19.63	19.42	19.23
3000	31.84	31.22	30.68	30.21	29.80	29.44	29.12	28.84
4000	42.45	41.62	40.90	40.28	39.73	39.25	38.83	38.46
5000	53.06	52.02	51.13	50.34	49.66	49.06	48.54	48.07
6000	63.67	62.43	61.35	60.41	59.59	58.87	58.24	57.68
7000	74.28	72.83	71.58	70.48	69.52	68.69	67.95	67.30
8000	84.89	83.24	81.80	80.55	79.45	78.50	77.65	76.91
9000	95.51	93.64	92.02	90.62	89.39	88.31	87.36	86.52
10000	106.12	104.04	102.25	100.68	99.32	98.12	97.07	96.14
11000	116.73	114.45	112.47	110.75	109.25	107.93	106.77	105.75
12000	127.34	124.85	122.70	120.82	119.18	117.74	116.48	115.36
13000	137.95	135.26	132.92	130.89	129.11	127.55	126.18	124.98
14000	148.56	145.66	143.15	140.96	139.04	137.37	135.89	134.59
15000	159.17	156.06	153.37	151.02	148.97	147.18	145.60	144.20
16000	169.78	166.47	163.59	161.09	158.90	156.99	155.30	153.82
17000	180.39	176.87	173.82	171.16	168.84	166.80	165.01	163.43
18000	191.01	187.28	184.04	181.23	178.77	176.61	174.71	173.04
19000	201.62	197.68	194.27	191.30	188.70	186.42	184.42	182.66
20000	212.23	208.08	204.49	201.36	198.63	196.23	194.13	192.27
21000	222.84	218.49	214.72	211.43	208.56	206.05	203.83	201.88
22000	233.45	228.89	224.94	221.50	218.49	215.86	213.54	211.50
23000	244.06	239.30	235.16	231.57	228.42	225.67	223.25	221.11
24000	254.67	249.70	245.39	241.63	238.35	235.48	232.95	230.72
25000	265.28	260.10	255.61	251.70	248.29	245.29	242.66	240.34
26000	275.90	270.51	265.84	261.77	258.22	255.10	252.36	249.95
27000	286.51	280.91	276.06	271.84	268.15	264.91	262.07	259.56
28000	297.12	291.31	286.29	281.91	278.08	274.73	271.78	269.18
29000	307.73	301.72	296.51	291.97	288.01	284.54	281.48	278.79
30000	318.34	312.12	306.73	302.04	297.94	294.35	291.19	288.40
31000	328.95	322.53	316.96	312.11	307.87	304.16	300.89	298.02
32000	339.56	332.93	327.18	322.18	317.80	313.97	310.60	307.63
33000	350.17	343.33	337.41	332.25	327.74	323.78	320.31	317.24
34000	360.78	353.74	347.63	342.31	337.67	333.59	330.01	326.86
35000	371.40	364.14	357.86	352.38	347.60	343.41	339.72	336.47
40000	424.45	416.16	408.98	402.72	397.25	392.46	388.25	384.54
45000	477.51	468.18	460.10	453.06	446.91	441.52	436.78	432.60
50000	530.56	520.20	511.22	503.40	496.57	490.58	485.31	480.67
55000	583.62	572.22	562.34	553.74	546.22	539.63	533.84	528.73
60000	636.67	624.24	613.46	604.08	595.88	588.69	582.37	576.80
65000	689.73	676.26	664.58	654.42	645.54	637.75	630.90	624.87
70000	742.79	728.28	715.71	704.76	695.19	686.81	679.43	672.93
75000	795.84	780.30	766.83	755.10	744.85	735.86	727.96	721.00
80000	848.90	832.32	817.95	805.44	794.50	784.92	776.49	769.07
85000	901.95	884.34	869.07	855.78	844.16	833.98	825.02	817.13
90000	955.01	936.36	920.19	906.12	893.82	883.03	873.55	865.20
95000	1008.07	988.38	971.31	956.46	943.47	932.09	922.09	913.26
100000	1061.12	1040.40	1022.43	1006.80	993.13	981.15	970.62	961.33
105000	1114.18	1092.42	1073.56	1057.14	1042.79	1030.21	1019.15	1009.40
110000	1167.23	1144.44	1124.68	1107.47	1092.44	1079.26	1067.68	1057.46
115000	1220.29	1196.46	1175.80	1157.81	1142.10	1128.32	1116.21	1105.53
120000	1273.34	1248.48	1226.92	1208.15	1191.75	1177.38	1164.74	1153.60
125000	1326.40	1300.50	1278.04	1258.49	1241.41	1226.44	1213.27	1201.66
130000	1379.46	1352.52	1329.16	1308.83	1291.07	1275.49	1261.80	1249.73
135000	1432.51	1404.54	1380.28	1359.17	1340.72	1324.55	1310.33	1297.79
140000	1485.57	1456.55	1431.41	1409.51	1390.38	1373.61	1358.86	1345.86
145000	1538.62	1508.57	1482.53	1459.85	1440.04	1422.66	1407.39	1393.93
150000	1591.68	1560.59	1533.65	1510.19	1489.69	1471.72	1455.92	1441.99
155000	1644.74	1612.61	1584.77	1560.53	1539.35	1520.78	1504.45	1490.06
160000	1697.79	1664.63	1635.89	1610.87	1589.00	1569.84	1552.98	1538.13

AMOUNT OF LOAN	NUMBER OF YEARS IN TERM 25	26	27	28	29	30	35	40
$ 50	.48	.48	.47	.47	.47	.47	.46	.45
100	.96	.95	.94	.94	.93	.93	.91	.90
200	1.91	1.90	1.88	1.87	1.86	1.85	1.82	1.80
300	2.86	2.84	2.82	2.81	2.79	2.78	2.73	2.70
400	3.82	3.79	3.76	3.74	3.72	3.70	3.64	3.60
500	4.77	4.73	4.70	4.67	4.65	4.63	4.54	4.50
600	5.72	5.68	5.64	5.61	5.58	5.55	5.45	5.40
700	6.68	6.63	6.58	6.54	6.51	6.47	6.36	6.29
800	7.63	7.57	7.52	7.47	7.43	7.40	7.27	7.19
900	8.58	8.52	8.46	8.41	8.36	8.32	8.18	8.09
1000	9.54	9.46	9.40	9.34	9.29	9.25	9.08	8.99
2000	19.07	18.92	18.79	18.68	18.58	18.49	18.16	17.97
3000	28.60	28.38	28.19	28.02	27.86	27.73	27.24	26.96
4000	38.13	37.84	37.58	37.35	37.15	36.97	36.32	35.94
5000	47.66	47.30	46.98	46.69	46.44	46.21	45.40	44.93
6000	57.19	56.76	56.37	56.03	55.72	55.45	54.47	53.91
7000	66.72	66.22	65.76	65.36	65.01	64.69	63.55	62.90
8000	76.25	75.67	75.16	74.70	74.29	73.93	72.63	71.88
9000	85.79	85.13	84.55	84.04	83.58	83.17	81.71	80.87
10000	95.32	94.59	93.95	93.38	92.87	92.41	90.79	89.85
11000	104.85	104.05	103.34	102.71	102.15	101.66	99.86	98.84
12000	114.38	113.51	112.74	112.05	111.44	110.90	108.94	107.82
13000	123.91	122.97	122.13	121.39	120.73	120.14	118.02	116.81
14000	133.44	132.43	131.52	130.72	130.01	129.38	127.10	125.79
15000	142.97	141.88	140.92	140.06	139.30	138.62	136.18	134.78
16000	152.50	151.34	150.31	149.40	148.58	147.86	145.25	143.76
17000	162.04	160.80	159.71	158.74	157.87	157.10	154.33	152.75
18000	171.57	170.26	169.10	168.07	167.16	166.34	163.41	161.73
19000	181.10	179.72	178.50	177.41	176.44	175.58	172.49	170.72
20000	190.63	189.18	187.89	186.75	185.73	184.82	181.57	179.70
21000	200.16	198.64	197.28	196.08	195.02	194.07	190.64	188.68
22000	209.69	208.09	206.68	205.42	204.30	203.31	199.72	197.67
23000	219.22	217.55	216.07	214.76	213.59	212.55	208.80	206.65
24000	228.75	227.01	225.47	224.09	222.87	221.79	217.88	215.64
25000	238.29	236.47	234.86	233.43	232.16	231.03	226.96	224.62
26000	247.82	245.93	244.26	242.77	241.45	240.27	236.03	233.61
27000	257.35	255.39	253.65	252.11	250.73	249.51	245.11	242.59
28000	266.88	264.85	263.04	261.44	260.02	258.75	254.19	251.58
29000	276.41	274.31	272.44	270.78	269.31	267.99	263.27	260.56
30000	285.94	283.76	281.83	280.12	278.59	277.23	272.35	269.55
31000	295.47	293.22	291.23	289.45	287.88	286.48	281.43	278.53
32000	305.00	302.68	300.62	298.79	297.16	295.72	290.50	287.52
33000	314.54	312.14	310.02	308.13	306.45	304.96	299.58	296.50
34000	324.07	321.60	319.41	317.47	315.74	314.20	308.66	305.49
35000	333.60	331.06	328.80	326.80	325.02	323.44	317.74	314.47
40000	381.25	378.35	375.78	373.49	371.45	369.64	363.13	359.39
45000	428.91	425.64	422.75	420.17	417.89	415.85	408.52	404.32
50000	476.57	472.94	469.72	466.86	464.32	462.05	453.91	449.24
55000	524.22	520.23	516.69	513.54	510.75	508.26	499.30	494.17
60000	571.88	567.52	563.66	560.23	557.18	554.46	544.69	539.09
65000	619.54	614.82	610.63	606.92	603.61	600.67	590.08	584.01
70000	667.19	662.11	657.60	653.60	650.04	646.87	635.47	628.94
75000	714.85	709.40	704.57	700.29	696.47	693.08	680.86	673.86
80000	762.50	756.70	751.55	746.97	742.90	739.28	726.25	718.78
85000	810.16	803.99	798.52	793.66	789.34	785.49	771.64	763.71
90000	857.82	851.28	845.49	840.34	835.77	831.69	817.03	808.63
95000	905.47	898.57	892.46	887.03	882.20	877.90	862.42	853.56
100000	953.13	945.87	939.43	933.71	928.63	924.10	907.81	898.48
105000	1000.78	993.16	986.40	980.40	975.06	970.31	953.20	943.40
110000	1048.44	1040.45	1033.37	1027.08	1021.49	1016.51	998.59	988.33
115000	1096.10	1087.75	1080.34	1073.77	1067.92	1062.72	1043.98	1033.25
120000	1143.75	1135.04	1127.32	1120.45	1114.35	1108.92	1089.37	1078.17
125000	1191.41	1182.33	1174.29	1167.14	1160.79	1155.13	1134.76	1123.10
130000	1239.07	1229.63	1221.26	1213.83	1207.22	1201.33	1180.15	1168.02
135000	1286.72	1276.92	1268.23	1260.51	1253.65	1247.54	1225.55	1212.95
140000	1334.38	1324.21	1315.20	1307.20	1300.08	1293.74	1270.94	1257.87
145000	1382.03	1371.51	1362.17	1353.88	1346.51	1339.95	1316.33	1302.79
150000	1429.69	1418.80	1409.14	1400.57	1392.94	1386.15	1361.72	1347.72
155000	1477.35	1466.09	1456.11	1447.25	1439.37	1432.36	1407.11	1392.64
160000	1525.00	1513.39	1503.09	1493.94	1485.80	1478.56	1452.50	1437.56

10¾% MONTHLY AMORTIZING PAYMENTS

AMOUNT OF LOAN	NUMBER OF YEARS IN TERM							
	1	1-1/2	2	3	4	5	6	7
$ 50	4.42	3.03	2.33	1.64	1.29	1.09	.95	.85
100	8.83	6.05	4.65	3.27	2.58	2.17	1.90	1.70
200	17.66	12.09	9.30	6.53	5.15	4.33	3.79	3.40
300	26.48	18.13	13.95	9.79	7.72	6.49	5.68	5.10
400	35.31	24.17	18.60	13.05	10.29	8.65	7.57	6.80
500	44.14	30.21	23.25	16.32	12.87	10.81	9.46	8.50
600	52.96	36.25	27.90	19.58	15.44	12.98	11.35	10.20
700	61.79	42.29	32.55	22.84	18.01	15.14	13.24	11.90
800	70.62	48.33	37.20	26.10	20.58	17.30	15.13	13.60
900	79.44	54.37	41.85	29.36	23.16	19.46	17.02	15.30
1000	88.27	60.41	46.50	32.63	25.73	21.62	18.91	17.00
2000	176.54	120.81	92.99	65.25	51.45	43.24	37.82	33.99
3000	264.80	181.21	139.48	97.87	77.18	64.86	56.72	50.98
4000	353.07	241.62	185.97	130.49	102.90	86.48	75.63	67.97
5000	441.33	302.02	232.46	163.11	128.63	108.09	94.54	84.96
6000	529.60	362.42	278.96	195.73	154.35	129.71	113.44	101.95
7000	617.86	422.83	325.45	228.35	180.07	151.33	132.35	118.94
8000	706.13	483.23	371.94	260.97	205.80	172.95	151.26	135.94
9000	794.39	543.63	418.43	293.59	231.52	194.57	170.16	152.93
10000	882.66	604.03	464.92	326.21	257.25	216.18	189.07	169.92
11000	970.92	664.44	511.42	358.83	282.97	237.80	207.97	186.91
12000	1059.19	724.84	557.91	391.45	308.70	259.42	226.88	203.90
13000	1147.45	785.24	604.40	424.07	334.42	281.04	245.79	220.89
14000	1235.72	845.65	650.89	456.69	360.14	302.66	264.69	237.88
15000	1323.98	906.05	697.38	489.31	385.87	324.27	283.60	254.87
16000	1412.25	966.45	743.87	521.93	411.59	345.89	302.51	271.87
17000	1500.51	1026.86	790.37	554.55	437.32	367.51	321.41	288.86
18000	1588.78	1087.26	836.86	587.17	463.04	389.13	340.32	305.85
19000	1677.04	1147.66	883.35	619.79	488.77	410.75	359.22	322.84
20000	1765.31	1208.06	929.84	652.41	514.49	432.36	378.13	339.83
21000	1853.57	1268.47	976.33	685.03	540.21	453.98	397.04	356.82
22000	1941.84	1328.87	1022.83	717.65	565.94	475.60	415.94	373.81
23000	2030.10	1389.27	1069.32	750.28	591.66	497.22	434.85	390.80
24000	2118.37	1449.68	1115.81	782.90	617.39	518.84	453.76	407.80
25000	2206.63	1510.08	1162.30	815.52	643.11	540.45	472.66	424.79
26000	2294.90	1570.48	1208.79	848.14	668.84	562.07	491.57	441.78
27000	2383.16	1630.89	1255.29	880.76	694.56	583.69	510.47	458.77
28000	2471.43	1691.29	1301.78	913.38	720.28	605.31	529.38	475.76
29000	2559.69	1751.69	1348.27	946.00	746.01	626.93	548.29	492.75
30000	2647.96	1812.09	1394.76	978.62	771.73	648.54	567.19	509.74
31000	2736.22	1872.50	1441.25	1011.24	797.46	670.16	586.10	526.73
32000	2824.49	1932.90	1487.74	1043.86	823.18	691.78	605.01	543.73
33000	2912.75	1993.30	1534.24	1076.48	848.91	713.40	623.91	560.72
34000	3001.02	2053.71	1580.73	1109.10	874.63	735.02	642.82	577.71
35000	3089.28	2114.11	1627.22	1141.72	900.35	756.63	661.72	594.70
40000	3530.61	2416.12	1859.68	1304.82	1028.98	864.72	756.26	679.66
45000	3971.93	2718.14	2092.14	1467.93	1157.60	972.81	850.79	764.61
50000	4413.26	3020.15	2324.60	1631.03	1286.22	1080.90	945.32	849.57
55000	4854.58	3322.17	2557.06	1794.13	1414.84	1188.99	1039.85	934.52
60000	5295.91	3624.18	2789.52	1957.23	1543.46	1297.08	1134.38	1019.48
65000	5737.24	3926.20	3021.98	2120.33	1672.08	1405.17	1228.91	1104.44
70000	6178.56	4228.21	3254.43	2283.44	1800.70	1513.26	1323.44	1189.39
75000	6619.89	4530.23	3486.89	2446.54	1929.33	1621.35	1417.98	1274.35
80000	7061.21	4832.24	3719.35	2609.64	2057.95	1729.44	1512.51	1359.31
85000	7502.54	5134.26	3951.81	2772.74	2186.57	1837.53	1607.04	1444.26
90000	7943.86	5436.27	4184.27	2935.85	2315.19	1945.62	1701.57	1529.22
95000	8385.19	5738.29	4416.73	3098.95	2443.81	2053.71	1796.10	1614.18
100000	8826.51	6040.30	4649.19	3262.05	2572.43	2161.80	1890.63	1699.13
105000	9267.84	6342.32	4881.65	3425.15	2701.05	2269.89	1985.16	1784.09
110000	9709.16	6644.33	5114.11	3588.25	2829.68	2377.98	2079.70	1869.04
115000	10150.49	6946.35	5346.57	3751.36	2958.30	2486.07	2174.23	1954.00
120000	10591.82	7248.36	5579.03	3914.46	3086.92	2594.16	2268.76	2038.96
125000	11033.14	7550.38	5811.49	4077.56	3215.54	2702.25	2363.29	2123.91
130000	11474.47	7852.39	6043.95	4240.66	3344.16	2810.34	2457.82	2208.87
135000	11915.79	8154.41	6276.41	4403.77	3472.78	2918.43	2552.35	2293.83
140000	12357.12	8456.42	6508.86	4566.87	3601.40	3026.52	2646.88	2378.78
145000	12798.44	8758.44	6741.32	4729.97	3730.03	3134.61	2741.42	2463.74
150000	13239.77	9060.45	6973.78	4893.07	3858.65	3242.70	2835.95	2548.70
155000	13681.09	9362.47	7206.24	5056.18	3987.27	3350.79	2930.48	2633.65
160000	14122.42	9664.48	7438.70	5219.28	4115.89	3458.88	3025.01	2718.61

AMOUNT OF LOAN	NUMBER OF YEARS IN TERM 8	9	10	11	12	14	15	16
$ 50	.78	.73	.69	.65	.62	.58	.57	.55
100	1.56	1.45	1.37	1.30	1.24	1.16	1.13	1.10
200	3.12	2.90	2.73	2.59	2.48	2.31	2.25	2.19
300	4.68	4.35	4.10	3.89	3.72	3.47	3.37	3.28
400	6.23	5.80	5.46	5.18	4.96	4.62	4.49	4.38
500	7.79	7.25	6.82	6.48	6.20	5.77	5.61	5.47
600	9.35	8.70	8.19	7.77	7.44	6.93	6.73	6.56
700	10.91	10.15	9.55	9.07	8.68	8.08	7.85	7.66
800	12.46	11.60	10.91	10.36	9.92	9.23	8.97	8.75
900	14.02	13.04	12.28	11.66	11.15	10.39	10.09	9.84
1000	15.58	14.49	13.64	12.95	12.39	11.54	11.21	10.94
2000	31.15	28.98	27.27	25.90	24.78	23.08	22.42	21.87
3000	46.73	43.47	40.91	38.85	37.17	34.62	33.63	32.80
4000	62.30	57.96	54.54	51.80	49.56	46.15	44.84	43.73
5000	77.87	72.45	68.17	64.74	61.95	57.69	56.05	54.66
6000	93.45	86.93	81.81	77.69	74.33	69.23	67.26	65.59
7000	109.02	101.42	95.44	90.64	86.72	80.76	78.47	76.52
8000	124.60	115.91	109.08	103.59	99.11	92.30	89.68	87.45
9000	140.17	130.40	122.71	116.54	111.50	103.84	100.89	98.38
10000	155.74	144.89	136.34	129.48	123.89	115.37	112.10	109.31
11000	171.32	159.37	149.98	142.43	136.27	126.91	123.31	120.24
12000	186.89	173.86	163.61	155.38	148.66	138.45	134.52	131.17
13000	202.47	188.35	177.25	168.33	161.05	149.99	145.73	142.10
14000	218.04	202.84	190.88	181.28	173.44	161.52	156.94	153.03
15000	233.61	217.33	204.51	194.22	185.83	173.06	168.15	163.97
16000	249.19	231.81	218.15	207.17	198.21	184.60	179.36	174.90
17000	264.76	246.30	231.78	220.12	210.60	196.13	190.57	185.83
18000	280.34	260.79	245.41	233.07	222.99	207.67	201.78	196.76
19000	295.91	275.28	259.05	246.02	235.38	219.21	212.99	207.69
20000	311.48	289.77	272.68	258.96	247.77	230.74	224.19	218.62
21000	327.06	304.25	286.32	271.91	260.15	242.28	235.40	229.55
22000	342.63	318.74	299.95	284.86	272.54	253.82	246.61	240.48
23000	358.20	333.23	313.58	297.81	284.93	265.36	257.82	251.41
24000	373.78	347.72	327.22	310.76	297.32	276.89	269.03	262.34
25000	389.35	362.21	340.85	323.70	309.71	288.43	280.24	273.27
26000	404.93	376.69	354.49	336.65	322.09	299.97	291.45	284.20
27000	420.50	391.18	368.12	349.60	334.48	311.50	302.66	295.13
28000	436.07	405.67	381.75	362.55	346.87	323.04	313.87	306.06
29000	451.65	420.16	395.39	375.50	359.26	334.58	325.08	317.00
30000	467.22	434.65	409.02	388.44	371.65	346.11	336.29	327.93
31000	482.80	449.13	422.65	401.39	384.03	357.65	347.50	338.86
32000	498.37	463.62	436.29	414.34	396.42	369.19	358.71	349.79
33000	513.94	478.11	449.92	427.29	408.81	380.72	369.92	360.72
34000	529.52	492.60	463.56	440.24	421.20	392.26	381.13	371.65
35000	545.09	507.09	477.19	453.18	433.59	403.80	392.34	382.58
40000	622.96	579.53	545.36	517.92	495.53	461.48	448.38	437.23
45000	700.83	651.97	613.53	582.66	557.47	519.17	504.43	491.89
50000	778.70	724.41	681.70	647.40	619.41	576.85	560.48	546.54
55000	856.57	796.85	749.87	712.14	681.35	634.54	616.53	601.19
60000	934.44	869.29	818.04	776.88	743.29	692.22	672.57	655.85
65000	1012.31	941.73	886.21	841.62	805.23	749.91	728.62	710.50
70000	1090.18	1014.17	954.38	906.36	867.17	807.59	784.67	765.15
75000	1168.05	1086.61	1022.55	971.10	929.11	865.28	840.72	819.81
80000	1245.92	1159.05	1090.71	1035.84	991.05	922.96	896.76	874.46
85000	1323.79	1231.49	1158.88	1100.58	1052.99	980.65	952.81	929.11
90000	1401.66	1303.93	1227.05	1165.32	1114.93	1038.33	1008.86	983.77
95000	1479.53	1376.37	1295.22	1230.06	1176.87	1096.02	1064.91	1038.42
100000	1557.40	1448.81	1363.39	1294.80	1238.81	1153.70	1120.95	1093.07
105000	1635.26	1521.25	1431.56	1359.54	1300.75	1211.39	1177.00	1147.73
110000	1713.13	1593.69	1499.73	1424.28	1362.69	1269.07	1233.05	1202.38
115000	1791.00	1666.13	1567.90	1489.02	1424.63	1326.76	1289.10	1257.04
120000	1868.87	1738.57	1636.07	1553.76	1486.57	1384.44	1345.14	1311.69
125000	1946.74	1811.01	1704.24	1618.50	1548.51	1442.12	1401.19	1366.34
130000	2024.61	1883.45	1772.41	1683.24	1610.45	1499.81	1457.24	1421.00
135000	2102.48	1955.89	1840.58	1747.98	1672.39	1557.49	1513.28	1475.65
140000	2180.35	2028.33	1908.75	1812.72	1734.33	1615.18	1569.33	1530.30
145000	2258.22	2100.77	1976.92	1877.46	1796.27	1672.86	1625.38	1584.96
150000	2336.09	2173.21	2045.09	1942.20	1858.21	1730.55	1681.43	1639.61
155000	2413.96	2245.65	2113.25	2006.94	1920.15	1788.23	1737.47	1694.26
160000	2491.83	2318.09	2181.42	2071.68	1982.09	1845.92	1793.52	1748.92

MONTHLY AMORTIZING PAYMENTS

AMOUNT OF LOAN	NUMBER OF YEARS IN TERM 17	18	19	20	21	22	23	24
$ 50	.54	.53	.52	.51	.51	.50	.49	.49
100	1.07	1.05	1.04	1.02	1.01	.99	.98	.98
200	2.14	2.10	2.07	2.04	2.01	1.98	1.96	1.95
300	3.21	3.15	3.10	3.05	3.01	2.97	2.94	2.92
400	4.28	4.20	4.13	4.07	4.01	3.96	3.92	3.89
500	5.35	5.25	5.16	5.08	5.01	4.95	4.90	4.86
600	6.42	6.30	6.19	6.10	6.02	5.94	5.88	5.83
700	7.49	7.35	7.22	7.11	7.02	6.93	6.86	6.80
800	8.56	8.39	8.25	8.13	8.02	7.92	7.84	7.77
900	9.63	9.44	9.28	9.14	9.02	8.91	8.82	8.74
1000	10.70	10.49	10.31	10.16	10.02	9.90	9.80	9.71
2000	21.39	20.98	20.62	20.31	20.04	19.80	19.59	19.41
3000	32.08	31.46	30.93	30.46	30.06	29.70	29.39	29.11
4000	42.77	41.95	41.23	40.61	40.07	39.60	39.18	38.81
5000	53.46	52.43	51.54	50.77	50.09	49.50	48.97	48.51
6000	64.16	62.92	61.85	60.92	60.11	59.39	58.77	58.22
7000	74.85	73.41	72.16	71.07	70.12	69.29	68.56	67.92
8000	85.54	83.89	82.46	81.22	80.14	79.19	78.36	77.62
9000	96.23	94.38	92.77	91.38	90.16	89.09	88.15	87.32
10000	106.92	104.86	103.08	101.53	100.17	98.99	97.94	97.02
11000	117.61	115.35	113.39	111.68	110.19	108.88	107.74	106.73
12000	128.31	125.84	123.69	121.83	120.21	118.78	117.53	116.43
13000	139.00	136.32	134.00	131.98	130.22	128.68	127.32	126.13
14000	149.69	146.81	144.31	142.14	140.24	138.58	137.12	135.83
15000	160.38	157.29	154.62	152.29	150.26	148.48	146.91	145.53
16000	171.07	167.78	164.92	162.44	160.27	158.37	156.71	155.24
17000	181.77	178.26	175.23	172.59	170.29	168.27	166.50	164.94
18000	192.46	188.75	185.54	182.75	180.31	178.17	176.29	174.64
19000	203.15	199.24	195.85	192.90	190.32	188.07	186.09	184.34
20000	213.84	209.72	206.15	203.05	200.34	197.97	195.88	194.04
21000	224.53	220.21	216.46	213.20	210.36	207.87	205.68	203.75
22000	235.22	230.69	226.77	223.36	220.37	217.76	215.47	213.45
23000	245.92	241.18	237.08	233.51	230.39	227.66	225.26	223.15
24000	256.61	251.67	247.38	243.66	240.41	237.56	235.06	232.85
25000	267.30	262.15	257.69	253.81	250.42	247.46	244.85	242.55
26000	277.99	272.64	268.00	263.96	260.44	257.36	254.64	252.26
27000	288.68	283.12	278.31	274.12	270.46	267.25	264.44	261.96
28000	299.37	293.61	288.61	284.27	280.48	277.15	274.23	271.66
29000	310.07	304.09	298.92	294.42	290.49	287.05	284.03	281.36
30000	320.76	314.58	309.23	304.57	300.51	296.95	293.82	291.06
31000	331.45	325.07	319.54	314.73	310.53	306.85	303.61	300.77
32000	342.14	335.55	329.84	324.88	320.54	316.74	313.41	310.47
33000	352.83	346.04	340.15	335.03	330.56	326.64	323.20	320.17
34000	363.53	356.52	350.46	345.18	340.58	336.54	332.99	329.87
35000	374.22	367.01	360.77	355.34	350.59	346.44	342.79	339.57
40000	427.68	419.44	412.30	406.10	400.68	395.93	391.76	388.08
45000	481.14	471.87	463.84	456.86	450.76	445.42	440.73	436.59
50000	534.59	524.30	515.38	507.62	500.84	494.91	489.70	485.10
55000	588.05	576.73	566.92	558.38	550.93	544.40	538.67	533.61
60000	641.51	629.16	618.45	609.14	601.01	593.89	587.63	582.12
65000	694.97	681.59	669.99	659.90	651.10	643.38	636.60	630.63
70000	748.43	734.01	721.53	710.67	701.18	692.87	685.57	679.14
75000	801.89	786.44	773.07	761.43	751.26	742.36	734.54	727.65
80000	855.35	838.87	824.60	812.19	801.35	791.85	783.51	776.16
85000	908.81	891.30	876.14	862.95	851.43	841.34	832.48	824.67
90000	962.27	943.73	927.68	913.71	901.52	890.83	881.45	873.18
95000	1015.72	996.16	979.21	964.47	951.60	940.32	930.42	921.69
100000	1069.18	1048.59	1030.75	1015.23	1001.68	989.81	979.39	970.20
105000	1122.64	1101.02	1082.29	1066.00	1051.77	1039.31	1028.36	1018.71
110000	1176.10	1153.45	1133.83	1116.76	1101.85	1088.80	1077.33	1067.22
115000	1229.56	1205.88	1185.36	1167.52	1151.94	1138.29	1126.29	1115.73
120000	1283.02	1258.31	1236.90	1218.28	1202.02	1187.78	1175.26	1164.24
125000	1336.48	1310.74	1288.44	1269.04	1252.10	1237.27	1224.23	1212.75
130000	1389.94	1363.17	1339.98	1319.80	1302.19	1286.76	1273.20	1261.26
135000	1443.40	1415.59	1391.51	1370.56	1352.27	1336.25	1322.17	1309.77
140000	1496.85	1468.02	1443.05	1421.33	1402.36	1385.74	1371.14	1358.28
145000	1550.31	1520.45	1494.59	1472.09	1452.44	1435.23	1420.11	1406.79
150000	1603.77	1572.88	1546.13	1522.85	1502.52	1484.72	1469.08	1455.30
155000	1657.23	1625.31	1597.66	1573.61	1552.61	1534.21	1518.05	1503.81
160000	1710.69	1677.74	1649.20	1624.37	1602.69	1583.70	1567.02	1552.32

AMOUNT OF LOAN	25	26	27	28	29	30	35	40
	NUMBER OF YEARS IN TERM							
$ 50	.49	.48	.48	.48	.47	.47	.46	.46
100	.97	.96	.95	.95	.94	.94	.92	.91
200	1.93	1.91	1.90	1.89	1.88	1.87	1.84	1.82
300	2.89	2.87	2.85	2.83	2.82	2.81	2.76	2.73
400	3.85	3.82	3.80	3.78	3.76	3.74	3.68	3.64
500	4.82	4.78	4.75	4.72	4.69	4.67	4.59	4.55
600	5.78	5.73	5.70	5.66	5.63	5.61	5.51	5.46
700	6.74	6.69	6.65	6.61	6.57	6.54	6.43	6.36
800	7.70	7.64	7.59	7.55	7.51	7.47	7.35	7.27
900	8.66	8.60	8.54	8.49	8.45	8.41	8.26	8.18
1000	9.63	9.55	9.49	9.43	9.38	9.34	9.18	9.09
2000	19.25	19.10	18.98	18.86	18.76	18.67	18.36	18.17
3000	28.87	28.65	28.46	28.29	28.14	28.01	27.53	27.26
4000	38.49	38.20	37.95	37.72	37.52	37.34	36.71	36.34
5000	48.11	47.75	47.43	47.15	46.90	46.68	45.88	45.42
6000	57.73	57.30	56.92	56.58	56.28	56.01	55.06	54.51
7000	67.35	66.85	66.41	66.01	65.66	65.35	64.23	63.59
8000	76.97	76.40	75.89	75.44	75.04	74.68	73.41	72.68
9000	86.59	85.95	85.38	84.87	84.42	84.02	82.58	81.76
10000	96.21	95.50	94.86	94.30	93.80	93.35	91.76	90.84
11000	105.84	105.05	104.35	103.73	103.18	102.69	100.93	99.93
12000	115.46	114.60	113.83	113.16	112.56	112.02	110.11	109.01
13000	125.08	124.15	123.32	122.59	121.94	121.36	119.28	118.10
14000	134.70	133.69	132.81	132.02	131.32	130.69	128.46	127.18
15000	144.32	143.24	142.29	141.45	140.70	140.03	137.63	136.26
16000	153.94	152.79	151.78	150.88	150.07	149.36	146.81	145.35
17000	163.56	162.34	161.26	160.30	159.45	158.70	155.98	154.43
18000	173.18	171.89	170.75	169.73	168.83	168.03	165.16	163.52
19000	182.80	181.44	180.23	179.16	178.21	177.37	174.33	172.60
20000	192.42	190.99	189.72	188.59	187.59	186.70	183.51	181.68
21000	202.04	200.54	199.21	198.02	196.97	196.04	192.68	190.77
22000	211.67	210.09	208.69	207.45	206.35	205.37	201.86	199.85
23000	221.29	219.64	218.18	216.88	215.73	214.71	211.03	208.94
24000	230.91	229.19	227.66	226.31	225.11	224.04	220.21	218.02
25000	240.53	238.74	237.15	235.74	234.49	233.38	229.38	227.10
26000	250.15	248.29	246.63	245.17	243.87	242.71	238.56	236.19
27000	259.77	257.83	256.12	254.60	253.25	252.04	247.73	245.27
28000	269.39	267.38	265.61	264.03	262.63	261.38	256.91	254.36
29000	279.01	276.93	275.09	273.46	272.01	270.71	266.08	263.44
30000	288.63	286.48	284.58	282.89	281.39	280.05	275.26	272.52
31000	298.25	296.03	294.06	292.32	290.76	289.38	284.43	281.61
32000	307.87	305.58	303.55	301.75	300.14	298.72	293.61	290.69
33000	317.50	315.13	313.03	311.18	309.52	308.05	302.78	299.78
34000	327.12	324.68	322.52	320.60	318.90	317.39	311.96	308.86
35000	336.74	334.23	332.01	330.03	328.28	326.72	321.13	317.94
40000	384.84	381.97	379.43	377.18	375.18	373.40	367.01	363.36
45000	432.95	429.72	426.86	424.33	422.08	420.07	412.88	408.78
50000	481.05	477.47	474.29	471.47	468.97	466.75	458.76	454.20
55000	529.16	525.21	521.72	518.62	515.87	513.42	504.63	499.62
60000	577.26	572.96	569.15	565.77	562.77	560.09	550.51	545.04
65000	625.37	620.71	616.58	612.92	609.66	606.77	596.38	590.46
70000	673.47	668.45	664.01	660.06	656.56	653.44	642.26	635.88
75000	721.57	716.20	711.44	707.21	703.46	700.12	688.13	681.30
80000	769.68	763.94	758.86	754.36	750.35	746.79	734.01	726.72
85000	817.78	811.69	806.29	801.50	797.25	793.46	779.88	772.14
90000	865.89	859.44	853.72	848.65	844.15	840.14	825.76	817.56
95000	913.99	907.18	901.15	895.80	891.04	886.81	871.63	862.98
100000	962.10	954.93	948.58	942.94	937.94	933.49	917.51	908.40
105000	1010.20	1002.68	996.01	990.09	984.84	980.16	963.38	953.82
110000	1058.31	1050.42	1043.44	1037.24	1031.73	1026.83	1009.26	999.24
115000	1106.41	1098.17	1090.86	1084.39	1078.63	1073.51	1055.13	1044.66
120000	1154.52	1145.91	1138.29	1131.53	1125.53	1120.18	1101.01	1090.08
125000	1202.62	1193.66	1185.72	1178.68	1172.42	1166.86	1146.88	1135.50
130000	1250.73	1241.41	1233.15	1225.83	1219.32	1213.53	1192.76	1180.92
135000	1298.83	1289.15	1280.58	1272.97	1266.22	1260.20	1238.63	1226.34
140000	1346.93	1336.90	1328.01	1320.12	1313.11	1306.88	1284.51	1271.76
145000	1395.04	1384.65	1375.44	1367.27	1360.01	1353.55	1330.38	1317.18
150000	1443.14	1432.39	1422.87	1414.41	1406.91	1400.23	1376.26	1362.60
155000	1491.25	1480.14	1470.29	1461.56	1453.80	1446.90	1422.13	1408.02
160000	1539.35	1527.88	1517.72	1508.71	1500.70	1493.58	1468.01	1453.44

MONTHLY AMORTIZING PAYMENTS

AMOUNT OF LOAN	NUMBER OF YEARS IN TERM							
	1	1-1/2	2	3	4	5	6	7
$ 50	4.42	3.03	2.33	1.64	1.29	1.09	.95	.86
100	8.84	6.05	4.66	3.27	2.58	2.17	1.90	1.71
200	17.67	12.10	9.31	6.54	5.16	4.34	3.80	3.42
300	26.50	18.14	13.97	9.81	7.74	6.51	5.70	5.12
400	35.33	24.19	18.62	13.08	10.32	8.68	7.59	6.83
500	44.17	30.24	23.28	16.34	12.90	10.85	9.49	8.53
600	53.00	36.28	27.93	19.61	15.48	13.01	11.39	10.24
700	61.83	42.33	32.59	22.88	18.05	15.18	13.28	11.94
800	70.66	48.37	37.24	26.15	20.63	17.35	15.18	13.65
900	79.50	54.42	41.90	29.42	23.21	19.52	17.08	15.36
1000	88.33	60.47	46.55	32.68	25.79	21.69	18.98	17.06
2000	176.65	120.93	93.10	65.36	51.57	43.37	37.95	34.12
3000	264.98	181.39	139.65	98.04	77.36	65.05	56.92	51.18
4000	353.30	241.85	186.20	130.72	103.14	86.73	75.89	68.23
5000	441.62	302.31	232.75	163.40	128.93	108.41	94.86	85.29
6000	529.95	362.77	279.30	196.08	154.71	130.09	113.83	102.35
7000	618.27	423.23	325.85	228.76	180.50	151.77	132.80	119.40
8000	706.59	483.69	372.40	261.44	206.28	173.45	151.77	136.46
9000	794.92	544.15	418.95	294.12	232.07	195.13	170.74	153.52
10000	883.24	604.61	465.50	326.80	257.85	216.81	189.71	170.57
11000	971.56	665.07	512.05	359.48	283.64	238.49	208.68	187.63
12000	1059.89	725.53	558.60	392.16	309.42	260.17	227.65	204.69
13000	1148.21	785.99	605.15	424.84	335.21	281.85	246.62	221.74
14000	1236.53	846.46	651.70	457.52	360.99	303.53	265.59	238.80
15000	1324.86	906.92	698.25	490.20	386.78	325.21	284.56	255.86
16000	1413.18	967.38	744.80	522.88	412.56	346.89	303.53	272.91
17000	1501.50	1027.84	791.35	555.56	438.35	368.57	322.50	289.97
18000	1589.83	1088.30	837.90	588.24	464.13	390.25	341.47	307.03
19000	1678.15	1148.76	884.45	620.92	489.92	411.93	360.44	324.08
20000	1766.47	1209.22	931.00	653.60	515.70	433.61	379.41	341.14
21000	1854.80	1269.68	977.55	686.28	541.49	455.29	398.38	358.20
22000	1943.12	1330.14	1024.10	718.96	567.27	476.97	417.35	375.25
23000	2031.44	1390.60	1070.65	751.63	593.06	498.65	436.32	392.31
24000	2119.77	1451.06	1117.20	784.31	618.84	520.33	455.29	409.37
25000	2208.09	1511.52	1163.75	816.99	644.63	542.01	474.26	426.42
26000	2296.41	1571.98	1210.30	849.67	670.41	563.69	493.23	443.48
27000	2384.74	1632.45	1256.85	882.35	696.20	585.37	512.20	460.54
28000	2473.06	1692.91	1303.40	915.03	721.98	607.05	531.17	477.59
29000	2561.38	1753.37	1349.95	947.71	747.77	628.73	550.14	494.65
30000	2649.71	1813.83	1396.50	980.39	773.55	650.41	569.11	511.71
31000	2738.03	1874.29	1443.05	1013.07	799.34	672.09	588.08	528.77
32000	2826.35	1934.75	1489.60	1045.75	825.12	693.77	607.05	545.82
33000	2914.68	1995.21	1536.15	1078.43	850.91	715.45	626.02	562.88
34000	3003.00	2055.67	1582.70	1111.11	876.69	737.13	644.99	579.94
35000	3091.32	2116.13	1629.25	1143.79	902.48	758.81	663.96	596.99
40000	3532.94	2418.43	1862.00	1307.19	1031.40	867.21	758.81	682.28
45000	3974.56	2720.74	2094.75	1470.58	1160.32	975.61	853.66	767.56
50000	4416.17	3023.04	2327.50	1633.98	1289.25	1084.01	948.51	852.84
55000	4857.79	3325.35	2560.25	1797.38	1418.17	1192.41	1043.36	938.13
60000	5299.41	3627.65	2792.99	1960.78	1547.10	1300.81	1138.21	1023.41
65000	5741.02	3929.95	3025.74	2124.18	1676.02	1409.21	1233.06	1108.70
70000	6182.64	4232.26	3258.49	2287.57	1804.95	1517.61	1327.91	1193.98
75000	6624.26	4534.56	3491.24	2450.97	1933.87	1626.02	1422.76	1279.26
80000	7065.87	4836.86	3723.99	2614.37	2062.79	1734.42	1517.61	1364.55
85000	7507.49	5139.17	3956.74	2777.77	2191.72	1842.82	1612.46	1449.83
90000	7949.11	5441.47	4189.49	2941.16	2320.64	1951.22	1707.32	1535.12
95000	8390.72	5743.78	4422.24	3104.56	2449.57	2059.62	1802.17	1620.40
100000	8832.34	6046.08	4654.99	3267.96	2578.49	2168.02	1897.02	1705.68
105000	9273.96	6348.38	4887.74	3431.36	2707.42	2276.42	1991.87	1790.97
110000	9715.57	6650.69	5120.49	3594.76	2836.34	2384.82	2086.72	1876.25
115000	10157.19	6952.99	5353.23	3758.15	2965.26	2493.22	2181.57	1961.54
120000	10598.81	7255.29	5585.98	3921.55	3094.19	2601.62	2276.42	2046.82
125000	11040.43	7557.60	5818.73	4084.95	3223.11	2710.02	2371.27	2132.10
130000	11482.04	7859.90	6051.48	4248.35	3352.04	2818.42	2466.12	2217.39
135000	11923.66	8162.21	6284.23	4411.74	3480.96	2926.82	2560.97	2302.67
140000	12365.28	8464.51	6516.98	4575.14	3609.89	3035.22	2655.82	2387.95
145000	12806.89	8766.81	6749.73	4738.54	3738.81	3143.62	2750.67	2473.24
150000	13248.51	9069.12	6982.48	4901.94	3867.73	3252.03	2845.52	2558.52
155000	13690.13	9371.42	7215.23	5065.34	3996.66	3360.43	2940.37	2643.81
160000	14131.74	9673.72	7447.98	5228.73	4125.58	3468.83	3035.22	2729.09

AMOUNT OF LOAN	8	9	10	11	12	14	15	16
	NUMBER OF YEARS IN TERM							
$ 50	.79	.73	.69	.66	.63	.59	.57	.56
100	1.57	1.46	1.38	1.31	1.25	1.17	1.13	1.11
200	3.13	2.92	2.75	2.61	2.50	2.33	2.26	2.21
300	4.70	4.37	4.12	3.91	3.74	3.49	3.39	3.31
400	6.26	5.83	5.49	5.21	4.99	4.65	4.52	4.41
500	7.83	7.28	6.86	6.52	6.24	5.81	5.65	5.51
600	9.39	8.74	8.23	7.82	7.48	6.97	6.78	6.61
700	10.95	10.19	9.60	9.12	8.73	8.13	7.91	7.71
800	12.52	11.65	10.97	10.42	9.97	9.30	9.04	8.81
900	14.08	13.11	12.34	11.72	11.22	10.46	10.16	9.91
1000	15.65	14.56	13.71	13.03	12.47	11.62	11.29	11.02
2000	31.29	29.12	27.41	26.05	24.93	23.23	22.58	22.03
3000	46.93	43.68	41.12	39.07	37.39	34.85	33.87	33.04
4000	62.57	58.23	54.82	52.09	49.85	46.46	45.16	44.05
5000	78.21	72.79	68.53	65.11	62.31	58.07	56.44	55.06
6000	93.85	87.35	82.23	78.13	74.78	69.69	67.73	66.07
7000	109.49	101.90	95.94	91.15	87.24	81.30	79.02	77.08
8000	125.13	116.46	109.64	104.17	99.70	92.91	90.31	88.09
9000	140.77	131.02	123.34	117.19	112.16	104.53	101.59	99.10
10000	156.42	145.57	137.05	130.21	124.62	116.14	112.88	110.11
11000	172.06	160.13	150.75	143.23	137.08	127.75	124.17	121.12
12000	187.70	174.69	164.46	156.25	149.55	139.37	135.46	132.13
13000	203.34	189.24	178.16	169.27	162.01	150.98	146.74	143.14
14000	218.98	203.80	191.87	182.29	174.47	162.60	158.03	154.15
15000	234.62	218.36	205.57	195.31	186.93	174.21	169.32	165.16
16000	250.26	232.91	219.27	208.33	199.39	185.82	180.61	176.17
17000	265.90	247.47	232.98	221.35	211.85	197.44	191.89	187.18
18000	281.54	262.03	246.68	234.37	224.32	209.05	203.18	198.19
19000	297.19	276.59	260.39	247.39	236.78	220.66	214.47	209.20
20000	312.83	291.14	274.09	260.41	249.24	232.28	225.76	220.21
21000	328.47	305.70	287.80	273.43	261.70	243.89	237.04	231.22
22000	344.11	320.26	301.50	286.45	274.16	255.50	248.33	242.23
23000	359.75	334.81	315.20	299.47	286.62	267.12	259.62	253.24
24000	375.39	349.37	328.91	312.49	299.09	278.73	270.91	264.25
25000	391.03	363.93	342.61	325.51	311.55	290.35	282.20	275.26
26000	406.67	378.48	356.32	338.53	324.01	301.96	293.48	286.27
27000	422.31	393.04	370.02	351.55	336.47	313.57	304.77	297.28
28000	437.96	407.60	383.73	364.57	348.93	325.19	316.06	308.29
29000	453.60	422.15	397.43	377.59	361.39	336.80	327.35	319.30
30000	469.24	436.71	411.14	390.61	373.86	348.41	338.63	330.31
31000	484.88	451.27	424.84	403.63	386.32	360.03	349.92	341.32
32000	500.52	465.82	438.54	416.65	398.78	371.64	361.21	352.33
33000	516.16	480.38	452.25	429.67	411.24	383.25	372.50	363.34
34000	531.80	494.94	465.95	442.69	423.70	394.87	383.78	374.35
35000	547.44	509.49	479.66	455.71	436.16	406.48	395.07	385.36
40000	625.65	582.28	548.18	520.81	498.47	464.55	451.51	440.41
45000	703.85	655.06	616.70	585.91	560.78	522.62	507.95	495.47
50000	782.06	727.85	685.22	651.01	623.09	580.69	564.39	550.52
55000	860.26	800.63	753.74	716.11	685.40	638.75	620.82	605.57
60000	938.47	873.42	822.27	781.21	747.71	696.82	677.26	660.62
65000	1016.68	946.20	890.79	846.31	810.01	754.89	733.70	715.67
70000	1094.88	1018.98	959.31	911.41	872.32	812.96	790.14	770.72
75000	1173.09	1091.77	1027.83	976.51	934.63	871.03	846.58	825.77
80000	1251.29	1164.55	1096.35	1041.61	996.94	929.10	903.01	880.82
85000	1329.50	1237.34	1164.87	1106.71	1059.25	987.16	959.45	935.87
90000	1407.70	1310.12	1233.40	1171.81	1121.56	1045.23	1015.89	990.93
95000	1485.91	1382.91	1301.92	1236.91	1183.87	1103.30	1072.33	1045.98
100000	1564.11	1455.69	1370.44	1302.01	1246.17	1161.37	1128.77	1101.03
105000	1642.32	1528.47	1438.96	1367.11	1308.48	1219.44	1185.20	1156.08
110000	1720.52	1601.26	1507.48	1432.21	1370.79	1277.50	1241.64	1211.13
115000	1798.73	1674.04	1576.00	1497.31	1433.10	1335.57	1298.08	1266.18
120000	1876.94	1746.83	1644.53	1562.41	1495.41	1393.64	1354.52	1321.23
125000	1955.14	1819.61	1713.05	1627.51	1557.72	1451.71	1410.96	1376.28
130000	2033.35	1892.40	1781.57	1692.61	1620.02	1509.78	1467.39	1431.33
135000	2111.55	1965.18	1850.09	1757.71	1682.33	1567.85	1523.83	1486.39
140000	2189.76	2037.96	1918.61	1822.81	1744.64	1625.91	1580.27	1541.44
145000	2267.96	2110.75	1987.13	1887.91	1806.95	1683.98	1636.71	1596.49
150000	2346.17	2183.53	2055.66	1953.02	1869.26	1742.05	1693.15	1651.54
155000	2424.37	2256.32	2124.18	2018.12	1931.57	1800.12	1749.58	1706.59
160000	2502.58	2329.10	2192.70	2083.22	1993.88	1858.19	1806.02	1761.64

MONTHLY AMORTIZING PAYMENTS

AMOUNT OF LOAN	NUMBER OF YEARS IN TERM							
	17	18	19	20	21	22	23	24
$ 50	.54	.53	.52	.52	.51	.50	.50	.49
100	1.08	1.06	1.04	1.03	1.02	1.00	.99	.98
200	2.16	2.12	2.08	2.05	2.03	2.00	1.98	1.96
300	3.24	3.18	3.12	3.08	3.04	3.00	2.97	2.94
400	4.31	4.23	4.16	4.10	4.05	4.00	3.96	3.92
500	5.39	5.29	5.20	5.12	5.06	5.00	4.95	4.90
600	6.47	6.35	6.24	6.15	6.07	6.00	5.93	5.88
700	7.55	7.40	7.28	7.17	7.08	6.99	6.92	6.86
800	8.62	8.46	8.32	8.19	8.09	7.99	7.91	7.84
900	9.70	9.52	9.36	9.22	9.10	8.99	8.90	8.82
1000	10.78	10.57	10.40	10.24	10.11	9.99	9.89	9.80
2000	21.55	21.14	20.79	20.48	20.21	19.98	19.77	19.59
3000	32.32	31.71	31.18	30.72	30.31	29.96	29.65	29.38
4000	43.10	42.28	41.57	40.95	40.42	39.95	39.53	39.17
5000	53.87	52.85	51.96	51.19	50.52	49.93	49.41	48.96
6000	64.64	63.41	62.35	61.43	60.62	59.92	59.30	58.75
7000	75.41	73.98	72.74	71.66	70.72	69.90	69.18	68.54
8000	86.19	84.55	83.13	81.90	80.83	79.89	79.06	78.33
9000	96.96	95.12	93.52	92.14	90.93	89.87	88.94	88.12
10000	107.73	105.69	103.91	102.37	101.03	99.86	98.82	97.91
11000	118.50	116.25	114.31	112.61	111.13	109.84	108.70	107.71
12000	129.28	126.82	124.70	122.85	121.24	119.83	118.59	117.50
13000	140.05	137.39	135.09	133.09	131.34	129.81	128.47	127.29
14000	150.82	147.96	145.48	143.32	141.44	139.80	138.35	137.08
15000	161.59	158.53	155.87	153.56	151.54	149.78	148.23	146.87
16000	172.37	169.09	166.26	163.80	161.65	159.77	158.11	156.66
17000	183.14	179.66	176.65	174.03	171.75	169.75	168.00	166.45
18000	193.91	190.23	187.04	184.27	181.85	179.74	177.88	176.24
19000	204.69	200.80	197.43	194.51	191.95	189.72	187.76	186.03
20000	215.46	211.37	207.82	204.74	202.06	199.71	197.64	195.82
21000	226.23	221.93	218.21	214.98	212.16	209.69	207.52	205.62
22000	237.00	232.50	228.61	225.22	222.26	219.68	217.40	215.41
23000	247.78	243.07	239.00	235.45	232.37	229.66	227.29	225.20
24000	258.55	253.64	249.39	245.69	242.47	239.65	237.17	234.99
25000	269.32	264.21	259.78	255.93	252.57	249.63	247.05	244.78
26000	280.09	274.77	270.17	266.17	262.67	259.62	256.93	254.57
27000	290.87	285.34	280.56	276.40	272.78	269.60	266.81	264.36
28000	301.64	295.91	290.95	286.64	282.88	279.59	276.70	274.15
29000	312.41	306.48	301.34	296.88	292.98	289.57	286.58	283.94
30000	323.18	317.05	311.73	307.11	303.08	299.56	296.46	293.73
31000	333.96	327.61	322.12	317.35	313.19	309.54	306.34	303.53
32000	344.73	338.18	332.51	327.59	323.29	319.53	316.22	313.32
33000	355.50	348.75	342.91	337.82	333.39	329.51	326.10	323.11
34000	366.28	359.32	353.30	348.06	343.49	339.50	335.99	332.90
35000	377.05	369.89	363.69	358.30	353.60	349.48	345.87	342.69
40000	430.91	422.73	415.64	409.48	404.11	399.41	395.28	391.64
45000	484.77	475.57	467.60	460.67	454.62	449.33	444.69	440.60
50000	538.64	528.41	519.55	511.85	505.14	499.26	494.10	489.55
55000	592.50	581.25	571.51	563.04	555.65	549.18	543.50	538.51
60000	646.36	634.09	623.46	614.22	606.16	599.11	592.91	587.46
65000	700.23	686.93	675.41	665.41	656.67	649.03	642.32	636.42
70000	754.09	739.77	727.37	716.59	707.19	698.96	691.73	685.37
75000	807.95	792.61	779.32	767.78	757.70	748.88	741.14	734.33
80000	861.82	845.45	831.28	818.96	808.21	798.81	790.55	783.28
85000	915.68	898.29	883.23	870.15	858.73	848.73	839.96	832.24
90000	969.54	951.13	935.19	921.33	909.24	898.66	889.37	881.19
95000	1023.41	1003.97	987.14	972.52	959.75	948.58	938.78	930.15
100000	1077.27	1056.81	1039.10	1023.70	1010.27	998.51	988.19	979.10
105000	1131.13	1109.65	1091.05	1074.88	1060.78	1048.43	1037.60	1028.06
110000	1185.00	1162.49	1143.01	1126.07	1111.29	1098.36	1087.00	1077.01
115000	1238.86	1215.33	1194.96	1177.25	1161.81	1148.28	1136.41	1125.97
120000	1292.72	1268.17	1246.92	1228.44	1212.32	1198.21	1185.82	1174.92
125000	1346.59	1321.01	1298.87	1279.62	1262.83	1248.13	1235.23	1223.88
130000	1400.45	1373.85	1350.82	1330.81	1313.34	1298.06	1284.64	1272.83
135000	1454.31	1426.69	1402.78	1381.99	1363.86	1347.98	1334.05	1321.79
140000	1508.18	1479.53	1454.73	1433.18	1414.37	1397.91	1383.46	1370.74
145000	1562.04	1532.37	1506.69	1484.36	1464.88	1447.83	1432.87	1419.70
150000	1615.90	1585.21	1558.64	1535.55	1515.40	1497.76	1482.28	1468.65
155000	1669.77	1638.05	1610.60	1586.73	1565.91	1547.68	1531.69	1517.61
160000	1723.63	1690.89	1662.55	1637.92	1616.42	1597.61	1581.10	1566.56

AMOUNT OF LOAN	NUMBER OF YEARS IN TERM							
	25	26	27	28	29	30	35	40
$ 50	.49	.49	.48	.48	.48	.48	.47	.46
100	.98	.97	.96	.96	.95	.95	.93	.92
200	1.95	1.93	1.92	1.91	1.90	1.89	1.86	1.84
300	2.92	2.90	2.88	2.86	2.85	2.83	2.79	2.76
400	3.89	3.86	3.84	3.81	3.79	3.78	3.71	3.68
500	4.86	4.83	4.79	4.77	4.74	4.72	4.64	4.60
600	5.83	5.79	5.75	5.72	5.69	5.66	5.57	5.52
700	6.80	6.75	6.71	6.67	6.64	6.61	6.50	6.43
800	7.77	7.72	7.67	7.62	7.58	7.55	7.42	7.35
900	8.74	8.68	8.62	8.57	8.53	8.49	8.35	8.27
1000	9.72	9.65	9.58	9.53	9.48	9.43	9.28	9.19
2000	19.43	19.29	19.16	19.05	18.95	18.86	18.55	18.37
3000	29.14	28.93	28.74	28.57	28.42	28.29	27.82	27.56
4000	38.85	38.57	38.31	38.09	37.90	37.72	37.09	36.74
5000	48.56	48.21	47.89	47.61	47.37	47.15	46.37	45.92
6000	58.27	57.85	57.47	57.14	56.84	56.58	55.64	55.11
7000	67.98	67.49	67.05	66.66	66.31	66.01	64.91	64.29
8000	77.69	77.13	76.62	76.18	75.79	75.44	74.18	73.47
9000	87.40	86.77	86.20	85.70	85.26	84.87	83.45	82.66
10000	97.11	96.41	95.78	95.22	94.73	94.29	92.73	91.84
11000	106.82	106.05	105.36	104.75	104.20	103.72	102.00	101.02
12000	116.54	115.69	114.93	114.27	113.68	113.15	111.27	110.21
13000	126.25	125.33	124.51	123.79	123.15	122.58	120.54	119.39
14000	135.96	134.97	134.09	133.31	132.62	132.01	129.82	128.57
15000	145.67	144.61	143.67	142.83	142.10	141.44	139.09	137.76
16000	155.38	154.25	153.24	152.36	151.57	150.87	148.36	146.94
17000	165.09	163.89	162.82	161.88	161.04	160.30	157.63	156.12
18000	174.80	173.53	172.40	171.40	170.51	169.73	166.90	165.31
19000	184.51	183.17	181.98	180.92	179.99	179.15	176.18	174.49
20000	194.22	192.81	191.55	190.44	189.46	188.58	185.45	183.67
21000	203.93	202.45	201.13	199.97	198.93	198.01	194.72	192.86
22000	213.64	212.09	210.71	209.49	208.40	207.44	203.99	202.04
23000	223.36	221.73	220.29	219.01	217.88	216.87	213.27	211.22
24000	233.07	231.37	229.86	228.53	227.35	226.30	222.54	220.41
25000	242.78	241.01	239.44	238.05	236.82	235.73	231.81	229.59
26000	252.49	250.65	249.02	247.58	246.29	245.16	241.08	238.77
27000	262.20	260.29	258.60	257.10	255.77	254.59	250.35	247.96
28000	271.91	269.93	268.17	266.62	265.24	264.01	259.63	257.14
29000	281.62	279.57	277.75	276.14	274.71	273.44	268.90	266.32
30000	291.33	289.21	287.33	285.66	284.19	282.87	278.17	275.51
31000	301.04	298.85	296.91	295.19	293.66	292.30	287.44	284.69
32000	310.75	308.49	306.48	304.71	303.13	301.73	296.72	293.87
33000	320.46	318.13	316.06	314.23	312.60	311.16	305.99	303.06
34000	330.18	327.77	325.64	323.75	322.08	320.59	315.26	312.24
35000	339.89	337.41	335.22	333.27	331.55	330.02	324.53	321.42
40000	388.44	385.61	383.10	380.88	378.91	377.16	370.89	367.34
45000	437.00	433.81	430.99	428.49	426.28	424.31	417.25	413.26
50000	485.55	482.01	478.88	476.10	473.64	471.45	463.61	459.17
55000	534.10	530.21	526.77	523.71	521.00	518.59	509.98	505.09
60000	582.66	578.41	574.65	571.32	568.37	565.74	556.34	551.01
65000	631.21	626.61	622.54	618.93	615.73	612.88	602.70	596.92
70000	679.77	674.81	670.43	666.54	663.09	660.03	649.06	642.84
75000	728.32	723.01	718.32	714.15	710.46	707.17	695.42	688.76
80000	776.88	771.21	766.20	761.76	757.82	754.32	741.78	734.67
85000	825.43	819.42	814.09	809.37	805.18	801.46	788.14	780.59
90000	873.99	867.62	861.98	856.98	852.55	848.61	834.50	826.51
95000	922.54	915.82	909.87	904.59	899.91	895.75	880.86	872.43
100000	971.09	964.02	957.75	952.20	947.27	942.90	927.22	918.34
105000	1019.65	1012.22	1005.64	999.81	994.64	990.04	973.59	964.26
110000	1068.20	1060.42	1053.53	1047.42	1042.00	1037.18	1019.95	1010.18
115000	1116.76	1108.62	1101.42	1095.03	1089.36	1084.33	1066.31	1056.09
120000	1165.31	1156.82	1149.30	1142.64	1136.73	1131.47	1112.67	1102.01
125000	1213.87	1205.02	1197.19	1190.25	1184.09	1178.62	1159.03	1147.93
130000	1262.42	1253.22	1245.08	1237.86	1231.45	1225.76	1205.39	1193.84
135000	1310.98	1301.42	1292.97	1285.47	1278.82	1272.91	1251.75	1239.76
140000	1359.53	1349.62	1340.85	1333.08	1326.18	1320.05	1298.11	1285.68
145000	1408.08	1397.82	1388.74	1380.69	1373.55	1367.20	1344.47	1331.59
150000	1456.64	1446.02	1436.63	1428.30	1420.91	1414.34	1390.83	1377.51
155000	1505.19	1494.22	1484.52	1475.91	1468.27	1461.48	1437.20	1423.43
160000	1553.75	1542.42	1532.40	1523.52	1515.64	1508.63	1483.56	1469.34

11% MONTHLY AMORTIZING PAYMENTS

AMOUNT OF LOAN	NUMBER OF YEARS IN TERM							
	1	1-1/2	2	3	4	5	6	7
$ 50	4.42	3.03	2.34	1.64	1.30	1.09	.96	.86
100	8.84	6.06	4.67	3.28	2.59	2.18	1.91	1.72
200	17.68	12.11	9.33	6.55	5.17	4.35	3.81	3.43
300	26.52	18.16	13.99	9.83	7.76	6.53	5.72	5.14
400	35.36	24.21	18.65	13.10	10.34	8.70	7.62	6.85
500	44.20	30.26	23.31	16.37	12.93	10.88	9.52	8.57
600	53.03	36.32	27.97	19.65	15.51	13.05	11.43	10.28
700	61.87	42.37	32.63	22.92	18.10	15.22	13.33	11.99
800	70.71	48.42	37.29	26.20	20.68	17.40	15.23	13.70
900	79.55	54.47	41.95	29.47	23.27	19.57	17.14	15.42
1000	88.39	60.52	46.61	32.74	25.85	21.75	19.04	17.13
2000	176.77	121.04	93.22	65.48	51.70	43.49	38.07	34.25
3000	265.15	181.56	139.83	98.22	77.54	65.23	57.11	51.37
4000	353.53	242.08	186.44	130.96	103.39	86.97	76.14	68.49
5000	441.91	302.60	233.04	163.70	129.23	108.72	95.18	85.62
6000	530.29	363.12	279.65	196.44	155.08	130.46	114.21	102.74
7000	618.68	423.63	326.26	229.18	180.92	152.20	133.24	119.86
8000	707.06	484.15	372.87	261.91	206.77	173.94	152.28	136.98
9000	795.44	544.67	419.48	294.65	232.61	195.69	171.31	154.11
10000	883.82	605.19	466.08	327.39	258.46	217.43	190.35	171.23
11000	972.20	665.71	512.69	360.13	284.31	239.17	209.38	188.35
12000	1060.58	726.23	559.30	392.87	310.15	260.91	228.41	205.47
13000	1148.97	786.75	605.91	425.61	336.00	282.66	247.45	222.60
14000	1237.35	847.26	652.51	458.35	361.84	304.40	266.48	239.72
15000	1325.73	907.78	699.12	491.09	387.69	326.14	285.52	256.84
16000	1414.11	968.30	745.73	523.82	413.53	347.88	304.55	273.96
17000	1502.49	1028.82	792.34	556.56	439.38	369.63	323.58	291.09
18000	1590.87	1089.34	838.95	589.30	465.22	391.37	342.62	308.21
19000	1679.26	1149.86	885.55	622.04	491.07	413.11	361.65	325.33
20000	1767.64	1210.38	932.16	654.78	516.92	434.85	380.69	342.45
21000	1856.02	1270.89	978.77	687.52	542.76	456.60	399.72	359.58
22000	1944.40	1331.41	1025.38	720.26	568.61	478.34	418.75	376.70
23000	2032.78	1391.93	1071.99	753.00	594.45	500.08	437.79	393.82
24000	2121.16	1452.45	1118.59	785.73	620.30	521.82	456.82	410.94
25000	2209.55	1512.97	1165.20	818.47	646.14	543.57	475.86	428.07
26000	2297.93	1573.49	1211.81	851.21	671.99	565.31	494.89	445.19
27000	2386.31	1634.01	1258.42	883.95	697.83	587.05	513.93	462.31
28000	2474.69	1694.52	1305.02	916.69	723.68	608.79	532.96	479.43
29000	2563.07	1755.04	1351.63	949.43	749.53	630.54	551.99	496.56
30000	2651.45	1815.56	1398.24	982.17	775.37	652.28	571.03	513.68
31000	2739.84	1876.08	1444.85	1014.91	801.22	674.02	590.06	530.80
32000	2828.22	1936.60	1491.46	1047.64	827.06	695.76	609.10	547.92
33000	2916.60	1997.12	1538.06	1080.38	852.91	717.50	628.13	565.05
34000	3004.98	2057.64	1584.67	1113.12	878.75	739.25	647.16	582.17
35000	3093.36	2118.15	1631.28	1145.86	904.60	760.99	666.20	599.29
40000	3535.27	2420.75	1864.32	1309.55	1033.83	869.70	761.37	684.90
45000	3977.18	2723.34	2097.36	1473.25	1163.05	978.41	856.54	770.51
50000	4419.09	3025.93	2330.40	1636.94	1292.28	1087.13	951.71	856.13
55000	4861.00	3328.52	2563.44	1800.63	1421.51	1195.84	1046.88	941.74
60000	5302.90	3631.12	2796.48	1964.33	1550.74	1304.55	1142.05	1027.35
65000	5744.81	3933.71	3029.51	2128.02	1679.96	1413.26	1237.22	1112.96
70000	6186.72	4236.30	3262.55	2291.72	1809.19	1521.97	1332.39	1198.58
75000	6628.63	4538.90	3495.59	2455.41	1938.42	1630.69	1427.56	1284.19
80000	7070.54	4841.49	3728.63	2619.10	2067.65	1739.40	1522.73	1369.80
85000	7512.45	5144.08	3961.67	2782.80	2196.87	1848.11	1617.90	1455.41
90000	7954.35	5446.67	4194.71	2946.49	2326.10	1956.82	1713.07	1541.02
95000	8396.26	5749.27	4427.75	3110.18	2455.33	2065.54	1808.24	1626.64
100000	8838.17	6051.86	4660.79	3273.88	2584.56	2174.25	1903.41	1712.25
105000	9280.08	6354.45	4893.83	3437.57	2713.78	2282.96	1998.58	1797.86
110000	9721.99	6657.04	5126.87	3601.26	2843.01	2391.67	2093.75	1883.47
115000	10163.90	6959.64	5359.91	3764.96	2972.24	2500.38	2188.92	1969.09
120000	10605.80	7262.23	5592.95	3928.65	3101.47	2609.10	2284.09	2054.70
125000	11047.71	7564.82	5825.98	4092.34	3230.70	2717.81	2379.26	2140.31
130000	11489.62	7867.42	6059.02	4256.04	3359.92	2826.52	2474.44	2225.92
135000	11931.53	8170.01	6292.06	4419.73	3489.15	2935.23	2569.61	2311.53
140000	12373.44	8472.60	6525.10	4583.43	3618.38	3043.94	2664.78	2397.15
145000	12815.35	8775.19	6758.14	4747.12	3747.61	3152.66	2759.95	2482.76
150000	13257.25	9077.79	6991.18	4910.81	3876.83	3261.37	2855.12	2568.37
155000	13699.16	9380.38	7224.22	5074.51	4006.06	3370.08	2950.29	2653.98
160000	14141.07	9682.97	7457.26	5238.20	4135.29	3478.79	3045.46	2739.59

MONTHLY AMORTIZING PAYMENTS 11%

AMOUNT OF LOAN	NUMBER OF YEARS IN TERM							
	8	9	10	11	12	14	15	16
$ 50	.79	.74	.69	.66	.63	.59	.57	.56
100	1.58	1.47	1.38	1.31	1.26	1.17	1.14	1.11
200	3.15	2.93	2.76	2.62	2.51	2.34	2.28	2.22
300	4.72	4.39	4.14	3.93	3.77	3.51	3.41	3.33
400	6.29	5.86	5.51	5.24	5.02	4.68	4.55	4.44
500	7.86	7.32	6.89	6.55	6.27	5.85	5.69	5.55
600	9.43	8.78	8.27	7.86	7.53	7.02	6.82	6.66
700	11.00	10.24	9.65	9.17	8.78	8.19	7.96	7.77
800	12.57	11.71	11.02	10.48	10.03	9.36	9.10	8.88
900	14.14	13.17	12.40	11.79	11.29	10.53	10.23	9.99
1000	15.71	14.63	13.78	13.10	12.54	11.70	11.37	11.10
2000	31.42	29.26	27.56	26.19	25.08	23.39	22.74	22.19
3000	47.13	43.88	41.33	39.28	37.61	35.08	34.10	33.28
4000	62.84	58.51	55.11	52.37	50.15	46.77	45.47	44.37
5000	78.55	73.13	68.88	65.47	62.68	58.46	56.83	55.46
6000	94.26	87.76	82.66	78.56	75.22	70.15	68.20	66.55
7000	109.96	102.39	96.43	91.65	87.75	81.84	79.57	77.64
8000	125.67	117.01	110.21	104.74	100.29	93.53	90.93	88.73
9000	141.38	131.64	123.98	117.84	112.82	105.22	102.30	99.82
10000	157.09	146.26	137.76	130.93	125.36	116.91	113.66	110.91
11000	172.80	160.89	151.53	144.02	137.90	128.60	125.03	122.00
12000	188.51	175.52	165.31	157.11	150.43	140.29	136.40	133.09
13000	204.21	190.14	179.08	170.21	162.97	151.98	147.76	144.18
14000	219.92	204.77	192.86	183.30	175.50	163.67	159.13	155.27
15000	235.63	219.39	206.63	196.39	188.04	175.36	170.49	166.36
16000	251.34	234.02	220.41	209.48	200.57	187.05	181.86	177.45
17000	267.05	248.64	234.18	222.57	213.11	198.74	193.23	188.54
18000	282.76	263.27	247.96	235.67	225.64	210.43	204.59	199.63
19000	298.47	277.90	261.73	248.76	238.18	222.13	215.96	210.72
20000	314.17	292.52	275.51	261.85	250.72	233.82	227.32	221.81
21000	329.88	307.15	289.28	274.94	263.25	245.51	238.69	232.90
22000	345.59	321.77	303.06	288.04	275.79	257.20	250.06	243.99
23000	361.30	336.40	316.83	301.13	288.32	268.89	261.42	255.08
24000	377.01	351.03	330.61	314.22	300.86	280.58	272.79	266.17
25000	392.72	365.65	344.38	327.31	313.39	292.27	284.15	277.26
26000	408.42	380.28	358.16	340.41	325.93	303.96	295.52	288.35
27000	424.13	394.90	371.93	353.50	338.46	315.65	306.89	299.44
28000	439.84	409.53	385.71	366.59	351.00	327.34	318.25	310.53
29000	455.55	424.15	399.48	379.68	363.54	339.03	329.62	321.62
30000	471.26	438.78	413.26	392.78	376.07	350.72	340.98	332.71
31000	486.97	453.41	427.03	405.87	388.61	362.41	352.35	343.80
32000	502.67	468.03	440.81	418.96	401.14	374.10	363.72	354.89
33000	518.38	482.66	454.58	432.05	413.68	385.79	375.08	365.98
34000	534.09	497.28	468.36	445.14	426.21	397.48	386.45	377.07
35000	549.80	511.91	482.13	458.24	438.75	409.17	397.81	388.16
40000	628.34	585.04	551.01	523.70	501.43	467.63	454.64	443.61
45000	706.88	658.17	619.88	589.16	564.10	526.08	511.47	499.06
50000	785.43	731.30	688.76	654.62	626.78	584.53	568.30	554.51
55000	863.97	804.43	757.63	720.08	689.46	642.98	625.13	609.96
60000	942.51	877.56	826.51	785.55	752.14	701.44	681.96	665.41
65000	1021.05	950.69	895.38	851.01	814.82	759.89	738.79	720.86
70000	1099.59	1023.82	964.26	916.47	877.49	818.34	795.62	776.31
75000	1178.14	1096.94	1033.13	981.93	940.17	876.80	852.45	831.76
80000	1256.68	1170.07	1102.01	1047.39	1002.85	935.25	909.28	887.21
85000	1335.22	1243.20	1170.88	1112.85	1065.53	993.70	966.11	942.66
90000	1413.76	1316.33	1239.76	1178.32	1128.20	1052.15	1022.94	998.11
95000	1492.31	1389.46	1308.63	1243.78	1190.88	1110.61	1079.77	1053.56
100000	1570.85	1462.59	1377.51	1309.24	1253.56	1169.06	1136.60	1109.01
105000	1649.39	1535.72	1446.38	1374.70	1316.24	1227.51	1193.43	1164.46
110000	1727.93	1608.85	1515.26	1440.16	1378.92	1285.96	1250.26	1219.91
115000	1806.47	1681.98	1584.13	1505.63	1441.59	1344.42	1307.09	1275.36
120000	1885.02	1755.11	1653.01	1571.09	1504.27	1402.87	1363.92	1330.81
125000	1963.56	1828.24	1721.88	1636.55	1566.95	1461.32	1420.75	1386.26
130000	2042.10	1901.37	1790.76	1702.01	1629.63	1519.78	1477.58	1441.71
135000	2120.64	1974.50	1859.63	1767.47	1692.30	1578.23	1534.41	1497.16
140000	2199.18	2047.63	1928.51	1832.93	1754.98	1636.68	1591.24	1552.61
145000	2277.73	2120.75	1997.38	1898.40	1817.66	1695.13	1648.07	1608.06
150000	2356.27	2193.88	2066.26	1963.86	1880.34	1753.59	1704.90	1663.51
155000	2434.81	2267.01	2135.13	2029.32	1943.02	1812.04	1761.73	1718.96
160000	2513.35	2340.14	2204.01	2094.78	2005.69	1870.49	1818.56	1774.41

MONTHLY AMORTIZING PAYMENTS

AMOUNT OF LOAN	NUMBER OF YEARS IN TERM							
	17	18	19	20	21	22	23	24
$ 50	.55	.54	.53	.52	.51	.51	.50	.50
100	1.09	1.07	1.05	1.04	1.02	1.01	1.00	.99
200	2.18	2.14	2.10	2.07	2.04	2.02	2.00	1.98
300	3.26	3.20	3.15	3.10	3.06	3.03	3.00	2.97
400	4.35	4.27	4.19	4.13	4.08	4.03	3.99	3.96
500	5.43	5.33	5.24	5.17	5.10	5.04	4.99	4.95
600	6.52	6.40	6.29	6.20	6.12	6.05	5.99	5.93
700	7.60	7.46	7.34	7.23	7.14	7.06	6.98	6.92
800	8.69	8.53	8.38	8.26	8.16	8.06	7.98	7.91
900	9.77	9.59	9.43	9.29	9.17	9.07	8.98	8.90
1000	10.86	10.66	10.48	10.33	10.19	10.08	9.98	9.89
2000	21.71	21.31	20.95	20.65	20.38	20.15	19.95	19.77
3000	32.57	31.96	31.43	30.97	30.57	30.22	29.92	29.65
4000	43.42	42.61	41.90	41.29	40.76	40.29	39.89	39.53
5000	54.27	53.26	52.38	51.61	50.95	50.37	49.86	49.41
6000	65.13	63.91	62.85	61.94	61.14	60.44	59.83	59.29
7000	75.98	74.56	73.33	72.26	71.33	70.51	69.80	69.17
8000	86.84	85.21	83.80	82.58	81.51	80.58	79.77	79.05
9000	97.69	95.86	94.28	92.90	91.70	90.66	89.74	88.93
10000	108.54	106.51	104.75	103.22	101.89	100.73	99.71	98.81
11000	119.40	117.16	115.23	113.55	112.08	110.80	109.68	108.69
12000	130.25	127.81	125.70	123.87	122.27	120.87	119.65	118.57
13000	141.10	138.46	136.18	134.19	132.46	130.94	129.62	128.45
14000	151.96	149.11	146.65	144.51	142.65	141.02	139.59	138.33
15000	162.81	159.76	157.12	154.83	152.84	151.09	149.56	148.21
16000	173.67	170.41	167.60	165.16	163.02	161.16	159.53	158.09
17000	184.52	181.06	178.07	175.48	173.21	171.23	169.50	167.97
18000	195.37	191.71	188.55	185.80	183.40	181.31	179.47	177.85
19000	206.23	202.36	199.02	196.12	193.59	191.38	189.44	187.73
20000	217.08	213.01	209.50	206.44	203.78	201.45	199.41	197.61
21000	227.93	223.67	219.97	216.76	213.97	211.52	209.38	207.49
22000	238.79	234.32	230.45	227.09	224.16	221.59	219.35	217.37
23000	249.64	244.97	240.92	237.41	234.35	231.67	229.32	227.25
24000	260.50	255.62	251.40	247.73	244.53	241.74	239.29	237.13
25000	271.35	266.27	261.87	258.05	254.72	251.81	249.26	247.01
26000	282.20	276.92	272.35	268.37	264.91	261.88	259.23	256.89
27000	293.06	287.57	282.82	278.70	275.10	271.96	269.20	266.77
28000	303.91	298.22	293.29	289.02	285.29	282.03	279.17	276.65
29000	314.77	308.87	303.77	299.34	295.48	292.10	289.14	286.53
30000	325.62	319.52	314.24	309.66	305.67	302.17	299.11	296.41
31000	336.47	330.17	324.72	319.98	315.85	312.24	309.08	306.29
32000	347.33	340.82	335.19	330.31	326.04	322.32	319.05	316.17
33000	358.18	351.47	345.67	340.63	336.23	332.39	329.02	326.05
34000	369.03	362.12	356.14	350.95	346.42	342.46	338.99	335.93
35000	379.89	372.77	366.62	361.27	356.61	352.53	348.96	345.81
40000	434.16	426.02	418.99	412.88	407.55	402.89	398.81	395.22
45000	488.43	479.28	471.36	464.49	458.50	453.26	448.66	444.62
50000	542.70	532.53	523.74	516.10	509.44	503.62	498.51	494.02
55000	596.96	585.78	576.11	567.71	560.38	553.98	548.36	543.42
60000	651.23	639.03	628.48	619.32	611.33	604.34	598.21	592.82
65000	705.50	692.29	680.86	670.93	662.27	654.70	648.06	642.22
70000	759.77	745.54	733.23	722.54	713.21	705.06	697.91	691.62
75000	814.04	798.79	785.60	774.15	764.16	755.42	747.76	741.02
80000	868.31	852.04	837.98	825.76	815.10	805.78	797.61	790.43
85000	922.58	905.30	890.35	877.37	866.05	856.14	847.46	839.83
90000	976.85	958.55	942.72	928.97	916.99	906.51	897.31	889.23
95000	1031.12	1011.80	995.10	980.58	967.93	956.87	947.16	938.63
100000	1085.39	1065.05	1047.47	1032.19	1018.88	1007.23	997.01	988.03
105000	1139.65	1118.31	1099.84	1083.80	1069.82	1057.59	1046.86	1037.43
110000	1193.92	1171.56	1152.22	1135.41	1120.76	1107.95	1096.71	1086.83
115000	1248.19	1224.81	1204.59	1187.02	1171.71	1158.31	1146.56	1136.24
120000	1302.46	1278.06	1256.96	1238.63	1222.65	1208.67	1196.41	1185.64
125000	1356.73	1331.32	1309.33	1290.24	1273.59	1259.03	1246.27	1235.04
130000	1411.00	1384.57	1361.71	1341.85	1324.54	1309.40	1296.12	1284.44
135000	1465.27	1437.82	1414.08	1393.46	1375.48	1359.76	1345.97	1333.84
140000	1519.54	1491.07	1466.45	1445.07	1426.42	1410.12	1395.82	1383.24
145000	1573.81	1544.33	1518.83	1496.68	1477.37	1460.48	1445.67	1432.64
150000	1628.08	1597.58	1571.20	1548.29	1528.31	1510.84	1495.52	1482.04
155000	1682.34	1650.83	1623.57	1599.90	1579.25	1561.20	1545.37	1531.45
160000	1736.61	1704.08	1675.95	1651.51	1630.20	1611.56	1595.22	1580.85

AMOUNT OF LOAN	NUMBER OF YEARS IN TERM							
	25	26	27	28	29	30	35	40
$ 50	.50	.49	.49	.49	.48	.48	.47	.47
100	.99	.98	.97	.97	.96	.96	.94	.93
200	1.97	1.95	1.94	1.93	1.92	1.91	1.88	1.86
300	2.95	2.92	2.91	2.89	2.87	2.86	2.82	2.79
400	3.93	3.90	3.87	3.85	3.83	3.81	3.75	3.72
500	4.91	4.87	4.84	4.81	4.79	4.77	4.69	4.65
600	5.89	5.84	5.81	5.77	5.74	5.72	5.63	5.57
700	6.87	6.82	6.77	6.74	6.70	6.67	6.56	6.50
800	7.85	7.79	7.74	7.70	7.66	7.62	7.50	7.43
900	8.83	8.76	8.71	8.66	8.61	8.58	8.44	8.36
1000	9.81	9.74	9.67	9.62	9.57	9.53	9.37	9.29
2000	19.61	19.47	19.34	19.23	19.14	19.05	18.74	18.57
3000	29.41	29.20	29.01	28.85	28.70	28.57	28.11	27.85
4000	39.21	38.93	38.68	38.46	38.27	38.10	37.48	37.14
5000	49.01	48.66	48.35	48.08	47.84	47.62	46.85	46.42
6000	58.81	58.39	58.02	57.69	57.40	57.14	56.22	55.70
7000	68.61	68.12	67.69	67.31	66.97	66.67	65.59	64.99
8000	78.41	77.86	77.36	76.92	76.54	76.19	74.96	74.27
9000	88.22	87.59	87.03	86.54	86.10	85.71	84.33	83.55
10000	98.02	97.32	96.70	96.15	95.67	95.24	93.70	92.83
11000	107.82	107.05	106.37	105.77	105.23	104.76	103.07	102.12
12000	117.62	116.78	116.04	115.38	114.80	114.28	112.44	111.40
13000	127.42	126.51	125.71	125.00	124.37	123.81	121.81	120.68
14000	137.22	136.24	135.38	134.61	133.93	133.33	131.18	129.97
15000	147.02	145.97	145.05	144.23	143.50	142.85	140.55	139.25
16000	156.82	155.71	154.72	153.84	153.07	152.38	149.92	148.53
17000	166.62	165.44	164.39	163.46	162.63	161.90	159.29	157.82
18000	176.43	175.17	174.06	173.07	172.20	171.42	168.66	167.10
19000	186.23	184.90	183.73	182.69	181.76	180.95	178.03	176.38
20000	196.03	194.63	193.40	192.30	191.33	190.47	187.40	185.66
21000	205.83	204.36	203.06	201.92	200.90	199.99	196.77	194.95
22000	215.63	214.09	212.73	211.53	210.46	209.52	206.14	204.23
23000	225.43	223.82	222.40	221.15	220.03	219.04	215.51	213.51
24000	235.23	233.56	232.07	230.76	229.60	228.56	224.87	222.80
25000	245.03	243.29	241.74	240.37	239.16	238.09	234.24	232.08
26000	254.83	253.02	251.41	249.99	248.73	247.61	243.61	241.36
27000	264.64	262.75	261.08	259.60	258.29	257.13	252.98	250.64
28000	274.44	272.48	270.75	269.22	267.86	266.66	262.35	259.93
29000	284.24	282.21	280.42	278.83	277.43	276.18	271.72	269.21
30000	294.04	291.94	290.09	288.45	286.99	285.70	281.09	278.49
31000	303.84	301.67	299.76	298.06	296.56	295.23	290.46	287.78
32000	313.64	311.41	309.43	307.68	306.13	304.75	299.83	297.06
33000	323.44	321.14	319.10	317.29	315.69	314.27	309.20	306.34
34000	333.24	330.87	328.77	326.91	325.26	323.79	318.57	315.63
35000	343.04	340.60	338.44	336.52	334.83	333.32	327.94	324.91
40000	392.05	389.26	386.79	384.60	382.66	380.93	374.79	371.32
45000	441.06	437.91	435.13	432.67	430.49	428.55	421.64	417.74
50000	490.06	486.57	483.48	480.74	478.32	476.17	468.48	464.15
55000	539.07	535.23	531.83	528.82	526.15	523.78	515.33	510.57
60000	588.07	583.88	580.18	576.89	573.98	571.40	562.18	556.98
65000	637.08	632.54	628.52	624.97	621.81	619.02	609.03	603.40
70000	686.08	681.19	676.87	673.04	669.65	666.63	655.88	649.81
75000	735.09	729.85	725.22	721.11	717.48	714.25	702.72	696.23
80000	784.10	778.51	773.57	769.19	765.31	761.86	749.57	742.64
85000	833.10	827.16	821.91	817.26	813.14	809.48	796.42	789.06
90000	882.11	875.82	870.26	865.34	860.97	857.10	843.27	835.47
95000	931.11	924.48	918.61	913.41	908.80	904.71	890.11	881.88
100000	980.12	973.13	966.96	961.48	956.63	952.33	936.96	928.30
105000	1029.12	1021.79	1015.30	1009.56	1004.47	999.94	983.81	974.71
110000	1078.13	1070.45	1063.65	1057.63	1052.30	1047.56	1030.66	1021.13
115000	1127.14	1119.10	1112.00	1105.71	1100.13	1095.18	1077.51	1067.54
120000	1176.14	1167.76	1160.35	1153.78	1147.96	1142.79	1124.35	1113.96
125000	1225.15	1216.41	1208.69	1201.85	1195.79	1190.41	1171.20	1160.37
130000	1274.15	1265.07	1257.04	1249.93	1243.62	1238.03	1218.05	1206.79
135000	1323.16	1313.73	1305.39	1298.00	1291.45	1285.64	1264.90	1253.20
140000	1372.16	1362.38	1353.74	1346.08	1339.29	1333.26	1311.75	1299.62
145000	1421.17	1411.04	1402.08	1394.15	1387.12	1380.87	1358.59	1346.03
150000	1470.17	1459.70	1450.43	1442.22	1434.95	1428.49	1405.44	1392.45
155000	1519.18	1508.35	1498.78	1490.30	1482.78	1476.11	1452.29	1438.86
160000	1568.19	1557.01	1547.13	1538.37	1530.61	1523.72	1499.14	1485.28

MONTHLY AMORTIZING PAYMENTS

AMOUNT OF LOAN	NUMBER OF YEARS IN TERM 1	1-1/2	2	3	4	5	6	7
$ 50	4.43	3.03	2.34	1.64	1.30	1.10	.96	.86
100	8.85	6.06	4.67	3.28	2.60	2.19	1.91	1.72
200	17.69	12.12	9.34	6.56	5.19	4.37	3.82	3.44
300	26.54	18.18	14.00	9.84	7.78	6.55	5.73	5.16
400	35.38	24.24	18.67	13.12	10.37	8.73	7.64	6.88
500	44.22	30.29	23.34	16.40	12.96	10.91	9.55	8.60
600	53.07	36.35	28.00	19.68	15.55	13.09	11.46	10.32
700	61.91	42.41	32.67	22.96	18.14	15.27	13.37	12.04
800	70.76	48.47	37.34	26.24	20.73	17.45	15.28	13.76
900	79.60	54.52	42.00	29.52	23.32	19.63	17.19	15.47
1000	88.44	60.58	46.67	32.80	25.91	21.81	19.10	17.19
2000	176.88	121.16	93.34	65.60	51.82	43.61	38.20	34.38
3000	265.32	181.73	140.00	98.40	77.72	65.42	57.30	51.57
4000	353.76	242.31	186.67	131.20	103.63	87.22	76.40	68.76
5000	442.20	302.89	233.33	163.99	129.54	109.03	95.50	85.95
6000	530.64	363.46	280.00	196.79	155.44	130.83	114.59	103.13
7000	619.08	424.04	326.67	229.59	181.35	152.64	133.69	120.32
8000	707.52	484.62	373.33	262.39	207.26	174.44	152.79	137.51
9000	795.96	545.19	420.00	295.19	233.16	196.25	171.89	154.70
10000	884.40	605.77	466.66	327.98	259.07	218.05	190.99	171.89
11000	972.84	666.35	513.33	360.78	284.97	239.86	210.08	189.08
12000	1061.28	726.92	560.00	393.58	310.88	261.66	229.18	206.26
13000	1149.72	787.50	606.66	426.38	336.79	283.47	248.28	223.45
14000	1238.16	848.07	653.33	459.18	362.69	305.27	267.38	240.64
15000	1326.60	908.65	699.99	491.97	388.60	327.08	286.48	257.83
16000	1415.04	969.23	746.66	524.77	414.51	348.88	305.58	275.02
17000	1503.48	1029.80	793.33	557.57	440.41	370.69	324.67	292.20
18000	1591.92	1090.38	839.99	590.37	466.32	392.49	343.77	309.39
19000	1680.36	1150.96	886.66	623.17	492.22	414.30	362.87	326.58
20000	1768.80	1211.53	933.32	655.96	518.13	436.10	381.97	343.77
21000	1857.24	1272.11	979.99	688.76	544.04	457.91	401.07	360.96
22000	1945.68	1332.69	1026.65	721.56	569.94	479.71	420.16	378.15
23000	2034.12	1393.26	1073.32	754.36	595.85	501.52	439.26	395.33
24000	2122.56	1453.84	1119.99	787.16	621.76	523.32	458.36	412.52
25000	2211.00	1514.41	1166.65	819.95	647.66	545.13	477.46	429.71
26000	2299.44	1574.99	1213.32	852.75	673.57	566.93	496.56	446.90
27000	2387.88	1635.57	1259.98	885.55	699.47	588.73	515.66	464.09
28000	2476.32	1696.14	1306.65	918.35	725.38	610.54	534.75	481.28
29000	2564.76	1756.72	1353.32	951.15	751.29	632.34	553.85	498.46
30000	2653.20	1817.30	1399.98	983.94	777.19	654.15	572.95	515.65
31000	2741.64	1877.87	1446.65	1016.74	803.10	675.95	592.05	532.84
32000	2830.08	1938.45	1493.31	1049.54	829.01	697.76	611.15	550.03
33000	2918.52	1999.03	1539.98	1082.34	854.91	719.56	630.24	567.22
34000	3006.96	2059.60	1586.65	1115.14	880.82	741.37	649.34	584.40
35000	3095.40	2120.18	1633.31	1147.93	906.72	763.17	668.44	601.59
40000	3537.60	2423.06	1866.64	1311.92	1036.26	872.20	763.93	687.53
45000	3979.80	2725.94	2099.97	1475.91	1165.79	981.22	859.42	773.48
50000	4422.00	3028.82	2333.30	1639.90	1295.32	1090.25	954.91	859.42
55000	4864.20	3331.71	2566.63	1803.89	1424.85	1199.27	1050.40	945.36
60000	5306.40	3634.59	2799.96	1967.88	1554.38	1308.29	1145.89	1031.30
65000	5748.60	3937.47	3033.29	2131.87	1683.91	1417.32	1241.39	1117.24
70000	6190.80	4240.35	3266.62	2295.86	1813.44	1526.34	1336.88	1203.18
75000	6633.00	4543.23	3499.95	2459.85	1942.98	1635.37	1432.37	1289.12
80000	7075.20	4846.11	3733.28	2623.84	2072.51	1744.39	1527.86	1375.06
85000	7517.40	5149.00	3966.61	2787.83	2202.04	1853.41	1623.35	1461.00
90000	7959.60	5451.88	4199.94	2951.82	2331.57	1962.44	1718.84	1546.95
95000	8401.80	5754.76	4433.26	3115.81	2461.10	2071.46	1814.33	1632.89
100000	8844.00	6057.64	4666.59	3279.80	2590.63	2180.49	1909.82	1718.83
105000	9286.20	6360.52	4899.92	3443.79	2720.16	2289.51	2005.31	1804.77
110000	9728.40	6663.41	5133.25	3607.78	2849.69	2398.53	2100.80	1890.71
115000	10170.60	6966.29	5366.58	3771.77	2979.23	2507.56	2196.29	1976.65
120000	10612.80	7269.17	5599.91	3935.76	3108.76	2616.58	2291.78	2062.59
125000	11055.00	7572.05	5833.24	4099.75	3238.29	2725.61	2387.28	2148.53
130000	11497.20	7874.93	6066.57	4263.74	3367.82	2834.63	2482.77	2234.48
135000	11939.40	8177.81	6299.90	4427.73	3497.35	2943.65	2578.26	2320.42
140000	12381.60	8480.70	6533.23	4591.72	3626.88	3052.68	2673.75	2406.36
145000	12823.80	8783.58	6766.56	4755.71	3756.41	3161.70	2769.24	2492.30
150000	13266.00	9086.46	6999.89	4919.70	3885.95	3270.73	2864.73	2578.24
155000	13708.20	9389.34	7233.22	5083.69	4015.48	3379.75	2960.22	2664.18
160000	14150.40	9692.22	7466.55	5247.68	4145.01	3488.78	3055.71	2750.12

AMOUNT OF LOAN	NUMBER OF YEARS IN TERM							
	8	9	10	11	12	14	15	16
$ 50	.79	.74	.70	.66	.64	.59	.58	.56
100	1.58	1.47	1.39	1.32	1.27	1.18	1.15	1.12
200	3.16	2.94	2.77	2.64	2.53	2.36	2.29	2.24
300	4.74	4.41	4.16	3.95	3.79	3.54	3.44	3.36
400	6.32	5.88	5.54	5.27	5.05	4.71	4.58	4.47
500	7.89	7.35	6.93	6.59	6.31	5.89	5.73	5.59
600	9.47	8.82	8.31	7.90	7.57	7.07	6.87	6.71
700	11.05	10.29	9.70	9.22	8.83	8.24	8.02	7.82
800	12.63	11.76	11.08	10.54	10.09	9.42	9.16	8.94
900	14.20	13.23	12.47	11.85	11.35	10.60	10.31	10.06
1000	15.78	14.70	13.85	13.17	12.61	11.77	11.45	11.18
2000	31.56	29.40	27.70	26.33	25.22	23.54	22.89	22.35
3000	47.33	44.09	41.54	39.50	37.83	35.31	34.34	33.52
4000	63.11	58.79	55.39	52.66	50.44	47.08	45.78	44.69
5000	78.88	73.48	69.23	65.83	63.05	58.84	57.23	55.86
6000	94.66	88.18	83.08	78.99	75.66	70.61	68.67	67.03
7000	110.44	102.87	96.93	92.16	88.27	82.38	80.12	78.20
8000	126.21	117.57	110.77	105.32	100.88	94.15	91.56	89.37
9000	141.99	132.26	124.62	118.49	113.49	105.91	103.01	100.54
10000	157.76	146.96	138.46	131.65	126.10	117.68	114.45	111.71
11000	173.54	161.65	152.31	144.82	138.71	129.45	125.90	122.88
12000	189.32	176.35	166.16	157.98	151.32	141.22	137.34	134.05
13000	205.09	191.04	180.00	171.15	163.93	152.98	148.78	145.22
14000	220.87	205.74	193.85	184.31	176.54	164.75	160.23	156.39
15000	236.64	220.43	207.69	197.48	189.15	176.52	171.67	167.56
16000	252.42	235.13	221.54	210.64	201.76	188.29	183.12	178.73
17000	268.20	249.82	235.38	223.81	214.37	200.06	194.56	189.90
18000	283.97	264.52	249.23	236.97	226.98	211.82	206.01	201.07
19000	299.75	279.21	263.08	250.14	239.59	223.59	217.45	212.24
20000	315.52	293.91	276.92	263.30	252.20	235.36	228.90	223.41
21000	331.30	308.60	290.77	276.47	264.81	247.13	240.34	234.58
22000	347.08	323.30	304.61	289.63	277.42	258.89	251.79	245.75
23000	362.85	337.99	318.46	302.80	290.03	270.66	263.23	256.92
24000	378.63	352.69	332.31	315.96	302.64	282.43	274.68	268.09
25000	394.40	367.38	346.15	329.13	315.25	294.20	286.12	279.26
26000	410.18	382.08	360.00	342.29	327.86	305.96	297.56	290.43
27000	425.95	396.77	373.84	355.46	340.47	317.73	309.01	301.60
28000	441.73	411.47	387.69	368.62	353.07	329.50	320.45	312.77
29000	457.51	426.16	401.53	381.79	365.68	341.27	331.90	323.94
30000	473.28	440.86	415.38	394.95	378.29	353.04	343.34	335.11
31000	489.06	455.55	429.23	408.11	390.90	364.80	354.79	346.28
32000	504.83	470.25	443.07	421.28	403.51	376.57	366.23	357.45
33000	520.61	484.94	456.92	434.44	416.12	388.34	377.68	368.62
34000	536.39	499.64	470.76	447.61	428.73	400.11	389.12	379.79
35000	552.16	514.33	484.61	460.77	441.34	411.87	400.57	390.96
40000	631.04	587.81	553.84	526.60	504.39	470.71	457.79	446.81
45000	709.92	661.28	623.07	592.42	567.44	529.55	515.01	502.66
50000	788.80	734.76	692.30	658.25	630.49	588.39	572.23	558.51
55000	867.68	808.23	761.53	724.07	693.53	647.23	629.46	614.36
60000	946.56	881.71	830.76	789.89	756.58	706.07	686.68	670.21
65000	1025.44	955.18	899.99	855.72	819.63	764.90	743.90	726.06
70000	1104.32	1028.66	969.21	921.54	882.68	823.74	801.13	781.91
75000	1183.20	1102.13	1038.44	987.37	945.73	882.58	858.35	837.76
80000	1262.08	1175.61	1107.67	1053.19	1008.78	941.42	915.57	893.61
85000	1340.96	1249.08	1176.90	1119.02	1071.82	1000.26	972.79	949.46
90000	1419.84	1322.56	1246.13	1184.84	1134.87	1059.10	1030.02	1005.31
95000	1498.72	1396.03	1315.36	1250.66	1197.92	1117.94	1087.24	1061.16
100000	1577.60	1469.51	1384.59	1316.49	1260.97	1176.77	1144.46	1117.01
105000	1656.48	1542.99	1453.82	1382.31	1324.02	1235.61	1201.69	1172.86
110000	1735.36	1616.46	1523.05	1448.14	1387.06	1294.45	1258.91	1228.71
115000	1814.24	1689.94	1592.28	1513.96	1450.11	1353.29	1316.13	1284.56
120000	1893.12	1763.41	1661.51	1579.78	1513.16	1412.13	1373.36	1340.41
125000	1972.00	1836.89	1730.74	1645.61	1576.21	1470.97	1430.58	1396.26
130000	2050.88	1910.36	1799.97	1711.43	1639.26	1529.80	1487.80	1452.11
135000	2129.75	1983.84	1869.20	1777.26	1702.31	1588.64	1545.02	1507.96
140000	2208.63	2057.31	1938.42	1843.08	1765.35	1647.48	1602.25	1563.81
145000	2287.51	2130.79	2007.65	1908.91	1828.40	1706.32	1659.47	1619.66
150000	2366.39	2204.26	2076.88	1974.73	1891.45	1765.16	1716.69	1675.51
155000	2445.27	2277.74	2146.11	2040.55	1954.50	1824.00	1773.92	1731.36
160000	2524.15	2351.21	2215.34	2106.38	2017.55	1882.84	1831.14	1787.21

MONTHLY AMORTIZING PAYMENTS

AMOUNT OF LOAN	NUMBER OF YEARS IN TERM							
	17	18	19	20	21	22	23	24
$ 50	.55	.54	.53	.53	.52	.51	.51	.50
100	1.10	1.08	1.06	1.05	1.03	1.02	1.01	1.00
200	2.19	2.15	2.12	2.09	2.06	2.04	2.02	2.00
300	3.29	3.22	3.17	3.13	3.09	3.05	3.02	3.00
400	4.38	4.30	4.23	4.17	4.12	4.07	4.03	3.99
500	5.47	5.37	5.28	5.21	5.14	5.08	5.03	4.99
600	6.57	6.44	6.34	6.25	6.17	6.10	6.04	5.99
700	7.66	7.52	7.40	7.29	7.20	7.12	7.05	6.98
800	8.75	8.59	8.45	8.33	8.23	8.13	8.05	7.98
900	9.85	9.66	9.51	9.37	9.25	9.15	9.06	8.98
1000	10.94	10.74	10.56	10.41	10.28	10.16	10.06	9.97
2000	21.88	21.47	21.12	20.82	20.56	20.32	20.12	19.94
3000	32.81	32.20	31.68	31.23	30.83	30.48	30.18	29.91
4000	43.75	42.94	42.24	41.63	41.11	40.64	40.24	39.88
5000	54.68	53.67	52.80	52.04	51.38	50.80	50.30	49.85
6000	65.62	64.40	63.36	62.45	61.66	60.96	60.36	59.82
7000	76.55	75.14	73.92	72.85	71.93	71.12	70.42	69.79
8000	87.49	85.87	84.47	83.26	82.21	81.28	80.47	79.76
9000	98.42	96.60	95.03	93.67	92.48	91.44	90.53	89.73
10000	109.36	107.34	105.59	104.08	102.76	101.60	100.59	99.70
11000	120.29	118.07	116.15	114.48	113.03	111.76	110.65	109.67
12000	131.23	128.80	126.71	124.89	123.31	121.92	120.71	119.64
13000	142.16	139.54	137.27	135.30	133.58	132.08	130.77	129.61
14000	153.10	150.27	147.83	145.70	143.86	142.24	140.83	139.58
15000	164.03	161.00	158.38	156.11	154.13	152.40	150.88	149.55
16000	174.97	171.74	168.94	166.52	164.41	162.56	160.94	159.52
17000	185.90	182.47	179.50	176.93	174.68	172.72	171.00	169.49
18000	196.84	193.20	190.06	187.33	184.96	182.88	181.06	179.46
19000	207.77	203.94	200.62	197.74	195.23	193.04	191.12	189.43
20000	218.71	214.67	211.18	208.15	205.51	203.20	201.18	199.40
21000	229.64	225.40	221.74	218.55	215.78	213.36	211.24	209.37
22000	240.58	236.14	232.29	228.96	226.06	223.52	221.29	219.34
23000	251.51	246.87	242.85	239.37	236.33	233.68	231.35	229.31
24000	262.45	257.60	253.41	249.78	246.61	243.84	241.41	239.28
25000	273.39	268.34	263.97	260.18	256.88	254.00	251.47	249.25
26000	284.32	279.07	274.53	270.59	267.16	264.16	261.53	259.22
27000	295.26	289.80	285.09	281.00	277.43	274.32	271.59	269.19
28000	306.19	300.54	295.65	291.40	287.71	284.48	281.65	279.16
29000	317.13	311.27	306.21	301.81	297.98	294.64	291.70	289.13
30000	328.06	322.00	316.76	312.22	308.26	304.80	301.76	299.10
31000	339.00	332.73	327.32	322.62	318.53	314.96	311.82	309.07
32000	349.93	343.47	337.88	333.03	328.81	325.12	321.88	319.04
33000	360.87	354.20	348.44	343.44	339.08	335.28	331.94	329.01
34000	371.80	364.93	359.00	353.85	349.36	345.44	342.00	338.98
35000	382.74	375.67	369.56	364.25	359.63	355.59	352.06	348.95
40000	437.41	429.33	422.35	416.29	411.01	406.39	402.35	398.80
45000	492.09	483.00	475.14	468.32	462.38	457.19	452.64	448.65
50000	546.77	536.67	527.94	520.36	513.76	507.99	502.94	498.50
55000	601.44	590.33	580.73	572.39	565.13	558.79	553.23	548.34
60000	656.12	644.00	633.52	624.43	616.51	609.59	603.52	598.19
65000	710.79	697.66	686.32	676.47	667.88	660.39	653.82	648.04
70000	765.47	751.33	739.11	728.50	719.26	711.18	704.11	697.89
75000	820.15	805.00	791.90	780.54	770.64	761.98	754.40	747.74
80000	874.82	858.66	844.70	832.57	822.01	812.78	804.69	797.59
85000	929.50	912.33	897.49	884.61	873.39	863.58	854.99	847.44
90000	984.17	965.99	950.28	936.64	924.76	914.38	905.28	897.29
95000	1038.85	1019.66	1003.07	988.68	976.14	965.18	955.57	947.14
100000	1093.53	1073.33	1055.87	1040.71	1027.51	1015.98	1005.87	996.99
105000	1148.20	1126.99	1108.66	1092.75	1078.89	1066.77	1056.16	1046.84
110000	1202.88	1180.66	1161.45	1144.78	1130.26	1117.57	1106.45	1096.68
115000	1257.55	1234.33	1214.25	1196.82	1181.64	1168.37	1156.75	1146.53
120000	1312.23	1287.99	1267.04	1248.86	1233.01	1219.17	1207.04	1196.38
125000	1366.91	1341.66	1319.83	1300.89	1284.39	1269.97	1257.33	1246.23
130000	1421.58	1395.32	1372.63	1352.93	1335.76	1320.77	1307.63	1296.08
135000	1476.26	1448.99	1425.42	1404.96	1387.14	1371.57	1357.92	1345.93
140000	1530.93	1502.66	1478.21	1457.00	1438.52	1422.36	1408.21	1395.78
145000	1585.61	1556.32	1531.01	1509.03	1489.89	1473.16	1458.50	1445.63
150000	1640.29	1609.99	1583.80	1561.07	1541.27	1523.96	1508.80	1495.48
155000	1694.96	1663.65	1636.59	1613.10	1592.64	1574.76	1559.09	1545.33
160000	1749.64	1717.32	1689.39	1665.14	1644.02	1625.56	1609.38	1595.17

AMOUNT OF LOAN	25	26	27	28	29	30	35	40
	NUMBER OF YEARS IN TERM							
$ 50	.50	.50	.49	.49	.49	.49	.48	.47
100	.99	.99	.98	.98	.97	.97	.95	.94
200	1.98	1.97	1.96	1.95	1.94	1.93	1.90	1.88
300	2.97	2.95	2.93	2.92	2.90	2.89	2.85	2.82
400	3.96	3.93	3.91	3.89	3.87	3.85	3.79	3.76
500	4.95	4.92	4.89	4.86	4.84	4.81	4.74	4.70
600	5.94	5.90	5.86	5.83	5.80	5.78	5.69	5.63
700	6.93	6.88	6.84	6.80	6.77	6.74	6.63	6.57
800	7.92	7.86	7.81	7.77	7.73	7.70	7.58	7.51
900	8.91	8.85	8.79	8.74	8.70	8.66	8.53	8.45
1000	9.90	9.83	9.77	9.71	9.67	9.62	9.47	9.39
2000	19.79	19.65	19.53	19.42	19.33	19.24	18.94	18.77
3000	29.68	29.47	29.29	29.13	28.99	28.86	28.41	28.15
4000	39.57	39.30	39.05	38.84	38.65	38.48	37.87	37.54
5000	49.46	49.12	48.81	48.54	48.31	48.09	47.34	46.92
6000	59.35	58.94	58.58	58.25	57.97	57.71	56.81	56.30
7000	69.25	68.76	68.34	67.96	67.63	67.33	66.28	65.68
8000	79.14	78.59	78.10	77.67	77.29	76.95	75.74	75.07
9000	89.03	88.41	87.86	87.38	86.95	86.57	85.21	84.45
10000	98.92	98.23	97.62	97.08	96.61	96.18	94.68	93.83
11000	108.81	108.05	107.38	106.79	106.27	105.80	104.14	103.21
12000	118.70	117.88	117.15	116.50	115.93	115.42	113.61	112.60
13000	128.60	127.70	126.91	126.21	125.59	125.04	123.08	121.98
14000	138.49	137.52	136.67	135.92	135.25	134.65	132.55	131.36
15000	148.38	147.35	146.43	145.62	144.91	144.27	142.01	140.75
16000	158.27	157.17	156.19	155.33	154.57	153.89	151.48	150.13
17000	168.16	166.99	165.96	165.04	164.23	163.51	160.95	159.51
18000	178.05	176.81	175.72	174.75	173.89	173.13	170.41	168.89
19000	187.95	186.64	185.48	184.45	183.55	182.74	179.88	178.28
20000	197.84	196.46	195.24	194.16	193.21	192.36	189.35	187.66
21000	207.73	206.28	205.00	203.87	202.87	201.98	198.82	197.04
22000	217.62	216.10	214.76	213.58	212.53	211.60	208.28	206.42
23000	227.51	225.93	224.53	223.29	222.19	221.21	217.75	215.81
24000	237.40	235.75	234.29	232.99	231.85	230.83	227.22	225.19
25000	247.30	245.57	244.05	242.70	241.51	240.45	236.68	234.57
26000	257.19	255.39	253.81	252.41	251.17	250.07	246.15	243.95
27000	267.08	265.22	263.57	262.12	260.83	259.69	255.62	253.34
28000	276.97	275.04	273.33	271.83	270.49	269.30	265.09	262.72
29000	286.86	284.86	283.10	281.53	280.15	278.92	274.55	272.10
30000	296.75	294.69	292.86	291.24	289.81	288.54	284.02	281.49
31000	306.65	304.51	302.62	300.95	299.47	298.16	293.49	290.87
32000	316.54	314.33	312.38	310.66	309.13	307.77	302.95	300.25
33000	326.43	324.15	322.14	320.37	318.79	317.39	312.42	309.63
34000	336.32	333.98	331.91	330.07	328.45	327.01	321.89	319.02
35000	346.21	343.80	341.67	339.78	338.11	336.63	331.36	328.40
40000	395.67	392.91	390.48	388.32	386.41	384.72	378.69	375.31
45000	445.13	442.03	439.28	436.86	434.71	432.81	426.03	422.23
50000	494.59	491.14	488.09	485.40	483.01	480.90	473.36	469.14
55000	544.04	540.25	536.90	533.94	531.31	528.98	520.70	516.05
60000	593.50	589.37	585.71	582.48	579.61	577.07	568.03	562.97
65000	642.96	638.48	634.52	631.02	627.91	625.16	615.37	609.88
70000	692.42	687.59	683.33	679.56	676.22	673.25	662.71	656.79
75000	741.88	736.71	732.14	728.10	724.52	721.34	710.04	703.71
80000	791.34	785.82	780.95	776.64	772.82	769.43	757.38	750.62
85000	840.79	834.93	829.76	825.17	821.12	817.52	804.71	797.53
90000	890.25	884.05	878.56	873.71	869.42	865.61	852.05	844.45
95000	939.71	933.16	927.37	922.25	917.72	913.70	899.39	891.36
100000	989.17	982.27	976.18	970.79	966.02	961.79	946.72	938.27
105000	1038.63	1031.39	1024.99	1019.33	1014.32	1009.87	994.06	985.19
110000	1088.08	1080.50	1073.80	1067.87	1062.62	1057.96	1041.39	1032.10
115000	1137.54	1129.61	1122.61	1116.41	1110.92	1106.05	1088.73	1079.01
120000	1187.00	1178.73	1171.42	1164.95	1159.22	1154.14	1136.06	1125.93
125000	1236.46	1227.84	1220.23	1213.49	1207.52	1202.23	1183.40	1172.84
130000	1285.92	1276.95	1269.04	1262.03	1255.82	1250.32	1230.74	1219.75
135000	1335.38	1326.07	1317.84	1310.57	1304.12	1298.41	1278.07	1266.67
140000	1384.83	1375.18	1366.65	1359.11	1352.43	1346.50	1325.41	1313.58
145000	1434.29	1424.29	1415.46	1407.65	1400.73	1394.59	1372.74	1360.49
150000	1483.75	1473.41	1464.27	1456.19	1449.03	1442.68	1420.08	1407.41
155000	1533.21	1522.52	1513.08	1504.73	1497.33	1490.76	1467.41	1454.32
160000	1582.67	1571.63	1561.89	1553.27	1545.63	1538.85	1514.75	1501.23

MONTHLY AMORTIZING PAYMENTS

AMOUNT OF LOAN	NUMBER OF YEARS IN TERM 1	1-1/2	2	3	4	5	6	7
$ 50	4.43	3.04	2.34	1.65	1.30	1.10	.96	.87
100	8.85	6.07	4.68	3.29	2.60	2.19	1.92	1.73
200	17.70	12.13	9.35	6.58	5.20	4.38	3.84	3.46
300	26.55	18.20	14.02	9.86	7.80	6.57	5.75	5.18
400	35.40	24.26	18.69	13.15	10.39	8.75	7.67	6.91
500	44.25	30.32	23.37	16.43	12.99	10.94	9.59	8.63
600	53.10	36.39	28.04	19.72	15.59	13.13	11.50	10.36
700	61.95	42.45	32.71	23.01	18.18	15.31	13.42	12.08
800	70.80	48.51	37.38	26.29	20.78	17.50	15.33	13.81
900	79.65	54.58	42.06	29.58	23.38	19.69	17.25	15.53
1000	88.50	60.64	46.73	32.86	25.97	21.87	19.17	17.26
2000	177.00	121.27	93.45	65.72	51.94	43.74	38.33	34.51
3000	265.50	181.91	140.18	98.58	77.91	65.61	57.49	51.77
4000	354.00	242.54	186.90	131.43	103.87	87.47	76.65	69.02
5000	442.50	303.18	233.62	164.29	129.84	109.34	95.82	86.28
6000	530.99	363.81	280.35	197.15	155.81	131.21	114.98	103.53
7000	619.49	424.44	327.07	230.01	181.77	153.08	134.14	120.78
8000	707.99	485.08	373.80	262.86	207.74	174.94	153.30	138.04
9000	796.49	545.71	420.52	295.72	233.71	196.81	172.47	155.29
10000	884.99	606.35	467.24	328.58	259.68	218.68	191.63	172.55
11000	973.49	666.98	513.97	361.43	285.64	240.55	210.79	189.80
12000	1061.98	727.62	560.69	394.29	311.61	262.41	229.95	207.06
13000	1150.48	788.25	607.42	427.15	337.58	284.28	249.12	224.31
14000	1238.98	848.88	654.14	460.01	363.54	306.15	268.28	241.56
15000	1327.48	909.52	700.86	492.86	389.51	328.01	287.44	258.82
16000	1415.98	970.15	747.59	525.72	415.48	349.88	306.60	276.07
17000	1504.48	1030.79	794.31	558.58	441.45	371.75	325.77	293.33
18000	1592.97	1091.42	841.04	591.44	467.41	393.62	344.93	310.58
19000	1681.47	1152.06	887.76	624.29	493.38	415.48	364.09	327.83
20000	1769.97	1212.69	934.48	657.15	519.35	437.35	383.25	345.09
21000	1858.47	1273.32	981.21	690.01	545.31	459.22	402.41	362.34
22000	1946.97	1333.96	1027.93	722.86	571.28	481.09	421.58	379.60
23000	2035.47	1394.59	1074.66	755.72	597.25	502.95	440.74	396.85
24000	2123.96	1455.23	1121.38	788.58	623.22	524.82	459.90	414.11
25000	2212.46	1515.86	1168.10	821.44	649.18	546.69	479.06	431.36
26000	2300.96	1576.49	1214.83	854.29	675.15	568.56	498.23	448.61
27000	2389.46	1637.13	1261.55	887.15	701.12	590.42	517.39	465.87
28000	2477.96	1697.76	1308.28	920.01	727.08	612.29	536.55	483.12
29000	2566.46	1758.40	1355.00	952.86	753.05	634.16	555.71	500.38
30000	2654.95	1819.03	1401.72	985.72	779.02	656.02	574.88	517.63
31000	2743.45	1879.67	1448.45	1018.58	804.99	677.89	594.04	534.88
32000	2831.95	1940.30	1495.17	1051.44	830.95	699.76	613.20	552.14
33000	2920.45	2000.93	1541.90	1084.29	856.92	721.63	632.36	569.39
34000	3008.95	2061.57	1588.62	1117.15	882.89	743.49	651.53	586.65
35000	3097.45	2122.20	1635.34	1150.01	908.85	765.36	670.69	603.90
40000	3539.94	2425.37	1868.96	1314.29	1038.69	874.70	766.50	690.17
45000	3982.43	2728.55	2102.58	1478.58	1168.52	984.03	862.31	776.44
50000	4424.92	3031.72	2336.20	1642.87	1298.36	1093.37	958.12	862.71
55000	4867.41	3334.89	2569.82	1807.15	1428.20	1202.71	1053.94	948.98
60000	5309.90	3638.06	2803.44	1971.44	1558.03	1312.04	1149.75	1035.26
65000	5752.40	3941.23	3037.06	2135.73	1687.87	1421.38	1245.56	1121.53
70000	6194.89	4244.40	3270.68	2300.01	1817.70	1530.72	1341.37	1207.80
75000	6637.38	4547.57	3504.30	2464.30	1947.54	1640.05	1437.18	1294.07
80000	7079.87	4850.74	3737.92	2628.58	2077.37	1749.39	1532.99	1380.34
85000	7522.36	5153.91	3971.54	2792.87	2207.21	1858.73	1628.81	1466.61
90000	7964.85	5457.09	4205.16	2957.16	2337.04	1968.06	1724.62	1552.88
95000	8407.34	5760.26	4438.78	3121.44	2466.88	2077.40	1820.43	1639.15
100000	8849.84	6063.43	4672.40	3285.73	2596.71	2186.74	1916.24	1725.42
105000	9292.33	6366.60	4906.02	3450.01	2726.55	2296.07	2012.05	1811.69
110000	9734.82	6669.77	5139.64	3614.30	2856.39	2405.41	2107.87	1897.96
115000	10177.31	6972.94	5373.26	3778.59	2986.22	2514.75	2203.68	1984.23
120000	10619.80	7276.11	5606.88	3942.87	3116.06	2624.08	2299.49	2070.51
125000	11062.29	7579.28	5840.50	4107.16	3245.89	2733.42	2395.30	2156.78
130000	11504.79	7882.45	6074.12	4271.45	3375.73	2842.76	2491.11	2243.05
135000	11947.28	8185.63	6307.74	4435.73	3505.56	2952.09	2586.93	2329.32
140000	12389.77	8488.80	6541.36	4600.02	3635.40	3061.43	2682.74	2415.59
145000	12832.26	8791.97	6774.98	4764.30	3765.23	3170.76	2778.55	2501.86
150000	13274.75	9095.14	7008.60	4928.59	3895.07	3280.10	2874.36	2588.13
155000	13717.24	9398.31	7242.22	5092.88	4024.91	3389.44	2970.17	2674.40
160000	14159.74	9701.48	7475.84	5257.16	4154.74	3498.77	3065.98	2760.67

AMOUNT OF LOAN	NUMBER OF YEARS IN TERM							
	8	9	10	11	12	14	15	16
$ 50	.80	.74	.70	.67	.64	.60	.58	.57
100	1.59	1.48	1.40	1.33	1.27	1.19	1.16	1.13
200	3.17	2.96	2.79	2.65	2.54	2.37	2.31	2.26
300	4.76	4.43	4.18	3.98	3.81	3.56	3.46	3.38
400	6.34	5.91	5.57	5.30	5.08	4.74	4.61	4.51
500	7.93	7.39	6.96	6.62	6.35	5.93	5.77	5.63
600	9.51	8.86	8.36	7.95	7.62	7.11	6.92	6.76
700	11.10	10.34	9.75	9.27	8.88	8.30	8.07	7.88
800	12.68	11.82	11.14	10.60	10.15	9.48	9.22	9.01
900	14.26	13.29	12.53	11.92	11.42	10.67	10.38	10.13
1000	15.85	14.77	13.92	13.24	12.69	11.85	11.53	11.26
2000	31.69	29.53	27.84	26.48	25.37	23.70	23.05	22.51
3000	47.54	44.30	41.76	39.72	38.06	35.54	34.58	33.76
4000	63.38	59.06	55.67	52.96	50.74	47.39	46.10	45.01
5000	79.22	73.83	69.59	66.19	63.42	59.23	57.62	56.26
6000	95.07	88.59	83.51	79.43	76.11	71.08	69.15	67.51
7000	110.91	103.36	97.42	92.67	88.79	82.92	80.67	78.76
8000	126.75	118.12	111.34	105.91	101.48	94.77	92.19	90.01
9000	142.60	132.88	125.26	119.14	114.16	106.61	103.72	101.26
10000	158.44	147.65	139.17	132.38	126.84	118.46	115.24	112.51
11000	174.28	162.41	153.09	145.62	139.53	130.30	126.76	123.76
12000	190.13	177.18	167.01	158.86	152.21	142.15	138.29	135.01
13000	205.97	191.94	180.92	172.09	164.90	153.99	149.81	146.26
14000	221.82	206.71	194.84	185.33	177.58	165.84	161.33	157.51
15000	237.66	221.47	208.76	198.57	190.26	177.68	172.86	168.76
16000	253.50	236.24	222.68	211.81	202.95	189.53	184.38	180.01
17000	269.35	251.00	236.59	225.04	215.63	201.37	195.90	191.26
18000	285.19	265.76	250.51	238.28	228.32	213.22	207.43	202.51
19000	301.03	280.53	264.43	251.52	241.00	225.06	218.95	213.76
20000	316.88	295.29	278.34	264.76	253.68	236.91	230.47	225.01
21000	332.72	310.06	292.26	277.99	266.37	248.75	242.00	236.26
22000	348.56	324.82	306.18	291.23	279.05	260.60	253.52	247.51
23000	364.41	339.59	320.09	304.47	291.74	272.44	265.04	258.76
24000	380.25	354.35	334.01	317.71	304.42	284.29	276.57	270.01
25000	396.09	369.12	347.93	330.94	317.10	296.13	288.09	281.26
26000	411.94	383.88	361.84	344.18	329.79	307.98	299.61	292.51
27000	427.78	398.64	375.76	357.42	342.47	319.82	311.14	303.76
28000	443.63	413.41	389.68	370.66	355.16	331.67	322.66	315.01
29000	459.47	428.17	403.59	383.89	367.84	343.51	334.18	326.26
30000	475.31	442.94	417.51	397.13	380.52	355.36	345.71	337.51
31000	491.16	457.70	431.43	410.37	393.21	367.20	357.23	348.77
32000	507.00	472.47	445.35	423.61	405.89	379.05	368.76	360.02
33000	522.84	487.23	459.26	436.84	418.57	390.89	380.28	371.27
34000	538.69	502.00	473.18	450.08	431.26	402.74	391.80	382.52
35000	554.53	516.76	487.10	463.32	443.94	414.58	403.33	393.77
40000	633.75	590.58	556.68	529.51	507.36	473.81	460.94	450.02
45000	712.97	664.40	626.27	595.69	570.78	533.03	518.56	506.27
50000	792.18	738.23	695.85	661.88	634.20	592.26	576.18	562.52
55000	871.40	812.05	765.43	728.07	697.62	651.48	633.79	618.77
60000	950.62	885.87	835.02	794.26	761.04	710.71	691.41	675.02
65000	1029.84	959.69	904.60	860.44	824.46	769.94	749.03	731.28
70000	1109.06	1033.51	974.19	926.63	887.88	829.16	806.65	787.53
75000	1188.27	1107.34	1043.77	992.82	951.30	888.39	864.26	843.78
80000	1267.49	1181.16	1113.36	1059.01	1014.72	947.61	921.88	900.03
85000	1346.71	1254.98	1182.94	1125.19	1078.14	1006.84	979.50	956.28
90000	1425.93	1328.80	1252.53	1191.38	1141.56	1066.06	1037.12	1012.53
95000	1505.15	1402.62	1322.11	1257.57	1204.98	1125.29	1094.73	1068.79
100000	1584.36	1476.45	1391.69	1323.76	1268.40	1184.51	1152.35	1125.04
105000	1663.58	1550.27	1461.28	1389.94	1331.82	1243.74	1209.97	1181.29
110000	1742.80	1624.09	1530.86	1456.13	1395.24	1302.96	1267.58	1237.54
115000	1822.02	1697.91	1600.45	1522.32	1458.66	1362.19	1325.20	1293.79
120000	1901.24	1771.73	1670.03	1588.51	1522.08	1421.41	1382.82	1350.04
125000	1980.45	1845.56	1739.62	1654.70	1585.50	1480.64	1440.44	1406.30
130000	2059.67	1919.38	1809.20	1720.88	1648.92	1539.87	1498.05	1462.55
135000	2138.89	1993.20	1878.79	1787.07	1712.34	1599.09	1555.67	1518.80
140000	2218.11	2067.02	1948.37	1853.26	1775.76	1658.32	1613.29	1575.05
145000	2297.32	2140.84	2017.95	1919.45	1839.17	1717.54	1670.90	1631.30
150000	2376.54	2214.67	2087.54	1985.63	1902.59	1776.77	1728.52	1687.55
155000	2455.76	2288.49	2157.12	2051.82	1966.01	1835.99	1786.14	1743.81
160000	2534.98	2362.31	2226.71	2118.01	2029.43	1895.22	1843.76	1800.06

11¼% MONTHLY AMORTIZING PAYMENTS

AMOUNT OF LOAN	NUMBER OF YEARS IN TERM							
	17	18	19	20	21	22	23	24
$ 50	.56	.55	.54	.53	.52	.52	.51	.51
100	1.11	1.09	1.07	1.05	1.04	1.03	1.02	1.01
200	2.21	2.17	2.13	2.10	2.08	2.05	2.03	2.02
300	3.31	3.25	3.20	3.15	3.11	3.08	3.05	3.02
400	4.41	4.33	4.26	4.20	4.15	4.10	4.06	4.03
500	5.51	5.41	5.33	5.25	5.19	5.13	5.08	5.03
600	6.62	6.49	6.39	6.30	6.22	6.15	6.09	6.04
700	7.72	7.58	7.46	7.35	7.26	7.18	7.11	7.05
800	8.82	8.66	8.52	8.40	8.29	8.20	8.12	8.05
900	9.92	9.74	9.58	9.45	9.33	9.23	9.14	9.06
1000	11.02	10.82	10.65	10.50	10.37	10.25	10.15	10.06
2000	22.04	21.64	21.29	20.99	20.73	20.50	20.30	20.12
3000	33.06	32.45	31.93	31.48	31.09	30.75	30.45	30.18
4000	44.07	43.27	42.58	41.98	41.45	40.99	40.59	40.24
5000	55.09	54.09	53.22	52.47	51.81	51.24	50.74	50.30
6000	66.11	64.90	63.86	62.96	62.18	61.49	60.89	60.36
7000	77.12	75.72	74.51	73.45	72.54	71.74	71.04	70.42
8000	88.14	86.53	85.15	83.95	82.90	81.98	81.18	80.48
9000	99.16	97.35	95.79	94.44	93.26	92.23	91.33	90.54
10000	110.17	108.17	106.43	104.93	103.62	102.48	101.48	100.60
11000	121.19	118.98	117.08	115.42	113.98	112.73	111.63	110.66
12000	132.21	129.80	127.72	125.92	124.35	122.97	121.77	120.72
13000	143.22	140.62	138.36	136.41	134.71	133.22	131.92	130.78
14000	154.24	151.43	149.01	146.90	145.07	143.47	142.07	140.84
15000	165.26	162.25	159.65	157.39	155.43	153.72	152.22	150.90
16000	176.27	173.06	170.29	167.89	165.79	163.96	162.36	160.96
17000	187.29	183.88	180.93	178.38	176.15	174.21	172.51	171.02
18000	198.31	194.70	191.58	188.87	186.52	184.46	182.66	181.08
19000	209.33	205.51	202.22	199.36	196.88	194.71	192.81	191.14
20000	220.34	216.33	212.86	209.86	207.24	204.95	202.95	201.20
21000	231.36	227.15	223.51	220.35	217.60	215.20	213.10	211.26
22000	242.38	237.96	234.15	230.84	227.96	225.45	223.25	221.32
23000	253.39	248.78	244.79	241.33	238.32	235.70	233.40	231.38
24000	264.41	259.59	255.43	251.83	248.69	245.94	243.54	241.44
25000	275.43	270.41	266.08	262.32	259.05	256.19	253.69	251.50
26000	286.44	281.23	276.72	272.81	269.41	266.44	263.84	261.56
27000	297.46	292.04	287.36	283.30	279.77	276.69	273.99	271.61
28000	308.48	302.86	298.01	293.80	290.13	286.93	284.13	281.67
29000	319.49	313.67	308.65	304.29	300.49	297.18	294.28	291.73
30000	330.51	324.49	319.29	314.78	310.86	307.43	304.43	301.79
31000	341.53	335.31	329.93	325.27	321.22	317.68	314.58	311.85
32000	352.54	346.12	340.58	335.77	331.58	327.92	324.72	321.91
33000	363.56	356.94	351.22	346.26	341.94	338.17	334.87	331.97
34000	374.58	367.76	361.86	356.75	352.30	348.42	345.02	342.03
35000	385.60	378.57	372.51	367.24	362.66	358.67	355.16	352.09
40000	440.68	432.65	425.72	419.71	414.47	409.90	405.90	402.39
45000	495.76	486.73	478.93	472.17	466.28	461.14	456.64	452.69
50000	550.85	540.82	532.15	524.63	518.09	512.38	507.38	502.99
55000	605.93	594.90	585.36	577.10	569.90	563.62	558.11	553.28
60000	661.02	648.98	638.58	629.56	621.71	614.85	608.85	603.58
65000	716.10	703.06	691.79	682.02	673.52	666.09	659.59	653.88
70000	771.19	757.14	745.01	734.48	725.32	717.33	710.32	704.18
75000	826.27	811.22	798.22	786.95	777.13	768.56	761.06	754.48
80000	881.35	865.30	851.44	839.41	828.94	819.80	811.80	804.77
85000	936.44	919.38	904.65	891.87	880.75	871.04	862.54	855.07
90000	991.52	973.46	957.86	944.34	932.56	922.28	913.27	905.37
95000	1046.61	1027.54	1011.08	996.80	984.37	973.51	964.01	955.67
100000	1101.69	1081.63	1064.29	1049.26	1036.18	1024.75	1014.75	1005.97
105000	1156.78	1135.71	1117.51	1101.72	1087.98	1075.99	1065.48	1056.26
110000	1211.86	1189.79	1170.72	1154.19	1139.79	1127.23	1116.22	1106.56
115000	1266.95	1243.87	1223.94	1206.65	1191.60	1178.46	1166.96	1156.86
120000	1322.03	1297.95	1277.15	1259.11	1243.41	1229.70	1217.70	1207.16
125000	1377.11	1352.03	1330.37	1311.58	1295.22	1280.94	1268.43	1257.46
130000	1432.20	1406.11	1383.58	1364.04	1347.03	1332.17	1319.17	1307.76
135000	1487.28	1460.19	1436.79	1416.50	1398.84	1383.41	1369.91	1358.05
140000	1542.37	1514.27	1490.01	1468.96	1450.64	1434.65	1420.64	1408.35
145000	1597.45	1568.35	1543.22	1521.43	1502.45	1485.89	1471.38	1458.65
150000	1652.54	1622.44	1596.44	1573.89	1554.26	1537.12	1522.12	1508.95
155000	1707.62	1676.52	1649.65	1626.35	1606.07	1588.36	1572.86	1559.25
160000	1762.70	1730.60	1702.87	1678.81	1657.88	1639.60	1623.59	1609.54

AMOUNT OF LOAN	NUMBER OF YEARS IN TERM							
	25	26	27	28	29	30	35	40
$ 50	.50	.50	.50	.50	.49	.49	.48	.48
100	1.00	1.00	.99	.99	.98	.98	.96	.95
200	2.00	1.99	1.98	1.97	1.96	1.95	1.92	1.90
300	3.00	2.98	2.96	2.95	2.93	2.92	2.87	2.85
400	4.00	3.97	3.95	3.93	3.91	3.89	3.83	3.80
500	5.00	4.96	4.93	4.91	4.88	4.86	4.79	4.75
600	5.99	5.95	5.92	5.89	5.86	5.83	5.74	5.69
700	6.99	6.95	6.90	6.87	6.83	6.80	6.70	6.64
800	7.99	7.94	7.89	7.85	7.81	7.78	7.66	7.59
900	8.99	8.93	8.87	8.83	8.78	8.75	8.61	8.54
1000	9.99	9.92	9.86	9.81	9.76	9.72	9.57	9.49
2000	19.97	19.83	19.71	19.61	19.51	19.43	19.13	18.97
3000	29.95	29.75	29.57	29.41	29.27	29.14	28.70	28.45
4000	39.93	39.66	39.42	39.21	39.02	38.86	38.26	37.94
5000	49.92	49.58	49.28	49.01	48.78	48.57	47.83	47.42
6000	59.90	59.49	59.13	58.81	58.53	58.28	57.39	56.90
7000	69.88	69.41	68.99	68.61	68.28	67.99	66.96	66.38
8000	79.86	79.32	78.84	78.41	78.04	77.71	76.52	75.87
9000	89.85	89.23	88.69	88.22	87.79	87.42	86.09	85.35
10000	99.83	99.15	98.55	98.02	97.55	97.13	95.65	94.83
11000	109.81	109.06	108.40	107.82	107.30	106.84	105.22	104.31
12000	119.79	118.98	118.26	117.62	117.06	116.56	114.78	113.80
13000	129.78	128.89	128.11	127.42	126.81	126.27	124.35	123.28
14000	139.76	138.81	137.97	137.22	136.56	135.98	133.91	132.76
15000	149.74	148.72	147.82	147.02	146.32	145.69	143.48	142.24
16000	159.72	158.63	157.67	156.82	156.07	155.41	153.04	151.73
17000	169.71	168.55	167.53	166.63	165.83	165.12	162.61	161.21
18000	179.69	178.46	177.38	176.43	175.58	174.83	172.17	170.69
19000	189.67	188.38	187.24	186.23	185.34	184.54	181.74	180.17
20000	199.65	198.29	197.09	196.03	195.09	194.26	191.30	189.66
21000	209.64	208.21	206.95	205.83	204.84	203.97	200.87	199.14
22000	219.62	218.12	216.80	215.63	214.60	213.68	210.43	208.62
23000	229.60	228.04	226.65	225.43	224.35	223.40	220.00	218.10
24000	239.58	237.95	236.51	235.23	234.11	233.11	229.56	227.59
25000	249.56	247.86	246.36	245.04	243.86	242.82	239.13	237.07
26000	259.55	257.78	256.22	254.84	253.62	252.53	248.69	246.55
27000	269.53	267.69	266.07	264.64	263.37	262.25	258.26	256.03
28000	279.51	277.61	275.93	274.44	273.12	271.96	267.82	265.52
29000	289.49	287.52	285.78	284.24	282.88	281.67	277.39	275.00
30000	299.48	297.44	295.63	294.04	292.63	291.38	286.95	284.48
31000	309.46	307.35	305.49	303.84	302.39	301.10	296.52	293.96
32000	319.44	317.26	315.34	313.64	312.14	310.81	306.08	303.45
33000	329.42	327.18	325.20	323.44	321.89	320.52	315.65	312.93
34000	339.41	337.09	335.05	333.25	331.65	330.23	325.21	322.41
35000	349.39	347.01	344.91	343.05	341.40	339.95	334.78	331.90
40000	399.30	396.58	394.18	392.05	390.17	388.51	382.60	379.31
45000	449.21	446.15	443.45	441.06	438.95	437.07	430.43	426.72
50000	499.12	495.72	492.72	490.07	487.72	485.64	478.25	474.13
55000	549.04	545.29	541.99	539.07	536.49	534.20	526.08	521.55
60000	598.95	594.87	591.26	588.08	585.26	582.76	573.90	568.96
65000	648.86	644.44	640.53	637.08	634.03	631.32	621.73	616.37
70000	698.77	694.01	689.81	686.09	682.80	679.89	669.55	663.79
75000	748.68	743.58	739.08	735.10	731.57	728.45	717.38	711.20
80000	798.60	793.15	788.35	784.10	780.34	777.01	765.20	758.61
85000	848.51	842.72	837.62	833.11	829.11	825.58	813.02	806.02
90000	898.42	892.30	886.89	882.11	877.89	874.14	860.85	853.44
95000	948.33	941.87	936.16	931.12	926.66	922.70	908.67	900.85
100000	998.24	991.44	985.43	980.13	975.43	971.27	956.50	948.26
105000	1048.16	1041.01	1034.71	1029.13	1024.20	1019.83	1004.32	995.68
110000	1098.07	1090.58	1083.98	1078.14	1072.97	1068.39	1052.15	1043.09
115000	1147.98	1140.16	1133.25	1127.14	1121.74	1116.96	1099.97	1090.50
120000	1197.89	1189.73	1182.52	1176.15	1170.51	1165.52	1147.80	1137.91
125000	1247.80	1239.30	1231.79	1225.16	1219.28	1214.08	1195.62	1185.33
130000	1297.72	1288.87	1281.06	1274.16	1268.06	1262.64	1243.45	1232.74
135000	1347.63	1338.44	1330.33	1323.17	1316.83	1311.21	1291.27	1280.15
140000	1397.54	1388.01	1379.61	1372.17	1365.60	1359.77	1339.10	1327.57
145000	1447.45	1437.59	1428.88	1421.18	1414.37	1408.33	1386.92	1374.98
150000	1497.36	1487.16	1478.15	1470.19	1463.14	1456.90	1434.75	1422.39
155000	1547.28	1536.73	1527.42	1519.19	1511.91	1505.46	1482.57	1469.80
160000	1597.19	1586.30	1576.69	1568.20	1560.68	1554.02	1530.40	1517.22

MONTHLY AMORTIZING PAYMENTS

AMOUNT OF LOAN	NUMBER OF YEARS IN TERM							
	1	1-1/2	2	3	4	5	6	7
$ 50	4.43	3.04	2.34	1.65	1.31	1.10	.97	.87
100	8.86	6.07	4.68	3.30	2.61	2.20	1.93	1.74
200	17.72	12.14	9.36	6.59	5.21	4.39	3.85	3.47
300	26.57	18.21	14.04	9.88	7.81	6.58	5.77	5.20
400	35.43	24.28	18.72	13.17	10.42	8.78	7.70	6.93
500	44.28	30.35	23.40	16.46	13.02	10.97	9.62	8.67
600	53.14	36.42	28.07	19.75	15.62	13.16	11.54	10.40
700	61.99	42.49	32.75	23.05	18.22	15.36	13.46	12.13
800	70.85	48.56	37.43	26.34	20.83	17.55	15.39	13.86
900	79.71	54.63	42.11	29.63	23.43	19.74	17.31	15.59
1000	88.56	60.70	46.79	32.92	26.03	21.93	19.23	17.33
2000	177.12	121.39	93.57	65.84	52.06	43.86	38.46	34.65
3000	265.68	182.08	140.35	98.75	78.09	65.79	57.69	51.97
4000	354.23	242.77	187.13	131.67	104.12	87.72	76.91	69.29
5000	442.79	303.47	233.92	164.59	130.15	109.65	96.14	86.61
6000	531.35	364.16	280.70	197.50	156.17	131.58	115.37	103.93
7000	619.90	424.85	327.48	230.42	182.20	153.51	134.59	121.25
8000	708.46	485.54	374.26	263.34	208.23	175.44	153.82	138.57
9000	797.02	546.23	421.04	296.25	234.26	197.37	173.05	155.89
10000	885.57	606.93	467.83	329.17	260.29	219.30	192.27	173.21
11000	974.13	667.62	514.61	362.09	286.31	241.23	211.50	190.53
12000	1062.69	728.31	561.39	395.00	312.34	263.16	230.73	207.85
13000	1151.24	789.00	608.17	427.92	338.37	285.09	249.95	225.17
14000	1239.80	849.69	654.95	460.84	364.40	307.02	269.18	242.49
15000	1328.36	910.39	701.74	493.75	390.43	328.95	288.41	259.81
16000	1416.91	971.08	748.52	526.67	416.45	350.88	307.63	277.13
17000	1505.47	1031.77	795.30	559.59	442.48	372.81	326.86	294.45
18000	1594.03	1092.46	842.08	592.50	468.51	394.74	346.09	311.77
19000	1682.58	1153.16	888.87	625.42	494.54	416.67	365.31	329.09
20000	1771.14	1213.85	935.65	658.34	520.57	438.60	384.54	346.41
21000	1859.70	1274.54	982.43	691.25	546.59	460.53	403.77	363.73
22000	1948.25	1335.23	1029.21	724.17	572.62	482.46	422.99	381.05
23000	2036.81	1395.92	1075.99	757.09	598.65	504.39	442.22	398.37
24000	2125.37	1456.62	1122.78	790.00	624.68	526.32	461.45	415.69
25000	2213.92	1517.31	1169.56	822.92	650.71	548.25	480.67	433.01
26000	2302.48	1578.00	1216.34	855.84	676.73	570.18	499.90	450.33
27000	2391.04	1638.69	1263.12	888.75	702.76	592.11	519.13	467.65
28000	2479.59	1699.38	1309.90	921.67	728.79	614.04	538.35	484.97
29000	2568.15	1760.08	1356.69	954.59	754.82	635.97	557.58	502.29
30000	2656.71	1820.77	1403.47	987.50	780.85	657.90	576.81	519.61
31000	2745.26	1881.46	1450.25	1020.42	806.87	679.83	596.03	536.93
32000	2833.82	1942.15	1497.03	1053.34	832.90	701.76	615.26	554.25
33000	2922.38	2002.84	1543.82	1086.25	858.93	723.69	634.49	571.57
34000	3010.93	2063.54	1590.60	1119.17	884.96	745.62	653.71	588.89
35000	3099.49	2124.23	1637.38	1152.09	910.99	767.55	672.94	606.21
40000	3542.27	2427.69	1871.29	1316.67	1041.13	877.20	769.07	692.81
45000	3985.06	2731.15	2105.20	1481.25	1171.27	986.85	865.21	779.42
50000	4427.84	3034.61	2339.11	1645.83	1301.41	1096.50	961.34	866.02
55000	4870.62	3338.07	2573.02	1810.42	1431.55	1206.15	1057.47	952.62
60000	5313.41	3641.53	2806.93	1975.00	1561.69	1315.80	1153.61	1039.22
65000	5756.19	3944.99	3040.84	2139.58	1691.83	1425.45	1249.74	1125.82
70000	6198.97	4248.45	3274.75	2304.17	1821.97	1535.10	1345.87	1212.42
75000	6641.76	4551.91	3508.66	2468.75	1952.11	1644.75	1442.01	1299.02
80000	7084.54	4855.37	3742.58	2633.33	2082.25	1754.40	1538.14	1385.62
85000	7527.32	5158.84	3976.49	2797.92	2212.39	1864.05	1634.27	1472.23
90000	7970.11	5462.30	4210.40	2962.50	2342.53	1973.70	1730.41	1558.83
95000	8412.89	5765.76	4444.31	3127.08	2472.67	2083.35	1826.54	1645.43
100000	8855.67	6069.22	4678.22	3291.66	2602.81	2193.00	1922.68	1732.03
105000	9298.46	6372.68	4912.13	3456.25	2732.95	2302.65	2018.81	1818.63
110000	9741.24	6676.14	5146.04	3620.83	2863.09	2412.29	2114.94	1905.23
115000	10184.02	6979.60	5379.95	3785.41	2993.23	2521.94	2211.08	1991.83
120000	10626.81	7283.06	5613.86	3950.00	3123.37	2631.59	2307.21	2078.43
125000	11069.59	7586.52	5847.77	4114.58	3253.51	2741.24	2403.34	2165.04
130000	11512.37	7889.98	6081.68	4279.16	3383.65	2850.89	2499.48	2251.64
135000	11955.16	8193.44	6315.59	4443.74	3513.79	2960.54	2595.61	2338.24
140000	12397.94	8496.90	6549.50	4608.33	3643.93	3070.19	2691.74	2424.84
145000	12840.72	8800.36	6783.41	4772.91	3774.07	3179.84	2787.88	2511.44
150000	13283.51	9103.82	7017.32	4937.49	3904.21	3289.49	2884.01	2598.04
155000	13726.29	9407.28	7251.24	5102.08	4034.35	3399.14	2980.14	2684.64
160000	14169.07	9710.74	7485.15	5266.66	4164.49	3508.79	3076.28	2771.24

AMOUNT OF LOAN	NUMBER OF YEARS IN TERM							
	8	9	10	11	12	14	15	16
$ 50	.80	.75	.70	.67	.64	.60	.59	.57
100	1.60	1.49	1.40	1.34	1.28	1.20	1.17	1.14
200	3.19	2.97	2.80	2.67	2.56	2.39	2.33	2.27
300	4.78	4.46	4.20	4.00	3.83	3.58	3.49	3.40
400	6.37	5.94	5.60	5.33	5.11	4.77	4.65	4.54
500	7.96	7.42	7.00	6.66	6.38	5.97	5.81	5.67
600	9.55	8.91	8.40	7.99	7.66	7.16	6.97	6.80
700	11.14	10.39	9.80	9.32	8.94	8.35	8.13	7.94
800	12.73	11.87	11.20	10.65	10.21	9.54	9.29	9.07
900	14.33	13.36	12.59	11.98	11.49	10.74	10.45	10.20
1000	15.92	14.84	13.99	13.32	12.76	11.93	11.61	11.34
2000	31.83	29.67	27.98	26.63	25.52	23.85	23.21	22.67
3000	47.74	44.51	41.97	39.94	38.28	35.77	34.81	34.00
4000	63.65	59.34	55.96	53.25	51.04	47.70	46.42	45.33
5000	79.56	74.17	69.95	66.56	63.80	59.62	58.02	56.66
6000	95.47	89.01	83.93	79.87	76.56	71.54	69.62	67.99
7000	111.38	103.84	97.92	93.18	89.31	83.46	81.22	79.32
8000	127.30	118.68	111.91	106.49	102.07	95.39	92.83	90.65
9000	143.21	133.51	125.90	119.80	114.83	107.31	104.43	101.98
10000	159.12	148.34	139.89	133.11	127.59	119.23	116.03	113.31
11000	175.03	163.18	153.87	146.42	140.35	131.15	127.63	124.64
12000	190.94	178.01	167.86	159.73	153.11	143.08	139.24	135.98
13000	206.85	192.85	181.85	173.04	165.86	155.00	150.84	147.31
14000	222.76	207.68	195.84	186.35	178.62	166.92	162.44	158.64
15000	238.68	222.51	209.83	199.66	191.38	178.85	174.04	169.97
16000	254.59	237.35	223.82	212.97	204.14	190.77	185.65	181.30
17000	270.50	252.18	237.80	226.28	216.90	202.69	197.25	192.63
18000	286.41	267.02	251.79	239.59	229.66	214.61	208.85	203.96
19000	302.32	281.85	265.78	252.90	242.42	226.54	220.45	215.29
20000	318.23	296.68	279.77	266.21	255.17	238.46	232.06	226.62
21000	334.14	311.52	293.76	279.52	267.93	250.38	243.66	237.95
22000	350.06	326.35	307.74	292.83	280.69	262.30	255.26	249.28
23000	365.97	341.19	321.73	306.14	293.45	274.23	266.86	260.61
24000	381.88	356.02	335.72	319.45	306.21	286.15	278.47	271.95
25000	397.79	370.85	349.71	332.77	318.97	298.07	290.07	283.28
26000	413.70	385.69	363.70	346.08	331.72	310.00	301.67	294.61
27000	429.61	400.52	377.68	359.39	344.48	321.92	313.27	305.94
28000	445.52	415.36	391.67	372.70	357.24	333.84	324.88	317.27
29000	461.44	430.19	405.66	386.01	370.00	345.76	336.48	328.60
30000	477.35	445.02	419.65	399.32	382.76	357.69	348.08	339.93
31000	493.26	459.86	433.64	412.63	395.52	369.61	359.68	351.26
32000	509.17	474.69	447.63	425.94	408.28	381.53	371.29	362.59
33000	525.08	489.53	461.61	439.25	421.03	393.45	382.89	373.92
34000	540.99	504.36	475.60	452.56	433.79	405.38	394.49	385.25
35000	556.90	519.19	489.59	465.87	446.55	417.30	406.09	396.59
40000	636.46	593.36	559.53	532.42	510.34	476.91	464.11	453.24
45000	716.02	667.53	629.47	598.97	574.13	536.53	522.12	509.89
50000	795.57	741.70	699.41	665.53	637.93	596.14	580.13	566.55
55000	875.13	815.87	769.35	732.08	701.72	655.75	638.15	623.20
60000	954.69	890.04	839.29	798.63	765.51	715.37	696.16	679.86
65000	1034.25	964.21	909.23	865.18	829.30	774.98	754.17	736.51
70000	1113.80	1038.38	979.17	931.73	893.10	834.59	812.18	793.17
75000	1193.36	1112.55	1049.11	998.29	956.89	894.21	870.20	849.82
80000	1272.92	1186.72	1119.06	1064.84	1020.68	953.82	928.21	906.47
85000	1352.47	1260.89	1189.00	1131.39	1084.47	1013.43	986.22	963.13
90000	1432.03	1335.06	1258.94	1197.94	1148.26	1073.05	1044.23	1019.78
95000	1511.59	1409.23	1328.88	1264.49	1212.06	1132.66	1102.25	1076.44
100000	1591.14	1483.40	1398.82	1331.05	1275.85	1192.27	1160.26	1133.09
105000	1670.70	1557.57	1468.76	1397.60	1339.64	1251.89	1218.27	1189.75
110000	1750.26	1631.74	1538.70	1464.15	1403.43	1311.50	1276.29	1246.40
115000	1829.82	1705.91	1608.64	1530.70	1467.23	1371.12	1334.30	1303.05
120000	1909.37	1780.08	1678.58	1597.25	1531.02	1430.73	1392.31	1359.71
125000	1988.93	1854.25	1748.52	1663.81	1594.81	1490.34	1450.32	1416.36
130000	2068.49	1928.42	1818.46	1730.36	1658.60	1549.96	1508.34	1473.02
135000	2148.04	2002.59	1888.40	1796.91	1722.39	1609.57	1566.35	1529.67
140000	2227.60	2076.76	1958.34	1863.46	1786.19	1669.18	1624.36	1586.33
145000	2307.16	2150.93	2028.28	1930.01	1849.98	1728.80	1682.37	1642.98
150000	2386.71	2225.10	2098.22	1996.57	1913.77	1788.41	1740.39	1699.63
155000	2466.27	2299.27	2168.16	2063.12	1977.56	1848.02	1798.40	1756.29
160000	2545.83	2373.44	2238.11	2129.67	2041.36	1907.64	1856.41	1812.94

MONTHLY AMORTIZING PAYMENTS

AMOUNT OF LOAN	NUMBER OF YEARS IN TERM							
	17	18	19	20	21	22	23	24
$ 50	.56	.55	.54	.53	.53	.52	.52	.51
100	1.11	1.09	1.08	1.06	1.05	1.04	1.03	1.02
200	2.22	2.18	2.15	2.12	2.09	2.07	2.05	2.03
300	3.33	3.27	3.22	3.18	3.14	3.11	3.08	3.05
400	4.44	4.36	4.30	4.24	4.18	4.14	4.10	4.06
500	5.55	5.45	5.37	5.29	5.23	5.17	5.12	5.08
600	6.66	6.54	6.44	6.35	6.27	6.21	6.15	6.09
700	7.77	7.63	7.51	7.41	7.32	7.24	7.17	7.11
800	8.88	8.72	8.59	8.47	8.36	8.27	8.19	8.12
900	9.99	9.81	9.66	9.53	9.41	9.31	9.22	9.14
1000	11.10	10.90	10.73	10.58	10.45	10.34	10.24	10.15
2000	22.20	21.80	21.46	21.16	20.90	20.68	20.48	20.30
3000	33.30	32.70	32.19	31.74	31.35	31.01	30.71	30.45
4000	44.40	43.60	42.91	42.32	41.80	41.35	40.95	40.60
5000	55.50	54.50	53.64	52.90	52.25	51.68	51.19	50.75
6000	66.60	65.40	64.37	63.47	62.70	62.02	61.42	60.90
7000	77.70	76.30	75.10	74.05	73.15	72.35	71.66	71.05
8000	88.80	87.20	85.82	84.63	83.59	82.69	81.90	81.20
9000	99.89	98.10	96.55	95.21	94.04	93.02	92.13	91.35
10000	110.99	109.00	107.28	105.79	104.49	103.36	102.37	101.50
11000	122.09	119.90	118.01	116.37	114.94	113.70	112.61	111.65
12000	133.19	130.80	128.73	126.94	125.39	124.03	122.84	121.80
13000	144.29	141.70	139.46	137.52	135.84	134.37	133.08	131.95
14000	155.39	152.60	150.19	148.10	146.29	144.70	143.32	142.10
15000	166.49	163.50	160.92	158.68	156.73	155.04	153.55	152.25
16000	177.59	174.40	171.64	169.26	167.18	165.37	163.79	162.40
17000	188.68	185.30	182.37	179.84	177.63	175.71	174.03	172.55
18000	199.78	196.20	193.10	190.41	188.08	186.04	184.26	182.70
19000	210.88	207.09	203.83	200.99	198.53	196.38	194.50	192.85
20000	221.98	217.99	214.55	211.57	208.98	206.71	204.73	203.00
21000	233.08	228.89	225.28	222.15	219.43	217.05	214.97	213.15
22000	244.18	239.79	236.01	232.73	229.87	227.39	225.21	223.30
23000	255.28	250.69	246.74	243.31	240.32	237.72	235.44	233.45
24000	266.38	261.59	257.46	253.88	250.77	248.06	245.68	243.60
25000	277.47	272.49	268.19	264.46	261.22	258.39	255.92	253.75
26000	288.57	283.39	278.92	275.04	271.67	268.73	266.15	263.90
27000	299.67	294.29	289.64	285.62	282.12	279.06	276.39	274.05
28000	310.77	305.19	300.37	296.20	292.57	289.40	286.63	284.20
29000	321.87	316.09	311.10	306.78	303.01	299.73	296.86	294.35
30000	332.97	326.99	321.83	317.35	313.46	310.07	307.10	304.50
31000	344.07	337.89	332.55	327.93	323.91	320.40	317.34	314.65
32000	355.17	348.79	343.28	338.51	334.36	330.74	327.57	324.80
33000	366.27	359.69	354.01	349.09	344.81	341.08	337.81	334.94
34000	377.36	370.59	364.74	359.67	355.26	351.41	348.05	345.09
35000	388.46	381.49	375.46	370.25	365.71	361.75	358.28	355.24
40000	443.96	435.98	429.10	423.14	417.95	413.42	409.46	405.99
45000	499.45	490.48	482.74	476.03	470.19	465.10	460.65	456.74
50000	554.94	544.98	536.38	528.92	522.44	516.78	511.83	507.49
55000	610.44	599.47	590.01	581.81	574.68	568.46	563.01	558.24
60000	665.93	653.97	643.65	634.70	626.92	620.13	614.19	608.99
65000	721.43	708.47	697.29	687.59	679.16	671.81	665.38	659.73
70000	776.92	762.97	750.92	740.49	731.41	723.49	716.56	710.48
75000	832.41	817.46	804.56	793.38	783.65	775.17	767.74	761.23
80000	887.91	871.96	858.20	846.27	835.89	826.84	818.92	811.98
85000	943.40	926.46	911.83	899.16	888.14	878.52	870.11	862.73
90000	998.90	980.96	965.47	952.05	940.38	930.20	921.29	913.48
95000	1054.39	1035.45	1019.11	1004.94	992.62	981.87	972.47	964.23
100000	1109.88	1089.95	1072.75	1057.83	1044.87	1033.55	1023.65	1014.97
105000	1165.38	1144.45	1126.38	1110.73	1097.11	1085.23	1074.84	1065.72
110000	1220.87	1198.94	1180.02	1163.62	1149.35	1136.91	1126.02	1116.47
115000	1276.37	1253.44	1233.66	1216.51	1201.60	1188.58	1177.20	1167.22
120000	1331.86	1307.94	1287.29	1269.40	1253.84	1240.26	1228.38	1217.97
125000	1387.35	1362.44	1340.93	1322.29	1306.08	1291.94	1279.57	1268.72
130000	1442.85	1416.93	1394.57	1375.18	1358.32	1343.62	1330.75	1319.46
135000	1498.34	1471.43	1448.20	1428.08	1410.57	1395.29	1381.93	1370.21
140000	1553.84	1525.93	1501.84	1480.97	1462.81	1446.97	1433.11	1420.96
145000	1609.33	1580.43	1555.48	1533.86	1515.05	1498.65	1484.30	1471.71
150000	1664.82	1634.92	1609.12	1586.75	1567.30	1550.33	1535.48	1522.46
155000	1720.32	1689.42	1662.75	1639.64	1619.54	1602.00	1586.66	1573.21
160000	1775.81	1743.92	1716.39	1692.53	1671.78	1653.68	1637.84	1623.96

AMOUNT OF LOAN	NUMBER OF YEARS IN TERM							
	25	26	27	28	29	30	35	40
$ 50	.51	.51	.50	.50	.50	.50	.49	.48
100	1.01	1.01	1.00	.99	.99	.99	.97	.96
200	2.02	2.01	1.99	1.98	1.97	1.97	1.94	1.92
300	3.03	3.01	2.99	2.97	2.96	2.95	2.90	2.88
400	4.03	4.01	3.98	3.96	3.94	3.93	3.87	3.84
500	5.04	5.01	4.98	4.95	4.93	4.91	4.84	4.80
600	6.05	6.01	5.97	5.94	5.91	5.89	5.80	5.75
700	7.06	7.01	6.97	6.93	6.90	6.87	6.77	6.71
800	8.06	8.01	7.96	7.92	7.88	7.85	7.74	7.67
900	9.07	9.01	8.96	8.91	8.87	8.83	8.70	8.63
1000	10.08	10.01	9.95	9.90	9.85	9.81	9.67	9.59
2000	20.15	20.02	19.90	19.79	19.70	19.62	19.33	19.17
3000	30.23	30.02	29.85	29.69	29.55	29.43	28.99	28.75
4000	40.30	40.03	39.79	39.58	39.40	39.24	38.66	38.34
5000	50.37	50.04	49.74	49.48	49.25	49.04	48.32	47.92
6000	60.45	60.04	59.69	59.37	59.10	58.85	57.98	57.50
7000	70.52	70.05	69.63	69.27	68.94	68.66	67.65	67.08
8000	80.59	80.06	79.58	79.16	78.79	78.47	77.31	76.67
9000	90.67	90.06	89.53	89.06	88.64	88.27	86.97	86.25
10000	100.74	100.07	99.48	98.95	98.49	98.08	96.63	95.83
11000	110.81	110.07	109.42	108.85	108.34	107.89	106.30	105.41
12000	120.89	120.08	119.37	118.74	118.19	117.70	115.96	115.00
13000	130.96	130.09	129.32	128.64	128.04	127.50	125.62	124.58
14000	141.03	140.09	139.26	138.53	137.88	137.31	135.29	134.16
15000	151.11	150.10	149.21	148.43	147.73	147.12	144.95	143.74
16000	161.18	160.11	159.16	158.32	157.58	156.93	154.61	153.33
17000	171.25	170.11	169.11	168.22	167.43	166.74	164.27	162.91
18000	181.33	180.12	179.05	178.11	177.28	176.54	173.94	172.49
19000	191.40	190.12	189.00	188.01	187.13	186.35	183.60	182.07
20000	201.47	200.13	198.95	197.90	196.98	196.16	193.26	191.66
21000	211.55	210.14	208.89	207.80	206.82	205.97	202.93	201.24
22000	221.62	220.14	218.84	217.69	216.67	215.77	212.59	210.82
23000	231.69	230.15	228.79	227.59	226.52	225.58	222.25	220.41
24000	241.77	240.16	238.73	237.48	236.37	235.39	231.91	229.99
25000	251.84	250.16	248.68	247.37	246.22	245.20	241.58	239.57
26000	261.91	260.17	258.63	257.27	256.07	255.00	251.24	249.15
27000	271.99	270.17	268.58	267.16	265.92	264.81	260.90	258.74
28000	282.06	280.18	278.52	277.06	275.76	274.62	270.57	268.32
29000	292.13	290.19	288.47	286.95	285.61	284.43	280.23	277.90
30000	302.21	300.19	298.42	296.85	295.46	294.23	289.89	287.48
31000	312.28	310.20	308.36	306.74	305.31	304.04	299.56	297.07
32000	322.35	320.21	318.31	316.64	315.16	313.85	309.22	306.65
33000	332.43	330.21	328.26	326.53	325.01	323.66	318.88	316.23
34000	342.50	340.22	338.21	336.43	334.86	333.47	328.54	325.81
35000	352.57	350.22	348.15	346.32	344.70	343.27	338.21	335.40
40000	402.94	400.26	397.89	395.80	393.95	392.31	386.52	383.31
45000	453.31	450.29	447.62	445.27	443.19	441.35	434.84	431.22
50000	503.68	500.32	497.36	494.74	492.43	490.39	483.15	479.14
55000	554.04	550.35	547.09	544.22	541.68	539.43	531.47	527.05
60000	604.41	600.38	596.83	593.69	590.92	588.46	579.78	574.96
65000	654.78	650.41	646.56	643.17	640.16	637.50	628.09	622.88
70000	705.14	700.44	696.30	692.64	689.40	686.54	676.41	670.79
75000	755.51	750.48	746.03	742.11	738.65	735.58	724.72	718.70
80000	805.88	800.51	795.77	791.59	787.89	784.62	773.04	766.61
85000	856.25	850.54	845.51	841.06	837.13	833.66	821.35	814.53
90000	906.61	900.57	895.24	890.54	886.38	882.69	869.67	862.44
95000	956.98	950.60	944.98	940.01	935.62	931.73	917.98	910.35
100000	1007.35	1000.63	994.71	989.48	984.86	980.77	966.30	958.27
105000	1057.71	1050.66	1044.45	1038.96	1034.10	1029.81	1014.61	1006.18
110000	1108.08	1100.69	1094.18	1088.43	1083.35	1078.85	1062.93	1054.09
115000	1158.45	1150.73	1143.92	1137.91	1132.59	1127.88	1111.24	1102.01
120000	1208.81	1200.76	1193.65	1187.38	1181.83	1176.92	1159.55	1149.92
125000	1259.18	1250.79	1243.39	1236.85	1231.08	1225.96	1207.87	1197.83
130000	1309.55	1300.82	1293.12	1286.33	1280.32	1275.00	1256.18	1245.75
135000	1359.92	1350.85	1342.86	1335.80	1329.56	1324.04	1304.50	1293.66
140000	1410.28	1400.88	1392.59	1385.27	1378.80	1373.08	1352.81	1341.57
145000	1460.65	1450.91	1442.33	1434.75	1428.05	1422.11	1401.13	1389.49
150000	1511.02	1500.95	1492.06	1484.22	1477.29	1471.15	1449.44	1437.40
155000	1561.38	1550.98	1541.80	1533.70	1526.53	1520.19	1497.76	1485.31
160000	1611.75	1601.01	1591.54	1583.17	1575.77	1569.23	1546.07	1533.22

MONTHLY AMORTIZING PAYMENTS

AMOUNT OF LOAN	NUMBER OF YEARS IN TERM							
	1	1-1/2	2	3	4	5	6	7
$ 50	4.44	3.04	2.35	1.65	1.31	1.10	.97	.87
100	8.87	6.08	4.69	3.30	2.61	2.20	1.93	1.74
200	17.73	12.16	9.37	6.60	5.22	4.40	3.86	3.48
300	26.59	18.23	14.06	9.90	7.83	6.60	5.79	5.22
400	35.45	24.31	18.74	13.20	10.44	8.80	7.72	6.96
500	44.31	30.38	23.43	16.49	13.05	11.00	9.65	8.70
600	53.17	36.46	28.11	19.79	15.66	13.20	11.58	10.44
700	62.04	42.53	32.79	23.09	18.27	15.40	13.51	12.18
800	70.90	48.61	37.48	26.39	20.88	17.60	15.44	13.91
900	79.76	54.68	42.16	29.68	23.49	19.80	17.37	15.65
1000	88.62	60.76	46.85	32.98	26.09	22.00	19.30	17.39
2000	177.24	121.51	93.69	65.96	52.18	43.99	38.59	34.78
3000	265.85	182.26	140.53	98.93	78.27	65.98	57.88	52.16
4000	354.47	243.01	187.37	131.91	104.36	87.98	77.17	69.55
5000	443.08	303.76	234.21	164.89	130.45	109.97	96.46	86.94
6000	531.70	364.51	281.05	197.86	156.54	131.96	115.75	104.32
7000	620.31	425.26	327.89	230.84	182.63	153.95	135.04	121.71
8000	708.93	486.01	374.73	263.81	208.72	175.95	154.33	139.10
9000	797.54	546.76	421.57	296.79	234.81	197.94	173.63	156.48
10000	886.16	607.51	468.41	329.77	260.90	219.93	192.92	173.87
11000	974.77	668.26	515.25	362.74	286.98	241.92	212.21	191.26
12000	1063.39	729.01	562.09	395.72	313.07	263.92	231.50	208.64
13000	1152.00	789.76	608.93	428.69	339.16	285.91	250.79	226.03
14000	1240.62	850.51	655.77	461.67	365.25	307.90	270.08	243.42
15000	1329.23	911.26	702.61	494.65	391.34	329.89	289.37	260.80
16000	1417.85	972.01	749.45	527.62	417.43	351.89	308.66	278.19
17000	1506.46	1032.76	796.29	560.60	443.52	373.88	327.95	295.57
18000	1595.08	1093.51	843.13	593.57	469.61	395.87	347.25	312.96
19000	1683.69	1154.26	889.97	626.55	495.70	417.86	366.54	330.35
20000	1772.31	1215.01	936.81	659.53	521.79	439.86	385.83	347.73
21000	1860.92	1275.76	983.65	692.50	547.87	461.85	405.12	365.12
22000	1949.54	1336.51	1030.49	725.48	573.96	483.84	424.41	382.51
23000	2038.15	1397.26	1077.33	758.45	600.05	505.83	443.70	399.89
24000	2126.77	1458.01	1124.17	791.43	626.14	527.83	462.99	417.28
25000	2215.38	1518.76	1171.01	824.41	652.23	549.82	482.28	434.67
26000	2304.00	1579.51	1217.85	857.38	678.32	571.81	501.58	452.05
27000	2392.61	1640.26	1264.69	890.36	704.41	593.81	520.87	469.44
28000	2481.23	1701.01	1311.53	923.33	730.50	615.80	540.16	486.83
29000	2569.84	1761.76	1358.37	956.31	756.59	637.79	559.45	504.21
30000	2658.46	1822.51	1405.21	989.29	782.68	659.78	578.74	521.60
31000	2747.07	1883.26	1452.05	1022.26	808.76	681.78	598.03	538.99
32000	2835.69	1944.01	1498.90	1055.24	834.85	703.77	617.32	556.37
33000	2924.30	2004.76	1545.74	1088.21	860.94	725.76	636.61	573.76
34000	3012.92	2065.51	1592.58	1121.19	887.03	747.75	655.90	591.14
35000	3101.53	2126.26	1639.42	1154.17	913.12	769.75	675.20	608.53
40000	3544.61	2430.01	1873.62	1319.05	1043.57	879.71	771.65	695.46
45000	3987.68	2733.76	2107.82	1483.93	1174.01	989.67	868.11	782.40
50000	4430.76	3037.51	2342.02	1648.81	1304.46	1099.64	964.56	869.33
55000	4873.83	3341.26	2576.22	1813.69	1434.90	1209.60	1061.02	956.26
60000	5316.91	3645.01	2810.42	1978.57	1565.35	1319.56	1157.47	1043.19
65000	5759.98	3948.76	3044.63	2143.45	1695.79	1429.52	1253.93	1130.12
70000	6203.06	4252.51	3278.83	2308.33	1826.24	1539.49	1350.39	1217.06
75000	6646.13	4556.26	3513.03	2473.21	1956.68	1649.45	1446.84	1303.99
80000	7089.21	4860.01	3747.23	2638.09	2087.13	1759.41	1543.30	1390.92
85000	7532.28	5163.76	3981.43	2802.97	2217.57	1869.38	1639.75	1477.85
90000	7975.36	5467.51	4215.63	2967.85	2348.02	1979.34	1736.21	1564.79
95000	8418.44	5771.26	4449.83	3132.73	2478.46	2089.30	1832.66	1651.72
100000	8861.51	6075.01	4684.04	3297.61	2608.91	2199.27	1929.12	1738.65
105000	9304.59	6378.76	4918.24	3462.49	2739.35	2309.23	2025.58	1825.58
110000	9747.66	6682.51	5152.44	3627.37	2869.80	2419.19	2122.03	1912.52
115000	10190.74	6986.26	5386.64	3792.25	3000.24	2529.15	2218.49	1999.45
120000	10633.81	7290.01	5620.84	3957.13	3130.69	2639.12	2314.94	2086.38
125000	11076.89	7593.76	5855.04	4122.01	3261.13	2749.08	2411.40	2173.31
130000	11519.96	7897.51	6089.25	4286.89	3391.58	2859.04	2507.86	2260.24
135000	11963.04	8201.26	6323.45	4451.77	3522.02	2969.01	2604.31	2347.18
140000	12406.11	8505.01	6557.65	4616.65	3652.47	3078.97	2700.77	2434.11
145000	12849.19	8808.76	6791.85	4781.53	3782.91	3188.93	2797.22	2521.04
150000	13292.26	9112.51	7026.05	4946.41	3913.36	3298.90	2893.68	2607.97
155000	13735.34	9416.26	7260.25	5111.29	4043.80	3408.86	2990.13	2694.91
160000	14178.41	9720.01	7494.46	5276.17	4174.25	3518.82	3086.59	2781.84

AMOUNT OF LOAN	NUMBER OF YEARS IN TERM							
	8	9	10	11	12	14	15	16
$ 50	.80	.75	.71	.67	.65	.61	.59	.58
100	1.60	1.50	1.41	1.34	1.29	1.21	1.17	1.15
200	3.20	2.99	2.82	2.68	2.57	2.41	2.34	2.29
300	4.80	4.48	4.22	4.02	3.85	3.61	3.51	3.43
400	6.40	5.97	5.63	5.36	5.14	4.81	4.68	4.57
500	7.99	7.46	7.03	6.70	6.42	6.01	5.85	5.71
600	9.59	8.95	8.44	8.04	7.70	7.21	7.01	6.85
700	11.19	10.44	9.85	9.37	8.99	8.41	8.18	7.99
800	12.79	11.93	11.25	10.71	10.27	9.61	9.35	9.13
900	14.39	13.42	12.66	12.05	11.55	10.81	10.52	10.28
1000	15.98	14.91	14.06	13.39	12.84	12.01	11.69	11.42
2000	31.96	29.81	28.12	26.77	25.67	24.01	23.37	22.83
3000	47.94	44.72	42.18	40.16	38.50	36.01	35.05	34.24
4000	63.92	59.62	56.24	53.54	51.34	48.01	46.73	45.65
5000	79.90	74.52	70.30	66.92	64.17	60.01	58.41	57.06
6000	95.88	89.43	84.36	80.31	77.00	72.01	70.10	68.47
7000	111.86	104.33	98.42	93.69	89.84	84.01	81.78	79.89
8000	127.84	119.23	112.48	107.07	102.67	96.01	93.46	91.30
9000	143.82	134.14	126.54	120.46	115.50	108.01	105.14	102.71
10000	159.80	149.04	140.60	133.84	128.34	120.01	116.82	114.12
11000	175.78	163.95	154.66	147.22	141.17	132.01	128.51	125.53
12000	191.76	178.85	168.72	160.61	154.00	144.01	140.19	136.94
13000	207.74	193.75	182.78	173.99	166.84	156.01	151.87	148.36
14000	223.72	208.66	196.84	187.37	179.67	168.01	163.55	159.77
15000	239.70	223.56	210.90	200.76	192.50	180.01	175.23	171.18
16000	255.67	238.46	224.96	214.14	205.34	192.01	186.92	182.59
17000	271.65	253.37	239.02	227.52	218.17	204.01	198.60	194.00
18000	287.63	268.27	253.08	240.91	231.00	216.01	210.28	205.41
19000	303.61	283.17	267.14	254.29	243.84	228.02	221.96	216.83
20000	319.59	298.08	281.20	267.68	256.67	240.02	233.64	228.24
21000	335.57	312.98	295.26	281.06	269.50	252.02	245.32	239.65
22000	351.55	327.89	309.31	294.44	282.33	264.02	257.01	251.06
23000	367.53	342.79	323.37	307.83	295.17	276.02	268.69	262.47
24000	383.51	357.69	337.43	321.21	308.00	288.02	280.37	273.88
25000	399.49	372.60	351.49	334.59	320.83	300.02	292.05	285.30
26000	415.47	387.50	365.55	347.98	333.67	312.02	303.73	296.71
27000	431.45	402.40	379.61	361.36	346.50	324.02	315.42	308.12
28000	447.43	417.31	393.67	374.74	359.33	336.02	327.10	319.53
29000	463.41	432.21	407.73	388.13	372.17	348.02	338.78	330.94
30000	479.39	447.11	421.79	401.51	385.00	360.02	350.46	342.35
31000	495.37	462.02	435.85	414.89	397.83	372.02	362.14	353.77
32000	511.34	476.92	449.91	428.28	410.67	384.02	373.83	365.18
33000	527.32	491.83	463.97	441.66	423.50	396.02	385.51	376.59
34000	543.30	506.73	478.03	455.04	436.33	408.02	397.19	388.00
35000	559.28	521.63	492.09	468.43	449.17	420.02	408.87	399.41
40000	639.18	596.15	562.39	535.35	513.33	480.03	467.28	456.47
45000	719.08	670.67	632.68	602.26	577.50	540.03	525.69	513.53
50000	798.97	745.19	702.98	669.18	641.66	600.03	584.10	570.59
55000	878.87	819.71	773.28	736.10	705.83	660.04	642.51	627.65
60000	958.77	894.22	843.58	803.02	769.99	720.04	700.92	684.70
65000	1038.66	968.74	913.88	869.93	834.16	780.04	759.33	741.76
70000	1118.56	1043.26	984.17	936.85	898.33	840.04	817.74	798.82
75000	1198.46	1117.78	1054.47	1003.77	962.49	900.05	876.15	855.88
80000	1278.35	1192.30	1124.77	1070.69	1026.66	960.05	934.56	912.94
85000	1358.25	1266.82	1195.07	1137.60	1090.82	1020.05	992.97	970.00
90000	1438.15	1341.33	1265.36	1204.52	1154.99	1080.05	1051.38	1027.05
95000	1518.05	1415.85	1335.66	1271.44	1219.16	1140.06	1109.79	1084.11
100000	1597.94	1490.37	1405.96	1338.36	1283.32	1200.06	1168.19	1141.17
105000	1677.84	1564.89	1476.26	1405.27	1347.49	1260.06	1226.60	1198.23
110000	1757.74	1639.41	1546.55	1472.19	1411.65	1320.07	1285.01	1255.29
115000	1837.63	1713.93	1616.85	1539.11	1475.82	1380.07	1343.42	1312.34
120000	1917.53	1788.44	1687.15	1606.03	1539.98	1440.07	1401.83	1369.40
125000	1997.43	1862.96	1757.45	1672.94	1604.15	1500.07	1460.24	1426.46
130000	2077.32	1937.48	1827.75	1739.86	1668.32	1560.08	1518.65	1483.52
135000	2157.22	2012.00	1898.04	1806.78	1732.48	1620.08	1577.06	1540.58
140000	2237.12	2086.52	1968.34	1873.70	1796.65	1680.08	1635.47	1597.64
145000	2317.01	2161.04	2038.64	1940.61	1860.81	1740.09	1693.88	1654.69
150000	2396.91	2235.55	2108.94	2007.53	1924.98	1800.09	1752.29	1711.75
155000	2476.81	2310.07	2179.23	2074.45	1989.15	1860.09	1810.70	1768.81
160000	2556.70	2384.59	2249.53	2141.37	2053.31	1920.09	1869.11	1825.87

AMOUNT OF LOAN	NUMBER OF YEARS IN TERM							
	17	18	19	20	21	22	23	24
$ 50	.56	.55	.55	.54	.53	.53	.52	.52
100	1.12	1.10	1.09	1.07	1.06	1.05	1.04	1.03
200	2.24	2.20	2.17	2.14	2.11	2.09	2.07	2.05
300	3.36	3.30	3.25	3.20	3.17	3.13	3.10	3.08
400	4.48	4.40	4.33	4.27	4.22	4.17	4.14	4.10
500	5.60	5.50	5.41	5.34	5.27	5.22	5.17	5.13
600	6.71	6.59	6.49	6.40	6.33	6.26	6.20	6.15
700	7.83	7.69	7.57	7.47	7.38	7.30	7.23	7.17
800	8.95	8.79	8.65	8.54	8.43	8.34	8.27	8.20
900	10.07	9.89	9.74	9.60	9.49	9.39	9.30	9.22
1000	11.19	10.99	10.82	10.67	10.54	10.43	10.33	10.25
2000	22.37	21.97	21.63	21.33	21.08	20.85	20.66	20.49
3000	33.55	32.95	32.44	32.00	31.61	31.28	30.98	30.73
4000	44.73	43.94	43.25	42.66	42.15	41.70	41.31	40.97
5000	55.91	54.92	54.07	53.33	52.68	52.12	51.63	51.21
6000	67.09	65.90	64.88	63.99	63.22	62.55	61.96	61.45
7000	78.27	76.89	75.69	74.66	73.76	72.97	72.29	71.69
8000	89.45	87.87	86.50	85.32	84.29	83.39	82.61	81.93
9000	100.63	98.85	97.31	95.98	94.83	93.82	92.94	92.17
10000	111.81	109.83	108.13	106.65	105.36	104.24	103.26	102.41
11000	123.00	120.82	118.94	117.31	115.90	114.67	113.59	112.65
12000	134.18	131.80	129.75	127.98	126.43	125.09	123.91	122.89
13000	145.36	142.78	140.56	138.64	136.97	135.51	134.24	133.13
14000	156.54	153.77	151.38	149.31	147.51	145.94	144.57	143.37
15000	167.72	164.75	162.19	159.97	158.04	156.36	154.89	153.61
16000	178.90	175.73	173.00	170.63	168.58	166.78	165.22	163.85
17000	190.08	186.72	183.81	181.30	179.11	177.21	175.54	174.09
18000	201.26	197.70	194.62	191.96	189.65	187.63	185.87	184.33
19000	212.44	208.68	205.44	202.63	200.18	198.06	196.20	194.57
20000	223.62	219.66	216.25	213.29	210.72	208.48	206.52	204.81
21000	234.81	230.65	227.06	223.96	221.26	218.90	216.85	215.05
22000	245.99	241.63	237.87	234.62	231.79	229.33	227.17	225.29
23000	257.17	252.61	248.69	245.28	242.33	239.75	237.50	235.53
24000	268.35	263.60	259.50	255.95	252.86	250.17	247.82	245.77
25000	279.53	274.58	270.31	266.61	263.40	260.60	258.15	256.01
26000	290.71	285.56	281.12	277.28	273.94	271.02	268.48	266.25
27000	301.89	296.54	291.93	287.94	284.47	281.45	278.80	276.49
28000	313.07	307.53	302.75	298.61	295.01	291.87	289.13	286.73
29000	324.25	318.51	313.56	309.27	305.54	302.29	299.45	296.97
30000	335.43	329.49	324.37	319.93	316.08	312.72	309.78	307.21
31000	346.61	340.48	335.18	330.60	326.61	323.14	320.11	317.45
32000	357.80	351.46	345.99	341.26	337.15	333.56	330.43	327.69
33000	368.98	362.44	356.81	351.93	347.69	343.99	340.76	337.93
34000	380.16	373.43	367.62	362.59	358.22	354.41	351.08	348.17
35000	391.34	384.41	378.43	373.26	368.76	364.84	361.41	358.41
40000	447.24	439.32	432.49	426.58	421.44	416.95	413.04	409.61
45000	503.15	494.24	486.55	479.90	474.11	469.07	464.67	460.81
50000	559.05	549.15	540.61	533.22	526.79	521.19	516.30	512.01
55000	614.96	604.07	594.67	586.54	579.47	573.31	567.92	563.21
60000	670.86	658.98	648.74	639.86	632.15	625.43	619.55	614.41
65000	726.77	713.90	702.80	693.18	684.83	677.55	671.18	665.61
70000	782.67	768.81	756.86	746.51	737.51	729.67	722.81	716.81
75000	838.58	823.73	810.92	799.83	790.19	781.79	774.44	768.01
80000	894.48	878.64	864.98	853.15	842.87	833.90	826.07	819.21
85000	950.39	933.56	919.04	906.47	895.55	886.02	877.70	870.41
90000	1006.29	988.47	973.10	959.79	948.22	938.14	929.33	921.61
95000	1062.20	1043.39	1027.16	1013.11	1000.90	990.26	980.96	972.81
100000	1118.10	1098.30	1081.22	1066.43	1053.58	1042.38	1032.59	1024.01
105000	1174.01	1153.22	1135.28	1119.76	1106.26	1094.50	1084.22	1075.21
110000	1229.91	1208.13	1189.34	1173.08	1158.94	1146.62	1135.84	1126.41
115000	1285.82	1263.04	1243.41	1226.40	1211.62	1198.74	1187.47	1177.61
120000	1341.72	1317.96	1297.47	1279.72	1264.30	1250.85	1239.10	1228.81
125000	1397.63	1372.87	1351.53	1333.04	1316.98	1302.97	1290.73	1280.01
130000	1453.53	1427.79	1405.59	1386.36	1369.66	1355.09	1342.36	1331.21
135000	1509.43	1482.70	1459.65	1439.69	1422.33	1407.21	1393.99	1382.41
140000	1565.34	1537.62	1513.71	1493.01	1475.01	1459.33	1445.62	1433.61
145000	1621.24	1592.53	1567.77	1546.33	1527.69	1511.45	1497.25	1484.81
150000	1677.15	1647.45	1621.83	1599.65	1580.37	1563.57	1548.88	1536.01
155000	1733.05	1702.36	1675.89	1652.97	1633.05	1615.68	1600.51	1587.21
160000	1788.96	1757.28	1729.95	1706.29	1685.73	1667.80	1652.14	1638.41

MONTHLY AMORTIZING PAYMENTS 11½%

AMOUNT OF LOAN	NUMBER OF YEARS IN TERM							
	25	26	27	28	29	30	35	40
$ 50	.51	.51	.51	.50	.50	.50	.49	.49
100	1.02	1.01	1.01	1.00	1.00	1.00	.98	.97
200	2.04	2.02	2.01	2.00	1.99	1.99	1.96	1.94
300	3.05	3.03	3.02	3.00	2.99	2.98	2.93	2.91
400	4.07	4.04	4.02	4.00	3.98	3.97	3.91	3.88
500	5.09	5.05	5.03	5.00	4.98	4.96	4.89	4.85
600	6.10	6.06	6.03	6.00	5.97	5.95	5.86	5.81
700	7.12	7.07	7.03	7.00	6.97	6.94	6.84	6.78
800	8.14	8.08	8.04	8.00	7.96	7.93	7.81	7.75
900	9.15	9.09	9.04	8.99	8.95	8.92	8.79	8.72
1000	10.17	10.10	10.05	9.99	9.95	9.91	9.77	9.69
2000	20.33	20.20	20.09	19.98	19.89	19.81	19.53	19.37
3000	30.50	30.30	30.13	29.97	29.83	29.71	29.29	29.05
4000	40.66	40.40	40.17	39.96	39.78	39.62	39.05	38.74
5000	50.83	50.50	50.21	49.95	49.72	49.52	48.81	48.42
6000	60.99	60.60	60.25	59.94	59.66	59.42	58.57	58.10
7000	71.16	70.69	70.29	69.93	69.61	69.33	68.33	67.78
8000	81.32	80.79	80.33	79.91	79.55	79.23	78.09	77.47
9000	91.49	90.89	90.37	89.90	89.49	89.13	87.85	87.15
10000	101.65	100.99	100.41	99.89	99.44	99.03	97.62	96.83
11000	111.82	111.09	110.45	109.88	109.38	108.94	107.38	106.52
12000	121.98	121.19	120.49	119.87	119.32	118.84	117.14	116.20
13000	132.15	131.28	130.53	129.86	129.27	128.74	126.90	125.88
14000	142.31	141.38	140.57	139.85	139.21	138.65	136.66	135.56
15000	152.48	151.48	150.61	149.83	149.15	148.55	146.42	145.25
16000	162.64	161.58	160.65	159.82	159.09	158.45	156.18	154.93
17000	172.80	171.68	170.69	169.81	169.04	168.35	165.94	164.61
18000	182.97	181.78	180.73	179.80	178.98	178.26	175.70	174.30
19000	193.13	191.88	190.77	189.79	188.92	188.16	185.47	183.98
20000	203.30	201.97	200.81	199.78	198.87	198.06	195.23	193.66
21000	213.46	212.07	210.85	209.77	208.81	207.97	204.99	203.34
22000	223.63	222.17	220.89	219.75	218.75	217.87	214.75	213.03
23000	233.79	232.27	230.93	229.74	228.70	227.77	224.51	222.71
24000	243.96	242.37	240.97	239.73	238.64	237.67	234.27	232.39
25000	254.12	252.47	251.01	249.72	248.58	247.58	244.03	242.08
26000	264.29	262.56	261.05	259.71	258.53	257.48	253.79	251.76
27000	274.45	272.66	271.09	269.70	268.47	267.38	263.55	261.44
28000	284.62	282.76	281.13	279.69	278.41	277.29	273.32	271.12
29000	294.78	292.86	291.17	289.67	288.36	287.19	283.08	280.81
30000	304.95	302.96	301.21	299.66	298.30	297.09	292.84	290.49
31000	315.11	313.06	311.25	309.65	308.24	307.00	302.60	300.17
32000	325.28	323.16	321.29	319.64	318.18	316.90	312.36	309.86
33000	335.44	333.25	331.33	329.63	328.13	326.80	322.12	319.54
34000	345.60	343.35	341.37	339.62	338.07	336.70	331.88	329.22
35000	355.77	353.45	351.41	349.61	348.01	346.61	341.64	338.90
40000	406.59	403.94	401.61	399.55	397.73	396.12	390.45	387.32
45000	457.42	454.43	451.81	449.49	447.45	445.64	439.25	435.73
50000	508.24	504.93	502.01	499.43	497.16	495.15	488.06	484.15
55000	559.06	555.42	552.21	549.38	546.88	544.67	536.86	532.56
60000	609.89	605.91	602.41	599.32	596.59	594.18	585.67	580.97
65000	660.71	656.40	652.61	649.26	646.31	643.69	634.47	629.39
70000	711.53	706.90	702.81	699.21	696.02	693.21	683.28	677.80
75000	762.36	757.39	753.01	749.15	745.74	742.72	732.09	726.22
80000	813.18	807.88	803.21	799.09	795.45	792.24	780.89	774.63
85000	864.00	858.37	853.41	849.04	845.17	841.75	829.70	823.04
90000	914.83	908.86	903.61	898.98	894.89	891.27	878.50	871.46
95000	965.65	959.36	953.81	948.92	944.60	940.78	927.31	919.87
100000	1016.47	1009.85	1004.01	998.86	994.32	990.30	976.11	968.29
105000	1067.30	1060.34	1054.21	1048.81	1044.03	1039.81	1024.92	1016.70
110000	1118.12	1110.83	1104.41	1098.75	1093.75	1089.33	1073.72	1065.12
115000	1168.94	1161.33	1154.61	1148.69	1143.46	1138.84	1122.53	1113.53
120000	1219.77	1211.82	1204.81	1198.64	1193.18	1188.35	1171.33	1161.94
125000	1270.59	1262.31	1255.01	1248.58	1242.90	1237.87	1220.14	1210.36
130000	1321.41	1312.80	1305.22	1298.52	1292.61	1287.38	1268.94	1258.77
135000	1372.24	1363.29	1355.42	1348.47	1342.33	1336.90	1317.75	1307.19
140000	1423.06	1413.79	1405.62	1398.41	1392.04	1386.41	1366.56	1355.60
145000	1473.88	1464.28	1455.82	1448.35	1441.76	1435.93	1415.36	1404.01
150000	1524.71	1514.77	1506.02	1498.29	1491.47	1485.44	1464.17	1452.43
155000	1575.53	1565.26	1556.22	1548.24	1541.19	1534.96	1512.97	1500.84
160000	1626.36	1615.76	1606.42	1598.18	1590.90	1584.47	1561.78	1549.26

MONTHLY AMORTIZING PAYMENTS

AMOUNT OF LOAN	NUMBER OF YEARS IN TERM							
	1	1-1/2	2	3	4	5	6	7
$ 50	4.44	3.05	2.35	1.66	1.31	1.11	.97	.88
100	8.87	6.09	4.69	3.31	2.62	2.21	1.94	1.75
200	17.74	12.17	9.38	6.61	5.24	4.42	3.88	3.50
300	26.61	18.25	14.07	9.92	7.85	6.62	5.81	5.24
400	35.47	24.33	18.76	13.22	10.47	8.83	7.75	6.99
500	44.34	30.41	23.45	16.52	13.08	11.03	9.68	8.73
600	53.21	36.49	28.14	19.83	15.70	13.24	11.62	10.48
700	62.08	42.57	32.83	23.13	18.31	15.44	13.55	12.22
800	70.94	48.65	37.52	26.43	20.93	17.65	15.49	13.97
900	79.81	54.73	42.21	29.74	23.54	19.85	17.43	15.71
1000	88.68	60.81	46.90	33.04	26.16	22.06	19.36	17.46
2000	177.35	121.62	93.80	66.08	52.31	44.12	38.72	34.91
3000	266.03	182.43	140.70	99.11	78.46	66.17	58.07	52.36
4000	354.70	243.24	187.60	132.15	104.61	88.23	77.43	69.82
5000	443.37	304.04	234.50	165.18	130.76	110.28	96.78	87.27
6000	532.05	364.85	281.40	198.22	156.91	132.34	116.14	104.72
7000	620.72	425.66	328.29	231.25	183.06	154.39	135.50	122.17
8000	709.39	486.47	375.19	264.29	209.21	176.45	154.85	139.63
9000	798.07	547.28	422.09	297.32	235.36	198.50	174.21	157.08
10000	886.74	608.08	468.99	330.36	261.51	220.56	193.56	174.53
11000	975.41	668.89	515.89	363.40	287.66	242.61	212.92	191.99
12000	1064.09	729.70	562.79	396.43	313.81	264.67	232.27	209.44
13000	1152.76	790.51	609.69	429.47	339.96	286.73	251.63	226.89
14000	1241.43	851.32	656.58	462.50	366.11	308.78	270.99	244.34
15000	1330.11	912.12	703.48	495.54	392.26	330.84	290.34	261.80
16000	1418.78	972.93	750.38	528.57	418.41	352.89	309.70	279.25
17000	1507.45	1033.74	797.28	561.61	444.56	374.95	329.05	296.70
18000	1596.13	1094.55	844.18	594.64	470.71	397.00	348.41	314.16
19000	1684.80	1155.36	891.08	627.68	496.86	419.06	367.76	331.61
20000	1773.47	1216.16	937.98	660.71	523.01	441.11	387.12	349.06
21000	1862.15	1276.97	984.87	693.75	549.16	463.17	406.48	366.51
22000	1950.82	1337.78	1031.77	726.79	575.31	485.22	425.83	383.97
23000	2039.49	1398.59	1078.67	759.82	601.46	507.28	445.19	401.42
24000	2128.17	1459.40	1125.57	792.86	627.61	529.33	464.54	418.87
25000	2216.84	1520.20	1172.47	825.89	653.76	551.39	483.90	436.33
26000	2305.51	1581.01	1219.37	858.93	679.91	573.45	503.25	453.78
27000	2394.19	1641.82	1266.27	891.96	706.06	595.50	522.61	471.23
28000	2482.86	1702.63	1313.16	925.00	732.21	617.56	541.97	488.68
29000	2571.54	1763.44	1360.06	958.03	758.36	639.61	561.32	506.14
30000	2660.21	1824.24	1406.96	991.07	784.51	661.67	580.68	523.59
31000	2748.88	1885.05	1453.86	1024.11	810.66	683.72	600.03	541.04
32000	2837.56	1945.86	1500.76	1057.14	836.81	705.78	619.39	558.50
33000	2926.23	2006.67	1547.66	1090.18	862.96	727.83	638.74	575.95
34000	3014.90	2067.48	1594.56	1123.21	889.11	749.89	658.10	593.40
35000	3103.58	2128.28	1641.45	1156.25	915.26	771.94	677.46	610.85
40000	3546.94	2432.32	1875.95	1321.42	1046.01	882.22	774.23	698.12
45000	3990.31	2736.36	2110.44	1486.60	1176.76	992.50	871.01	785.38
50000	4433.68	3040.40	2344.93	1651.78	1307.51	1102.78	967.79	872.65
55000	4877.05	3344.44	2579.42	1816.96	1438.26	1213.05	1064.57	959.91
60000	5320.41	3648.48	2813.92	1982.13	1569.01	1323.33	1161.35	1047.17
65000	5763.78	3952.52	3048.41	2147.31	1699.76	1433.61	1258.13	1134.44
70000	6207.15	4256.56	3282.90	2312.49	1830.51	1543.88	1354.91	1221.70
75000	6650.51	4560.60	3517.40	2477.67	1961.26	1654.16	1451.68	1308.97
80000	7093.88	4864.64	3751.89	2642.84	2092.01	1764.44	1548.46	1396.23
85000	7537.25	5168.68	3986.38	2808.02	2222.76	1874.72	1645.24	1483.49
90000	7980.62	5472.72	4220.87	2973.20	2353.51	1984.99	1742.02	1570.76
95000	8423.98	5776.76	4455.37	3138.38	2484.26	2095.27	1838.80	1658.02
100000	8867.35	6080.80	4689.86	3303.55	2615.01	2205.55	1935.58	1745.29
105000	9310.72	6384.84	4924.35	3468.73	2745.76	2315.82	2032.36	1832.55
110000	9754.09	6688.88	5158.84	3633.91	2876.51	2426.10	2129.14	1919.82
115000	10197.45	6992.92	5393.34	3799.09	3007.27	2536.38	2225.91	2007.08
120000	10640.82	7296.96	5627.83	3964.26	3138.02	2646.65	2322.69	2094.34
125000	11084.19	7601.00	5862.32	4129.44	3268.77	2756.93	2419.47	2181.61
130000	11527.55	7905.04	6096.82	4294.62	3399.52	2867.21	2516.25	2268.87
135000	11970.92	8209.08	6331.31	4459.80	3530.27	2977.49	2613.03	2356.14
140000	12414.29	8513.12	6565.80	4624.97	3661.02	3087.76	2709.81	2443.40
145000	12857.66	8817.16	6800.29	4790.15	3791.77	3198.04	2806.59	2530.66
150000	13301.02	9121.20	7034.79	4955.33	3922.52	3308.32	2903.36	2617.93
155000	13744.39	9425.24	7269.28	5120.51	4053.27	3418.59	3000.14	2705.19
160000	14187.76	9729.28	7503.77	5285.68	4184.02	3528.87	3096.92	2792.46

AMOUNT OF LOAN	NUMBER OF YEARS IN TERM							
	8	9	10	11	12	14	15	16
$ 50	.81	.75	.71	.68	.65	.61	.59	.58
100	1.61	1.50	1.42	1.35	1.30	1.21	1.18	1.15
200	3.21	3.00	2.83	2.70	2.59	2.42	2.36	2.30
300	4.82	4.50	4.24	4.04	3.88	3.63	3.53	3.45
400	6.42	5.99	5.66	5.39	5.17	4.84	4.71	4.60
500	8.03	7.49	7.07	6.73	6.46	6.04	5.89	5.75
600	9.63	8.99	8.48	8.08	7.75	7.25	7.06	6.90
700	11.24	10.49	9.90	9.42	9.04	8.46	8.24	8.05
800	12.84	11.98	11.31	10.77	10.33	9.67	9.41	9.20
900	14.45	13.48	12.72	12.12	11.62	10.88	10.59	10.35
1000	16.05	14.98	14.14	13.46	12.91	12.08	11.77	11.50
2000	32.10	29.95	28.27	26.92	25.82	24.16	23.53	22.99
3000	48.15	44.93	42.40	40.38	38.73	36.24	35.29	34.48
4000	64.20	59.90	56.53	53.83	51.64	48.32	47.05	45.98
5000	80.24	74.87	70.66	67.29	64.55	60.40	58.81	57.47
6000	96.29	89.85	84.79	80.75	77.45	72.48	70.57	68.96
7000	112.34	104.82	98.92	94.20	90.36	84.56	82.34	80.45
8000	128.39	119.79	113.05	107.66	103.27	96.63	94.10	91.95
9000	144.43	134.77	127.19	121.12	116.18	108.71	105.86	103.44
10000	160.48	149.74	141.32	134.57	129.09	120.79	117.62	114.93
11000	176.53	164.71	155.45	148.03	141.99	132.87	129.38	126.42
12000	192.58	179.69	169.58	161.49	154.90	144.95	141.14	137.92
13000	208.62	194.66	183.71	174.94	167.81	157.03	152.90	149.41
14000	224.67	209.63	197.84	188.40	180.72	169.11	164.67	160.90
15000	240.72	224.61	211.97	201.86	193.63	181.18	176.43	172.40
16000	256.77	239.58	226.10	215.31	206.53	193.26	188.19	183.89
17000	272.81	254.56	240.23	228.77	219.44	205.34	199.95	195.38
18000	288.86	269.53	254.37	242.23	232.35	217.42	211.71	206.87
19000	304.91	284.50	268.50	255.68	245.26	229.50	223.47	218.37
20000	320.96	299.48	282.63	269.14	258.17	241.58	235.23	229.86
21000	337.00	314.45	296.76	282.60	271.08	253.66	247.00	241.35
22000	353.05	329.42	310.89	296.05	283.98	265.74	258.76	252.84
23000	369.10	344.40	325.02	309.51	296.89	277.81	270.52	264.34
24000	385.15	359.37	339.15	322.97	309.80	289.89	282.28	275.83
25000	401.19	374.34	353.28	336.42	322.71	301.97	294.04	287.32
26000	417.24	389.32	367.41	349.88	335.62	314.05	305.80	298.81
27000	433.29	404.29	381.55	363.34	348.52	326.13	317.57	310.31
28000	449.34	419.26	395.68	376.80	361.43	338.21	329.33	321.80
29000	465.38	434.24	409.81	390.25	374.34	350.29	341.09	333.29
30000	481.43	449.21	423.94	403.71	387.25	362.36	352.85	344.79
31000	497.48	464.18	438.07	417.17	400.16	374.44	364.61	356.28
32000	513.53	479.16	452.20	430.62	413.06	386.52	376.37	367.77
33000	529.57	494.13	466.33	444.08	425.97	398.60	388.13	379.26
34000	545.62	509.11	480.46	457.54	438.88	410.68	399.90	390.76
35000	561.67	524.08	494.60	470.99	451.79	422.76	411.66	402.25
40000	641.91	598.95	565.25	538.28	516.33	483.15	470.46	459.71
45000	722.14	673.81	635.91	605.56	580.87	543.54	529.27	517.18
50000	802.38	748.68	706.56	672.84	645.41	603.94	588.08	574.64
55000	882.62	823.55	777.22	740.13	709.95	664.33	646.89	632.10
60000	962.86	898.42	847.87	807.41	774.49	724.72	705.69	689.57
65000	1043.09	973.29	918.53	874.70	839.03	785.12	764.50	747.03
70000	1123.33	1048.15	989.19	941.98	903.57	845.51	823.31	804.49
75000	1203.57	1123.02	1059.84	1009.26	968.11	905.90	882.12	861.96
80000	1283.81	1197.89	1130.50	1076.55	1032.65	966.30	940.92	919.42
85000	1364.04	1272.76	1201.15	1143.83	1097.19	1026.69	999.73	976.88
90000	1444.28	1347.62	1271.81	1211.12	1161.73	1087.08	1058.54	1034.35
95000	1524.52	1422.49	1342.46	1278.40	1226.27	1147.48	1117.35	1091.81
100000	1604.76	1497.36	1413.12	1345.68	1290.82	1207.87	1176.15	1149.27
105000	1684.99	1572.23	1483.78	1412.97	1355.36	1268.26	1234.96	1206.74
110000	1765.23	1647.09	1554.43	1480.25	1419.90	1328.66	1293.77	1264.20
115000	1845.47	1721.96	1625.09	1547.54	1484.44	1389.05	1352.58	1321.66
120000	1925.71	1796.83	1695.74	1614.82	1548.98	1449.44	1411.38	1379.13
125000	2005.94	1871.70	1766.40	1682.10	1613.52	1509.84	1470.19	1436.59
130000	2086.18	1946.57	1837.05	1749.39	1678.06	1570.23	1529.00	1494.05
135000	2166.42	2021.43	1907.71	1816.67	1742.60	1630.62	1587.81	1551.52
140000	2246.66	2096.30	1978.37	1883.96	1807.14	1691.02	1646.61	1608.98
145000	2326.89	2171.17	2049.02	1951.24	1871.68	1751.41	1705.42	1666.44
150000	2407.13	2246.04	2119.68	2018.52	1936.22	1811.80	1764.23	1723.91
155000	2487.37	2320.90	2190.33	2085.81	2000.76	1872.19	1823.04	1781.37
160000	2567.61	2395.77	2260.99	2153.09	2065.30	1932.59	1881.84	1838.83

11⅝%

MONTHLY AMORTIZING PAYMENTS

AMOUNT OF LOAN	NUMBER OF YEARS IN TERM							
	17	18	19	20	21	22	23	24
$ 50	.57	.56	.55	.54	.54	.53	.53	.52
100	1.13	1.11	1.09	1.08	1.07	1.06	1.05	1.04
200	2.26	2.22	2.18	2.16	2.13	2.11	2.09	2.07
300	3.38	3.33	3.27	3.23	3.19	3.16	3.13	3.10
400	4.51	4.43	4.36	4.31	4.25	4.21	4.17	4.14
500	5.64	5.54	5.45	5.38	5.32	5.26	5.21	5.17
600	6.76	6.65	6.54	6.46	6.38	6.31	6.25	6.20
700	7.89	7.75	7.63	7.53	7.44	7.36	7.30	7.24
800	9.02	8.86	8.72	8.61	8.50	8.41	8.34	8.27
900	10.14	9.97	9.81	9.68	9.57	9.47	9.38	9.30
1000	11.27	11.07	10.90	10.76	10.63	10.52	10.42	10.34
2000	22.53	22.14	21.80	21.51	21.25	21.03	20.84	20.67
3000	33.80	33.21	32.70	32.26	31.87	31.54	31.25	31.00
4000	45.06	44.27	43.59	43.01	42.50	42.05	41.67	41.33
5000	56.32	55.34	54.49	53.76	53.12	52.57	52.08	51.66
6000	67.59	66.41	65.39	64.51	63.74	63.08	62.50	61.99
7000	78.85	77.47	76.29	75.26	74.37	73.59	72.91	72.32
8000	90.11	88.54	87.18	86.01	84.99	84.10	83.33	82.65
9000	101.38	99.61	98.08	96.76	95.61	94.62	93.74	92.98
10000	112.64	110.67	108.98	107.51	106.24	105.13	104.16	103.31
11000	123.90	121.74	119.87	118.26	116.86	115.64	114.57	113.64
12000	135.17	132.81	130.77	129.01	127.48	126.15	124.99	123.97
13000	146.43	143.87	141.67	139.76	138.11	136.66	135.41	134.30
14000	157.69	154.94	152.57	150.51	148.73	147.18	145.82	144.63
15000	168.96	166.01	163.46	161.26	159.35	157.69	156.24	154.96
16000	180.22	177.07	174.36	172.01	169.98	168.20	166.65	165.29
17000	191.48	188.14	185.26	182.76	180.60	178.71	177.07	175.63
18000	202.75	199.21	196.15	193.51	191.22	189.23	187.48	185.96
19000	214.01	210.27	207.05	204.27	201.85	199.74	197.90	196.29
20000	225.27	221.34	217.95	215.02	212.47	210.25	208.31	206.62
21000	236.54	232.41	228.85	225.77	223.09	220.76	218.73	216.95
22000	247.80	243.47	239.74	236.52	233.72	231.27	229.14	227.28
23000	259.06	254.54	250.64	247.27	244.34	241.79	239.56	237.61
24000	270.33	265.61	261.54	258.02	254.96	252.30	249.97	247.94
25000	281.59	276.67	272.44	268.77	265.58	262.81	260.39	258.27
26000	292.85	287.74	283.33	279.52	276.21	273.32	270.81	268.60
27000	304.12	298.81	294.23	290.27	286.83	283.84	281.22	278.93
28000	315.38	309.87	305.13	301.02	297.45	294.35	291.64	289.26
29000	326.64	320.94	316.02	311.77	308.08	304.86	302.05	299.59
30000	337.91	332.01	326.92	322.52	318.70	315.37	312.47	309.92
31000	349.17	343.07	337.82	333.27	329.32	325.89	322.88	320.25
32000	360.43	354.14	348.72	344.02	339.95	336.40	333.30	330.58
33000	371.70	365.21	359.61	354.77	350.57	346.91	343.71	340.91
34000	382.96	376.27	370.51	365.52	361.19	357.42	354.13	351.25
35000	394.22	387.34	381.41	376.27	371.82	367.93	364.54	361.58
40000	450.54	442.67	435.89	430.03	424.93	420.50	416.62	413.23
45000	506.86	498.01	490.38	483.78	478.05	473.06	468.70	464.88
50000	563.17	553.34	544.87	537.53	531.16	525.62	520.77	516.53
55000	619.49	608.67	599.35	591.29	584.28	578.18	572.85	568.19
60000	675.81	664.01	653.84	645.04	637.40	630.74	624.93	619.84
65000	732.13	719.34	708.32	698.79	690.51	683.30	677.01	671.49
70000	788.44	774.67	762.81	752.54	743.63	735.86	729.08	723.15
75000	844.76	830.01	817.30	806.30	796.74	788.43	781.16	774.80
80000	901.08	885.34	871.78	860.05	849.86	840.99	833.24	826.45
85000	957.39	940.68	926.27	913.80	902.98	893.55	885.31	878.11
90000	1013.71	996.01	980.75	967.55	956.09	946.11	937.39	929.76
95000	1070.03	1051.34	1035.24	1021.31	1009.21	998.67	989.47	981.41
100000	1126.34	1106.68	1089.73	1075.06	1062.32	1051.23	1041.54	1033.06
105000	1182.66	1162.01	1144.21	1128.81	1115.44	1103.79	1093.62	1084.72
110000	1238.98	1217.34	1198.70	1182.57	1168.56	1156.35	1145.70	1136.37
115000	1295.29	1272.68	1253.19	1236.32	1221.67	1208.92	1197.78	1188.02
120000	1351.61	1328.01	1307.67	1290.07	1274.79	1261.48	1249.85	1239.68
125000	1407.93	1383.34	1362.16	1343.82	1327.90	1314.04	1301.93	1291.33
130000	1464.25	1438.68	1416.64	1397.58	1381.02	1366.60	1354.01	1342.98
135000	1520.56	1494.01	1471.13	1451.33	1434.14	1419.16	1406.08	1394.64
140000	1576.88	1549.34	1525.62	1505.08	1487.25	1471.72	1458.16	1446.29
145000	1633.20	1604.68	1580.10	1558.84	1540.37	1524.28	1510.24	1497.94
150000	1689.51	1660.01	1634.59	1612.59	1593.48	1576.85	1562.31	1549.59
155000	1745.83	1715.35	1689.07	1666.34	1646.60	1629.41	1614.39	1601.25
160000	1802.15	1770.68	1743.56	1720.09	1699.72	1681.97	1666.47	1652.90

AMOUNT OF LOAN	NUMBER OF YEARS IN TERM 25	26	27	28	29	30	35	40
$ 50	.52	.51	.51	.51	.51	.50	.50	.49
100	1.03	1.02	1.02	1.01	1.01	1.00	.99	.98
200	2.06	2.04	2.03	2.02	2.01	2.00	1.98	1.96
300	3.08	3.06	3.04	3.03	3.02	3.00	2.96	2.94
400	4.11	4.08	4.06	4.04	4.02	4.00	3.95	3.92
500	5.13	5.10	5.07	5.05	5.02	5.00	4.93	4.90
600	6.16	6.12	6.08	6.05	6.03	6.00	5.92	5.87
700	7.18	7.14	7.10	7.06	7.03	7.00	6.91	6.85
800	8.21	8.16	8.11	8.07	8.04	8.00	7.89	7.83
900	9.24	9.18	9.12	9.08	9.04	9.00	8.88	8.81
1000	10.26	10.20	10.14	10.09	10.04	10.00	9.86	9.79
2000	20.52	20.39	20.27	20.17	20.08	20.00	19.72	19.57
3000	30.77	30.58	30.40	30.25	30.12	30.00	29.58	29.35
4000	41.03	40.77	40.54	40.34	40.16	40.00	39.44	39.14
5000	51.29	50.96	50.67	50.42	50.19	50.00	49.30	48.92
6000	61.54	61.15	60.80	60.50	60.23	60.00	59.16	58.70
7000	71.80	71.34	70.94	70.58	70.27	69.99	69.02	68.49
8000	82.05	81.53	81.07	80.67	80.31	79.99	78.88	78.27
9000	92.31	91.72	91.20	90.75	90.35	89.99	88.74	88.05
10000	102.57	101.91	101.34	100.83	100.38	99.99	98.60	97.84
11000	112.82	112.10	111.47	110.91	110.42	109.99	108.46	107.62
12000	123.08	122.30	121.60	121.00	120.46	119.99	118.32	117.40
13000	133.34	132.49	131.74	131.08	130.50	129.98	128.18	127.19
14000	143.59	142.68	141.87	141.16	140.54	139.98	138.04	136.97
15000	153.85	152.87	152.00	151.24	150.57	149.98	147.90	146.75
16000	164.10	163.06	162.14	161.33	160.61	159.98	157.76	156.54
17000	174.36	173.25	172.27	171.41	170.65	169.98	167.62	166.32
18000	184.62	183.44	182.40	181.49	180.69	179.98	177.47	176.10
19000	194.87	193.63	192.54	191.58	190.73	189.97	187.33	185.89
20000	205.13	203.82	202.67	201.66	200.76	199.97	197.19	195.67
21000	215.39	214.01	212.80	211.74	210.80	209.97	207.05	205.45
22000	225.64	224.20	222.94	221.82	220.84	219.97	216.91	215.23
23000	235.90	234.39	233.07	231.91	230.88	229.97	226.77	225.02
24000	246.15	244.59	243.20	241.99	240.91	239.97	236.63	234.80
25000	256.41	254.78	253.34	252.07	250.95	249.96	246.49	244.58
26000	266.67	264.97	263.47	262.15	260.99	259.96	256.35	254.37
27000	276.92	275.16	273.60	272.24	271.03	269.96	266.21	264.15
28000	287.18	285.35	283.74	282.32	281.07	279.96	276.07	273.93
29000	297.44	295.54	293.87	292.40	291.10	289.96	285.93	283.72
30000	307.69	305.73	304.00	302.48	301.14	299.96	295.79	293.50
31000	317.95	315.92	314.14	312.57	311.18	309.96	305.65	303.28
32000	328.20	326.11	324.27	322.65	321.22	319.95	315.51	313.07
33000	338.46	336.30	334.40	332.73	331.26	329.95	325.37	322.85
34000	348.72	346.49	344.54	342.81	341.29	339.95	335.23	332.63
35000	358.97	356.68	354.67	352.90	351.33	349.95	345.08	342.42
40000	410.25	407.64	405.34	403.31	401.52	399.94	394.38	391.33
45000	461.53	458.59	456.00	453.72	451.71	449.93	443.68	440.25
50000	512.82	509.55	506.67	504.14	501.90	499.92	492.98	489.16
55000	564.10	560.50	557.34	554.55	552.09	549.92	542.27	538.08
60000	615.38	611.46	608.00	604.96	602.28	599.91	591.57	586.99
65000	666.66	662.41	658.67	655.38	652.47	649.90	640.87	635.91
70000	717.94	713.36	709.34	705.79	702.66	699.89	690.16	684.83
75000	769.22	764.32	760.00	756.20	752.85	749.88	739.46	733.74
80000	820.50	815.27	810.67	806.62	803.04	799.88	788.76	782.66
85000	871.78	866.23	861.34	857.03	853.23	849.87	838.06	831.57
90000	923.06	917.18	912.00	907.44	903.42	899.86	887.35	880.49
95000	974.35	968.14	962.67	957.86	953.61	949.85	936.65	929.41
100000	1025.63	1019.09	1013.34	1008.27	1003.80	999.84	985.95	978.32
105000	1076.91	1070.04	1064.00	1058.68	1053.99	1049.84	1035.24	1027.24
110000	1128.19	1121.00	1114.67	1109.10	1104.17	1099.83	1084.54	1076.15
115000	1179.47	1171.95	1165.34	1159.51	1154.36	1149.82	1133.84	1125.07
120000	1230.75	1222.91	1216.00	1209.92	1204.55	1199.81	1183.14	1173.98
125000	1282.03	1273.86	1266.67	1260.33	1254.74	1249.80	1232.43	1222.90
130000	1333.31	1324.82	1317.34	1310.75	1304.93	1299.80	1281.73	1271.82
135000	1384.59	1375.77	1368.00	1361.16	1355.12	1349.79	1331.03	1320.73
140000	1435.87	1426.72	1418.67	1411.57	1405.31	1399.78	1380.32	1369.65
145000	1487.16	1477.68	1469.34	1461.99	1455.50	1449.77	1429.62	1418.56
150000	1538.44	1528.63	1520.00	1512.40	1505.69	1499.76	1478.92	1467.48
155000	1589.72	1579.59	1570.67	1562.81	1555.88	1549.76	1528.21	1516.39
160000	1641.00	1630.54	1621.34	1613.23	1606.07	1599.75	1577.51	1565.31

11¾% MONTHLY AMORTIZING PAYMENTS

AMOUNT OF LOAN	NUMBER OF YEARS IN TERM							
	1	1-1/2	2	3	4	5	6	7
$ 50	4.44	3.05	2.35	1.66	1.32	1.11	.98	.88
100	8.88	6.09	4.70	3.31	2.63	2.22	1.95	1.76
200	17.75	12.18	9.40	6.62	5.25	4.43	3.89	3.51
300	26.62	18.26	14.09	9.93	7.87	6.64	5.83	5.26
400	35.50	24.35	18.79	13.24	10.49	8.85	7.77	7.01
500	44.37	30.44	23.48	16.55	13.11	11.06	9.72	8.76
600	53.24	36.52	28.18	19.86	15.73	13.28	11.66	10.52
700	62.12	42.61	32.87	23.17	18.35	15.49	13.60	12.27
800	70.99	48.70	37.57	26.48	20.97	17.70	15.54	14.02
900	79.86	54.78	42.27	29.79	23.60	19.91	17.48	15.77
1000	88.74	60.87	46.96	33.10	26.22	22.12	19.43	17.52
2000	177.47	121.74	93.92	66.20	52.43	44.24	38.85	35.04
3000	266.20	182.60	140.88	99.29	78.64	66.36	58.27	52.56
4000	354.93	243.47	187.83	132.39	104.85	88.48	77.69	70.08
5000	443.66	304.33	234.79	165.48	131.06	110.60	97.11	87.60
6000	532.40	365.20	281.75	198.58	157.27	132.71	116.53	105.12
7000	621.13	426.07	328.70	231.67	183.48	154.83	135.95	122.64
8000	709.86	486.93	375.66	264.77	209.70	176.95	155.37	140.16
9000	798.59	547.80	422.62	297.86	235.91	199.07	174.79	157.68
10000	887.32	608.66	469.57	330.96	262.12	221.19	194.21	175.20
11000	976.06	669.53	516.53	364.05	288.33	243.31	213.63	192.72
12000	1064.79	730.40	563.49	397.15	314.54	265.42	233.05	210.24
13000	1153.52	791.26	610.44	430.24	340.75	287.54	252.47	227.76
14000	1242.25	852.13	657.40	463.34	366.96	309.66	271.89	245.28
15000	1330.98	912.99	704.36	496.43	393.17	331.78	291.31	262.79
16000	1419.72	973.86	751.31	529.53	419.39	353.90	310.73	280.31
17000	1508.45	1034.73	798.27	562.62	445.60	376.02	330.15	297.83
18000	1597.18	1095.59	845.23	595.72	471.81	398.13	349.57	315.35
19000	1685.91	1156.46	892.18	628.81	498.02	420.25	368.99	332.87
20000	1774.64	1217.32	939.14	661.91	524.23	442.37	388.41	350.39
21000	1863.37	1278.19	986.10	695.00	550.44	464.49	407.83	367.91
22000	1952.11	1339.06	1033.05	728.10	576.65	486.61	427.25	385.43
23000	2040.84	1399.92	1080.01	761.19	602.86	508.73	446.67	402.95
24000	2129.57	1460.79	1126.97	794.29	629.08	530.84	466.10	420.47
25000	2218.30	1521.65	1173.93	827.38	655.29	552.96	485.52	437.99
26000	2307.03	1582.52	1220.88	860.48	681.50	575.08	504.94	455.51
27000	2395.77	1643.39	1267.84	893.57	707.71	597.20	524.36	473.03
28000	2484.50	1704.25	1314.80	926.67	733.92	619.32	543.78	490.55
29000	2573.23	1765.12	1361.75	959.76	760.13	641.44	563.20	508.07
30000	2661.96	1825.98	1408.71	992.86	786.34	663.55	582.62	525.58
31000	2750.69	1886.85	1455.67	1025.95	812.55	685.67	602.04	543.10
32000	2839.43	1947.72	1502.62	1059.05	838.77	707.79	621.46	560.62
33000	2928.16	2008.58	1549.58	1092.14	864.98	729.91	640.88	578.14
34000	3016.89	2069.45	1596.54	1125.24	891.19	752.03	660.30	595.66
35000	3105.62	2130.31	1643.49	1158.33	917.40	774.15	679.72	613.18
40000	3549.28	2434.64	1878.28	1323.81	1048.46	884.74	776.82	700.78
45000	3992.94	2738.97	2113.06	1489.28	1179.51	995.33	873.92	788.37
50000	4436.60	3043.30	2347.85	1654.76	1310.57	1105.92	971.03	875.97
55000	4880.26	3347.63	2582.63	1820.23	1441.62	1216.51	1068.13	963.57
60000	5323.92	3651.96	2817.41	1985.71	1572.68	1327.10	1165.23	1051.16
65000	5767.58	3956.29	3052.20	2151.18	1703.74	1437.70	1262.33	1138.76
70000	6211.24	4260.62	3286.98	2316.66	1834.79	1548.29	1359.44	1226.36
75000	6654.90	4564.95	3521.77	2482.13	1965.85	1658.88	1456.54	1313.95
80000	7098.56	4869.28	3756.55	2647.61	2096.91	1769.47	1553.64	1401.55
85000	7542.21	5173.61	3991.33	2813.08	2227.96	1880.06	1650.74	1489.15
90000	7985.87	5477.94	4226.12	2978.56	2359.02	1990.65	1747.84	1576.74
95000	8429.53	5782.27	4460.90	3144.03	2490.07	2101.25	1844.95	1664.34
100000	8873.19	6086.60	4695.69	3309.51	2621.13	2211.84	1942.05	1751.94
105000	9316.85	6390.93	4930.47	3474.98	2752.19	2322.43	2039.15	1839.53
110000	9760.51	6695.26	5165.25	3640.46	2883.24	2433.02	2136.25	1927.13
115000	10204.17	6999.59	5400.04	3805.93	3014.30	2543.61	2233.35	2014.73
120000	10647.83	7303.92	5634.82	3971.41	3145.36	2654.20	2330.46	2102.32
125000	11091.49	7608.25	5869.61	4136.88	3276.41	2764.80	2427.56	2189.92
130000	11535.15	7912.58	6104.39	4302.36	3407.47	2875.39	2524.66	2277.52
135000	11978.81	8216.91	6339.17	4467.83	3538.52	2985.98	2621.76	2365.11
140000	12422.47	8521.24	6573.96	4633.31	3669.58	3096.57	2718.87	2452.71
145000	12866.13	8825.57	6808.74	4798.78	3800.64	3207.16	2815.97	2540.31
150000	13309.79	9129.90	7043.53	4964.26	3931.69	3317.75	2913.07	2627.90
155000	13753.45	9434.23	7278.31	5129.73	4062.75	3428.34	3010.17	2715.50
160000	14197.11	9738.56	7513.09	5295.21	4193.81	3538.94	3107.27	2803.10

MONTHLY AMORTIZING PAYMENTS 11¾%

AMOUNT OF LOAN	NUMBER OF YEARS IN TERM							
	8	9	10	11	12	14	15	16
$ 50	.81	.76	.72	.68	.65	.61	.60	.58
100	1.62	1.51	1.43	1.36	1.30	1.22	1.19	1.16
200	3.23	3.01	2.85	2.71	2.60	2.44	2.37	2.32
300	4.84	4.52	4.27	4.06	3.90	3.65	3.56	3.48
400	6.45	6.02	5.69	5.42	5.20	4.87	4.74	4.63
500	8.06	7.53	7.11	6.77	6.50	6.08	5.93	5.79
600	9.67	9.03	8.53	8.12	7.79	7.30	7.11	6.95
700	11.29	10.54	9.95	9.48	9.09	8.51	8.29	8.11
800	12.90	12.04	11.37	10.83	10.39	9.73	9.48	9.26
900	14.51	13.54	12.79	12.18	11.69	10.95	10.66	10.42
1000	16.12	15.05	14.21	13.54	12.99	12.16	11.85	11.58
2000	32.24	30.09	28.41	27.07	25.97	24.32	23.69	23.15
3000	48.35	45.14	42.61	40.60	38.95	36.48	35.53	34.73
4000	64.47	60.18	56.82	54.13	51.94	48.63	47.37	46.30
5000	80.58	75.22	71.02	67.66	64.92	60.79	59.21	57.87
6000	96.70	90.27	85.22	81.19	77.90	72.95	71.05	69.45
7000	112.82	105.31	99.43	94.72	90.89	85.10	82.89	81.02
8000	128.93	120.35	113.63	108.25	103.87	97.26	94.74	92.60
9000	145.05	135.40	127.83	121.78	116.85	109.42	106.58	104.17
10000	161.16	150.44	142.03	135.31	129.84	121.57	118.42	115.74
11000	177.28	165.48	156.24	148.84	142.82	133.73	130.26	127.32
12000	193.39	180.53	170.44	162.37	155.80	145.89	142.10	138.89
13000	209.51	195.57	184.64	175.90	168.79	158.05	153.94	150.47
14000	225.63	210.62	198.85	189.43	181.77	170.20	165.78	162.04
15000	241.74	225.66	213.05	202.96	194.75	182.36	177.62	173.61
16000	257.86	240.70	227.25	216.49	207.74	194.52	189.47	185.19
17000	273.97	255.75	241.46	230.02	220.72	206.67	201.31	196.76
18000	290.09	270.79	255.66	243.55	233.70	218.83	213.15	208.34
19000	306.21	285.83	269.86	257.08	246.69	230.99	224.99	219.91
20000	322.32	300.88	284.06	270.61	259.67	243.14	236.83	231.48
21000	338.44	315.92	298.27	284.14	272.65	255.30	248.67	243.06
22000	354.55	330.96	312.47	297.67	285.64	267.46	260.51	254.63
23000	370.67	346.01	326.67	311.20	298.62	279.62	272.36	266.21
24000	386.78	361.05	340.88	324.73	311.60	291.77	284.20	277.78
25000	402.90	376.10	355.08	338.26	324.59	303.93	296.04	289.35
26000	419.02	391.14	369.28	351.79	337.57	316.09	307.88	300.93
27000	435.13	406.18	383.48	365.32	350.55	328.24	319.72	312.50
28000	451.25	421.23	397.69	378.85	363.54	340.40	331.56	324.08
29000	467.36	436.27	411.89	392.38	376.52	352.56	343.40	335.65
30000	483.48	451.31	426.09	405.91	389.50	364.71	355.24	347.22
31000	499.59	466.36	440.30	419.44	402.49	376.87	367.09	358.80
32000	515.71	481.40	454.50	432.97	415.47	389.03	378.93	370.37
33000	531.83	496.44	468.70	446.50	428.45	401.18	390.77	381.95
34000	547.94	511.49	482.91	460.03	441.44	413.34	402.61	393.52
35000	564.06	526.53	497.11	473.57	454.42	425.50	414.45	405.09
40000	644.64	601.75	568.12	541.22	519.34	486.28	473.66	462.96
45000	725.22	676.97	639.14	608.87	584.25	547.07	532.86	520.83
50000	805.79	752.19	710.15	676.52	649.17	607.85	592.07	578.70
55000	886.37	827.40	781.17	744.17	714.08	668.64	651.28	636.57
60000	966.95	902.62	852.18	811.82	779.00	729.42	710.48	694.44
65000	1047.53	977.84	923.20	879.47	843.92	790.21	769.69	752.31
70000	1128.11	1053.06	994.21	947.13	908.83	850.99	828.90	810.18
75000	1208.69	1128.28	1065.23	1014.78	973.75	911.78	888.10	868.05
80000	1289.27	1203.49	1136.24	1082.43	1038.67	972.56	947.31	925.92
85000	1369.85	1278.71	1207.26	1150.08	1103.58	1033.35	1006.52	983.79
90000	1450.43	1353.93	1278.27	1217.73	1168.50	1094.13	1065.72	1041.66
95000	1531.01	1429.15	1349.28	1285.38	1233.41	1154.92	1124.93	1099.53
100000	1611.58	1504.37	1420.30	1353.03	1298.33	1215.70	1184.14	1157.40
105000	1692.16	1579.58	1491.31	1420.69	1363.25	1276.49	1243.34	1215.27
110000	1772.74	1654.80	1562.33	1488.34	1428.16	1337.27	1302.55	1273.14
115000	1853.32	1730.02	1633.34	1555.99	1493.08	1398.06	1361.76	1331.01
120000	1933.90	1805.24	1704.36	1623.64	1558.00	1458.84	1420.96	1388.88
125000	2014.48	1880.46	1775.37	1691.29	1622.91	1519.63	1480.17	1446.75
130000	2095.06	1955.67	1846.39	1758.94	1687.83	1580.41	1539.38	1504.62
135000	2175.64	2030.89	1917.40	1826.59	1752.74	1641.20	1598.58	1562.49
140000	2256.22	2106.11	1988.42	1894.25	1817.66	1701.98	1657.79	1620.36
145000	2336.80	2181.33	2059.43	1961.90	1882.58	1762.76	1717.00	1678.23
150000	2417.37	2256.55	2130.45	2029.55	1947.49	1823.55	1776.20	1736.10
155000	2497.95	2331.76	2201.46	2097.20	2012.41	1884.33	1835.41	1793.97
160000	2578.53	2406.98	2272.48	2164.85	2077.33	1945.12	1894.62	1851.84

MONTHLY AMORTIZING PAYMENTS

AMOUNT OF LOAN	NUMBER OF YEARS IN TERM							
	17	18	19	20	21	22	23	24
$ 50	.57	.56	.55	.55	.54	.54	.53	.53
100	1.14	1.12	1.10	1.09	1.08	1.07	1.06	1.05
200	2.27	2.24	2.20	2.17	2.15	2.13	2.11	2.09
300	3.41	3.35	3.30	3.26	3.22	3.19	3.16	3.13
400	4.54	4.47	4.40	4.34	4.29	4.25	4.21	4.17
500	5.68	5.58	5.50	5.42	5.36	5.31	5.26	5.22
600	6.81	6.70	6.59	6.51	6.43	6.37	6.31	6.26
700	7.95	7.81	7.69	7.59	7.50	7.43	7.36	7.30
800	9.08	8.93	8.79	8.67	8.57	8.49	8.41	8.34
900	10.22	10.04	9.89	9.76	9.64	9.55	9.46	9.38
1000	11.35	11.16	10.99	10.84	10.72	10.61	10.51	10.43
2000	22.70	22.31	21.97	21.68	21.43	21.21	21.02	20.85
3000	34.04	33.46	32.95	32.52	32.14	31.81	31.52	31.27
4000	45.39	44.61	43.94	43.35	42.85	42.41	42.03	41.69
5000	56.74	55.76	54.92	54.19	53.56	53.01	52.53	52.11
6000	68.08	66.91	65.90	65.03	64.27	63.61	63.04	62.53
7000	79.43	78.06	76.88	75.86	74.98	74.21	73.54	72.95
8000	90.77	89.21	87.87	86.70	85.69	84.81	84.05	83.38
9000	102.12	100.36	98.85	97.54	96.40	95.41	94.55	93.80
10000	113.47	111.51	109.83	108.38	107.11	106.02	105.06	104.22
11000	124.81	122.66	120.81	119.21	117.82	116.62	115.56	114.64
12000	136.16	133.81	131.80	130.05	128.54	127.22	126.07	125.06
13000	147.50	144.96	142.78	140.89	139.25	137.82	136.57	135.48
14000	158.85	156.12	153.76	151.72	149.96	148.42	147.08	145.90
15000	170.20	167.27	164.74	162.56	160.67	159.02	157.58	156.33
16000	181.54	178.42	175.73	173.40	171.38	169.62	168.09	166.75
17000	192.89	189.57	186.71	184.24	182.09	180.22	178.59	177.17
18000	204.23	200.72	197.69	195.07	192.80	190.82	189.10	187.59
19000	215.58	211.87	208.67	205.91	203.51	201.43	199.60	198.01
20000	226.93	223.02	219.66	216.75	214.22	212.03	210.11	208.43
21000	238.27	234.17	230.64	227.58	224.93	222.63	220.61	218.85
22000	249.62	245.32	241.62	238.42	235.64	233.23	231.12	229.28
23000	260.96	256.47	252.60	249.26	246.36	243.83	241.63	239.70
24000	272.31	267.62	263.59	260.09	257.07	254.43	252.13	250.12
25000	283.66	278.77	274.57	270.93	267.78	265.03	262.64	260.54
26000	295.00	289.92	285.55	281.77	278.49	275.63	273.14	270.96
27000	306.35	301.07	296.53	292.61	289.20	286.23	283.65	281.38
28000	317.69	312.23	307.52	303.44	299.91	296.83	294.15	291.80
29000	329.04	323.38	318.50	314.28	310.62	307.44	304.66	302.23
30000	340.39	334.53	329.48	325.12	321.33	318.04	315.16	312.65
31000	351.73	345.68	340.46	335.95	332.04	328.64	325.67	323.07
32000	363.08	356.83	351.45	346.79	342.75	339.24	336.17	333.49
33000	374.43	367.98	362.43	357.63	353.46	349.84	346.68	343.91
34000	385.77	379.13	373.41	368.47	364.17	360.44	357.18	354.33
35000	397.12	390.28	384.39	379.30	374.89	371.04	367.69	364.75
40000	453.85	446.03	439.31	433.49	428.44	424.05	420.21	416.86
45000	510.58	501.79	494.22	487.67	481.99	477.05	472.74	468.97
50000	567.31	557.54	549.13	541.86	535.55	530.06	525.27	521.08
55000	624.04	613.29	604.04	596.04	589.10	583.06	577.79	573.18
60000	680.77	669.05	658.96	650.23	642.66	636.07	630.32	625.29
65000	737.50	724.80	713.87	704.41	696.21	689.07	682.85	677.40
70000	794.23	780.56	768.78	758.60	749.77	742.08	735.37	729.50
75000	850.96	836.31	823.69	812.79	803.32	795.08	787.90	781.61
80000	907.69	892.06	878.61	866.97	856.88	848.09	840.42	833.72
85000	964.42	947.82	933.52	921.16	910.43	901.09	892.95	885.83
90000	1021.15	1003.57	988.43	975.34	963.98	954.10	945.48	937.93
95000	1077.88	1059.32	1043.34	1029.53	1017.54	1007.11	998.00	990.04
100000	1134.61	1115.08	1098.26	1083.71	1071.09	1060.11	1050.53	1042.15
105000	1191.34	1170.83	1153.17	1137.90	1124.65	1113.12	1103.05	1094.25
110000	1248.07	1226.58	1208.08	1192.08	1178.20	1166.12	1155.58	1146.36
115000	1304.80	1282.34	1262.99	1246.27	1231.76	1219.13	1208.11	1198.47
120000	1361.53	1338.09	1317.91	1300.45	1285.31	1272.13	1260.63	1250.58
125000	1418.26	1393.85	1372.82	1354.64	1338.86	1325.14	1313.16	1302.68
130000	1474.99	1449.60	1427.73	1408.82	1392.42	1378.14	1365.69	1354.79
135000	1531.72	1505.35	1482.64	1463.01	1445.97	1431.15	1418.21	1406.90
140000	1588.45	1561.11	1537.56	1517.19	1499.53	1484.15	1470.74	1459.00
145000	1645.18	1616.86	1592.47	1571.38	1553.08	1537.16	1523.26	1511.11
150000	1701.91	1672.61	1647.38	1625.57	1606.64	1590.16	1575.79	1563.22
155000	1758.64	1728.37	1702.29	1679.75	1660.19	1643.17	1628.32	1615.33
160000	1815.37	1784.12	1757.21	1733.94	1713.75	1696.17	1680.84	1667.43

MONTHLY AMORTIZING PAYMENTS 11¾%

AMOUNT OF LOAN	NUMBER OF YEARS IN TERM							
	25	26	27	28	29	30	35	40
$ 50	.52	.52	.52	.51	.51	.51	.50	.50
100	1.04	1.03	1.03	1.02	1.02	1.01	1.00	.99
200	2.07	2.06	2.05	2.04	2.03	2.02	2.00	1.98
300	3.11	3.09	3.07	3.06	3.04	3.03	2.99	2.97
400	4.14	4.12	4.10	4.08	4.06	4.04	3.99	3.96
500	5.18	5.15	5.12	5.09	5.07	5.05	4.98	4.95
600	6.21	6.18	6.14	6.11	6.08	6.06	5.98	5.94
700	7.25	7.20	7.16	7.13	7.10	7.07	6.98	6.92
800	8.28	8.23	8.19	8.15	8.11	8.08	7.97	7.91
900	9.32	9.26	9.21	9.16	9.12	9.09	8.97	8.90
1000	10.35	10.29	10.23	10.18	10.14	10.10	9.96	9.89
2000	20.70	20.57	20.46	20.36	20.27	20.19	19.92	19.77
3000	31.05	30.86	30.69	30.54	30.40	30.29	29.88	29.66
4000	41.40	41.14	40.91	40.71	40.54	40.38	39.84	39.54
5000	51.74	51.42	51.14	50.89	50.67	50.48	49.79	49.42
6000	62.09	61.71	61.37	61.07	60.80	60.57	59.75	59.31
7000	72.44	71.99	71.59	71.24	70.94	70.66	69.71	69.19
8000	82.79	82.27	81.82	81.42	81.07	80.76	79.67	79.07
9000	93.14	92.56	92.05	91.60	91.20	90.85	89.63	88.96
10000	103.48	102.84	102.27	101.77	101.33	100.95	99.58	98.84
11000	113.83	113.12	112.50	111.95	111.47	111.04	109.54	108.73
12000	124.18	123.41	122.73	122.13	121.60	121.13	119.50	118.61
13000	134.53	133.69	132.95	132.30	131.73	131.23	129.46	128.49
14000	144.88	143.97	143.18	142.48	141.87	141.32	139.42	138.38
15000	155.22	154.26	153.41	152.66	152.00	151.42	149.37	148.26
16000	165.57	164.54	163.63	162.84	162.13	161.51	159.33	158.14
17000	175.92	174.82	173.86	173.01	172.26	171.60	169.29	168.03
18000	186.27	185.11	184.09	183.19	182.40	181.70	179.25	177.91
19000	196.62	195.39	194.31	193.37	192.53	191.79	189.21	187.79
20000	206.96	205.68	204.54	203.54	202.66	201.89	199.16	197.68
21000	217.31	215.96	214.77	213.72	212.80	211.98	209.12	207.56
22000	227.66	226.24	225.00	223.90	222.93	222.08	219.08	217.45
23000	238.01	236.53	235.22	234.07	233.06	232.17	229.04	227.33
24000	248.36	246.81	245.45	244.25	243.20	242.26	239.00	237.21
25000	258.70	257.09	255.68	254.43	253.33	252.36	248.95	247.10
26000	269.05	267.38	265.90	264.60	263.46	262.45	258.91	256.98
27000	279.40	277.66	276.13	274.78	273.59	272.55	268.87	266.86
28000	289.75	287.94	286.36	284.96	283.73	282.64	278.83	276.75
29000	300.10	298.23	296.58	295.14	293.86	292.73	288.79	286.63
30000	310.44	308.51	306.81	305.31	303.99	302.83	298.74	296.51
31000	320.79	318.79	317.04	315.49	314.13	312.92	308.70	306.40
32000	331.14	329.08	327.26	325.67	324.26	323.02	318.66	316.28
33000	341.49	339.36	337.49	335.84	334.39	333.11	328.62	326.17
34000	351.84	349.64	347.72	346.02	344.52	343.20	338.57	336.05
35000	362.18	359.93	357.94	356.20	354.66	353.30	348.53	345.93
40000	413.92	411.35	409.08	407.08	405.32	403.77	398.32	395.35
45000	465.66	462.76	460.21	457.97	455.99	454.24	448.11	444.77
50000	517.40	514.18	511.35	508.85	506.65	504.71	497.90	494.19
55000	569.14	565.60	562.48	559.74	557.32	555.18	547.69	543.61
60000	620.88	617.02	613.61	610.62	607.98	605.65	597.48	593.02
65000	672.62	668.43	664.75	661.50	658.64	656.12	647.27	642.44
70000	724.36	719.85	715.88	712.39	709.31	706.59	697.06	691.86
75000	776.10	771.27	767.02	763.27	759.97	757.06	746.85	741.28
80000	827.84	822.69	818.15	814.16	810.64	807.53	796.64	790.70
85000	879.58	874.10	869.28	865.04	861.30	858.00	846.43	840.11
90000	931.32	925.52	920.42	915.93	911.97	908.47	896.22	889.53
95000	983.06	976.94	971.55	966.81	962.63	958.94	946.01	938.95
100000	1034.80	1028.36	1022.69	1017.70	1013.30	1009.41	995.80	988.37
105000	1086.54	1079.77	1073.82	1068.58	1063.96	1059.89	1045.59	1037.79
110000	1138.28	1131.19	1124.96	1119.47	1114.63	1110.36	1095.38	1087.21
115000	1190.02	1182.61	1176.09	1170.35	1165.29	1160.83	1145.17	1136.62
120000	1241.76	1234.03	1227.22	1221.23	1215.96	1211.30	1194.96	1186.04
125000	1293.50	1285.44	1278.36	1272.12	1266.62	1261.77	1244.75	1235.46
130000	1345.24	1336.86	1329.49	1323.00	1317.28	1312.24	1294.54	1284.88
135000	1396.98	1388.28	1380.63	1373.89	1367.95	1362.71	1344.33	1334.30
140000	1448.72	1439.70	1431.76	1424.77	1418.61	1413.18	1394.12	1383.71
145000	1500.46	1491.11	1482.89	1475.66	1469.28	1463.65	1443.91	1433.13
150000	1552.20	1542.53	1534.03	1526.54	1519.94	1514.12	1493.70	1482.55
155000	1603.94	1593.95	1585.16	1577.43	1570.61	1564.59	1543.49	1531.97
160000	1655.68	1645.37	1636.30	1628.31	1621.27	1615.06	1593.28	1581.39

MONTHLY AMORTIZING PAYMENTS

AMOUNT OF LOAN	NUMBER OF YEARS IN TERM 1	1-1/2	2	3	4	5	6	7
$ 50	4.44	3.05	2.36	1.66	1.32	1.11	.98	.88
100	8.88	6.10	4.71	3.32	2.63	2.22	1.95	1.76
200	17.76	12.19	9.41	6.64	5.26	4.44	3.90	3.52
300	26.64	18.28	14.11	9.95	7.89	6.66	5.85	5.28
400	35.52	24.37	18.81	13.27	10.51	8.88	7.80	7.04
500	44.40	30.47	23.51	16.58	13.14	11.10	9.75	8.80
600	53.28	36.56	28.21	19.90	15.77	13.31	11.70	10.56
700	62.16	42.65	32.92	23.21	18.40	15.53	13.64	12.32
800	71.04	48.74	37.62	26.53	21.02	17.75	15.59	14.07
900	79.92	54.84	42.32	29.84	23.65	19.97	17.54	15.83
1000	88.80	60.93	47.02	33.16	26.28	22.19	19.49	17.59
2000	177.59	121.85	94.04	66.31	52.55	44.37	38.98	35.18
3000	266.38	182.78	141.05	99.47	78.82	66.55	58.46	52.76
4000	355.17	243.70	188.07	132.62	105.10	88.73	77.95	70.35
5000	443.96	304.62	235.08	165.78	131.37	110.91	97.43	87.93
6000	532.75	365.55	282.10	198.93	157.64	133.09	116.92	105.52
7000	621.54	426.47	329.11	232.09	183.91	155.27	136.40	123.11
8000	710.33	487.40	376.13	265.24	210.19	177.46	155.89	140.69
9000	799.12	548.32	423.14	298.40	236.46	199.64	175.37	158.28
10000	887.91	609.24	470.16	331.55	262.73	221.82	194.86	175.86
11000	976.70	670.17	517.17	364.71	289.00	244.00	214.34	193.45
12000	1065.49	731.09	564.19	397.86	315.28	266.18	233.83	211.04
13000	1154.28	792.02	611.20	431.02	341.55	288.36	253.31	228.62
14000	1243.07	852.94	658.22	464.17	367.82	310.54	272.80	246.21
15000	1331.86	913.86	705.23	497.32	394.09	332.72	292.28	263.79
16000	1420.65	974.79	752.25	530.48	420.37	354.91	311.77	281.38
17000	1509.44	1035.71	799.26	563.63	446.64	377.09	331.25	298.97
18000	1598.23	1096.64	846.28	596.79	472.91	399.27	350.74	316.55
19000	1687.02	1157.56	893.29	629.94	499.18	421.45	370.22	334.14
20000	1775.81	1218.48	940.31	663.10	525.46	443.63	389.71	351.72
21000	1864.60	1279.41	987.32	696.25	551.73	465.81	409.20	369.31
22000	1953.39	1340.33	1034.34	729.41	578.00	487.99	428.68	386.90
23000	2042.18	1401.26	1081.35	762.56	604.27	510.18	448.17	404.48
24000	2130.97	1462.18	1128.37	795.72	630.55	532.36	467.65	422.07
25000	2219.76	1523.10	1175.38	828.87	656.82	554.54	487.14	439.65
26000	2308.55	1584.03	1222.40	862.03	683.09	576.72	506.62	457.24
27000	2397.34	1644.95	1269.41	895.18	709.36	598.90	526.11	474.83
28000	2486.13	1705.88	1316.43	928.33	735.64	621.08	545.59	492.41
29000	2574.92	1766.80	1363.44	961.49	761.91	643.26	565.08	510.00
30000	2663.71	1827.72	1410.46	994.64	788.18	665.44	584.56	527.58
31000	2752.51	1888.65	1457.47	1027.80	814.45	687.63	604.05	545.17
32000	2841.30	1949.57	1504.49	1060.95	840.73	709.81	623.53	562.76
33000	2930.09	2010.50	1551.50	1094.11	867.00	731.99	643.02	580.34
34000	3018.88	2071.42	1598.52	1127.26	893.27	754.17	662.50	597.93
35000	3107.67	2132.34	1645.53	1160.42	919.54	776.35	681.99	615.51
40000	3551.62	2436.96	1880.61	1326.19	1050.91	887.26	779.42	703.44
45000	3995.57	2741.58	2115.69	1491.96	1182.27	998.16	876.84	791.37
50000	4439.52	3046.20	2350.76	1657.74	1313.63	1109.07	974.27	879.30
55000	4883.47	3350.82	2585.84	1823.51	1444.99	1219.98	1071.69	967.23
60000	5327.42	3655.44	2820.91	1989.28	1576.36	1330.88	1169.12	1055.16
65000	5771.38	3960.06	3055.99	2155.06	1707.72	1441.79	1266.55	1143.09
70000	6215.33	4264.68	3291.06	2320.83	1839.08	1552.70	1363.97	1231.02
75000	6659.28	4569.30	3526.14	2486.60	1970.44	1663.60	1461.40	1318.95
80000	7103.23	4873.92	3761.21	2652.38	2101.81	1774.51	1558.83	1406.88
85000	7547.18	5178.54	3996.29	2818.15	2233.17	1885.42	1656.25	1494.81
90000	7991.13	5483.16	4231.37	2983.92	2364.53	1996.32	1753.68	1582.74
95000	8435.09	5787.78	4466.44	3149.70	2495.89	2107.23	1851.10	1670.67
100000	8879.04	6092.40	4701.52	3315.47	2627.26	2218.14	1948.53	1758.60
105000	9322.99	6397.02	4936.59	3481.24	2758.62	2329.04	2045.96	1846.53
110000	9766.94	6701.64	5171.67	3647.02	2889.98	2439.95	2143.38	1934.46
115000	10210.89	7006.26	5406.74	3812.79	3021.34	2550.86	2240.81	2022.39
120000	10654.84	7310.88	5641.82	3978.56	3152.71	2661.76	2338.24	2110.32
125000	11098.80	7615.50	5876.89	4144.33	3284.07	2772.67	2435.66	2198.25
130000	11542.75	7920.12	6111.97	4310.11	3415.43	2883.58	2533.09	2286.18
135000	11986.70	8224.74	6347.05	4475.88	3546.79	2994.48	2630.51	2374.11
140000	12430.65	8529.36	6582.12	4641.65	3678.16	3105.39	2727.94	2462.04
145000	12874.60	8833.98	6817.20	4807.43	3809.52	3216.30	2825.37	2549.97
150000	13318.55	9138.60	7052.27	4973.20	3940.88	3327.20	2922.79	2637.90
155000	13762.51	9443.22	7287.35	5138.97	4072.24	3438.11	3020.22	2725.83
160000	14206.46	9747.84	7522.42	5304.75	4203.61	3549.02	3117.65	2813.76

MONTHLY AMORTIZING PAYMENTS 11 7/8%

AMOUNT OF LOAN	NUMBER OF YEARS IN TERM							
	8	9	10	11	12	14	15	16
$ 50	.81	.76	.72	.69	.66	.62	.60	.59
100	1.62	1.52	1.43	1.37	1.31	1.23	1.20	1.17
200	3.24	3.03	2.86	2.73	2.62	2.45	2.39	2.34
300	4.86	4.54	4.29	4.09	3.92	3.68	3.58	3.50
400	6.48	6.05	5.71	5.45	5.23	4.90	4.77	4.67
500	8.10	7.56	7.14	6.81	6.53	6.12	5.97	5.83
600	9.72	9.07	8.57	8.17	7.84	7.35	7.16	7.00
700	11.33	10.58	10.00	9.53	9.15	8.57	8.35	8.16
800	12.95	12.10	11.42	10.89	10.45	9.79	9.54	9.33
900	14.57	13.61	12.85	12.25	11.76	11.02	10.73	10.49
1000	16.19	15.12	14.28	13.61	13.06	12.24	11.93	11.66
2000	32.37	30.23	28.55	27.21	26.12	24.48	23.85	23.32
3000	48.56	45.35	42.83	40.82	39.18	36.71	35.77	34.97
4000	64.74	60.46	57.10	54.42	52.24	48.95	47.69	46.63
5000	80.93	75.57	71.38	68.02	65.30	61.18	59.61	58.28
6000	97.11	90.69	85.65	81.63	78.36	73.42	71.53	69.94
7000	113.29	105.80	99.93	95.23	91.42	85.65	83.45	81.59
8000	129.48	120.92	114.20	108.84	104.47	97.89	95.38	93.25
9000	145.66	136.03	128.48	122.44	117.53	110.12	107.30	104.90
10000	161.85	151.14	142.75	136.04	130.59	122.36	119.22	116.56
11000	178.03	166.26	157.03	149.65	143.65	134.60	131.14	128.22
12000	194.22	181.37	171.30	163.25	156.71	146.83	143.06	139.87
13000	210.40	196.48	185.58	176.86	169.77	159.07	154.98	151.53
14000	226.58	211.60	199.85	190.46	182.83	171.30	166.90	163.18
15000	242.77	226.71	214.13	204.06	195.88	183.54	178.83	174.84
16000	258.95	241.83	228.40	217.67	208.94	195.77	190.75	186.49
17000	275.14	256.94	242.68	231.27	222.00	208.01	202.67	198.15
18000	291.32	272.05	256.95	244.88	235.06	220.24	214.59	209.80
19000	307.51	287.17	271.23	258.48	248.12	232.48	226.51	221.46
20000	323.69	302.28	285.50	272.08	261.18	244.72	238.43	233.11
21000	339.87	317.40	299.78	285.69	274.24	256.95	250.35	244.77
22000	356.06	332.51	314.05	299.29	287.29	269.19	262.28	256.43
23000	372.24	347.62	328.33	312.90	300.35	281.42	274.20	268.08
24000	388.43	362.74	342.60	326.50	313.41	293.66	286.12	279.74
25000	404.61	377.85	356.88	340.10	326.47	305.89	298.04	291.39
26000	420.80	392.96	371.15	353.71	339.53	318.13	309.96	303.05
27000	436.98	408.08	385.43	367.31	352.59	330.36	321.88	314.70
28000	453.16	423.19	399.70	380.92	365.65	342.60	333.80	326.36
29000	469.35	438.31	413.98	394.52	378.70	354.83	345.72	338.01
30000	485.53	453.42	428.25	408.12	391.76	367.07	357.65	349.67
31000	501.72	468.53	442.53	421.73	404.82	379.31	369.57	361.33
32000	517.90	483.65	456.80	435.33	417.88	391.54	381.49	372.98
33000	534.08	498.76	471.08	448.94	430.94	403.78	393.41	384.64
34000	550.27	513.88	485.35	462.54	444.00	416.01	405.33	396.29
35000	566.45	528.99	499.63	476.14	457.06	428.25	417.25	407.95
40000	647.37	604.56	571.00	544.16	522.35	489.43	476.86	466.22
45000	728.30	680.13	642.38	612.18	587.64	550.60	536.47	524.50
50000	809.22	755.70	713.75	680.20	652.94	611.78	596.07	582.78
55000	890.14	831.27	785.13	748.22	718.23	672.96	655.68	641.06
60000	971.06	906.83	856.50	816.24	783.52	734.14	715.29	699.33
65000	1051.98	982.40	927.88	884.26	848.82	795.31	774.89	757.61
70000	1132.90	1057.97	999.25	952.28	914.11	856.49	834.50	815.89
75000	1213.82	1133.54	1070.62	1020.30	979.40	917.67	894.11	874.17
80000	1294.74	1209.11	1142.00	1088.32	1044.69	978.85	953.72	932.44
85000	1375.67	1284.68	1213.37	1156.34	1109.99	1040.02	1013.32	990.72
90000	1456.59	1360.25	1284.75	1224.36	1175.28	1101.20	1072.93	1049.00
95000	1537.51	1435.82	1356.12	1292.38	1240.57	1162.38	1132.54	1107.28
100000	1618.43	1511.39	1427.50	1360.40	1305.87	1223.56	1192.14	1165.55
105000	1699.35	1586.96	1498.87	1428.42	1371.16	1284.73	1251.75	1223.83
110000	1780.27	1662.53	1570.25	1496.44	1436.45	1345.91	1311.36	1282.11
115000	1861.19	1738.10	1641.62	1564.46	1501.75	1407.09	1370.96	1340.39
120000	1942.11	1813.66	1713.00	1632.48	1567.04	1468.27	1430.57	1398.66
125000	2023.03	1889.23	1784.37	1700.50	1632.33	1529.44	1490.18	1456.94
130000	2103.96	1964.80	1855.75	1768.52	1697.63	1590.62	1549.78	1515.22
135000	2184.88	2040.37	1927.12	1836.54	1762.92	1651.80	1609.39	1573.50
140000	2265.80	2115.94	1998.49	1904.56	1828.21	1712.98	1669.00	1631.77
145000	2346.72	2191.51	2069.87	1972.58	1893.50	1774.15	1728.60	1690.05
150000	2427.64	2267.08	2141.24	2040.60	1958.80	1835.33	1788.21	1748.33
155000	2508.56	2342.65	2212.62	2108.62	2024.09	1896.51	1847.82	1806.61
160000	2589.48	2418.22	2283.99	2176.64	2089.38	1957.69	1907.43	1864.88

MONTHLY AMORTIZING PAYMENTS

AMOUNT OF LOAN	NUMBER OF YEARS IN TERM							
	17	18	19	20	21	22	23	24
$ 50	.58	.57	.56	.55	.54	.54	.53	.53
100	1.15	1.13	1.11	1.10	1.08	1.07	1.06	1.06
200	2.29	2.25	2.22	2.19	2.16	2.14	2.12	2.11
300	3.43	3.38	3.33	3.28	3.24	3.21	3.18	3.16
400	4.58	4.50	4.43	4.37	4.32	4.28	4.24	4.21
500	5.72	5.62	5.54	5.47	5.40	5.35	5.30	5.26
600	6.86	6.75	6.65	6.56	6.48	6.42	6.36	6.31
700	8.01	7.87	7.75	7.65	7.56	7.49	7.42	7.36
800	9.15	8.99	8.86	8.74	8.64	8.56	8.48	8.41
900	10.29	10.12	9.97	9.84	9.72	9.63	9.54	9.47
1000	11.43	11.24	11.07	10.93	10.80	10.70	10.60	10.52
2000	22.86	22.47	22.14	21.85	21.60	21.39	21.20	21.03
3000	34.29	33.71	33.21	32.78	32.40	32.08	31.79	31.54
4000	45.72	44.94	44.28	43.70	43.20	42.77	42.39	42.06
5000	57.15	56.18	55.35	54.62	54.00	53.46	52.98	52.57
6000	68.58	67.41	66.41	65.55	64.80	64.15	63.58	63.08
7000	80.01	78.65	77.48	76.47	75.60	74.84	74.17	73.59
8000	91.44	89.88	88.55	87.40	86.40	85.53	84.77	84.11
9000	102.87	101.12	99.62	98.32	97.19	96.22	95.36	94.62
10000	114.29	112.35	110.69	109.24	107.99	106.91	105.96	105.13
11000	125.72	123.59	121.75	120.17	118.79	117.60	116.55	115.64
12000	137.15	134.82	132.82	131.09	129.59	128.29	127.15	126.16
13000	148.58	146.06	143.89	142.01	140.39	138.98	137.74	136.67
14000	160.01	157.29	154.96	152.94	151.19	149.67	148.34	147.18
15000	171.44	168.53	166.03	163.86	161.99	160.36	158.93	157.69
16000	182.87	179.76	177.09	174.79	172.79	171.05	169.53	168.21
17000	194.30	191.00	188.16	185.71	183.58	181.74	180.13	178.72
18000	205.73	202.23	199.23	196.63	194.38	192.43	190.72	189.23
19000	217.16	213.47	210.30	207.56	205.18	203.12	201.32	199.74
20000	228.58	224.70	221.37	218.48	215.98	213.81	211.91	210.26
21000	240.01	235.94	232.43	229.41	226.78	224.50	222.51	220.77
22000	251.44	247.17	243.50	240.33	237.58	235.19	233.10	231.28
23000	262.87	258.41	254.57	251.25	248.38	245.88	243.70	241.79
24000	274.30	269.64	265.64	262.18	259.18	256.57	254.29	252.31
25000	285.73	280.88	276.71	273.10	269.98	267.26	264.89	262.82
26000	297.16	292.11	287.77	284.02	280.77	277.95	275.48	273.33
27000	308.59	303.35	298.84	294.95	291.57	288.64	286.08	283.84
28000	320.02	314.58	309.91	305.87	302.37	299.33	296.67	294.36
29000	331.45	325.82	320.98	316.80	313.17	310.02	307.27	304.87
30000	342.87	337.05	332.05	327.72	323.97	320.71	317.86	315.38
31000	354.30	348.29	343.11	338.64	334.77	331.40	328.46	325.89
32000	365.73	359.52	354.18	349.57	345.57	342.09	339.06	336.41
33000	377.16	370.76	365.25	360.49	356.37	352.78	349.65	346.92
34000	388.59	381.99	376.32	371.42	367.16	363.47	360.25	357.43
35000	400.02	393.23	387.39	382.34	377.96	374.16	370.84	367.94
40000	457.16	449.40	442.73	436.96	431.96	427.61	423.82	420.51
45000	514.31	505.58	498.07	491.58	485.95	481.06	476.79	473.07
50000	571.45	561.75	553.41	546.20	539.95	534.51	529.77	525.63
55000	628.60	617.93	608.75	600.82	593.94	587.96	582.75	578.19
60000	685.74	674.10	664.09	655.44	647.93	641.41	635.72	630.76
65000	742.89	730.28	719.43	710.05	701.93	694.86	688.70	683.32
70000	800.03	786.45	774.77	764.67	755.92	748.31	741.68	735.88
75000	857.18	842.63	830.11	819.29	809.92	801.76	794.65	788.44
80000	914.32	898.80	885.45	873.91	863.91	855.21	847.63	841.01
85000	971.47	954.98	940.79	928.53	917.90	908.66	900.61	893.57
90000	1028.61	1011.15	996.13	983.15	971.90	962.11	953.58	946.13
95000	1085.76	1067.33	1051.47	1037.77	1025.89	1015.56	1006.56	998.69
100000	1142.90	1123.50	1106.81	1092.39	1079.89	1069.01	1059.54	1051.26
105000	1200.05	1179.68	1162.15	1147.01	1133.88	1122.47	1112.51	1103.82
110000	1257.19	1235.85	1217.49	1201.63	1187.87	1175.92	1165.49	1156.38
115000	1314.34	1292.03	1272.83	1256.25	1241.87	1229.37	1218.47	1208.94
120000	1371.48	1348.20	1328.17	1310.87	1295.86	1282.82	1271.44	1261.51
125000	1428.63	1404.38	1383.51	1365.49	1349.86	1336.27	1324.42	1314.07
130000	1485.77	1460.55	1438.85	1420.10	1403.85	1389.72	1377.40	1366.63
135000	1542.92	1516.73	1494.19	1474.72	1457.84	1443.17	1430.37	1419.19
140000	1600.06	1572.90	1549.53	1529.34	1511.84	1496.62	1483.35	1471.76
145000	1657.21	1629.08	1604.87	1583.96	1565.83	1550.07	1536.33	1524.32
150000	1714.35	1685.25	1660.21	1638.58	1619.83	1603.52	1589.30	1576.88
155000	1771.50	1741.43	1715.55	1693.20	1673.82	1656.97	1642.28	1629.44
160000	1828.64	1797.60	1770.89	1747.82	1727.82	1710.42	1695.26	1682.01

MONTHLY AMORTIZING PAYMENTS 11⅞%

AMOUNT OF LOAN	NUMBER OF YEARS IN TERM							
	25	26	27	28	29	30	35	40
$ 50	.53	.52	.52	.52	.52	.51	.51	.50
100	1.05	1.04	1.04	1.03	1.03	1.02	1.01	1.00
200	2.09	2.08	2.07	2.06	2.05	2.04	2.02	2.00
300	3.14	3.12	3.10	3.09	3.07	3.06	3.02	3.00
400	4.18	4.16	4.13	4.11	4.10	4.08	4.03	4.00
500	5.22	5.19	5.17	5.14	5.12	5.10	5.03	5.00
600	6.27	6.23	6.20	6.17	6.14	6.12	6.04	6.00
700	7.31	7.27	7.23	7.19	7.16	7.14	7.04	6.99
800	8.36	8.31	8.26	8.22	8.19	8.16	8.05	7.99
900	9.40	9.34	9.29	9.25	9.21	9.18	9.06	8.99
1000	10.44	10.38	10.33	10.28	10.23	10.20	10.06	9.99
2000	20.88	20.76	20.65	20.55	20.46	20.39	20.12	19.97
3000	31.32	31.13	30.97	30.82	30.69	30.58	30.17	29.96
4000	41.76	41.51	41.29	41.09	40.92	40.77	40.23	39.94
5000	52.20	51.89	51.61	51.36	51.15	50.96	50.29	49.93
6000	62.64	62.26	61.93	61.63	61.37	61.15	60.34	59.91
7000	73.08	72.64	72.25	71.90	71.60	71.34	70.40	69.89
8000	83.52	83.02	82.57	82.18	81.83	81.53	80.46	79.88
9000	93.96	93.39	92.89	92.45	92.06	91.72	90.51	89.86
10000	104.40	103.77	103.21	102.72	102.29	101.91	100.57	99.85
11000	114.84	114.15	113.53	112.99	112.51	112.10	110.63	109.83
12000	125.28	124.52	123.85	123.26	122.74	122.29	120.68	119.82
13000	135.72	134.90	134.17	133.53	132.97	132.48	130.74	129.80
14000	146.16	145.27	144.49	143.80	143.20	142.67	140.80	139.78
15000	156.60	155.65	154.81	154.08	153.43	152.86	150.85	149.77
16000	167.04	166.03	165.13	164.35	163.66	163.05	160.91	159.75
17000	177.48	176.40	175.45	174.62	173.88	173.24	170.97	169.74
18000	187.92	186.78	185.77	184.89	184.11	183.43	181.02	179.72
19000	198.36	197.16	196.10	195.16	194.34	193.62	191.08	189.71
20000	208.80	207.53	206.42	205.43	204.57	203.81	201.14	199.69
21000	219.24	217.91	216.74	215.70	214.80	214.00	211.19	209.67
22000	229.68	228.29	227.06	225.98	225.02	224.19	221.25	219.66
23000	240.12	238.66	237.38	236.25	235.25	234.38	231.31	229.64
24000	250.56	249.04	247.70	246.52	245.48	244.57	241.36	239.63
25000	261.00	259.41	258.02	256.79	255.71	254.76	251.42	249.61
26000	271.44	269.79	268.34	267.06	265.94	264.95	261.48	259.60
27000	281.88	280.17	278.66	277.33	276.16	275.14	271.53	269.58
28000	292.32	290.54	288.98	287.60	286.39	285.33	281.59	279.56
29000	302.76	300.92	299.30	297.88	296.62	295.52	291.65	289.55
30000	313.20	311.30	309.62	308.15	306.85	305.71	301.70	299.53
31000	323.64	321.67	319.94	318.42	317.08	315.90	311.76	309.52
32000	334.08	332.05	330.26	328.69	327.31	326.09	321.82	319.50
33000	344.52	342.43	340.58	338.96	337.53	336.28	331.87	329.49
34000	354.96	352.80	350.90	349.23	347.76	346.47	341.93	339.47
35000	365.40	363.18	361.22	359.50	357.99	356.66	351.99	349.45
40000	417.60	415.06	412.83	410.86	409.13	407.61	402.27	399.38
45000	469.80	466.94	464.43	462.22	460.27	458.56	452.55	449.30
50000	522.00	518.82	516.03	513.58	511.41	509.51	502.84	499.22
55000	574.20	570.71	567.63	564.93	562.55	560.46	553.12	549.14
60000	626.40	622.59	619.24	616.29	613.69	611.41	603.40	599.06
65000	678.60	674.47	670.84	667.65	664.83	662.36	653.69	648.98
70000	730.80	726.35	722.44	719.00	715.98	713.31	703.97	698.90
75000	783.00	778.23	774.05	770.36	767.12	764.26	754.25	748.82
80000	835.20	830.12	825.65	821.72	818.26	815.21	804.54	798.75
85000	887.40	882.00	877.25	873.07	869.40	866.16	854.82	848.67
90000	939.60	933.88	928.85	924.43	920.54	917.11	905.10	898.59
95000	991.80	985.76	980.46	975.79	971.68	968.06	955.39	948.51
100000	1044.00	1037.64	1032.06	1027.15	1022.82	1019.01	1005.67	998.43
105000	1096.20	1089.53	1083.66	1078.50	1073.96	1069.96	1055.95	1048.35
110000	1148.40	1141.41	1135.26	1129.86	1125.10	1120.91	1106.23	1098.27
115000	1200.60	1193.29	1186.87	1181.22	1176.24	1171.86	1156.52	1148.19
120000	1252.80	1245.17	1238.47	1232.57	1227.38	1222.81	1206.80	1198.12
125000	1305.00	1297.05	1290.07	1283.93	1278.52	1273.76	1257.08	1248.04
130000	1357.20	1348.94	1341.68	1335.29	1329.66	1324.71	1307.37	1297.96
135000	1409.40	1400.82	1393.28	1386.65	1380.80	1375.66	1357.65	1347.88
140000	1461.60	1452.70	1444.88	1438.00	1431.95	1426.61	1407.93	1397.80
145000	1513.80	1504.58	1496.48	1489.36	1483.09	1477.56	1458.22	1447.72
150000	1566.00	1556.46	1548.09	1540.72	1534.23	1528.51	1508.50	1497.64
155000	1618.20	1608.35	1599.69	1592.07	1585.37	1579.46	1558.78	1547.56
160000	1670.40	1660.23	1651.29	1643.43	1636.51	1630.41	1609.07	1597.49

12% MONTHLY AMORTIZING PAYMENTS

AMOUNT OF LOAN	NUMBER OF YEARS IN TERM							
	1	1-1/2	2	3	4	5	6	7
$ 50	4.45	3.05	2.36	1.67	1.32	1.12	.98	.89
100	8.89	6.10	4.71	3.33	2.64	2.23	1.96	1.77
200	17.77	12.20	9.42	6.65	5.27	4.45	3.92	3.54
300	26.66	18.30	14.13	9.97	7.91	6.68	5.87	5.30
400	35.54	24.40	18.83	13.29	10.54	8.90	7.83	7.07
500	44.43	30.50	23.54	16.61	13.17	11.13	9.78	8.83
600	53.31	36.59	28.25	19.93	15.81	13.35	11.74	10.60
700	62.20	42.69	32.96	23.26	18.44	15.58	13.69	12.36
800	71.08	48.79	37.66	26.58	21.07	17.80	15.65	14.13
900	79.97	54.89	42.37	29.90	23.71	20.03	17.60	15.89
1000	88.85	60.99	47.08	33.22	26.34	22.25	19.56	17.66
2000	177.70	121.97	94.15	66.43	52.67	44.49	39.11	35.31
3000	266.55	182.95	141.23	99.65	79.01	66.74	58.66	52.96
4000	355.40	243.93	188.30	132.86	105.34	88.98	78.21	70.62
5000	444.25	304.92	235.37	166.08	131.67	111.23	97.76	88.27
6000	533.10	365.90	282.45	199.29	158.01	133.47	117.31	105.92
7000	621.95	426.88	329.52	232.51	184.34	155.72	136.86	123.57
8000	710.80	487.86	376.59	265.72	210.68	177.96	156.41	141.23
9000	799.64	548.84	423.67	298.93	237.01	200.21	175.96	158.88
10000	888.49	609.83	470.74	332.15	263.34	222.45	195.51	176.53
11000	977.34	670.81	517.81	365.36	289.68	244.69	215.06	194.19
12000	1066.19	731.79	564.89	398.58	316.01	266.94	234.61	211.84
13000	1155.04	792.77	611.96	431.79	342.34	289.18	254.16	229.49
14000	1243.89	853.75	659.03	465.01	368.68	311.43	273.71	247.14
15000	1332.74	914.74	706.11	498.22	395.01	333.67	293.26	264.80
16000	1421.59	975.72	753.18	531.43	421.35	355.92	312.81	282.45
17000	1510.43	1036.70	800.25	564.65	447.68	378.16	332.36	300.10
18000	1599.28	1097.68	847.33	597.86	474.01	400.41	351.91	317.75
19000	1688.13	1158.66	894.40	631.08	500.35	422.65	371.46	335.41
20000	1776.98	1219.65	941.47	664.29	526.68	444.89	391.01	353.06
21000	1865.83	1280.63	988.55	697.51	553.02	467.14	410.56	370.71
22000	1954.68	1341.61	1035.62	730.72	579.35	489.38	430.11	388.37
23000	2043.53	1402.59	1082.69	763.93	605.68	511.63	449.66	406.02
24000	2132.38	1463.57	1129.77	797.15	632.02	533.87	469.21	423.67
25000	2221.22	1524.56	1176.84	830.36	658.35	556.12	488.76	441.32
26000	2310.07	1585.54	1223.92	863.58	684.68	578.36	508.31	458.98
27000	2398.92	1646.52	1270.99	896.79	711.02	600.61	527.86	476.63
28000	2487.77	1707.50	1318.06	930.01	737.35	622.85	547.41	494.28
29000	2576.62	1768.48	1365.14	963.22	763.69	645.09	566.96	511.93
30000	2665.47	1829.47	1412.21	996.43	790.02	667.34	586.51	529.59
31000	2754.32	1890.45	1459.28	1029.65	816.35	689.58	606.06	547.24
32000	2843.17	1951.43	1506.36	1062.86	842.69	711.83	625.61	564.89
33000	2932.02	2012.41	1553.43	1096.08	869.02	734.07	645.16	582.55
34000	3020.86	2073.39	1600.50	1129.29	895.36	756.32	664.71	600.20
35000	3109.71	2134.38	1647.58	1162.51	921.69	778.56	684.26	617.85
40000	3553.96	2439.29	1882.94	1328.58	1053.36	889.78	782.01	706.11
45000	3998.20	2744.20	2118.31	1494.65	1185.03	1001.01	879.76	794.38
50000	4442.44	3049.11	2353.68	1660.72	1316.70	1112.23	977.51	882.64
55000	4886.69	3354.02	2589.05	1826.79	1448.37	1223.45	1075.27	970.91
60000	5330.93	3658.93	2824.41	1992.86	1580.04	1334.67	1173.02	1059.17
65000	5775.18	3963.84	3059.78	2158.94	1711.70	1445.89	1270.77	1147.43
70000	6219.42	4268.75	3295.15	2325.01	1843.37	1557.12	1368.52	1235.70
75000	6663.66	4573.66	3530.52	2491.08	1975.04	1668.34	1466.27	1323.96
80000	7107.91	4878.57	3765.88	2657.15	2106.71	1779.56	1564.02	1412.22
85000	7552.15	5183.48	4001.25	2823.22	2238.38	1890.78	1661.77	1500.49
90000	7996.40	5488.39	4236.62	2989.29	2370.05	2002.01	1759.52	1588.75
95000	8440.64	5793.30	4471.98	3155.36	2501.72	2113.23	1857.27	1677.01
100000	8884.88	6098.21	4707.35	3321.44	2633.39	2224.45	1955.02	1765.28
105000	9329.13	6403.12	4942.72	3487.51	2765.06	2335.67	2052.78	1853.54
110000	9773.37	6708.03	5178.09	3653.58	2896.73	2446.89	2150.53	1941.81
115000	10217.62	7012.94	5413.45	3819.65	3028.40	2558.12	2248.28	2030.07
120000	10661.86	7317.85	5648.82	3985.72	3160.07	2669.34	2346.03	2118.33
125000	11106.10	7622.76	5884.19	4151.79	3291.73	2780.56	2443.78	2206.60
130000	11550.35	7927.67	6119.56	4317.87	3423.40	2891.78	2541.53	2294.86
135000	11994.59	8232.58	6354.92	4483.94	3555.07	3003.01	2639.28	2383.12
140000	12438.84	8537.49	6590.29	4650.01	3686.74	3114.23	2737.03	2471.39
145000	12883.08	8842.40	6825.66	4816.08	3818.41	3225.45	2834.78	2559.65
150000	13327.32	9147.31	7061.03	4982.15	3950.08	3336.67	2932.53	2647.91
155000	13771.57	9452.22	7296.39	5148.22	4081.75	3447.89	3030.28	2736.18
160000	14215.81	9757.13	7531.76	5314.29	4213.42	3559.12	3128.04	2824.44

MONTHLY AMORTIZING PAYMENTS 12%

AMOUNT OF LOAN	NUMBER OF YEARS IN TERM							
	8	9	10	11	12	14	15	16
$ 50	.82	.76	.72	.69	.66	.62	.61	.59
100	1.63	1.52	1.44	1.37	1.32	1.24	1.21	1.18
200	3.26	3.04	2.87	2.74	2.63	2.47	2.41	2.35
300	4.88	4.56	4.31	4.11	3.95	3.70	3.61	3.53
400	6.51	6.08	5.74	5.48	5.26	4.93	4.81	4.70
500	8.13	7.60	7.18	6.84	6.57	6.16	6.01	5.87
600	9.76	9.12	8.61	8.21	7.89	7.39	7.21	7.05
700	11.38	10.63	10.05	9.58	9.20	8.63	8.41	8.22
800	13.01	12.15	11.48	10.95	10.51	9.86	9.61	9.39
900	14.63	13.67	12.92	12.32	11.83	11.09	10.81	10.57
1000	16.26	15.19	14.35	13.68	13.14	12.32	12.01	11.74
2000	32.51	30.37	28.70	27.36	26.27	24.63	24.01	23.48
3000	48.76	45.56	43.05	41.04	39.41	36.95	36.01	35.22
4000	65.02	60.74	57.39	54.72	52.54	49.26	48.01	46.95
5000	81.27	75.93	71.74	68.39	65.68	61.58	60.01	58.69
6000	97.52	91.11	86.09	82.07	78.81	73.89	72.02	70.43
7000	113.77	106.29	100.43	95.75	91.94	86.21	84.02	82.17
8000	130.03	121.48	114.78	109.43	105.08	98.52	96.02	93.90
9000	146.28	136.66	129.13	123.11	118.21	110.83	108.02	105.64
10000	162.53	151.85	143.48	136.78	131.35	123.15	120.02	117.38
11000	178.79	167.03	157.82	150.46	144.48	135.46	132.02	129.11
12000	195.04	182.22	172.17	164.14	157.62	147.78	144.03	140.85
13000	211.29	197.40	186.52	177.82	170.75	160.09	156.03	152.59
14000	227.54	212.58	200.86	191.50	183.88	172.41	168.03	164.33
15000	243.80	227.77	215.21	205.17	197.02	184.72	180.03	176.06
16000	260.05	242.95	229.56	218.85	210.15	197.03	192.03	187.80
17000	276.30	258.14	243.91	232.53	223.29	209.35	204.03	199.54
18000	292.56	273.32	258.25	246.21	236.42	221.66	216.04	211.28
19000	308.81	288.51	272.60	259.88	249.55	233.98	228.04	223.01
20000	325.06	303.69	286.95	273.56	262.69	246.29	240.04	234.75
21000	341.31	318.87	301.29	287.24	275.82	258.61	252.04	246.49
22000	357.57	334.06	315.64	300.92	288.96	270.92	264.04	258.22
23000	373.82	349.24	329.99	314.60	302.09	283.23	276.04	269.96
24000	390.07	364.43	344.34	328.27	315.23	295.55	288.05	281.70
25000	406.33	379.61	358.68	341.95	328.36	307.86	300.05	293.44
26000	422.58	394.80	373.03	355.63	341.49	320.18	312.05	305.17
27000	438.83	409.98	387.38	369.31	354.63	332.49	324.05	316.91
28000	455.08	425.16	401.72	382.99	367.76	344.81	336.05	328.65
29000	471.34	440.35	416.07	396.66	380.90	357.12	348.05	340.39
30000	487.59	455.53	430.42	410.34	394.03	369.43	360.06	352.12
31000	503.84	470.72	444.76	424.02	407.16	381.75	372.06	363.86
32000	520.10	485.90	459.11	437.70	420.30	394.06	384.06	375.60
33000	536.35	501.08	473.46	451.37	433.43	406.38	396.06	387.33
34000	552.60	516.27	487.81	465.05	446.57	418.69	408.06	399.07
35000	568.85	531.45	502.15	478.73	459.70	431.01	420.06	410.81
40000	650.12	607.37	573.89	547.12	525.37	492.58	480.07	469.50
45000	731.38	683.30	645.62	615.51	591.04	554.15	540.08	528.18
50000	812.65	759.22	717.36	683.90	656.71	615.72	600.09	586.87
55000	893.91	835.14	789.10	752.29	722.39	677.29	660.10	645.55
60000	975.18	911.06	860.83	820.68	788.06	738.86	720.11	704.24
65000	1056.44	986.98	932.57	889.07	853.73	800.43	780.11	762.93
70000	1137.70	1062.90	1004.30	957.46	919.40	862.01	840.12	821.61
75000	1218.97	1138.82	1076.04	1025.85	985.07	923.58	900.13	880.30
80000	1300.23	1214.74	1147.77	1094.24	1050.74	985.15	960.14	938.99
85000	1381.50	1290.66	1219.51	1162.62	1116.41	1046.72	1020.15	997.67
90000	1462.76	1366.59	1291.24	1231.01	1182.08	1108.29	1080.16	1056.36
95000	1544.02	1442.51	1362.98	1299.40	1247.75	1169.86	1140.16	1115.04
100000	1625.29	1518.43	1434.71	1367.79	1313.42	1231.43	1200.17	1173.73
105000	1706.55	1594.35	1506.45	1436.18	1379.10	1293.01	1260.18	1232.42
110000	1787.82	1670.27	1578.19	1504.57	1444.77	1354.58	1320.19	1291.10
115000	1869.08	1746.19	1649.92	1572.96	1510.44	1416.15	1380.20	1349.79
120000	1950.35	1822.11	1721.66	1641.35	1576.11	1477.72	1440.21	1408.48
125000	2031.61	1898.03	1793.39	1709.74	1641.78	1539.29	1500.22	1467.16
130000	2112.87	1973.96	1865.13	1778.13	1707.45	1600.86	1560.22	1525.85
135000	2194.14	2049.88	1936.86	1846.52	1773.12	1662.43	1620.23	1584.53
140000	2275.40	2125.80	2008.60	1914.91	1838.79	1724.01	1680.24	1643.22
145000	2356.67	2201.72	2080.33	1983.30	1904.46	1785.58	1740.25	1701.91
150000	2437.93	2277.64	2152.07	2051.69	1970.13	1847.15	1800.26	1760.59
155000	2519.20	2353.56	2223.80	2120.08	2035.80	1908.72	1860.27	1819.28
160000	2600.46	2429.48	2295.54	2188.47	2101.48	1970.29	1920.27	1877.97

MONTHLY AMORTIZING PAYMENTS

AMOUNT OF LOAN	NUMBER OF YEARS IN TERM							
	17	18	19	20	21	22	23	24
$ 50	.58	.57	.56	.56	.55	.54	.54	.54
100	1.16	1.14	1.12	1.11	1.09	1.08	1.07	1.07
200	2.31	2.27	2.24	2.21	2.18	2.16	2.14	2.13
300	3.46	3.40	3.35	3.31	3.27	3.24	3.21	3.19
400	4.61	4.53	4.47	4.41	4.36	4.32	4.28	4.25
500	5.76	5.66	5.58	5.51	5.45	5.39	5.35	5.31
600	6.91	6.80	6.70	6.61	6.54	6.47	6.42	6.37
700	8.06	7.93	7.81	7.71	7.63	7.55	7.48	7.43
800	9.21	9.06	8.93	8.81	8.71	8.63	8.55	8.49
900	10.37	10.19	10.04	9.91	9.80	9.71	9.62	9.55
1000	11.52	11.32	11.16	11.02	10.89	10.78	10.69	10.61
2000	23.03	22.64	22.31	22.03	21.78	21.56	21.38	21.21
3000	34.54	33.96	33.47	33.04	32.67	32.34	32.06	31.82
4000	46.05	45.28	44.62	44.05	43.55	43.12	42.75	42.42
5000	57.57	56.60	55.77	55.06	54.44	53.90	53.43	53.02
6000	69.08	67.92	66.93	66.07	65.33	64.68	64.12	63.63
7000	80.59	79.24	78.08	77.08	76.21	75.46	74.80	74.23
8000	92.10	90.56	89.24	88.09	87.10	86.24	85.49	84.84
9000	103.61	101.88	100.39	99.10	97.99	97.02	96.18	95.44
10000	115.13	113.20	111.54	110.11	108.87	107.80	106.86	106.04
11000	126.64	124.52	122.70	121.12	119.76	118.58	117.55	116.65
12000	138.15	135.84	133.85	132.14	130.65	129.36	128.23	127.25
13000	149.66	147.16	145.01	143.15	141.54	140.14	138.92	137.85
14000	161.18	158.48	156.16	154.16	152.42	150.92	149.60	148.46
15000	172.69	169.80	167.31	165.17	163.31	161.70	160.29	159.06
16000	184.20	181.12	178.47	176.18	174.20	172.48	170.98	169.67
17000	195.71	192.44	189.62	187.19	185.08	183.25	181.66	180.27
18000	207.22	203.76	200.77	198.20	195.97	194.03	192.35	190.87
19000	218.74	215.08	211.93	209.21	206.86	204.81	203.03	201.48
20000	230.25	226.40	223.08	220.22	217.74	215.59	213.72	212.08
21000	241.76	237.71	234.24	231.23	228.63	226.37	224.40	222.69
22000	253.27	249.03	245.39	242.24	239.52	237.15	235.09	233.29
23000	264.78	260.35	256.54	253.25	250.41	247.93	245.77	243.89
24000	276.30	271.67	267.70	264.27	261.29	258.71	256.46	254.50
25000	287.81	282.99	278.85	275.28	272.18	269.49	267.15	265.10
26000	299.32	294.31	290.01	286.29	283.07	280.27	277.83	275.70
27000	310.83	305.63	301.16	297.30	293.95	291.05	288.52	286.31
28000	322.35	316.95	312.31	308.31	304.84	301.83	299.20	296.91
29000	333.86	328.27	323.47	319.32	315.73	312.61	309.89	307.52
30000	345.37	339.59	334.62	330.33	326.61	323.39	320.57	318.12
31000	356.88	350.91	345.77	341.34	337.50	334.17	331.26	328.72
32000	368.39	362.23	356.93	352.35	348.39	344.95	341.95	339.33
33000	379.91	373.55	368.08	363.36	359.28	355.72	352.63	349.93
34000	391.42	384.87	379.24	374.37	370.16	366.50	363.32	360.53
35000	402.93	396.19	390.39	385.39	381.05	377.28	374.00	371.14
40000	460.49	452.79	446.16	440.44	435.48	431.18	427.43	424.16
45000	518.05	509.38	501.93	495.49	489.92	485.08	480.86	477.18
50000	575.61	565.98	557.70	550.55	544.35	538.97	534.29	530.20
55000	633.17	622.58	613.47	605.60	598.79	592.87	587.72	583.22
60000	690.73	679.18	669.24	660.66	653.22	646.77	641.14	636.23
65000	748.30	735.77	725.01	715.71	707.66	700.66	694.57	689.25
70000	805.86	792.37	780.77	770.77	762.09	754.56	748.00	742.27
75000	863.42	848.97	836.54	825.82	816.53	808.46	801.43	795.29
80000	920.98	905.57	892.31	880.87	870.96	862.36	854.86	848.31
85000	978.54	962.16	948.08	935.93	925.40	916.25	908.29	901.33
90000	1036.10	1018.76	1003.85	990.98	979.83	970.15	961.71	954.35
95000	1093.66	1075.36	1059.62	1046.04	1034.27	1024.05	1015.14	1007.37
100000	1151.22	1131.96	1115.39	1101.09	1088.70	1077.94	1068.57	1060.39
105000	1208.78	1188.55	1171.16	1156.15	1143.14	1131.84	1122.00	1113.41
110000	1266.34	1245.15	1226.93	1211.20	1197.57	1185.74	1175.43	1166.43
115000	1323.90	1301.75	1282.70	1266.25	1252.01	1239.63	1228.85	1219.44
120000	1381.46	1358.35	1338.47	1321.31	1306.44	1293.53	1282.28	1272.46
125000	1439.02	1414.94	1394.24	1376.36	1360.88	1347.43	1335.71	1325.48
130000	1496.59	1471.54	1450.01	1431.42	1415.31	1401.32	1389.14	1378.50
135000	1554.15	1528.14	1505.78	1486.47	1469.75	1455.22	1442.57	1431.52
140000	1611.71	1584.74	1561.54	1541.53	1524.18	1509.12	1496.00	1484.54
145000	1669.27	1641.33	1617.31	1596.58	1578.62	1563.02	1549.42	1537.56
150000	1726.83	1697.93	1673.08	1651.63	1633.05	1616.91	1602.85	1590.58
155000	1784.39	1754.53	1728.85	1706.69	1687.49	1670.81	1656.28	1643.60
160000	1841.95	1811.13	1784.62	1761.74	1741.92	1724.71	1709.71	1696.62

MONTHLY AMORTIZING PAYMENTS 12%

AMOUNT OF LOAN	NUMBER OF YEARS IN TERM							
	25	26	27	28	29	30	35	40
$ 50	.53	.53	.53	.52	.52	.52	.51	.51
100	1.06	1.05	1.05	1.04	1.04	1.03	1.02	1.01
200	2.11	2.10	2.09	2.08	2.07	2.06	2.04	2.02
300	3.16	3.15	3.13	3.11	3.10	3.09	3.05	3.03
400	4.22	4.19	4.17	4.15	4.13	4.12	4.07	4.04
500	5.27	5.24	5.21	5.19	5.17	5.15	5.08	5.05
600	6.32	6.29	6.25	6.22	6.20	6.18	6.10	6.06
700	7.38	7.33	7.30	7.26	7.23	7.21	7.11	7.06
800	8.43	8.38	8.34	8.30	8.26	8.23	8.13	8.07
900	9.48	9.43	9.38	9.33	9.30	9.26	9.14	9.08
1000	10.54	10.47	10.42	10.37	10.33	10.29	10.16	10.09
2000	21.07	20.94	20.83	20.74	20.65	20.58	20.32	20.17
3000	31.60	31.41	31.25	31.10	30.98	30.86	30.47	30.26
4000	42.13	41.88	41.66	41.47	41.30	41.15	40.63	40.34
5000	52.67	52.35	52.08	51.84	51.62	51.44	50.78	50.43
6000	63.20	62.82	62.49	62.20	61.95	61.72	60.94	60.51
7000	73.73	73.29	72.91	72.57	72.27	72.01	71.09	70.60
8000	84.26	83.76	83.32	82.93	82.59	82.29	81.25	80.68
9000	94.80	94.23	93.74	93.30	92.92	92.58	91.40	90.77
10000	105.33	104.70	104.15	103.67	103.24	102.87	101.56	100.85
11000	115.86	115.17	114.56	114.03	113.56	113.15	111.72	110.94
12000	126.39	125.64	124.98	124.40	123.89	123.44	121.87	121.02
13000	136.92	136.11	135.39	134.76	134.21	133.72	132.03	131.11
14000	147.46	146.58	145.81	145.13	144.54	144.01	142.18	141.19
15000	157.99	157.05	156.22	155.50	154.86	154.30	152.34	151.28
16000	168.52	167.52	166.64	165.86	165.18	164.58	162.49	161.36
17000	179.05	177.99	177.05	176.23	175.51	174.87	172.65	171.45
18000	189.59	188.46	187.47	186.60	185.83	185.16	182.80	181.53
19000	200.12	198.93	197.88	196.96	196.15	195.44	192.96	191.62
20000	210.65	209.40	208.29	207.33	206.48	205.73	203.11	201.70
21000	221.18	219.87	218.71	217.69	216.80	216.01	213.27	211.79
22000	231.71	230.33	229.12	228.06	227.12	226.30	223.43	221.87
23000	242.25	240.80	239.54	238.43	237.45	236.59	233.58	231.96
24000	252.78	251.27	249.95	248.79	247.77	246.87	243.74	242.04
25000	263.31	261.74	260.37	259.16	258.09	257.16	253.89	252.13
26000	273.84	272.21	270.78	269.52	268.42	267.44	264.05	262.21
27000	284.38	282.68	281.20	279.89	278.74	277.73	274.20	272.30
28000	294.91	293.15	291.61	290.26	289.07	288.02	284.36	282.38
29000	305.44	303.62	302.03	300.62	299.39	298.30	294.51	292.47
30000	315.97	314.09	312.44	310.99	309.71	308.59	304.67	302.55
31000	326.50	324.56	322.85	321.36	320.04	318.87	314.83	312.64
32000	337.04	335.03	333.27	331.72	330.36	329.16	324.98	322.72
33000	347.57	345.50	343.68	342.09	340.68	339.45	335.14	332.81
34000	358.10	355.97	354.10	352.45	351.01	349.73	345.29	342.89
35000	368.63	366.44	364.51	362.82	361.33	360.02	355.45	352.98
40000	421.29	418.79	416.58	414.65	412.95	411.45	406.22	403.40
45000	473.96	471.13	468.66	466.48	464.57	462.88	457.00	453.83
50000	526.62	523.48	520.73	518.31	516.18	514.31	507.78	504.25
55000	579.28	575.83	572.80	570.14	567.80	565.74	558.56	554.68
60000	631.94	628.18	624.87	621.97	619.42	617.17	609.33	605.10
65000	684.60	680.52	676.95	673.80	671.04	668.60	660.11	655.53
70000	737.26	732.87	729.02	725.63	722.66	720.03	710.89	705.95
75000	789.92	785.22	781.09	777.46	774.27	771.46	761.67	756.38
80000	842.58	837.57	833.16	829.30	825.89	822.90	812.44	806.80
85000	895.25	889.91	885.24	881.13	877.51	874.33	863.22	857.23
90000	947.91	942.26	937.31	932.96	929.13	925.76	914.00	907.65
95000	1000.57	994.61	989.38	984.79	980.75	977.19	964.78	958.08
100000	1053.23	1046.96	1041.45	1036.62	1032.36	1028.62	1015.55	1008.50
105000	1105.89	1099.31	1093.53	1088.45	1083.98	1080.05	1066.33	1058.93
110000	1158.55	1151.65	1145.60	1140.28	1135.60	1131.48	1117.11	1109.35
115000	1211.21	1204.00	1197.67	1192.11	1187.22	1182.91	1167.89	1159.78
120000	1263.87	1256.35	1249.74	1243.94	1238.84	1234.34	1218.66	1210.20
125000	1316.54	1308.70	1301.82	1295.77	1290.45	1285.77	1269.44	1260.63
130000	1369.20	1361.04	1353.89	1347.60	1342.07	1337.20	1320.22	1311.05
135000	1421.86	1413.39	1405.96	1399.43	1393.69	1388.63	1371.00	1361.48
140000	1474.52	1465.74	1458.03	1451.26	1445.31	1440.06	1421.77	1411.90
145000	1527.18	1518.09	1510.11	1503.09	1496.93	1491.49	1472.55	1462.33
150000	1579.84	1570.43	1562.18	1554.92	1548.54	1542.92	1523.33	1512.75
155000	1632.50	1622.78	1614.25	1606.76	1600.16	1594.35	1574.11	1563.18
160000	1685.16	1675.13	1666.32	1658.59	1651.78	1645.79	1624.88	1613.60

MONTHLY AMORTIZING PAYMENTS

AMOUNT OF LOAN	NUMBER OF YEARS IN TERM							
	1	2	3	4	5	6	7	8
$ 50	4.45	2.36	1.67	1.32	1.12	.99	.89	.82
100	8.90	4.72	3.33	2.64	2.24	1.97	1.78	1.64
200	17.79	9.43	6.66	5.28	4.47	3.93	3.55	3.27
300	26.68	14.14	9.99	7.92	6.70	5.89	5.32	4.90
400	35.57	18.86	13.31	10.56	8.93	7.85	7.09	6.53
500	44.46	23.57	16.64	13.20	11.16	9.81	8.86	8.17
600	53.35	28.28	19.97	15.84	13.39	11.77	10.64	9.80
700	62.24	33.00	23.30	18.48	15.62	13.74	12.41	11.43
800	71.13	37.71	26.62	21.12	17.85	15.70	14.18	13.06
900	80.02	42.42	29.95	23.76	20.08	17.66	15.95	14.69
1000	88.91	47.14	33.28	26.40	22.31	19.62	17.72	16.33
2000	177.82	94.27	66.55	52.80	44.62	39.24	35.44	32.65
3000	266.73	141.40	99.83	79.19	66.93	58.85	53.16	48.97
4000	355.63	188.53	133.10	105.59	89.24	78.47	70.88	65.29
5000	444.54	235.66	166.38	131.98	111.54	98.08	88.60	81.61
6000	533.45	282.80	199.65	158.38	133.85	117.70	106.32	97.93
7000	622.36	329.93	232.92	184.77	156.16	137.31	124.04	114.26
8000	711.26	377.06	266.20	211.17	178.47	156.93	141.76	130.58
9000	800.17	424.19	299.47	237.56	200.77	176.54	159.48	146.90
10000	889.08	471.32	332.75	263.96	223.08	196.16	177.20	163.22
11000	977.99	518.46	366.02	290.35	245.39	215.77	194.92	179.54
12000	1066.89	565.59	399.29	316.75	267.70	235.39	212.64	195.86
13000	1155.80	612.72	432.57	343.14	290.00	255.00	230.36	212.19
14000	1244.71	659.85	465.84	369.54	312.31	274.62	248.08	228.51
15000	1333.61	706.98	499.12	395.93	334.62	294.23	265.80	244.83
16000	1422.52	754.11	532.39	422.33	356.93	313.85	283.52	261.15
17000	1511.43	801.25	565.66	448.72	379.24	333.46	301.24	277.47
18000	1600.34	848.38	598.94	475.12	401.54	353.08	318.96	293.79
19000	1689.24	895.51	632.21	501.51	423.85	372.69	336.68	310.12
20000	1778.15	942.64	665.49	527.91	446.16	392.31	354.40	326.44
21000	1867.06	989.77	698.76	554.31	468.47	411.93	372.12	342.76
22000	1955.97	1036.91	732.03	580.70	490.77	431.54	389.84	359.08
23000	2044.87	1084.04	765.31	607.10	513.08	451.16	407.56	375.40
24000	2133.78	1131.17	798.58	633.49	535.39	470.77	425.28	391.72
25000	2222.69	1178.30	831.86	659.89	557.70	490.39	443.00	408.04
26000	2311.59	1225.43	865.13	686.28	580.00	510.00	460.72	424.37
27000	2400.50	1272.57	898.40	712.68	602.31	529.62	478.44	440.69
28000	2489.41	1319.70	931.68	739.07	624.62	549.23	496.16	457.01
29000	2578.32	1366.83	964.95	765.47	646.93	568.85	513.87	473.33
30000	2667.22	1413.96	998.23	791.86	669.23	588.46	531.59	489.65
31000	2756.13	1461.09	1031.50	818.26	691.54	608.08	549.31	505.97
32000	2845.04	1508.22	1064.77	844.65	713.85	627.69	567.03	522.30
33000	2933.95	1555.36	1098.05	871.05	736.16	647.31	584.75	538.62
34000	3022.85	1602.49	1131.32	897.44	758.47	666.92	602.47	554.94
35000	3111.76	1649.62	1164.60	923.84	780.77	686.54	620.19	571.26
40000	3556.30	1885.28	1330.97	1055.82	892.31	784.62	708.79	652.87
45000	4000.83	2120.94	1497.34	1187.79	1003.85	882.69	797.39	734.48
50000	4445.37	2356.60	1663.71	1319.77	1115.39	980.77	885.99	816.08
55000	4889.91	2592.26	1830.08	1451.74	1226.93	1078.84	974.59	897.69
60000	5334.44	2827.92	1996.45	1583.72	1338.46	1176.92	1063.18	979.30
65000	5778.98	3063.58	2162.82	1715.70	1450.00	1275.00	1151.78	1060.91
70000	6223.51	3299.24	2329.19	1847.67	1561.54	1373.07	1240.38	1142.52
75000	6668.05	3534.90	2495.56	1979.65	1673.08	1471.15	1328.98	1224.12
80000	7112.59	3770.55	2661.93	2111.63	1784.62	1569.23	1417.58	1305.73
85000	7557.12	4006.21	2828.30	2243.60	1896.16	1667.30	1506.18	1387.34
90000	8001.66	4241.87	2994.67	2375.58	2007.69	1765.38	1594.77	1468.95
95000	8446.20	4477.53	3161.04	2507.55	2119.23	1863.45	1683.37	1550.56
100000	8890.73	4713.19	3327.41	2639.53	2230.77	1961.53	1771.97	1632.16
105000	9335.27	4948.85	3493.78	2771.51	2342.31	2059.61	1860.57	1713.77
110000	9779.81	5184.51	3660.15	2903.48	2453.85	2157.68	1949.17	1795.38
115000	10224.34	5420.17	3826.52	3035.46	2565.39	2255.76	2037.76	1876.99
120000	10668.88	5655.83	3992.89	3167.44	2676.92	2353.84	2126.36	1958.60
125000	11113.41	5891.49	4159.26	3299.41	2788.46	2451.91	2214.96	2040.20
130000	11557.95	6127.15	4325.63	3431.39	2900.00	2549.99	2303.56	2121.81
135000	12002.49	6362.81	4492.00	3563.36	3011.54	2648.06	2392.16	2203.42
140000	12447.02	6598.47	4658.37	3695.34	3123.08	2746.14	2480.76	2285.03
145000	12891.56	6834.13	4824.74	3827.32	3234.62	2844.22	2569.35	2366.64
150000	13336.10	7069.79	4991.11	3959.29	3346.15	2942.29	2657.95	2448.24
155000	13780.63	7305.44	5157.48	4091.27	3457.69	3040.37	2746.55	2529.85
160000	14225.17	7541.10	5323.85	4223.25	3569.23	3138.45	2835.15	2611.46

MONTHLY AMORTIZING PAYMENTS 12 1/8%

AMOUNT OF LOAN	NUMBER OF YEARS IN TERM							
	9	10	15	20	25	30	35	40
$ 50	.77	.73	.61	.56	.54	.52	.52	.51
100	1.53	1.45	1.21	1.11	1.07	1.04	1.03	1.02
200	3.06	2.89	2.42	2.22	2.13	2.08	2.06	2.04
300	4.58	4.33	3.63	3.33	3.19	3.12	3.08	3.06
400	6.11	5.77	4.84	4.44	4.25	4.16	4.11	4.08
500	7.63	7.21	6.05	5.55	5.32	5.20	5.13	5.10
600	9.16	8.66	7.25	6.66	6.38	6.23	6.16	6.12
700	10.68	10.10	8.46	7.77	7.44	7.27	7.18	7.14
800	12.21	11.54	9.67	8.88	8.50	8.31	8.21	8.15
900	13.73	12.98	10.88	9.99	9.57	9.35	9.23	9.17
1000	15.26	14.42	12.09	11.10	10.63	10.39	10.26	10.19
2000	30.51	28.84	24.17	22.20	21.25	20.77	20.51	20.38
3000	45.77	43.26	36.25	33.30	31.88	31.15	30.77	30.56
4000	61.02	57.68	48.33	44.40	42.50	41.53	41.02	40.75
5000	76.28	72.10	60.42	55.50	53.13	51.92	51.28	50.93
6000	91.53	86.52	72.50	66.59	63.75	62.30	61.53	61.12
7000	106.79	100.94	84.58	77.69	74.38	72.68	71.79	71.31
8000	122.04	115.36	96.66	88.79	85.00	83.06	82.04	81.49
9000	137.30	129.78	108.74	99.89	95.63	93.45	92.30	91.68
10000	152.55	144.20	120.83	110.99	106.25	103.83	102.55	101.86
11000	167.81	158.62	132.91	122.08	116.88	114.21	112.80	112.05
12000	183.06	173.04	144.99	133.18	127.50	124.59	123.06	122.24
13000	198.32	187.46	157.07	144.28	138.13	134.98	133.31	132.42
14000	213.57	201.88	169.16	155.38	148.75	145.36	143.57	142.61
15000	228.83	216.30	181.24	166.48	159.38	155.74	153.82	152.79
16000	244.08	230.72	193.32	177.58	170.00	166.12	164.08	162.98
17000	259.34	245.14	205.40	188.67	180.63	176.51	174.33	173.16
18000	274.59	259.56	217.48	199.77	191.25	186.89	184.59	183.35
19000	289.85	273.97	229.57	210.87	201.87	197.27	194.84	193.54
20000	305.10	288.39	241.65	221.97	212.50	207.65	205.10	203.72
21000	320.36	302.81	253.73	233.07	223.12	218.04	215.35	213.91
22000	335.61	317.23	265.81	244.16	233.75	228.42	225.60	224.09
23000	350.87	331.65	277.90	255.26	244.37	238.80	235.86	234.28
24000	366.12	346.07	289.98	266.36	255.00	249.18	246.11	244.47
25000	381.38	360.49	302.06	277.46	265.62	259.57	256.37	254.65
26000	396.63	374.91	314.14	288.56	276.25	269.95	266.62	264.84
27000	411.88	389.33	326.22	299.65	286.87	280.33	276.88	275.02
28000	427.14	403.75	338.31	310.75	297.50	290.71	287.13	285.21
29000	442.39	418.17	350.39	321.85	308.12	301.10	297.39	295.40
30000	457.65	432.59	362.47	332.95	318.75	311.48	307.64	305.58
31000	472.90	447.01	374.55	344.05	329.37	321.86	317.90	315.77
32000	488.16	461.43	386.64	355.15	340.00	332.24	328.15	325.95
33000	503.41	475.85	398.72	366.24	350.62	342.63	338.40	336.14
34000	518.67	490.27	410.80	377.34	361.25	353.01	348.66	346.32
35000	533.92	504.69	422.88	388.44	371.87	363.39	358.91	356.51
40000	610.20	576.78	483.29	443.93	424.99	415.30	410.19	407.44
45000	686.47	648.88	543.70	499.42	478.12	467.22	461.46	458.37
50000	762.75	720.98	604.12	554.91	531.24	519.13	512.73	509.30
55000	839.02	793.07	664.53	610.40	584.36	571.04	564.00	560.23
60000	915.29	865.17	724.94	665.89	637.49	622.95	615.28	611.16
65000	991.57	937.27	785.35	721.38	690.61	674.86	666.55	662.09
70000	1067.84	1009.37	845.76	776.87	743.74	726.78	717.82	713.02
75000	1144.12	1081.46	906.17	832.36	796.86	778.69	769.09	763.95
80000	1220.39	1153.56	966.58	887.86	849.98	830.60	820.37	814.87
85000	1296.66	1225.66	1026.99	943.35	903.11	882.51	871.64	865.80
90000	1372.94	1297.76	1087.40	998.84	956.23	934.43	922.91	916.73
95000	1449.21	1369.85	1147.82	1054.33	1009.35	986.34	974.18	967.66
100000	1525.49	1441.95	1208.23	1109.82	1062.48	1038.25	1025.46	1018.59
105000	1601.76	1514.05	1268.64	1165.31	1115.60	1090.16	1076.73	1069.52
110000	1678.03	1586.14	1329.05	1220.80	1168.72	1142.07	1128.00	1120.45
115000	1754.31	1658.24	1389.46	1276.29	1221.85	1193.99	1179.28	1171.38
120000	1830.58	1730.34	1449.87	1331.78	1274.97	1245.90	1230.55	1222.31
125000	1906.86	1802.44	1510.28	1387.27	1328.10	1297.81	1281.82	1273.24
130000	1983.13	1874.53	1570.69	1442.76	1381.22	1349.72	1333.09	1324.17
135000	2059.40	1946.63	1631.10	1498.25	1434.34	1401.64	1384.37	1375.10
140000	2135.68	2018.73	1691.52	1553.74	1487.47	1453.55	1435.64	1426.03
145000	2211.95	2090.82	1751.93	1609.23	1540.59	1505.46	1486.91	1476.96
150000	2288.23	2162.92	1812.34	1664.72	1593.71	1557.37	1538.18	1527.89
155000	2364.50	2235.02	1872.75	1720.22	1646.84	1609.28	1589.46	1578.81
160000	2440.77	2307.12	1933.16	1775.71	1699.96	1661.20	1640.73	1629.74

MONTHLY AMORTIZING PAYMENTS

AMOUNT OF LOAN	NUMBER OF YEARS IN TERM							
	1	2	3	4	5	6	7	8
$ 50	4.45	2.36	1.67	1.33	1.12	.99	.89	.82
100	8.90	4.72	3.34	2.65	2.24	1.97	1.78	1.64
200	17.80	9.44	6.67	5.30	4.48	3.94	3.56	3.28
300	26.69	14.16	10.01	7.94	6.72	5.91	5.34	4.92
400	35.59	18.88	13.34	10.59	8.95	7.88	7.12	6.56
500	44.49	23.60	16.67	13.23	11.19	9.85	8.90	8.20
600	53.38	28.32	20.01	15.88	13.43	11.81	10.68	9.84
700	62.28	33.04	23.34	18.52	15.66	13.78	12.46	11.48
800	71.18	37.76	26.67	21.17	17.90	15.75	14.23	13.12
900	80.07	42.48	30.01	23.82	20.14	17.72	16.01	14.76
1000	88.97	47.20	33.34	26.46	22.38	19.69	17.79	16.40
2000	177.94	94.39	66.67	52.92	44.75	39.37	35.58	32.79
3000	266.90	141.58	100.01	79.38	67.12	59.05	53.37	49.18
4000	355.87	188.77	133.34	105.83	89.49	78.73	71.15	65.57
5000	444.83	235.96	166.67	132.29	111.86	98.41	88.94	81.96
6000	533.80	283.15	200.01	158.75	134.23	118.09	106.73	98.35
7000	622.77	330.34	233.34	185.20	156.60	137.77	124.51	114.74
8000	711.73	377.53	266.68	211.66	178.97	157.45	142.30	131.13
9000	800.70	424.72	300.01	238.12	201.34	177.13	160.09	147.52
10000	889.66	471.91	333.34	264.57	223.71	196.81	177.87	163.91
11000	978.63	519.10	366.68	291.03	246.09	216.49	195.66	180.30
12000	1067.59	566.29	400.01	317.49	268.46	236.17	213.45	196.69
13000	1156.56	613.48	433.34	343.94	290.83	255.85	231.23	213.08
14000	1245.53	660.67	466.68	370.40	313.20	275.53	249.02	229.47
15000	1334.49	707.86	500.01	396.86	335.57	295.21	266.81	245.86
16000	1423.46	755.05	533.35	423.31	357.94	314.89	284.59	262.25
17000	1512.42	802.24	566.68	449.77	380.31	334.57	302.38	278.64
18000	1601.39	849.43	600.01	476.23	402.68	354.25	320.17	295.03
19000	1690.35	896.62	633.35	502.68	425.05	373.93	337.95	311.42
20000	1779.32	943.81	666.68	529.14	447.42	393.61	355.74	327.82
21000	1868.29	991.00	700.02	555.60	469.80	413.29	373.53	344.21
22000	1957.25	1038.19	733.35	582.05	492.17	432.97	391.31	360.60
23000	2046.22	1085.38	766.68	608.51	514.54	452.66	409.10	376.99
24000	2135.18	1132.57	800.02	634.97	536.91	472.34	426.89	393.38
25000	2224.15	1179.76	833.35	661.42	559.28	492.02	444.67	409.77
26000	2313.12	1226.95	866.68	687.88	581.65	511.70	462.46	426.16
27000	2402.08	1274.14	900.02	714.34	604.02	531.38	480.25	442.55
28000	2491.05	1321.33	933.35	740.79	626.39	551.06	498.03	458.94
29000	2580.01	1368.52	966.69	767.25	648.76	570.74	515.82	475.33
30000	2668.98	1415.71	1000.02	793.71	671.13	590.42	533.61	491.72
31000	2757.94	1462.90	1033.35	820.16	693.51	610.10	551.39	508.11
32000	2846.91	1510.09	1066.69	846.62	715.88	629.78	569.18	524.50
33000	2935.88	1557.29	1100.02	873.08	738.25	649.46	586.97	540.89
34000	3024.84	1604.48	1133.36	899.53	760.62	669.14	604.75	557.28
35000	3113.81	1651.67	1166.69	925.99	782.99	688.82	622.54	573.67
40000	3558.64	1887.62	1333.36	1058.28	894.84	787.22	711.47	655.63
45000	4003.47	2123.57	1500.03	1190.56	1006.70	885.62	800.41	737.58
50000	4448.29	2359.52	1666.70	1322.84	1118.55	984.03	889.34	819.53
55000	4893.12	2595.47	1833.37	1455.13	1230.41	1082.43	978.27	901.48
60000	5337.95	2831.42	2000.04	1587.41	1342.26	1180.83	1067.21	983.44
65000	5782.78	3067.37	2166.70	1719.69	1454.12	1279.23	1156.14	1065.39
70000	6227.61	3303.33	2333.37	1851.98	1565.97	1377.64	1245.07	1147.34
75000	6672.44	3539.28	2500.04	1984.26	1677.83	1476.04	1334.01	1229.29
80000	7117.27	3775.23	2666.71	2116.55	1789.68	1574.44	1422.94	1311.25
85000	7562.10	4011.18	2833.38	2248.83	1901.54	1672.84	1511.88	1393.20
90000	8006.93	4247.13	3000.05	2381.11	2013.39	1771.24	1600.81	1475.15
95000	8451.75	4483.08	3166.72	2513.40	2125.25	1869.65	1689.74	1557.10
100000	8896.58	4719.04	3333.39	2645.68	2237.10	1968.05	1778.68	1639.06
105000	9341.41	4954.99	3500.06	2777.96	2348.96	2066.45	1867.61	1721.01
110000	9786.24	5190.94	3666.73	2910.25	2460.81	2164.85	1956.54	1802.96
115000	10231.07	5426.89	3833.40	3042.53	2572.67	2263.26	2045.48	1884.91
120000	10675.90	5662.84	4000.07	3174.82	2684.52	2361.66	2134.41	1966.87
125000	11120.73	5898.79	4166.74	3307.10	2796.38	2460.06	2223.34	2048.82
130000	11565.56	6134.74	4333.40	3439.38	2908.23	2558.46	2312.28	2130.77
135000	12010.39	6370.70	4500.07	3571.67	3020.09	2656.86	2401.21	2212.72
140000	12455.21	6606.65	4666.74	3703.95	3131.94	2755.27	2490.14	2294.68
145000	12900.04	6842.60	4833.41	3836.23	3243.80	2853.67	2579.08	2376.63
150000	13344.87	7078.55	5000.08	3968.52	3355.65	2952.07	2668.01	2458.58
155000	13789.70	7314.50	5166.75	4100.80	3467.51	3050.47	2756.94	2540.53
160000	14234.53	7550.45	5333.42	4233.09	3579.36	3148.88	2845.88	2622.49

AMOUNT OF LOAN	NUMBER OF YEARS IN TERM							
	9	10	15	20	25	30	35	40
$ 50	.77	.73	.61	.56	.54	.53	.52	.52
100	1.54	1.45	1.22	1.12	1.08	1.05	1.04	1.03
200	3.07	2.90	2.44	2.24	2.15	2.10	2.08	2.06
300	4.60	4.35	3.65	3.36	3.22	3.15	3.11	3.09
400	6.14	5.80	4.87	4.48	4.29	4.20	4.15	4.12
500	7.67	7.25	6.09	5.60	5.36	5.24	5.18	5.15
600	9.20	8.70	7.30	6.72	6.44	6.29	6.22	6.18
700	10.73	10.15	8.52	7.83	7.51	7.34	7.25	7.21
800	12.27	11.60	9.74	8.95	8.58	8.39	8.29	8.23
900	13.80	13.05	10.95	10.07	9.65	9.44	9.32	9.26
1000	15.33	14.50	12.17	11.19	10.72	10.48	10.36	10.29
2000	30.66	28.99	24.33	22.38	21.44	20.96	20.71	20.58
3000	45.98	43.48	36.49	33.56	32.16	31.44	31.07	30.87
4000	61.31	57.97	48.66	44.75	42.87	41.92	41.42	41.15
5000	76.63	72.46	60.82	55.93	53.59	52.40	51.77	51.44
6000	91.96	86.96	72.98	67.12	64.31	62.88	62.13	61.73
7000	107.28	101.45	85.15	78.30	75.03	73.36	72.48	72.01
8000	122.61	115.94	97.31	89.49	85.74	83.84	82.83	82.30
9000	137.93	130.43	109.47	100.68	96.46	94.32	93.19	92.59
10000	153.26	144.92	121.63	111.86	107.18	104.79	103.54	102.87
11000	168.59	159.42	133.80	123.05	117.90	115.27	113.90	113.16
12000	183.91	173.91	145.96	134.23	128.61	125.75	124.25	123.45
13000	199.24	188.40	158.12	145.42	139.33	136.23	134.60	133.73
14000	214.56	202.89	170.29	156.60	150.05	146.71	144.96	144.02
15000	229.89	217.38	182.45	167.79	160.77	157.19	155.31	154.31
16000	245.21	231.88	194.61	178.98	171.48	167.67	165.66	164.59
17000	260.54	246.37	206.78	190.16	182.20	178.15	176.02	174.88
18000	275.86	260.86	218.94	201.35	192.92	188.63	186.37	185.17
19000	291.19	275.35	231.10	212.53	203.64	199.11	196.73	195.46
20000	306.52	289.84	243.26	223.72	214.35	209.58	207.08	205.74
21000	321.84	304.34	255.43	234.90	225.07	220.06	217.43	216.03
22000	337.17	318.83	267.59	246.09	235.79	230.54	227.79	226.32
23000	352.49	333.32	279.75	257.27	246.51	241.02	238.14	236.60
24000	367.82	347.81	291.92	268.46	257.22	251.50	248.49	246.89
25000	383.14	362.30	304.08	279.65	267.94	261.98	258.85	257.18
26000	398.47	376.80	316.24	290.83	278.66	272.46	269.20	267.46
27000	413.79	391.29	328.41	302.02	289.38	282.94	279.56	277.75
28000	429.12	405.78	340.57	313.20	300.09	293.42	289.91	288.04
29000	444.45	420.27	352.73	324.39	310.81	303.89	300.26	298.32
30000	459.77	434.76	364.89	335.57	321.53	314.37	310.62	308.61
31000	475.10	449.26	377.06	346.76	332.25	324.85	320.97	318.90
32000	490.42	463.75	389.22	357.95	342.96	335.33	331.32	329.18
33000	505.75	478.24	401.38	369.13	353.68	345.81	341.68	339.47
34000	521.07	492.73	413.55	380.32	364.40	356.29	352.03	349.76
35000	536.40	507.22	425.71	391.50	375.12	366.77	362.38	360.05
40000	613.03	579.68	486.52	447.43	428.70	419.16	414.15	411.48
45000	689.65	652.14	547.34	503.36	482.29	471.56	465.92	462.91
50000	766.28	724.60	608.15	559.29	535.88	523.95	517.69	514.35
55000	842.91	797.06	668.97	615.22	589.46	576.35	569.46	565.78
60000	919.54	869.52	729.78	671.14	643.05	628.74	621.23	617.22
65000	996.17	941.98	790.60	727.07	696.64	681.14	673.00	668.65
70000	1072.79	1014.44	851.41	783.00	750.23	733.53	724.76	720.09
75000	1149.42	1086.90	912.23	838.93	803.81	785.93	776.53	771.52
80000	1226.05	1159.36	973.04	894.86	857.40	838.32	828.30	822.95
85000	1302.68	1231.82	1033.86	950.78	910.99	890.72	880.07	874.39
90000	1379.30	1304.28	1094.67	1006.71	964.57	943.11	931.84	925.82
95000	1455.93	1376.74	1155.49	1062.64	1018.16	995.51	983.61	977.26
100000	1532.56	1449.20	1216.30	1118.57	1071.75	1047.90	1035.38	1028.69
105000	1609.19	1521.66	1277.12	1174.50	1125.34	1100.30	1087.14	1080.13
110000	1685.82	1594.12	1337.93	1230.43	1178.92	1152.69	1138.91	1131.56
115000	1762.44	1666.58	1398.75	1286.35	1232.51	1205.09	1190.68	1182.99
120000	1839.07	1739.04	1459.56	1342.28	1286.10	1257.48	1242.45	1234.43
125000	1915.70	1811.50	1520.38	1398.21	1339.68	1309.88	1294.22	1285.86
130000	1992.33	1883.96	1581.19	1454.14	1393.27	1362.27	1345.99	1337.30
135000	2068.95	1956.42	1642.01	1510.07	1446.86	1414.67	1397.76	1388.73
140000	2145.58	2028.88	1702.82	1566.00	1500.45	1467.06	1449.52	1440.17
145000	2222.21	2101.34	1763.64	1621.92	1554.03	1519.45	1501.29	1491.60
150000	2298.84	2173.80	1824.45	1677.85	1607.62	1571.85	1553.06	1543.03
155000	2375.47	2246.26	1885.27	1733.78	1661.21	1624.24	1604.83	1594.47
160000	2452.09	2318.72	1946.08	1789.71	1714.80	1676.64	1656.60	1645.90

MONTHLY AMORTIZING PAYMENTS

AMOUNT OF LOAN	NUMBER OF YEARS IN TERM							
	1	2	3	4	5	6	7	8
$ 50	4.46	2.37	1.67	1.33	1.13	.99	.90	.83
100	8.91	4.73	3.34	2.66	2.25	1.98	1.79	1.65
200	17.81	9.45	6.68	5.31	4.49	3.95	3.58	3.30
300	26.71	14.18	10.02	7.96	6.74	5.93	5.36	4.94
400	35.61	18.90	13.36	10.61	8.98	7.90	7.15	6.59
500	44.52	23.63	16.70	13.26	11.22	9.88	8.93	8.23
600	53.42	28.35	20.04	15.92	13.47	11.85	10.72	9.88
700	62.32	33.08	23.38	18.57	15.71	13.83	12.50	11.53
800	71.22	37.80	26.72	21.22	17.95	15.80	14.29	13.17
900	80.13	42.53	30.06	23.87	20.20	17.78	16.07	14.82
1000	89.03	47.25	33.40	26.52	22.44	19.75	17.86	16.46
2000	178.05	94.50	66.79	53.04	44.87	39.50	35.71	32.92
3000	267.08	141.75	100.19	79.56	67.31	59.24	53.57	49.38
4000	356.10	189.00	133.58	106.08	89.74	78.99	71.42	65.84
5000	445.13	236.25	166.97	132.60	112.18	98.73	89.27	82.30
6000	534.15	283.50	200.37	159.11	134.61	118.48	107.13	98.76
7000	623.18	330.75	233.76	185.63	157.05	138.23	124.98	115.22
8000	712.20	378.00	267.15	212.15	179.48	157.97	142.84	131.68
9000	801.22	425.24	300.55	238.67	201.91	177.72	160.69	148.14
10000	890.25	472.49	333.94	265.19	224.35	197.46	178.54	164.60
11000	979.27	519.74	367.34	291.71	246.78	217.21	196.40	181.06
12000	1068.30	566.99	400.73	318.22	269.22	236.95	214.25	197.52
13000	1157.32	614.24	434.12	344.74	291.65	256.70	232.11	213.98
14000	1246.35	661.49	467.52	371.26	314.09	276.45	249.96	230.44
15000	1335.37	708.74	500.91	397.78	336.52	296.19	267.81	246.90
16000	1424.39	755.99	534.30	424.30	358.96	315.94	285.67	263.36
17000	1513.42	803.23	567.70	450.82	381.39	335.68	303.52	279.82
18000	1602.44	850.48	601.09	477.33	403.82	355.43	321.38	296.28
19000	1691.47	897.73	634.49	503.85	426.26	375.17	339.23	312.74
20000	1780.49	944.98	667.88	530.37	448.69	394.92	357.08	329.20
21000	1869.52	992.23	701.27	556.89	471.13	414.67	374.94	345.66
22000	1958.54	1039.48	734.67	583.41	493.56	434.41	392.79	362.12
23000	2047.56	1086.73	768.06	609.93	516.00	454.16	410.64	378.58
24000	2136.59	1133.98	801.45	636.44	538.43	473.90	428.50	395.04
25000	2225.61	1181.22	834.85	662.96	560.87	493.65	446.35	411.49
26000	2314.64	1228.47	868.24	689.48	583.30	513.39	464.21	427.95
27000	2403.66	1275.72	901.63	716.00	605.73	533.14	482.06	444.41
28000	2492.69	1322.97	935.03	742.52	628.17	552.89	499.91	460.87
29000	2581.71	1370.22	968.42	769.04	650.60	572.63	517.77	477.33
30000	2670.73	1417.47	1001.82	795.55	673.04	592.38	535.62	493.79
31000	2759.76	1464.72	1035.21	822.07	695.47	612.12	553.48	510.25
32000	2848.78	1511.97	1068.60	848.59	717.91	631.87	571.33	526.71
33000	2937.81	1559.21	1102.00	875.11	740.34	651.61	589.18	543.17
34000	3026.83	1606.46	1135.39	901.63	762.77	671.36	607.04	559.63
35000	3115.86	1653.71	1168.78	928.15	785.21	691.11	624.89	576.09
40000	3560.98	1889.96	1335.75	1060.74	897.38	789.83	714.16	658.39
45000	4006.10	2126.20	1502.72	1193.33	1009.55	888.56	803.43	740.69
50000	4451.22	2362.44	1669.69	1325.92	1121.73	987.29	892.70	822.98
55000	4896.34	2598.69	1836.66	1458.51	1233.90	1086.02	981.97	905.28
60000	5341.46	2834.93	2003.63	1591.10	1346.07	1184.75	1071.24	987.58
65000	5786.59	3071.18	2170.60	1723.70	1458.24	1283.48	1160.51	1069.88
70000	6231.71	3307.42	2337.56	1856.29	1570.41	1382.21	1249.78	1152.18
75000	6676.83	3543.66	2504.53	1988.88	1682.59	1480.94	1339.05	1234.47
80000	7121.95	3779.91	2671.50	2121.47	1794.76	1579.66	1428.32	1316.77
85000	7567.07	4016.15	2838.47	2254.06	1906.93	1678.39	1517.59	1399.07
90000	8012.19	4252.40	3005.44	2386.65	2019.10	1777.12	1606.86	1481.37
95000	8457.31	4488.64	3172.41	2519.25	2131.27	1875.85	1696.13	1563.67
100000	8902.44	4724.88	3339.38	2651.84	2243.45	1974.58	1785.40	1645.96
105000	9347.56	4961.13	3506.34	2784.43	2355.62	2073.31	1874.66	1728.26
110000	9792.68	5197.37	3673.31	2917.02	2467.79	2172.04	1963.93	1810.56
115000	10237.80	5433.62	3840.28	3049.61	2579.96	2270.77	2053.20	1892.86
120000	10682.92	5669.86	4007.25	3182.20	2692.13	2369.49	2142.47	1975.16
125000	11128.04	5906.10	4174.22	3314.80	2804.31	2468.22	2231.74	2057.45
130000	11573.17	6142.35	4341.19	3447.39	2916.48	2566.95	2321.01	2139.75
135000	12018.29	6378.59	4508.15	3579.98	3028.65	2665.68	2410.28	2222.05
140000	12463.41	6614.83	4675.12	3712.57	3140.82	2764.41	2499.55	2304.35
145000	12908.53	6851.08	4842.09	3845.16	3252.99	2863.14	2588.82	2386.64
150000	13353.65	7087.32	5009.06	3977.75	3365.17	2961.87	2678.09	2468.94
155000	13798.77	7323.57	5176.03	4110.35	3477.34	3060.60	2767.36	2551.24
160000	14243.89	7559.81	5343.00	4242.94	3589.51	3159.32	2856.63	2633.54

MONTHLY AMORTIZING PAYMENTS 12 3/8%

AMOUNT OF LOAN	9	10	15	20	25	30	35	40
	NUMBER OF YEARS IN TERM							
$ 50	.77	.73	.62	.57	.55	.53	.53	.52
100	1.54	1.46	1.23	1.13	1.09	1.06	1.05	1.04
200	3.08	2.92	2.45	2.26	2.17	2.12	2.10	2.08
300	4.62	4.37	3.68	3.39	3.25	3.18	3.14	3.12
400	6.16	5.83	4.90	4.51	4.33	4.24	4.19	4.16
500	7.70	7.29	6.13	5.64	5.41	5.29	5.23	5.20
600	9.24	8.74	7.35	6.77	6.49	6.35	6.28	6.24
700	10.78	10.20	8.58	7.90	7.57	7.41	7.32	7.28
800	12.32	11.66	9.80	9.02	8.65	8.47	8.37	8.32
900	13.86	13.11	11.02	10.15	9.73	9.52	9.41	9.35
1000	15.40	14.57	12.25	11.28	10.82	10.58	10.46	10.39
2000	30.80	29.13	24.49	22.55	21.63	21.16	20.91	20.78
3000	46.19	43.70	36.74	33.83	32.44	31.73	31.36	31.17
4000	61.59	58.26	48.98	45.10	43.25	42.31	41.82	41.56
5000	76.99	72.83	61.22	56.37	54.06	52.88	52.27	51.94
6000	92.38	87.39	73.47	67.65	64.87	63.46	62.72	62.33
7000	107.78	101.96	85.71	78.92	75.68	74.03	73.18	72.72
8000	123.18	116.52	97.96	90.19	86.49	84.61	83.63	83.11
9000	138.57	131.09	110.20	101.47	97.30	95.19	94.08	93.50
10000	153.97	145.65	122.44	112.74	108.11	105.76	104.54	103.88
11000	169.37	160.22	134.69	124.01	118.92	116.34	114.99	114.27
12000	184.76	174.78	146.93	135.29	129.73	126.91	125.44	124.66
13000	200.16	189.35	159.18	146.56	140.54	137.49	135.89	135.05
14000	215.56	203.91	171.42	157.83	151.35	148.06	146.35	145.44
15000	230.95	218.48	183.66	169.11	162.16	158.64	156.80	155.82
16000	246.35	233.04	195.91	180.38	172.97	169.22	167.25	166.21
17000	261.74	247.61	208.15	191.65	183.78	179.79	177.71	176.60
18000	277.14	262.17	220.40	202.93	194.59	190.37	188.16	186.99
19000	292.54	276.73	232.64	214.20	205.40	200.94	198.61	197.38
20000	307.93	291.30	244.88	225.47	216.21	211.52	209.07	207.76
21000	323.33	305.86	257.13	236.75	227.02	222.09	219.52	218.15
22000	338.73	320.43	269.37	248.02	237.83	232.67	229.97	228.54
23000	354.12	334.99	281.62	259.29	248.64	243.25	240.43	238.93
24000	369.52	349.56	293.86	270.57	259.45	253.82	250.88	249.32
25000	384.92	364.12	306.10	281.84	270.26	264.40	261.33	259.70
26000	400.31	378.69	318.35	293.11	281.07	274.97	271.78	270.09
27000	415.71	393.25	330.59	304.39	291.89	285.55	282.24	280.48
28000	431.11	407.82	342.84	315.66	302.70	296.12	292.69	290.87
29000	446.50	422.38	355.08	326.93	313.51	306.70	303.14	301.26
30000	461.90	436.95	367.32	338.21	324.32	317.28	313.60	311.64
31000	477.30	451.51	379.57	349.48	335.13	327.85	324.05	322.03
32000	492.69	466.08	391.81	360.75	345.94	338.43	334.50	332.42
33000	508.09	480.64	404.06	372.03	356.75	349.00	344.96	342.81
34000	523.48	495.21	416.30	383.30	367.56	359.58	355.41	353.20
35000	538.88	509.77	428.54	394.57	378.37	370.15	365.86	363.58
40000	615.86	582.59	489.76	450.94	432.42	423.03	418.13	415.52
45000	692.85	655.42	550.98	507.31	486.47	475.91	470.39	467.46
50000	769.83	728.24	612.20	563.68	540.52	528.79	522.66	519.40
55000	846.81	801.06	673.42	620.04	594.58	581.67	574.92	571.34
60000	923.79	873.89	734.64	676.41	648.63	634.55	627.19	623.28
65000	1000.78	946.71	795.86	732.78	702.68	687.42	679.45	675.22
70000	1077.76	1019.53	857.08	789.14	756.73	740.30	731.72	727.16
75000	1154.74	1092.36	918.30	845.51	810.78	793.18	783.98	779.10
80000	1231.72	1165.18	979.52	901.88	864.84	846.06	836.25	831.04
85000	1308.70	1238.01	1040.74	958.24	918.89	898.94	888.51	882.98
90000	1385.69	1310.83	1101.96	1014.61	972.94	951.82	940.78	934.92
95000	1462.67	1383.65	1163.18	1070.98	1026.99	1004.69	993.04	986.86
100000	1539.65	1456.48	1224.40	1127.35	1081.04	1057.57	1045.31	1038.80
105000	1616.63	1529.30	1285.62	1183.71	1135.09	1110.45	1097.58	1090.74
110000	1693.62	1602.12	1346.84	1240.08	1189.15	1163.33	1149.84	1142.68
115000	1770.60	1674.95	1408.06	1296.45	1243.20	1216.21	1202.11	1194.62
120000	1847.58	1747.77	1469.28	1352.81	1297.25	1269.09	1254.37	1246.56
125000	1924.56	1820.59	1530.50	1409.18	1351.30	1321.96	1306.64	1298.50
130000	2001.55	1893.42	1591.72	1465.55	1405.35	1374.84	1358.90	1350.44
135000	2078.53	1966.24	1652.94	1521.91	1459.41	1427.72	1411.17	1402.38
140000	2155.51	2039.06	1714.16	1578.28	1513.46	1480.60	1463.43	1454.32
145000	2232.49	2111.89	1775.38	1634.65	1567.51	1533.48	1515.70	1506.26
150000	2309.47	2184.71	1836.60	1691.02	1621.56	1586.36	1567.96	1558.20
155000	2386.46	2257.54	1897.82	1747.38	1675.61	1639.23	1620.23	1610.14
160000	2463.44	2330.36	1959.04	1803.75	1729.67	1692.11	1672.49	1662.08

AMOUNT OF LOAN	NUMBER OF YEARS IN TERM							
	1	2	3	4	5	6	7	8
$ 50	4.46	2.37	1.68	1.33	1.13	1.00	.90	.83
100	8.91	4.74	3.35	2.66	2.25	1.99	1.80	1.66
200	17.82	9.47	6.70	5.32	4.50	3.97	3.59	3.31
300	26.73	14.20	10.04	7.98	6.75	5.95	5.38	4.96
400	35.64	18.93	13.39	10.64	9.00	7.93	7.17	6.62
500	44.55	23.66	16.73	13.29	11.25	9.91	8.97	8.27
600	53.45	28.39	20.08	15.95	13.50	11.89	10.76	9.92
700	62.36	33.12	23.42	18.61	15.75	13.87	12.55	11.58
800	71.27	37.85	26.77	21.27	18.00	15.85	14.34	13.23
900	80.18	42.58	30.11	23.93	20.25	17.84	16.13	14.88
1000	89.09	47.31	33.46	26.58	22.50	19.82	17.93	16.53
2000	178.17	94.62	66.91	53.16	45.00	39.63	35.85	33.06
3000	267.25	141.93	100.37	79.74	67.50	59.44	53.77	49.59
4000	356.34	189.23	133.82	106.32	90.00	79.25	71.69	66.12
5000	445.42	236.54	167.27	132.90	112.49	99.06	89.61	82.65
6000	534.50	283.85	200.73	159.48	134.99	118.87	107.53	99.18
7000	623.59	331.16	234.18	186.06	157.49	138.68	125.45	115.71
8000	712.67	378.46	267.63	212.64	179.99	158.49	143.37	132.24
9000	801.75	425.77	301.09	239.22	202.49	178.31	161.30	148.76
10000	890.83	473.08	334.54	265.80	224.98	198.12	179.22	165.29
11000	979.92	520.39	367.99	292.38	247.48	217.93	197.14	181.82
12000	1069.00	567.69	401.45	318.96	269.98	237.74	215.06	198.35
13000	1158.08	615.00	434.90	345.54	292.48	257.55	232.98	214.88
14000	1247.17	662.31	468.36	372.12	314.98	277.36	250.90	231.41
15000	1336.25	709.61	501.81	398.70	337.47	297.17	268.82	247.94
16000	1425.33	756.92	535.26	425.28	359.97	316.98	286.74	264.47
17000	1514.41	804.23	568.72	451.86	382.47	336.80	304.67	280.99
18000	1603.50	851.54	602.17	478.44	404.97	356.61	322.59	297.52
19000	1692.58	898.84	635.62	505.02	427.47	376.42	340.51	314.05
20000	1781.66	946.15	669.08	531.60	449.96	396.23	358.43	330.58
21000	1870.75	993.46	702.53	558.18	472.46	416.04	376.35	347.11
22000	1959.83	1040.77	735.98	584.76	494.96	435.85	394.27	363.64
23000	2048.91	1088.07	769.44	611.34	517.46	455.66	412.19	380.17
24000	2137.99	1135.38	802.89	637.92	539.96	475.47	430.11	396.70
25000	2227.08	1182.69	836.35	664.50	562.45	495.28	448.04	413.23
26000	2316.16	1230.00	869.80	691.08	584.95	515.10	465.96	429.75
27000	2405.24	1277.30	903.25	717.66	607.45	534.91	483.88	446.28
28000	2494.33	1324.61	936.71	744.24	629.95	554.72	501.80	462.81
29000	2583.41	1371.92	970.16	770.82	652.45	574.53	519.72	479.34
30000	2672.49	1419.22	1003.61	797.40	674.94	594.34	537.64	495.87
31000	2761.57	1466.53	1037.07	823.98	697.44	614.15	555.56	512.40
32000	2850.66	1513.84	1070.52	850.56	719.94	633.96	573.48	528.93
33000	2939.74	1561.15	1103.97	877.14	742.44	653.77	591.41	545.46
34000	3028.82	1608.45	1137.43	903.72	764.93	673.59	609.33	561.98
35000	3117.91	1655.76	1170.88	930.30	787.43	693.40	627.25	578.51
40000	3563.32	1892.30	1338.15	1063.20	899.92	792.45	716.85	661.16
45000	4008.73	2128.83	1505.42	1196.10	1012.41	891.51	806.46	743.80
50000	4454.15	2365.37	1672.69	1329.00	1124.90	990.56	896.07	826.45
55000	4899.56	2601.91	1839.95	1461.90	1237.39	1089.62	985.67	909.09
60000	5344.98	2838.44	2007.22	1594.80	1349.88	1188.68	1075.28	991.73
65000	5790.39	3074.98	2174.49	1727.70	1462.37	1287.73	1164.89	1074.38
70000	6235.81	3311.52	2341.76	1860.60	1574.86	1386.79	1254.49	1157.02
75000	6681.22	3548.05	2509.03	1993.50	1687.35	1485.84	1344.10	1239.67
80000	7126.63	3784.59	2676.30	2126.40	1799.84	1584.90	1433.70	1322.31
85000	7572.05	4021.13	2843.56	2259.30	1912.33	1683.96	1523.31	1404.95
90000	8017.46	4257.66	3010.83	2392.20	2024.82	1783.01	1612.92	1487.60
95000	8462.88	4494.20	3178.10	2525.10	2137.31	1882.07	1702.52	1570.24
100000	8908.29	4730.74	3345.37	2658.00	2249.80	1981.12	1792.13	1652.89
105000	9353.71	4967.27	3512.64	2790.90	2362.29	2080.18	1881.74	1735.53
110000	9799.12	5203.81	3679.90	2923.80	2474.78	2179.23	1971.34	1818.17
115000	10244.53	5440.35	3847.17	3056.70	2587.27	2278.29	2060.95	1900.82
120000	10689.95	5676.88	4014.44	3189.60	2699.76	2377.35	2150.55	1983.46
125000	11135.36	5913.42	4181.71	3322.50	2812.25	2476.40	2240.16	2066.11
130000	11580.78	6149.96	4348.98	3455.40	2924.74	2575.46	2329.77	2148.75
135000	12026.19	6386.49	4516.24	3588.30	3037.23	2674.51	2419.37	2231.39
140000	12471.61	6623.03	4683.51	3721.20	3149.72	2773.57	2508.98	2314.04
145000	12917.02	6859.56	4850.78	3854.10	3262.21	2872.63	2598.58	2396.68
150000	13362.43	7096.10	5018.05	3987.00	3374.70	2971.68	2688.19	2479.33
155000	13807.85	7332.64	5185.32	4119.90	3487.19	3070.74	2777.80	2561.97
160000	14253.26	7569.17	5352.59	4252.80	3599.68	3169.79	2867.40	2644.61

MONTHLY AMORTIZING PAYMENTS 12½%

AMOUNT OF LOAN	9	10	15	20	25	30	35	40
	NUMBER OF YEARS IN TERM							
$ 50	.78	.74	.62	.57	.55	.54	.53	.53
100	1.55	1.47	1.24	1.14	1.10	1.07	1.06	1.05
200	3.10	2.93	2.47	2.28	2.19	2.14	2.12	2.10
300	4.65	4.40	3.70	3.41	3.28	3.21	3.17	3.15
400	6.19	5.86	4.94	4.55	4.37	4.27	4.23	4.20
500	7.74	7.32	6.17	5.69	5.46	5.34	5.28	5.25
600	9.29	8.79	7.40	6.82	6.55	6.41	6.34	6.30
700	10.83	10.25	8.63	7.96	7.64	7.48	7.39	7.35
800	12.38	11.72	9.87	9.09	8.73	8.54	8.45	8.40
900	13.93	13.18	11.10	10.23	9.82	9.61	9.50	9.45
1000	15.47	14.64	12.33	11.37	10.91	10.68	10.56	10.49
2000	30.94	29.28	24.66	22.73	21.81	21.35	21.11	20.98
3000	46.41	43.92	36.98	34.09	32.72	32.02	31.66	31.47
4000	61.88	58.56	49.31	45.45	43.62	42.70	42.22	41.96
5000	77.34	73.19	61.63	56.81	54.52	53.37	52.77	52.45
6000	92.81	87.83	73.96	68.17	65.43	64.04	63.32	62.94
7000	108.28	102.47	86.28	79.53	76.33	74.71	73.87	73.43
8000	123.75	117.11	98.61	90.90	87.23	85.39	84.43	83.92
9000	139.21	131.74	110.93	102.26	98.14	96.06	94.98	94.41
10000	154.68	146.38	123.26	113.62	109.04	106.73	105.53	104.90
11000	170.15	161.02	135.58	124.98	119.94	117.40	116.08	115.39
12000	185.62	175.66	147.91	136.34	130.85	128.08	126.64	125.88
13000	201.08	190.29	160.23	147.70	141.75	138.75	137.19	136.36
14000	216.55	204.93	172.56	159.06	152.65	149.42	147.74	146.85
15000	232.02	219.57	184.88	170.43	163.56	160.09	158.29	157.34
16000	247.49	234.21	197.21	181.79	174.46	170.77	168.85	167.83
17000	262.95	248.84	209.53	193.15	185.37	181.44	179.40	178.32
18000	278.42	263.48	221.86	204.51	196.27	192.11	189.95	188.81
19000	293.89	278.12	234.18	215.87	207.17	202.78	200.50	199.30
20000	309.36	292.76	246.51	227.23	218.08	213.46	211.06	209.79
21000	324.82	307.39	258.83	238.59	228.98	224.13	221.61	220.28
22000	340.29	322.03	271.16	249.96	239.88	234.80	232.16	230.77
23000	355.76	336.67	283.49	261.32	250.79	245.47	242.71	241.26
24000	371.23	351.31	295.81	272.68	261.69	256.15	253.27	251.75
25000	386.69	365.95	308.14	284.04	272.59	266.82	263.82	262.23
26000	402.16	380.58	320.46	295.40	283.50	277.49	274.37	272.72
27000	417.63	395.22	332.79	306.76	294.40	288.16	284.92	283.21
28000	433.10	409.86	345.11	318.12	305.30	298.84	295.48	293.70
29000	448.56	424.50	357.44	329.49	316.21	309.51	306.03	304.19
30000	464.03	439.13	369.76	340.85	327.11	320.18	316.58	314.68
31000	479.50	453.77	382.09	352.21	338.01	330.85	327.13	325.17
32000	494.97	468.41	394.41	363.57	348.92	341.53	337.69	335.66
33000	510.43	483.05	406.74	374.93	359.82	352.20	348.24	346.15
34000	525.90	497.68	419.06	386.29	370.73	362.87	358.79	356.64
35000	541.37	512.32	431.39	397.65	381.63	373.55	369.34	367.13
40000	618.71	585.51	493.01	454.46	436.15	426.91	422.11	419.57
45000	696.04	658.70	554.64	511.27	490.66	480.27	474.87	472.02
50000	773.38	731.89	616.27	568.08	545.18	533.63	527.63	524.46
55000	850.72	805.07	677.89	624.88	599.70	587.00	580.39	576.91
60000	928.06	878.26	739.52	681.69	654.22	640.36	633.16	629.36
65000	1005.40	951.45	801.14	738.50	708.74	693.72	685.92	681.80
70000	1082.73	1024.64	862.77	795.30	763.25	747.09	738.68	734.25
75000	1160.07	1097.83	924.40	852.11	817.77	800.45	791.45	786.69
80000	1237.41	1171.01	986.02	908.92	872.29	853.81	844.21	839.14
85000	1314.75	1244.20	1047.65	965.72	926.81	907.17	896.97	891.59
90000	1392.08	1317.39	1109.27	1022.53	981.32	960.54	949.73	944.03
95000	1469.42	1390.58	1170.90	1079.34	1035.84	1013.90	1002.50	996.48
100000	1546.76	1463.77	1232.53	1136.15	1090.36	1067.26	1055.26	1048.92
105000	1624.10	1536.95	1294.15	1192.95	1144.88	1120.63	1108.02	1101.37
110000	1701.44	1610.14	1355.78	1249.76	1199.39	1173.99	1160.78	1153.82
115000	1778.77	1683.33	1417.41	1306.57	1253.91	1227.35	1213.55	1206.26
120000	1856.11	1756.52	1479.03	1363.37	1308.43	1280.71	1266.31	1258.71
125000	1933.45	1829.71	1540.66	1420.18	1362.95	1334.08	1319.07	1311.15
130000	2010.79	1902.90	1602.28	1476.99	1417.47	1387.44	1371.84	1363.60
135000	2088.12	1976.08	1663.91	1533.79	1471.98	1440.80	1424.60	1416.05
140000	2165.46	2049.27	1725.54	1590.60	1526.50	1494.17	1477.36	1468.49
145000	2242.80	2122.46	1787.16	1647.41	1581.02	1547.53	1530.12	1520.94
150000	2320.14	2195.65	1848.79	1704.22	1635.54	1600.89	1582.89	1573.38
155000	2397.48	2268.84	1910.41	1761.02	1690.05	1654.25	1635.65	1625.83
160000	2474.81	2342.02	1972.04	1817.83	1744.57	1707.62	1688.41	1678.28

MONTHLY AMORTIZING PAYMENTS

AMOUNT OF LOAN	NUMBER OF YEARS IN TERM 1	2	3	4	5	6	7	8
$ 50	4.46	2.37	1.68	1.34	1.13	1.00	.90	.83
100	8.92	4.74	3.36	2.67	2.26	1.99	1.80	1.66
200	17.83	9.48	6.71	5.33	4.52	3.98	3.60	3.32
300	26.75	14.21	10.06	8.00	6.77	5.97	5.40	4.98
400	35.66	18.95	13.41	10.66	9.03	7.96	7.20	6.64
500	44.58	23.69	16.76	13.33	11.29	9.94	9.00	8.30
600	53.49	28.42	20.11	15.99	13.54	11.93	10.80	9.96
700	62.40	33.16	23.46	18.65	15.80	13.92	12.60	11.62
800	71.32	37.90	26.82	21.32	18.05	15.91	14.40	13.28
900	80.23	42.63	30.17	23.98	20.31	17.89	16.19	14.94
1000	89.15	47.37	33.52	26.65	22.57	19.88	17.99	16.60
2000	178.29	94.74	67.03	53.29	45.13	39.76	35.98	33.20
3000	267.43	142.10	100.55	79.93	67.69	59.64	53.97	49.80
4000	356.57	189.47	134.06	106.57	90.25	79.51	71.96	66.40
5000	445.71	236.83	167.57	133.21	112.81	99.39	89.95	83.00
6000	534.85	284.20	201.09	159.86	135.37	119.27	107.94	99.59
7000	624.00	331.57	234.60	186.50	157.94	139.14	125.93	116.19
8000	713.14	378.93	268.11	213.14	180.50	159.02	143.91	132.79
9000	802.28	426.30	301.63	239.78	203.06	178.90	161.90	149.39
10000	891.42	473.66	335.14	266.42	225.62	198.77	179.89	165.99
11000	980.56	521.03	368.65	293.06	248.18	218.65	197.88	182.59
12000	1069.70	568.40	402.17	319.71	270.74	238.53	215.87	199.18
13000	1158.84	615.76	435.68	346.35	293.31	258.40	233.86	215.78
14000	1247.99	663.13	469.20	372.99	315.87	278.28	251.85	232.38
15000	1337.13	710.49	502.71	399.63	338.43	298.16	269.84	248.98
16000	1426.27	757.86	536.22	426.27	360.99	318.03	287.82	265.58
17000	1515.41	805.22	569.74	452.91	383.55	337.91	305.81	282.17
18000	1604.55	852.59	603.25	479.56	406.11	357.79	323.80	298.77
19000	1693.69	899.96	636.76	506.20	428.67	377.66	341.79	315.37
20000	1782.83	947.32	670.28	532.84	451.24	397.54	359.78	331.97
21000	1871.98	994.69	703.79	559.48	473.80	417.42	377.77	348.57
22000	1961.12	1042.05	737.30	586.12	496.36	437.29	395.76	365.17
23000	2050.26	1089.42	770.82	612.77	518.92	457.17	413.75	381.76
24000	2139.40	1136.79	804.33	639.41	541.48	477.05	431.73	398.36
25000	2228.54	1184.15	837.85	666.05	564.04	496.92	449.72	414.96
26000	2317.68	1231.52	871.36	692.69	586.61	516.80	467.71	431.56
27000	2406.82	1278.88	904.87	719.33	609.17	536.68	485.70	448.16
28000	2495.97	1326.25	938.39	745.97	631.73	556.55	503.69	464.75
29000	2585.11	1373.62	971.90	772.62	654.29	576.43	521.68	481.35
30000	2674.25	1420.98	1005.41	799.26	676.85	596.31	539.67	497.95
31000	2763.39	1468.35	1038.93	825.90	699.41	616.18	557.66	514.55
32000	2852.53	1515.71	1072.44	852.54	721.98	636.06	575.64	531.15
33000	2941.67	1563.08	1105.95	879.18	744.54	655.94	593.63	547.75
34000	3030.81	1610.44	1139.47	905.82	767.10	675.81	611.62	564.34
35000	3119.96	1657.81	1172.98	932.47	789.66	695.69	629.61	580.94
40000	3565.66	1894.64	1340.55	1065.67	902.47	795.07	719.55	663.93
45000	4011.37	2131.47	1508.12	1198.88	1015.28	894.46	809.50	746.92
50000	4457.08	2368.30	1675.69	1332.09	1128.08	993.84	899.44	829.91
55000	4902.78	2605.13	1843.25	1465.30	1240.89	1093.23	989.38	912.91
60000	5348.49	2841.96	2010.82	1598.51	1353.70	1192.61	1079.33	995.90
65000	5794.20	3078.79	2178.39	1731.72	1466.51	1291.99	1169.27	1078.89
70000	6239.91	3315.62	2345.96	1864.93	1579.31	1391.38	1259.21	1161.88
75000	6685.61	3552.45	2513.53	1998.14	1692.12	1490.76	1349.16	1244.87
80000	7131.32	3789.27	2681.09	2131.34	1804.93	1590.14	1439.10	1327.86
85000	7577.03	4026.10	2848.66	2264.55	1917.74	1689.53	1529.05	1410.85
90000	8022.73	4262.93	3016.23	2397.76	2030.55	1788.91	1618.99	1493.84
95000	8468.44	4499.76	3183.80	2530.97	2143.35	1888.29	1708.93	1576.83
100000	8914.15	4736.59	3351.37	2664.18	2256.16	1987.68	1798.88	1659.82
105000	9359.86	4973.42	3518.93	2797.39	2368.97	2087.06	1888.82	1742.81
110000	9805.56	5210.25	3686.50	2930.60	2481.78	2186.45	1978.76	1825.81
115000	10251.27	5447.08	3854.07	3063.81	2594.59	2285.83	2068.71	1908.80
120000	10696.98	5683.91	4021.64	3197.01	2707.39	2385.21	2158.65	1991.79
125000	11142.68	5920.74	4189.21	3330.22	2820.20	2484.60	2248.59	2074.78
130000	11588.39	6157.57	4356.77	3463.43	2933.01	2583.98	2338.54	2157.77
135000	12034.10	6394.40	4524.34	3596.64	3045.82	2683.36	2428.48	2240.76
140000	12479.81	6631.23	4691.91	3729.85	3158.62	2782.75	2518.42	2323.75
145000	12925.51	6868.06	4859.48	3863.06	3271.43	2882.13	2608.37	2406.74
150000	13371.22	7104.89	5027.05	3996.27	3384.24	2981.51	2698.31	2489.73
155000	13816.93	7341.72	5194.61	4129.48	3497.05	3080.90	2788.26	2572.72
160000	14262.63	7578.54	5362.18	4262.68	3609.86	3180.28	2878.20	2655.72

MONTHLY AMORTIZING PAYMENTS 12 5/8%

AMOUNT OF LOAN	NUMBER OF YEARS IN TERM							
	9	10	15	20	25	30	35	40
$ 50	.78	.74	.63	.58	.55	.54	.54	.53
100	1.56	1.48	1.25	1.15	1.10	1.08	1.07	1.06
200	3.11	2.95	2.49	2.29	2.20	2.16	2.14	2.12
300	4.67	4.42	3.73	3.44	3.30	3.24	3.20	3.18
400	6.22	5.89	4.97	4.58	4.40	4.31	4.27	4.24
500	7.77	7.36	6.21	5.73	5.50	5.39	5.33	5.30
600	9.33	8.83	7.45	6.87	6.60	6.47	6.40	6.36
700	10.88	10.30	8.69	8.02	7.70	7.54	7.46	7.42
800	12.44	11.77	9.93	9.16	8.80	8.62	8.53	8.48
900	13.99	13.24	11.17	10.31	9.90	9.70	9.59	9.54
1000	15.54	14.72	12.41	11.45	11.00	10.77	10.66	10.60
2000	31.08	29.43	24.82	22.90	22.00	21.54	21.31	21.19
3000	46.62	44.14	37.23	34.35	33.00	32.31	31.96	31.78
4000	62.16	58.85	49.63	45.80	43.99	43.08	42.61	42.37
5000	77.70	73.56	62.04	57.25	54.99	53.85	53.27	52.96
6000	93.24	88.27	74.45	68.70	65.99	64.62	63.92	63.55
7000	108.78	102.98	86.85	80.15	76.98	75.39	74.57	74.14
8000	124.32	117.69	99.26	91.60	87.98	86.16	85.22	84.73
9000	139.85	132.40	111.67	103.05	98.98	96.93	95.87	95.32
10000	155.39	147.11	124.07	114.50	109.97	107.70	106.53	105.91
11000	170.93	161.82	136.48	125.95	120.97	118.47	117.18	116.50
12000	186.47	176.53	148.89	137.40	131.97	129.24	127.83	127.09
13000	202.01	191.24	161.29	148.85	142.97	140.01	138.48	137.68
14000	217.55	205.95	173.70	160.30	153.96	150.78	149.14	148.27
15000	233.09	220.67	186.11	171.75	164.96	161.55	159.79	158.86
16000	248.63	235.38	198.51	183.20	175.96	172.32	170.44	169.45
17000	264.16	250.09	210.92	194.65	186.95	183.09	181.09	180.04
18000	279.70	264.80	223.33	206.10	197.95	193.86	191.74	190.63
19000	295.24	279.51	235.73	217.55	208.95	204.63	202.40	201.22
20000	310.78	294.22	248.14	229.00	219.94	215.40	213.05	211.82
21000	326.32	308.93	260.55	240.45	230.94	226.17	223.70	222.41
22000	341.86	323.64	272.95	251.90	241.94	236.94	234.35	233.00
23000	357.40	338.35	285.36	263.35	252.93	247.71	245.01	243.59
24000	372.94	353.06	297.77	274.80	263.93	258.48	255.66	254.18
25000	388.48	367.77	310.17	286.25	274.93	269.25	266.31	264.77
26000	404.01	382.48	322.58	297.70	285.93	280.02	276.96	275.36
27000	419.55	397.19	334.99	309.15	296.92	290.79	287.61	285.95
28000	435.09	411.90	347.39	320.60	307.92	301.56	298.27	296.54
29000	450.63	426.62	359.80	332.04	318.92	312.33	308.92	307.13
30000	466.17	441.33	372.21	343.49	329.91	323.09	319.57	317.72
31000	481.71	456.04	384.61	354.94	340.91	333.86	330.22	328.31
32000	497.25	470.75	397.02	366.39	351.91	344.63	340.87	338.90
33000	512.79	485.46	409.43	377.84	362.90	355.40	351.53	349.49
34000	528.32	500.17	421.83	389.29	373.90	366.17	362.18	360.08
35000	543.86	514.88	434.24	400.74	384.90	376.94	372.83	370.67
40000	621.56	588.43	496.27	457.99	439.88	430.79	426.09	423.63
45000	699.25	661.99	558.31	515.24	494.87	484.64	479.35	476.58
50000	776.95	735.54	620.34	572.49	549.85	538.49	532.61	529.53
55000	854.64	809.09	682.37	629.74	604.84	592.34	585.87	582.48
60000	932.33	882.65	744.41	686.98	659.82	646.18	639.14	635.44
65000	1010.03	956.20	806.44	744.23	714.81	700.03	692.40	688.39
70000	1087.72	1029.75	868.47	801.48	769.79	753.88	745.66	741.34
75000	1165.42	1103.31	930.51	858.73	824.77	807.73	798.92	794.29
80000	1243.11	1176.86	992.54	915.98	879.76	861.58	852.18	847.25
85000	1320.80	1250.42	1054.57	973.22	934.74	915.43	905.44	900.20
90000	1398.50	1323.97	1116.61	1030.47	989.73	969.27	958.70	953.15
95000	1476.19	1397.52	1178.64	1087.72	1044.71	1023.12	1011.96	1006.10
100000	1553.89	1471.08	1240.67	1144.97	1099.70	1076.97	1065.22	1059.06
105000	1631.58	1544.63	1302.71	1202.22	1154.68	1130.82	1118.48	1112.01
110000	1709.27	1618.18	1364.74	1259.47	1209.67	1184.67	1171.74	1164.96
115000	1786.97	1691.74	1426.77	1316.71	1264.65	1238.52	1225.01	1217.92
120000	1864.66	1765.29	1488.81	1373.96	1319.64	1292.36	1278.27	1270.87
125000	1942.36	1838.84	1550.84	1431.21	1374.62	1346.21	1331.53	1323.82
130000	2020.05	1912.40	1612.87	1488.46	1429.61	1400.06	1384.79	1376.77
135000	2097.74	1985.95	1674.91	1545.71	1484.59	1453.91	1438.05	1429.73
140000	2175.44	2059.50	1736.94	1602.96	1539.57	1507.76	1491.31	1482.68
145000	2253.13	2133.06	1798.97	1660.20	1594.56	1561.61	1544.57	1535.63
150000	2330.83	2206.61	1861.01	1717.45	1649.54	1615.45	1597.83	1588.58
155000	2408.52	2280.16	1923.04	1774.70	1704.53	1669.30	1651.09	1641.54
160000	2486.21	2353.72	1985.07	1831.95	1759.51	1723.15	1704.35	1694.49

AMOUNT OF LOAN	1	2	3	4	5	6	7	8
	NUMBER OF YEARS IN TERM							
$ 50	4.47	2.38	1.68	1.34	1.14	1.00	.91	.84
100	8.93	4.75	3.36	2.68	2.27	2.00	1.81	1.67
200	17.85	9.49	6.72	5.35	4.53	3.99	3.62	3.34
300	26.77	14.23	10.08	8.02	6.79	5.99	5.42	5.01
400	35.69	18.97	13.43	10.69	9.06	7.98	7.23	6.67
500	44.61	23.72	16.79	13.36	11.32	9.98	9.03	8.34
600	53.53	28.46	20.15	16.03	13.58	11.97	10.84	10.01
700	62.45	33.20	23.51	18.70	15.84	13.96	12.64	11.67
800	71.37	37.94	26.86	21.37	18.11	15.96	14.45	13.34
900	80.29	42.69	30.22	24.04	20.37	17.95	16.26	15.01
1000	89.21	47.43	33.58	26.71	22.63	19.95	18.06	16.67
2000	178.41	94.85	67.15	53.41	45.26	39.89	36.12	33.34
3000	267.61	142.28	100.73	80.12	67.88	59.83	54.17	50.01
4000	356.81	189.70	134.30	106.82	90.51	79.77	72.23	66.68
5000	446.01	237.13	167.87	133.52	113.13	99.72	90.29	83.34
6000	535.21	284.55	201.45	160.23	135.76	119.66	108.34	100.01
7000	624.41	331.98	235.02	186.93	158.38	139.60	126.40	116.68
8000	713.61	379.40	268.59	213.63	181.01	159.54	144.46	133.35
9000	802.81	426.83	302.17	240.34	203.63	179.49	162.51	150.01
10000	892.01	474.25	335.74	267.04	226.26	199.43	180.57	166.68
11000	981.21	521.67	369.32	293.74	248.88	219.37	198.62	183.35
12000	1070.41	569.10	402.89	320.45	271.51	239.31	216.68	200.02
13000	1159.61	616.52	436.46	347.15	294.13	259.26	234.74	216.69
14000	1248.81	663.95	470.04	373.86	316.76	279.20	252.79	233.35
15000	1338.01	711.37	503.61	400.56	339.38	299.14	270.85	250.02
16000	1427.21	758.80	537.18	427.26	362.01	319.08	288.91	266.69
17000	1516.41	806.22	570.76	453.97	384.64	339.03	306.96	283.36
18000	1605.61	853.65	604.33	480.67	407.26	358.97	325.02	300.02
19000	1694.81	901.07	637.90	507.37	429.89	378.91	343.08	316.69
20000	1784.01	948.49	671.48	534.08	452.51	398.85	361.13	333.36
21000	1873.21	995.92	705.05	560.78	475.14	418.80	379.19	350.03
22000	1962.41	1043.34	738.63	587.48	497.76	438.74	397.24	366.69
23000	2051.61	1090.77	772.20	614.19	520.39	458.68	415.30	383.36
24000	2140.81	1138.19	805.77	640.89	543.01	478.62	433.36	400.03
25000	2230.01	1185.62	839.35	667.59	565.64	498.56	451.41	416.70
26000	2319.21	1233.04	872.92	694.30	588.26	518.51	469.47	433.37
27000	2408.41	1280.47	906.49	721.00	610.89	538.45	487.53	450.03
28000	2497.61	1327.89	940.07	747.71	633.51	558.39	505.58	466.70
29000	2586.81	1375.31	973.64	774.41	656.14	578.33	523.64	483.37
30000	2676.01	1422.74	1007.21	801.11	678.76	598.28	541.69	500.04
31000	2765.21	1470.16	1040.79	827.82	701.39	618.22	559.75	516.70
32000	2854.41	1517.59	1074.36	854.52	724.01	638.16	577.81	533.37
33000	2943.61	1565.01	1107.94	881.22	746.64	658.10	595.86	550.04
34000	3032.81	1612.44	1141.51	907.93	769.27	678.05	613.92	566.71
35000	3122.01	1659.86	1175.08	934.63	791.89	697.99	631.98	583.38
40000	3568.01	1896.98	1342.95	1068.15	905.02	797.70	722.26	666.71
45000	4014.01	2134.11	1510.82	1201.67	1018.14	897.41	812.54	750.05
50000	4460.01	2371.23	1678.69	1335.18	1131.27	997.13	902.82	833.39
55000	4906.01	2608.35	1846.56	1468.70	1244.40	1096.84	993.10	916.73
60000	5352.01	2845.47	2014.42	1602.22	1357.52	1196.55	1083.38	1000.07
65000	5798.01	3082.60	2182.29	1735.74	1470.65	1296.26	1173.67	1083.41
70000	6244.01	3319.72	2350.16	1869.26	1583.78	1395.97	1263.95	1166.75
75000	6690.01	3556.84	2518.03	2002.77	1696.90	1495.69	1354.23	1250.08
80000	7136.01	3793.96	2685.90	2136.29	1810.03	1595.40	1444.51	1333.42
85000	7582.01	4031.09	2853.77	2269.81	1923.16	1695.11	1534.79	1416.76
90000	8028.01	4268.21	3021.63	2403.33	2036.28	1794.82	1625.07	1500.10
95000	8474.01	4505.33	3189.50	2536.85	2149.41	1894.53	1715.36	1583.44
100000	8920.01	4742.45	3357.37	2670.36	2262.54	1994.25	1805.64	1666.78
105000	9366.01	4979.58	3525.24	2803.88	2375.66	2093.96	1895.92	1750.12
110000	9812.01	5216.70	3693.11	2937.40	2488.79	2193.67	1986.20	1833.45
115000	10258.01	5453.82	3860.98	3070.92	2601.91	2293.38	2076.48	1916.79
120000	10704.01	5690.94	4028.84	3204.43	2715.04	2393.09	2166.76	2000.13
125000	11150.01	5928.07	4196.71	3337.95	2828.17	2492.81	2257.05	2083.47
130000	11596.01	6165.19	4364.58	3471.47	2941.29	2592.52	2347.33	2166.81
135000	12042.01	6402.31	4532.45	3604.99	3054.42	2692.23	2437.61	2250.15
140000	12488.01	6639.43	4700.32	3738.51	3167.55	2791.94	2527.89	2333.49
145000	12934.01	6876.55	4868.19	3872.02	3280.67	2891.65	2618.17	2416.82
150000	13380.01	7113.68	5036.05	4005.54	3393.80	2991.37	2708.45	2500.16
155000	13826.01	7350.80	5203.92	4139.06	3506.93	3091.08	2798.74	2583.50
160000	14272.01	7587.92	5371.79	4272.58	3620.05	3190.79	2889.02	2666.84

MONTHLY AMORTIZING PAYMENTS 12¾%

AMOUNT OF LOAN	NUMBER OF YEARS IN TERM 9	10	15	20	25	30	35	40
$ 50	.79	.74	.63	.58	.56	.55	.54	.54
100	1.57	1.48	1.25	1.16	1.11	1.09	1.08	1.07
200	3.13	2.96	2.50	2.31	2.22	2.18	2.16	2.14
300	4.69	4.44	3.75	3.47	3.33	3.27	3.23	3.21
400	6.25	5.92	5.00	4.62	4.44	4.35	4.31	4.28
500	7.81	7.40	6.25	5.77	5.55	5.44	5.38	5.35
600	9.37	8.88	7.50	6.93	6.66	6.53	6.46	6.42
700	10.93	10.35	8.75	8.08	7.77	7.61	7.53	7.49
800	12.49	11.83	10.00	9.24	8.88	8.70	8.61	8.56
900	14.05	13.31	11.24	10.39	9.99	9.79	9.68	9.63
1000	15.62	14.79	12.49	11.54	11.10	10.87	10.76	10.70
2000	31.23	29.57	24.98	23.08	22.19	21.74	21.51	21.39
3000	46.84	44.36	37.47	34.62	33.28	32.61	32.26	32.08
4000	62.45	59.14	49.96	46.16	44.37	43.47	43.01	42.77
5000	78.06	73.92	62.45	57.70	55.46	54.34	53.76	53.46
6000	93.67	88.71	74.94	69.23	66.55	65.21	64.52	64.16
7000	109.28	103.49	87.42	80.77	77.64	76.07	75.27	74.85
8000	124.89	118.28	99.91	92.31	88.73	86.94	86.02	85.54
9000	140.50	133.06	112.40	103.85	99.82	97.81	96.77	96.23
10000	156.11	147.84	124.89	115.39	110.91	108.67	107.52	106.92
11000	171.72	162.63	137.38	126.92	122.00	119.54	118.28	117.62
12000	187.33	177.41	149.87	138.46	133.09	130.41	129.03	128.31
13000	202.94	192.20	162.35	150.00	144.18	141.28	139.78	139.00
14000	218.55	206.98	174.84	161.54	155.27	152.14	150.53	149.69
15000	234.16	221.76	187.33	173.08	166.36	163.01	161.28	160.38
16000	249.77	236.55	199.82	184.61	177.45	173.88	172.04	171.08
17000	265.38	251.33	212.31	196.15	188.54	184.74	182.79	181.77
18000	280.99	266.12	224.80	207.69	199.63	195.61	193.54	192.46
19000	296.60	280.90	237.28	219.23	210.72	206.48	204.29	203.15
20000	312.21	295.68	249.77	230.77	221.82	217.34	215.04	213.84
21000	327.82	310.47	262.26	242.31	232.91	228.21	225.80	224.54
22000	343.43	325.25	274.75	253.84	244.00	239.08	236.55	235.23
23000	359.04	340.04	287.24	265.38	255.09	249.94	247.30	245.92
24000	374.65	354.82	299.73	276.92	266.18	260.81	258.05	256.61
25000	390.26	369.60	312.21	288.46	277.27	271.68	268.80	267.30
26000	405.87	384.39	324.70	300.00	288.36	282.55	279.56	278.00
27000	421.48	399.17	337.19	311.53	299.45	293.41	290.31	288.69
28000	437.09	413.96	349.68	323.07	310.54	304.28	301.06	299.38
29000	452.70	428.74	362.17	334.61	321.63	315.15	311.81	310.07
30000	468.31	443.52	374.66	346.15	332.72	326.01	322.56	320.76
31000	483.92	458.31	387.14	357.69	343.81	336.88	333.32	331.46
32000	499.53	473.09	399.63	369.22	354.90	347.75	344.07	342.15
33000	515.14	487.88	412.12	380.76	365.99	358.61	354.82	352.84
34000	530.75	502.66	424.61	392.30	377.08	369.48	365.57	363.53
35000	546.36	517.44	437.10	403.84	388.17	380.35	376.32	374.22
40000	624.41	591.36	499.54	461.53	443.63	434.68	430.08	427.68
45000	702.47	665.28	561.98	519.22	499.08	489.02	483.84	481.14
50000	780.52	739.20	624.42	576.91	554.53	543.35	537.60	534.60
55000	858.57	813.12	686.87	634.60	609.98	597.69	591.36	588.06
60000	936.62	887.04	749.31	692.29	665.44	652.02	645.12	641.52
65000	1014.67	960.96	811.75	749.98	720.89	706.36	698.88	694.98
70000	1092.72	1034.88	874.19	807.67	776.34	760.69	752.64	748.44
75000	1170.77	1108.80	936.63	865.36	831.79	815.02	806.40	801.90
80000	1248.82	1182.72	999.07	923.05	887.25	869.36	860.16	855.36
85000	1326.87	1256.64	1061.52	980.74	942.70	923.69	913.92	908.82
90000	1404.93	1330.56	1123.96	1038.44	998.15	978.03	967.68	962.28
95000	1482.98	1404.48	1186.40	1096.13	1053.60	1032.36	1021.44	1015.74
100000	1561.03	1478.40	1248.84	1153.82	1109.06	1086.70	1075.20	1069.20
105000	1639.08	1552.32	1311.28	1211.51	1164.51	1141.03	1128.96	1122.66
110000	1717.13	1626.24	1373.73	1269.20	1219.96	1195.37	1182.72	1176.12
115000	1795.18	1700.16	1436.17	1326.89	1275.42	1249.70	1236.48	1229.58
120000	1873.23	1774.08	1498.61	1384.58	1330.87	1304.04	1290.24	1283.04
125000	1951.28	1848.00	1561.05	1442.27	1386.32	1358.37	1344.00	1336.50
130000	2029.34	1921.92	1623.49	1499.96	1441.77	1412.71	1397.76	1389.96
135000	2107.39	1995.84	1685.93	1557.65	1497.23	1467.04	1451.52	1443.42
140000	2185.44	2069.76	1748.38	1615.34	1552.68	1521.38	1505.28	1496.88
145000	2263.49	2143.68	1810.82	1673.03	1608.13	1575.71	1559.04	1550.34
150000	2341.54	2217.60	1873.26	1730.72	1663.58	1630.04	1612.80	1603.80
155000	2419.59	2291.52	1935.70	1788.41	1719.04	1684.38	1666.56	1657.26
160000	2497.64	2365.44	1998.14	1846.10	1774.49	1738.71	1720.32	1710.72

MONTHLY AMORTIZING PAYMENTS

AMOUNT OF LOAN	NUMBER OF YEARS IN TERM 1	2	3	4	5	6	7	8
$ 50	4.47	2.38	1.69	1.34	1.14	1.01	.91	.84
100	8.93	4.75	3.37	2.68	2.27	2.01	1.82	1.68
200	17.86	9.50	6.73	5.36	4.54	4.01	3.63	3.35
300	26.78	14.25	10.10	8.03	6.81	6.01	5.44	5.03
400	35.71	19.00	13.46	10.71	9.08	8.01	7.25	6.70
500	44.63	23.75	16.82	13.39	11.35	10.01	9.07	8.37
600	53.56	28.49	20.19	16.06	13.62	12.01	10.88	10.05
700	62.49	33.24	23.55	18.74	15.89	14.01	12.69	11.72
800	71.41	37.99	26.91	21.42	18.16	16.01	14.50	13.39
900	80.34	42.74	30.28	24.09	20.43	18.01	16.32	15.07
1000	89.26	47.49	33.64	26.77	22.69	20.01	18.13	16.74
2000	178.52	94.97	67.27	53.54	45.38	40.02	36.25	33.48
3000	267.78	142.45	100.91	80.30	68.07	60.03	54.38	50.22
4000	357.04	189.94	134.54	107.07	90.76	80.04	72.50	66.95
5000	446.30	237.42	168.17	133.83	113.45	100.05	90.63	83.69
6000	535.56	284.90	201.81	160.60	136.14	120.05	108.75	100.43
7000	624.82	332.39	235.44	187.36	158.83	140.06	126.87	117.17
8000	714.07	379.87	269.08	214.13	181.52	160.07	145.00	133.90
9000	803.33	427.35	302.71	240.89	204.21	180.08	163.12	150.64
10000	892.59	474.84	336.34	267.66	226.90	200.09	181.25	167.38
11000	981.85	522.32	369.98	294.43	249.59	220.10	199.37	184.12
12000	1071.11	569.80	403.61	321.19	272.27	240.10	217.49	200.85
13000	1160.37	617.29	437.24	347.96	294.96	260.11	235.62	217.59
14000	1249.63	664.77	470.88	374.72	317.65	280.12	253.74	234.33
15000	1338.88	712.25	504.51	401.49	340.34	300.13	271.87	251.07
16000	1428.14	759.74	538.15	428.25	363.03	320.14	289.99	267.80
17000	1517.40	807.22	571.78	455.02	385.72	340.14	308.11	284.54
18000	1606.66	854.70	605.41	481.78	408.41	360.15	326.24	301.28
19000	1695.92	902.18	639.05	508.55	431.10	380.16	344.36	318.02
20000	1785.18	949.67	672.68	535.31	453.79	400.17	362.49	334.75
21000	1874.44	997.15	706.31	562.08	476.48	420.18	380.61	351.49
22000	1963.70	1044.63	739.95	588.85	499.17	440.19	398.73	368.23
23000	2052.95	1092.12	773.58	615.61	521.86	460.19	416.86	384.97
24000	2142.21	1139.60	807.22	642.38	544.54	480.20	434.98	401.70
25000	2231.47	1187.08	840.85	669.14	567.23	500.21	453.11	418.44
26000	2320.73	1234.57	874.48	695.91	589.92	520.22	471.23	435.18
27000	2409.99	1282.05	908.12	722.67	612.61	540.23	489.36	451.92
28000	2499.25	1329.53	941.75	749.44	635.30	560.23	507.48	468.65
29000	2588.51	1377.02	975.38	776.20	657.99	580.24	525.60	485.39
30000	2677.76	1424.50	1009.02	802.97	680.68	600.25	543.73	502.13
31000	2767.02	1471.98	1042.65	829.74	703.37	620.26	561.85	518.86
32000	2856.28	1519.47	1076.29	856.50	726.06	640.27	579.98	535.60
33000	2945.54	1566.95	1109.92	883.27	748.75	660.28	598.10	552.34
34000	3034.80	1614.43	1143.55	910.03	771.44	680.28	616.22	569.08
35000	3124.06	1661.91	1177.19	936.80	794.12	700.29	634.35	585.81
40000	3570.35	1899.33	1345.36	1070.62	907.57	800.33	724.97	669.50
45000	4016.64	2136.75	1513.52	1204.45	1021.02	900.37	815.59	753.19
50000	4462.94	2374.16	1681.69	1338.28	1134.46	1000.41	906.21	836.88
55000	4909.23	2611.58	1849.86	1472.11	1247.91	1100.46	996.83	920.56
60000	5355.52	2848.99	2018.03	1605.93	1361.35	1200.50	1087.45	1004.25
65000	5801.82	3086.41	2186.20	1739.76	1474.80	1300.54	1178.07	1087.94
70000	6248.11	3323.82	2354.37	1873.59	1588.24	1400.58	1268.69	1171.62
75000	6694.40	3561.24	2522.54	2007.42	1701.69	1500.62	1359.31	1255.31
80000	7140.70	3798.66	2690.71	2141.24	1815.14	1600.66	1449.93	1339.00
85000	7586.99	4036.07	2858.88	2275.07	1928.58	1700.70	1540.55	1422.69
90000	8033.28	4273.49	3027.04	2408.90	2042.03	1800.74	1631.17	1506.37
95000	8479.58	4510.90	3195.21	2542.73	2155.47	1900.78	1721.79	1590.06
100000	8925.87	4748.32	3363.38	2676.55	2268.92	2000.82	1812.41	1673.75
105000	9372.16	4985.73	3531.55	2810.38	2382.36	2100.87	1903.03	1757.43
110000	9818.46	5223.15	3699.72	2944.21	2495.81	2200.91	1993.65	1841.12
115000	10264.75	5460.57	3867.89	3078.04	2609.26	2300.95	2084.27	1924.81
120000	10711.04	5697.98	4036.06	3211.86	2722.70	2400.99	2174.89	2008.49
125000	11157.34	5935.40	4204.23	3345.69	2836.15	2501.03	2265.51	2092.18
130000	11603.63	6172.81	4372.40	3479.52	2949.59	2601.07	2356.13	2175.87
135000	12049.92	6410.23	4540.56	3613.35	3063.04	2701.11	2446.76	2259.56
140000	12496.21	6647.64	4708.73	3747.17	3176.48	2801.15	2537.38	2343.24
145000	12942.51	6885.06	4876.90	3881.00	3289.93	2901.19	2628.00	2426.93
150000	13388.80	7122.47	5045.07	4014.83	3403.38	3001.23	2718.62	2510.62
155000	13835.09	7359.89	5213.24	4148.66	3516.82	3101.27	2809.24	2594.30
160000	14281.39	7597.31	5381.41	4282.48	3630.27	3201.32	2899.86	2677.99

MONTHLY AMORTIZING PAYMENTS 12 7/8%

AMOUNT OF LOAN	NUMBER OF YEARS IN TERM							
	9	10	15	20	25	30	35	40
$ 50	.79	.75	.63	.59	.56	.55	.55	.54
100	1.57	1.49	1.26	1.17	1.12	1.10	1.09	1.08
200	3.14	2.98	2.52	2.33	2.24	2.20	2.18	2.16
300	4.71	4.46	3.78	3.49	3.36	3.29	3.26	3.24
400	6.28	5.95	5.03	4.66	4.48	4.39	4.35	4.32
500	7.85	7.43	6.29	5.82	5.60	5.49	5.43	5.40
600	9.41	8.92	7.55	6.98	6.72	6.58	6.52	6.48
700	10.98	10.41	8.80	8.14	7.83	7.68	7.60	7.56
800	12.55	11.89	10.06	9.31	8.95	8.78	8.69	8.64
900	14.12	13.38	11.32	10.47	10.07	9.87	9.77	9.72
1000	15.69	14.86	12.58	11.63	11.19	10.97	10.86	10.80
2000	31.37	29.72	25.15	23.26	22.37	21.93	21.71	21.59
3000	47.05	44.58	37.72	34.89	33.56	32.90	32.56	32.39
4000	62.73	59.43	50.29	46.51	44.74	43.86	43.41	43.18
5000	78.41	74.29	62.86	58.14	55.93	54.83	54.26	53.97
6000	94.10	89.15	75.43	69.77	67.11	65.79	65.12	64.77
7000	109.78	104.01	88.00	81.39	78.30	76.76	75.97	75.56
8000	125.46	118.86	100.57	93.02	89.48	87.72	86.82	86.35
9000	141.14	133.72	113.14	104.65	100.66	98.68	97.67	97.15
10000	156.82	148.58	125.71	116.27	111.85	109.65	108.52	107.94
11000	172.51	163.44	138.28	127.90	123.03	120.61	119.38	118.73
12000	188.19	178.29	150.85	139.53	134.22	131.58	130.23	129.53
13000	203.87	193.15	163.42	151.15	145.40	142.54	141.08	140.32
14000	219.55	208.01	175.99	162.78	156.59	153.51	151.93	151.11
15000	235.23	222.87	188.56	174.41	167.77	164.47	162.78	161.91
16000	250.91	237.72	201.13	186.03	178.95	175.44	173.64	172.70
17000	266.60	252.58	213.70	197.66	190.14	186.40	184.49	183.49
18000	282.28	267.44	226.27	209.29	201.32	197.36	195.34	194.29
19000	297.96	282.30	238.84	220.91	212.51	208.33	206.19	205.08
20000	313.64	297.15	251.41	232.54	223.69	219.29	217.04	215.88
21000	329.32	312.01	263.98	244.17	234.88	230.26	227.89	226.67
22000	345.01	326.87	276.55	255.80	246.06	241.22	238.75	237.46
23000	360.69	341.73	289.12	267.42	257.24	252.19	249.60	248.26
24000	376.37	356.58	301.69	279.05	268.43	263.15	260.45	259.05
25000	392.05	371.44	314.26	290.68	279.61	274.11	271.30	269.84
26000	407.73	386.30	326.83	302.30	290.80	285.08	282.15	280.64
27000	423.41	401.16	339.40	313.93	301.98	296.04	293.01	291.43
28000	439.10	416.01	351.97	325.56	313.17	307.01	303.86	302.22
29000	454.78	430.87	364.54	337.18	324.35	317.97	314.71	313.02
30000	470.46	445.73	377.11	348.81	335.54	328.94	325.56	323.81
31000	486.14	460.59	389.68	360.44	346.72	339.90	336.41	334.60
32000	501.82	475.44	402.25	372.06	357.90	350.87	347.27	345.40
33000	517.51	490.30	414.82	383.69	369.09	361.83	358.12	356.19
34000	533.19	505.16	427.39	395.32	380.27	372.79	368.97	366.98
35000	548.87	520.02	439.96	406.94	391.46	383.76	379.82	377.78
40000	627.28	594.30	502.82	465.08	447.38	438.58	434.08	431.75
45000	705.69	668.59	565.67	523.21	503.30	493.40	488.34	485.71
50000	784.10	742.88	628.52	581.35	559.22	548.22	542.60	539.68
55000	862.51	817.16	691.37	639.48	615.14	603.05	596.86	593.65
60000	940.91	891.45	754.22	697.61	671.07	657.87	651.12	647.62
65000	1019.32	965.74	817.07	755.75	726.99	712.69	705.38	701.58
70000	1097.73	1040.03	879.92	813.88	782.91	767.51	759.64	755.55
75000	1176.14	1114.31	942.78	872.02	838.83	822.33	813.90	809.52
80000	1254.55	1188.60	1005.63	930.15	894.75	877.16	868.16	863.49
85000	1332.96	1262.89	1068.48	988.28	950.67	931.98	922.41	917.45
90000	1411.37	1337.17	1131.33	1046.42	1006.60	986.80	976.67	971.42
95000	1489.78	1411.46	1194.18	1104.55	1062.52	1041.62	1030.93	1025.39
100000	1568.19	1485.75	1257.03	1162.69	1118.44	1096.44	1085.19	1079.36
105000	1646.60	1560.04	1319.88	1220.82	1174.36	1151.26	1139.45	1133.32
110000	1725.01	1634.32	1382.74	1278.96	1230.28	1206.09	1193.71	1187.29
115000	1803.41	1708.61	1445.59	1337.09	1286.20	1260.91	1247.97	1241.26
120000	1881.82	1782.90	1508.44	1395.22	1342.13	1315.73	1302.23	1295.23
125000	1960.23	1857.18	1571.29	1453.36	1398.05	1370.55	1356.49	1349.19
130000	2038.64	1931.47	1634.14	1511.49	1453.97	1425.37	1410.75	1403.16
135000	2117.05	2005.76	1696.99	1569.63	1509.89	1480.20	1465.01	1457.13
140000	2195.46	2080.05	1759.84	1627.76	1565.81	1535.02	1519.27	1511.10
145000	2273.87	2154.33	1822.70	1685.89	1621.73	1589.84	1573.53	1565.06
150000	2352.28	2228.62	1885.55	1744.03	1677.66	1644.66	1627.79	1619.03
155000	2430.69	2302.91	1948.40	1802.16	1733.58	1699.48	1682.05	1673.00
160000	2509.10	2377.19	2011.25	1860.30	1789.50	1754.31	1736.31	1726.97

13% MONTHLY AMORTIZING PAYMENTS

AMOUNT OF LOAN	NUMBER OF YEARS IN TERM							
	1	2	3	4	5	6	7	8
$ 50	4.47	2.38	1.69	1.35	1.14	1.01	.91	.85
100	8.94	4.76	3.37	2.69	2.28	2.01	1.82	1.69
200	17.87	9.51	6.74	5.37	4.56	4.02	3.64	3.37
300	26.80	14.27	10.11	8.05	6.83	6.03	5.46	5.05
400	35.73	19.02	13.48	10.74	9.11	8.03	7.28	6.73
500	44.66	23.78	16.85	13.42	11.38	10.04	9.10	8.41
600	53.60	28.53	20.22	16.10	13.66	12.05	10.92	10.09
700	62.53	33.28	23.59	18.78	15.93	14.06	12.74	11.77
800	71.46	38.04	26.96	21.47	18.21	16.06	14.56	13.45
900	80.39	42.79	30.33	24.15	20.48	18.07	16.38	15.13
1000	89.32	47.55	33.70	26.83	22.76	20.08	18.20	16.81
2000	178.64	95.09	67.39	53.66	45.51	40.15	36.39	33.62
3000	267.96	142.63	101.09	80.49	68.26	60.23	54.58	50.43
4000	357.27	190.17	134.78	107.31	91.02	80.30	72.77	67.23
5000	446.59	237.71	168.47	134.14	113.77	100.38	90.96	84.04
6000	535.91	285.26	202.17	160.97	136.52	120.45	109.16	100.85
7000	625.23	332.80	235.86	187.80	159.28	140.52	127.35	117.66
8000	714.54	380.34	269.56	214.62	182.03	160.60	145.54	134.46
9000	803.86	427.88	303.25	241.45	204.78	180.67	163.73	151.27
10000	893.18	475.42	336.94	268.28	227.54	200.75	181.92	168.08
11000	982.50	522.97	370.64	295.11	250.29	220.82	200.12	184.88
12000	1071.81	570.51	404.33	321.93	273.04	240.89	218.31	201.69
13000	1161.13	618.05	438.03	348.76	295.79	260.97	236.50	218.50
14000	1250.45	665.59	471.72	375.59	318.55	281.04	254.69	235.31
15000	1339.76	713.13	505.41	402.42	341.30	301.12	272.88	252.11
16000	1429.08	760.67	539.11	429.24	364.05	321.19	291.08	268.92
17000	1518.40	808.22	572.80	456.07	386.81	341.26	309.27	285.73
18000	1607.72	855.76	606.50	482.90	409.56	361.34	327.46	302.54
19000	1697.03	903.30	640.19	509.73	432.31	381.41	345.65	319.34
20000	1786.35	950.84	673.88	536.55	455.07	401.49	363.84	336.15
21000	1875.67	998.38	707.58	563.38	477.82	421.56	382.04	352.96
22000	1964.99	1045.93	741.27	590.21	500.57	441.64	400.23	369.76
23000	2054.30	1093.47	774.97	617.04	523.33	461.71	418.42	386.57
24000	2143.62	1141.01	808.66	643.86	546.08	481.78	436.61	403.38
25000	2232.94	1188.55	842.35	670.69	568.83	501.86	454.80	420.19
26000	2322.25	1236.09	876.05	697.52	591.58	521.93	473.00	436.99
27000	2411.57	1283.63	909.74	724.35	614.34	542.01	491.19	453.80
28000	2500.89	1331.18	943.44	751.17	637.09	562.08	509.38	470.61
29000	2590.21	1378.72	977.13	778.00	659.84	582.15	527.57	487.42
30000	2679.52	1426.26	1010.82	804.83	682.60	602.23	545.76	504.22
31000	2768.84	1473.80	1044.52	831.66	705.35	622.30	563.96	521.03
32000	2858.16	1521.34	1078.21	858.48	728.10	642.38	582.15	537.84
33000	2947.48	1568.89	1111.91	885.31	750.86	662.45	600.34	554.64
34000	3036.79	1616.43	1145.60	912.14	773.61	682.52	618.53	571.45
35000	3126.11	1663.97	1179.29	938.97	796.36	702.60	636.72	588.26
40000	3572.70	1901.68	1347.76	1073.10	910.13	802.97	727.68	672.30
45000	4019.28	2139.39	1516.23	1207.24	1023.89	903.34	818.64	756.33
50000	4465.87	2377.10	1684.70	1341.38	1137.66	1003.71	909.60	840.37
55000	4912.46	2614.81	1853.17	1475.52	1251.42	1104.08	1000.56	924.40
60000	5359.04	2852.51	2021.64	1609.65	1365.19	1204.45	1091.52	1008.44
65000	5805.63	3090.22	2190.11	1743.79	1478.95	1304.82	1182.48	1092.48
70000	6252.21	3327.93	2358.58	1877.93	1592.72	1405.19	1273.44	1176.51
75000	6698.80	3565.64	2527.05	2012.07	1706.49	1505.56	1364.40	1260.55
80000	7145.39	3803.35	2695.52	2146.20	1820.25	1605.93	1455.36	1344.59
85000	7591.97	4041.06	2863.99	2280.34	1934.02	1706.30	1546.32	1428.62
90000	8038.56	4278.77	3032.46	2414.48	2047.78	1806.67	1637.28	1512.66
95000	8485.15	4516.48	3200.93	2548.62	2161.55	1907.04	1728.24	1596.69
100000	8931.73	4754.19	3369.40	2682.75	2275.31	2007.42	1819.20	1680.73
105000	9378.32	4991.90	3537.87	2816.89	2389.08	2107.79	1910.16	1764.77
110000	9824.91	5229.61	3706.34	2951.03	2502.84	2208.16	2001.12	1848.80
115000	10271.49	5467.31	3874.81	3085.17	2616.61	2308.53	2092.08	1932.84
120000	10718.08	5705.02	4043.28	3219.30	2730.37	2408.90	2183.04	2016.88
125000	11164.66	5942.73	4211.75	3353.44	2844.14	2509.27	2274.00	2100.91
130000	11611.25	6180.44	4380.22	3487.58	2957.90	2609.64	2364.96	2184.95
135000	12057.84	6418.15	4548.69	3621.72	3071.67	2710.01	2455.92	2268.98
140000	12504.42	6655.86	4717.16	3755.85	3185.44	2810.38	2546.88	2353.02
145000	12951.01	6893.57	4885.63	3889.99	3299.20	2910.75	2637.84	2437.06
150000	13397.60	7131.28	5054.10	4024.13	3412.97	3011.12	2728.80	2521.09
155000	13844.18	7368.99	5222.57	4158.27	3526.73	3111.49	2819.76	2605.13
160000	14290.77	7606.70	5391.04	4292.40	3640.50	3211.86	2910.72	2689.17

MONTHLY AMORTIZING PAYMENTS 13%

AMOUNT OF LOAN	NUMBER OF YEARS IN TERM							
	9	10	15	20	25	30	35	40
$ 50	.79	.75	.64	.59	.57	.56	.55	.55
100	1.58	1.50	1.27	1.18	1.13	1.11	1.10	1.09
200	3.16	2.99	2.54	2.35	2.26	2.22	2.20	2.18
300	4.73	4.48	3.80	3.52	3.39	3.32	3.29	3.27
400	6.31	5.98	5.07	4.69	4.52	4.43	4.39	4.36
500	7.88	7.47	6.33	5.86	5.64	5.54	5.48	5.45
600	9.46	8.96	7.60	7.03	6.77	6.64	6.58	6.54
700	11.03	10.46	8.86	8.21	7.90	7.75	7.67	7.63
800	12.61	11.95	10.13	9.38	9.03	8.85	8.77	8.72
900	14.18	13.44	11.39	10.55	10.16	9.96	9.86	9.81
1000	15.76	14.94	12.66	11.72	11.28	11.07	10.96	10.90
2000	31.51	29.87	25.31	23.44	22.56	22.13	21.91	21.80
3000	47.27	44.80	37.96	35.15	33.84	33.19	32.86	32.69
4000	63.02	59.73	50.61	46.87	45.12	44.25	43.81	43.59
5000	78.77	74.66	63.27	58.58	56.40	55.31	54.76	54.48
6000	94.53	89.59	75.92	70.30	67.68	66.38	65.72	65.38
7000	110.28	104.52	88.57	82.02	78.95	77.44	76.67	76.27
8000	126.03	119.45	101.22	93.73	90.23	88.50	87.62	87.17
9000	141.79	134.38	113.88	105.45	101.51	99.56	98.57	98.06
10000	157.54	149.32	126.53	117.16	112.79	110.62	109.52	108.96
11000	173.29	164.25	139.18	128.88	124.07	121.69	120.48	119.85
12000	189.05	179.18	151.83	140.59	135.35	132.75	131.43	130.75
13000	204.80	194.11	164.49	152.31	146.62	143.81	142.38	141.64
14000	220.56	209.04	177.14	164.03	157.90	154.87	153.33	152.54
15000	236.31	223.97	189.79	175.74	169.18	165.93	164.28	163.43
16000	252.06	238.90	202.44	187.46	180.46	177.00	175.24	174.33
17000	267.82	253.83	215.10	199.17	191.74	188.06	186.19	185.22
18000	283.57	268.76	227.75	210.89	203.02	199.12	197.14	196.12
19000	299.32	283.70	240.40	222.60	214.29	210.18	208.09	207.01
20000	315.08	298.63	253.05	234.32	225.57	221.24	219.04	217.91
21000	330.83	313.56	265.71	246.04	236.85	232.31	230.00	228.80
22000	346.58	328.49	278.36	257.75	248.13	243.37	240.95	239.70
23000	362.34	343.42	291.01	269.47	259.41	254.43	251.90	250.59
24000	378.09	358.35	303.66	281.18	270.69	265.49	262.85	261.49
25000	393.84	373.28	316.32	292.90	281.96	276.55	273.80	272.38
26000	409.60	388.21	328.97	304.61	293.24	287.62	284.76	283.28
27000	425.35	403.14	341.62	316.33	304.52	298.68	295.71	294.17
28000	441.11	418.08	354.27	328.05	315.80	309.74	306.66	305.07
29000	456.86	433.01	366.93	339.76	327.08	320.80	317.61	315.96
30000	472.61	447.94	379.58	351.48	338.36	331.86	328.56	326.86
31000	488.37	462.87	392.23	363.19	349.63	342.93	339.51	337.75
32000	504.12	477.80	404.88	374.91	360.91	353.99	350.47	348.65
33000	519.87	492.73	417.53	386.62	372.19	365.05	361.42	359.54
34000	535.63	507.66	430.19	398.34	383.47	376.11	372.37	370.44
35000	551.38	522.59	442.84	410.06	394.75	387.17	383.32	381.33
40000	630.15	597.25	506.10	468.64	451.14	442.48	438.08	435.81
45000	708.92	671.90	569.36	527.21	507.53	497.79	492.84	490.29
50000	787.68	746.56	632.63	585.79	563.92	553.10	547.60	544.76
55000	866.45	821.21	695.89	644.37	620.31	608.41	602.36	599.24
60000	945.22	895.87	759.15	702.95	676.71	663.72	657.12	653.71
65000	1023.99	970.52	822.41	761.53	733.10	719.03	711.88	708.19
70000	1102.76	1045.18	885.67	820.11	789.49	774.34	766.64	762.66
75000	1181.52	1119.84	948.94	878.69	845.88	829.65	821.40	817.14
80000	1260.29	1194.49	1012.20	937.27	902.27	884.96	876.16	871.62
85000	1339.06	1269.15	1075.46	995.84	958.67	940.27	930.92	926.09
90000	1417.83	1343.80	1138.72	1054.42	1015.06	995.58	985.68	980.57
95000	1496.60	1418.46	1201.99	1113.00	1071.45	1050.89	1040.44	1035.04
100000	1575.36	1493.11	1265.25	1171.58	1127.84	1106.20	1095.20	1089.52
105000	1654.13	1567.77	1328.51	1230.16	1184.23	1161.51	1149.96	1143.99
110000	1732.90	1642.42	1391.77	1288.74	1240.62	1216.82	1204.72	1198.47
115000	1811.67	1717.08	1455.03	1347.32	1297.02	1272.13	1259.48	1252.95
120000	1890.44	1791.73	1518.30	1405.90	1353.41	1327.44	1314.24	1307.42
125000	1969.20	1866.39	1581.56	1464.47	1409.80	1382.75	1369.00	1361.90
130000	2047.97	1941.04	1644.82	1523.05	1466.19	1438.06	1423.76	1416.37
135000	2126.74	2015.70	1708.08	1581.63	1522.58	1493.37	1478.52	1470.85
140000	2205.51	2090.36	1771.34	1640.21	1578.97	1548.68	1533.28	1525.32
145000	2284.28	2165.01	1834.61	1698.79	1635.37	1603.99	1588.04	1579.80
150000	2363.04	2239.67	1897.87	1757.37	1691.76	1659.30	1642.79	1634.28
155000	2441.81	2314.32	1961.13	1815.95	1748.15	1714.61	1697.55	1688.75
160000	2520.58	2388.98	2024.39	1874.53	1804.54	1769.92	1752.31	1743.23

MONTHLY AMORTIZING PAYMENTS

AMOUNT OF LOAN	NUMBER OF YEARS IN TERM 1	2	3	4	5	6	7	8
$ 50	4.47	2.39	1.69	1.35	1.15	1.01	.92	.85
100	8.94	4.77	3.38	2.69	2.29	2.02	1.83	1.69
200	17.88	9.53	6.76	5.38	4.57	4.03	3.66	3.38
300	26.82	14.29	10.13	8.07	6.85	6.05	5.48	5.07
400	35.76	19.05	13.51	10.76	9.13	8.06	7.31	6.76
500	44.69	23.81	16.88	13.45	11.41	10.08	9.13	8.44
600	53.63	28.57	20.26	16.14	13.70	12.09	10.96	10.13
700	62.57	33.33	23.63	18.83	15.98	14.10	12.79	11.82
800	71.51	38.09	27.01	21.52	18.26	16.12	14.61	13.51
900	80.44	42.85	30.38	24.21	20.54	18.13	16.44	15.19
1000	89.38	47.61	33.76	26.89	22.82	20.15	18.26	16.88
2000	178.76	95.21	67.51	53.78	45.64	40.29	36.52	33.76
3000	268.13	142.81	101.27	80.67	68.46	60.43	54.78	50.64
4000	357.51	190.41	135.02	107.56	91.27	80.57	73.04	67.51
5000	446.88	238.01	168.78	134.45	114.09	100.71	91.30	84.39
6000	536.26	285.61	202.53	161.34	136.91	120.85	109.56	101.27
7000	625.64	333.21	236.28	188.23	159.72	140.99	127.82	118.15
8000	715.01	380.81	270.04	215.12	182.54	161.13	146.08	135.02
9000	804.39	428.41	303.79	242.01	205.36	181.27	164.34	151.90
10000	893.76	476.01	337.55	268.90	228.18	201.41	182.60	168.78
11000	983.14	523.61	371.30	295.79	250.99	221.55	200.86	185.65
12000	1072.52	571.21	405.06	322.68	273.81	241.69	219.12	202.53
13000	1161.89	618.81	438.81	349.57	296.63	261.83	237.38	219.41
14000	1251.27	666.41	472.56	376.46	319.44	281.97	255.64	236.29
15000	1340.64	714.01	506.32	403.35	342.26	302.11	273.90	253.16
16000	1430.02	761.61	540.07	430.24	365.08	322.25	292.16	270.04
17000	1519.40	809.21	573.83	457.13	387.90	342.39	310.42	286.92
18000	1608.77	856.82	607.58	484.02	410.71	362.53	328.68	303.80
19000	1698.15	904.42	641.33	510.91	433.53	382.67	346.94	320.67
20000	1787.52	952.02	675.09	537.80	456.35	402.81	365.20	337.55
21000	1876.90	999.62	708.84	564.69	479.16	422.95	383.46	354.43
22000	1966.28	1047.22	742.60	591.58	501.98	443.09	401.72	371.30
23000	2055.65	1094.82	776.35	618.47	524.80	463.23	419.98	388.18
24000	2145.03	1142.42	810.11	645.35	547.62	483.37	438.24	405.06
25000	2234.40	1190.02	843.86	672.24	570.43	503.51	456.50	421.94
26000	2323.78	1237.62	877.61	699.13	593.25	523.65	474.76	438.81
27000	2413.16	1285.22	911.37	726.02	616.07	543.79	493.02	455.69
28000	2502.53	1332.82	945.12	752.91	638.88	563.93	511.28	472.57
29000	2591.91	1380.42	978.88	779.80	661.70	584.07	529.54	489.45
30000	2681.28	1428.02	1012.63	806.69	684.52	604.21	547.80	506.32
31000	2770.66	1475.62	1046.38	833.58	707.34	624.35	566.06	523.20
32000	2860.03	1523.22	1080.14	860.47	730.15	644.49	584.32	540.08
33000	2949.41	1570.82	1113.89	887.36	752.97	664.63	602.58	556.95
34000	3038.79	1618.42	1147.65	914.25	775.79	684.77	620.84	573.83
35000	3128.16	1666.02	1181.40	941.14	798.60	704.91	639.10	590.71
40000	3575.04	1904.03	1350.17	1075.59	912.69	805.61	730.40	675.10
45000	4021.92	2142.03	1518.94	1210.04	1026.78	906.31	821.70	759.48
50000	4468.80	2380.03	1687.71	1344.48	1140.86	1007.01	913.00	843.87
55000	4915.68	2618.04	1856.49	1478.93	1254.95	1107.71	1004.30	928.25
60000	5362.56	2856.04	2025.26	1613.38	1369.03	1208.41	1095.60	1012.64
65000	5809.44	3094.04	2194.03	1747.83	1483.12	1309.11	1186.90	1097.03
70000	6256.32	3332.04	2362.80	1882.28	1597.20	1409.81	1278.20	1181.41
75000	6703.20	3570.05	2531.57	2016.72	1711.29	1510.52	1369.50	1265.80
80000	7150.08	3808.05	2700.34	2151.17	1825.37	1611.22	1460.80	1350.19
85000	7596.96	4046.05	2869.11	2285.62	1939.46	1711.92	1552.10	1434.57
90000	8043.84	4284.06	3037.88	2420.07	2053.55	1812.62	1643.40	1518.96
95000	8490.72	4522.06	3206.65	2554.51	2167.63	1913.32	1734.70	1603.34
100000	8937.60	4760.06	3375.42	2688.96	2281.72	2014.02	1826.00	1687.73
105000	9384.48	4998.06	3544.20	2823.41	2395.80	2114.72	1917.30	1772.12
110000	9831.36	5236.07	3712.97	2957.86	2509.89	2215.42	2008.60	1856.50
115000	10278.24	5474.07	3881.74	3092.31	2623.97	2316.12	2099.90	1940.89
120000	10725.12	5712.07	4050.51	3226.75	2738.06	2416.82	2191.20	2025.28
125000	11172.00	5950.07	4219.28	3361.20	2852.14	2517.52	2282.50	2109.66
130000	11618.88	6188.08	4388.05	3495.65	2966.23	2618.22	2373.80	2194.05
135000	12065.76	6426.08	4556.82	3630.10	3080.32	2718.92	2465.10	2278.43
140000	12512.64	6664.08	4725.59	3764.55	3194.40	2819.62	2556.40	2362.82
145000	12959.52	6902.09	4894.36	3898.99	3308.49	2920.33	2647.70	2447.21
150000	13406.39	7140.09	5063.13	4033.44	3422.57	3021.03	2739.00	2531.59
155000	13853.27	7378.09	5231.90	4167.89	3536.66	3121.73	2830.30	2615.98
160000	14300.15	7616.09	5400.68	4302.34	3650.74	3222.43	2921.60	2700.37

AMOUNT OF LOAN	9	10	15	20	25	30	35	40
	NUMBER OF YEARS IN TERM							
$ 50	.80	.76	.64	.60	.57	.56	.56	.55
100	1.59	1.51	1.28	1.19	1.14	1.12	1.11	1.10
200	3.17	3.01	2.55	2.37	2.28	2.24	2.22	2.20
300	4.75	4.51	3.83	3.55	3.42	3.35	3.32	3.30
400	6.34	6.01	5.10	4.73	4.55	4.47	4.43	4.40
500	7.92	7.51	6.37	5.91	5.69	5.58	5.53	5.50
600	9.50	9.01	7.65	7.09	6.83	6.70	6.64	6.60
700	11.08	10.51	8.92	8.27	7.97	7.82	7.74	7.70
800	12.67	12.01	10.19	9.45	9.10	8.93	8.85	8.80
900	14.25	13.51	11.47	10.63	10.24	10.05	9.95	9.90
1000	15.83	15.01	12.74	11.81	11.38	11.16	11.06	11.00
2000	31.66	30.01	25.47	23.61	22.75	22.32	22.11	22.00
3000	47.48	45.02	38.21	35.42	34.12	33.48	33.16	33.00
4000	63.31	60.02	50.94	47.22	45.50	44.64	44.21	43.99
5000	79.13	75.03	63.68	59.03	56.87	55.80	55.27	54.99
6000	94.96	90.03	76.41	70.83	68.24	66.96	66.32	65.99
7000	110.78	105.04	89.15	82.64	79.61	78.12	77.37	76.98
8000	126.61	120.04	101.88	94.44	90.99	89.28	88.42	87.98
9000	142.43	135.05	114.62	106.25	102.36	100.44	99.47	98.98
10000	158.26	150.05	127.35	118.05	113.73	111.60	110.53	109.97
11000	174.09	165.06	140.09	129.86	125.10	122.76	121.58	120.97
12000	189.91	180.06	152.82	141.66	136.48	133.92	132.63	131.97
13000	205.74	195.07	165.56	153.47	147.85	145.08	143.68	142.96
14000	221.56	210.07	178.29	165.27	159.22	156.24	154.73	153.96
15000	237.39	225.08	191.03	177.08	170.59	167.40	165.79	164.96
16000	253.21	240.08	203.76	188.88	181.97	178.56	176.84	175.95
17000	269.04	255.09	216.50	200.69	193.34	189.72	187.89	186.95
18000	284.86	270.09	229.23	212.49	204.71	200.88	198.94	197.95
19000	300.69	285.10	241.97	224.30	216.08	212.04	210.00	208.95
20000	316.52	300.10	254.70	236.10	227.46	223.20	221.05	219.94
21000	332.34	315.11	267.44	247.91	238.83	234.36	232.10	230.94
22000	348.17	330.11	280.17	259.71	250.20	245.52	243.15	241.94
23000	363.99	345.12	292.90	271.52	261.57	256.68	254.20	252.93
24000	379.82	360.12	305.64	283.32	272.95	267.84	265.26	263.93
25000	395.64	375.13	318.37	295.13	284.32	279.00	276.31	274.93
26000	411.47	390.13	331.11	306.93	295.69	290.16	287.36	285.92
27000	427.29	405.14	343.84	318.74	307.06	301.32	298.41	296.92
28000	443.12	420.14	356.58	330.54	318.44	312.48	309.46	307.92
29000	458.95	435.15	369.31	342.35	329.81	323.64	320.52	318.91
30000	474.77	450.15	382.05	354.15	341.18	334.80	331.57	329.91
31000	490.60	465.16	394.78	365.96	352.55	345.96	342.62	340.91
32000	506.42	480.16	407.52	377.76	363.93	357.12	353.67	351.90
33000	522.25	495.17	420.25	389.57	375.30	368.28	364.72	362.90
34000	538.07	510.17	432.99	401.37	386.67	379.44	375.78	373.90
35000	553.90	525.18	445.72	413.18	398.05	390.60	386.83	384.90
40000	633.03	600.20	509.40	472.20	454.91	446.40	442.09	439.88
45000	712.15	675.23	573.07	531.23	511.77	502.20	497.35	494.86
50000	791.28	750.25	636.74	590.25	568.63	557.99	552.61	549.85
55000	870.41	825.27	700.42	649.28	625.50	613.79	607.87	604.83
60000	949.54	900.30	764.09	708.30	682.36	669.59	663.13	659.82
65000	1028.66	975.32	827.77	767.32	739.22	725.39	718.39	714.80
70000	1107.79	1050.35	891.44	826.35	796.09	781.19	773.65	769.79
75000	1186.92	1125.37	955.11	885.37	852.95	836.99	828.91	824.77
80000	1266.05	1200.40	1018.79	944.40	909.81	892.79	884.17	879.75
85000	1345.17	1275.42	1082.46	1003.42	966.67	948.59	939.43	934.74
90000	1424.30	1350.45	1146.14	1062.45	1023.54	1004.39	994.70	989.72
95000	1503.43	1425.47	1209.81	1121.47	1080.40	1060.18	1049.96	1044.71
100000	1582.56	1500.49	1273.48	1180.50	1137.26	1115.98	1105.22	1099.69
105000	1661.68	1575.52	1337.16	1239.52	1194.13	1171.78	1160.48	1154.68
110000	1740.81	1650.54	1400.83	1298.55	1250.99	1227.58	1215.74	1209.66
115000	1819.94	1725.57	1464.50	1357.57	1307.85	1283.38	1271.00	1264.65
120000	1899.07	1800.59	1528.18	1416.60	1364.71	1339.18	1326.26	1319.63
125000	1978.19	1875.62	1591.85	1475.62	1421.58	1394.98	1381.52	1374.61
130000	2057.32	1950.64	1655.53	1534.64	1478.44	1450.78	1436.78	1429.60
135000	2136.45	2025.67	1719.20	1593.67	1535.30	1506.58	1492.04	1484.58
140000	2215.58	2100.69	1782.87	1652.69	1592.17	1562.37	1547.30	1539.57
145000	2294.71	2175.71	1846.55	1711.72	1649.03	1618.17	1602.56	1594.55
150000	2373.83	2250.74	1910.22	1770.74	1705.89	1673.97	1657.82	1649.54
155000	2452.96	2325.76	1973.90	1829.77	1762.75	1729.77	1713.08	1704.52
160000	2532.09	2400.79	2037.57	1888.79	1819.62	1785.57	1768.34	1759.50

AMOUNT OF LOAN	NUMBER OF YEARS IN TERM							
	1	2	3	4	5	6	7	8
$ 50	4.48	2.39	1.70	1.35	1.15	1.02	.92	.85
100	8.95	4.77	3.39	2.70	2.29	2.03	1.84	1.70
200	17.89	9.54	6.77	5.40	4.58	4.05	3.67	3.39
300	26.84	14.30	10.15	8.09	6.87	6.07	5.50	5.09
400	35.78	19.07	13.53	10.79	9.16	8.09	7.34	6.78
500	44.72	23.83	16.91	13.48	11.45	10.11	9.17	8.48
600	53.67	28.60	20.29	16.18	13.73	12.13	11.00	10.17
700	62.61	33.37	23.68	18.87	16.02	14.15	12.83	11.87
800	71.55	38.13	27.06	21.57	18.31	16.17	14.67	13.56
900	80.50	42.90	30.44	24.26	20.60	18.19	16.50	15.26
1000	89.44	47.66	33.82	26.96	22.89	20.21	18.33	16.95
2000	178.87	95.32	67.63	53.91	45.77	40.42	36.66	33.90
3000	268.31	142.98	101.45	80.86	68.65	60.62	54.99	50.85
4000	357.74	190.64	135.26	107.81	91.53	80.83	73.32	67.79
5000	447.18	238.30	169.08	134.76	114.41	101.04	91.65	84.74
6000	536.61	285.96	202.89	161.72	137.29	121.24	109.97	101.69
7000	626.05	333.62	236.71	188.67	160.17	141.45	128.30	118.64
8000	715.48	381.28	270.52	215.62	183.06	161.66	146.63	135.58
9000	804.92	428.94	304.34	242.57	205.94	181.86	164.96	152.53
10000	894.35	476.60	338.15	269.52	228.82	202.07	183.29	169.48
11000	983.79	524.26	371.96	296.47	251.70	222.27	201.61	186.43
12000	1073.22	571.92	405.78	323.43	274.58	242.48	219.94	203.37
13000	1162.65	619.58	439.59	350.38	297.46	262.69	238.27	220.32
14000	1252.09	667.24	473.41	377.33	320.34	282.89	256.60	237.27
15000	1341.52	714.90	507.22	404.28	343.22	303.10	274.93	254.22
16000	1430.96	762.55	541.04	431.23	366.11	323.31	293.26	271.16
17000	1520.39	810.21	574.85	458.18	388.99	343.51	311.58	288.11
18000	1609.83	857.87	608.67	485.14	411.87	363.72	329.91	305.06
19000	1699.26	905.53	642.48	512.09	434.75	383.92	348.24	322.01
20000	1788.70	953.19	676.29	539.04	457.63	404.13	366.57	338.95
21000	1878.13	1000.85	710.11	565.99	480.51	424.34	384.90	355.90
22000	1967.57	1048.51	743.92	592.94	503.39	444.54	403.22	372.85
23000	2057.00	1096.17	777.74	619.90	526.27	464.75	421.55	389.80
24000	2146.44	1143.83	811.55	646.85	549.16	484.96	439.88	406.74
25000	2235.87	1191.49	845.37	673.80	572.04	505.16	458.21	423.69
26000	2325.30	1239.15	879.18	700.75	594.92	525.37	476.54	440.64
27000	2414.74	1286.81	913.00	727.70	617.80	545.57	494.87	457.58
28000	2504.17	1334.47	946.81	754.65	640.68	565.78	513.19	474.53
29000	2593.61	1382.13	980.63	781.61	663.56	585.99	531.52	491.48
30000	2683.04	1429.79	1014.44	808.56	686.44	606.19	549.85	508.43
31000	2772.48	1477.44	1048.25	835.51	709.32	626.40	568.18	525.37
32000	2861.91	1525.10	1082.07	862.46	732.21	646.61	586.51	542.32
33000	2951.35	1572.76	1115.88	889.41	755.09	666.81	604.83	559.27
34000	3040.78	1620.42	1149.70	916.36	777.97	687.02	623.16	576.22
35000	3130.22	1668.08	1183.51	943.32	800.85	707.23	641.49	593.16
40000	3577.39	1906.38	1352.58	1078.07	915.26	808.26	733.13	677.90
45000	4024.56	2144.68	1521.66	1212.83	1029.66	909.29	824.77	762.64
50000	4471.74	2382.97	1690.73	1347.59	1144.07	1010.32	916.41	847.38
55000	4918.91	2621.27	1859.80	1482.35	1258.47	1111.35	1008.05	932.11
60000	5366.08	2859.57	2028.87	1617.11	1372.88	1212.38	1099.69	1016.85
65000	5813.25	3097.86	2197.95	1751.87	1487.29	1313.41	1191.33	1101.59
70000	6260.43	3336.16	2367.02	1886.63	1601.69	1414.45	1282.98	1186.32
75000	6707.60	3574.46	2536.09	2021.39	1716.10	1515.48	1374.62	1271.06
80000	7154.77	3812.75	2705.16	2156.14	1830.51	1616.51	1466.26	1355.80
85000	7601.95	4051.05	2874.24	2290.90	1944.91	1717.54	1557.90	1440.53
90000	8049.12	4289.35	3043.31	2425.66	2059.32	1818.57	1649.54	1525.27
95000	8496.29	4527.64	3212.38	2560.42	2173.72	1919.60	1741.18	1610.01
100000	8943.47	4765.94	3381.45	2695.18	2288.13	2020.63	1832.82	1694.75
105000	9390.64	5004.24	3550.53	2829.94	2402.54	2121.67	1924.46	1779.48
110000	9837.81	5242.53	3719.60	2964.70	2516.94	2222.70	2016.10	1864.22
115000	10284.99	5480.83	3888.67	3099.46	2631.35	2323.73	2107.74	1948.96
120000	10732.16	5719.13	4057.74	3234.21	2745.76	2424.76	2199.38	2033.69
125000	11179.33	5957.42	4226.82	3368.97	2860.16	2525.79	2291.02	2118.43
130000	11626.50	6195.72	4395.89	3503.73	2974.57	2626.82	2382.66	2203.17
135000	12073.68	6434.02	4564.96	3638.49	3088.97	2727.85	2474.31	2287.90
140000	12520.85	6672.31	4734.03	3773.25	3203.38	2828.89	2565.95	2372.64
145000	12968.02	6910.61	4903.11	3908.01	3317.79	2929.92	2657.59	2457.38
150000	13415.20	7148.91	5072.18	4042.77	3432.19	3030.95	2749.23	2542.12
155000	13862.37	7387.20	5241.25	4177.53	3546.60	3131.98	2840.87	2626.85
160000	14309.54	7625.50	5410.32	4312.28	3661.01	3233.01	2932.51	2711.59

AMOUNT OF LOAN	NUMBER OF YEARS IN TERM 9	10	15	20	25	30	35	40
$ 50	.80	.76	.65	.60	.58	.57	.56	.56
100	1.59	1.51	1.29	1.19	1.15	1.13	1.12	1.11
200	3.18	3.02	2.57	2.38	2.30	2.26	2.24	2.22
300	4.77	4.53	3.85	3.57	3.45	3.38	3.35	3.33
400	6.36	6.04	5.13	4.76	4.59	4.51	4.47	4.44
500	7.95	7.54	6.41	5.95	5.74	5.63	5.58	5.55
600	9.54	9.05	7.70	7.14	6.89	6.76	6.70	6.66
700	11.13	10.56	8.98	8.33	8.03	7.89	7.81	7.77
800	12.72	12.07	10.26	9.52	9.18	9.01	8.93	8.88
900	14.31	13.58	11.54	10.71	10.33	10.14	10.04	9.99
1000	15.90	15.08	12.82	11.90	11.47	11.26	11.16	11.10
2000	31.80	30.16	25.64	23.79	22.94	22.52	22.31	22.20
3000	47.70	45.24	38.46	35.69	34.41	33.78	33.46	33.30
4000	63.60	60.32	51.27	47.58	45.87	45.04	44.61	44.40
5000	79.49	75.40	64.09	59.48	57.34	56.29	55.77	55.50
6000	95.39	90.48	76.91	71.37	68.81	67.55	66.92	66.60
7000	111.29	105.56	89.73	83.27	80.27	78.81	78.07	77.70
8000	127.19	120.64	102.54	95.16	91.74	90.07	89.22	88.79
9000	143.08	135.72	115.36	107.05	103.21	101.32	100.38	99.89
10000	158.98	150.79	128.18	118.95	114.68	112.58	111.53	110.99
11000	174.88	165.87	141.00	130.84	126.14	123.84	122.68	122.09
12000	190.78	180.95	153.81	142.74	137.61	135.10	133.83	133.19
13000	206.67	196.03	166.63	154.63	149.08	146.36	144.99	144.29
14000	222.57	211.11	179.45	166.53	160.54	157.61	156.14	155.39
15000	238.47	226.19	192.27	178.42	172.01	168.87	167.29	166.49
16000	254.37	241.27	205.08	190.31	183.48	180.13	178.44	177.58
17000	270.26	256.35	217.90	202.21	194.94	191.39	189.60	188.68
18000	286.16	271.43	230.72	214.10	206.41	202.64	200.75	199.78
19000	302.06	286.50	243.53	226.00	217.88	213.90	211.90	210.88
20000	317.96	301.58	256.35	237.89	229.35	225.16	223.05	221.98
21000	333.85	316.66	269.17	249.79	240.81	236.42	234.21	233.08
22000	349.75	331.74	281.99	261.68	252.28	247.68	245.36	244.18
23000	365.65	346.82	294.80	273.57	263.75	258.93	256.51	255.28
24000	381.55	361.90	307.62	285.47	275.21	270.19	267.66	266.37
25000	397.45	376.98	320.44	297.36	286.68	281.45	278.82	277.47
26000	413.34	392.06	333.26	309.26	298.15	292.71	289.97	288.57
27000	429.24	407.14	346.07	321.15	309.61	303.96	301.12	299.67
28000	445.14	422.21	358.89	333.05	321.08	315.22	312.27	310.77
29000	461.04	437.29	371.71	344.94	332.55	326.48	323.43	321.87
30000	476.93	452.37	384.53	356.83	344.02	337.74	334.58	332.97
31000	492.83	467.45	397.34	368.73	355.48	348.99	345.73	344.06
32000	508.73	482.53	410.16	380.62	366.95	360.25	356.88	355.16
33000	524.63	497.61	422.98	392.52	378.42	371.51	368.03	366.26
34000	540.52	512.69	435.80	404.41	389.88	382.77	379.19	377.36
35000	556.42	527.77	448.61	416.31	401.35	394.03	390.34	388.46
40000	635.91	603.16	512.70	475.78	458.69	450.31	446.10	443.95
45000	715.40	678.56	576.79	535.25	516.02	506.60	501.86	499.45
50000	794.89	753.95	640.87	594.72	573.36	562.89	557.63	554.94
55000	874.37	829.34	704.96	654.19	630.69	619.18	613.39	610.43
60000	953.86	904.74	769.05	713.66	688.03	675.47	669.15	665.93
65000	1033.35	980.13	833.13	773.13	745.36	731.76	724.91	721.42
70000	1112.84	1055.53	897.22	832.61	802.70	788.05	780.67	776.91
75000	1192.33	1130.92	961.31	892.08	860.03	844.34	836.44	832.41
80000	1271.81	1206.32	1025.39	951.55	917.37	900.62	892.20	887.90
85000	1351.30	1281.71	1089.48	1011.02	974.70	956.91	947.96	943.39
90000	1430.79	1357.11	1153.57	1070.49	1032.04	1013.20	1003.72	998.89
95000	1510.28	1432.50	1217.65	1129.96	1089.37	1069.49	1059.49	1054.38
100000	1589.77	1507.89	1281.74	1189.44	1146.71	1125.78	1115.25	1109.87
105000	1669.25	1583.29	1345.83	1248.91	1204.04	1182.07	1171.01	1165.37
110000	1748.74	1658.68	1409.92	1308.38	1261.38	1238.36	1226.77	1220.86
115000	1828.23	1734.08	1474.00	1367.85	1318.71	1294.64	1282.53	1276.36
120000	1907.72	1809.47	1538.09	1427.32	1376.05	1350.93	1338.30	1331.85
125000	1987.21	1884.87	1602.18	1486.79	1433.38	1407.22	1394.06	1387.34
130000	2066.70	1960.26	1666.26	1546.26	1490.72	1463.51	1449.82	1442.84
135000	2146.18	2035.66	1730.35	1605.74	1548.05	1519.80	1505.58	1498.33
140000	2225.67	2111.05	1794.44	1665.21	1605.39	1576.09	1561.34	1553.82
145000	2305.16	2186.44	1858.52	1724.68	1662.72	1632.38	1617.11	1609.32
150000	2384.65	2261.84	1922.61	1784.15	1720.06	1688.67	1672.87	1664.81
155000	2464.14	2337.23	1986.70	1843.62	1777.39	1744.95	1728.63	1720.30
160000	2543.62	2412.63	2050.78	1903.09	1834.73	1801.24	1784.39	1775.80

AMOUNT OF LOAN	NUMBER OF YEARS IN TERM							
	1	2	3	4	5	6	7	8
$ 50	4.48	2.39	1.70	1.36	1.15	1.02	.92	.86
100	8.95	4.78	3.39	2.71	2.30	2.03	1.84	1.71
200	17.90	9.55	6.78	5.41	4.59	4.06	3.68	3.41
300	26.85	14.32	10.17	8.11	6.89	6.09	5.52	5.11
400	35.80	19.09	13.55	10.81	9.18	8.11	7.36	6.81
500	44.75	23.86	16.94	13.51	11.48	10.14	9.20	8.51
600	53.70	28.64	20.33	16.21	13.77	12.17	11.04	10.22
700	62.65	33.41	23.72	18.91	16.07	14.20	12.88	11.92
800	71.60	38.18	27.10	21.62	18.36	16.22	14.72	13.62
900	80.55	42.95	30.49	24.32	20.66	18.25	16.56	15.32
1000	89.50	47.72	33.88	27.02	22.95	20.28	18.40	17.02
2000	178.99	95.44	67.75	54.03	45.90	40.55	36.80	34.04
3000	268.48	143.16	101.63	81.05	68.84	60.82	55.19	51.06
4000	357.98	190.88	135.50	108.06	91.79	81.10	73.59	68.08
5000	447.47	238.60	169.38	135.07	114.73	101.37	91.99	85.09
6000	536.96	286.31	203.25	162.09	137.68	121.64	110.38	102.11
7000	626.46	334.03	237.13	189.10	160.62	141.91	128.78	119.13
8000	715.95	381.75	271.00	216.12	183.57	162.19	147.18	136.15
9000	805.44	429.47	304.88	243.13	206.51	182.46	165.57	153.16
10000	894.94	477.19	338.75	270.14	229.46	202.73	183.97	170.18
11000	984.43	524.90	372.63	297.16	252.41	223.00	202.37	187.20
12000	1073.92	572.62	406.50	324.17	275.35	243.28	220.76	204.22
13000	1163.42	620.34	440.38	351.19	298.30	263.55	239.16	221.24
14000	1252.91	668.06	474.25	378.20	321.24	283.82	257.56	238.25
15000	1342.40	715.78	508.13	405.21	344.19	304.09	275.95	255.27
16000	1431.90	763.50	542.00	432.23	367.13	324.37	294.35	272.29
17000	1521.39	811.21	575.88	459.24	390.08	344.64	312.74	289.31
18000	1610.88	858.93	609.75	486.26	413.02	364.91	331.14	306.32
19000	1700.38	906.65	643.63	513.27	435.97	385.18	349.54	323.34
20000	1789.87	954.37	677.50	540.28	458.91	405.46	367.93	340.36
21000	1879.36	1002.09	711.38	567.30	481.86	425.73	386.33	357.38
22000	1968.86	1049.80	745.25	594.31	504.81	446.00	404.73	374.39
23000	2058.35	1097.52	779.13	621.33	527.75	466.27	423.12	391.41
24000	2147.84	1145.24	813.00	648.34	550.70	486.55	441.52	408.43
25000	2237.34	1192.96	846.88	675.35	573.64	506.82	459.92	425.45
26000	2326.83	1240.68	880.75	702.37	596.59	527.09	478.31	442.47
27000	2416.32	1288.40	914.63	729.38	619.53	547.36	496.71	459.48
28000	2505.82	1336.11	948.50	756.40	642.48	567.64	515.11	476.50
29000	2595.31	1383.83	982.38	783.41	665.42	587.91	533.50	493.52
30000	2684.80	1431.55	1016.25	810.42	688.37	608.18	551.90	510.54
31000	2774.30	1479.27	1050.13	837.44	711.32	628.45	570.30	527.55
32000	2863.79	1526.99	1084.00	864.45	734.26	648.73	588.69	544.57
33000	2953.28	1574.70	1117.88	891.47	757.21	669.00	607.09	561.59
34000	3042.78	1622.42	1151.75	918.48	780.15	689.27	625.48	578.61
35000	3132.27	1670.14	1185.63	945.49	803.10	709.54	643.88	595.62
40000	3579.74	1908.73	1355.00	1080.56	917.82	810.91	735.86	680.71
45000	4027.20	2147.32	1524.37	1215.63	1032.55	912.27	827.85	765.80
50000	4474.67	2385.91	1693.75	1350.70	1147.28	1013.63	919.83	850.89
55000	4922.14	2624.50	1863.12	1485.77	1262.01	1115.00	1011.81	935.98
60000	5369.60	2863.09	2032.50	1620.84	1376.73	1216.36	1103.79	1021.07
65000	5817.07	3101.68	2201.87	1755.91	1491.46	1317.72	1195.77	1106.16
70000	6264.54	3340.28	2371.25	1890.98	1606.19	1419.08	1287.76	1191.24
75000	6712.00	3578.87	2540.62	2026.05	1720.92	1520.45	1379.74	1276.33
80000	7159.47	3817.46	2709.99	2161.12	1835.64	1621.81	1471.72	1361.42
85000	7606.94	4056.05	2879.37	2296.19	1950.37	1723.17	1563.70	1446.51
90000	8054.40	4294.64	3048.74	2431.26	2065.10	1824.54	1655.69	1531.60
95000	8501.87	4533.23	3218.12	2566.33	2179.83	1925.90	1747.67	1616.69
100000	8949.34	4771.82	3387.49	2701.40	2294.55	2027.26	1839.65	1701.78
105000	9396.80	5010.41	3556.87	2836.47	2409.28	2128.62	1931.63	1786.86
110000	9844.27	5249.00	3726.24	2971.54	2524.01	2229.99	2023.62	1871.95
115000	10291.74	5487.59	3895.61	3106.61	2638.74	2331.35	2115.60	1957.04
120000	10739.20	5726.18	4064.99	3241.68	2753.46	2432.71	2207.58	2042.13
125000	11186.67	5964.77	4234.36	3376.75	2868.19	2534.08	2299.56	2127.22
130000	11634.14	6203.36	4403.74	3511.82	2982.92	2635.44	2391.54	2212.31
135000	12081.60	6441.96	4573.11	3646.89	3097.65	2736.80	2483.53	2297.40
140000	12529.07	6680.55	4742.49	3781.96	3212.37	2838.16	2575.51	2382.48
145000	12976.53	6919.14	4911.86	3917.03	3327.10	2939.53	2667.49	2467.57
150000	13424.00	7157.73	5081.23	4052.10	3441.83	3040.89	2759.47	2552.66
155000	13871.47	7396.32	5250.61	4187.17	3556.56	3142.25	2851.46	2637.75
160000	14318.93	7634.91	5419.98	4322.24	3671.28	3243.62	2943.44	2722.84

MONTHLY AMORTIZING PAYMENTS 13 3/8%

AMOUNT OF LOAN	9	10	15	20	25	30	35	40
	NUMBER OF YEARS IN TERM							
$ 50	.80	.76	.65	.60	.58	.57	.57	.57
100	1.60	1.52	1.30	1.20	1.16	1.14	1.13	1.13
200	3.20	3.04	2.59	2.40	2.32	2.28	2.26	2.25
300	4.80	4.55	3.88	3.60	3.47	3.41	3.38	3.37
400	6.39	6.07	5.17	4.80	4.63	4.55	4.51	4.49
500	7.99	7.58	6.46	6.00	5.79	5.68	5.63	5.61
600	9.59	9.10	7.75	7.20	6.94	6.82	6.76	6.73
700	11.18	10.61	9.04	8.39	8.10	7.95	7.88	7.85
800	12.78	12.13	10.33	9.59	9.25	9.09	9.01	8.97
900	14.38	13.64	11.62	10.79	10.41	10.23	10.13	10.09
1000	15.97	15.16	12.91	11.99	11.57	11.36	11.26	11.21
2000	31.94	30.31	25.81	23.97	23.13	22.72	22.51	22.41
3000	47.91	45.46	38.71	35.96	34.69	34.07	33.76	33.61
4000	63.88	60.62	51.61	47.94	46.25	45.43	45.02	44.81
5000	79.85	75.77	64.51	59.92	57.81	56.78	56.27	56.01
6000	95.82	90.92	77.41	71.91	69.37	68.14	67.52	67.21
7000	111.79	106.08	90.31	83.89	80.94	79.50	78.77	78.41
8000	127.76	121.23	103.21	95.88	92.50	90.85	90.03	89.61
9000	143.73	136.38	116.11	107.86	104.06	102.21	101.28	100.81
10000	159.70	151.54	129.01	119.84	115.62	113.56	112.53	112.01
11000	175.67	166.69	141.91	131.83	127.18	124.92	123.79	123.21
12000	191.64	181.84	154.81	143.81	138.74	136.28	135.04	134.41
13000	207.61	196.99	167.71	155.80	150.31	147.63	146.29	145.61
14000	223.58	212.15	180.61	167.78	161.87	158.99	157.54	156.81
15000	239.55	227.30	193.51	179.76	173.43	170.34	168.80	168.01
16000	255.52	242.45	206.41	191.75	184.99	181.70	180.05	179.21
17000	271.49	257.61	219.31	203.73	196.55	193.05	191.30	190.42
18000	287.46	272.76	232.21	215.72	208.11	204.41	202.56	201.62
19000	303.43	287.91	245.11	227.70	219.68	215.77	213.81	212.82
20000	319.40	303.07	258.01	239.68	231.24	227.12	225.06	224.02
21000	335.37	318.22	270.91	251.67	242.80	238.48	236.31	235.22
22000	351.34	333.37	283.81	263.65	254.36	249.83	247.57	246.42
23000	367.31	348.53	296.71	275.64	265.92	261.19	258.82	257.62
24000	383.28	363.68	309.61	287.62	277.48	272.55	270.07	268.82
25000	399.25	378.83	322.51	299.60	289.05	283.90	281.33	280.02
26000	415.22	393.98	335.41	311.59	300.61	295.26	292.58	291.22
27000	431.19	409.14	348.31	323.57	312.17	306.61	303.83	302.42
28000	447.16	424.29	361.21	335.55	323.73	317.97	315.08	313.62
29000	463.13	439.44	374.11	347.54	335.29	329.32	326.34	324.82
30000	479.10	454.60	387.01	359.52	346.85	340.68	337.59	336.02
31000	495.07	469.75	399.91	371.51	358.42	352.04	348.84	347.22
32000	511.04	484.90	412.81	383.49	369.98	363.39	360.10	358.42
33000	527.01	500.06	425.71	395.47	381.54	374.75	371.35	369.63
34000	542.98	515.21	438.61	407.46	393.10	386.10	382.60	380.83
35000	558.95	530.36	451.51	419.44	404.66	397.46	393.85	392.03
40000	638.80	606.13	516.01	479.36	462.47	454.24	450.12	448.03
45000	718.65	681.89	580.51	539.28	520.28	511.02	506.38	504.03
50000	798.50	757.66	645.01	599.20	578.09	567.80	562.65	560.04
55000	878.35	833.42	709.51	659.12	635.89	624.58	618.91	616.04
60000	958.20	909.19	774.01	719.04	693.70	681.36	675.18	672.04
65000	1038.05	984.95	838.52	778.96	751.51	738.14	731.44	728.04
70000	1117.90	1060.72	903.02	838.88	809.32	794.91	787.70	784.05
75000	1197.75	1136.49	967.52	898.80	867.13	851.69	843.97	840.05
80000	1277.60	1212.25	1032.02	958.72	924.94	908.47	900.23	896.05
85000	1357.44	1288.02	1096.52	1018.64	982.74	965.25	956.50	952.06
90000	1437.29	1363.78	1161.02	1078.56	1040.55	1022.03	1012.76	1008.06
95000	1517.14	1439.55	1225.52	1138.48	1098.36	1078.81	1069.03	1064.06
100000	1596.99	1515.31	1290.02	1198.40	1156.17	1135.59	1125.29	1120.07
105000	1676.84	1591.08	1354.52	1258.32	1213.98	1192.37	1181.55	1176.07
110000	1756.69	1666.84	1419.02	1318.24	1271.78	1249.15	1237.82	1232.07
115000	1836.54	1742.61	1483.52	1378.16	1329.59	1305.93	1294.08	1288.08
120000	1916.39	1818.37	1548.02	1438.08	1387.40	1362.71	1350.35	1344.08
125000	1996.24	1894.14	1612.53	1497.99	1445.21	1419.49	1406.61	1400.08
130000	2076.09	1969.90	1677.03	1557.91	1503.02	1476.27	1462.88	1456.08
135000	2155.94	2045.67	1741.53	1617.83	1560.82	1533.04	1519.14	1512.09
140000	2235.79	2121.43	1806.03	1677.75	1618.63	1589.82	1575.40	1568.09
145000	2315.64	2197.20	1870.53	1737.67	1676.44	1646.60	1631.67	1624.09
150000	2395.49	2272.97	1935.03	1797.59	1734.25	1703.38	1687.93	1680.10
155000	2475.34	2348.73	1999.53	1857.51	1792.06	1760.16	1744.20	1736.10
160000	2555.19	2424.50	2064.03	1917.43	1849.87	1816.94	1800.46	1792.10

13½%

MONTHLY AMORTIZING PAYMENTS

AMOUNT OF LOAN	NUMBER OF YEARS IN TERM							
	1	2	3	4	5	6	7	8
$ 50	4.48	2.39	1.70	1.36	1.16	1.02	.93	.86
100	8.96	4.78	3.40	2.71	2.31	2.04	1.85	1.71
200	17.92	9.56	6.79	5.42	4.61	4.07	3.70	3.42
300	26.87	14.34	10.19	8.13	6.91	6.11	5.54	5.13
400	35.83	19.12	13.58	10.84	9.21	8.14	7.39	6.84
500	44.78	23.89	16.97	13.54	11.51	10.17	9.24	8.55
600	53.74	28.67	20.37	16.25	13.81	12.21	11.08	10.26
700	62.69	33.45	23.76	18.96	16.11	14.24	12.93	11.97
800	71.65	38.23	27.15	21.67	18.41	16.28	14.78	13.68
900	80.60	43.00	30.55	24.37	20.71	18.31	16.62	15.38
1000	89.56	47.78	33.94	27.08	23.01	20.34	18.47	17.09
2000	179.11	95.56	67.88	54.16	46.02	40.68	36.93	34.18
3000	268.66	143.34	101.81	81.23	69.03	61.02	55.40	51.27
4000	358.21	191.11	135.75	108.31	92.04	81.36	73.86	68.36
5000	447.77	238.89	169.68	135.39	115.05	101.70	92.33	85.45
6000	537.32	286.67	203.62	162.46	138.06	122.04	110.79	102.53
7000	626.87	334.44	237.55	189.54	161.07	142.38	129.26	119.62
8000	716.42	382.22	271.49	216.62	184.08	162.72	147.72	136.71
9000	805.97	430.00	305.42	243.69	207.09	183.06	166.19	153.80
10000	895.53	477.78	339.36	270.77	230.10	203.39	184.65	170.89
11000	985.08	525.55	373.29	297.84	253.11	223.73	203.12	187.97
12000	1074.63	573.33	407.23	324.92	276.12	244.07	221.58	205.06
13000	1164.18	621.11	441.16	352.00	299.13	264.41	240.05	222.15
14000	1253.73	668.88	475.10	379.07	322.14	284.75	258.51	239.24
15000	1343.29	716.66	509.03	406.15	345.15	305.09	276.98	256.33
16000	1432.84	764.44	542.97	433.23	368.16	325.43	295.44	273.42
17000	1522.39	812.21	576.90	460.30	391.17	345.77	313.91	290.50
18000	1611.94	859.99	610.84	487.38	414.18	366.11	332.37	307.59
19000	1701.49	907.77	644.78	514.46	437.19	386.45	350.84	324.68
20000	1791.05	955.55	678.71	541.53	460.20	406.78	369.30	341.77
21000	1880.60	1003.32	712.65	568.61	483.21	427.12	387.77	358.86
22000	1970.15	1051.10	746.58	595.68	506.22	447.46	406.23	375.94
23000	2059.70	1098.88	780.52	622.76	529.23	467.80	424.70	393.03
24000	2149.25	1146.65	814.45	649.84	552.24	488.14	443.16	410.12
25000	2238.81	1194.43	848.39	676.91	575.25	508.48	461.63	427.21
26000	2328.36	1242.21	882.32	703.99	598.26	528.82	480.09	444.30
27000	2417.91	1289.98	916.26	731.07	621.27	549.16	498.56	461.39
28000	2507.46	1337.76	950.19	758.14	644.28	569.50	517.02	478.47
29000	2597.01	1385.54	984.13	785.22	667.29	589.83	535.49	495.56
30000	2686.57	1433.32	1018.06	812.29	690.30	610.17	553.95	512.65
31000	2776.12	1481.09	1052.00	839.37	713.31	630.51	572.42	529.74
32000	2865.67	1528.87	1085.93	866.45	736.32	650.85	590.88	546.83
33000	2955.22	1576.65	1119.87	893.52	759.33	671.19	609.35	563.91
34000	3044.77	1624.42	1153.80	920.60	782.34	691.53	627.81	581.00
35000	3134.33	1672.20	1187.74	947.68	805.35	711.87	646.28	598.09
40000	3582.09	1911.09	1357.42	1083.06	920.40	813.56	738.60	683.53
45000	4029.85	2149.97	1527.09	1218.44	1035.45	915.26	830.93	768.97
50000	4477.61	2388.86	1696.77	1353.82	1150.50	1016.95	923.25	854.41
55000	4925.37	2627.74	1866.45	1489.20	1265.55	1118.65	1015.57	939.85
60000	5373.13	2866.63	2036.12	1624.58	1380.60	1220.34	1107.90	1025.29
65000	5820.89	3105.51	2205.80	1759.97	1495.64	1322.04	1200.22	1110.74
70000	6268.65	3344.40	2375.48	1895.35	1610.69	1423.73	1292.55	1196.18
75000	6716.41	3583.28	2545.15	2030.73	1725.74	1525.43	1384.87	1281.62
80000	7164.17	3822.17	2714.83	2166.11	1840.79	1627.12	1477.20	1367.06
85000	7611.93	4061.05	2884.50	2301.49	1955.84	1728.82	1569.52	1452.50
90000	8059.69	4299.94	3054.18	2436.87	2070.89	1830.51	1661.85	1537.94
95000	8507.45	4538.82	3223.86	2572.26	2185.94	1932.21	1754.17	1623.38
100000	8955.21	4777.71	3393.53	2707.64	2300.99	2033.90	1846.49	1708.82
105000	9402.97	5016.59	3563.21	2843.02	2416.04	2135.60	1938.82	1794.26
110000	9850.73	5255.48	3732.89	2978.40	2531.09	2237.29	2031.14	1879.70
115000	10298.49	5494.36	3902.56	3113.78	2646.14	2338.99	2123.47	1965.14
120000	10746.25	5733.25	4072.24	3249.16	2761.19	2440.68	2215.79	2050.58
125000	11194.01	5972.13	4241.92	3384.55	2876.24	2542.38	2308.12	2136.02
130000	11641.77	6211.02	4411.59	3519.93	2991.28	2644.07	2400.44	2221.47
135000	12089.53	6449.90	4581.27	3655.31	3106.33	2745.76	2492.77	2306.91
140000	12537.29	6688.79	4750.95	3790.69	3221.38	2847.46	2585.09	2392.35
145000	12985.05	6927.67	4920.62	3926.07	3336.43	2949.15	2677.41	2477.79
150000	13432.81	7166.56	5090.30	4061.45	3451.48	3050.85	2769.74	2563.23
155000	13880.57	7405.44	5259.97	4196.84	3566.53	3152.54	2862.06	2648.67
160000	14328.33	7644.33	5429.65	4332.22	3681.58	3254.24	2954.39	2734.11

AMOUNT OF LOAN	NUMBER OF YEARS IN TERM							
	9	10	15	20	25	30	35	40
$ 50	.81	.77	.65	.61	.59	.58	.57	.57
100	1.61	1.53	1.30	1.21	1.17	1.15	1.14	1.14
200	3.21	3.05	2.60	2.42	2.34	2.30	2.28	2.27
300	4.82	4.57	3.90	3.63	3.50	3.44	3.41	3.40
400	6.42	6.10	5.20	4.83	4.67	4.59	4.55	4.53
500	8.03	7.62	6.50	6.04	5.83	5.73	5.68	5.66
600	9.63	9.14	7.79	7.25	7.00	6.88	6.82	6.79
700	11.23	10.66	9.09	8.46	8.16	8.02	7.95	7.92
800	12.84	12.19	10.39	9.66	9.33	9.17	9.09	9.05
900	14.44	13.71	11.69	10.87	10.50	10.31	10.22	10.18
1000	16.05	15.23	12.99	12.08	11.66	11.46	11.36	11.31
2000	32.09	30.46	25.97	24.15	23.32	22.91	22.71	22.61
3000	48.13	45.69	38.95	36.23	34.97	34.37	34.07	33.91
4000	64.17	60.91	51.94	48.30	46.63	45.82	45.42	45.22
5000	80.22	76.14	64.92	60.37	58.29	57.28	56.77	56.52
6000	96.26	91.37	77.90	72.45	69.94	68.73	68.13	67.82
7000	112.30	106.60	90.89	84.52	81.60	80.18	79.48	79.12
8000	128.34	121.82	103.87	96.59	93.26	91.64	90.83	90.43
9000	144.39	137.05	116.85	108.67	104.91	103.09	102.19	101.73
10000	160.43	152.28	129.84	120.74	116.57	114.55	113.54	113.03
11000	176.47	167.51	142.82	132.82	128.23	126.00	124.89	124.33
12000	192.51	182.73	155.80	144.89	139.88	137.45	136.25	135.64
13000	208.56	197.96	168.79	156.96	151.54	148.91	147.60	146.94
14000	224.60	213.19	181.77	169.04	163.20	160.36	158.95	158.24
15000	240.64	228.42	194.75	181.11	174.85	171.82	170.31	169.54
16000	256.68	243.64	207.74	193.18	186.51	183.27	181.66	180.85
17000	272.72	258.87	220.72	205.26	198.16	194.73	193.01	192.15
18000	288.77	274.10	233.70	217.33	209.82	206.18	204.37	203.45
19000	304.81	289.33	246.69	229.41	221.48	217.63	215.72	214.75
20000	320.85	304.55	259.67	241.48	233.13	229.09	227.07	226.06
21000	336.89	319.78	272.65	253.55	244.79	240.54	238.43	237.36
22000	352.94	335.01	285.64	265.63	256.45	252.00	249.78	248.66
23000	368.98	350.24	298.62	277.70	268.10	263.45	261.13	259.97
24000	385.02	365.46	311.60	289.77	279.76	274.90	272.49	271.27
25000	401.06	380.69	324.58	301.85	291.42	286.36	283.84	282.57
26000	417.11	395.92	337.57	313.92	303.07	297.81	295.19	293.87
27000	433.15	411.15	350.55	326.00	314.73	309.27	306.55	305.18
28000	449.19	426.37	363.53	338.07	326.39	320.72	317.90	316.48
29000	465.23	441.60	376.52	350.14	338.04	332.17	329.25	327.78
30000	481.27	456.83	389.50	362.22	349.70	343.63	340.61	339.08
31000	497.32	472.06	402.48	374.29	361.35	355.08	351.96	350.39
32000	513.36	487.28	415.47	386.36	373.01	366.54	363.31	361.69
33000	529.40	502.51	428.45	398.44	384.67	377.99	374.67	372.99
34000	545.44	517.74	441.43	410.51	396.32	389.45	386.02	384.29
35000	561.49	532.97	454.42	422.59	407.98	400.90	397.37	395.60
40000	641.70	609.10	519.33	482.95	466.26	458.17	454.14	452.11
45000	721.91	685.24	584.25	543.32	524.55	515.44	510.91	508.62
50000	802.12	761.38	649.16	603.69	582.83	572.71	567.68	565.14
55000	882.33	837.51	714.08	664.06	641.11	629.98	624.44	621.65
60000	962.54	913.65	779.00	724.43	699.39	687.25	681.21	678.16
65000	1042.76	989.79	843.91	784.80	757.67	744.52	737.98	734.67
70000	1122.97	1065.93	908.83	845.17	815.96	801.79	794.74	791.19
75000	1203.18	1142.06	973.74	905.54	874.24	859.06	851.51	847.70
80000	1283.39	1218.20	1038.66	965.90	932.52	916.33	908.28	904.21
85000	1363.60	1294.34	1103.58	1026.27	990.80	973.61	965.04	960.73
90000	1443.81	1370.47	1168.49	1086.64	1049.09	1030.88	1021.81	1017.24
95000	1524.02	1446.61	1233.41	1147.01	1107.37	1088.15	1078.58	1073.75
100000	1604.24	1522.75	1298.32	1207.38	1165.65	1145.42	1135.35	1130.27
105000	1684.45	1598.89	1363.24	1267.75	1223.93	1202.69	1192.11	1186.78
110000	1764.66	1675.02	1428.16	1328.12	1282.21	1259.96	1248.88	1243.29
115000	1844.87	1751.16	1493.07	1388.49	1340.50	1317.23	1305.65	1299.81
120000	1925.08	1827.30	1557.99	1448.85	1398.78	1374.50	1362.41	1356.32
125000	2005.29	1903.43	1622.90	1509.22	1457.06	1431.77	1419.18	1412.83
130000	2085.51	1979.57	1687.82	1569.59	1515.34	1489.04	1475.95	1469.34
135000	2165.72	2055.71	1752.74	1629.96	1573.63	1546.31	1532.71	1525.86
140000	2245.93	2131.85	1817.65	1690.33	1631.91	1603.58	1589.48	1582.37
145000	2326.14	2207.98	1882.57	1750.70	1690.19	1660.85	1646.25	1638.88
150000	2406.35	2284.12	1947.48	1811.07	1748.47	1718.12	1703.02	1695.40
155000	2486.56	2360.26	2012.40	1871.44	1806.75	1775.39	1759.78	1751.91
160000	2566.78	2436.39	2077.31	1931.80	1865.04	1832.66	1816.55	1808.42

13 5/8% MONTHLY AMORTIZING PAYMENTS

AMOUNT OF LOAN	NUMBER OF YEARS IN TERM							
	1	2	3	4	5	6	7	8
$ 50	4.49	2.40	1.70	1.36	1.16	1.03	.93	.86
100	8.97	4.79	3.40	2.72	2.31	2.05	1.86	1.72
200	17.93	9.57	6.80	5.43	4.62	4.09	3.71	3.44
300	26.89	14.36	10.20	8.15	6.93	6.13	5.57	5.15
400	35.85	19.14	13.60	10.86	9.23	8.17	7.42	6.87
500	44.81	23.92	17.00	13.57	11.54	10.21	9.27	8.58
600	53.77	28.71	20.40	16.29	13.85	12.25	11.13	10.30
700	62.73	33.49	23.80	19.00	16.16	14.29	12.98	12.02
800	71.69	38.27	27.20	21.72	18.46	16.33	14.83	13.73
900	80.65	43.06	30.60	24.43	20.77	18.37	16.69	15.45
1000	89.62	47.84	34.00	27.14	23.08	20.41	18.54	17.16
2000	179.23	95.68	68.00	54.28	46.15	40.82	37.07	34.32
3000	268.84	143.51	101.99	81.42	69.23	61.22	55.61	51.48
4000	358.45	191.35	135.99	108.56	92.30	81.63	74.14	68.64
5000	448.06	239.18	169.98	135.70	115.38	102.03	92.67	85.80
6000	537.67	287.02	203.98	162.84	138.45	122.44	111.21	102.96
7000	627.28	334.86	237.98	189.98	161.53	142.84	129.74	120.12
8000	716.89	382.69	271.97	217.11	184.60	163.25	148.27	137.28
9000	806.50	430.53	305.97	244.25	207.67	183.65	166.81	154.43
10000	896.11	478.36	339.96	271.39	230.75	204.06	185.34	171.59
11000	985.72	526.20	373.96	298.53	253.82	224.47	203.87	188.75
12000	1075.33	574.04	407.95	325.67	276.90	244.87	222.41	205.91
13000	1164.94	621.87	441.95	352.81	299.97	265.28	240.94	223.07
14000	1254.56	669.71	475.95	379.95	323.05	285.68	259.47	240.23
15000	1344.17	717.54	509.94	407.09	346.12	306.09	278.01	257.39
16000	1433.78	765.38	543.94	434.22	369.19	326.49	296.54	274.55
17000	1523.39	813.22	577.93	461.36	392.27	346.90	315.07	291.70
18000	1613.00	861.05	611.93	488.50	415.34	367.30	333.61	308.86
19000	1702.61	908.89	645.92	515.64	438.42	387.71	352.14	326.02
20000	1792.22	956.72	679.92	542.78	461.49	408.11	370.67	343.18
21000	1881.83	1004.56	713.92	569.92	484.57	428.52	389.21	360.34
22000	1971.44	1052.40	747.91	597.06	507.64	448.93	407.74	377.50
23000	2061.05	1100.23	781.91	624.20	530.71	469.33	426.27	394.66
24000	2150.66	1148.07	815.90	651.33	553.79	489.74	444.81	411.82
25000	2240.27	1195.90	849.90	678.47	576.86	510.14	463.34	428.97
26000	2329.88	1243.74	883.90	705.61	599.94	530.55	481.88	446.13
27000	2419.50	1291.57	917.89	732.75	623.01	550.95	500.41	463.29
28000	2509.11	1339.41	951.89	759.89	646.09	571.36	518.94	480.45
29000	2598.72	1387.25	985.88	787.03	669.16	591.76	537.48	497.61
30000	2688.33	1435.08	1019.88	814.17	692.23	612.17	556.01	514.77
31000	2777.94	1482.92	1053.87	841.31	715.31	632.57	574.54	531.93
32000	2867.55	1530.75	1087.87	868.44	738.38	652.98	593.08	549.09
33000	2957.16	1578.59	1121.87	895.58	761.46	673.39	611.61	566.24
34000	3046.77	1626.43	1155.86	922.72	784.53	693.79	630.14	583.40
35000	3136.38	1674.26	1189.86	949.86	807.61	714.20	648.68	600.56
40000	3584.44	1913.44	1359.84	1085.55	922.98	816.22	741.34	686.36
45000	4032.49	2152.62	1529.82	1221.25	1038.35	918.25	834.01	772.15
50000	4480.54	2391.80	1699.79	1356.94	1153.72	1020.28	926.68	857.94
55000	4928.60	2630.98	1869.77	1492.64	1269.09	1122.31	1019.35	943.74
60000	5376.65	2870.16	2039.75	1628.33	1384.46	1224.33	1112.01	1029.53
65000	5824.70	3109.34	2209.73	1764.02	1499.83	1326.36	1204.68	1115.32
70000	6272.76	3348.52	2379.71	1899.72	1615.21	1428.39	1297.35	1201.12
75000	6720.81	3587.70	2549.69	2035.41	1730.58	1530.42	1390.02	1286.91
80000	7168.87	3826.88	2719.67	2171.10	1845.95	1632.44	1482.68	1372.71
85000	7616.92	4066.06	2889.65	2306.80	1961.32	1734.47	1575.35	1458.50
90000	8064.97	4305.24	3059.63	2442.49	2076.69	1836.50	1668.02	1544.29
95000	8513.03	4544.42	3229.60	2578.19	2192.06	1938.53	1760.68	1630.09
100000	8961.08	4783.60	3399.58	2713.88	2307.43	2040.55	1853.35	1715.88
105000	9409.14	5022.78	3569.56	2849.57	2422.81	2142.58	1946.02	1801.68
110000	9857.19	5261.96	3739.54	2985.27	2538.18	2244.61	2038.69	1887.47
115000	10305.24	5501.14	3909.52	3120.96	2653.55	2346.63	2131.35	1973.26
120000	10753.30	5740.32	4079.50	3256.65	2768.92	2448.66	2224.02	2059.06
125000	11201.35	5979.49	4249.48	3392.35	2884.29	2550.69	2316.69	2144.85
130000	11649.40	6218.67	4419.46	3528.04	2999.66	2652.72	2409.36	2230.64
135000	12097.46	6457.85	4589.44	3663.73	3115.03	2754.74	2502.02	2316.44
140000	12545.51	6697.03	4759.41	3799.43	3230.41	2856.77	2594.69	2402.23
145000	12993.57	6936.21	4929.39	3935.12	3345.78	2958.80	2687.36	2488.03
150000	13441.62	7175.39	5099.37	4070.82	3461.15	3060.83	2780.03	2573.82
155000	13889.67	7414.57	5269.35	4206.51	3576.52	3162.85	2872.69	2659.61
160000	14337.73	7653.75	5439.33	4342.20	3691.89	3264.88	2965.36	2745.41

AMOUNT OF LOAN	NUMBER OF YEARS IN TERM							
	9	10	15	20	25	30	35	40
$ 50	.81	.77	.66	.61	.59	.58	.58	.58
100	1.62	1.54	1.31	1.22	1.18	1.16	1.15	1.15
200	3.23	3.07	2.62	2.44	2.36	2.32	2.30	2.29
300	4.84	4.60	3.92	3.65	3.53	3.47	3.44	3.43
400	6.45	6.13	5.23	4.87	4.71	4.63	4.59	4.57
500	8.06	7.66	6.54	6.09	5.88	5.78	5.73	5.71
600	9.67	9.19	7.84	7.30	7.06	6.94	6.88	6.85
700	11.29	10.72	9.15	8.52	8.23	8.09	8.02	7.99
800	12.90	12.25	10.46	9.74	9.41	9.25	9.17	9.13
900	14.51	13.78	11.76	10.95	10.58	10.40	10.31	10.27
1000	16.12	15.31	13.07	12.17	11.76	11.56	11.46	11.41
2000	32.23	30.61	26.14	24.33	23.51	23.11	22.91	22.81
3000	48.35	45.91	39.20	36.50	35.26	34.66	34.37	34.22
4000	64.46	61.21	52.27	48.66	47.01	46.22	45.82	45.62
5000	80.58	76.51	65.34	60.82	58.76	57.77	57.28	57.03
6000	96.69	91.82	78.40	72.99	70.51	69.32	68.73	68.43
7000	112.81	107.12	91.47	85.15	82.27	80.87	80.18	79.84
8000	128.92	122.42	104.54	97.32	94.02	92.43	91.64	91.24
9000	145.04	137.72	117.60	109.48	105.77	103.98	103.09	102.65
10000	161.15	153.02	130.67	121.64	117.52	115.53	114.55	114.05
11000	177.27	168.33	143.74	133.81	129.27	127.08	126.00	125.46
12000	193.38	183.63	156.80	145.97	141.02	138.64	137.45	136.86
13000	209.50	198.93	169.87	158.13	152.77	150.19	148.91	148.27
14000	225.61	214.23	182.93	170.30	164.53	161.74	160.36	159.67
15000	241.73	229.53	196.00	182.46	176.28	173.29	171.82	171.08
16000	257.84	244.84	209.07	194.63	188.03	184.85	183.27	182.48
17000	273.96	260.14	222.13	206.79	199.78	196.40	194.72	193.88
18000	290.07	275.44	235.20	218.95	211.53	207.95	206.18	205.29
19000	306.19	290.74	248.27	231.12	223.28	219.50	217.63	216.69
20000	322.30	306.04	261.33	243.28	235.03	231.06	229.09	228.10
21000	338.42	321.35	274.40	255.44	246.79	242.61	240.54	239.50
22000	354.53	336.65	287.47	267.61	258.54	254.16	251.99	250.91
23000	370.65	351.95	300.53	279.77	270.29	265.71	263.45	262.31
24000	386.76	367.25	313.60	291.94	282.04	277.27	274.90	273.72
25000	402.88	382.55	326.67	304.10	293.79	288.82	286.36	285.12
26000	418.99	397.86	339.73	316.26	305.54	300.37	297.81	296.53
27000	435.11	413.16	352.80	328.43	317.29	311.92	309.26	307.93
28000	451.22	428.46	365.86	340.59	329.05	323.48	320.72	319.34
29000	467.34	443.76	378.93	352.75	340.80	335.03	332.17	330.74
30000	483.45	459.06	392.00	364.92	352.55	346.58	343.63	342.15
31000	499.57	474.37	405.06	377.08	364.30	358.13	355.08	353.55
32000	515.68	489.67	418.13	389.25	376.05	369.69	366.54	364.96
33000	531.80	504.97	431.20	401.41	387.80	381.24	377.99	376.36
34000	547.91	520.27	444.26	413.57	399.55	392.79	389.44	387.76
35000	564.03	535.57	457.33	425.74	411.31	404.34	400.90	399.17
40000	644.60	612.08	522.66	486.56	470.06	462.11	458.17	456.19
45000	725.18	688.59	587.99	547.38	528.82	519.87	515.44	513.22
50000	805.75	765.10	653.33	608.19	587.58	577.63	572.71	570.24
55000	886.33	841.61	718.66	669.01	646.34	635.40	629.98	627.26
60000	966.90	918.12	783.99	729.83	705.09	693.16	687.25	684.29
65000	1047.47	994.63	849.32	790.65	763.85	750.92	744.52	741.31
70000	1128.05	1071.14	914.65	851.47	822.61	808.68	801.79	798.33
75000	1208.62	1147.65	979.99	912.29	881.36	866.45	859.06	855.36
80000	1289.20	1224.16	1045.32	973.11	940.12	924.21	916.33	912.38
85000	1369.77	1300.67	1110.65	1033.93	998.88	981.97	973.60	969.40
90000	1450.35	1377.18	1175.98	1094.75	1057.64	1039.73	1030.87	1026.43
95000	1530.92	1453.69	1241.32	1155.57	1116.39	1097.50	1088.14	1083.45
100000	1611.50	1530.20	1306.65	1216.38	1175.15	1155.26	1145.41	1140.47
105000	1692.07	1606.71	1371.98	1277.20	1233.91	1213.02	1202.68	1197.50
110000	1772.65	1683.22	1437.31	1338.02	1292.67	1270.79	1259.95	1254.52
115000	1853.22	1759.73	1502.64	1398.84	1351.42	1328.55	1317.22	1311.54
120000	1933.79	1836.24	1567.98	1459.66	1410.18	1386.31	1374.49	1368.57
125000	2014.37	1912.75	1633.31	1520.48	1468.94	1444.07	1431.76	1425.59
130000	2094.94	1989.26	1698.64	1581.30	1527.69	1501.84	1489.03	1482.62
135000	2175.52	2065.77	1763.97	1642.12	1586.45	1559.60	1546.30	1539.64
140000	2256.09	2142.28	1829.30	1702.94	1645.21	1617.36	1603.58	1596.66
145000	2336.67	2218.79	1894.64	1763.76	1703.97	1675.12	1660.85	1653.69
150000	2417.24	2295.30	1959.97	1824.57	1762.72	1732.89	1718.12	1710.71
155000	2497.82	2371.81	2025.30	1885.39	1821.48	1790.65	1775.39	1767.73
160000	2578.39	2448.32	2090.63	1946.21	1880.24	1848.41	1832.66	1824.76

MONTHLY AMORTIZING PAYMENTS

AMOUNT OF LOAN	NUMBER OF YEARS IN TERM							
	1	2	3	4	5	6	7	8
$ 50	4.49	2.40	1.71	1.37	1.16	1.03	.94	.87
100	8.97	4.79	3.41	2.73	2.32	2.05	1.87	1.73
200	17.94	9.58	6.82	5.45	4.63	4.10	3.73	3.45
300	26.91	14.37	10.22	8.17	6.95	6.15	5.59	5.17
400	35.87	19.16	13.63	10.89	9.26	8.19	7.45	6.90
500	44.84	23.95	17.03	13.61	11.57	10.24	9.31	8.62
600	53.81	28.74	20.44	16.33	13.89	12.29	11.17	10.34
700	62.77	33.53	23.84	19.05	16.20	14.34	13.03	12.07
800	71.74	38.32	27.25	21.77	18.52	16.38	14.89	13.79
900	80.71	43.11	30.66	24.49	20.83	18.43	16.75	15.51
1000	89.67	47.90	34.06	27.21	23.14	20.48	18.61	17.23
2000	179.34	95.79	68.12	54.41	46.28	40.95	37.21	34.46
3000	269.01	143.69	102.17	81.61	69.42	61.42	55.81	51.69
4000	358.68	191.58	136.23	108.81	92.56	81.89	74.41	68.92
5000	448.35	239.48	170.29	136.01	115.70	102.37	93.02	86.15
6000	538.02	287.37	204.34	163.21	138.84	122.84	111.62	103.38
7000	627.69	335.27	238.40	190.41	161.98	143.31	130.22	120.61
8000	717.36	383.16	272.46	217.61	185.12	163.78	148.82	137.84
9000	807.03	431.06	306.51	244.82	208.25	184.25	167.42	155.07
10000	896.70	478.95	340.57	272.02	231.39	204.73	186.03	172.30
11000	986.37	526.85	374.62	299.22	254.53	225.20	204.63	189.53
12000	1076.04	574.74	408.68	326.42	277.67	245.67	223.23	206.76
13000	1165.71	622.64	442.74	353.62	300.81	266.14	241.83	223.99
14000	1255.38	670.53	476.79	380.82	323.95	286.61	260.44	241.22
15000	1345.05	718.43	510.85	408.02	347.09	307.09	279.04	258.45
16000	1434.72	766.32	544.91	435.22	370.23	327.56	297.64	275.68
17000	1524.39	814.22	578.96	462.43	393.37	348.03	316.24	292.91
18000	1614.06	862.11	613.02	489.63	416.50	368.50	334.84	310.14
19000	1703.73	910.01	647.08	516.83	439.64	388.98	353.45	327.37
20000	1793.40	957.90	681.13	544.03	462.78	409.45	372.05	344.60
21000	1883.07	1005.80	715.19	571.23	485.92	429.92	390.65	361.83
22000	1972.73	1053.69	749.24	598.43	509.06	450.39	409.25	379.05
23000	2062.40	1101.59	783.30	625.63	532.20	470.86	427.86	396.28
24000	2152.07	1149.48	817.36	652.83	555.34	491.34	446.46	413.51
25000	2241.74	1197.38	851.41	680.04	578.48	511.81	465.06	430.74
26000	2331.41	1245.27	885.47	707.24	601.61	532.28	483.66	447.97
27000	2421.08	1293.17	919.53	734.44	624.75	552.75	502.26	465.20
28000	2510.75	1341.06	953.58	761.64	647.89	573.22	520.87	482.43
29000	2600.42	1388.96	987.64	788.84	671.03	593.70	539.47	499.66
30000	2690.09	1436.85	1021.69	816.04	694.17	614.17	558.07	516.89
31000	2779.76	1484.75	1055.75	843.24	717.31	634.64	576.67	534.12
32000	2869.43	1532.64	1089.81	870.44	740.45	655.11	595.27	551.35
33000	2959.10	1580.54	1123.86	897.65	763.59	675.58	613.88	568.58
34000	3048.77	1628.43	1157.92	924.85	786.73	696.06	632.48	585.81
35000	3138.44	1676.33	1191.98	952.05	809.86	716.53	651.08	603.04
40000	3586.79	1915.80	1362.26	1088.05	925.56	818.89	744.09	689.19
45000	4035.13	2155.27	1532.54	1224.06	1041.25	921.25	837.10	775.33
50000	4483.48	2394.75	1702.82	1360.07	1156.95	1023.61	930.11	861.48
55000	4931.83	2634.22	1873.10	1496.07	1272.64	1125.97	1023.12	947.63
60000	5380.18	2873.70	2043.38	1632.08	1388.34	1228.33	1116.14	1033.78
65000	5828.52	3113.17	2213.67	1768.09	1504.03	1330.69	1209.15	1119.92
70000	6276.87	3352.65	2383.95	1904.09	1619.72	1433.05	1302.16	1206.07
75000	6725.22	3592.12	2554.23	2040.10	1735.42	1535.41	1395.17	1292.22
80000	7173.57	3831.59	2724.51	2176.10	1851.11	1637.77	1488.18	1378.37
85000	7621.92	4071.07	2894.79	2312.11	1966.81	1740.13	1581.19	1464.51
90000	8070.26	4310.54	3065.07	2448.12	2082.50	1842.50	1674.20	1550.66
95000	8518.61	4550.02	3235.36	2584.12	2198.20	1944.86	1767.21	1636.81
100000	8966.96	4789.49	3405.64	2720.13	2313.89	2047.22	1860.22	1722.96
105000	9415.31	5028.97	3575.92	2856.13	2429.58	2149.58	1953.23	1809.11
110000	9863.65	5268.44	3746.20	2992.14	2545.28	2251.94	2046.24	1895.25
115000	10312.00	5507.91	3916.48	3128.15	2660.97	2354.30	2139.26	1981.40
120000	10760.35	5747.39	4086.76	3264.15	2776.67	2456.66	2232.27	2067.55
125000	11208.70	5986.86	4257.05	3400.16	2892.36	2559.02	2325.28	2153.70
130000	11657.04	6226.34	4427.33	3536.17	3008.05	2661.38	2418.29	2239.84
135000	12105.39	6465.81	4597.61	3672.17	3123.75	2763.74	2511.30	2325.99
140000	12553.74	6705.29	4767.89	3808.18	3239.44	2866.10	2604.31	2412.14
145000	13002.09	6944.76	4938.17	3944.18	3355.14	2968.46	2697.32	2498.29
150000	13450.43	7184.23	5108.45	4080.19	3470.83	3070.82	2790.33	2584.43
155000	13898.78	7423.71	5278.74	4216.20	3586.53	3173.18	2883.34	2670.58
160000	14347.13	7663.18	5449.02	4352.20	3702.22	3275.54	2976.35	2756.73

AMOUNT OF LOAN	NUMBER OF YEARS IN TERM							
	9	10	15	20	25	30	35	40
$ 50	.81	.77	.66	.62	.60	.59	.58	.58
100	1.62	1.54	1.32	1.23	1.19	1.17	1.16	1.16
200	3.24	3.08	2.63	2.46	2.37	2.34	2.32	2.31
300	4.86	4.62	3.95	3.68	3.56	3.50	3.47	3.46
400	6.48	6.16	5.26	4.91	4.74	4.67	4.63	4.61
500	8.10	7.69	6.58	6.13	5.93	5.83	5.78	5.76
600	9.72	9.23	7.89	7.36	7.11	7.00	6.94	6.91
700	11.34	10.77	9.21	8.58	8.30	8.16	8.09	8.06
800	12.96	12.31	10.52	9.81	9.48	9.33	9.25	9.21
900	14.57	13.84	11.84	11.03	10.67	10.49	10.40	10.36
1000	16.19	15.38	13.15	12.26	11.85	11.66	11.56	11.51
2000	32.38	30.76	26.30	24.51	23.70	23.31	23.11	23.02
3000	48.57	46.14	39.45	36.77	35.54	34.96	34.67	34.53
4000	64.76	61.51	52.60	49.02	47.39	46.61	46.22	46.03
5000	80.94	76.89	65.75	61.28	59.24	58.26	57.78	57.54
6000	97.13	92.27	78.90	73.53	71.08	69.91	69.33	69.05
7000	113.32	107.64	92.05	85.78	82.93	81.56	80.89	80.55
8000	129.51	123.02	105.20	98.04	94.78	93.21	92.44	92.06
9000	145.69	138.40	118.35	110.29	106.62	104.87	104.00	103.57
10000	161.88	153.77	131.50	122.55	118.47	116.52	115.55	115.07
11000	178.07	169.15	144.65	134.80	130.32	128.17	127.11	126.58
12000	194.26	184.53	157.80	147.05	142.16	139.82	138.66	138.09
13000	210.44	199.90	170.95	159.31	154.01	151.47	150.22	149.59
14000	226.63	215.28	184.10	171.56	165.86	163.12	161.77	161.10
15000	242.82	230.66	197.25	183.82	177.70	174.77	173.33	172.61
16000	259.01	246.03	210.40	196.07	189.55	186.42	184.88	184.11
17000	275.20	261.41	223.55	208.32	201.40	198.07	196.44	195.62
18000	291.38	276.79	236.70	220.58	213.24	209.73	207.99	207.13
19000	307.57	292.16	249.85	232.83	225.09	221.38	219.55	218.64
20000	323.76	307.54	263.00	245.09	236.94	233.03	231.10	230.14
21000	339.95	322.92	276.15	257.34	248.78	244.68	242.66	241.65
22000	356.13	338.29	289.30	269.59	260.63	256.33	254.21	253.16
23000	372.32	353.67	302.45	281.85	272.48	267.98	265.77	264.66
24000	388.51	369.05	315.60	294.10	284.32	279.63	277.32	276.17
25000	404.70	384.42	328.75	306.36	296.17	291.28	288.88	287.68
26000	420.88	399.80	341.90	318.61	308.02	302.93	300.43	299.18
27000	437.07	415.18	355.05	330.86	319.86	314.59	311.99	310.69
28000	453.26	430.55	368.20	343.12	331.71	326.24	323.54	322.20
29000	469.45	445.93	381.35	355.37	343.56	337.89	335.10	333.70
30000	485.64	461.31	394.50	367.63	355.40	349.54	346.65	345.21
31000	501.82	476.68	407.65	379.88	367.25	361.19	358.21	356.72
32000	518.01	492.06	420.80	392.13	379.10	372.84	369.76	368.22
33000	534.20	507.44	433.95	404.39	390.94	384.49	381.32	379.73
34000	550.39	522.81	447.10	416.64	402.79	396.14	392.87	391.24
35000	566.57	538.19	460.25	428.90	414.64	407.79	404.42	402.74
40000	647.51	615.07	526.00	490.17	473.87	466.05	462.20	460.28
45000	728.45	691.96	591.75	551.44	533.10	524.31	519.97	517.81
50000	809.39	768.84	657.50	612.71	592.34	582.56	577.75	575.35
55000	890.33	845.72	723.25	673.98	651.57	640.82	635.52	632.88
60000	971.27	922.61	789.00	735.25	710.80	699.07	693.30	690.42
65000	1052.20	999.49	854.75	796.52	770.04	757.33	751.07	747.95
70000	1133.14	1076.37	920.50	857.79	829.27	815.58	808.84	805.48
75000	1214.08	1153.26	986.25	919.06	888.50	873.84	866.62	863.02
80000	1295.02	1230.14	1051.99	980.33	947.74	932.10	924.39	920.55
85000	1375.96	1307.02	1117.74	1041.60	1006.97	990.35	982.17	978.09
90000	1456.90	1383.91	1183.49	1102.87	1066.20	1048.61	1039.94	1035.62
95000	1537.83	1460.79	1249.24	1164.14	1125.44	1106.86	1097.72	1093.16
100000	1618.77	1537.67	1314.99	1225.41	1184.67	1165.12	1155.49	1150.69
105000	1699.71	1614.56	1380.74	1286.68	1243.90	1223.37	1213.26	1208.22
110000	1780.65	1691.44	1446.49	1347.95	1303.14	1281.63	1271.04	1265.76
115000	1861.59	1768.32	1512.24	1409.22	1362.37	1339.88	1328.81	1323.29
120000	1942.53	1845.21	1577.99	1470.49	1421.60	1398.14	1386.59	1380.83
125000	2023.46	1922.09	1643.74	1531.76	1480.84	1456.40	1444.36	1438.36
130000	2104.40	1998.97	1709.49	1593.03	1540.07	1514.65	1502.14	1495.90
135000	2185.34	2075.86	1775.24	1654.30	1599.30	1572.91	1559.91	1553.43
140000	2266.28	2152.74	1840.99	1715.57	1658.54	1631.16	1617.68	1610.96
145000	2347.22	2229.62	1906.74	1776.84	1717.77	1689.42	1675.46	1668.50
150000	2428.16	2306.51	1972.49	1838.11	1777.00	1747.67	1733.23	1726.03
155000	2509.09	2383.39	2038.24	1899.38	1836.24	1805.93	1791.01	1783.57
160000	2590.03	2460.27	2103.98	1960.65	1895.47	1864.19	1848.78	1841.10

MONTHLY AMORTIZING PAYMENTS

AMOUNT OF LOAN	NUMBER OF YEARS IN TERM							
	1	2	3	4	5	6	7	8
$ 50	4.49	2.40	1.71	1.37	1.17	1.03	.94	.87
100	8.98	4.80	3.42	2.73	2.33	2.06	1.87	1.74
200	17.95	9.60	6.83	5.46	4.65	4.11	3.74	3.47
300	26.92	14.39	10.24	8.18	6.97	6.17	5.61	5.20
400	35.90	19.19	13.65	10.91	9.29	8.22	7.47	6.93
500	44.87	23.98	17.06	13.64	11.61	10.27	9.34	8.66
600	53.84	28.78	20.48	16.36	13.93	12.33	11.21	10.39
700	62.81	33.57	23.89	19.09	16.25	14.38	13.07	12.12
800	71.79	38.37	27.30	21.82	18.57	16.44	14.94	13.85
900	80.76	43.16	30.71	24.54	20.89	18.49	16.81	15.58
1000	89.73	47.96	34.12	27.27	23.21	20.54	18.68	17.31
2000	179.46	95.91	68.24	54.53	46.41	41.08	37.35	34.61
3000	269.19	143.87	102.36	81.80	69.62	61.62	56.02	51.91
4000	358.92	191.82	136.47	109.06	92.82	82.16	74.69	69.21
5000	448.65	239.77	170.59	136.32	116.02	102.70	93.36	86.51
6000	538.37	287.73	204.71	163.59	139.23	123.24	112.03	103.81
7000	628.10	335.68	238.82	190.85	162.43	143.78	130.70	121.11
8000	717.83	383.64	272.94	218.12	185.63	164.32	149.37	138.41
9000	807.56	431.59	307.06	245.38	208.84	184.85	168.04	155.71
10000	897.29	479.54	341.17	272.64	232.04	205.39	186.72	173.01
11000	987.02	527.50	375.29	299.91	255.24	225.93	205.39	190.31
12000	1076.74	575.45	409.41	327.17	278.45	246.47	224.06	207.61
13000	1166.47	623.41	443.53	354.43	301.65	267.01	242.73	224.91
14000	1256.20	671.36	477.64	381.70	324.85	287.55	261.40	242.21
15000	1345.93	719.31	511.76	408.96	348.06	308.09	280.07	259.51
16000	1435.66	767.27	545.88	436.23	371.26	328.63	298.74	276.81
17000	1525.39	815.22	579.99	463.49	394.46	349.17	317.41	294.11
18000	1615.11	863.17	614.11	490.75	417.67	369.70	336.08	311.41
19000	1704.84	911.13	648.23	518.02	440.87	390.24	354.75	328.71
20000	1794.57	959.08	682.34	545.28	464.07	410.78	373.43	346.01
21000	1884.30	1007.04	716.46	572.55	487.28	431.32	392.10	363.31
22000	1974.03	1054.99	750.58	599.81	510.48	451.86	410.77	380.61
23000	2063.76	1102.94	784.69	627.07	533.69	472.40	429.44	397.92
24000	2153.48	1150.90	818.81	654.34	556.89	492.94	448.11	415.22
25000	2243.21	1198.85	852.93	681.60	580.09	513.48	466.78	432.52
26000	2332.94	1246.81	887.05	708.86	603.30	534.02	485.45	449.82
27000	2422.67	1294.76	921.16	736.13	626.50	554.55	504.12	467.12
28000	2512.40	1342.71	955.28	763.39	649.70	575.09	522.79	484.42
29000	2602.13	1390.67	989.40	790.66	672.91	595.63	541.46	501.72
30000	2691.85	1438.62	1023.51	817.92	696.11	616.17	560.14	519.02
31000	2781.58	1486.57	1057.63	845.18	719.31	636.71	578.81	536.32
32000	2871.31	1534.53	1091.75	872.45	742.52	657.25	597.48	553.62
33000	2961.04	1582.48	1125.86	899.71	765.72	677.79	616.15	570.92
34000	3050.77	1630.44	1159.98	926.97	788.92	698.33	634.82	588.22
35000	3140.50	1678.39	1194.10	954.24	812.13	718.87	653.49	605.52
40000	3589.14	1918.16	1364.68	1090.56	928.14	821.56	746.85	692.02
45000	4037.78	2157.93	1535.27	1226.88	1044.16	924.25	840.20	778.52
50000	4486.42	2397.70	1705.85	1363.20	1160.18	1026.95	933.56	865.03
55000	4935.06	2637.47	1876.44	1499.51	1276.20	1129.64	1026.91	951.53
60000	5383.70	2877.24	2047.02	1635.83	1392.21	1232.34	1120.27	1038.03
65000	5832.35	3117.01	2217.61	1772.15	1508.23	1335.03	1213.62	1124.53
70000	6280.99	3356.77	2388.19	1908.47	1624.25	1437.73	1306.98	1211.04
75000	6729.63	3596.54	2558.78	2044.79	1740.27	1540.42	1400.33	1297.54
80000	7178.27	3836.31	2729.36	2181.11	1856.28	1643.11	1493.69	1384.04
85000	7626.91	4076.08	2899.95	2317.43	1972.30	1745.81	1587.04	1470.54
90000	8075.55	4315.85	3070.53	2453.75	2088.32	1848.50	1680.40	1557.04
95000	8524.19	4555.62	3241.12	2590.07	2204.34	1951.20	1773.75	1643.55
100000	8972.84	4795.39	3411.70	2726.39	2320.35	2053.89	1867.11	1730.05
105000	9421.48	5035.16	3582.28	2862.71	2436.37	2156.59	1960.46	1816.55
110000	9870.12	5274.93	3752.87	2999.02	2552.39	2259.28	2053.82	1903.05
115000	10318.76	5514.70	3923.45	3135.34	2668.41	2361.97	2147.17	1989.56
120000	10767.40	5754.47	4094.04	3271.66	2784.42	2464.67	2240.53	2076.06
125000	11216.04	5994.24	4264.62	3407.98	2900.44	2567.36	2333.88	2162.56
130000	11664.69	6234.01	4435.21	3544.30	3016.46	2670.06	2427.24	2249.06
135000	12113.33	6473.78	4605.79	3680.62	3132.48	2772.75	2520.59	2335.56
140000	12561.97	6713.54	4776.38	3816.94	3248.49	2875.45	2613.95	2422.07
145000	13010.61	6953.31	4946.96	3953.26	3364.51	2978.14	2707.30	2508.57
150000	13459.25	7193.08	5117.55	4089.58	3480.53	3080.83	2800.66	2595.07
155000	13907.89	7432.85	5288.13	4225.90	3596.55	3183.53	2894.01	2681.57
160000	14356.54	7672.62	5458.72	4362.22	3712.56	3286.22	2987.37	2768.08

AMOUNT OF LOAN	NUMBER OF YEARS IN TERM 9	10	15	20	25	30	35	40
$ 50	.82	.78	.67	.62	.60	.59	.59	.59
100	1.63	1.55	1.33	1.24	1.20	1.18	1.17	1.17
200	3.26	3.10	2.65	2.47	2.39	2.35	2.34	2.33
300	4.88	4.64	3.98	3.71	3.59	3.53	3.50	3.49
400	6.51	6.19	5.30	4.94	4.78	4.70	4.67	4.65
500	8.14	7.73	6.62	6.18	5.98	5.88	5.83	5.81
600	9.76	9.28	7.95	7.41	7.17	7.05	7.00	6.97
700	11.39	10.82	9.27	8.65	8.36	8.23	8.16	8.13
800	13.01	12.37	10.59	9.88	9.56	9.40	9.33	9.29
900	14.64	13.91	11.92	11.12	10.75	10.58	10.50	10.45
1000	16.27	15.46	13.24	12.35	11.95	11.75	11.66	11.61
2000	32.53	30.91	26.47	24.69	23.89	23.50	23.32	23.22
3000	48.79	46.36	39.71	37.04	35.83	35.25	34.97	34.83
4000	65.05	61.81	52.94	49.38	47.77	47.00	46.63	46.44
5000	81.31	77.26	66.17	61.73	59.72	58.75	58.28	58.05
6000	97.57	92.71	79.41	74.07	71.66	70.50	69.94	69.66
7000	113.83	108.17	92.64	86.42	83.60	82.25	81.60	81.27
8000	130.09	123.62	105.87	98.76	95.54	94.00	93.25	92.88
9000	146.35	139.07	119.11	111.11	107.48	105.75	104.91	104.49
10000	162.61	154.52	132.34	123.45	119.43	117.50	116.56	116.10
11000	178.87	169.97	145.57	135.79	131.37	129.25	128.22	127.70
12000	195.13	185.42	158.81	148.14	143.31	141.00	139.87	139.31
13000	211.39	200.88	172.04	160.48	155.25	152.75	151.53	150.92
14000	227.65	216.33	185.27	172.83	167.19	164.50	163.19	162.53
15000	243.91	231.78	198.51	185.17	179.14	176.25	174.84	174.14
16000	260.17	247.23	211.74	197.52	191.08	188.00	186.50	185.75
17000	276.44	262.68	224.98	209.86	203.02	199.75	198.15	197.36
18000	292.70	278.13	238.21	222.21	214.96	211.50	209.81	208.97
19000	308.96	293.58	251.44	234.55	226.90	223.25	221.46	220.58
20000	325.22	309.04	264.68	246.90	238.85	235.00	233.12	232.19
21000	341.48	324.49	277.91	259.24	250.79	246.75	244.78	243.80
22000	357.74	339.94	291.14	271.58	262.73	258.50	256.43	255.40
23000	374.00	355.39	304.38	283.93	274.67	270.25	268.09	267.01
24000	390.26	370.84	317.61	296.27	286.61	282.00	279.74	278.62
25000	406.52	386.29	330.84	308.62	298.56	293.75	291.40	290.23
26000	422.78	401.75	344.08	320.96	310.50	305.50	303.05	301.84
27000	439.04	417.20	357.31	333.31	322.44	317.25	314.71	313.45
28000	455.30	432.65	370.54	345.65	334.38	329.00	326.37	325.06
29000	471.56	448.10	383.78	358.00	346.32	340.75	338.02	336.67
30000	487.82	463.55	397.01	370.34	358.27	352.50	349.68	348.28
31000	504.08	479.00	410.24	382.69	370.21	364.25	361.33	359.89
32000	520.34	494.46	423.48	395.03	382.15	376.00	372.99	371.50
33000	536.61	509.91	436.71	407.37	394.09	387.75	384.64	383.10
34000	552.87	525.36	449.95	419.72	406.03	399.50	396.30	394.71
35000	569.13	540.81	463.18	432.06	417.98	411.25	407.96	406.32
40000	650.43	618.07	529.35	493.79	477.69	470.00	466.23	464.37
45000	731.73	695.33	595.51	555.51	537.40	528.75	524.51	522.41
50000	813.04	772.58	661.68	617.23	597.11	587.50	582.79	580.46
55000	894.34	849.84	727.85	678.95	656.82	646.25	641.07	638.50
60000	975.64	927.10	794.02	740.68	716.53	705.00	699.35	696.55
65000	1056.94	1004.36	860.18	802.40	776.24	763.75	757.63	754.60
70000	1138.25	1081.62	926.35	864.12	835.95	822.49	815.91	812.64
75000	1219.55	1158.87	992.52	925.84	895.66	881.24	874.19	870.69
80000	1300.85	1236.13	1058.69	987.57	955.37	939.99	932.46	928.73
85000	1382.16	1313.39	1124.86	1049.29	1015.08	998.74	990.74	986.78
90000	1463.46	1390.65	1191.02	1111.01	1074.79	1057.49	1049.02	1044.82
95000	1544.76	1467.90	1257.19	1172.73	1134.50	1116.24	1107.30	1102.87
100000	1626.07	1545.16	1323.36	1234.46	1194.21	1174.99	1165.58	1160.91
105000	1707.37	1622.42	1389.53	1296.18	1253.92	1233.74	1223.86	1218.96
110000	1788.67	1699.68	1455.69	1357.90	1313.63	1292.49	1282.14	1277.00
115000	1869.97	1776.94	1521.86	1419.63	1373.34	1351.24	1340.41	1335.05
120000	1951.28	1854.19	1588.03	1481.35	1433.05	1409.99	1398.69	1393.10
125000	2032.58	1931.45	1654.20	1543.07	1492.76	1468.74	1456.97	1451.14
130000	2113.88	2008.71	1720.36	1604.79	1552.47	1527.49	1515.25	1509.19
135000	2195.19	2085.97	1786.53	1666.52	1612.18	1586.23	1573.53	1567.23
140000	2276.49	2163.23	1852.70	1728.24	1671.89	1644.98	1631.81	1625.28
145000	2357.79	2240.48	1918.87	1789.96	1731.60	1703.73	1690.09	1683.32
150000	2439.10	2317.74	1985.04	1851.68	1791.31	1762.48	1748.37	1741.37
155000	2520.40	2395.00	2051.20	1913.41	1851.02	1821.23	1806.64	1799.41
160000	2601.70	2472.26	2117.37	1975.13	1910.73	1879.98	1864.92	1857.46

MONTHLY AMORTIZING PAYMENTS

AMOUNT OF LOAN	NUMBER OF YEARS IN TERM 1	2	3	4	5	6	7	8
$ 50	4.49	2.41	1.71	1.37	1.17	1.04	.94	.87
100	8.98	4.81	3.42	2.74	2.33	2.07	1.88	1.74
200	17.96	9.61	6.84	5.47	4.66	4.13	3.75	3.48
300	26.94	14.41	10.26	8.20	6.99	6.19	5.63	5.22
400	35.92	19.21	13.68	10.94	9.31	8.25	7.50	6.95
500	44.90	24.01	17.09	13.67	11.64	10.31	9.38	8.69
600	53.88	28.81	20.51	16.40	13.97	12.37	11.25	10.43
700	62.86	33.61	23.93	19.13	16.29	14.43	13.12	12.17
800	71.83	38.42	27.35	21.87	18.62	16.49	15.00	13.90
900	80.81	43.22	30.76	24.60	20.95	18.55	16.87	15.64
1000	89.79	48.02	34.18	27.33	23.27	20.61	18.75	17.38
2000	179.58	96.03	68.36	54.66	46.54	41.22	37.49	34.75
3000	269.37	144.04	102.54	81.98	69.81	61.82	56.23	52.12
4000	359.15	192.06	136.72	109.31	93.08	82.43	74.97	69.49
5000	448.94	240.07	170.89	136.64	116.35	103.03	93.71	86.86
6000	538.73	288.08	205.07	163.96	139.61	123.64	112.45	104.23
7000	628.51	336.10	239.25	191.29	162.88	144.25	131.19	121.61
8000	718.30	384.11	273.43	218.62	186.15	164.85	149.93	138.98
9000	808.09	432.12	307.60	245.94	209.42	185.46	168.67	156.35
10000	897.88	480.13	341.78	273.27	232.69	206.06	187.41	173.72
11000	987.66	528.15	375.96	300.60	255.96	226.67	206.15	191.09
12000	1077.45	576.16	410.14	327.92	279.22	247.27	224.89	208.46
13000	1167.24	624.17	444.31	355.25	302.49	267.88	243.63	225.83
14000	1257.02	672.19	478.49	382.58	325.76	288.49	262.37	243.21
15000	1346.81	720.20	512.67	409.90	349.03	309.09	281.11	260.58
16000	1436.60	768.21	546.85	437.23	372.30	329.70	299.85	277.95
17000	1526.39	816.22	581.02	464.56	395.57	350.30	318.59	295.32
18000	1616.17	864.24	615.20	491.88	418.83	370.91	337.33	312.69
19000	1705.96	912.25	649.38	519.21	442.10	391.51	356.07	330.06
20000	1795.75	960.26	683.56	546.53	465.37	412.12	374.81	347.44
21000	1885.53	1008.28	717.74	573.86	488.64	432.73	393.55	364.81
22000	1975.32	1056.29	751.91	601.19	511.91	453.33	412.29	382.18
23000	2065.11	1104.30	786.09	628.51	535.17	473.94	431.03	399.55
24000	2154.90	1152.31	820.27	655.84	558.44	494.54	449.77	416.92
25000	2244.68	1200.33	854.45	683.17	581.71	515.15	468.51	434.29
26000	2334.47	1248.34	888.62	710.49	604.98	535.75	487.25	451.66
27000	2424.26	1296.35	922.80	737.82	628.25	556.36	505.99	469.04
28000	2514.04	1344.37	956.98	765.15	651.52	576.97	524.73	486.41
29000	2603.83	1392.38	991.16	792.47	674.78	597.57	543.47	503.78
30000	2693.62	1440.39	1025.33	819.80	698.05	618.18	562.21	521.15
31000	2783.41	1488.40	1059.51	847.13	721.32	638.78	580.95	538.52
32000	2873.19	1536.42	1093.69	874.45	744.59	659.39	599.69	555.89
33000	2962.98	1584.43	1127.87	901.78	767.86	679.99	618.43	573.26
34000	3052.77	1632.44	1162.04	929.11	791.13	700.60	637.17	590.64
35000	3142.55	1680.46	1196.22	956.43	814.39	721.21	655.91	608.01
40000	3591.49	1920.52	1367.11	1093.06	930.74	824.23	749.61	694.87
45000	4040.43	2160.58	1538.00	1229.70	1047.08	927.26	843.31	781.72
50000	4489.36	2400.65	1708.89	1366.33	1163.42	1030.29	937.01	868.58
55000	4938.30	2640.71	1879.77	1502.96	1279.76	1133.32	1030.71	955.44
60000	5387.23	2880.78	2050.66	1639.59	1396.10	1236.35	1124.41	1042.30
65000	5836.17	3120.84	2221.55	1776.23	1512.44	1339.38	1218.11	1129.15
70000	6285.10	3360.91	2392.44	1912.86	1628.78	1442.41	1311.81	1216.01
75000	6734.04	3600.97	2563.33	2049.49	1745.12	1545.44	1405.51	1302.87
80000	7182.97	3841.04	2734.22	2186.12	1861.47	1648.46	1499.21	1389.73
85000	7631.91	4081.10	2905.10	2322.76	1977.81	1751.49	1592.91	1476.58
90000	8080.85	4321.16	3075.99	2459.39	2094.15	1854.52	1686.61	1563.44
95000	8529.78	4561.23	3246.88	2596.02	2210.49	1957.55	1780.31	1650.30
100000	8978.72	4801.29	3417.77	2732.65	2326.83	2060.58	1874.01	1737.16
105000	9427.65	5041.36	3588.66	2869.29	2443.17	2163.61	1967.71	1824.01
110000	9876.59	5281.42	3759.54	3005.92	2559.51	2266.64	2061.41	1910.87
115000	10325.52	5521.49	3930.43	3142.55	2675.85	2369.67	2155.11	1997.73
120000	10774.46	5761.55	4101.32	3279.18	2792.20	2472.69	2248.81	2084.59
125000	11223.39	6001.62	4272.21	3415.81	2908.54	2575.72	2342.51	2171.44
130000	11672.33	6241.68	4443.10	3552.45	3024.88	2678.75	2436.21	2258.30
135000	12121.27	6481.74	4613.99	3689.08	3141.22	2781.78	2529.91	2345.16
140000	12570.20	6721.81	4784.87	3825.71	3257.56	2884.81	2623.61	2432.02
145000	13019.14	6961.87	4955.76	3962.34	3373.90	2987.84	2717.31	2518.87
150000	13468.07	7201.94	5126.65	4098.98	3490.24	3090.87	2811.01	2605.73
155000	13917.01	7442.00	5297.54	4235.61	3606.58	3193.89	2904.71	2692.59
160000	14365.94	7682.07	5468.43	4372.24	3722.93	3296.92	2998.41	2779.45

AMOUNT OF LOAN	NUMBER OF YEARS IN TERM							
	9	10	15	20	25	30	35	40
$ 50	.82	.78	.67	.63	.61	.60	.59	.59
100	1.64	1.56	1.34	1.25	1.21	1.19	1.18	1.18
200	3.27	3.11	2.67	2.49	2.41	2.37	2.36	2.35
300	4.91	4.66	4.00	3.74	3.62	3.56	3.53	3.52
400	6.54	6.22	5.33	4.98	4.82	4.74	4.71	4.69
500	8.17	7.77	6.66	6.22	6.02	5.93	5.88	5.86
600	9.81	9.32	8.00	7.47	7.23	7.11	7.06	7.03
700	11.44	10.87	9.33	8.71	8.43	8.30	8.23	8.20
800	13.07	12.43	10.66	9.95	9.64	9.48	9.41	9.37
900	14.71	13.98	11.99	11.20	10.84	10.67	10.59	10.55
1000	16.34	15.53	13.32	12.44	12.04	11.85	11.76	11.72
2000	32.67	31.06	26.64	24.88	24.08	23.70	23.52	23.43
3000	49.01	46.58	39.96	37.31	36.12	35.55	35.28	35.14
4000	65.34	62.11	53.27	49.75	48.16	47.40	47.03	46.85
5000	81.67	77.64	66.59	62.18	60.19	59.25	58.79	58.56
6000	98.01	93.16	79.91	74.62	72.23	71.10	70.55	70.27
7000	114.34	108.69	93.23	87.05	84.27	82.95	82.30	81.98
8000	130.67	124.22	106.54	99.49	96.31	94.79	94.06	93.70
9000	147.01	139.74	119.86	111.92	108.34	106.64	105.82	105.41
10000	163.34	155.27	133.18	124.36	120.38	118.49	117.57	117.12
11000	179.68	170.80	146.50	136.79	132.42	130.34	129.33	128.83
12000	196.01	186.32	159.81	149.23	144.46	142.19	141.09	140.54
13000	212.34	201.85	173.13	161.66	156.49	154.04	152.84	152.25
14000	228.68	217.38	186.45	174.10	168.53	165.89	164.60	163.96
15000	245.01	232.90	199.77	186.53	180.57	177.74	176.36	175.68
16000	261.34	248.43	213.08	198.97	192.61	189.58	188.11	187.39
17000	277.68	263.96	226.40	211.40	204.64	201.43	199.87	199.10
18000	294.01	279.48	239.72	223.84	216.68	213.28	211.63	210.81
19000	310.35	295.01	253.04	236.27	228.72	225.13	223.38	222.52
20000	326.68	310.54	266.35	248.71	240.76	236.98	235.14	234.23
21000	343.01	326.06	279.67	261.14	252.79	248.83	246.90	245.94
22000	359.35	341.59	292.99	273.58	264.83	260.68	258.65	257.66
23000	375.68	357.12	306.31	286.01	276.87	272.53	270.41	269.37
24000	392.01	372.64	319.62	298.45	288.91	284.37	282.17	281.08
25000	408.35	388.17	332.94	310.89	300.95	296.22	293.92	292.79
26000	424.68	403.70	346.26	323.32	312.98	308.07	305.68	304.50
27000	441.01	419.22	359.58	335.76	325.02	319.92	317.44	316.21
28000	457.35	434.75	372.89	348.19	337.06	331.77	329.19	327.92
29000	473.68	450.28	386.21	360.63	349.10	343.62	340.95	339.64
30000	490.02	465.80	399.53	373.06	361.13	355.47	352.71	351.35
31000	506.35	481.33	412.84	385.50	373.17	367.32	364.46	363.06
32000	522.68	496.86	426.16	397.93	385.21	379.16	376.22	374.77
33000	539.02	512.38	439.48	410.37	397.25	391.01	387.98	386.48
34000	555.35	527.91	452.80	422.80	409.28	402.86	399.73	398.19
35000	571.68	543.44	466.11	435.24	421.32	414.71	411.49	409.90
40000	653.35	621.07	532.70	497.41	481.51	473.95	470.27	468.46
45000	735.02	698.70	599.29	559.59	541.70	533.20	529.06	527.02
50000	816.69	776.34	665.88	621.77	601.89	592.44	587.84	585.58
55000	898.36	853.97	732.46	683.94	662.07	651.68	646.63	644.13
60000	980.03	931.60	799.05	746.12	722.26	710.93	705.41	702.69
65000	1061.70	1009.24	865.64	808.29	782.45	770.17	764.19	761.25
70000	1143.36	1086.87	932.22	870.47	842.64	829.42	822.98	819.80
75000	1225.03	1164.50	998.81	932.65	902.83	888.66	881.76	878.36
80000	1306.70	1242.14	1065.40	994.82	963.01	947.90	940.54	936.92
85000	1388.37	1319.77	1131.99	1057.00	1023.20	1007.15	999.33	995.47
90000	1470.04	1397.40	1198.57	1119.17	1083.39	1066.39	1058.11	1054.03
95000	1551.71	1475.04	1265.16	1181.35	1143.58	1125.63	1116.89	1112.59
100000	1633.38	1552.67	1331.75	1243.53	1203.77	1184.88	1175.68	1171.15
105000	1715.04	1630.30	1398.33	1305.70	1263.95	1244.12	1234.46	1229.70
110000	1796.71	1707.94	1464.92	1367.88	1324.14	1303.36	1293.25	1288.26
115000	1878.38	1785.57	1531.51	1430.05	1384.33	1362.61	1352.03	1346.82
120000	1960.05	1863.20	1598.09	1492.23	1444.52	1421.85	1410.81	1405.37
125000	2041.72	1940.84	1664.68	1554.41	1504.71	1481.09	1469.60	1463.93
130000	2123.39	2018.47	1731.27	1616.58	1564.89	1540.34	1528.38	1522.49
135000	2205.05	2096.10	1797.86	1678.76	1625.08	1599.58	1587.16	1581.04
140000	2286.72	2173.74	1864.44	1740.93	1685.27	1658.83	1645.95	1639.60
145000	2368.39	2251.37	1931.03	1803.11	1745.46	1718.07	1704.73	1698.16
150000	2450.06	2329.00	1997.62	1865.29	1805.65	1777.31	1763.51	1756.72
155000	2531.73	2406.63	2064.20	1927.46	1865.83	1836.56	1822.30	1815.27
160000	2613.40	2484.27	2130.79	1989.64	1926.02	1895.80	1881.08	1873.83

MONTHLY AMORTIZING PAYMENTS

AMOUNT OF LOAN	NUMBER OF YEARS IN TERM							
	1	2	3	4	5	6	7	8
$ 50	4.50	2.41	1.72	1.37	1.17	1.04	.95	.88
100	8.99	4.81	3.43	2.74	2.34	2.07	1.89	1.75
200	17.97	9.62	6.85	5.48	4.67	4.14	3.77	3.49
300	26.96	14.43	10.28	8.22	7.00	6.21	5.65	5.24
400	35.94	19.23	13.70	10.96	9.34	8.27	7.53	6.98
500	44.93	24.04	17.12	13.70	11.67	10.34	9.41	8.73
600	53.91	28.85	20.55	16.44	14.00	12.41	11.29	10.47
700	62.90	33.66	23.97	19.18	16.34	14.48	13.17	12.21
800	71.88	38.46	27.40	21.92	18.67	16.54	15.05	13.96
900	80.87	43.27	30.82	24.66	21.00	18.61	16.93	15.70
1000	89.85	48.08	34.24	27.39	23.34	20.68	18.81	17.45
2000	179.70	96.15	68.48	54.78	46.67	41.35	37.62	34.89
3000	269.54	144.22	102.72	82.17	70.00	62.02	56.43	52.33
4000	359.39	192.29	136.96	109.56	93.34	82.70	75.24	69.78
5000	449.23	240.36	171.20	136.95	116.67	103.37	94.05	87.22
6000	539.08	288.44	205.44	164.34	140.00	124.04	112.86	104.66
7000	628.93	336.51	239.67	191.73	163.34	144.71	131.67	122.10
8000	718.77	384.58	273.91	219.12	186.67	165.39	150.48	139.55
9000	808.62	432.65	308.15	246.51	210.00	186.06	169.29	156.99
10000	898.46	480.72	342.39	273.90	233.34	206.73	188.10	174.43
11000	988.31	528.80	376.63	301.29	256.67	227.41	206.91	191.87
12000	1078.16	576.87	410.87	328.68	280.00	248.08	225.71	209.32
13000	1168.00	624.94	445.10	356.06	303.34	268.75	244.52	226.76
14000	1257.85	673.01	479.34	383.45	326.67	289.42	263.33	244.20
15000	1347.69	721.08	513.58	410.84	350.00	310.10	282.14	261.65
16000	1437.54	769.16	547.82	438.23	373.33	330.77	300.95	279.09
17000	1527.39	817.23	582.06	465.62	396.67	351.44	319.76	296.53
18000	1617.23	865.30	616.30	493.01	420.00	372.11	338.57	313.97
19000	1707.08	913.37	650.53	520.40	443.33	392.79	357.38	331.42
20000	1796.92	961.44	684.77	547.79	466.67	413.46	376.19	348.86
21000	1886.77	1009.52	719.01	575.18	490.00	434.13	395.00	366.30
22000	1976.62	1057.59	753.25	602.57	513.33	454.81	413.81	383.74
23000	2066.46	1105.66	787.49	629.96	536.67	475.48	432.62	401.19
24000	2156.31	1153.73	821.73	657.35	560.00	496.15	451.42	418.63
25000	2246.15	1201.80	855.96	684.74	583.33	516.82	470.23	436.07
26000	2336.00	1249.88	890.20	712.12	606.67	537.50	489.04	453.52
27000	2425.85	1297.95	924.44	739.51	630.00	558.17	507.85	470.96
28000	2515.69	1346.02	958.68	766.90	653.33	578.84	526.66	488.40
29000	2605.54	1394.09	992.92	794.29	676.67	599.51	545.47	505.84
30000	2695.38	1442.16	1027.16	821.68	700.00	620.19	564.28	523.29
31000	2785.23	1490.24	1061.39	849.07	723.33	640.86	583.09	540.73
32000	2875.08	1538.31	1095.63	876.46	746.66	661.53	601.90	558.17
33000	2964.92	1586.38	1129.87	903.85	770.00	682.21	620.71	575.61
34000	3054.77	1634.45	1164.11	931.24	793.33	702.88	639.52	593.06
35000	3144.61	1682.52	1198.35	958.63	816.66	723.55	658.32	610.50
40000	3593.84	1922.88	1369.54	1095.57	933.33	826.91	752.37	697.71
45000	4043.07	2163.24	1540.73	1232.52	1049.99	930.28	846.42	784.93
50000	4492.30	2403.60	1711.92	1369.47	1166.66	1033.64	940.46	872.14
55000	4941.53	2643.96	1883.12	1506.41	1283.33	1137.01	1034.51	959.35
60000	5390.76	2884.32	2054.31	1643.36	1399.99	1240.37	1128.55	1046.57
65000	5839.99	3124.68	2225.50	1780.30	1516.66	1343.73	1222.60	1133.78
70000	6289.22	3365.04	2396.69	1917.25	1633.32	1447.10	1316.64	1221.00
75000	6738.45	3605.40	2567.88	2054.20	1749.99	1550.46	1410.69	1308.21
80000	7187.68	3845.76	2739.07	2191.14	1866.65	1653.82	1504.74	1395.42
85000	7636.91	4086.12	2910.27	2328.09	1983.32	1757.19	1598.78	1482.64
90000	8086.14	4326.48	3081.46	2465.03	2099.98	1860.55	1692.83	1569.85
95000	8535.37	4566.84	3252.65	2601.98	2216.65	1963.91	1786.87	1657.06
100000	8984.60	4807.20	3423.84	2738.93	2333.32	2067.28	1880.92	1744.28
105000	9433.83	5047.56	3595.03	2875.87	2449.98	2170.64	1974.96	1831.49
110000	9883.06	5287.92	3766.23	3012.82	2566.65	2274.01	2069.01	1918.70
115000	10332.29	5528.28	3937.42	3149.77	2683.31	2377.37	2163.06	2005.92
120000	10781.52	5768.64	4108.61	3286.71	2799.98	2480.73	2257.10	2093.13
125000	11230.75	6009.00	4279.80	3423.66	2916.64	2584.10	2351.15	2180.34
130000	11679.98	6249.36	4450.99	3560.60	3033.31	2687.46	2445.19	2267.56
135000	12129.21	6489.72	4622.19	3697.55	3149.97	2790.82	2539.24	2354.77
140000	12578.44	6730.08	4793.38	3834.50	3266.64	2894.19	2633.28	2441.99
145000	13027.67	6970.44	4964.57	3971.44	3383.31	2997.55	2727.33	2529.20
150000	13476.90	7210.80	5135.76	4108.39	3499.97	3100.91	2821.37	2616.41
155000	13926.13	7451.16	5306.95	4245.33	3616.64	3204.28	2915.42	2703.63
160000	14375.36	7691.52	5478.14	4382.28	3733.30	3307.64	3009.47	2790.84

MONTHLY AMORTIZING PAYMENTS 14 1/8%

AMOUNT OF LOAN	NUMBER OF YEARS IN TERM 9	10	15	20	25	30	35	40
$ 50	.83	.79	.68	.63	.61	.60	.60	.60
100	1.65	1.57	1.35	1.26	1.22	1.20	1.19	1.19
200	3.29	3.13	2.69	2.51	2.43	2.39	2.38	2.37
300	4.93	4.69	4.03	3.76	3.65	3.59	3.56	3.55
400	6.57	6.25	5.37	5.02	4.86	4.78	4.75	4.73
500	8.21	7.81	6.71	6.27	6.07	5.98	5.93	5.91
600	9.85	9.37	8.05	7.52	7.29	7.17	7.12	7.09
700	11.49	10.93	9.39	8.77	8.50	8.37	8.31	8.27
800	13.13	12.49	10.73	10.03	9.71	9.56	9.49	9.46
900	14.77	14.05	12.07	11.28	10.93	10.76	10.68	10.64
1000	16.41	15.61	13.41	12.53	12.14	11.95	11.86	11.82
2000	32.82	31.21	26.81	25.06	24.27	23.90	23.72	23.63
3000	49.23	46.81	40.21	37.58	36.41	35.85	35.58	35.45
4000	65.63	62.41	53.61	50.11	48.54	47.80	47.44	47.26
5000	82.04	78.01	67.01	62.64	60.67	59.74	59.29	59.07
6000	98.45	93.62	80.41	75.16	72.81	71.69	71.15	70.89
7000	114.85	109.22	93.82	87.69	84.94	83.64	83.01	82.70
8000	131.26	124.82	107.22	100.21	97.07	95.59	94.87	94.52
9000	147.67	140.42	120.62	112.74	109.21	107.53	106.73	106.33
10000	164.07	156.02	134.02	125.27	121.34	119.48	118.58	118.14
11000	180.48	171.63	147.42	137.79	133.47	131.43	130.44	129.96
12000	196.89	187.23	160.82	150.32	145.61	143.38	142.30	141.77
13000	213.30	202.83	174.22	162.84	157.74	155.33	154.16	153.58
14000	229.70	218.43	187.63	175.37	169.87	167.27	166.01	165.40
15000	246.11	234.03	201.03	187.90	182.01	179.22	177.87	177.21
16000	262.52	249.64	214.43	200.42	194.14	191.17	189.73	189.03
17000	278.92	265.24	227.83	212.95	206.27	203.12	201.59	200.84
18000	295.33	280.84	241.23	225.47	218.41	215.06	213.45	212.65
19000	311.74	296.44	254.63	238.00	230.54	227.01	225.30	224.47
20000	328.14	312.04	268.04	250.53	242.67	238.96	237.16	236.28
21000	344.55	327.64	281.44	263.05	254.81	250.91	249.02	248.09
22000	360.96	343.25	294.84	275.58	266.94	262.85	260.88	259.91
23000	377.37	358.85	308.24	288.11	279.07	274.80	272.74	271.72
24000	393.77	374.45	321.64	300.63	291.21	286.75	284.59	283.54
25000	410.18	390.05	335.04	313.16	303.34	298.70	296.45	295.35
26000	426.59	405.65	348.44	325.68	315.47	310.65	308.31	307.16
27000	442.99	421.26	361.85	338.21	327.61	322.59	320.17	318.98
28000	459.40	436.86	375.25	350.74	339.74	334.54	332.02	330.79
29000	475.81	452.46	388.65	363.26	351.87	346.49	343.88	342.60
30000	492.21	468.06	402.05	375.79	364.01	358.44	355.74	354.42
31000	508.62	483.66	415.45	388.31	376.14	370.38	367.60	366.23
32000	525.03	499.27	428.85	400.84	388.27	382.33	379.46	378.05
33000	541.43	514.87	442.25	413.37	400.41	394.28	391.31	389.86
34000	557.84	530.47	455.66	425.89	412.54	406.23	403.17	401.67
35000	574.25	546.07	469.06	438.42	424.67	418.18	415.03	413.49
40000	656.28	624.08	536.07	501.05	485.34	477.91	474.32	472.56
45000	738.32	702.09	603.07	563.68	546.01	537.65	533.61	531.63
50000	820.35	780.10	670.08	626.31	606.67	597.39	592.90	590.69
55000	902.39	858.11	737.09	688.94	667.34	657.13	652.19	649.76
60000	984.42	936.12	804.10	751.57	728.01	716.87	711.47	708.83
65000	1066.46	1014.13	871.10	814.20	788.67	776.61	770.76	767.90
70000	1148.49	1092.14	938.11	876.83	849.34	836.35	830.05	826.97
75000	1230.53	1170.15	1005.12	939.46	910.01	896.08	889.34	886.04
80000	1312.56	1248.16	1072.13	1002.09	970.67	955.82	948.63	945.11
85000	1394.60	1326.17	1139.13	1064.72	1031.34	1015.56	1007.92	1004.18
90000	1476.63	1404.18	1206.14	1127.35	1092.01	1075.30	1067.21	1063.25
95000	1558.67	1482.18	1273.15	1189.98	1152.67	1135.04	1126.50	1122.31
100000	1640.70	1560.19	1340.16	1252.61	1213.34	1194.78	1185.79	1181.38
105000	1722.74	1638.20	1407.16	1315.25	1274.01	1254.52	1245.08	1240.45
110000	1804.77	1716.21	1474.17	1377.88	1334.67	1314.25	1304.37	1299.52
115000	1886.81	1794.22	1541.18	1440.51	1395.34	1373.99	1363.66	1358.59
120000	1968.84	1872.23	1608.19	1503.14	1456.01	1433.73	1422.94	1417.66
125000	2050.88	1950.24	1675.19	1565.77	1516.67	1493.47	1482.23	1476.73
130000	2132.91	2028.25	1742.20	1628.40	1577.34	1553.21	1541.52	1535.80
135000	2214.94	2106.26	1809.21	1691.03	1638.01	1612.95	1600.81	1594.87
140000	2296.98	2184.27	1876.22	1753.66	1698.67	1672.69	1660.10	1653.93
145000	2379.01	2262.28	1943.22	1816.29	1759.34	1732.43	1719.39	1713.00
150000	2461.05	2340.29	2010.23	1878.92	1820.01	1792.16	1778.68	1772.07
155000	2543.08	2418.30	2077.24	1941.55	1880.68	1851.90	1837.97	1831.14
160000	2625.12	2496.31	2144.25	2004.18	1941.34	1911.64	1897.26	1890.21

AMOUNT OF LOAN	NUMBER OF YEARS IN TERM							
	1	2	3	4	5	6	7	8
$ 50	4.50	2.41	1.72	1.38	1.17	1.04	.95	.88
100	9.00	4.82	3.43	2.75	2.34	2.08	1.89	1.76
200	17.99	9.63	6.86	5.50	4.68	4.15	3.78	3.51
300	26.98	14.44	10.29	8.24	7.02	6.23	5.67	5.26
400	35.97	19.26	13.72	10.99	9.36	8.30	7.56	7.01
500	44.96	24.07	17.15	13.73	11.70	10.37	9.44	8.76
600	53.95	28.88	20.58	16.48	14.04	12.45	11.33	10.51
700	62.94	33.70	24.01	19.22	16.38	14.52	13.22	12.26
800	71.93	38.51	27.44	21.97	18.72	16.60	15.11	14.02
900	80.92	43.32	30.87	24.71	21.06	18.67	17.00	15.77
1000	89.91	48.14	34.30	27.46	23.40	20.74	18.88	17.52
2000	179.81	96.27	68.60	54.91	46.80	41.48	37.76	35.03
3000	269.72	144.40	102.90	82.36	70.20	62.22	56.64	52.55
4000	359.62	192.53	137.20	109.81	93.60	82.96	75.52	70.06
5000	449.53	240.66	171.50	137.27	117.00	103.70	94.40	87.58
6000	539.43	288.79	205.80	164.72	140.39	124.44	113.28	105.09
7000	629.34	336.92	240.10	192.17	163.79	145.18	132.15	122.60
8000	719.24	385.05	274.40	219.62	187.19	165.92	151.03	140.12
9000	809.15	433.18	308.70	247.07	210.59	186.66	169.91	157.63
10000	899.05	481.32	343.00	274.53	233.99	207.40	188.79	175.15
11000	988.96	529.45	377.30	301.98	257.38	228.14	207.67	192.66
12000	1078.86	577.58	411.60	329.43	280.78	248.88	226.55	210.17
13000	1168.77	625.71	445.89	356.88	304.18	269.62	245.42	227.69
14000	1258.67	673.84	480.19	384.33	327.58	290.36	264.30	245.20
15000	1348.58	721.97	514.49	411.79	350.98	311.10	283.18	262.72
16000	1438.48	770.10	548.79	439.24	374.37	331.84	302.06	280.23
17000	1528.39	818.23	583.09	466.69	397.77	352.58	320.94	297.74
18000	1618.29	866.36	617.39	494.14	421.17	373.32	339.82	315.26
19000	1708.20	914.50	651.69	521.59	444.57	394.06	358.69	332.77
20000	1798.10	962.63	685.99	549.05	467.97	414.80	377.57	350.29
21000	1888.01	1010.76	720.29	576.50	491.36	435.54	396.45	367.80
22000	1977.91	1058.89	754.59	603.95	514.76	456.28	415.33	385.31
23000	2067.82	1107.02	788.89	631.40	538.16	477.02	434.21	402.83
24000	2157.72	1155.15	823.19	658.85	561.56	497.76	453.09	420.34
25000	2247.62	1203.28	857.48	686.31	584.96	518.50	471.96	437.86
26000	2337.53	1251.41	891.78	713.76	608.35	539.24	490.84	455.37
27000	2427.43	1299.54	926.08	741.21	631.75	559.98	509.72	472.89
28000	2517.34	1347.67	960.38	768.66	655.15	580.72	528.60	490.40
29000	2607.24	1395.81	994.68	796.11	678.55	601.46	547.48	507.91
30000	2697.15	1443.94	1028.98	823.57	701.95	622.20	566.36	525.43
31000	2787.05	1492.07	1063.28	851.02	725.34	642.94	585.24	542.94
32000	2876.96	1540.20	1097.58	878.47	748.74	663.68	604.11	560.46
33000	2966.86	1588.33	1131.88	905.92	772.14	684.42	622.99	577.97
34000	3056.77	1636.46	1166.18	933.37	795.54	705.16	641.87	595.48
35000	3146.67	1684.59	1200.48	960.83	818.94	725.90	660.75	613.00
40000	3596.20	1925.25	1371.97	1098.09	935.93	829.60	755.14	700.57
45000	4045.72	2165.90	1543.47	1235.35	1052.92	933.30	849.53	788.14
50000	4495.24	2406.56	1714.96	1372.61	1169.91	1037.00	943.92	875.71
55000	4944.77	2647.21	1886.46	1509.87	1286.90	1140.70	1038.32	963.28
60000	5394.29	2887.87	2057.96	1647.13	1403.89	1244.40	1132.71	1050.85
65000	5843.82	3128.52	2229.45	1784.39	1520.88	1348.09	1227.10	1138.42
70000	6293.34	3369.18	2400.95	1921.65	1637.87	1451.79	1321.49	1225.99
75000	6742.86	3609.84	2572.44	2058.91	1754.86	1555.49	1415.88	1313.56
80000	7192.39	3850.49	2743.94	2196.17	1871.85	1659.19	1510.28	1401.13
85000	7641.91	4091.15	2915.44	2333.43	1988.84	1762.89	1604.67	1488.70
90000	8091.44	4331.80	3086.93	2470.69	2105.83	1866.59	1699.06	1576.27
95000	8540.96	4572.46	3258.43	2607.95	2222.82	1970.29	1793.45	1663.84
100000	8990.48	4813.11	3429.92	2745.21	2339.81	2073.99	1887.84	1751.41
105000	9440.01	5053.77	3601.42	2882.47	2456.80	2177.69	1982.24	1838.98
110000	9889.53	5294.42	3772.91	3019.73	2573.79	2281.39	2076.63	1926.55
115000	10339.06	5535.08	3944.41	3156.99	2690.78	2385.09	2171.02	2014.12
120000	10788.58	5775.73	4115.91	3294.25	2807.77	2488.79	2265.41	2101.69
125000	11238.10	6016.39	4287.40	3431.51	2924.76	2592.49	2359.80	2189.26
130000	11687.63	6257.04	4458.90	3568.77	3041.75	2696.18	2454.20	2276.84
135000	12137.15	6497.70	4630.39	3706.03	3158.74	2799.88	2548.59	2364.41
140000	12586.68	6738.35	4801.89	3843.29	3275.73	2903.58	2642.98	2451.98
145000	13036.20	6979.01	4973.39	3980.55	3392.72	3007.28	2737.37	2539.55
150000	13485.72	7219.67	5144.88	4117.81	3509.71	3110.98	2831.76	2627.12
155000	13935.25	7460.32	5316.38	4255.07	3626.70	3214.68	2926.16	2714.69
160000	14384.77	7700.98	5487.87	4392.33	3743.70	3318.38	3020.55	2802.26

AMOUNT OF LOAN	NUMBER OF YEARS IN TERM							
	9	10	15	20	25	30	35	40
$ 50	.83	.79	.68	.64	.62	.61	.60	.60
100	1.65	1.57	1.35	1.27	1.23	1.21	1.20	1.20
200	3.30	3.14	2.70	2.53	2.45	2.41	2.40	2.39
300	4.95	4.71	4.05	3.79	3.67	3.62	3.59	3.58
400	6.60	6.28	5.40	5.05	4.90	4.82	4.79	4.77
500	8.25	7.84	6.75	6.31	6.12	6.03	5.98	5.96
600	9.89	9.41	8.10	7.58	7.34	7.23	7.18	7.15
700	11.54	10.98	9.45	8.84	8.57	8.44	8.38	8.35
800	13.19	12.55	10.79	10.10	9.79	9.64	9.57	9.54
900	14.84	14.11	12.14	11.36	11.01	10.85	10.77	10.73
1000	16.49	15.68	13.49	12.62	12.23	12.05	11.96	11.92
2000	32.97	31.36	26.98	25.24	24.46	24.10	23.92	23.84
3000	49.45	47.04	40.46	37.86	36.69	36.15	35.88	35.75
4000	65.93	62.71	53.95	50.47	48.92	48.19	47.84	47.67
5000	82.41	78.39	67.43	63.09	61.15	60.24	59.80	59.59
6000	98.89	94.07	80.92	75.71	73.38	72.29	71.76	71.50
7000	115.37	109.75	94.41	88.33	85.61	84.33	83.72	83.42
8000	131.85	125.42	107.89	100.94	97.84	96.38	95.68	95.33
9000	148.33	141.10	121.38	113.56	110.07	108.43	107.64	107.25
10000	164.81	156.78	134.86	126.18	122.30	120.47	119.60	119.17
11000	181.29	172.46	148.35	138.79	134.53	132.52	131.55	131.08
12000	197.77	188.13	161.83	151.41	146.76	144.57	143.51	143.00
13000	214.25	203.81	175.32	164.03	158.99	156.61	155.47	154.92
14000	230.73	219.49	188.81	176.65	171.21	168.66	167.43	166.83
15000	247.21	235.16	202.29	189.26	183.44	180.71	179.39	178.75
16000	263.69	250.84	215.78	201.88	195.67	192.75	191.35	190.66
17000	280.17	266.52	229.26	214.50	207.90	204.80	203.31	202.58
18000	296.65	282.20	242.75	227.11	220.13	216.85	215.27	214.50
19000	313.13	297.87	256.24	239.73	232.36	228.90	227.23	226.41
20000	329.61	313.55	269.72	252.35	244.59	240.94	239.19	238.33
21000	346.09	329.23	283.21	264.97	256.82	252.99	251.14	250.25
22000	362.57	344.91	296.69	277.58	269.05	265.04	263.10	262.16
23000	379.05	360.58	310.18	290.20	281.28	277.08	275.06	274.08
24000	395.53	376.26	323.66	302.82	293.51	289.13	287.02	285.99
25000	412.01	391.94	337.15	315.43	305.74	301.18	298.98	297.91
26000	428.49	407.62	350.64	328.05	317.97	313.22	310.94	309.83
27000	444.98	423.29	364.12	340.67	330.20	325.27	322.90	321.74
28000	461.46	438.97	377.61	353.29	342.42	337.32	334.86	333.66
29000	477.94	454.65	391.09	365.90	354.65	349.36	346.82	345.58
30000	494.42	470.32	404.58	378.52	366.88	361.41	358.78	357.49
31000	510.90	486.00	418.06	391.14	379.11	373.46	370.73	369.41
32000	527.38	501.68	431.55	403.76	391.34	385.50	382.69	381.32
33000	543.86	517.36	445.04	416.37	403.57	397.55	394.65	393.24
34000	560.34	533.03	458.52	428.99	415.80	409.60	406.61	405.16
35000	576.82	548.71	472.01	441.61	428.03	421.65	418.57	417.07
40000	659.22	627.10	539.44	504.69	489.18	481.88	478.37	476.65
45000	741.62	705.48	606.87	567.78	550.32	542.11	538.16	536.24
50000	824.02	783.87	674.29	630.86	611.47	602.35	597.96	595.82
55000	906.43	862.26	741.72	693.95	672.62	662.58	657.75	655.40
60000	988.83	940.64	809.15	757.04	733.76	722.82	717.55	714.98
65000	1071.23	1019.03	876.58	820.12	794.91	783.05	777.34	774.56
70000	1153.63	1097.42	944.01	883.21	856.05	843.29	837.14	834.14
75000	1236.03	1175.80	1011.44	946.29	917.20	903.52	896.93	893.72
80000	1318.44	1254.19	1078.87	1009.38	978.35	963.75	956.73	953.30
85000	1400.84	1332.58	1146.30	1072.47	1039.49	1023.99	1016.52	1012.88
90000	1483.24	1410.96	1213.73	1135.55	1100.64	1084.22	1076.32	1072.47
95000	1565.64	1489.35	1281.16	1198.64	1161.79	1144.46	1136.11	1132.05
100000	1648.04	1567.74	1348.58	1261.72	1222.93	1204.69	1195.91	1191.63
105000	1730.45	1646.12	1416.01	1324.81	1284.08	1264.93	1255.70	1251.21
110000	1812.85	1724.51	1483.44	1387.90	1345.23	1325.16	1315.50	1310.79
115000	1895.25	1802.90	1550.87	1450.98	1406.37	1385.40	1375.29	1370.37
120000	1977.65	1881.28	1618.30	1514.07	1467.52	1445.63	1435.09	1429.95
125000	2060.05	1959.67	1685.73	1577.15	1528.66	1505.86	1494.88	1489.53
130000	2142.45	2038.06	1753.16	1640.24	1589.81	1566.10	1554.68	1549.12
135000	2224.86	2116.44	1820.59	1703.33	1650.96	1626.33	1614.47	1608.70
140000	2307.26	2194.83	1888.02	1766.41	1712.10	1686.57	1674.27	1668.28
145000	2389.66	2273.22	1955.45	1829.50	1773.25	1746.80	1734.06	1727.86
150000	2472.06	2351.60	2022.87	1892.58	1834.40	1807.04	1793.86	1787.44
155000	2554.46	2429.99	2090.30	1955.67	1895.54	1867.27	1853.65	1847.02
160000	2636.87	2508.37	2157.73	2018.76	1956.69	1927.50	1913.45	1906.60

MONTHLY AMORTIZING PAYMENTS

AMOUNT OF LOAN	NUMBER OF YEARS IN TERM							
	1	2	3	4	5	6	7	8
$ 50	4.50	2.41	1.72	1.38	1.18	1.05	.95	.88
100	9.00	4.82	3.44	2.76	2.35	2.09	1.90	1.76
200	18.00	9.64	6.88	5.51	4.70	4.17	3.79	3.52
300	26.99	14.46	10.31	8.26	7.04	6.25	5.69	5.28
400	35.99	19.28	13.75	11.01	9.39	8.33	7.58	7.04
500	44.99	24.10	17.19	13.76	11.74	10.41	9.48	8.80
600	53.98	28.92	20.62	16.51	14.08	12.49	11.37	10.56
700	62.98	33.74	24.06	19.27	16.43	14.57	13.27	12.31
800	71.98	38.56	27.49	22.02	18.78	16.65	15.16	14.07
900	80.97	43.38	30.93	24.77	21.12	18.73	17.06	15.83
1000	89.97	48.20	34.37	27.52	23.47	20.81	18.95	17.59
2000	179.93	96.39	68.73	55.03	46.93	41.62	37.90	35.18
3000	269.90	144.58	103.09	82.55	70.39	62.43	56.85	52.76
4000	359.86	192.77	137.45	110.06	93.86	83.23	75.80	70.35
5000	449.82	240.96	171.81	137.58	117.32	104.04	94.74	87.93
6000	539.79	289.15	206.17	165.09	140.78	124.85	113.69	105.52
7000	629.75	337.34	240.53	192.61	164.25	145.65	132.64	123.10
8000	719.71	385.53	274.89	220.12	187.71	166.46	151.59	140.69
9000	809.68	433.72	309.25	247.64	211.17	187.27	170.54	158.28
10000	899.64	481.91	343.61	275.15	234.64	208.08	189.48	175.86
11000	989.61	530.10	377.97	302.67	258.10	228.88	208.43	193.45
12000	1079.57	578.29	412.33	330.18	281.56	249.69	227.38	211.03
13000	1169.53	626.48	446.69	357.70	305.03	270.50	246.33	228.62
14000	1259.50	674.67	481.05	385.21	328.49	291.30	265.27	246.20
15000	1349.46	722.86	515.41	412.73	351.95	312.11	284.22	263.79
16000	1439.42	771.05	549.77	440.24	375.41	332.92	303.17	281.37
17000	1529.39	819.24	584.13	467.76	398.88	353.73	322.12	298.96
18000	1619.35	867.43	618.49	495.27	422.34	374.53	341.07	316.55
19000	1709.31	915.62	652.85	522.79	445.80	395.34	360.01	334.13
20000	1799.28	963.81	687.21	550.30	469.27	416.15	378.96	351.72
21000	1889.24	1012.00	721.57	577.82	492.73	436.95	397.91	369.30
22000	1979.21	1060.19	755.93	605.33	516.19	457.76	416.86	386.89
23000	2069.17	1108.38	790.29	632.85	539.66	478.57	435.80	404.47
24000	2159.13	1156.57	824.65	660.36	563.12	499.37	454.75	422.06
25000	2249.10	1204.76	859.01	687.88	586.58	520.18	473.70	439.64
26000	2339.06	1252.95	893.37	715.39	610.05	540.99	492.65	457.23
27000	2429.02	1301.14	927.73	742.91	633.51	561.80	511.60	474.82
28000	2518.99	1349.33	962.09	770.42	656.97	582.60	530.54	492.40
29000	2608.95	1397.52	996.45	797.94	680.44	603.41	549.49	509.99
30000	2698.91	1445.71	1030.81	825.45	703.90	624.22	568.44	527.57
31000	2788.88	1493.90	1065.17	852.97	727.36	645.02	587.39	545.16
32000	2878.84	1542.09	1099.53	880.48	750.82	665.83	606.33	562.74
33000	2968.81	1590.28	1133.89	908.00	774.29	686.64	625.28	580.33
34000	3058.77	1638.47	1168.25	935.51	797.75	707.45	644.23	597.92
35000	3148.73	1686.66	1202.61	963.03	821.21	728.25	663.18	615.50
40000	3598.55	1927.61	1374.41	1100.60	938.53	832.29	757.92	703.43
45000	4048.37	2168.57	1546.21	1238.18	1055.85	936.32	852.66	791.36
50000	4498.19	2409.52	1718.01	1375.75	1173.16	1040.36	947.39	879.28
55000	4948.01	2650.47	1889.81	1513.33	1290.48	1144.39	1042.13	967.21
60000	5397.82	2891.42	2061.61	1650.90	1407.79	1248.43	1136.87	1055.14
65000	5847.64	3132.37	2233.41	1788.48	1525.11	1352.46	1231.61	1143.07
70000	6297.46	3373.32	2405.21	1926.05	1642.42	1456.50	1326.35	1231.00
75000	6747.28	3614.27	2577.01	2063.63	1759.74	1560.54	1421.09	1318.92
80000	7197.10	3855.22	2748.81	2201.20	1877.05	1664.57	1515.83	1406.85
85000	7646.92	4096.17	2920.61	2338.78	1994.37	1768.61	1610.57	1494.78
90000	8096.73	4337.13	3092.41	2476.35	2111.69	1872.64	1705.31	1582.71
95000	8546.55	4578.08	3264.21	2613.93	2229.00	1976.68	1800.04	1670.64
100000	8996.37	4819.03	3436.01	2751.50	2346.32	2080.71	1894.78	1758.56
105000	9446.19	5059.98	3607.81	2889.08	2463.63	2184.75	1989.52	1846.49
110000	9896.01	5300.93	3779.61	3026.65	2580.95	2288.78	2084.26	1934.42
115000	10345.83	5541.88	3951.41	3164.23	2698.26	2392.82	2179.00	2022.35
120000	10795.64	5782.83	4123.21	3301.80	2815.58	2496.85	2273.74	2110.28
125000	11245.46	6023.78	4295.01	3439.37	2932.90	2600.89	2368.48	2198.20
130000	11695.28	6264.73	4466.81	3576.95	3050.21	2704.92	2463.22	2286.13
135000	12145.10	6505.69	4638.61	3714.52	3167.53	2808.96	2557.96	2374.06
140000	12594.92	6746.64	4810.41	3852.10	3284.84	2913.00	2652.69	2461.99
145000	13044.74	6987.59	4982.21	3989.67	3402.16	3017.03	2747.43	2549.92
150000	13494.55	7228.54	5154.01	4127.25	3519.47	3121.07	2842.17	2637.84
155000	13944.37	7469.49	5325.81	4264.82	3636.79	3225.10	2936.91	2725.77
160000	14394.19	7710.44	5497.61	4402.40	3754.10	3329.14	3031.65	2813.70

AMOUNT OF LOAN	9	10	15	20	25	30	35	40
	NUMBER OF YEARS IN TERM							
$ 50	.83	.79	.68	.64	.62	.61	.61	.61
100	1.66	1.58	1.36	1.28	1.24	1.22	1.21	1.21
200	3.32	3.16	2.72	2.55	2.47	2.43	2.42	2.41
300	4.97	4.73	4.08	3.82	3.70	3.65	3.62	3.61
400	6.63	6.31	5.43	5.09	4.94	4.86	4.83	4.81
500	8.28	7.88	6.79	6.36	6.17	6.08	6.04	6.01
600	9.94	9.46	8.15	7.63	7.40	7.29	7.24	7.22
700	11.59	11.03	9.50	8.90	8.63	8.51	8.45	8.42
800	13.25	12.61	10.86	10.17	9.87	9.72	9.65	9.62
900	14.90	14.18	12.22	11.44	11.10	10.94	10.86	10.82
1000	16.56	15.76	13.58	12.71	12.33	12.15	12.07	12.02
2000	33.11	31.51	27.15	25.42	24.66	24.30	24.13	24.04
3000	49.67	47.26	40.72	38.13	36.98	36.44	36.19	36.06
4000	66.22	63.02	54.29	50.84	49.31	48.59	48.25	48.08
5000	82.77	78.77	67.86	63.55	61.63	60.74	60.31	60.10
6000	99.33	94.52	81.43	76.26	73.96	72.88	72.37	72.12
7000	115.88	110.28	95.00	88.96	86.28	85.03	84.43	84.14
8000	132.44	126.03	108.57	101.67	98.61	97.17	96.49	96.15
9000	148.99	141.78	122.14	114.38	110.93	109.32	108.55	108.17
10000	165.54	157.53	135.71	127.09	123.26	121.47	120.61	120.19
11000	182.10	173.29	149.28	139.80	135.58	133.61	132.67	132.21
12000	198.65	189.04	162.85	152.51	147.91	145.76	144.73	144.23
13000	215.21	204.79	176.42	165.22	160.23	157.90	156.79	156.25
14000	231.76	220.55	189.99	177.92	172.56	170.05	168.85	168.27
15000	248.31	236.30	203.56	190.63	184.89	182.20	180.91	180.29
16000	264.87	252.05	217.13	203.34	197.21	194.34	192.97	192.30
17000	281.42	267.80	230.70	216.05	209.54	206.49	205.03	204.32
18000	297.98	283.56	244.27	228.76	221.86	218.64	217.09	216.34
19000	314.53	299.31	257.84	241.47	234.19	230.78	229.15	228.36
20000	331.08	315.06	271.41	254.17	246.51	242.93	241.21	240.38
21000	347.64	330.82	284.98	266.88	258.84	255.07	253.27	252.40
22000	364.19	346.57	298.55	279.59	271.16	267.22	265.33	264.42
23000	380.75	362.32	312.12	292.30	283.49	279.37	277.39	276.44
24000	397.30	378.07	325.69	305.01	295.81	291.51	289.45	288.45
25000	413.85	393.83	339.26	317.72	308.14	303.66	301.51	300.47
26000	430.41	409.58	352.83	330.43	320.46	315.80	313.57	312.49
27000	446.96	425.33	366.40	343.13	332.79	327.95	325.63	324.51
28000	463.52	441.09	379.97	355.84	345.12	340.10	337.69	336.53
29000	480.07	456.84	393.54	368.55	357.44	352.24	349.75	348.55
30000	496.62	472.59	407.11	381.26	369.77	364.39	361.81	360.57
31000	513.18	488.35	420.68	393.97	382.09	376.54	373.87	372.59
32000	529.73	504.10	434.25	406.68	394.42	388.68	385.94	384.60
33000	546.29	519.85	447.82	419.38	406.74	400.83	398.00	396.62
34000	562.84	535.60	461.40	432.09	419.07	412.97	410.06	408.64
35000	579.39	551.36	474.97	444.80	431.39	425.12	422.12	420.66
40000	662.16	630.12	542.82	508.34	493.02	485.85	482.42	480.75
45000	744.93	708.89	610.67	571.89	554.65	546.58	542.72	540.85
50000	827.70	787.65	678.52	635.43	616.27	607.31	603.02	600.94
55000	910.47	866.41	746.37	698.97	677.90	668.04	663.32	661.04
60000	993.24	945.18	814.22	762.51	739.53	728.77	723.62	721.13
65000	1076.01	1023.94	882.07	826.06	801.15	789.50	783.93	781.22
70000	1158.78	1102.71	949.93	889.60	862.78	850.24	844.23	841.32
75000	1241.55	1181.47	1017.78	953.14	924.41	910.97	904.53	901.41
80000	1324.32	1260.24	1085.63	1016.68	986.03	971.70	964.83	961.50
85000	1407.09	1339.00	1153.48	1080.23	1047.66	1032.43	1025.13	1021.60
90000	1489.86	1417.77	1221.33	1143.77	1109.29	1093.16	1085.43	1081.69
95000	1572.63	1496.53	1289.18	1207.31	1170.91	1153.89	1145.74	1141.79
100000	1655.40	1575.30	1357.03	1270.85	1232.54	1214.62	1206.04	1201.88
105000	1738.17	1654.06	1424.89	1334.40	1294.17	1275.35	1266.34	1261.97
110000	1820.94	1732.82	1492.74	1397.94	1355.80	1336.08	1326.64	1322.07
115000	1903.71	1811.59	1560.59	1461.48	1417.42	1396.81	1386.94	1382.16
120000	1986.48	1890.35	1628.44	1525.02	1479.05	1457.54	1447.24	1442.25
125000	2069.25	1969.12	1696.29	1588.57	1540.68	1518.27	1507.54	1502.35
130000	2152.02	2047.88	1764.14	1652.11	1602.30	1579.00	1567.85	1562.44
135000	2234.79	2126.65	1832.00	1715.65	1663.93	1639.74	1628.15	1622.54
140000	2317.56	2205.41	1899.85	1779.19	1725.56	1700.47	1688.45	1682.63
145000	2400.33	2284.18	1967.70	1842.74	1787.18	1761.20	1748.75	1742.72
150000	2483.10	2362.94	2035.55	1906.28	1848.81	1821.93	1809.05	1802.82
155000	2565.87	2441.71	2103.40	1969.82	1910.44	1882.66	1869.35	1862.91
160000	2648.64	2520.47	2171.25	2033.36	1972.06	1943.39	1929.66	1923.00

MONTHLY AMORTIZING PAYMENTS

AMOUNT OF LOAN	NUMBER OF YEARS IN TERM							
	1	2	3	4	5	6	7	8
$ 50	4.51	2.42	1.73	1.38	1.18	1.05	.96	.89
100	9.01	4.83	3.45	2.76	2.36	2.09	1.91	1.77
200	18.01	9.65	6.89	5.52	4.71	4.18	3.81	3.54
300	27.01	14.48	10.33	8.28	7.06	6.27	5.71	5.30
400	36.01	19.30	13.77	11.04	9.42	8.35	7.61	7.07
500	45.02	24.13	17.22	13.79	11.77	10.44	9.51	8.83
600	54.02	28.95	20.66	16.55	14.12	12.53	11.42	10.60
700	63.02	33.78	24.10	19.31	16.47	14.62	13.32	12.37
800	72.02	38.60	27.54	22.07	18.83	16.70	15.22	14.13
900	81.03	43.43	30.98	24.83	21.18	18.79	17.12	15.90
1000	90.03	48.25	34.43	27.58	23.53	20.88	19.02	17.66
2000	180.05	96.50	68.85	55.16	47.06	41.75	38.04	35.32
3000	270.07	144.75	103.27	82.74	70.59	62.63	57.06	52.98
4000	360.10	193.00	137.69	110.32	94.12	83.50	76.07	70.63
5000	450.12	241.25	172.11	137.89	117.65	104.38	95.09	88.29
6000	540.14	289.50	206.53	165.47	141.17	125.25	114.11	105.95
7000	630.16	337.75	240.95	193.05	164.70	146.13	133.13	123.61
8000	720.19	386.00	275.37	220.63	188.23	167.00	152.14	141.26
9000	810.21	434.25	309.79	248.21	211.76	187.87	171.16	158.92
10000	900.23	482.50	344.21	275.78	235.29	208.75	190.18	176.58
11000	990.25	530.75	378.64	303.36	258.82	229.62	209.20	194.23
12000	1080.28	579.00	413.06	330.94	282.34	250.50	228.21	211.89
13000	1170.30	627.25	447.48	358.52	305.87	271.37	247.23	229.55
14000	1260.32	675.50	481.90	386.10	329.40	292.25	266.25	247.21
15000	1350.34	723.75	516.32	413.67	352.93	313.12	285.26	264.86
16000	1440.37	772.00	550.74	441.25	376.46	334.00	304.28	282.52
17000	1530.39	820.25	585.16	468.83	399.99	354.87	323.30	300.18
18000	1620.41	868.49	619.58	496.41	423.51	375.74	342.32	317.84
19000	1710.43	916.74	654.00	523.99	447.04	396.62	361.33	335.49
20000	1800.46	964.99	688.42	551.56	470.57	417.49	380.35	353.15
21000	1890.48	1013.24	722.85	579.14	494.10	438.37	399.37	370.81
22000	1980.50	1061.49	757.27	606.72	517.63	459.24	418.39	388.46
23000	2070.52	1109.74	791.69	634.30	541.16	480.12	437.40	406.12
24000	2160.55	1157.99	826.11	661.88	564.68	500.99	456.42	423.78
25000	2250.57	1206.24	860.53	689.45	588.21	521.87	475.44	441.44
26000	2340.59	1254.49	894.95	717.03	611.74	542.74	494.45	459.09
27000	2430.61	1302.74	929.37	744.61	635.27	563.61	513.47	476.75
28000	2520.64	1350.99	963.79	772.19	658.80	584.49	532.49	494.41
29000	2610.66	1399.24	998.21	799.77	682.33	605.36	551.51	512.07
30000	2700.68	1447.49	1032.63	827.34	705.85	626.24	570.52	529.72
31000	2790.70	1495.74	1067.06	854.92	729.38	647.11	589.54	547.38
32000	2880.73	1543.99	1101.48	882.50	752.91	667.99	608.56	565.04
33000	2970.75	1592.24	1135.90	910.08	776.44	688.86	627.58	582.69
34000	3060.77	1640.49	1170.32	937.66	799.97	709.74	646.59	600.35
35000	3150.79	1688.73	1204.74	965.23	823.49	730.61	665.61	618.01
40000	3600.91	1929.98	1376.84	1103.12	941.14	834.98	760.70	706.30
45000	4051.02	2171.23	1548.95	1241.01	1058.78	939.35	855.78	794.58
50000	4501.13	2412.48	1721.05	1378.90	1176.42	1043.73	950.87	882.87
55000	4951.25	2653.72	1893.16	1516.79	1294.06	1148.10	1045.96	971.15
60000	5401.36	2894.97	2065.26	1654.68	1411.70	1252.47	1141.04	1059.44
65000	5851.47	3136.22	2237.37	1792.57	1529.34	1356.84	1236.13	1147.73
70000	6301.58	3377.46	2409.47	1930.46	1646.98	1461.21	1331.22	1236.01
75000	6751.70	3618.71	2581.58	2068.35	1764.63	1565.59	1426.30	1324.30
80000	7201.81	3859.96	2753.68	2206.24	1882.27	1669.96	1521.39	1412.59
85000	7651.92	4101.21	2925.79	2344.13	1999.91	1774.33	1616.48	1500.87
90000	8102.03	4342.45	3097.89	2482.02	2117.55	1878.70	1711.56	1589.16
95000	8552.15	4583.70	3270.00	2619.91	2235.19	1983.08	1806.65	1677.44
100000	9002.26	4824.95	3442.10	2757.80	2352.83	2087.45	1901.74	1765.73
105000	9452.37	5066.19	3614.21	2895.69	2470.47	2191.82	1996.82	1854.02
110000	9902.49	5307.44	3786.31	3033.58	2588.12	2296.19	2091.91	1942.30
115000	10352.60	5548.69	3958.42	3171.47	2705.76	2400.56	2186.99	2030.59
120000	10802.71	5789.94	4130.52	3309.36	2823.40	2504.94	2282.08	2118.88
125000	11252.82	6031.18	4302.63	3447.25	2941.04	2609.31	2377.17	2207.16
130000	11702.94	6272.43	4474.73	3585.14	3058.68	2713.68	2472.25	2295.45
135000	12153.05	6513.68	4646.84	3723.03	3176.32	2818.05	2567.34	2383.73
140000	12603.16	6754.92	4818.94	3860.92	3293.96	2922.42	2662.43	2472.02
145000	13053.27	6996.17	4991.05	3998.81	3411.61	3026.80	2757.51	2560.31
150000	13503.39	7237.42	5163.15	4136.70	3529.25	3131.17	2852.60	2648.59
155000	13953.50	7478.67	5335.26	4274.59	3646.89	3235.54	2947.69	2736.88
160000	14403.61	7719.91	5507.36	4412.48	3764.53	3339.91	3042.77	2825.17

MONTHLY AMORTIZING PAYMENTS 14 1/2%

AMOUNT OF LOAN	NUMBER OF YEARS IN TERM							
	9	10	15	20	25	30	35	40
$ 50	.84	.80	.69	.64	.63	.62	.61	.61
100	1.67	1.59	1.37	1.28	1.25	1.23	1.22	1.22
200	3.33	3.17	2.74	2.56	2.49	2.45	2.44	2.43
300	4.99	4.75	4.10	3.84	3.73	3.68	3.65	3.64
400	6.66	6.34	5.47	5.12	4.97	4.90	4.87	4.85
500	8.32	7.92	6.83	6.40	6.22	6.13	6.09	6.07
600	9.98	9.50	8.20	7.68	7.46	7.35	7.30	7.28
700	11.64	11.09	9.56	8.96	8.70	8.58	8.52	8.49
800	13.31	12.67	10.93	10.24	9.94	9.80	9.73	9.70
900	14.97	14.25	12.29	11.52	11.18	11.03	10.95	10.91
1000	16.63	15.83	13.66	12.80	12.43	12.25	12.17	12.13
2000	33.26	31.66	27.32	25.60	24.85	24.50	24.33	24.25
3000	49.89	47.49	40.97	38.40	37.27	36.74	36.49	36.37
4000	66.52	63.32	54.63	51.20	49.69	48.99	48.65	48.49
5000	83.14	79.15	68.28	64.00	62.11	61.23	60.81	60.61
6000	99.77	94.98	81.94	76.80	74.53	73.48	72.98	72.73
7000	116.40	110.81	95.59	89.60	86.96	85.72	85.14	84.85
8000	133.03	126.63	109.25	102.40	99.38	97.97	97.30	96.98
9000	149.65	142.46	122.90	115.20	111.80	110.22	109.46	109.10
10000	166.28	158.29	136.56	128.00	124.22	122.46	121.62	121.22
11000	182.91	174.12	150.21	140.80	136.64	134.71	133.78	133.34
12000	199.54	189.95	163.87	153.60	149.06	146.95	145.95	145.46
13000	216.17	205.78	177.52	166.40	161.49	159.20	158.11	157.58
14000	232.79	221.61	191.18	179.20	173.91	171.44	170.27	169.70
15000	249.42	237.44	204.83	192.00	186.33	183.69	182.43	181.82
16000	266.05	253.26	218.49	204.80	198.75	195.93	194.59	193.95
17000	282.68	269.09	232.14	217.60	211.17	208.18	206.75	206.07
18000	299.30	284.92	245.80	230.40	223.59	220.43	218.92	218.19
19000	315.93	300.75	259.45	243.20	236.02	232.67	231.08	230.31
20000	332.56	316.58	273.11	256.00	248.44	244.92	243.24	242.43
21000	349.19	332.41	286.76	268.80	260.86	257.16	255.40	254.55
22000	365.81	348.24	300.42	281.60	273.28	269.41	267.56	266.67
23000	382.44	364.06	314.07	294.40	285.70	281.65	279.72	278.80
24000	399.07	379.89	327.73	307.20	298.12	293.90	291.89	290.92
25000	415.70	395.72	341.38	320.00	310.55	306.14	304.05	303.04
26000	432.33	411.55	355.04	332.80	322.97	318.39	316.21	315.16
27000	448.95	427.38	368.69	345.60	335.39	330.64	328.37	327.28
28000	465.58	443.21	382.35	358.40	347.81	342.88	340.53	339.40
29000	482.21	459.04	396.00	371.20	360.23	355.13	352.69	351.52
30000	498.84	474.87	409.66	384.00	372.65	367.37	364.86	363.64
31000	515.46	490.69	423.31	396.80	385.08	379.62	377.02	375.77
32000	532.09	506.52	436.97	409.60	397.50	391.86	389.18	387.89
33000	548.72	522.35	450.62	422.40	409.92	404.11	401.34	400.01
34000	565.35	538.18	464.28	435.20	422.34	416.35	413.50	412.13
35000	581.98	554.01	477.93	448.00	434.76	428.60	425.66	424.25
40000	665.11	633.15	546.21	512.00	496.87	489.83	486.47	484.86
45000	748.25	712.30	614.48	576.00	558.98	551.06	547.28	545.46
50000	831.39	791.44	682.76	640.00	621.09	612.28	608.09	606.07
55000	914.53	870.58	751.03	704.00	683.19	673.51	668.90	666.68
60000	997.67	949.73	819.31	768.00	745.30	734.74	729.71	727.28
65000	1080.81	1028.87	887.58	832.00	807.41	795.97	790.52	787.89
70000	1163.95	1108.01	955.86	896.00	869.52	857.19	851.32	848.50
75000	1247.08	1187.16	1024.13	960.00	931.63	918.42	912.13	909.10
80000	1330.22	1266.30	1092.41	1024.00	993.74	979.65	972.94	969.71
85000	1413.36	1345.44	1160.68	1088.00	1055.84	1040.88	1033.75	1030.32
90000	1496.50	1424.59	1228.96	1152.00	1117.95	1102.11	1094.56	1090.92
95000	1579.64	1503.73	1297.23	1216.00	1180.06	1163.33	1155.37	1151.53
100000	1662.78	1582.87	1365.51	1280.00	1242.17	1224.56	1216.18	1212.14
105000	1745.92	1662.02	1433.78	1344.00	1304.28	1285.79	1276.98	1272.74
110000	1829.05	1741.16	1502.06	1408.00	1366.38	1347.02	1337.79	1333.35
115000	1912.19	1820.30	1570.33	1472.00	1428.49	1408.24	1398.60	1393.96
120000	1995.33	1899.45	1638.61	1536.00	1490.60	1469.47	1459.41	1454.56
125000	2078.47	1978.59	1706.88	1600.00	1552.71	1530.70	1520.22	1515.17
130000	2161.61	2057.73	1775.16	1664.00	1614.82	1591.93	1581.03	1575.78
135000	2244.75	2136.88	1843.43	1728.00	1676.92	1653.16	1641.84	1636.38
140000	2327.89	2216.02	1911.71	1792.00	1739.03	1714.38	1702.64	1696.99
145000	2411.02	2295.16	1979.98	1856.00	1801.14	1775.61	1763.45	1757.60
150000	2494.16	2374.31	2048.26	1920.00	1863.25	1836.84	1824.26	1818.20
155000	2577.30	2453.45	2116.53	1984.00	1925.36	1898.07	1885.07	1878.81
160000	2660.44	2532.59	2184.81	2048.00	1987.47	1959.29	1945.88	1939.42

MONTHLY AMORTIZING PAYMENTS

AMOUNT OF LOAN	NUMBER OF YEARS IN TERM							
	1	2	3	4	5	6	7	8
$ 50	4.51	2.42	1.73	1.39	1.18	1.05	.96	.89
100	9.01	4.84	3.45	2.77	2.36	2.10	1.91	1.78
200	18.02	9.67	6.90	5.53	4.72	4.19	3.82	3.55
300	27.03	14.50	10.35	8.30	7.08	6.29	5.73	5.32
400	36.04	19.33	13.80	11.06	9.44	8.38	7.64	7.10
500	45.05	24.16	17.25	13.83	11.80	10.48	9.55	8.87
600	54.05	28.99	20.69	16.59	14.16	12.57	11.46	10.64
700	63.06	33.82	24.14	19.35	16.52	14.66	13.37	12.42
800	72.07	38.65	27.59	22.12	18.88	16.76	15.27	14.19
900	81.08	43.48	31.04	24.88	21.24	18.85	17.18	15.96
1000	90.09	48.31	34.49	27.65	23.60	20.95	19.09	17.73
2000	180.17	96.62	68.97	55.29	47.19	41.89	38.18	35.46
3000	270.25	144.93	103.45	82.93	70.79	62.83	57.27	53.19
4000	360.33	193.24	137.93	110.57	94.38	83.77	76.35	70.92
5000	450.41	241.55	172.41	138.21	117.97	104.71	95.44	88.65
6000	540.49	289.86	206.90	165.85	141.57	125.66	114.53	106.38
7000	630.58	338.17	241.38	193.49	165.16	146.60	133.61	124.11
8000	720.66	386.47	275.86	221.13	188.75	167.54	152.70	141.84
9000	810.74	434.78	310.34	248.77	212.35	188.48	171.79	159.57
10000	900.82	483.09	344.82	276.42	235.94	209.42	190.87	177.30
11000	990.90	531.40	379.31	304.06	259.53	230.37	209.96	195.02
12000	1080.98	579.71	413.79	331.70	283.13	251.31	229.05	212.75
13000	1171.06	628.02	448.27	359.34	306.72	272.25	248.14	230.48
14000	1261.15	676.33	482.75	386.98	330.31	293.19	267.22	248.21
15000	1351.23	724.64	517.23	414.62	353.91	314.13	286.31	265.94
16000	1441.31	772.94	551.72	442.26	377.50	335.08	305.40	283.67
17000	1531.39	821.25	586.20	469.90	401.10	356.02	324.48	301.40
18000	1621.47	869.56	620.68	497.54	424.69	376.96	343.57	319.13
19000	1711.55	917.87	655.16	525.18	448.28	397.90	362.66	336.86
20000	1801.63	966.18	689.64	552.83	471.88	418.84	381.74	354.59
21000	1891.72	1014.49	724.13	580.47	495.47	439.78	400.83	372.32
22000	1981.80	1062.80	758.61	608.11	519.06	460.73	419.92	390.04
23000	2071.88	1111.10	793.09	635.75	542.66	481.67	439.01	407.77
24000	2161.96	1159.41	827.57	663.39	566.25	502.61	458.09	425.50
25000	2252.04	1207.72	862.05	691.03	589.84	523.55	477.18	443.23
26000	2342.12	1256.03	896.54	718.67	613.44	544.49	496.27	460.96
27000	2432.20	1304.34	931.02	746.31	637.03	565.44	515.35	478.69
28000	2522.29	1352.65	965.50	773.95	660.62	586.38	534.44	496.42
29000	2612.37	1400.96	999.98	801.59	684.22	607.32	553.53	514.15
30000	2702.45	1449.27	1034.46	829.24	707.81	628.26	572.61	531.88
31000	2792.53	1497.57	1068.95	856.88	731.40	649.20	591.70	549.61
32000	2882.61	1545.88	1103.43	884.52	755.00	670.15	610.79	567.34
33000	2972.69	1594.19	1137.91	912.16	778.59	691.09	629.87	585.06
34000	3062.77	1642.50	1172.39	939.80	802.19	712.03	648.96	602.79
35000	3152.86	1690.81	1206.87	967.44	825.78	732.97	668.05	620.52
40000	3603.26	1932.35	1379.28	1105.65	943.75	837.68	763.48	709.17
45000	4053.67	2173.90	1551.69	1243.85	1061.71	942.39	858.92	797.81
50000	4504.08	2415.44	1724.10	1382.06	1179.68	1047.10	954.35	886.46
55000	4954.49	2656.98	1896.51	1520.26	1297.65	1151.81	1049.79	975.10
60000	5404.89	2898.53	2068.92	1658.47	1415.62	1256.52	1145.22	1063.75
65000	5855.30	3140.07	2241.33	1796.67	1533.59	1361.23	1240.66	1152.39
70000	6305.71	3381.61	2413.74	1934.88	1651.55	1465.94	1336.09	1241.04
75000	6756.11	3623.16	2586.15	2073.08	1769.52	1570.65	1431.53	1329.69
80000	7206.52	3864.70	2758.56	2211.29	1887.49	1675.36	1526.96	1418.33
85000	7656.93	4106.24	2930.97	2349.49	2005.46	1780.07	1622.40	1506.98
90000	8107.34	4347.79	3103.38	2487.70	2123.42	1884.78	1717.83	1595.62
95000	8557.74	4589.33	3275.79	2625.90	2241.39	1989.49	1813.27	1684.27
100000	9008.15	4830.87	3448.20	2764.11	2359.36	2094.19	1908.70	1772.91
105000	9458.56	5072.42	3620.61	2902.31	2477.33	2198.90	2004.14	1861.56
110000	9908.97	5313.96	3793.02	3040.52	2595.29	2303.61	2099.57	1950.20
115000	10359.37	5555.50	3965.43	3178.72	2713.26	2408.32	2195.01	2038.85
120000	10809.78	5797.05	4137.84	3316.93	2831.23	2513.03	2290.44	2127.49
125000	11260.19	6038.59	4310.25	3455.13	2949.20	2617.74	2385.88	2216.14
130000	11710.59	6280.13	4482.66	3593.34	3067.17	2722.45	2481.31	2304.78
135000	12161.00	6521.68	4655.07	3731.54	3185.13	2827.16	2576.75	2393.43
140000	12611.41	6763.22	4827.48	3869.75	3303.10	2931.87	2672.18	2482.07
145000	13061.82	7004.76	4999.89	4007.95	3421.07	3036.58	2767.61	2570.72
150000	13512.22	7246.31	5172.30	4146.16	3539.04	3141.29	2863.05	2659.37
155000	13962.63	7487.85	5344.71	4284.36	3657.00	3246.00	2958.48	2748.01
160000	14413.04	7729.39	5517.12	4422.57	3774.97	3350.71	3053.92	2836.66

MONTHLY AMORTIZING PAYMENTS 14 5/8%

AMOUNT OF LOAN	NUMBER OF YEARS IN TERM 9	10	15	20	25	30	35	40
$ 50	.84	.80	.69	.65	.63	.62	.62	.62
100	1.68	1.60	1.38	1.29	1.26	1.24	1.23	1.23
200	3.35	3.19	2.75	2.58	2.51	2.47	2.46	2.45
300	5.02	4.78	4.13	3.87	3.76	3.71	3.68	3.67
400	6.69	6.37	5.50	5.16	5.01	4.94	4.91	4.89
500	8.36	7.96	6.87	6.45	6.26	6.18	6.14	6.12
600	10.03	9.55	8.25	7.74	7.52	7.41	7.36	7.34
700	11.70	11.14	9.62	9.03	8.77	8.65	8.59	8.56
800	13.37	12.73	11.00	10.32	10.02	9.88	9.82	9.78
900	15.04	14.32	12.37	11.61	11.27	11.12	11.04	11.01
1000	16.71	15.91	13.74	12.90	12.52	12.35	12.27	12.23
2000	33.41	31.81	27.48	25.79	25.04	24.70	24.53	24.45
3000	50.11	47.72	41.22	38.68	37.56	37.04	36.79	36.68
4000	66.81	63.62	54.96	51.57	50.08	49.39	49.06	48.90
5000	83.51	79.53	68.70	64.46	62.60	61.73	61.32	61.12
6000	100.21	95.43	82.44	77.36	75.11	74.08	73.58	73.35
7000	116.92	111.34	96.18	90.25	87.63	86.42	85.85	85.57
8000	133.62	127.24	109.92	103.14	100.15	98.77	98.11	97.80
9000	150.32	143.15	123.66	116.03	112.67	111.11	110.37	110.02
10000	167.02	159.05	137.40	128.92	125.19	123.46	122.64	122.24
11000	183.72	174.96	151.14	141.81	137.70	135.80	134.90	134.47
12000	200.42	190.86	164.88	154.71	150.22	148.15	147.16	146.69
13000	217.13	206.77	178.62	167.60	162.74	160.49	159.43	158.92
14000	233.83	222.67	192.36	180.49	175.26	172.84	171.69	171.14
15000	250.53	238.57	206.10	193.38	187.78	185.18	183.95	183.36
16000	267.23	254.48	219.84	206.27	200.29	197.53	196.22	195.59
17000	283.93	270.38	233.58	219.16	212.81	209.87	208.48	207.81
18000	300.63	286.29	247.32	232.06	225.33	222.22	220.74	220.04
19000	317.34	302.19	261.06	244.95	237.85	234.56	233.01	232.26
20000	334.04	318.10	274.80	257.84	250.37	246.91	245.27	244.48
21000	350.74	334.00	288.54	270.73	262.88	259.25	257.53	256.71
22000	367.44	349.91	302.28	283.62	275.40	271.60	269.80	268.93
23000	384.14	365.81	316.02	296.51	287.92	283.94	282.06	281.16
24000	400.84	381.72	329.76	309.41	300.44	296.29	294.32	293.38
25000	417.55	397.62	343.50	322.30	312.96	308.63	306.58	305.60
26000	434.25	413.53	357.24	335.19	325.47	320.98	318.85	317.83
27000	450.95	429.43	370.98	348.08	337.99	333.32	331.11	330.05
28000	467.65	445.33	384.72	360.97	350.51	345.67	343.37	342.28
29000	484.35	461.24	398.46	373.86	363.03	358.01	355.64	354.50
30000	501.05	477.14	412.20	386.76	375.55	370.36	367.90	366.72
31000	517.76	493.05	425.94	399.65	388.06	382.70	380.16	378.95
32000	534.46	508.95	439.68	412.54	400.58	395.05	392.43	391.17
33000	551.16	524.86	453.42	425.43	413.10	407.39	404.69	403.40
34000	567.86	540.76	467.16	438.32	425.62	419.74	416.95	415.62
35000	584.56	556.67	480.90	451.21	438.14	432.08	429.22	427.84
40000	668.07	636.19	549.60	515.67	500.73	493.81	490.53	488.96
45000	751.58	715.71	618.30	580.13	563.32	555.53	551.85	550.08
50000	835.09	795.24	687.00	644.59	625.91	617.26	613.16	611.20
55000	918.59	874.76	755.70	709.05	688.50	678.99	674.48	672.32
60000	1002.10	954.28	824.40	773.51	751.09	740.71	735.80	733.44
65000	1085.61	1033.81	893.10	837.96	813.68	802.44	797.11	794.56
70000	1169.12	1113.33	961.80	902.42	876.27	864.16	858.43	855.68
75000	1252.63	1192.85	1030.50	966.88	938.86	925.89	919.74	916.80
80000	1336.14	1272.37	1099.20	1031.34	1001.45	987.61	981.06	977.92
85000	1419.64	1351.90	1167.90	1095.80	1064.04	1049.34	1042.38	1039.04
90000	1503.15	1431.42	1236.60	1160.26	1126.63	1111.06	1103.69	1100.16
95000	1586.66	1510.94	1305.30	1224.71	1189.22	1172.79	1165.01	1161.28
100000	1670.17	1590.47	1374.00	1289.17	1251.81	1234.51	1226.32	1222.40
105000	1753.68	1669.99	1442.70	1353.63	1314.40	1296.24	1287.64	1283.52
110000	1837.18	1749.51	1511.40	1418.09	1376.99	1357.97	1348.96	1344.64
115000	1920.69	1829.04	1580.10	1482.55	1439.58	1419.69	1410.27	1405.76
120000	2004.20	1908.56	1648.80	1547.01	1502.17	1481.42	1471.59	1466.88
125000	2087.71	1988.08	1717.50	1611.46	1564.76	1543.14	1532.90	1528.00
130000	2171.22	2067.61	1786.19	1675.92	1627.35	1604.87	1594.22	1589.12
135000	2254.73	2147.13	1854.89	1740.38	1689.94	1666.59	1655.53	1650.24
140000	2338.23	2226.65	1923.59	1804.84	1752.53	1728.32	1716.85	1711.36
145000	2421.74	2306.18	1992.29	1869.30	1815.12	1790.04	1778.17	1772.48
150000	2505.25	2385.70	2060.99	1933.76	1877.71	1851.77	1839.48	1833.60
155000	2588.76	2465.22	2129.69	1998.21	1940.30	1913.49	1900.80	1894.72
160000	2672.27	2544.74	2198.39	2062.67	2002.89	1975.22	1962.11	1955.84

MONTHLY AMORTIZING PAYMENTS

AMOUNT OF LOAN	NUMBER OF YEARS IN TERM							
	1	2	3	4	5	6	7	8
$ 50	4.51	2.42	1.73	1.39	1.19	1.06	.96	.90
100	9.02	4.84	3.46	2.78	2.37	2.11	1.92	1.79
200	18.03	9.68	6.91	5.55	4.74	4.21	3.84	3.57
300	27.05	14.52	10.37	8.32	7.10	6.31	5.75	5.35
400	36.06	19.35	13.82	11.09	9.47	8.41	7.67	7.13
500	45.08	24.19	17.28	13.86	11.83	10.51	9.58	8.91
600	54.09	29.03	20.73	16.63	14.20	12.61	11.50	10.69
700	63.10	33.86	24.19	19.40	16.57	14.71	13.41	12.47
800	72.12	38.70	27.64	22.17	18.93	16.81	15.33	14.25
900	81.13	43.54	31.09	24.94	21.30	18.91	17.25	16.03
1000	90.15	48.37	34.55	27.71	23.66	21.01	19.16	17.81
2000	180.29	96.74	69.09	55.41	47.32	42.02	38.32	35.61
3000	270.43	145.11	103.63	83.12	70.98	63.03	57.48	53.41
4000	360.57	193.48	138.18	110.82	94.64	84.04	76.63	71.21
5000	450.71	241.84	172.72	138.53	118.30	105.05	95.79	89.01
6000	540.85	290.21	207.26	166.23	141.96	126.06	114.95	106.81
7000	630.99	338.58	241.81	193.93	165.62	147.07	134.10	124.61
8000	721.13	386.95	276.35	221.64	189.28	168.08	153.26	142.41
9000	811.27	435.32	310.89	249.34	212.94	189.09	172.42	160.21
10000	901.41	483.68	345.44	277.05	236.59	210.10	191.57	178.02
11000	991.55	532.05	379.98	304.75	260.25	231.11	210.73	195.82
12000	1081.69	580.42	414.52	332.46	283.91	252.12	229.89	213.62
13000	1171.83	628.79	449.06	360.16	307.57	273.13	249.04	231.42
14000	1261.97	677.16	483.61	387.86	331.23	294.14	268.20	249.22
15000	1352.11	725.52	518.15	415.57	354.89	315.15	287.36	267.02
16000	1442.25	773.89	552.69	443.27	378.55	336.16	306.51	284.82
17000	1532.39	822.26	587.24	470.98	402.21	357.17	325.67	302.62
18000	1622.53	870.63	621.78	498.68	425.87	378.18	344.83	320.42
19000	1712.67	919.00	656.32	526.38	449.52	399.19	363.98	338.22
20000	1802.81	967.36	690.87	554.09	473.18	420.19	383.14	356.03
21000	1892.95	1015.73	725.41	581.79	496.84	441.20	402.30	373.83
22000	1983.09	1064.10	759.95	609.50	520.50	462.21	421.45	391.63
23000	2073.23	1112.47	794.49	637.20	544.16	483.22	440.61	409.43
24000	2163.37	1160.84	829.04	664.91	567.82	504.23	459.77	427.23
25000	2253.51	1209.20	863.58	692.61	591.48	525.24	478.92	445.03
26000	2343.66	1257.57	898.12	720.31	615.14	546.25	498.08	462.83
27000	2433.80	1305.94	932.67	748.02	638.80	567.26	517.24	480.63
28000	2523.94	1354.31	967.21	775.72	662.45	588.27	536.39	498.43
29000	2614.08	1402.68	1001.75	803.43	686.11	609.28	555.55	516.23
30000	2704.22	1451.04	1036.30	831.13	709.77	630.29	574.71	534.04
31000	2794.36	1499.41	1070.84	858.83	733.43	651.30	593.86	551.84
32000	2884.50	1547.78	1105.38	886.54	757.09	672.31	613.02	569.64
33000	2974.64	1596.15	1139.92	914.24	780.75	693.32	632.18	587.44
34000	3064.78	1644.52	1174.47	941.95	804.41	714.33	651.33	605.24
35000	3154.92	1692.88	1209.01	969.65	828.07	735.34	670.49	623.04
40000	3605.62	1934.72	1381.73	1108.17	946.36	840.38	766.28	712.05
45000	4056.32	2176.56	1554.44	1246.69	1064.66	945.43	862.06	801.05
50000	4507.02	2418.40	1727.16	1385.21	1182.95	1050.48	957.84	890.06
55000	4957.73	2660.24	1899.87	1523.74	1301.24	1155.53	1053.63	979.06
60000	5408.43	2902.08	2072.59	1662.26	1419.54	1260.57	1149.41	1068.07
65000	5859.13	3143.92	2245.30	1800.78	1537.83	1365.62	1245.19	1157.07
70000	6309.83	3385.76	2418.02	1939.30	1656.13	1470.67	1340.98	1246.08
75000	6760.53	3627.60	2590.73	2077.82	1774.42	1575.72	1436.76	1335.08
80000	7211.24	3869.44	2763.45	2216.34	1892.72	1680.76	1532.55	1424.09
85000	7661.94	4111.28	2936.16	2354.86	2011.01	1785.81	1628.33	1513.09
90000	8112.64	4353.12	3108.88	2493.38	2129.31	1890.86	1724.11	1602.10
95000	8563.34	4594.96	3281.59	2631.90	2247.60	1995.91	1819.90	1691.10
100000	9014.04	4836.80	3454.31	2770.42	2365.90	2100.95	1915.68	1780.11
105000	9464.75	5078.64	3627.02	2908.94	2484.19	2206.00	2011.46	1869.11
110000	9915.45	5320.48	3799.74	3047.47	2602.48	2311.05	2107.25	1958.12
115000	10366.15	5562.32	3972.45	3185.99	2720.78	2416.10	2203.03	2047.12
120000	10816.85	5804.16	4145.17	3324.51	2839.07	2521.14	2298.82	2136.13
125000	11267.55	6046.00	4317.88	3463.03	2957.37	2626.19	2394.60	2225.13
130000	11718.26	6287.84	4490.60	3601.55	3075.66	2731.24	2490.38	2314.14
135000	12168.96	6529.68	4663.31	3740.07	3193.96	2836.29	2586.17	2403.14
140000	12619.66	6771.52	4836.03	3878.59	3312.25	2941.33	2681.95	2492.15
145000	13070.36	7013.36	5008.74	4017.11	3430.55	3046.38	2777.74	2581.15
150000	13521.06	7255.20	5181.46	4155.63	3548.84	3151.43	2873.52	2670.16
155000	13971.76	7497.04	5354.17	4294.15	3667.14	3256.47	2969.30	2759.17
160000	14422.47	7738.88	5526.89	4432.67	3785.43	3361.52	3065.09	2848.17

AMOUNT OF LOAN	NUMBER OF YEARS IN TERM 9	10	15	20	25	30	35	40
$ 50	.84	.80	.70	.65	.64	.63	.62	.62
100	1.68	1.60	1.39	1.30	1.27	1.25	1.24	1.24
200	3.36	3.20	2.77	2.60	2.53	2.49	2.48	2.47
300	5.04	4.80	4.15	3.90	3.79	3.74	3.71	3.70
400	6.72	6.40	5.54	5.20	5.05	4.98	4.95	4.94
500	8.39	8.00	6.92	6.50	6.31	6.23	6.19	6.17
600	10.07	9.59	8.30	7.80	7.57	7.47	7.42	7.40
700	11.75	11.19	9.68	9.09	8.84	8.72	8.66	8.63
800	13.43	12.79	11.07	10.39	10.10	9.96	9.90	9.87
900	15.10	14.39	12.45	11.69	11.36	11.21	11.13	11.10
1000	16.78	15.99	13.83	12.99	12.62	12.45	12.37	12.33
2000	33.56	31.97	27.66	25.97	25.23	24.89	24.73	24.66
3000	50.33	47.95	41.48	38.96	37.85	37.34	37.10	36.99
4000	67.11	63.93	55.31	51.94	50.46	49.78	49.46	49.31
5000	83.88	79.91	69.13	64.92	63.08	62.23	61.83	61.64
6000	100.66	95.89	82.96	77.91	75.69	74.67	74.19	73.97
7000	117.43	111.87	96.78	90.89	88.31	87.12	86.56	86.29
8000	134.21	127.85	110.61	103.87	100.92	99.56	98.92	98.62
9000	150.99	143.83	124.43	116.86	113.54	112.01	111.29	110.95
10000	167.76	159.81	138.26	129.84	126.15	124.45	123.65	123.27
11000	184.54	175.79	152.08	142.82	138.77	136.90	136.02	135.60
12000	201.31	191.77	165.91	155.81	151.38	149.34	148.38	147.93
13000	218.09	207.75	179.73	168.79	164.00	161.79	160.75	160.25
14000	234.86	223.74	193.56	181.77	176.61	174.23	173.11	172.58
15000	251.64	239.72	207.38	194.76	189.22	186.68	185.48	184.91
16000	268.42	255.70	221.21	207.74	201.84	199.12	197.84	197.23
17000	285.19	271.68	235.03	220.73	214.45	211.57	210.21	209.56
18000	301.97	287.66	248.86	233.71	227.07	224.01	222.57	221.89
19000	318.74	303.64	262.68	246.69	239.68	236.46	234.94	234.21
20000	335.52	319.62	276.51	259.68	252.30	248.90	247.30	246.54
21000	352.29	335.60	290.33	272.66	264.91	261.34	259.66	258.87
22000	369.07	351.58	304.16	285.64	277.53	273.79	272.03	271.19
23000	385.85	367.56	317.98	298.63	290.14	286.23	284.39	283.52
24000	402.62	383.54	331.81	311.61	302.76	298.68	296.76	295.85
25000	419.40	399.52	345.63	324.59	315.37	311.12	309.12	308.17
26000	436.17	415.50	359.46	337.58	327.99	323.57	321.49	320.50
27000	452.95	431.49	373.28	350.56	340.60	336.01	333.85	332.83
28000	469.72	447.47	387.11	363.54	353.22	348.46	346.22	345.15
29000	486.50	463.45	400.93	376.53	365.83	360.90	358.58	357.48
30000	503.28	479.43	414.76	389.51	378.44	373.35	370.95	369.81
31000	520.05	495.41	428.58	402.50	391.06	385.79	383.31	382.13
32000	536.83	511.39	442.41	415.48	403.67	398.24	395.68	394.46
33000	553.60	527.37	456.23	428.46	416.29	410.68	408.04	406.79
34000	570.38	543.35	470.06	441.45	428.90	423.13	420.41	419.11
35000	587.15	559.33	483.88	454.43	441.52	435.57	432.77	431.44
40000	671.03	639.23	553.01	519.35	504.59	497.80	494.59	493.07
45000	754.91	719.14	622.13	584.26	567.66	560.02	556.42	554.71
50000	838.79	799.04	691.26	649.18	630.74	622.24	618.24	616.34
55000	922.67	878.95	760.38	714.10	693.81	684.47	680.07	677.97
60000	1006.55	958.85	829.51	779.02	756.88	746.69	741.89	739.61
65000	1090.43	1038.75	898.63	843.94	819.96	808.91	803.71	801.24
70000	1174.30	1118.66	967.76	908.85	883.03	871.14	865.54	862.87
75000	1258.18	1198.56	1036.88	973.77	946.10	933.36	927.36	924.51
80000	1342.06	1278.46	1106.01	1038.69	1009.18	995.59	989.18	986.14
85000	1425.94	1358.37	1175.13	1103.61	1072.25	1057.81	1051.01	1047.77
90000	1509.82	1438.27	1244.26	1168.52	1135.32	1120.03	1112.83	1109.41
95000	1593.70	1518.18	1313.38	1233.44	1198.40	1182.26	1174.66	1171.04
100000	1677.58	1598.08	1382.51	1298.36	1261.47	1244.48	1236.48	1232.67
105000	1761.45	1677.98	1451.63	1363.28	1324.54	1306.70	1298.30	1294.31
110000	1845.33	1757.89	1520.76	1428.20	1387.62	1368.93	1360.13	1355.94
115000	1929.21	1837.79	1589.88	1493.11	1450.69	1431.15	1421.95	1417.57
120000	2013.09	1917.69	1659.01	1558.03	1513.76	1493.38	1483.77	1479.21
125000	2096.97	1997.60	1728.13	1622.95	1576.84	1555.60	1545.60	1540.84
130000	2180.85	2077.50	1797.26	1687.87	1639.91	1617.82	1607.42	1602.47
135000	2264.73	2157.41	1866.39	1752.78	1702.98	1680.05	1669.25	1664.11
140000	2348.60	2237.31	1935.51	1817.70	1766.06	1742.27	1731.07	1725.74
145000	2432.48	2317.21	2004.64	1882.62	1829.13	1804.49	1792.89	1787.37
150000	2516.36	2397.12	2073.76	1947.54	1892.20	1866.72	1854.72	1849.01
155000	2600.24	2477.02	2142.89	2012.46	1955.28	1928.94	1916.54	1910.64
160000	2684.12	2556.92	2212.01	2077.37	2018.35	1991.17	1978.36	1972.27

MONTHLY AMORTIZING PAYMENTS

AMOUNT OF LOAN	NUMBER OF YEARS IN TERM							
	1	2	3	4	5	6	7	8
$ 50	4.51	2.43	1.74	1.39	1.19	1.06	.97	.90
100	9.02	4.85	3.47	2.78	2.38	2.11	1.93	1.79
200	18.04	9.69	6.93	5.56	4.75	4.22	3.85	3.58
300	27.06	14.53	10.39	8.34	7.12	6.33	5.77	5.37
400	36.08	19.38	13.85	11.11	9.49	8.44	7.70	7.15
500	45.10	24.22	17.31	13.89	11.87	10.54	9.62	8.94
600	54.12	29.06	20.77	16.67	14.24	12.65	11.54	10.73
700	63.14	33.90	24.23	19.44	16.61	14.76	13.46	12.52
800	72.16	38.75	27.69	22.22	18.98	16.87	15.39	14.30
900	81.18	43.59	31.15	25.00	21.36	18.97	17.31	16.09
1000	90.20	48.43	34.61	27.77	23.73	21.08	19.23	17.88
2000	180.40	96.86	69.21	55.54	47.45	42.16	38.46	35.75
3000	270.60	145.29	103.82	83.31	71.18	63.24	57.69	53.62
4000	360.80	193.71	138.42	111.07	94.90	84.31	76.91	71.50
5000	451.00	242.14	173.03	138.84	118.63	105.39	96.14	89.37
6000	541.20	290.57	207.63	166.61	142.35	126.47	115.37	107.24
7000	631.40	339.00	242.23	194.38	166.08	147.55	134.59	125.12
8000	721.60	387.42	276.84	222.14	189.80	168.62	153.82	142.99
9000	811.80	435.85	311.44	249.91	213.52	189.70	173.05	160.86
10000	902.00	484.28	346.05	277.68	237.25	210.78	192.27	178.74
11000	992.20	532.71	380.65	305.45	260.97	231.85	211.50	196.61
12000	1082.40	581.13	415.25	333.21	284.70	252.93	230.73	214.48
13000	1172.60	629.56	449.86	360.98	308.42	274.01	249.95	232.36
14000	1262.80	677.99	484.46	388.75	332.15	295.09	269.18	250.23
15000	1353.00	726.41	519.07	416.52	355.87	316.16	288.41	268.10
16000	1443.19	774.84	553.67	444.28	379.59	337.24	307.63	285.98
17000	1533.39	823.27	588.28	472.05	403.32	358.32	326.86	303.85
18000	1623.59	871.70	622.88	499.82	427.04	379.39	346.09	321.72
19000	1713.79	920.12	657.48	527.59	450.77	400.47	365.31	339.59
20000	1803.99	968.55	692.09	555.35	474.49	421.55	384.54	357.47
21000	1894.19	1016.98	726.69	583.12	498.22	442.63	403.77	375.34
22000	1984.39	1065.41	761.30	610.89	521.94	463.70	422.99	393.21
23000	2074.59	1113.83	795.90	638.66	545.67	484.78	442.22	411.09
24000	2164.79	1162.26	830.50	666.42	569.39	505.86	461.45	428.96
25000	2254.99	1210.69	865.11	694.19	593.11	526.93	480.67	446.83
26000	2345.19	1259.11	899.71	721.96	616.84	548.01	499.90	464.71
27000	2435.39	1307.54	934.32	749.73	640.56	569.09	519.13	482.58
28000	2525.59	1355.97	968.92	777.49	664.29	590.17	538.35	500.45
29000	2615.79	1404.40	1003.53	805.26	688.01	611.24	557.58	518.33
30000	2705.99	1452.82	1038.13	833.03	711.74	632.32	576.81	536.20
31000	2796.18	1501.25	1072.73	860.80	735.46	653.40	596.03	554.07
32000	2886.38	1549.68	1107.34	888.56	759.18	674.48	615.26	571.95
33000	2976.58	1598.11	1141.94	916.33	782.91	695.55	634.49	589.82
34000	3066.78	1646.53	1176.55	944.10	806.63	716.63	653.71	607.69
35000	3156.98	1694.96	1211.15	971.86	830.36	737.71	672.94	625.57
40000	3607.98	1937.10	1384.17	1110.70	948.98	843.09	769.07	714.93
45000	4058.98	2179.23	1557.19	1249.54	1067.60	948.48	865.21	804.30
50000	4509.97	2421.37	1730.21	1388.38	1186.22	1053.86	961.34	893.66
55000	4960.97	2663.51	1903.23	1527.21	1304.85	1159.25	1057.47	983.03
60000	5411.97	2905.64	2076.25	1666.05	1423.47	1264.64	1153.61	1072.39
65000	5862.96	3147.78	2249.27	1804.89	1542.09	1370.02	1249.74	1161.76
70000	6313.96	3389.91	2422.30	1943.72	1660.71	1475.41	1345.87	1251.13
75000	6764.96	3632.05	2595.32	2082.56	1779.33	1580.79	1442.01	1340.49
80000	7215.95	3874.19	2768.34	2221.40	1897.95	1686.18	1538.14	1429.86
85000	7666.95	4116.32	2941.36	2360.24	2016.58	1791.57	1634.27	1519.22
90000	8117.95	4358.46	3114.38	2499.07	2135.20	1896.95	1730.41	1608.59
95000	8568.94	4600.60	3287.40	2637.91	2253.82	2002.34	1826.54	1697.95
100000	9019.94	4842.73	3460.42	2776.75	2372.44	2107.72	1922.67	1787.32
105000	9470.94	5084.87	3633.44	2915.58	2491.06	2213.11	2018.81	1876.69
110000	9921.93	5327.01	3806.46	3054.42	2609.69	2318.50	2114.94	1966.05
115000	10372.93	5569.14	3979.48	3193.26	2728.31	2423.88	2211.07	2055.42
120000	10823.93	5811.28	4152.50	3332.10	2846.93	2529.27	2307.21	2144.78
125000	11274.92	6053.41	4325.52	3470.93	2965.55	2634.65	2403.34	2234.15
130000	11725.92	6295.55	4498.54	3609.77	3084.17	2740.04	2499.47	2323.51
135000	12176.92	6537.69	4671.56	3748.61	3202.79	2845.43	2595.61	2412.88
140000	12627.91	6779.82	4844.59	3887.44	3321.42	2950.81	2691.74	2502.25
145000	13078.91	7021.96	5017.61	4026.28	3440.04	3056.20	2787.88	2591.61
150000	13529.91	7264.10	5190.63	4165.12	3558.66	3161.58	2884.01	2680.98
155000	13980.90	7506.23	5363.65	4303.96	3677.28	3266.97	2980.14	2770.34
160000	14431.90	7748.37	5536.67	4442.79	3795.90	3372.36	3076.28	2859.71

AMOUNT OF LOAN	NUMBER OF YEARS IN TERM							
	9	10	15	20	25	30	35	40
$ 50	.85	.81	.70	.66	.64	.63	.63	.63
100	1.69	1.61	1.40	1.31	1.28	1.26	1.25	1.25
200	3.37	3.22	2.79	2.62	2.55	2.51	2.50	2.49
300	5.06	4.82	4.18	3.93	3.82	3.77	3.74	3.73
400	6.74	6.43	5.57	5.24	5.09	5.02	4.99	4.98
500	8.43	8.03	6.96	6.54	6.36	6.28	6.24	6.22
600	10.11	9.64	8.35	7.85	7.63	7.53	7.48	7.46
700	11.80	11.24	9.74	9.16	8.90	8.79	8.73	8.71
800	13.48	12.85	11.13	10.47	10.17	10.04	9.98	9.95
900	15.17	14.46	12.52	11.77	11.45	11.30	11.22	11.19
1000	16.85	16.06	13.92	13.08	12.72	12.55	12.47	12.43
2000	33.70	32.12	27.83	26.16	25.43	25.09	24.94	24.86
3000	50.55	48.18	41.74	39.23	38.14	37.64	37.40	37.29
4000	67.40	64.23	55.65	52.31	50.85	50.18	49.87	49.72
5000	84.25	80.29	69.56	65.38	63.56	62.73	62.34	62.15
6000	101.10	96.35	83.47	78.46	76.27	75.27	74.80	74.58
7000	117.95	112.40	97.38	91.53	88.98	87.82	87.27	87.01
8000	134.80	128.46	111.29	104.61	101.70	100.36	99.74	99.44
9000	151.65	144.52	125.20	117.69	114.41	112.91	112.20	111.87
10000	168.50	160.58	139.11	130.76	127.12	125.45	124.67	124.30
11000	185.35	176.63	153.02	143.84	139.83	137.99	137.14	136.73
12000	202.20	192.69	166.93	156.91	152.54	150.54	149.60	149.16
13000	219.05	208.75	180.84	169.99	165.25	163.08	162.07	161.59
14000	235.90	224.80	194.75	183.06	177.96	175.63	174.53	174.02
15000	252.75	240.86	208.66	196.14	190.68	188.17	187.00	186.45
16000	269.60	256.92	222.57	209.22	203.39	200.72	199.47	198.88
17000	286.45	272.97	236.48	222.29	216.10	213.26	211.93	211.31
18000	303.30	289.03	250.39	235.37	228.81	225.81	224.40	223.73
19000	320.15	305.09	264.30	248.44	241.52	238.35	236.87	236.16
20000	337.00	321.15	278.21	261.52	254.23	250.90	249.33	248.59
21000	353.85	337.20	292.12	274.59	266.94	263.44	261.80	261.02
22000	370.70	353.26	306.03	287.67	279.66	275.98	274.27	273.45
23000	387.55	369.32	319.94	300.74	292.37	288.53	286.73	285.88
24000	404.40	385.37	333.85	313.82	305.08	301.07	299.20	298.31
25000	421.25	401.43	347.76	326.90	317.79	313.62	311.66	310.74
26000	438.10	417.49	361.67	339.97	330.50	326.16	324.13	323.17
27000	454.95	433.54	375.58	353.05	343.21	338.71	336.60	335.60
28000	471.80	449.60	389.49	366.12	355.92	351.25	349.06	348.03
29000	488.65	465.66	403.41	379.20	368.64	363.80	361.53	360.46
30000	505.50	481.72	417.32	392.27	381.35	376.34	374.00	372.89
31000	522.35	497.77	431.23	405.35	394.06	388.89	386.46	385.32
32000	539.20	513.83	445.14	418.43	406.77	401.43	398.93	397.75
33000	556.05	529.89	459.05	431.50	419.48	413.97	411.40	410.18
34000	572.90	545.94	472.96	444.58	432.19	426.52	423.86	422.61
35000	589.75	562.00	486.87	457.65	444.90	439.06	436.33	435.04
40000	674.00	642.29	556.42	523.03	508.46	501.79	498.66	497.18
45000	758.25	722.57	625.97	588.41	572.02	564.51	560.99	559.33
50000	842.50	802.86	695.52	653.79	635.57	627.23	623.32	621.48
55000	926.75	883.14	765.07	719.16	699.13	689.95	685.66	683.62
60000	1011.00	963.43	834.63	784.54	762.69	752.68	747.99	745.77
65000	1095.25	1043.71	904.18	849.92	826.25	815.40	810.32	807.92
70000	1179.50	1124.00	973.73	915.30	889.80	878.12	872.65	870.07
75000	1263.75	1204.28	1043.28	980.68	953.36	940.85	934.98	932.21
80000	1348.00	1284.57	1112.83	1046.06	1016.92	1003.57	997.32	994.36
85000	1432.25	1364.85	1182.39	1111.43	1080.47	1066.29	1059.65	1056.51
90000	1516.50	1445.14	1251.94	1176.81	1144.03	1129.01	1121.98	1118.65
95000	1600.75	1525.42	1321.49	1242.19	1207.59	1191.74	1184.31	1180.80
100000	1685.00	1605.71	1391.04	1307.57	1271.14	1254.46	1246.64	1242.95
105000	1769.25	1685.99	1460.59	1372.95	1334.70	1317.18	1308.98	1305.10
110000	1853.50	1766.28	1530.14	1438.32	1398.26	1379.90	1371.31	1367.24
115000	1937.75	1846.56	1599.70	1503.70	1461.82	1442.63	1433.64	1429.39
120000	2022.00	1926.85	1669.25	1569.08	1525.37	1505.35	1495.97	1491.54
125000	2106.25	2007.13	1738.80	1634.46	1588.93	1568.07	1558.30	1553.68
130000	2190.50	2087.42	1808.35	1699.84	1652.49	1630.80	1620.64	1615.83
135000	2274.75	2167.70	1877.90	1765.22	1716.04	1693.52	1682.97	1677.98
140000	2359.00	2247.99	1947.45	1830.59	1779.60	1756.24	1745.30	1740.13
145000	2443.25	2328.27	2017.01	1895.97	1843.16	1818.96	1807.63	1802.27
150000	2527.50	2408.56	2086.56	1961.35	1906.71	1881.69	1869.96	1864.42
155000	2611.75	2488.85	2156.11	2026.73	1970.27	1944.41	1932.30	1926.57
160000	2696.00	2569.13	2225.66	2092.11	2033.83	2007.13	1994.63	1988.71

MONTHLY AMORTIZING PAYMENTS

AMOUNT OF LOAN	NUMBER OF YEARS IN TERM							
	1	2	3	4	5	6	7	8
$ 50	4.52	2.43	1.74	1.40	1.19	1.06	.97	.90
100	9.03	4.85	3.47	2.79	2.38	2.12	1.93	1.80
200	18.06	9.70	6.94	5.57	4.76	4.23	3.86	3.59
300	27.08	14.55	10.40	8.35	7.14	6.35	5.79	5.39
400	36.11	19.40	13.87	11.14	9.52	8.46	7.72	7.18
500	45.13	24.25	17.34	13.92	11.90	10.58	9.65	8.98
600	54.16	29.10	20.80	16.70	14.28	12.69	11.58	10.77
700	63.19	33.95	24.27	19.49	16.66	14.81	13.51	12.57
800	72.21	38.79	27.74	22.27	19.04	16.92	15.44	14.36
900	81.24	43.64	31.20	25.05	21.42	19.04	17.37	16.16
1000	90.26	48.49	34.67	27.84	23.79	21.15	19.30	17.95
2000	180.52	96.98	69.34	55.67	47.58	42.30	38.60	35.90
3000	270.78	145.46	104.00	83.50	71.37	63.44	57.90	53.84
4000	361.04	193.95	138.67	111.33	95.16	84.59	77.19	71.79
5000	451.30	242.44	173.33	139.16	118.95	105.73	96.49	89.73
6000	541.55	290.92	208.00	166.99	142.74	126.88	115.79	107.68
7000	631.81	339.41	242.66	194.82	166.53	148.02	135.08	125.62
8000	722.07	387.90	277.33	222.65	190.32	169.17	154.38	143.57
9000	812.33	436.38	311.99	250.48	214.11	190.31	173.68	161.51
10000	902.59	484.87	346.66	278.31	237.90	211.46	192.97	179.46
11000	992.85	533.36	381.32	306.14	261.69	232.60	212.27	197.40
12000	1083.10	581.84	415.99	333.97	285.48	253.75	231.57	215.35
13000	1173.36	630.33	450.65	361.80	309.27	274.89	250.86	233.30
14000	1263.62	678.82	485.32	389.64	333.06	296.04	270.16	251.24
15000	1353.88	727.30	519.98	417.47	356.85	317.18	289.46	269.19
16000	1444.14	775.79	554.65	445.30	380.64	338.33	308.75	287.13
17000	1534.40	824.28	589.32	473.13	404.43	359.47	328.05	305.08
18000	1624.65	872.76	623.98	500.96	428.22	380.62	347.35	323.02
19000	1714.91	921.25	658.65	528.79	452.01	401.76	366.64	340.97
20000	1805.17	969.74	693.31	556.62	475.80	422.91	385.94	358.91
21000	1895.43	1018.22	727.98	584.45	499.59	444.05	405.24	376.86
22000	1985.69	1066.71	762.64	612.28	523.38	465.20	424.53	394.80
23000	2075.95	1115.20	797.31	640.11	547.17	486.34	443.83	412.75
24000	2166.20	1163.68	831.97	667.94	570.96	507.49	463.13	430.69
25000	2256.46	1212.17	866.64	695.77	594.75	528.63	482.42	448.64
26000	2346.72	1260.66	901.30	723.60	618.54	549.78	501.72	466.59
27000	2436.98	1309.14	935.97	751.44	642.33	570.92	521.02	484.53
28000	2527.24	1357.63	970.63	779.27	666.12	592.07	540.31	502.48
29000	2617.50	1406.12	1005.30	807.10	689.91	613.21	559.61	520.42
30000	2707.75	1454.60	1039.96	834.93	713.70	634.36	578.91	538.37
31000	2798.01	1503.09	1074.63	862.76	737.49	655.50	598.20	556.31
32000	2888.27	1551.58	1109.30	890.59	761.28	676.65	617.50	574.26
33000	2978.53	1600.06	1143.96	918.42	785.07	697.79	636.80	592.20
34000	3068.79	1648.55	1178.63	946.25	808.86	718.94	656.09	610.15
35000	3159.05	1697.04	1213.29	974.08	832.65	740.08	675.39	628.09
40000	3610.34	1939.47	1386.62	1113.23	951.60	845.81	771.88	717.82
45000	4061.63	2181.90	1559.94	1252.39	1070.55	951.53	868.36	807.55
50000	4512.92	2424.34	1733.27	1391.54	1189.50	1057.26	964.84	897.28
55000	4964.21	2666.77	1906.60	1530.70	1308.45	1162.98	1061.33	987.00
60000	5415.50	2909.20	2079.92	1669.85	1427.40	1268.71	1157.81	1076.73
65000	5866.80	3151.64	2253.25	1809.00	1546.35	1374.43	1254.29	1166.46
70000	6318.09	3394.07	2426.58	1948.16	1665.30	1480.16	1350.78	1256.18
75000	6769.38	3636.50	2599.90	2087.31	1784.25	1585.88	1447.26	1345.91
80000	7220.67	3878.94	2773.23	2226.46	1903.20	1691.61	1543.75	1435.64
85000	7671.96	4121.37	2946.56	2365.62	2022.15	1797.33	1640.23	1525.36
90000	8123.25	4363.80	3119.88	2504.77	2141.10	1903.06	1736.71	1615.09
95000	8574.54	4606.24	3293.21	2643.93	2260.05	2008.78	1833.20	1704.82
100000	9025.84	4848.67	3466.54	2783.08	2379.00	2114.51	1929.68	1794.55
105000	9477.13	5091.10	3639.86	2922.23	2497.95	2220.23	2026.16	1884.27
110000	9928.42	5333.54	3813.19	3061.39	2616.90	2325.96	2122.65	1974.00
115000	10379.71	5575.97	3986.52	3200.54	2735.85	2431.68	2219.13	2063.73
120000	10831.00	5818.40	4159.84	3339.69	2854.80	2537.41	2315.62	2153.45
125000	11282.29	6060.84	4333.17	3478.85	2973.75	2643.13	2412.10	2243.18
130000	11733.59	6303.27	4506.50	3618.00	3092.70	2748.86	2508.58	2332.91
135000	12184.88	6545.70	4679.82	3757.16	3211.65	2854.58	2605.07	2422.63
140000	12636.17	6788.14	4853.15	3896.31	3330.60	2960.31	2701.55	2512.36
145000	13087.46	7030.57	5026.48	4035.46	3449.54	3066.03	2798.03	2602.09
150000	13538.75	7273.00	5199.80	4174.62	3568.49	3171.76	2894.52	2691.82
155000	13990.04	7515.44	5373.13	4313.77	3687.44	3277.48	2991.00	2781.54
160000	14441.33	7757.87	5546.46	4452.92	3806.39	3383.21	3087.49	2871.27

AMOUNT OF LOAN	NUMBER OF YEARS IN TERM							
	9	10	15	20	25	30	35	40
$ 50	.85	.81	.70	.66	.65	.64	.63	.63
100	1.70	1.62	1.40	1.32	1.29	1.27	1.26	1.26
200	3.39	3.23	2.80	2.64	2.57	2.53	2.52	2.51
300	5.08	4.85	4.20	3.96	3.85	3.80	3.78	3.76
400	6.77	6.46	5.60	5.27	5.13	5.06	5.03	5.02
500	8.47	8.07	7.00	6.59	6.41	6.33	6.29	6.27
600	10.16	9.69	8.40	7.91	7.69	7.59	7.55	7.52
700	11.85	11.30	9.80	9.22	8.97	8.86	8.80	8.78
800	13.54	12.91	11.20	10.54	10.25	10.12	10.06	10.03
900	15.24	14.53	12.60	11.86	11.53	11.38	11.32	11.28
1000	16.93	16.14	14.00	13.17	12.81	12.65	12.57	12.54
2000	33.85	32.27	28.00	26.34	25.62	25.29	25.14	25.07
3000	50.78	48.41	41.99	39.51	38.43	37.94	37.71	37.60
4000	67.70	64.54	55.99	52.68	51.24	50.58	50.28	50.13
5000	84.63	80.67	69.98	65.84	64.05	63.23	62.85	62.67
6000	101.55	96.81	83.98	79.01	76.85	75.87	75.41	75.20
7000	118.48	112.94	97.98	92.18	89.66	88.52	87.98	87.73
8000	135.40	129.07	111.97	105.35	102.47	101.16	100.55	100.26
9000	152.32	145.21	125.97	118.52	115.28	113.80	113.12	112.80
10000	169.25	161.34	139.96	131.68	128.09	126.45	125.69	125.33
11000	186.17	177.47	153.96	144.85	140.90	139.09	138.25	137.86
12000	203.10	193.61	167.96	158.02	153.70	151.74	150.82	150.39
13000	220.02	209.74	181.95	171.19	166.51	164.38	163.39	162.92
14000	236.95	225.87	195.95	184.36	179.32	177.03	175.96	175.46
15000	253.87	242.01	209.94	197.52	192.13	189.67	188.53	187.99
16000	270.79	258.14	223.94	210.69	204.94	202.32	201.10	200.52
17000	287.72	274.27	237.93	223.86	217.75	214.96	213.66	213.05
18000	304.64	290.41	251.93	237.03	230.55	227.60	226.23	225.59
19000	321.57	306.54	265.93	250.20	243.36	240.25	238.80	238.12
20000	338.49	322.67	279.92	263.36	256.17	252.89	251.37	250.65
21000	355.42	338.81	293.92	276.53	268.98	265.54	263.94	263.18
22000	372.34	354.94	307.91	289.70	281.79	278.18	276.50	275.71
23000	389.26	371.08	321.91	302.87	294.60	290.83	289.07	288.25
24000	406.19	387.21	335.91	316.03	307.40	303.47	301.64	300.78
25000	423.11	403.34	349.90	329.20	320.21	316.12	314.21	313.31
26000	440.04	419.48	363.90	342.37	333.02	328.76	326.78	325.84
27000	456.96	435.61	377.89	355.54	345.83	341.40	339.34	338.38
28000	473.89	451.74	391.89	368.71	358.64	354.05	351.91	350.91
29000	490.81	467.88	405.89	381.87	371.45	366.69	364.48	363.44
30000	507.74	484.01	419.88	395.04	384.25	379.34	377.05	375.97
31000	524.66	500.14	433.88	408.21	397.06	391.98	389.62	388.50
32000	541.58	516.28	447.87	421.38	409.87	404.63	402.19	401.04
33000	558.51	532.41	461.87	434.55	422.68	417.27	414.75	413.57
34000	575.43	548.54	475.86	447.71	435.49	429.92	427.32	426.10
35000	592.36	564.68	489.86	460.88	448.30	442.56	439.89	438.63
40000	676.98	645.34	559.84	526.72	512.34	505.78	502.73	501.29
45000	761.60	726.01	629.82	592.56	576.38	569.00	565.57	563.96
50000	846.22	806.68	699.80	658.40	640.42	632.23	628.41	626.62
55000	930.84	887.35	769.78	724.24	704.46	695.45	691.25	689.28
60000	1015.47	968.01	839.76	790.08	768.50	758.67	754.09	751.94
65000	1100.09	1048.68	909.74	855.92	832.54	821.89	816.93	814.60
70000	1184.71	1129.35	979.72	921.76	896.59	885.12	879.77	877.26
75000	1269.33	1210.02	1049.70	987.60	960.63	948.34	942.61	939.92
80000	1353.95	1290.68	1119.67	1053.44	1024.67	1011.56	1005.46	1002.58
85000	1438.57	1371.35	1189.65	1119.28	1088.71	1074.78	1068.30	1065.25
90000	1523.20	1452.02	1259.63	1185.12	1152.75	1138.00	1131.14	1127.91
95000	1607.82	1532.69	1329.61	1250.96	1216.79	1201.23	1193.98	1190.57
100000	1692.44	1613.35	1399.59	1316.79	1280.84	1264.45	1256.82	1253.23
105000	1777.06	1694.02	1469.57	1382.63	1344.88	1327.67	1319.66	1315.89
110000	1861.68	1774.69	1539.55	1448.47	1408.92	1390.89	1382.50	1378.55
115000	1946.30	1855.36	1609.53	1514.31	1472.96	1454.12	1445.34	1441.21
120000	2030.93	1936.02	1679.51	1580.15	1537.00	1517.34	1508.18	1503.87
125000	2115.55	2016.69	1749.49	1645.99	1601.04	1580.56	1571.02	1566.54
130000	2200.17	2097.36	1819.47	1711.83	1665.08	1643.78	1633.86	1629.20
135000	2284.79	2178.03	1889.45	1777.67	1729.13	1707.00	1696.70	1691.86
140000	2369.41	2258.69	1959.43	1843.51	1793.17	1770.23	1759.54	1754.52
145000	2454.03	2339.36	2029.41	1909.35	1857.21	1833.45	1822.38	1817.18
150000	2538.66	2420.03	2099.39	1975.19	1921.25	1896.67	1885.22	1879.84
155000	2623.28	2500.70	2169.37	2041.03	1985.29	1959.89	1948.07	1942.50
160000	2707.90	2581.36	2239.34	2106.87	2049.33	2023.12	2010.91	2005.16

MONTHLY AMORTIZING PAYMENTS

AMOUNT OF LOAN	NUMBER OF YEARS IN TERM							
	1	2	3	4	5	6	7	8
$ 50	4.52	2.43	1.74	1.40	1.20	1.07	.97	.91
100	9.04	4.86	3.48	2.79	2.39	2.13	1.94	1.81
200	18.07	9.71	6.95	5.58	4.78	4.25	3.88	3.61
300	27.10	14.57	10.42	8.37	7.16	6.37	5.82	5.41
400	36.13	19.42	13.90	11.16	9.55	8.49	7.75	7.21
500	45.16	24.28	17.37	13.95	11.93	10.61	9.69	9.01
600	54.20	29.13	20.84	16.74	14.32	12.73	11.63	10.82
700	63.23	33.99	24.31	19.53	16.70	14.85	13.56	12.62
800	72.26	38.84	27.79	22.32	19.09	16.98	15.50	14.42
900	81.29	43.70	31.26	25.11	21.48	19.10	17.44	16.22
1000	90.32	48.55	34.73	27.90	23.86	21.22	19.37	18.02
2000	180.64	97.10	69.46	55.79	47.72	42.43	38.74	36.04
3000	270.96	145.64	104.18	83.69	71.57	63.64	58.11	54.06
4000	361.27	194.19	138.91	111.58	95.43	84.86	77.47	72.08
5000	451.59	242.74	173.64	139.48	119.28	106.07	96.84	90.09
6000	541.91	291.28	208.36	167.37	143.14	127.28	116.21	108.11
7000	632.23	339.83	243.09	195.26	166.99	148.50	135.57	126.13
8000	722.54	388.37	277.82	223.16	190.85	169.71	154.94	144.15
9000	812.86	436.92	312.54	251.05	214.71	190.92	174.31	162.17
10000	903.18	485.47	347.27	278.95	238.56	212.13	193.67	180.18
11000	993.50	534.01	382.00	306.84	262.42	233.35	213.04	198.20
12000	1083.81	582.56	416.72	334.73	286.27	254.56	232.41	216.22
13000	1174.13	631.10	451.45	362.63	310.13	275.77	251.78	234.24
14000	1264.45	679.65	486.18	390.52	333.98	296.99	271.14	252.25
15000	1354.76	728.20	520.90	418.42	357.84	318.20	290.51	270.27
16000	1445.08	776.74	555.63	446.31	381.69	339.41	309.88	288.29
17000	1535.40	825.29	590.36	474.21	405.55	360.63	329.24	306.31
18000	1625.72	873.83	625.08	502.10	429.41	381.84	348.61	324.33
19000	1716.03	922.38	659.81	529.99	453.26	403.05	367.98	342.34
20000	1806.35	970.93	694.54	557.89	477.12	424.26	387.34	360.36
21000	1896.67	1019.47	729.26	585.78	500.97	445.48	406.71	378.38
22000	1986.99	1068.02	763.99	613.68	524.83	466.69	426.08	396.40
23000	2077.30	1116.56	798.72	641.57	548.68	487.90	445.44	414.41
24000	2167.62	1165.11	833.44	669.46	572.54	509.12	464.81	432.43
25000	2257.94	1213.66	868.17	697.36	596.39	530.33	484.18	450.45
26000	2348.25	1262.20	902.90	725.25	620.25	551.54	503.55	468.47
27000	2438.57	1310.75	937.62	753.15	644.11	572.75	522.91	486.49
28000	2528.89	1359.29	972.35	781.04	667.96	593.97	542.28	504.50
29000	2619.21	1407.84	1007.08	808.94	691.82	615.18	561.65	522.52
30000	2709.52	1456.39	1041.80	836.83	715.67	636.39	581.01	540.54
31000	2799.84	1504.93	1076.53	864.72	739.53	657.61	600.38	558.56
32000	2890.16	1553.48	1111.26	892.62	763.38	678.82	619.75	576.58
33000	2980.48	1602.02	1145.98	920.51	787.24	700.03	639.11	594.59
34000	3070.79	1650.57	1180.71	948.41	811.10	721.25	658.48	612.61
35000	3161.11	1699.12	1215.44	976.30	834.95	742.46	677.85	630.63
40000	3612.70	1941.85	1389.07	1115.77	954.23	848.52	774.68	720.72
45000	4064.28	2184.58	1562.70	1255.24	1073.51	954.59	871.52	810.81
50000	4515.87	2427.31	1736.33	1394.71	1192.78	1060.65	968.35	900.90
55000	4967.46	2670.04	1909.97	1534.18	1312.06	1166.72	1065.19	990.98
60000	5419.04	2912.77	2083.60	1673.65	1431.34	1272.78	1162.02	1081.07
65000	5870.63	3155.50	2257.23	1813.12	1550.62	1378.85	1258.86	1171.16
70000	6322.22	3398.23	2430.87	1952.60	1669.90	1484.91	1355.69	1261.25
75000	6773.80	3640.96	2604.50	2092.07	1789.17	1590.98	1452.53	1351.34
80000	7225.39	3883.69	2778.13	2231.54	1908.45	1697.04	1549.36	1441.43
85000	7676.98	4126.42	2951.76	2371.01	2027.73	1803.11	1646.20	1531.52
90000	8128.56	4369.15	3125.40	2510.48	2147.01	1909.17	1743.03	1621.61
95000	8580.15	4611.88	3299.03	2649.95	2266.29	2015.24	1839.87	1711.70
100000	9031.74	4854.61	3472.66	2789.42	2385.56	2121.30	1936.70	1801.79
105000	9483.32	5097.34	3646.30	2928.89	2504.84	2227.37	2033.54	1891.88
110000	9934.91	5340.07	3819.93	3068.36	2624.12	2333.43	2130.37	1981.96
115000	10386.50	5582.80	3993.56	3207.83	2743.40	2439.49	2227.20	2072.05
120000	10838.08	5825.53	4167.19	3347.30	2862.68	2545.56	2324.04	2162.14
125000	11289.67	6068.26	4340.83	3486.77	2981.95	2651.62	2420.87	2252.23
130000	11741.25	6310.99	4514.46	3626.24	3101.23	2757.69	2517.71	2342.32
135000	12192.84	6553.72	4688.09	3765.72	3220.51	2863.75	2614.54	2432.41
140000	12644.43	6796.45	4861.73	3905.19	3339.79	2969.82	2711.38	2522.50
145000	13096.01	7039.18	5035.36	4044.66	3459.07	3075.88	2808.21	2612.59
150000	13547.60	7281.91	5208.99	4184.13	3578.34	3181.95	2905.05	2702.68
155000	13999.19	7524.64	5382.62	4323.60	3697.62	3288.01	3001.88	2792.77
160000	14450.77	7767.37	5556.26	4463.07	3816.90	3394.08	3098.72	2882.86

AMOUNT OF LOAN	NUMBER OF YEARS IN TERM							
	9	10	15	20	25	30	35	40
$ 50	.85	.82	.71	.67	.65	.64	.64	.64
100	1.70	1.63	1.41	1.33	1.30	1.28	1.27	1.27
200	3.40	3.25	2.82	2.66	2.59	2.55	2.54	2.53
300	5.10	4.87	4.23	3.98	3.88	3.83	3.81	3.80
400	6.80	6.49	5.64	5.31	5.17	5.10	5.07	5.06
500	8.50	8.11	7.05	6.64	6.46	6.38	6.34	6.32
600	10.20	9.73	8.45	7.96	7.75	7.65	7.61	7.59
700	11.90	11.35	9.86	9.29	9.04	8.93	8.87	8.85
800	13.60	12.97	11.27	10.61	10.33	10.20	10.14	10.11
900	15.30	14.59	12.68	11.94	11.62	11.48	11.41	11.38
1000	17.00	16.22	14.09	13.27	12.91	12.75	12.67	12.64
2000	34.00	32.43	28.17	26.53	25.82	25.49	25.34	25.28
3000	51.00	48.64	42.25	39.79	38.72	38.24	38.01	37.91
4000	68.00	64.85	56.33	53.05	51.63	50.98	50.68	50.55
5000	85.00	81.06	70.41	66.31	64.53	63.73	63.35	63.18
6000	102.00	97.27	84.49	79.57	77.44	76.47	76.02	75.82
7000	119.00	113.48	98.58	92.83	90.34	89.22	88.69	88.45
8000	136.00	129.69	112.66	106.09	103.25	101.96	101.36	101.09
9000	153.00	145.90	126.74	119.35	116.15	114.71	114.03	113.72
10000	169.99	162.11	140.82	132.61	129.06	127.45	126.70	126.36
11000	186.99	178.32	154.90	145.87	141.96	140.19	139.37	138.99
12000	203.99	194.53	168.98	159.13	154.87	152.94	152.04	151.63
13000	220.99	210.74	183.07	172.39	167.77	165.68	164.71	164.26
14000	237.99	226.95	197.15	185.65	180.68	178.43	177.38	176.90
15000	254.99	243.16	211.23	198.91	193.59	191.17	190.05	189.53
16000	271.99	259.37	225.31	212.17	206.49	203.92	202.72	202.17
17000	288.99	275.58	239.39	225.43	219.40	216.66	215.39	214.80
18000	305.99	291.79	253.47	238.69	232.30	229.41	228.06	227.44
19000	322.98	308.00	267.56	251.95	245.21	242.15	240.73	240.07
20000	339.98	324.21	281.64	265.21	258.11	254.89	253.40	252.71
21000	356.98	340.42	295.72	278.47	271.02	267.64	266.07	265.34
22000	373.98	356.63	309.80	291.73	283.92	280.38	278.74	277.98
23000	390.98	372.84	323.88	304.99	296.83	293.13	291.41	290.61
24000	407.98	389.05	337.96	318.25	309.73	305.87	304.08	303.25
25000	424.98	405.26	352.04	331.51	322.64	318.62	316.75	315.88
26000	441.98	421.47	366.13	344.77	335.54	331.36	329.42	328.52
27000	458.98	437.68	380.21	358.03	348.45	344.11	342.09	341.15
28000	475.97	453.89	394.29	371.29	361.36	356.85	354.76	353.79
29000	492.97	470.10	408.37	384.56	374.26	369.59	367.43	366.42
30000	509.97	486.31	422.45	397.82	387.17	382.34	380.10	379.06
31000	526.97	502.52	436.53	411.08	400.07	395.08	392.77	391.69
32000	543.97	518.73	450.62	424.34	412.98	407.83	405.44	404.33
33000	560.97	534.94	464.70	437.60	425.88	420.57	418.11	416.96
34000	577.97	551.15	478.78	450.86	438.79	433.32	430.78	429.60
35000	594.97	567.36	492.86	464.12	451.69	446.06	443.45	442.23
40000	679.96	648.41	563.27	530.42	516.22	509.78	506.80	505.41
45000	764.96	729.46	633.68	596.72	580.75	573.51	570.15	568.58
50000	849.95	810.51	704.08	663.02	645.27	637.23	633.50	631.76
55000	934.94	891.56	774.49	729.32	709.80	700.95	696.85	694.94
60000	1019.94	972.61	844.90	795.63	774.33	764.67	760.20	758.11
65000	1104.93	1053.66	915.31	861.93	838.85	828.39	823.55	821.29
70000	1189.93	1134.71	985.72	928.23	903.38	892.12	886.90	884.46
75000	1274.92	1215.76	1056.12	994.53	967.91	955.84	950.25	947.64
80000	1359.92	1296.82	1126.53	1060.83	1032.43	1019.56	1013.60	1010.81
85000	1444.91	1377.87	1196.94	1127.13	1096.96	1083.28	1076.95	1073.99
90000	1529.91	1458.92	1267.35	1193.44	1161.49	1147.01	1140.30	1137.16
95000	1614.90	1539.97	1337.76	1259.74	1226.01	1210.73	1203.65	1200.34
100000	1699.89	1621.02	1408.16	1326.04	1290.54	1274.45	1267.00	1263.52
105000	1784.89	1702.07	1478.57	1392.34	1355.07	1338.17	1330.35	1326.69
110000	1869.88	1783.12	1548.98	1458.64	1419.60	1401.90	1393.70	1389.87
115000	1954.88	1864.17	1619.39	1524.95	1484.12	1465.62	1457.05	1453.04
120000	2039.87	1945.22	1689.80	1591.25	1548.65	1529.34	1520.40	1516.22
125000	2124.87	2026.27	1760.20	1657.55	1613.18	1593.06	1583.75	1579.39
130000	2209.86	2107.32	1830.61	1723.85	1677.70	1656.78	1647.10	1642.57
135000	2294.86	2188.37	1901.02	1790.15	1742.23	1720.51	1710.45	1705.74
140000	2379.85	2269.42	1971.43	1856.45	1806.76	1784.23	1773.80	1768.92
145000	2464.84	2350.47	2041.83	1922.76	1871.28	1847.95	1837.15	1832.10
150000	2549.84	2431.52	2112.24	1989.06	1935.81	1911.67	1900.50	1895.27
155000	2634.83	2512.58	2182.65	2055.36	2000.34	1975.40	1963.85	1958.45
160000	2719.83	2593.63	2253.06	2121.66	2064.86	2039.12	2027.20	2021.62

MONTHLY AMORTIZING PAYMENTS

AMOUNT OF LOAN	NUMBER OF YEARS IN TERM							
	1	2	3	4	5	6	7	8
$ 50	4.52	2.44	1.74	1.40	1.20	1.07	.98	.91
100	9.04	4.87	3.48	2.80	2.40	2.13	1.95	1.81
200	18.08	9.73	6.96	5.60	4.79	4.26	3.89	3.62
300	27.12	14.59	10.44	8.39	7.18	6.39	5.84	5.43
400	36.16	19.45	13.92	11.19	9.57	8.52	7.78	7.24
500	45.19	24.31	17.40	13.98	11.97	10.65	9.72	9.05
600	54.23	29.17	20.88	16.78	14.36	12.77	11.67	10.86
700	63.27	34.03	24.36	19.58	16.75	14.90	13.61	12.67
800	72.31	38.89	27.84	22.37	19.14	17.03	15.55	14.48
900	81.34	43.75	31.31	25.17	21.53	19.16	17.50	16.29
1000	90.38	48.61	34.79	27.96	23.93	21.29	19.44	18.10
2000	180.76	97.22	69.58	55.92	47.85	42.57	38.88	36.19
3000	271.13	145.82	104.37	83.88	71.77	63.85	58.32	54.28
4000	361.51	194.43	139.16	111.84	95.69	85.13	77.75	72.37
5000	451.89	243.03	173.94	139.79	119.61	106.41	97.19	90.46
6000	542.26	291.64	208.73	167.75	143.53	127.69	116.63	108.55
7000	632.64	340.24	243.52	195.71	167.45	148.97	136.07	126.64
8000	723.02	388.85	278.31	223.67	191.38	170.25	155.50	144.73
9000	813.39	437.45	313.10	251.62	215.30	191.53	174.94	162.82
10000	903.77	486.06	347.88	279.58	239.22	212.82	194.38	180.91
11000	994.14	534.67	382.67	307.54	263.14	234.10	213.82	199.00
12000	1084.52	583.27	417.46	335.50	287.06	255.38	233.25	217.09
13000	1174.90	631.88	452.25	363.45	310.98	276.66	252.69	235.18
14000	1265.27	680.48	487.04	391.41	334.90	297.94	272.13	253.27
15000	1355.65	729.09	521.82	419.37	358.83	319.22	291.56	271.36
16000	1446.03	777.69	556.61	447.33	382.75	340.50	311.00	289.45
17000	1536.40	826.30	591.40	475.28	406.67	361.78	330.44	307.54
18000	1626.78	874.90	626.19	503.24	430.59	383.06	349.88	325.63
19000	1717.16	923.51	660.97	531.20	454.51	404.34	369.31	343.72
20000	1807.53	972.12	695.76	559.16	478.43	425.63	388.75	361.81
21000	1897.91	1020.72	730.55	587.12	502.35	446.91	408.19	379.90
22000	1988.28	1069.33	765.34	615.07	526.27	468.19	427.63	397.99
23000	2078.66	1117.93	800.13	643.03	550.20	489.47	447.06	416.08
24000	2169.04	1166.54	834.91	670.99	574.12	510.75	466.50	434.17
25000	2259.41	1215.14	869.70	698.95	598.04	532.03	485.94	452.26
26000	2349.79	1263.75	904.49	726.90	621.96	553.31	505.37	470.35
27000	2440.17	1312.35	939.28	754.86	645.88	574.59	524.81	488.44
28000	2530.54	1360.96	974.07	782.82	669.80	595.87	544.25	506.54
29000	2620.92	1409.56	1008.85	810.78	693.72	617.15	563.69	524.63
30000	2711.29	1458.17	1043.64	838.73	717.65	638.44	583.12	542.72
31000	2801.67	1506.78	1078.43	866.69	741.57	659.72	602.56	560.81
32000	2892.05	1555.38	1113.22	894.65	765.49	681.00	622.00	578.90
33000	2982.42	1603.99	1148.01	922.61	789.41	702.28	641.44	596.99
34000	3072.80	1652.59	1182.79	950.56	813.33	723.56	660.87	615.08
35000	3163.18	1701.20	1217.58	978.52	837.25	744.84	680.31	633.17
40000	3615.06	1944.23	1391.52	1118.31	956.86	851.25	777.50	723.62
45000	4066.94	2187.25	1565.46	1258.10	1076.47	957.65	874.68	814.07
50000	4518.82	2430.28	1739.40	1397.89	1196.07	1064.06	971.87	904.52
55000	4970.70	2673.31	1913.34	1537.68	1315.68	1170.46	1069.06	994.98
60000	5422.58	2916.34	2087.28	1677.46	1435.29	1276.87	1166.24	1085.43
65000	5874.47	3159.36	2261.22	1817.25	1554.89	1383.27	1263.43	1175.88
70000	6326.35	3402.39	2435.16	1957.04	1674.50	1489.68	1360.61	1266.33
75000	6778.23	3645.42	2609.10	2096.83	1794.11	1596.08	1457.80	1356.78
80000	7230.11	3888.45	2783.04	2236.62	1913.71	1702.49	1554.99	1447.23
85000	7681.99	4131.47	2956.97	2376.40	2033.32	1808.89	1652.17	1537.69
90000	8133.87	4374.50	3130.91	2516.19	2152.93	1915.30	1749.36	1628.14
95000	8585.76	4617.53	3304.85	2655.98	2272.53	2021.70	1846.55	1718.59
100000	9037.64	4860.56	3478.79	2795.77	2392.14	2128.11	1943.73	1809.04
105000	9489.52	5103.58	3652.73	2935.56	2511.75	2234.51	2040.92	1899.49
110000	9941.40	5346.61	3826.67	3075.35	2631.35	2340.92	2138.11	1989.95
115000	10393.28	5589.64	4000.61	3215.13	2750.96	2447.32	2235.29	2080.40
120000	10845.16	5832.67	4174.55	3354.92	2870.57	2553.73	2332.48	2170.85
125000	11297.05	6075.69	4348.49	3494.71	2990.17	2660.13	2429.67	2261.30
130000	11748.93	6318.72	4522.43	3634.50	3109.78	2766.54	2526.85	2351.75
135000	12200.81	6561.75	4696.37	3774.29	3229.39	2872.94	2624.04	2442.20
140000	12652.69	6804.78	4870.31	3914.07	3349.00	2979.35	2721.22	2532.66
145000	13104.57	7047.80	5044.25	4053.86	3468.60	3085.75	2818.41	2623.11
150000	13556.45	7290.83	5218.19	4193.65	3588.21	3192.16	2915.60	2713.56
155000	14008.33	7533.86	5392.13	4333.44	3707.82	3298.56	3012.78	2804.01
160000	14460.22	7776.89	5566.07	4473.23	3827.42	3404.97	3109.97	2894.46

MONTHLY AMORTIZING PAYMENTS 15¼%

AMOUNT OF LOAN	9	10	15	20	25	30	35	40
	NUMBER OF YEARS IN TERM							
$ 50	.86	.82	.71	.67	.66	.65	.64	.64
100	1.71	1.63	1.42	1.34	1.31	1.29	1.28	1.28
200	3.42	3.26	2.84	2.68	2.61	2.57	2.56	2.55
300	5.13	4.89	4.26	4.01	3.91	3.86	3.84	3.83
400	6.83	6.52	5.67	5.35	5.21	5.14	5.11	5.10
500	8.54	8.15	7.09	6.68	6.51	6.43	6.39	6.37
600	10.25	9.78	8.51	8.02	7.81	7.71	7.67	7.65
700	11.96	11.41	9.92	9.35	9.11	9.00	8.95	8.92
800	13.66	13.03	11.34	10.69	10.41	10.28	10.22	10.20
900	15.37	14.66	12.76	12.02	11.71	11.57	11.50	11.47
1000	17.08	16.29	14.17	13.36	13.01	12.85	12.78	12.74
2000	34.15	32.58	28.34	26.71	26.01	25.69	25.55	25.48
3000	51.23	48.87	42.51	40.06	39.01	38.54	38.32	38.22
4000	68.30	65.15	56.67	53.42	52.02	51.38	51.09	50.96
5000	85.37	81.44	70.84	66.77	65.02	64.23	63.86	63.70
6000	102.45	97.73	85.01	80.12	78.02	77.07	76.64	76.43
7000	119.52	114.01	99.18	93.48	91.02	89.92	89.41	89.17
8000	136.59	130.30	113.34	106.83	104.03	102.76	102.18	101.91
9000	153.67	146.59	127.51	120.18	117.03	115.61	114.95	114.65
10000	170.74	162.87	141.68	133.53	130.03	128.45	127.72	127.39
11000	187.81	179.16	155.85	146.89	143.03	141.30	140.50	140.12
12000	204.89	195.45	170.01	160.24	156.04	154.14	153.27	152.86
13000	221.96	211.74	184.18	173.59	169.04	166.98	166.04	165.60
14000	239.04	228.02	198.35	186.95	182.04	179.83	178.81	178.34
15000	256.11	244.31	212.52	200.30	195.04	192.67	191.58	191.08
16000	273.18	260.60	226.68	213.65	208.05	205.52	204.35	203.81
17000	290.26	276.88	240.85	227.01	221.05	218.36	217.13	216.55
18000	307.33	293.17	255.02	240.36	234.05	231.21	229.90	229.29
19000	324.40	309.46	269.19	253.71	247.05	244.05	242.67	242.03
20000	341.48	325.74	283.35	267.06	260.06	256.90	255.44	254.77
21000	358.55	342.03	297.52	280.42	273.06	269.74	268.21	267.50
22000	375.62	358.32	311.69	293.77	286.06	282.59	280.99	280.24
23000	392.70	374.60	325.86	307.12	299.06	295.43	293.76	292.98
24000	409.77	390.89	340.02	320.48	312.07	308.28	306.53	305.72
25000	426.85	407.18	354.19	333.83	325.07	321.12	319.30	318.46
26000	443.92	423.47	368.36	347.18	338.07	333.96	332.07	331.19
27000	460.99	439.75	382.53	360.54	351.07	346.81	344.84	343.93
28000	478.07	456.04	396.69	373.89	364.08	359.65	357.62	356.67
29000	495.14	472.33	410.86	387.24	377.08	372.50	370.39	369.41
30000	512.21	488.61	425.03	400.59	390.08	385.34	383.16	382.15
31000	529.29	504.90	439.20	413.95	403.09	398.19	395.93	394.88
32000	546.36	521.19	453.36	427.30	416.09	411.03	408.70	407.62
33000	563.43	537.47	467.53	440.65	429.09	423.88	421.48	420.36
34000	580.51	553.76	481.70	454.01	442.09	436.72	434.25	433.10
35000	597.58	570.05	495.87	467.36	455.10	449.57	447.02	445.84
40000	682.95	651.48	566.70	534.12	520.11	513.79	510.88	509.53
45000	768.32	732.92	637.54	600.89	585.12	578.01	574.74	573.22
50000	853.69	814.35	708.38	667.65	650.13	642.23	638.60	636.91
55000	939.05	895.79	779.22	734.42	715.15	706.46	702.46	700.60
60000	1024.42	977.22	850.05	801.18	780.16	770.68	766.32	764.29
65000	1109.79	1058.66	920.89	867.95	845.17	834.90	830.17	827.98
70000	1195.16	1140.09	991.73	934.71	910.19	899.13	894.03	891.67
75000	1280.53	1221.53	1062.57	1001.48	975.20	963.35	957.89	955.36
80000	1365.89	1302.96	1133.40	1068.24	1040.21	1027.57	1021.75	1019.05
85000	1451.26	1384.39	1204.24	1135.01	1105.22	1091.79	1085.61	1082.74
90000	1536.63	1465.83	1275.08	1201.77	1170.24	1156.02	1149.47	1146.43
95000	1622.00	1547.26	1345.92	1268.54	1235.25	1220.24	1213.33	1210.12
100000	1707.37	1628.70	1416.75	1335.30	1300.26	1284.46	1277.19	1273.81
105000	1792.73	1710.13	1487.59	1402.07	1365.28	1348.69	1341.05	1337.50
110000	1878.10	1791.57	1558.43	1468.83	1430.29	1412.91	1404.91	1401.19
115000	1963.47	1873.00	1629.27	1535.60	1495.30	1477.13	1468.77	1464.88
120000	2048.84	1954.44	1700.10	1602.36	1560.31	1541.36	1532.63	1528.57
125000	2134.21	2035.87	1770.94	1669.13	1625.33	1605.58	1596.48	1592.26
130000	2219.57	2117.31	1841.78	1735.89	1690.34	1669.80	1660.34	1655.95
135000	2304.94	2198.74	1912.62	1802.66	1755.35	1734.02	1724.20	1719.64
140000	2390.31	2280.18	1983.45	1869.42	1820.37	1798.25	1788.06	1783.33
145000	2475.68	2361.61	2054.29	1936.19	1885.38	1862.47	1851.92	1847.02
150000	2561.05	2443.05	2125.13	2002.95	1950.39	1926.69	1915.78	1910.71
155000	2646.41	2524.48	2195.97	2069.72	2015.41	1990.92	1979.64	1974.40
160000	2731.78	2605.91	2266.80	2136.48	2080.42	2055.14	2043.50	2038.09

MONTHLY AMORTIZING PAYMENTS

AMOUNT OF LOAN	NUMBER OF YEARS IN TERM							
	1	2	3	4	5	6	7	8
$ 50	4.53	2.44	1.75	1.41	1.20	1.07	.98	.91
100	9.05	4.87	3.49	2.81	2.40	2.14	1.96	1.82
200	18.09	9.74	6.97	5.61	4.80	4.27	3.91	3.64
300	27.14	14.60	10.46	8.41	7.20	6.41	5.86	5.45
400	36.18	19.47	13.94	11.21	9.60	8.54	7.81	7.27
500	45.22	24.34	17.43	14.02	12.00	10.68	9.76	9.09
600	54.27	29.20	20.91	16.82	14.40	12.81	11.71	10.90
700	63.31	34.07	24.40	19.62	16.80	14.95	13.66	12.72
800	72.35	38.94	27.88	22.42	19.19	17.08	15.61	14.54
900	81.40	43.80	31.37	25.22	21.59	19.22	17.56	16.35
1000	90.44	48.67	34.85	28.03	23.99	21.35	19.51	18.17
2000	180.88	97.34	69.70	56.05	47.98	42.70	39.02	36.33
3000	271.31	146.00	104.55	84.07	71.97	64.05	58.53	54.49
4000	361.75	194.67	139.40	112.09	95.95	85.40	78.04	72.66
5000	452.18	243.33	174.25	140.11	119.94	106.75	97.54	90.82
6000	542.62	292.00	209.10	168.13	143.93	128.10	117.05	108.98
7000	633.05	340.66	243.95	196.15	167.92	149.45	136.56	127.15
8000	723.49	389.33	278.80	224.17	191.90	170.80	156.07	145.31
9000	813.92	437.99	313.65	252.20	215.89	192.15	175.57	163.47
10000	904.36	486.66	348.50	280.22	239.88	213.50	195.08	181.64
11000	994.79	535.32	383.35	308.24	263.86	234.85	214.59	199.80
12000	1085.23	583.99	418.20	336.26	287.85	256.20	234.10	217.96
13000	1175.66	632.65	453.05	364.28	311.84	277.54	253.61	236.12
14000	1266.10	681.32	487.89	392.30	335.83	298.89	273.11	254.29
15000	1356.54	729.98	522.74	420.32	359.81	320.24	292.62	272.45
16000	1446.97	778.65	557.59	448.34	383.80	341.59	312.13	290.61
17000	1537.41	827.31	592.44	476.37	407.79	362.94	331.64	308.78
18000	1627.84	875.98	627.29	504.39	431.78	384.29	351.14	326.94
19000	1718.28	924.64	662.14	532.41	455.76	405.64	370.65	345.10
20000	1808.71	973.31	696.99	560.43	479.75	426.99	390.16	363.27
21000	1899.15	1021.97	731.84	588.45	503.74	448.34	409.67	381.43
22000	1989.58	1070.64	766.69	616.47	527.72	469.69	429.18	399.59
23000	2080.02	1119.30	801.54	644.49	551.71	491.04	448.68	417.76
24000	2170.45	1167.97	836.39	672.51	575.70	512.39	468.19	435.92
25000	2260.89	1216.63	871.24	700.54	599.69	533.73	487.70	454.08
26000	2351.32	1265.30	906.09	728.56	623.67	555.08	507.21	472.24
27000	2441.76	1313.96	940.93	756.58	647.66	576.43	526.71	490.41
28000	2532.20	1362.63	975.78	784.60	671.65	597.78	546.22	508.57
29000	2622.63	1411.29	1010.63	812.62	695.63	619.13	565.73	526.73
30000	2713.07	1459.96	1045.48	840.64	719.62	640.48	585.24	544.90
31000	2803.50	1508.62	1080.33	868.66	743.61	661.83	604.75	563.06
32000	2893.94	1557.29	1115.18	896.68	767.60	683.18	624.25	581.22
33000	2984.37	1605.95	1150.03	924.70	791.58	704.53	643.76	599.39
34000	3074.81	1654.62	1184.88	952.73	815.57	725.88	663.27	617.55
35000	3165.24	1703.28	1219.73	980.75	839.56	747.23	682.78	635.71
40000	3617.42	1946.61	1393.97	1120.85	959.49	853.97	780.31	726.53
45000	4069.60	2189.93	1568.22	1260.96	1079.43	960.72	877.85	817.34
50000	4521.77	2433.26	1742.47	1401.07	1199.37	1067.46	975.39	908.16
55000	4973.95	2676.58	1916.71	1541.17	1319.30	1174.21	1072.93	998.97
60000	5426.13	2919.91	2090.96	1681.28	1439.24	1280.96	1170.47	1089.79
65000	5878.30	3163.23	2265.21	1821.38	1559.17	1387.70	1268.01	1180.60
70000	6330.48	3406.56	2439.45	1961.49	1679.11	1494.45	1365.55	1271.42
75000	6782.66	3649.88	2613.70	2101.60	1799.05	1601.19	1463.09	1362.24
80000	7234.83	3893.21	2787.94	2241.70	1918.98	1707.94	1560.62	1453.05
85000	7687.01	4136.53	2962.19	2381.81	2038.92	1814.69	1658.16	1543.87
90000	8139.19	4379.86	3136.44	2521.91	2158.86	1921.43	1755.70	1634.68
95000	8591.36	4623.18	3310.68	2662.02	2278.79	2028.18	1853.24	1725.50
100000	9043.54	4866.51	3484.93	2802.13	2398.73	2134.92	1950.78	1816.31
105000	9495.72	5109.83	3659.18	2942.23	2518.66	2241.67	2048.32	1907.13
110000	9947.89	5353.16	3833.42	3082.34	2638.60	2348.42	2145.86	1997.94
115000	10400.07	5596.48	4007.67	3222.44	2758.54	2455.16	2243.40	2088.76
120000	10852.25	5839.81	4181.91	3362.55	2878.47	2561.91	2340.93	2179.57
125000	11304.42	6083.13	4356.16	3502.66	2998.41	2668.65	2438.47	2270.39
130000	11756.60	6326.46	4530.41	3642.76	3118.34	2775.40	2536.01	2361.20
135000	12208.78	6569.78	4704.65	3782.87	3238.28	2882.15	2633.55	2452.02
140000	12660.96	6813.11	4878.90	3922.97	3358.22	2988.89	2731.09	2542.84
145000	13113.13	7056.43	5053.15	4063.08	3478.15	3095.64	2828.63	2633.65
150000	13565.31	7299.76	5227.39	4203.19	3598.09	3202.38	2926.17	2724.47
155000	14017.49	7543.08	5401.64	4343.29	3718.02	3309.13	3023.71	2815.28
160000	14469.66	7786.41	5575.88	4483.40	3837.96	3415.88	3121.24	2906.10

AMOUNT OF LOAN	NUMBER OF YEARS IN TERM							
	9	10	15	20	25	30	35	40
$ 50	.86	.82	.72	.68	.66	.65	.65	.65
100	1.72	1.64	1.43	1.35	1.31	1.30	1.29	1.29
200	3.43	3.28	2.86	2.69	2.62	2.59	2.58	2.57
300	5.15	4.91	4.28	4.04	3.93	3.89	3.87	3.86
400	6.86	6.55	5.71	5.38	5.24	5.18	5.15	5.14
500	8.58	8.19	7.13	6.73	6.55	6.48	6.44	6.43
600	10.29	9.82	8.56	8.07	7.86	7.77	7.73	7.71
700	12.01	11.46	9.98	9.42	9.17	9.07	9.02	8.99
800	13.72	13.10	11.41	10.76	10.48	10.36	10.30	10.28
900	15.44	14.73	12.83	12.11	11.79	11.66	11.59	11.56
1000	17.15	16.37	14.26	13.45	13.10	12.95	12.88	12.85
2000	34.30	32.73	28.51	26.90	26.20	25.89	25.75	25.69
3000	51.45	49.10	42.77	40.34	39.30	38.84	38.63	38.53
4000	68.60	65.46	57.02	53.79	52.40	51.78	51.50	51.37
5000	85.75	81.82	71.27	67.23	65.50	64.73	64.37	64.21
6000	102.90	98.19	85.53	80.68	78.60	77.67	77.25	77.05
7000	120.04	114.55	99.78	94.13	91.70	90.62	90.12	89.89
8000	137.19	130.92	114.03	107.57	104.80	103.56	103.00	102.73
9000	154.34	147.28	128.29	121.02	117.90	116.51	115.87	115.57
10000	171.49	163.64	142.54	134.46	131.00	129.45	128.74	128.41
11000	188.64	180.01	156.79	147.91	144.10	142.40	141.62	141.26
12000	205.79	196.37	171.05	161.35	157.20	155.34	154.49	154.10
13000	222.94	212.74	185.30	174.80	170.30	168.29	167.36	166.94
14000	240.08	229.10	199.56	188.25	183.40	181.23	180.24	179.78
15000	257.23	245.46	213.81	201.69	196.50	194.18	193.11	192.62
16000	274.38	261.83	228.06	215.14	209.60	207.12	205.99	205.46
17000	291.53	278.19	242.32	228.58	222.70	220.07	218.86	218.30
18000	308.68	294.56	256.57	242.03	235.80	233.01	231.73	231.14
19000	325.83	310.92	270.82	255.48	248.90	245.96	244.61	243.98
20000	342.97	327.28	285.08	268.92	262.00	258.90	257.48	256.82
21000	360.12	343.65	299.33	282.37	275.10	271.85	270.35	269.67
22000	377.27	360.01	313.58	295.81	288.20	284.79	283.23	282.51
23000	394.42	376.37	327.84	309.26	301.30	297.74	296.10	295.35
24000	411.57	392.74	342.09	322.70	314.40	310.68	308.98	308.19
25000	428.72	409.10	356.35	336.15	327.50	323.63	321.85	321.03
26000	445.87	425.47	370.60	349.60	340.60	336.57	334.72	333.87
27000	463.01	441.83	384.85	363.04	353.70	349.52	347.60	346.71
28000	480.16	458.19	399.11	376.49	366.80	362.46	360.47	359.55
29000	497.31	474.56	413.36	389.93	379.90	375.40	373.35	372.39
30000	514.46	490.92	427.61	403.38	393.00	388.35	386.22	385.23
31000	531.61	507.29	441.87	416.83	406.10	401.29	399.09	398.08
32000	548.76	523.65	456.12	430.27	419.20	414.24	411.97	410.92
33000	565.91	540.01	470.37	443.72	432.30	427.18	424.84	423.76
34000	583.05	556.38	484.63	457.16	445.40	440.13	437.71	436.60
35000	600.20	572.74	498.88	470.61	458.50	453.07	450.59	449.44
40000	685.94	654.56	570.15	537.84	524.00	517.80	514.96	513.64
45000	771.69	736.38	641.42	605.07	589.50	582.52	579.33	577.85
50000	857.43	818.20	712.69	672.30	655.00	647.25	643.70	642.05
55000	943.17	900.02	783.95	739.52	720.50	711.97	708.06	706.26
60000	1028.91	981.84	855.22	806.75	786.00	776.69	772.43	770.46
65000	1114.66	1063.66	926.49	873.98	851.50	841.42	836.80	834.67
70000	1200.40	1145.48	997.76	941.21	917.00	906.14	901.17	898.87
75000	1286.14	1227.30	1069.03	1008.44	982.50	970.87	965.54	963.08
80000	1371.88	1309.12	1140.29	1075.67	1048.00	1035.59	1029.91	1027.28
85000	1457.63	1390.94	1211.56	1142.90	1113.50	1100.32	1094.28	1091.49
90000	1543.37	1472.76	1282.83	1210.13	1179.00	1165.04	1158.65	1155.69
95000	1629.11	1554.58	1354.10	1277.36	1244.50	1229.76	1223.02	1219.90
100000	1714.85	1636.40	1425.37	1344.59	1310.00	1294.49	1287.39	1284.10
105000	1800.60	1718.22	1496.63	1411.81	1375.50	1359.21	1351.75	1348.31
110000	1886.34	1800.04	1567.90	1479.04	1441.00	1423.94	1416.12	1412.51
115000	1972.08	1881.85	1639.17	1546.27	1506.50	1488.66	1480.49	1476.72
120000	2057.82	1963.67	1710.44	1613.50	1572.00	1553.38	1544.86	1540.92
125000	2143.57	2045.49	1781.71	1680.73	1637.50	1618.11	1609.23	1605.13
130000	2229.31	2127.31	1852.97	1747.96	1703.00	1682.83	1673.60	1669.33
135000	2315.05	2209.13	1924.24	1815.19	1768.50	1747.56	1737.97	1733.54
140000	2400.79	2290.95	1995.51	1882.42	1834.00	1812.28	1802.34	1797.74
145000	2486.54	2372.77	2066.78	1949.65	1899.50	1877.00	1866.71	1861.95
150000	2572.28	2454.59	2138.05	2016.88	1965.00	1941.73	1931.08	1926.15
155000	2658.02	2536.41	2209.31	2084.11	2030.50	2006.45	1995.44	1990.36
160000	2743.76	2618.23	2280.58	2151.33	2096.00	2071.18	2059.81	2054.56

AMOUNT OF LOAN	NUMBER OF YEARS IN TERM							
	1	2	3	4	5	6	7	8
$ 50	4.53	2.44	1.75	1.41	1.21	1.08	.98	.92
100	9.05	4.88	3.50	2.81	2.41	2.15	1.96	1.83
200	18.10	9.75	6.99	5.62	4.82	4.29	3.92	3.65
300	27.15	14.62	10.48	8.43	7.22	6.43	5.88	5.48
400	36.20	19.49	13.97	11.24	9.63	8.57	7.84	7.30
500	45.25	24.37	17.46	14.05	12.03	10.71	9.79	9.12
600	54.30	29.24	20.95	16.86	14.44	12.86	11.75	10.95
700	63.35	34.11	24.44	19.66	16.84	15.00	13.71	12.77
800	72.40	38.98	27.93	22.47	19.25	17.14	15.67	14.59
900	81.45	43.86	31.42	25.28	21.65	19.28	17.63	16.42
1000	90.50	48.73	34.92	28.09	24.06	21.42	19.58	18.24
2000	180.99	97.45	69.83	56.17	48.11	42.84	39.16	36.48
3000	271.49	146.18	104.74	84.26	72.16	64.26	58.74	54.71
4000	361.98	194.90	139.65	112.34	96.22	85.67	78.32	72.95
5000	452.48	243.63	174.56	140.43	120.27	107.09	97.90	91.18
6000	542.97	292.35	209.47	168.51	144.32	128.51	117.48	109.42
7000	633.47	341.08	244.38	196.60	168.38	149.93	137.05	127.66
8000	723.96	389.80	279.29	224.68	192.43	171.34	156.63	145.89
9000	814.45	438.53	314.20	252.77	216.48	192.76	176.21	164.13
10000	904.95	487.25	349.11	280.85	240.54	214.18	195.79	182.36
11000	995.44	535.97	384.02	308.94	264.59	235.60	215.37	200.60
12000	1085.94	584.70	418.93	337.02	288.64	257.01	234.95	218.84
13000	1176.43	633.42	453.84	365.11	312.70	278.43	254.52	237.07
14000	1266.93	682.15	488.75	393.19	336.75	299.85	274.10	255.31
15000	1357.42	730.87	523.67	421.28	360.80	321.27	293.68	273.54
16000	1447.92	779.60	558.58	449.36	384.86	342.68	313.26	291.78
17000	1538.41	828.32	593.49	477.45	408.91	364.10	332.84	310.02
18000	1628.90	877.05	628.40	505.53	432.96	385.52	352.42	328.25
19000	1719.40	925.77	663.31	533.62	457.02	406.94	371.99	346.49
20000	1809.89	974.50	698.22	561.70	481.07	428.35	391.57	364.72
21000	1900.39	1023.22	733.13	589.79	505.12	449.77	411.15	382.96
22000	1990.88	1071.94	768.04	617.87	529.18	471.19	430.73	401.20
23000	2081.38	1120.67	802.95	645.96	553.23	492.61	450.31	419.43
24000	2171.87	1169.39	837.86	674.04	577.28	514.02	469.89	437.67
25000	2262.37	1218.12	872.77	702.13	601.33	535.44	489.46	455.90
26000	2352.86	1266.84	907.68	730.21	625.39	556.86	509.04	474.14
27000	2443.35	1315.57	942.59	758.30	649.44	578.28	528.62	492.37
28000	2533.85	1364.29	977.50	786.38	673.49	599.69	548.20	510.61
29000	2624.34	1413.02	1012.41	814.47	697.55	621.11	567.78	528.85
30000	2714.84	1461.74	1047.33	842.55	721.60	642.53	587.36	547.08
31000	2805.33	1510.47	1082.24	870.64	745.65	663.95	606.93	565.32
32000	2895.83	1559.19	1117.15	898.72	769.71	685.36	626.51	583.55
33000	2986.32	1607.91	1152.06	926.81	793.76	706.78	646.09	601.79
34000	3076.82	1656.64	1186.97	954.89	817.81	728.20	665.67	620.03
35000	3167.31	1705.36	1221.88	982.98	841.87	749.62	685.25	638.26
40000	3619.78	1948.99	1396.43	1123.40	962.13	856.70	783.14	729.44
45000	4072.25	2192.61	1570.99	1263.82	1082.40	963.79	881.03	820.62
50000	4524.73	2436.23	1745.54	1404.25	1202.66	1070.88	978.92	911.80
55000	4977.20	2679.85	1920.09	1544.67	1322.93	1177.97	1076.81	1002.98
60000	5429.67	2923.48	2094.65	1685.10	1443.20	1285.05	1174.71	1094.16
65000	5882.14	3167.10	2269.20	1825.52	1563.46	1392.14	1272.60	1185.34
70000	6334.61	3410.72	2443.75	1965.95	1683.73	1499.23	1370.49	1276.52
75000	6787.09	3654.35	2618.31	2106.37	1803.99	1606.32	1468.38	1367.70
80000	7239.56	3897.97	2792.86	2246.79	1924.26	1713.40	1566.27	1458.88
85000	7692.03	4141.59	2967.41	2387.22	2044.53	1820.49	1664.16	1550.06
90000	8144.50	4385.21	3141.97	2527.64	2164.79	1927.58	1762.06	1641.24
95000	8596.97	4628.84	3316.52	2668.07	2285.06	2034.67	1859.95	1732.42
100000	9049.45	4872.46	3491.07	2808.49	2405.32	2141.75	1957.84	1823.60
105000	9501.92	5116.08	3665.63	2948.92	2525.59	2248.84	2055.73	1914.78
110000	9954.39	5359.70	3840.18	3089.34	2645.86	2355.93	2153.62	2005.96
115000	10406.86	5603.33	4014.73	3229.76	2766.12	2463.02	2251.51	2097.14
120000	10859.33	5846.95	4189.29	3370.19	2886.39	2570.10	2349.41	2188.32
125000	11311.81	6090.57	4363.84	3510.61	3006.65	2677.19	2447.30	2279.50
130000	11764.28	6334.20	4538.39	3651.04	3126.92	2784.28	2545.19	2370.67
135000	12216.75	6577.82	4712.95	3791.46	3247.19	2891.37	2643.08	2461.85
140000	12669.22	6821.44	4887.50	3931.89	3367.45	2998.45	2740.97	2553.03
145000	13121.70	7065.06	5062.05	4072.31	3487.72	3105.54	2838.87	2644.21
150000	13574.17	7308.69	5236.61	4212.73	3607.98	3212.63	2936.76	2735.39
155000	14026.64	7552.31	5411.16	4353.16	3728.25	3319.72	3034.65	2826.57
160000	14479.11	7795.93	5585.71	4493.58	3848.52	3426.80	3132.54	2917.75

MONTHLY AMORTIZING PAYMENTS 15½%

AMOUNT OF LOAN	NUMBER OF YEARS IN TERM 9	10	15	20	25	30	35	40
$ 50	.87	.83	.72	.68	.66	.66	.65	.65
100	1.73	1.65	1.44	1.36	1.32	1.31	1.30	1.30
200	3.45	3.29	2.87	2.71	2.64	2.61	2.60	2.59
300	5.17	4.94	4.31	4.07	3.96	3.92	3.90	3.89
400	6.89	6.58	5.74	5.42	5.28	5.22	5.20	5.18
500	8.62	8.23	7.17	6.77	6.60	6.53	6.49	6.48
600	10.34	9.87	8.61	8.13	7.92	7.83	7.79	7.77
700	12.06	11.51	10.04	9.48	9.24	9.14	9.09	9.07
800	13.78	13.16	11.48	10.84	10.56	10.44	10.39	10.36
900	15.51	14.80	12.91	12.19	11.88	11.75	11.68	11.65
1000	17.23	16.45	14.34	13.54	13.20	13.05	12.98	12.95
2000	34.45	32.89	28.68	27.08	26.40	26.10	25.96	25.89
3000	51.68	49.33	43.02	40.62	39.60	39.14	38.93	38.84
4000	68.90	65.77	57.36	54.16	52.79	52.19	51.91	51.78
5000	86.12	82.21	71.70	67.70	65.99	65.23	64.88	64.72
6000	103.35	98.65	86.04	81.24	79.19	78.28	77.86	77.67
7000	120.57	115.09	100.38	94.78	92.39	91.32	90.84	90.61
8000	137.79	131.53	114.72	108.32	105.58	104.37	103.81	103.56
9000	155.02	147.97	129.06	121.85	118.78	117.41	116.79	116.50
10000	172.24	164.42	143.40	135.39	131.98	130.46	129.76	129.44
11000	189.46	180.86	157.74	148.93	145.18	143.50	142.74	142.39
12000	206.69	197.30	172.08	162.47	158.37	156.55	155.72	155.33
13000	223.91	213.74	186.42	176.01	171.57	169.59	168.69	168.28
14000	241.13	230.18	200.76	189.55	184.77	182.64	181.67	181.22
15000	258.36	246.62	215.10	203.09	197.97	195.68	194.64	194.16
16000	275.58	263.06	229.44	216.63	211.16	208.73	207.62	207.11
17000	292.80	279.50	243.78	230.16	224.36	221.77	220.59	220.05
18000	310.03	295.94	258.12	243.70	237.56	234.82	233.57	233.00
19000	327.25	312.39	272.46	257.24	250.76	247.86	246.55	245.94
20000	344.48	328.83	286.80	270.78	263.95	260.91	259.52	258.88
21000	361.70	345.27	301.14	284.32	277.15	273.95	272.50	271.83
22000	378.92	361.71	315.48	297.86	290.35	287.00	285.47	284.77
23000	396.15	378.15	329.82	311.40	303.55	300.04	298.45	297.72
24000	413.37	394.59	344.16	324.94	316.74	313.09	311.43	310.66
25000	430.59	411.03	358.50	338.48	329.94	326.13	324.40	323.60
26000	447.82	427.47	372.84	352.01	343.14	339.18	337.38	336.55
27000	465.04	443.91	387.18	365.55	356.34	352.22	350.35	349.49
28000	482.26	460.35	401.52	379.09	369.53	365.27	363.33	362.44
29000	499.49	476.80	415.86	392.63	382.73	378.31	376.30	375.38
30000	516.71	493.24	430.20	406.17	395.93	391.36	389.28	388.32
31000	533.93	509.68	444.54	419.71	409.13	404.41	402.26	401.27
32000	551.16	526.12	458.88	433.25	422.32	417.45	415.23	414.21
33000	568.38	542.56	473.22	446.79	435.52	430.50	428.21	427.16
34000	585.60	559.00	487.56	460.32	448.72	443.54	441.18	440.10
35000	602.83	575.44	501.90	473.86	461.92	456.59	454.16	453.04
40000	688.95	657.65	573.60	541.56	527.90	521.81	519.04	517.76
45000	775.06	739.85	645.30	609.25	593.89	587.04	583.92	582.48
50000	861.18	822.06	717.00	676.95	659.88	652.26	648.80	647.20
55000	947.30	904.26	788.70	744.64	725.86	717.49	713.68	711.92
60000	1033.42	986.47	860.40	812.33	791.85	782.72	778.56	776.64
65000	1119.53	1068.67	932.10	880.03	857.84	847.94	843.44	841.36
70000	1205.65	1150.88	1003.80	947.72	923.83	913.17	908.31	906.08
75000	1291.77	1233.08	1075.50	1015.42	989.81	978.39	973.19	970.80
80000	1377.89	1315.29	1147.20	1083.11	1055.80	1043.62	1038.07	1035.52
85000	1464.00	1397.49	1218.90	1150.80	1121.79	1108.84	1102.95	1100.24
90000	1550.12	1479.70	1290.60	1218.50	1187.78	1174.07	1167.83	1164.96
95000	1636.24	1561.91	1362.30	1286.19	1253.76	1239.30	1232.71	1229.68
100000	1722.36	1644.11	1434.00	1353.89	1319.75	1304.52	1297.59	1294.40
105000	1808.48	1726.32	1505.69	1421.58	1385.74	1369.75	1362.47	1359.12
110000	1894.59	1808.52	1577.39	1489.27	1451.72	1434.97	1427.35	1423.84
115000	1980.71	1890.73	1649.09	1556.97	1517.71	1500.20	1492.23	1488.56
120000	2066.83	1972.93	1720.79	1624.66	1583.70	1565.43	1557.11	1553.28
125000	2152.95	2055.14	1792.49	1692.36	1649.69	1630.65	1621.99	1618.00
130000	2239.06	2137.34	1864.19	1760.05	1715.67	1695.88	1686.87	1682.72
135000	2325.18	2219.55	1935.89	1827.74	1781.66	1761.10	1751.74	1747.44
140000	2411.30	2301.75	2007.59	1895.44	1847.65	1826.33	1816.62	1812.16
145000	2497.42	2383.96	2079.29	1963.13	1913.64	1891.55	1881.50	1876.88
150000	2583.53	2466.16	2150.99	2030.83	1979.62	1956.78	1946.38	1941.60
155000	2669.65	2548.37	2222.69	2098.52	2045.61	2022.01	2011.26	2006.32
160000	2755.77	2630.57	2294.39	2166.21	2111.60	2087.23	2076.14	2071.04

MONTHLY AMORTIZING PAYMENTS

AMOUNT OF LOAN	NUMBER OF YEARS IN TERM							
	1	2	3	4	5	6	7	8
$ 50	4.53	2.44	1.75	1.41	1.21	1.08	.99	.92
100	9.06	4.88	3.50	2.82	2.42	2.15	1.97	1.84
200	18.12	9.76	7.00	5.63	4.83	4.30	3.93	3.67
300	27.17	14.64	10.50	8.45	7.24	6.45	5.90	5.50
400	36.23	19.52	13.99	11.26	9.65	8.60	7.86	7.33
500	45.28	24.40	17.49	14.08	12.06	10.75	9.83	9.16
600	54.34	29.28	20.99	16.89	14.48	12.90	11.79	10.99
700	63.39	34.15	24.49	19.71	16.89	15.05	13.76	12.82
800	72.45	39.03	27.98	22.52	19.30	17.19	15.72	14.65
900	81.50	43.91	31.48	25.34	21.71	19.34	17.69	16.48
1000	90.56	48.79	34.98	28.15	24.12	21.49	19.65	18.31
2000	181.11	97.57	69.95	56.30	48.24	42.98	39.30	36.62
3000	271.67	146.36	104.92	84.45	72.36	64.46	58.95	54.93
4000	362.22	195.14	139.89	112.60	96.48	85.95	78.60	73.24
5000	452.77	243.93	174.87	140.75	120.60	107.43	98.25	91.55
6000	543.33	292.71	209.84	168.90	144.72	128.92	117.90	109.86
7000	633.88	341.49	244.81	197.05	168.84	150.41	137.55	128.17
8000	724.43	390.28	279.78	225.19	192.96	171.89	157.20	146.48
9000	814.99	439.06	314.75	253.34	217.08	193.38	176.85	164.79
10000	905.54	487.85	349.73	281.49	241.20	214.86	196.50	183.09
11000	996.09	536.63	384.70	309.64	265.32	236.35	216.14	201.40
12000	1086.65	585.41	419.67	337.79	289.44	257.84	235.79	219.71
13000	1177.20	634.20	454.64	365.94	313.56	279.32	255.44	238.02
14000	1267.75	682.98	489.62	394.09	337.67	300.81	275.09	256.33
15000	1358.31	731.77	524.59	422.23	361.79	322.29	294.74	274.64
16000	1448.86	780.55	559.56	450.38	385.91	343.78	314.39	292.95
17000	1539.41	829.34	594.53	478.53	410.03	365.27	334.04	311.26
18000	1629.97	878.12	629.50	506.68	434.15	386.75	353.69	329.57
19000	1720.52	926.90	664.48	534.83	458.27	408.24	373.34	347.87
20000	1811.07	975.69	699.45	562.98	482.39	429.72	392.99	366.18
21000	1901.63	1024.47	734.42	591.13	506.51	451.21	412.64	384.49
22000	1992.18	1073.26	769.39	619.27	530.63	472.69	432.28	402.80
23000	2082.74	1122.04	804.37	647.42	554.75	494.18	451.93	421.11
24000	2173.29	1170.82	839.34	675.57	578.87	515.67	471.58	439.42
25000	2263.84	1219.61	874.31	703.72	602.99	537.15	491.23	457.73
26000	2354.40	1268.39	909.28	731.87	627.11	558.64	510.88	476.04
27000	2444.95	1317.18	944.25	760.02	651.22	580.12	530.53	494.35
28000	2535.50	1365.96	979.23	788.17	675.34	601.61	550.18	512.65
29000	2626.06	1414.74	1014.20	816.31	699.46	623.10	569.83	530.96
30000	2716.61	1463.53	1049.17	844.46	723.58	644.58	589.48	549.27
31000	2807.16	1512.31	1084.14	872.61	747.70	666.07	609.13	567.58
32000	2897.72	1561.10	1119.11	900.76	771.82	687.55	628.78	585.89
33000	2988.27	1609.88	1154.09	928.91	795.94	709.04	648.42	604.20
34000	3078.82	1658.67	1189.06	957.06	820.06	730.53	668.07	622.51
35000	3169.38	1707.45	1224.03	985.21	844.18	752.01	687.72	640.82
40000	3622.14	1951.37	1398.89	1125.95	964.78	859.44	785.97	732.36
45000	4074.91	2195.29	1573.75	1266.69	1085.37	966.87	884.21	823.91
50000	4527.68	2439.21	1748.61	1407.43	1205.97	1074.30	982.46	915.45
55000	4980.45	2683.13	1923.47	1548.18	1326.56	1181.73	1080.70	1007.00
60000	5433.21	2927.05	2098.34	1688.92	1447.16	1289.16	1178.95	1098.54
65000	5885.98	3170.97	2273.20	1829.66	1567.76	1396.59	1277.20	1190.08
70000	6338.75	3414.89	2448.06	1970.41	1688.35	1504.02	1375.44	1281.63
75000	6791.52	3658.81	2622.92	2111.15	1808.95	1611.45	1473.69	1373.17
80000	7244.28	3902.73	2797.78	2251.89	1929.55	1718.88	1571.93	1464.72
85000	7697.05	4146.66	2972.64	2392.64	2050.14	1826.31	1670.18	1556.26
90000	8149.82	4390.58	3147.50	2533.38	2170.74	1933.74	1768.42	1647.81
95000	8602.59	4634.50	3322.36	2674.12	2291.33	2041.17	1866.67	1739.35
100000	9055.35	4878.42	3497.22	2814.86	2411.93	2148.60	1964.91	1830.90
105000	9508.12	5122.34	3672.08	2955.61	2532.53	2256.02	2063.16	1922.44
110000	9960.89	5366.26	3846.94	3096.35	2653.12	2363.45	2161.40	2013.99
115000	10413.66	5610.18	4021.81	3237.09	2773.72	2470.88	2259.65	2105.53
120000	10866.42	5854.10	4196.67	3377.84	2894.32	2578.31	2357.89	2197.08
125000	11319.19	6098.02	4371.53	3518.58	3014.91	2685.74	2456.14	2288.62
130000	11771.96	6341.94	4546.39	3659.32	3135.51	2793.17	2554.39	2380.16
135000	12224.73	6585.86	4721.25	3800.06	3256.10	2900.60	2652.63	2471.71
140000	12677.49	6829.78	4896.11	3940.81	3376.70	3008.03	2750.88	2563.25
145000	13130.26	7073.70	5070.97	4081.55	3497.30	3115.46	2849.12	2654.80
150000	13583.03	7317.62	5245.83	4222.29	3617.89	3222.89	2947.37	2746.34
155000	14035.80	7561.54	5420.69	4363.04	3738.49	3330.32	3045.61	2837.89
160000	14488.56	7805.46	5595.55	4503.78	3859.09	3437.75	3143.86	2929.43

AMOUNT OF LOAN	NUMBER OF YEARS IN TERM							
	9	10	15	20	25	30	35	40
$ 50	.87	.83	.73	.69	.67	.66	.66	.66
100	1.73	1.66	1.45	1.37	1.33	1.32	1.31	1.31
200	3.46	3.31	2.89	2.73	2.66	2.63	2.62	2.61
300	5.19	4.96	4.33	4.09	3.99	3.95	3.93	3.92
400	6.92	6.61	5.78	5.46	5.32	5.26	5.24	5.22
500	8.65	8.26	7.22	6.82	6.65	6.58	6.54	6.53
600	10.38	9.92	8.66	8.18	7.98	7.89	7.85	7.83
700	12.11	11.57	10.10	9.55	9.31	9.21	9.16	9.14
800	13.84	13.22	11.55	10.91	10.64	10.52	10.47	10.44
900	15.57	14.87	12.99	12.27	11.97	11.84	11.78	11.75
1000	17.30	16.52	14.43	13.64	13.30	13.15	13.08	13.05
2000	34.60	33.04	28.86	27.27	26.60	26.30	26.16	26.10
3000	51.90	49.56	43.28	40.90	39.89	39.44	39.24	39.15
4000	69.20	66.08	57.71	54.53	53.19	52.59	52.32	52.19
5000	86.50	82.60	72.14	68.16	66.48	65.73	65.39	65.24
6000	103.80	99.12	86.56	81.80	79.78	78.88	78.47	78.29
7000	121.10	115.63	100.99	95.43	93.07	92.02	91.55	91.33
8000	138.39	132.15	115.42	109.06	106.37	105.17	104.63	104.38
9000	155.69	148.67	129.84	122.69	119.66	118.32	117.71	117.43
10000	172.99	165.19	144.27	136.32	132.96	131.46	130.78	130.48
11000	190.29	181.71	158.70	149.96	146.25	144.61	143.86	143.52
12000	207.59	198.23	173.12	163.59	159.55	157.75	156.94	156.57
13000	224.89	214.74	187.55	177.22	172.84	170.90	170.02	169.62
14000	242.19	231.26	201.97	190.85	186.14	184.04	183.10	182.66
15000	259.49	247.78	216.40	204.48	199.43	197.19	196.17	195.71
16000	276.78	264.30	230.83	218.12	212.73	210.33	209.25	208.76
17000	294.08	280.82	245.25	231.75	226.02	223.48	222.33	221.80
18000	311.38	297.34	259.68	245.38	239.32	236.63	235.41	234.85
19000	328.68	313.85	274.11	259.01	252.61	249.77	248.49	247.90
20000	345.98	330.37	288.53	272.64	265.91	262.92	261.56	260.95
21000	363.28	346.89	302.96	286.28	279.20	276.06	274.64	273.99
22000	380.58	363.41	317.39	299.91	292.50	289.21	287.72	287.04
23000	397.88	379.93	331.81	313.54	305.79	302.35	300.80	300.09
24000	415.17	396.45	346.24	327.17	319.09	315.50	313.88	313.13
25000	432.47	412.96	360.66	340.80	332.38	328.65	326.95	326.18
26000	449.77	429.48	375.09	354.44	345.68	341.79	340.03	339.23
27000	467.07	446.00	389.52	368.07	358.97	354.94	353.11	352.28
28000	484.37	462.52	403.94	381.70	372.27	368.08	366.19	365.32
29000	501.67	479.04	418.37	395.33	385.56	381.23	379.27	378.37
30000	518.97	495.56	432.80	408.96	398.86	394.37	392.34	391.42
31000	536.27	512.07	447.22	422.60	412.15	407.52	405.42	404.46
32000	553.56	528.59	461.65	436.23	425.45	420.66	418.50	417.51
33000	570.86	545.11	476.08	449.86	438.74	433.81	431.58	430.56
34000	588.16	561.63	490.50	463.49	452.04	446.96	444.66	443.60
35000	605.46	578.15	504.93	477.12	465.33	460.10	457.73	456.65
40000	691.95	660.74	577.06	545.28	531.81	525.83	523.12	521.89
45000	778.45	743.33	649.19	613.44	598.28	591.56	588.51	587.12
50000	864.94	825.92	721.32	681.60	664.76	657.29	653.90	652.36
55000	951.43	908.52	793.46	749.76	731.24	723.01	719.29	717.59
60000	1037.93	991.11	865.59	817.92	797.71	788.74	784.68	782.83
65000	1124.42	1073.70	937.72	886.08	864.19	854.47	850.07	848.06
70000	1210.92	1156.29	1009.85	954.24	930.66	920.20	915.46	913.30
75000	1297.41	1238.88	1081.98	1022.40	997.14	985.93	980.85	978.53
80000	1383.90	1321.47	1154.12	1090.56	1063.61	1051.65	1046.24	1043.77
85000	1470.40	1404.07	1226.25	1158.72	1130.09	1117.38	1111.63	1109.00
90000	1556.89	1486.66	1298.38	1226.88	1196.56	1183.11	1177.02	1174.24
95000	1643.38	1569.25	1370.51	1295.04	1263.04	1248.84	1242.41	1239.48
100000	1729.88	1651.84	1442.64	1363.20	1329.52	1314.57	1307.80	1304.71
105000	1816.37	1734.43	1514.78	1431.36	1395.99	1380.30	1373.19	1369.95
110000	1902.86	1817.03	1586.91	1499.52	1462.47	1446.02	1438.58	1435.18
115000	1989.36	1899.62	1659.04	1567.68	1528.94	1511.75	1503.97	1500.42
120000	2075.85	1982.21	1731.17	1635.84	1595.42	1577.48	1569.36	1565.65
125000	2162.34	2064.80	1803.30	1704.00	1661.89	1643.21	1634.75	1630.89
130000	2248.84	2147.39	1875.44	1772.16	1728.37	1708.94	1700.14	1696.12
135000	2335.33	2229.98	1947.57	1840.32	1794.84	1774.66	1765.53	1761.36
140000	2421.83	2312.58	2019.70	1908.48	1861.32	1840.39	1830.92	1826.59
145000	2508.32	2395.17	2091.83	1976.64	1927.80	1906.12	1896.31	1891.83
150000	2594.81	2477.76	2163.96	2044.80	1994.27	1971.85	1961.70	1957.06
155000	2681.31	2560.35	2236.10	2112.96	2060.75	2037.58	2027.09	2022.30
160000	2767.80	2642.94	2308.23	2181.12	2127.22	2103.30	2092.48	2087.53

AMOUNT OF LOAN	NUMBER OF YEARS IN TERM							
	1	2	3	4	5	6	7	8
$ 50	4.54	2.45	1.76	1.42	1.21	1.08	.99	.92
100	9.07	4.89	3.51	2.83	2.42	2.16	1.98	1.84
200	18.13	9.77	7.01	5.65	4.84	4.32	3.95	3.68
300	27.19	14.66	10.52	8.47	7.26	6.47	5.92	5.52
400	36.25	19.54	14.02	11.29	9.68	8.63	7.89	7.36
500	45.31	24.43	17.52	14.11	12.10	10.78	9.86	9.20
600	54.37	29.31	21.03	16.93	14.52	12.94	11.84	11.03
700	63.43	34.20	24.53	19.75	16.93	15.09	13.81	12.87
800	72.50	39.08	28.03	22.57	19.35	17.25	15.78	14.71
900	81.56	43.96	31.54	25.40	21.77	19.40	17.75	16.55
1000	90.62	48.85	35.04	28.22	24.19	21.56	19.72	18.39
2000	181.23	97.69	70.07	56.43	48.38	43.11	39.44	36.77
3000	271.84	146.54	105.11	84.64	72.56	64.67	59.16	55.15
4000	362.46	195.38	140.14	112.85	96.75	86.22	78.88	73.53
5000	453.07	244.22	175.17	141.07	120.93	107.78	98.60	91.92
6000	543.68	293.07	210.21	169.28	145.12	129.33	118.32	110.30
7000	634.29	341.91	245.24	197.49	169.30	150.89	138.04	128.68
8000	724.91	390.75	280.27	225.70	193.49	172.44	157.76	147.06
9000	815.52	439.60	315.31	253.92	217.67	193.99	177.48	165.44
10000	906.13	488.44	350.34	282.13	241.86	215.55	197.20	183.83
11000	996.74	537.29	385.38	310.34	266.04	237.10	216.92	202.21
12000	1087.36	586.13	420.41	338.55	290.23	258.66	236.64	220.59
13000	1177.97	634.97	455.44	366.77	314.42	280.21	256.36	238.97
14000	1268.58	683.82	490.48	394.98	338.60	301.77	276.08	257.35
15000	1359.19	732.66	525.51	423.19	362.79	323.32	295.80	275.74
16000	1449.81	781.50	560.54	451.40	386.97	344.88	315.52	294.12
17000	1540.42	830.35	595.58	479.62	411.16	366.43	335.24	312.50
18000	1631.03	879.19	630.61	507.83	435.34	387.98	354.96	330.88
19000	1721.64	928.04	665.65	536.04	459.53	409.54	374.68	349.26
20000	1812.26	976.88	700.68	564.25	483.71	431.09	394.40	367.65
21000	1902.87	1025.72	735.71	592.47	507.90	452.65	414.12	386.03
22000	1993.48	1074.57	770.75	620.68	532.08	474.20	433.84	404.41
23000	2084.09	1123.41	805.78	648.89	556.27	495.76	453.56	422.79
24000	2174.71	1172.25	840.81	677.10	580.46	517.31	473.28	441.17
25000	2265.32	1221.10	875.85	705.32	604.64	538.87	493.00	459.56
26000	2355.93	1269.94	910.88	733.53	628.83	560.42	512.72	477.94
27000	2446.55	1318.79	945.92	761.74	653.01	581.97	532.44	496.32
28000	2537.16	1367.63	980.95	789.95	677.20	603.53	552.16	514.70
29000	2627.77	1416.47	1015.98	818.16	701.38	625.08	571.88	533.08
30000	2718.38	1465.32	1051.02	846.38	725.57	646.64	591.60	551.47
31000	2809.00	1514.16	1086.05	874.59	749.75	668.19	611.32	569.85
32000	2899.61	1563.00	1121.08	902.80	773.94	689.75	631.04	588.23
33000	2990.22	1611.85	1156.12	931.01	798.12	711.30	650.76	606.61
34000	3080.83	1660.69	1191.15	959.23	822.31	732.86	670.48	625.00
35000	3171.45	1709.54	1226.19	987.44	846.49	754.41	690.20	643.38
40000	3624.51	1953.75	1401.35	1128.50	967.42	862.18	788.80	735.29
45000	4077.57	2197.97	1576.52	1269.56	1088.35	969.95	887.40	827.20
50000	4530.63	2442.19	1751.69	1410.63	1209.28	1077.73	986.00	919.11
55000	4983.70	2686.41	1926.86	1551.69	1330.20	1185.50	1084.60	1011.02
60000	5436.76	2930.63	2102.03	1692.75	1451.13	1293.27	1183.20	1102.93
65000	5889.82	3174.85	2277.20	1833.81	1572.06	1401.04	1281.80	1194.84
70000	6342.89	3419.07	2452.37	1974.87	1692.98	1508.82	1380.40	1286.75
75000	6795.95	3663.29	2627.53	2115.94	1813.91	1616.59	1479.00	1378.66
80000	7249.01	3907.50	2802.70	2257.00	1934.84	1724.36	1577.60	1470.57
85000	7702.08	4151.72	2977.87	2398.06	2055.77	1832.13	1676.20	1562.48
90000	8155.14	4395.94	3153.04	2539.12	2176.69	1939.90	1774.80	1654.39
95000	8608.20	4640.16	3328.21	2680.18	2297.62	2047.68	1873.40	1746.30
100000	9061.26	4884.38	3503.38	2821.25	2418.55	2155.45	1972.00	1838.21
105000	9514.33	5128.60	3678.55	2962.31	2539.47	2263.22	2070.60	1930.12
110000	9967.39	5372.82	3853.72	3103.37	2660.40	2370.99	2169.20	2022.03
115000	10420.45	5617.04	4028.88	3244.43	2781.33	2478.76	2267.80	2113.94
120000	10873.52	5861.25	4204.05	3385.49	2902.26	2586.54	2366.40	2205.85
125000	11326.58	6105.47	4379.22	3526.56	3023.18	2694.31	2465.00	2297.76
130000	11779.64	6349.69	4554.39	3667.62	3144.11	2802.08	2563.60	2389.67
135000	12232.71	6593.91	4729.56	3808.68	3265.04	2909.85	2662.20	2481.58
140000	12685.77	6838.13	4904.73	3949.74	3385.96	3017.63	2760.80	2573.49
145000	13138.83	7082.35	5079.90	4090.80	3506.89	3125.40	2859.40	2665.40
150000	13591.89	7326.57	5255.06	4231.87	3627.82	3233.17	2958.00	2757.31
155000	14044.96	7570.79	5430.23	4372.93	3748.75	3340.94	3056.60	2849.22
160000	14498.02	7815.00	5605.40	4513.99	3869.67	3448.71	3155.20	2941.14

AMOUNT OF LOAN	NUMBER OF YEARS IN TERM 9	10	15	20	25	30	35	40
$ 50	.87	.83	.73	.69	.67	.67	.66	.66
100	1.74	1.66	1.46	1.38	1.34	1.33	1.32	1.32
200	3.48	3.32	2.91	2.75	2.68	2.65	2.64	2.64
300	5.22	4.98	4.36	4.12	4.02	3.98	3.96	3.95
400	6.95	6.64	5.81	5.50	5.36	5.30	5.28	5.27
500	8.69	8.30	7.26	6.87	6.70	6.63	6.60	6.58
600	10.43	9.96	8.71	8.24	8.04	7.95	7.91	7.90
700	12.17	11.62	10.16	9.61	9.38	9.28	9.23	9.21
800	13.90	13.28	11.62	10.99	10.72	10.60	10.55	10.53
900	15.64	14.94	13.07	12.36	12.06	11.93	11.87	11.84
1000	17.38	16.60	14.52	13.73	13.40	13.25	13.19	13.16
2000	34.75	33.20	29.03	27.46	26.79	26.50	26.37	26.31
3000	52.13	49.79	43.54	41.18	40.18	39.74	39.55	39.46
4000	69.50	66.39	58.06	54.91	53.58	52.99	52.73	52.61
5000	86.88	82.98	72.57	68.63	66.97	66.24	65.91	65.76
6000	104.25	99.58	87.08	82.36	80.36	79.48	79.09	78.91
7000	121.62	116.18	101.60	96.08	93.76	92.73	92.27	92.06
8000	139.00	132.77	116.11	109.81	107.15	105.97	105.45	105.21
9000	156.37	149.37	130.62	123.53	120.54	119.22	118.63	118.36
10000	173.75	165.96	145.14	137.26	133.93	132.47	131.81	131.51
11000	191.12	182.56	159.65	150.98	147.33	145.71	144.99	144.66
12000	208.49	199.16	174.16	164.71	160.72	158.96	158.17	157.81
13000	225.87	215.75	188.68	178.43	174.11	172.21	171.35	170.96
14000	243.24	232.35	203.19	192.16	187.51	185.45	184.53	184.11
15000	260.62	248.94	217.70	205.89	200.90	198.70	197.71	197.26
16000	277.99	265.54	232.21	219.61	214.29	211.94	210.89	210.41
17000	295.36	282.13	246.73	233.34	227.68	225.19	224.07	223.56
18000	312.74	298.73	261.24	247.06	241.08	238.44	237.25	236.71
19000	330.11	315.33	275.75	260.79	254.47	251.68	250.43	249.86
20000	347.49	331.92	290.27	274.51	267.86	264.93	263.61	263.01
21000	364.86	348.52	304.78	288.24	281.26	278.17	276.79	276.16
22000	382.23	365.11	319.29	301.96	294.65	291.42	289.97	289.31
23000	399.61	381.71	333.81	315.69	308.04	304.67	303.15	302.46
24000	416.98	398.31	348.32	329.41	321.43	317.91	316.33	315.61
25000	434.36	414.90	362.83	343.14	334.83	331.16	329.51	328.76
26000	451.73	431.50	377.35	356.86	348.22	344.41	342.69	341.91
27000	469.10	448.09	391.86	370.59	361.61	357.65	355.87	355.06
28000	486.48	464.69	406.37	384.31	375.01	370.90	369.05	368.21
29000	503.85	481.28	420.88	398.04	388.40	384.14	382.23	381.36
30000	521.23	497.88	435.40	411.77	401.79	397.39	395.41	394.51
31000	538.60	514.48	449.91	425.49	415.18	410.64	408.59	407.66
32000	555.98	531.07	464.42	439.22	428.58	423.88	421.77	420.81
33000	573.35	547.67	478.94	452.94	441.97	437.13	434.95	433.96
34000	590.72	564.26	493.45	466.67	455.36	450.37	448.13	447.11
35000	608.10	580.86	507.96	480.39	468.76	463.62	461.31	460.26
40000	694.97	663.84	580.53	549.02	535.72	529.85	527.21	526.01
45000	781.84	746.82	653.09	617.65	602.69	596.08	593.11	591.76
50000	868.71	829.80	725.66	686.27	669.65	662.31	659.01	657.51
55000	955.58	912.78	798.22	754.90	736.61	728.54	724.91	723.26
60000	1042.45	995.76	870.79	823.53	803.58	794.78	790.81	789.01
65000	1129.32	1078.74	943.36	892.15	870.54	861.01	856.71	854.77
70000	1216.19	1161.71	1015.92	960.78	937.51	927.24	922.61	920.52
75000	1303.06	1244.69	1088.49	1029.41	1004.47	993.47	988.52	986.27
80000	1389.93	1327.67	1161.05	1098.03	1071.44	1059.70	1054.42	1052.02
85000	1476.80	1410.65	1233.62	1166.66	1138.40	1125.93	1120.32	1117.77
90000	1563.67	1493.63	1306.18	1235.29	1205.37	1192.16	1186.22	1183.52
95000	1650.54	1576.61	1378.75	1303.91	1272.33	1258.39	1252.12	1249.27
100000	1737.41	1659.59	1451.31	1372.54	1339.29	1324.62	1318.02	1315.02
105000	1824.28	1742.57	1523.88	1441.17	1406.26	1390.85	1383.92	1380.77
110000	1911.15	1825.55	1596.44	1509.79	1473.22	1457.08	1449.82	1446.52
115000	1998.02	1908.53	1669.01	1578.42	1540.19	1523.31	1515.72	1512.27
120000	2084.89	1991.51	1741.57	1647.05	1607.15	1589.55	1581.62	1578.02
125000	2171.76	2074.49	1814.14	1715.67	1674.12	1655.78	1647.52	1643.77
130000	2258.63	2157.47	1886.71	1784.30	1741.08	1722.01	1713.42	1709.53
135000	2345.50	2240.44	1959.27	1852.93	1808.05	1788.24	1779.32	1775.28
140000	2432.38	2323.42	2031.84	1921.55	1875.01	1854.47	1845.22	1841.03
145000	2519.25	2406.40	2104.40	1990.18	1941.97	1920.70	1911.12	1906.78
150000	2606.12	2489.38	2176.97	2058.81	2008.94	1986.93	1977.03	1972.53
155000	2692.99	2572.36	2249.53	2127.43	2075.90	2053.16	2042.93	2038.28
160000	2779.86	2655.34	2322.10	2196.06	2142.87	2119.39	2108.83	2104.03

MONTHLY AMORTIZING PAYMENTS

AMOUNT OF LOAN	NUMBER OF YEARS IN TERM							
	1	2	3	4	5	6	7	8
$ 50	4.54	2.45	1.76	1.42	1.22	1.09	.99	.93
100	9.07	4.90	3.51	2.83	2.43	2.17	1.98	1.85
200	18.14	9.79	7.02	5.66	4.86	4.33	3.96	3.70
300	27.21	14.68	10.53	8.49	7.28	6.49	5.94	5.54
400	36.27	19.57	14.04	11.32	9.71	8.65	7.92	7.39
500	45.34	24.46	17.55	14.14	12.13	10.82	9.90	9.23
600	54.41	29.35	21.06	16.97	14.56	12.98	11.88	11.08
700	63.48	34.24	24.57	19.80	16.98	15.14	13.86	12.92
800	72.54	39.13	28.08	22.63	19.41	17.30	15.84	14.77
900	81.61	44.02	31.59	25.45	21.83	19.47	17.82	16.61
1000	90.68	48.91	35.10	28.28	24.26	21.63	19.80	18.46
2000	181.35	97.81	70.20	56.56	48.51	43.25	39.59	36.92
3000	272.02	146.72	105.29	84.83	72.76	64.87	59.38	55.37
4000	362.69	195.62	140.39	113.11	97.01	86.50	79.17	73.83
5000	453.36	244.52	175.48	141.39	121.26	108.12	98.96	92.28
6000	544.04	293.43	210.58	169.66	145.52	129.74	118.75	110.74
7000	634.71	342.33	245.67	197.94	169.77	151.37	138.54	129.19
8000	725.38	391.23	280.77	226.22	194.02	172.99	158.33	147.65
9000	816.05	440.14	315.86	254.49	218.27	194.61	178.12	166.10
10000	906.72	489.04	350.96	282.77	242.52	216.24	197.91	184.56
11000	997.39	537.94	386.05	311.04	266.77	237.86	217.71	203.01
12000	1088.07	586.85	421.15	339.32	291.03	259.48	237.50	221.47
13000	1178.74	635.75	456.24	367.60	315.28	281.11	257.29	239.92
14000	1269.41	684.65	491.34	395.87	339.53	302.73	277.08	258.38
15000	1360.08	733.56	526.44	424.15	363.78	324.35	296.87	276.84
16000	1450.75	782.46	561.53	452.43	388.03	345.97	316.66	295.29
17000	1541.42	831.36	596.63	480.70	412.28	367.60	336.45	313.75
18000	1632.10	880.27	631.72	508.98	436.54	389.22	356.24	332.20
19000	1722.77	929.17	666.82	537.25	460.79	410.84	376.03	350.66
20000	1813.44	978.07	701.91	565.53	485.04	432.47	395.82	369.11
21000	1904.11	1026.98	737.01	593.81	509.29	454.09	415.61	387.57
22000	1994.78	1075.88	772.10	622.08	533.54	475.71	435.41	406.02
23000	2085.45	1124.78	807.20	650.36	557.79	497.34	455.20	424.48
24000	2176.13	1173.69	842.29	678.64	582.05	518.96	474.99	442.93
25000	2266.80	1222.59	877.39	706.91	606.30	540.58	494.78	461.39
26000	2357.47	1271.49	912.48	735.19	630.55	562.21	514.57	479.84
27000	2448.14	1320.40	947.58	763.47	654.80	583.83	534.36	498.30
28000	2538.81	1369.30	982.67	791.74	679.05	605.45	554.15	516.75
29000	2629.48	1418.20	1017.77	820.02	703.30	627.07	573.94	535.21
30000	2720.16	1467.11	1052.87	848.29	727.56	648.70	593.73	553.67
31000	2810.83	1516.01	1087.96	876.57	751.81	670.32	613.52	572.12
32000	2901.50	1564.91	1123.06	904.85	776.06	691.94	633.31	590.58
33000	2992.17	1613.82	1158.15	933.12	800.31	713.57	653.11	609.03
34000	3082.84	1662.72	1193.25	961.40	824.56	735.19	672.90	627.49
35000	3173.52	1711.62	1228.34	989.68	848.81	756.81	692.69	645.94
40000	3626.87	1956.14	1403.82	1131.06	970.07	864.93	791.64	738.22
45000	4080.23	2200.66	1579.30	1272.44	1091.33	973.04	890.60	830.50
50000	4533.59	2445.18	1754.77	1413.82	1212.59	1081.16	989.55	922.77
55000	4986.95	2689.69	1930.25	1555.20	1333.85	1189.27	1088.51	1015.05
60000	5440.31	2934.21	2105.73	1696.58	1455.11	1297.39	1187.46	1107.33
65000	5893.67	3178.73	2281.20	1837.96	1576.36	1405.51	1286.42	1199.60
70000	6347.03	3423.24	2456.68	1979.35	1697.62	1513.62	1385.37	1291.88
75000	6800.38	3667.76	2632.16	2120.73	1818.88	1621.74	1484.33	1384.16
80000	7253.74	3912.28	2807.63	2262.11	1940.14	1729.85	1583.28	1476.43
85000	7707.10	4156.79	2983.11	2403.49	2061.40	1837.97	1682.23	1568.71
90000	8160.46	4401.31	3158.59	2544.87	2182.66	1946.08	1781.19	1660.99
95000	8613.82	4645.83	3334.06	2686.25	2303.92	2054.20	1880.14	1753.26
100000	9067.18	4890.35	3509.54	2827.64	2425.17	2162.31	1979.10	1845.54
105000	9520.54	5134.86	3685.02	2969.02	2546.43	2270.43	2078.05	1937.82
110000	9973.89	5379.38	3860.49	3110.40	2667.69	2378.54	2177.01	2030.09
115000	10427.25	5623.90	4035.97	3251.78	2788.95	2486.66	2275.96	2122.37
120000	10880.61	5868.41	4211.45	3393.16	2910.21	2594.77	2374.92	2214.65
125000	11333.97	6112.93	4386.92	3534.54	3031.47	2702.89	2473.87	2306.92
130000	11787.33	6357.45	4562.40	3675.92	3152.72	2811.01	2572.83	2399.20
135000	12240.69	6601.96	4737.88	3817.31	3273.98	2919.12	2671.78	2491.48
140000	12694.05	6846.48	4913.35	3958.69	3395.24	3027.24	2770.74	2583.75
145000	13147.40	7091.00	5088.83	4100.07	3516.50	3135.35	2869.69	2676.03
150000	13600.76	7335.52	5264.31	4241.45	3637.76	3243.47	2968.65	2768.31
155000	14054.12	7580.03	5439.78	4382.83	3759.02	3351.58	3067.60	2860.58
160000	14507.48	7824.55	5615.26	4524.21	3880.28	3459.70	3166.55	2952.86

AMOUNT OF LOAN	NUMBER OF YEARS IN TERM							
	9	10	15	20	25	30	35	40
$ 50	.88	.84	.73	.70	.68	.67	.67	.67
100	1.75	1.67	1.46	1.39	1.35	1.34	1.33	1.33
200	3.49	3.34	2.92	2.77	2.70	2.67	2.66	2.66
300	5.24	5.01	4.38	4.15	4.05	4.01	3.99	3.98
400	6.98	6.67	5.84	5.53	5.40	5.34	5.32	5.31
500	8.73	8.34	7.30	6.91	6.75	6.68	6.65	6.63
600	10.47	10.01	8.76	8.30	8.10	8.01	7.97	7.96
700	12.22	11.68	10.22	9.68	9.45	9.35	9.30	9.28
800	13.96	13.34	11.68	11.06	10.80	10.68	10.63	10.61
900	15.71	15.01	13.14	12.44	12.15	12.02	11.96	11.93
1000	17.45	16.68	14.60	13.82	13.50	13.35	13.29	13.26
2000	34.90	33.35	29.20	27.64	26.99	26.70	26.57	26.51
3000	52.35	50.03	43.80	41.46	40.48	40.05	39.85	39.76
4000	69.80	66.70	58.40	55.28	53.97	53.39	53.13	53.02
5000	87.25	83.37	73.00	69.10	67.46	66.74	66.42	66.27
6000	104.70	100.05	87.60	82.92	80.95	80.09	79.70	79.52
7000	122.15	116.72	102.20	96.74	94.44	93.43	92.98	92.78
8000	139.60	133.39	116.80	110.56	107.93	106.78	106.26	106.03
9000	157.05	150.07	131.40	124.37	121.42	120.13	119.55	119.28
10000	174.50	166.74	146.00	138.19	134.91	133.47	132.83	132.54
11000	191.95	183.41	160.60	152.01	148.40	146.82	146.11	145.79
12000	209.40	200.09	175.20	165.83	161.89	160.17	159.39	159.04
13000	226.85	216.76	189.80	179.65	175.39	173.51	172.68	172.30
14000	244.30	233.43	204.40	193.47	188.88	186.86	185.96	185.55
15000	261.75	250.11	219.00	207.29	202.37	200.21	199.24	198.80
16000	279.20	266.78	233.60	221.11	215.86	213.55	212.52	212.06
17000	296.65	283.45	248.20	234.93	229.35	226.90	225.81	225.31
18000	314.10	300.13	262.80	248.74	242.84	240.25	239.09	238.56
19000	331.55	316.80	277.40	262.56	256.33	253.59	252.37	251.82
20000	349.00	333.47	292.00	276.38	269.82	266.94	265.65	265.07
21000	366.45	350.15	306.60	290.20	283.31	280.29	278.94	278.32
22000	383.90	366.82	321.20	304.02	296.80	293.64	292.22	291.58
23000	401.35	383.50	335.80	317.84	310.29	306.98	305.50	304.83
24000	418.79	400.17	350.40	331.66	323.78	320.33	318.78	318.08
25000	436.24	416.84	365.00	345.48	337.28	333.68	332.06	331.34
26000	453.69	433.52	379.60	359.30	350.77	347.02	345.35	344.59
27000	471.14	450.19	394.20	373.11	364.26	360.37	358.63	357.84
28000	488.59	466.86	408.80	386.93	377.75	373.72	371.91	371.10
29000	506.04	483.54	423.40	400.75	391.24	387.06	385.19	384.35
30000	523.49	500.21	438.00	414.57	404.73	400.41	398.48	397.60
31000	540.94	516.88	452.60	428.39	418.22	413.76	411.76	410.86
32000	558.39	533.56	467.20	442.21	431.71	427.10	425.04	424.11
33000	575.84	550.23	481.80	456.03	445.20	440.45	438.32	437.36
34000	593.29	566.90	496.40	469.85	458.69	453.80	451.61	450.62
35000	610.74	583.58	511.00	483.67	472.18	467.14	464.89	463.87
40000	697.99	666.94	584.00	552.76	539.64	533.88	531.30	530.14
45000	785.24	750.31	657.00	621.85	607.09	600.61	597.71	596.40
50000	872.48	833.68	730.00	690.95	674.55	667.35	664.12	662.67
55000	959.73	917.05	803.00	760.04	742.00	734.08	730.54	728.94
60000	1046.98	1000.41	876.00	829.14	809.45	800.81	796.95	795.20
65000	1134.23	1083.78	949.00	898.23	876.91	867.55	863.36	861.47
70000	1221.48	1167.15	1022.00	967.33	944.36	934.28	929.77	927.74
75000	1308.72	1250.52	1095.00	1036.42	1011.82	1001.02	996.18	994.00
80000	1395.97	1333.88	1168.00	1105.51	1079.27	1067.75	1062.60	1060.27
85000	1483.22	1417.25	1241.00	1174.61	1146.73	1134.48	1129.01	1126.54
90000	1570.47	1500.62	1314.00	1243.70	1214.18	1201.22	1195.42	1192.80
95000	1657.72	1583.99	1387.00	1312.80	1281.63	1267.95	1261.83	1259.07
100000	1744.96	1667.35	1460.00	1381.89	1349.09	1334.69	1328.24	1325.34
105000	1832.21	1750.72	1533.00	1450.99	1416.54	1401.42	1394.66	1391.60
110000	1919.46	1834.09	1606.00	1520.08	1484.00	1468.16	1461.07	1457.87
115000	2006.71	1917.46	1679.00	1589.17	1551.45	1534.89	1527.48	1524.13
120000	2093.95	2000.82	1752.00	1658.27	1618.90	1601.62	1593.89	1590.40
125000	2181.20	2084.19	1825.00	1727.36	1686.36	1668.36	1660.30	1656.67
130000	2268.45	2167.56	1898.00	1796.46	1753.81	1735.09	1726.71	1722.93
135000	2355.70	2250.93	1971.00	1865.55	1821.27	1801.83	1793.13	1789.20
140000	2442.95	2334.29	2044.00	1934.65	1888.72	1868.56	1859.54	1855.47
145000	2530.19	2417.66	2117.00	2003.74	1956.17	1935.29	1925.95	1921.73
150000	2617.44	2501.03	2190.00	2072.83	2023.63	2002.03	1992.36	1988.00
155000	2704.69	2584.40	2263.00	2141.93	2091.08	2068.76	2058.77	2054.27
160000	2791.94	2667.76	2336.00	2211.02	2158.54	2135.50	2125.19	2120.53

16% MONTHLY AMORTIZING PAYMENTS

AMOUNT OF LOAN	NUMBER OF YEARS IN TERM 1	2	3	4	5	6	7	8
$ 50	4.54	2.45	1.76	1.42	1.22	1.09	1.00	.93
100	9.08	4.90	3.52	2.84	2.44	2.17	1.99	1.86
200	18.15	9.80	7.04	5.67	4.87	4.34	3.98	3.71
300	27.22	14.69	10.55	8.51	7.30	6.51	5.96	5.56
400	36.30	19.59	14.07	11.34	9.73	8.68	7.95	7.42
500	45.37	24.49	17.58	14.18	12.16	10.85	9.94	9.27
600	54.44	29.38	21.10	17.01	14.60	13.02	11.92	11.12
700	63.52	34.28	24.61	19.84	17.03	15.19	13.91	12.98
800	72.59	39.18	28.13	22.68	19.46	17.36	15.89	14.83
900	81.66	44.07	31.65	25.51	21.89	19.53	17.88	16.68
1000	90.74	48.97	35.16	28.35	24.32	21.70	19.87	18.53
2000	181.47	97.93	70.32	56.69	48.64	43.39	39.73	37.06
3000	272.20	146.89	105.48	85.03	72.96	65.08	59.59	55.59
4000	362.93	195.86	140.63	113.37	97.28	86.77	79.45	74.12
5000	453.66	244.82	175.79	141.71	121.60	108.46	99.32	92.65
6000	544.39	293.78	210.95	170.05	145.91	130.16	119.18	111.18
7000	635.12	342.75	246.10	198.39	170.23	151.85	139.04	129.71
8000	725.85	391.71	281.26	226.73	194.55	173.54	158.90	148.24
9000	816.58	440.67	316.42	255.07	218.87	195.23	178.76	166.76
10000	907.31	489.64	351.58	283.41	243.19	216.92	198.63	185.29
11000	998.04	538.60	386.73	311.75	267.50	238.62	218.49	203.82
12000	1088.78	587.56	421.89	340.09	291.82	260.31	238.35	222.35
13000	1179.51	636.53	457.05	368.43	316.14	282.00	258.21	240.88
14000	1270.24	685.49	492.20	396.77	340.46	303.69	278.07	259.41
15000	1360.97	734.45	527.36	425.11	364.78	325.38	297.94	277.94
16000	1451.70	783.41	562.52	453.45	389.09	347.07	317.80	296.47
17000	1542.43	832.38	597.67	481.79	413.41	368.77	337.66	314.99
18000	1633.16	881.34	632.83	510.13	437.73	390.46	357.52	333.52
19000	1723.89	930.30	667.99	538.47	462.05	412.15	377.38	352.05
20000	1814.62	979.27	703.15	566.81	486.37	433.84	397.25	370.58
21000	1905.35	1028.23	738.30	595.15	510.68	455.53	417.11	389.11
22000	1996.08	1077.19	773.46	623.49	535.00	477.23	436.97	407.64
23000	2086.81	1126.16	808.62	651.83	559.32	498.92	456.83	426.17
24000	2177.55	1175.12	843.77	680.17	583.64	520.61	476.69	444.70
25000	2268.28	1224.08	878.93	708.51	607.96	542.30	496.56	463.22
26000	2359.01	1273.05	914.09	736.85	632.27	563.99	516.42	481.75
27000	2449.74	1322.01	949.24	765.19	656.59	585.68	536.28	500.28
28000	2540.47	1370.97	984.40	793.53	680.91	607.38	556.14	518.81
29000	2631.20	1419.94	1019.56	821.87	705.23	629.07	576.00	537.34
30000	2721.93	1468.90	1054.72	850.21	729.55	650.76	595.87	555.87
31000	2812.66	1517.86	1089.87	878.55	753.86	672.45	615.73	574.40
32000	2903.39	1566.82	1125.03	906.89	778.18	694.14	635.59	592.93
33000	2994.12	1615.79	1160.19	935.23	802.50	715.84	655.45	611.45
34000	3084.85	1664.75	1195.34	963.57	826.82	737.53	675.32	629.98
35000	3175.59	1713.71	1230.50	991.91	851.14	759.22	695.18	648.51
40000	3629.24	1958.53	1406.29	1133.62	972.73	867.68	794.49	741.16
45000	4082.89	2203.34	1582.07	1275.32	1094.32	976.14	893.80	833.80
50000	4536.55	2448.16	1757.86	1417.02	1215.91	1084.60	993.11	926.44
55000	4990.20	2692.98	1933.64	1558.72	1337.50	1193.06	1092.42	1019.09
60000	5443.86	2937.79	2109.43	1700.42	1459.09	1301.52	1191.73	1111.73
65000	5897.51	3182.61	2285.21	1842.12	1580.68	1409.97	1291.04	1204.38
70000	6351.17	3427.42	2461.00	1983.82	1702.27	1518.43	1390.35	1297.02
75000	6804.82	3672.24	2636.78	2125.53	1823.86	1626.89	1489.66	1389.66
80000	7258.47	3917.05	2812.57	2267.23	1945.45	1735.35	1588.97	1482.31
85000	7712.13	4161.87	2988.35	2408.93	2067.04	1843.81	1688.28	1574.95
90000	8165.78	4406.68	3164.14	2550.63	2188.63	1952.27	1787.59	1667.60
95000	8619.44	4651.50	3339.92	2692.33	2310.22	2060.73	1886.90	1760.24
100000	9073.09	4896.32	3515.71	2834.03	2431.81	2169.19	1986.21	1852.88
105000	9526.75	5141.13	3691.49	2975.73	2553.40	2277.65	2085.52	1945.53
110000	9980.40	5385.95	3867.28	3117.44	2674.99	2386.11	2184.83	2038.17
115000	10434.05	5630.76	4043.06	3259.14	2796.58	2494.57	2284.14	2130.82
120000	10887.71	5875.58	4218.85	3400.84	2918.17	2603.03	2383.45	2223.46
125000	11341.36	6120.39	4394.63	3542.54	3039.76	2711.49	2482.76	2316.10
130000	11795.02	6365.21	4570.42	3684.24	3161.35	2819.94	2582.07	2408.75
135000	12248.67	6610.02	4746.20	3825.94	3282.94	2928.40	2681.38	2501.39
140000	12702.33	6854.84	4921.99	3967.64	3404.53	3036.86	2780.69	2594.04
145000	13155.98	7099.66	5097.77	4109.35	3526.12	3145.32	2880.00	2686.68
150000	13609.63	7344.47	5273.56	4251.05	3647.71	3253.78	2979.31	2779.32
155000	14063.29	7589.29	5449.35	4392.75	3769.30	3362.24	3078.62	2871.97
160000	14516.94	7834.10	5625.13	4534.45	3890.89	3470.70	3177.94	2964.61

AMOUNT OF LOAN	NUMBER OF YEARS IN TERM							
	9	10	15	20	25	30	35	40
$ 50	.88	.84	.74	.70	.68	.68	.67	.67
100	1.76	1.68	1.47	1.40	1.36	1.35	1.34	1.34
200	3.51	3.36	2.94	2.79	2.72	2.69	2.68	2.68
300	5.26	5.03	4.41	4.18	4.08	4.04	4.02	4.01
400	7.02	6.71	5.88	5.57	5.44	5.38	5.36	5.35
500	8.77	8.38	7.35	6.96	6.80	6.73	6.70	6.68
600	10.52	10.06	8.82	8.35	8.16	8.07	8.04	8.02
700	12.27	11.73	10.29	9.74	9.52	9.42	9.37	9.35
800	14.03	13.41	11.75	11.14	10.88	10.76	10.71	10.69
900	15.78	15.08	13.22	12.53	12.23	12.11	12.05	12.03
1000	17.53	16.76	14.69	13.92	13.59	13.45	13.39	13.36
2000	35.06	33.51	29.38	27.83	27.18	26.90	26.77	26.72
3000	52.58	50.26	44.07	41.74	40.77	40.35	40.16	40.07
4000	70.11	67.01	58.75	55.66	54.36	53.80	53.54	53.43
5000	87.63	83.76	73.44	69.57	67.95	67.24	66.93	66.79
6000	105.16	100.51	88.13	83.48	81.54	80.69	80.31	80.14
7000	122.68	117.26	102.81	97.39	95.13	94.14	93.70	93.50
8000	140.21	134.02	117.50	111.31	108.72	107.59	107.08	106.86
9000	157.73	150.77	132.19	125.22	122.30	121.03	120.47	120.21
10000	175.26	167.52	146.88	139.13	135.89	134.48	133.85	133.57
11000	192.78	184.27	161.56	153.04	149.48	147.93	147.24	146.93
12000	210.31	201.02	176.25	166.96	163.07	161.38	160.62	160.28
13000	227.83	217.77	190.94	180.87	176.66	174.82	174.01	173.64
14000	245.36	234.52	205.62	194.78	190.25	188.27	187.39	187.00
15000	262.88	251.27	220.31	208.69	203.84	201.72	200.78	200.35
16000	280.41	268.03	235.00	222.61	217.43	215.17	214.16	213.71
17000	297.93	284.78	249.68	236.52	231.02	228.61	227.54	227.07
18000	315.46	301.53	264.37	250.43	244.60	242.06	240.93	240.42
19000	332.98	318.28	279.06	264.34	258.19	255.51	254.31	253.78
20000	350.51	335.03	293.75	278.26	271.78	268.96	267.70	267.13
21000	368.04	351.78	308.43	292.17	285.37	282.40	281.08	280.49
22000	385.56	368.53	323.12	306.08	298.96	295.85	294.47	293.85
23000	403.09	385.29	337.81	319.99	312.55	309.30	307.85	307.20
24000	420.61	402.04	352.49	333.91	326.14	322.75	321.24	320.56
25000	438.14	418.79	367.18	347.82	339.73	336.19	334.62	333.92
26000	455.66	435.54	381.87	361.73	353.32	349.64	348.01	347.27
27000	473.19	452.29	396.55	375.64	366.90	363.09	361.39	360.63
28000	490.71	469.04	411.24	389.56	380.49	376.54	374.78	373.99
29000	508.24	485.79	425.93	403.47	394.08	389.98	388.16	387.34
30000	525.76	502.54	440.62	417.38	407.67	403.43	401.55	400.70
31000	543.29	519.30	455.30	431.29	421.26	416.88	414.93	414.06
32000	560.81	536.05	469.99	445.21	434.85	430.33	428.32	427.41
33000	578.34	552.80	484.68	459.12	448.44	443.77	441.70	440.77
34000	595.86	569.55	499.36	473.03	462.03	457.22	455.08	454.13
35000	613.39	586.30	514.05	486.94	475.62	470.67	468.47	467.48
40000	701.02	670.06	587.49	556.51	543.56	537.91	535.39	534.26
45000	788.64	753.81	660.92	626.07	611.50	605.15	602.32	601.05
50000	876.27	837.57	734.36	695.63	679.45	672.38	669.24	667.83
55000	963.89	921.33	807.79	765.20	747.39	739.62	736.16	734.61
60000	1051.52	1005.08	881.23	834.76	815.34	806.86	803.09	801.39
65000	1139.15	1088.84	954.66	904.32	883.28	874.10	870.01	868.18
70000	1226.77	1172.60	1028.10	973.88	951.23	941.33	936.93	934.96
75000	1314.40	1256.35	1101.53	1043.45	1019.17	1008.57	1003.86	1001.74
80000	1402.03	1340.11	1174.97	1113.01	1087.12	1075.81	1070.78	1068.52
85000	1489.65	1423.87	1248.40	1182.57	1155.06	1143.05	1137.70	1135.31
90000	1577.28	1507.62	1321.84	1252.14	1223.00	1210.29	1204.63	1202.09
95000	1664.90	1591.38	1395.27	1321.70	1290.95	1277.52	1271.55	1268.87
100000	1752.53	1675.14	1468.71	1391.26	1358.89	1344.76	1338.47	1335.65
105000	1840.16	1758.89	1542.14	1460.82	1426.84	1412.00	1405.40	1402.44
110000	1927.78	1842.65	1615.58	1530.39	1494.78	1479.24	1472.32	1469.22
115000	2015.41	1926.41	1689.01	1599.95	1562.73	1546.48	1539.24	1536.00
120000	2103.04	2010.16	1762.45	1669.51	1630.67	1613.71	1606.17	1602.78
125000	2190.66	2093.92	1835.88	1739.07	1698.62	1680.95	1673.09	1669.57
130000	2278.29	2177.68	1909.32	1808.64	1766.56	1748.19	1740.02	1736.35
135000	2365.91	2261.43	1982.75	1878.20	1834.50	1815.43	1806.94	1803.13
140000	2453.54	2345.19	2056.19	1947.76	1902.45	1882.66	1873.86	1869.91
145000	2541.17	2428.95	2129.62	2017.33	1970.39	1949.90	1940.79	1936.70
150000	2628.79	2512.70	2203.06	2086.89	2038.34	2017.14	2007.71	2003.48
155000	2716.42	2596.46	2276.49	2156.45	2106.28	2084.38	2074.63	2070.26
160000	2804.05	2680.21	2349.93	2226.01	2174.23	2151.62	2141.56	2137.04

AMOUNT OF LOAN	NUMBER OF YEARS IN TERM							
	1	2	3	4	5	6	7	8
$ 50	4.54	2.46	1.77	1.43	1.22	1.09	1.00	.94
100	9.08	4.91	3.53	2.85	2.44	2.18	2.00	1.87
200	18.16	9.81	7.05	5.69	4.88	4.36	3.99	3.73
300	27.24	14.71	10.57	8.53	7.32	6.53	5.98	5.59
400	36.32	19.61	14.09	11.37	9.76	8.71	7.98	7.45
500	45.40	24.52	17.61	14.21	12.20	10.89	9.97	9.31
600	54.48	29.42	21.14	17.05	14.64	13.06	11.96	11.17
700	63.56	34.32	24.66	19.89	17.07	15.24	13.96	13.03
800	72.64	39.22	28.18	22.73	19.51	17.41	15.95	14.89
900	81.72	44.13	31.70	25.57	21.95	19.59	17.94	16.75
1000	90.80	49.03	35.22	28.41	24.39	21.77	19.94	18.61
2000	181.59	98.05	70.44	56.81	48.77	43.53	39.87	37.21
3000	272.38	147.07	105.66	85.22	73.16	65.29	59.80	55.81
4000	363.17	196.10	140.88	113.62	97.54	87.05	79.74	74.41
5000	453.96	245.12	176.10	142.03	121.93	108.81	99.67	93.02
6000	544.75	294.14	211.32	170.43	146.31	130.57	119.60	111.62
7000	635.54	343.17	246.54	198.84	170.70	152.33	139.54	130.22
8000	726.33	392.19	281.76	227.24	195.08	174.09	159.47	148.82
9000	817.12	441.21	316.97	255.64	219.47	195.85	179.40	167.43
10000	907.91	490.23	352.19	284.05	243.85	217.61	199.34	186.03
11000	998.70	539.26	387.41	312.45	268.23	239.37	219.27	204.63
12000	1089.49	588.28	422.63	340.86	292.62	261.13	239.20	223.23
13000	1180.28	637.30	457.85	369.26	317.00	282.89	259.14	241.84
14000	1271.07	686.33	493.07	397.67	341.39	304.66	279.07	260.44
15000	1361.86	735.35	528.29	426.07	365.77	326.42	299.00	279.04
16000	1452.65	784.37	563.51	454.47	390.16	348.18	318.94	297.64
17000	1543.44	833.39	598.72	482.88	414.54	369.94	338.87	316.25
18000	1634.23	882.42	633.94	511.28	438.93	391.70	358.80	334.85
19000	1725.02	931.44	669.16	539.69	463.31	413.46	378.74	353.45
20000	1815.81	980.46	704.38	568.09	487.70	435.22	398.67	372.05
21000	1906.60	1029.49	739.60	596.50	512.08	456.98	418.60	390.65
22000	1997.39	1078.51	774.82	624.90	536.46	478.74	438.54	409.26
23000	2088.18	1127.53	810.04	653.30	560.85	500.50	458.47	427.86
24000	2178.97	1176.55	845.26	681.71	585.23	522.26	478.40	446.46
25000	2269.76	1225.58	880.47	710.11	609.62	544.02	498.34	465.06
26000	2360.55	1274.60	915.69	738.52	634.00	565.78	518.27	483.67
27000	2451.34	1323.62	950.91	766.92	658.39	587.54	538.20	502.27
28000	2542.13	1372.65	986.13	795.33	682.77	609.31	558.14	520.87
29000	2632.92	1421.67	1021.35	823.73	707.16	631.07	578.07	539.47
30000	2723.71	1470.69	1056.57	852.14	731.54	652.83	598.00	558.08
31000	2814.50	1519.71	1091.79	880.54	755.93	674.59	617.94	576.68
32000	2905.29	1568.74	1127.01	908.94	780.31	696.35	637.87	595.28
33000	2996.08	1617.76	1162.22	937.35	804.69	718.11	657.80	613.88
34000	3086.87	1666.78	1197.44	965.75	829.08	739.87	677.74	632.49
35000	3177.66	1715.81	1232.66	994.16	853.46	761.63	697.67	651.09
40000	3631.61	1960.92	1408.76	1136.18	975.39	870.43	797.34	744.10
45000	4085.56	2206.03	1584.85	1278.20	1097.31	979.24	897.00	837.11
50000	4539.51	2451.15	1760.94	1420.22	1219.23	1088.04	996.67	930.12
55000	4993.46	2696.26	1937.04	1562.24	1341.15	1196.84	1096.34	1023.14
60000	5447.41	2941.38	2113.13	1704.27	1463.08	1305.65	1196.00	1116.15
65000	5901.36	3186.49	2289.23	1846.29	1585.00	1414.45	1295.67	1209.16
70000	6355.31	3431.61	2465.32	1988.31	1706.92	1523.26	1395.34	1302.17
75000	6809.26	3676.72	2641.41	2130.33	1828.84	1632.06	1495.00	1395.18
80000	7263.21	3921.83	2817.51	2272.35	1950.77	1740.86	1594.67	1488.19
85000	7717.16	4166.95	2993.60	2414.37	2072.69	1849.67	1694.34	1581.21
90000	8171.11	4412.06	3169.69	2556.40	2194.61	1958.47	1794.00	1674.22
95000	8625.06	4657.18	3345.79	2698.42	2316.53	2067.27	1893.67	1767.23
100000	9079.01	4902.29	3521.88	2840.44	2438.46	2176.08	1993.34	1860.24
105000	9532.96	5147.41	3697.98	2982.46	2560.38	2284.88	2093.00	1953.25
110000	9986.91	5392.52	3874.07	3124.48	2682.30	2393.68	2192.67	2046.27
115000	10440.86	5637.63	4050.16	3266.50	2804.23	2502.49	2292.34	2139.28
120000	10894.81	5882.75	4226.26	3408.53	2926.15	2611.29	2392.00	2232.29
125000	11348.76	6127.86	4402.35	3550.55	3048.07	2720.10	2491.67	2325.30
130000	11802.71	6372.98	4578.45	3692.57	3169.99	2828.90	2591.34	2418.31
135000	12256.66	6618.09	4754.54	3834.59	3291.92	2937.70	2691.00	2511.32
140000	12710.61	6863.21	4930.63	3976.61	3413.84	3046.51	2790.67	2604.34
145000	13164.56	7108.32	5106.73	4118.63	3535.76	3155.31	2890.34	2697.35
150000	13618.51	7353.43	5282.82	4260.66	3657.68	3264.11	2990.00	2790.36
155000	14072.46	7598.55	5458.92	4402.68	3779.61	3372.92	3089.67	2883.37
160000	14526.41	7843.66	5635.01	4544.70	3901.53	3481.72	3189.34	2976.38

AMOUNT OF LOAN	NUMBER OF YEARS IN TERM 9	10	15	20	25	30	35	40
$ 50	.89	.85	.74	.71	.69	.68	.68	.68
100	1.77	1.69	1.48	1.41	1.37	1.36	1.35	1.35
200	3.53	3.37	2.96	2.81	2.74	2.71	2.70	2.70
300	5.29	5.05	4.44	4.21	4.11	4.07	4.05	4.04
400	7.05	6.74	5.91	5.61	5.48	5.42	5.40	5.39
500	8.81	8.42	7.39	7.01	6.85	6.78	6.75	6.73
600	10.57	10.10	8.87	8.41	8.22	8.13	8.10	8.08
700	12.33	11.79	10.35	9.81	9.59	9.49	9.45	9.43
800	14.09	13.47	11.82	11.21	10.95	10.84	10.79	10.77
900	15.85	15.15	13.30	12.61	12.32	12.20	12.14	12.12
1000	17.61	16.83	14.78	14.01	13.69	13.55	13.49	13.46
2000	35.21	33.66	29.55	28.02	27.38	27.10	26.98	26.92
3000	52.81	50.49	44.33	42.02	41.07	40.65	40.47	40.38
4000	70.41	67.32	59.10	56.03	54.75	54.20	53.95	53.84
5000	88.01	84.15	73.88	70.04	68.44	67.75	67.44	67.30
6000	105.61	100.98	88.65	84.04	82.13	81.30	80.93	80.76
7000	123.21	117.81	103.42	98.05	95.81	94.84	94.41	94.22
8000	140.81	134.64	118.20	112.06	109.50	108.39	107.90	107.68
9000	158.41	151.47	132.97	126.06	123.19	121.94	121.39	121.14
10000	176.02	168.30	147.75	140.07	136.88	135.49	134.88	134.60
11000	193.62	185.13	162.52	154.08	150.56	149.04	148.36	148.06
12000	211.22	201.96	177.30	168.08	164.25	162.59	161.85	161.52
13000	228.82	218.79	192.07	182.09	177.94	176.13	175.34	174.98
14000	246.42	235.62	206.84	196.09	191.62	189.68	188.82	188.44
15000	264.02	252.44	221.62	210.10	205.31	203.23	202.31	201.90
16000	281.62	269.27	236.39	224.11	219.00	216.78	215.80	215.36
17000	299.22	286.10	251.17	238.11	232.69	230.33	229.29	228.82
18000	316.82	302.93	265.94	252.12	246.37	243.88	242.77	242.28
19000	334.43	319.76	280.72	266.13	260.06	257.42	256.26	255.74
20000	352.03	336.59	295.49	280.13	273.75	270.97	269.75	269.20
21000	369.63	353.42	310.26	294.14	287.43	284.52	283.23	282.66
22000	387.23	370.25	325.04	308.15	301.12	298.07	296.72	296.12
23000	404.83	387.08	339.81	322.15	314.81	311.62	310.21	309.58
24000	422.43	403.91	354.59	336.16	328.50	325.17	323.69	323.04
25000	440.03	420.74	369.36	350.17	342.18	338.72	337.18	336.50
26000	457.63	437.57	384.14	364.17	355.87	352.26	350.67	349.96
27000	475.23	454.40	398.91	378.18	369.56	365.81	364.16	363.42
28000	492.84	471.23	413.68	392.18	383.24	379.36	377.64	376.88
29000	510.44	488.05	428.46	406.19	396.93	392.91	391.13	390.34
30000	528.04	504.88	443.23	420.20	410.62	406.46	404.62	403.80
31000	545.64	521.71	458.01	434.20	424.30	420.01	418.10	417.26
32000	563.24	538.54	472.78	448.21	437.99	433.55	431.59	430.72
33000	580.84	555.37	487.56	462.22	451.68	447.10	445.08	444.18
34000	598.44	572.20	502.33	476.22	465.37	460.65	458.57	457.64
35000	616.04	589.03	517.10	490.23	479.05	474.20	472.05	471.09
40000	704.05	673.18	590.98	560.26	547.49	541.94	539.49	538.39
45000	792.05	757.32	664.85	630.29	615.92	609.68	606.92	605.69
50000	880.06	841.47	738.72	700.33	684.36	677.43	674.36	672.99
55000	968.06	925.62	812.59	770.36	752.79	745.17	741.79	740.29
60000	1056.07	1009.76	886.46	840.39	821.23	812.91	809.23	807.59
65000	1144.07	1093.91	960.33	910.42	889.67	880.65	876.66	874.89
70000	1232.08	1178.06	1034.20	980.45	958.10	948.39	944.10	942.18
75000	1320.09	1262.20	1108.07	1050.49	1026.54	1016.14	1011.54	1009.48
80000	1408.09	1346.35	1181.95	1120.52	1094.97	1083.88	1078.97	1076.78
85000	1496.10	1430.49	1255.82	1190.55	1163.41	1151.62	1146.41	1144.08
90000	1584.10	1514.64	1329.69	1260.58	1231.84	1219.36	1213.84	1211.38
95000	1672.11	1598.79	1403.56	1330.62	1300.28	1287.10	1281.28	1278.68
100000	1760.11	1682.93	1477.43	1400.65	1368.71	1354.85	1348.71	1345.98
105000	1848.12	1767.08	1551.30	1470.68	1437.15	1422.59	1416.15	1413.27
110000	1936.12	1851.23	1625.17	1540.71	1505.58	1490.33	1483.58	1480.57
115000	2024.13	1935.37	1699.04	1610.74	1574.02	1558.07	1551.02	1547.87
120000	2112.13	2019.52	1772.92	1680.78	1642.46	1625.81	1618.45	1615.17
125000	2200.14	2103.67	1846.79	1750.81	1710.89	1693.56	1685.89	1682.47
130000	2288.14	2187.81	1920.66	1820.84	1779.33	1761.30	1753.32	1749.77
135000	2376.15	2271.96	1994.53	1890.87	1847.76	1829.04	1820.76	1817.07
140000	2464.16	2356.11	2068.40	1960.90	1916.20	1896.78	1888.19	1884.36
145000	2552.16	2440.25	2142.27	2030.94	1984.63	1964.52	1955.63	1951.66
150000	2640.17	2524.40	2216.14	2100.97	2053.07	2032.27	2023.07	2018.96
155000	2728.17	2608.55	2290.01	2171.00	2121.50	2100.01	2090.50	2086.26
160000	2816.18	2692.69	2363.89	2241.03	2189.94	2167.75	2157.94	2153.56

AMOUNT OF LOAN	NUMBER OF YEARS IN TERM							
	1	2	3	4	5	6	7	8
$ 50	4.55	2.46	1.77	1.43	1.23	1.10	1.01	.94
100	9.09	4.91	3.53	2.85	2.45	2.19	2.01	1.87
200	18.17	9.82	7.06	5.70	4.90	4.37	4.01	3.74
300	27.26	14.73	10.59	8.55	7.34	6.55	6.01	5.61
400	36.34	19.64	14.12	11.39	9.79	8.74	8.01	7.48
500	45.43	24.55	17.65	14.24	12.23	10.92	10.01	9.34
600	54.51	29.45	21.17	17.09	14.68	13.10	12.01	11.21
700	63.60	34.36	24.70	19.93	17.12	15.29	14.01	13.08
800	72.68	39.27	28.23	22.78	19.57	17.47	16.01	14.95
900	81.77	44.18	31.76	25.63	22.01	19.65	18.01	16.81
1000	90.85	49.09	35.29	28.47	24.46	21.83	20.01	18.68
2000	181.70	98.17	70.57	56.94	48.91	43.66	40.01	37.36
3000	272.55	147.25	105.85	85.41	73.36	65.49	60.02	56.03
4000	363.40	196.34	141.13	113.88	97.81	87.32	80.02	74.71
5000	454.25	245.42	176.41	142.35	122.26	109.15	100.03	93.39
6000	545.10	294.50	211.69	170.82	146.71	130.98	120.03	112.06
7000	635.95	343.58	246.97	199.28	171.16	152.81	140.04	130.74
8000	726.80	392.67	282.25	227.75	195.61	174.64	160.04	149.41
9000	817.65	441.75	317.53	256.22	220.06	196.47	180.05	168.09
10000	908.50	490.83	352.81	284.69	244.52	218.30	200.05	186.77
11000	999.35	539.91	388.09	313.16	268.97	240.13	220.06	205.44
12000	1090.20	589.00	423.37	341.63	293.42	261.96	240.06	224.12
13000	1181.04	638.08	458.65	370.10	317.87	283.79	260.07	242.79
14000	1271.89	687.16	493.93	398.56	342.32	305.62	280.07	261.47
15000	1362.74	736.24	529.21	427.03	366.77	327.45	300.08	280.15
16000	1453.59	785.33	564.49	455.50	391.22	349.28	320.08	298.82
17000	1544.44	834.41	599.77	483.97	415.67	371.11	340.09	317.50
18000	1635.29	883.49	635.06	512.44	440.12	392.94	360.09	336.17
19000	1726.14	932.58	670.34	540.91	464.58	414.77	380.09	354.85
20000	1816.99	981.66	705.62	569.37	489.03	436.60	400.10	373.53
21000	1907.84	1030.74	740.90	597.84	513.48	458.43	420.10	392.20
22000	1998.69	1079.82	776.18	626.31	537.93	480.26	440.11	410.88
23000	2089.54	1128.91	811.46	654.78	562.38	502.09	460.11	429.56
24000	2180.39	1177.99	846.74	683.25	586.83	523.92	480.12	448.23
25000	2271.24	1227.07	882.02	711.72	611.28	545.75	500.12	466.91
26000	2362.08	1276.15	917.30	740.19	635.73	567.58	520.13	485.58
27000	2452.93	1325.24	952.58	768.65	660.18	589.41	540.13	504.26
28000	2543.78	1374.32	987.86	797.12	684.64	611.24	560.14	522.94
29000	2634.63	1423.40	1023.14	825.59	709.09	633.07	580.14	541.61
30000	2725.48	1472.48	1058.42	854.06	733.54	654.90	600.15	560.29
31000	2816.33	1521.57	1093.70	882.53	757.99	676.73	620.15	578.96
32000	2907.18	1570.65	1128.98	911.00	782.44	698.56	640.16	597.64
33000	2998.03	1619.73	1164.26	939.46	806.89	720.39	660.16	616.32
34000	3088.88	1668.81	1199.54	967.93	831.34	742.22	680.17	634.99
35000	3179.73	1717.90	1234.83	996.40	855.79	764.05	700.17	653.67
40000	3633.97	1963.31	1411.23	1138.74	978.05	873.19	800.19	747.05
45000	4088.22	2208.72	1587.63	1281.09	1100.30	982.34	900.22	840.43
50000	4542.47	2454.14	1764.03	1423.43	1222.56	1091.49	1000.24	933.81
55000	4996.71	2699.55	1940.44	1565.77	1344.81	1200.64	1100.26	1027.19
60000	5450.96	2944.96	2116.84	1708.11	1467.07	1309.79	1200.29	1120.57
65000	5905.20	3190.38	2293.24	1850.46	1589.33	1418.94	1300.31	1213.95
70000	6359.45	3435.79	2469.65	1992.80	1711.58	1528.09	1400.33	1307.33
75000	6813.70	3681.20	2646.05	2135.14	1833.84	1637.23	1500.36	1400.71
80000	7267.94	3926.62	2822.45	2277.48	1956.09	1746.38	1600.38	1494.09
85000	7722.19	4172.03	2998.85	2419.83	2078.35	1855.53	1700.41	1587.47
90000	8176.43	4417.44	3175.26	2562.17	2200.60	1964.68	1800.43	1680.85
95000	8630.68	4662.86	3351.66	2704.51	2322.86	2073.83	1900.45	1774.23
100000	9084.93	4908.27	3528.06	2846.85	2445.11	2182.98	2000.48	1867.61
105000	9539.17	5153.68	3704.47	2989.20	2567.37	2292.13	2100.50	1960.99
110000	9993.42	5399.10	3880.87	3131.54	2689.62	2401.27	2200.52	2054.37
115000	10447.66	5644.51	4057.27	3273.88	2811.88	2510.42	2300.55	2147.76
120000	10901.91	5889.92	4233.67	3416.22	2934.14	2619.57	2400.57	2241.14
125000	11356.16	6135.34	4410.08	3558.57	3056.39	2728.72	2500.59	2334.52
130000	11810.40	6380.75	4586.48	3700.91	3178.65	2837.87	2600.62	2427.90
135000	12264.65	6626.16	4762.88	3843.25	3300.90	2947.02	2700.64	2521.28
140000	12718.89	6871.58	4939.29	3985.59	3423.16	3056.17	2800.66	2614.66
145000	13173.14	7116.99	5115.69	4127.93	3545.41	3165.31	2900.69	2708.04
150000	13627.39	7362.40	5292.09	4270.28	3667.67	3274.46	3000.71	2801.42
155000	14081.63	7607.82	5468.50	4412.62	3789.92	3383.61	3100.74	2894.80
160000	14535.88	7853.23	5644.90	4554.96	3912.18	3492.76	3200.76	2988.18

AMOUNT OF LOAN	NUMBER OF YEARS IN TERM							
	9	10	15	20	25	30	35	40
$ 50	.89	.85	.75	.71	.69	.69	.68	.68
100	1.77	1.70	1.49	1.42	1.38	1.37	1.36	1.36
200	3.54	3.39	2.98	2.83	2.76	2.73	2.72	2.72
300	5.31	5.08	4.46	4.24	4.14	4.10	4.08	4.07
400	7.08	6.77	5.95	5.65	5.52	5.46	5.44	5.43
500	8.84	8.46	7.44	7.06	6.90	6.83	6.80	6.79
600	10.61	10.15	8.92	8.47	8.28	8.19	8.16	8.14
700	12.38	11.84	10.41	9.88	9.65	9.56	9.52	9.50
800	14.15	13.53	11.89	11.29	11.03	10.92	10.88	10.86
900	15.91	15.22	13.38	12.70	12.41	12.29	12.24	12.21
1000	17.68	16.91	14.87	14.11	13.79	13.65	13.59	13.57
2000	35.36	33.82	29.73	28.21	27.58	27.30	27.18	27.13
3000	53.04	50.73	44.59	42.31	41.36	40.95	40.77	40.69
4000	70.71	67.63	59.45	56.41	55.15	54.60	54.36	54.26
5000	88.39	84.54	74.31	70.51	68.93	68.25	67.95	67.82
6000	106.07	101.45	89.18	84.61	82.72	81.90	81.54	81.38
7000	123.74	118.36	104.04	98.71	96.50	95.55	95.13	94.95
8000	141.42	135.26	118.90	112.81	110.29	109.20	108.72	108.51
9000	159.10	152.17	133.76	126.91	124.07	122.85	122.31	122.07
10000	176.78	169.08	148.62	141.01	137.86	136.50	135.90	135.63
11000	194.45	185.99	163.48	155.11	151.64	150.15	149.49	149.20
12000	212.13	202.89	178.35	169.21	165.43	163.80	163.08	162.76
13000	229.81	219.80	193.21	183.31	179.22	177.45	176.67	176.32
14000	247.48	236.71	208.07	197.41	193.00	191.10	190.26	189.89
15000	265.16	253.62	222.93	211.51	206.79	204.75	203.85	203.45
16000	282.84	270.52	237.79	225.61	220.57	218.39	217.44	217.01
17000	300.51	287.43	252.65	239.71	234.36	232.04	231.03	230.58
18000	318.19	304.34	267.52	253.81	248.14	245.69	244.62	244.14
19000	335.87	321.25	282.38	267.91	261.93	259.34	258.21	257.70
20000	353.55	338.15	297.24	282.01	275.71	272.99	271.79	271.26
21000	371.22	355.06	312.10	296.11	289.50	286.64	285.38	284.83
22000	388.90	371.97	326.96	310.22	303.28	300.29	298.97	298.39
23000	406.58	388.88	341.82	324.32	317.07	313.94	312.56	311.95
24000	424.25	405.78	356.69	338.42	330.85	327.59	326.15	325.52
25000	441.93	422.69	371.55	352.52	344.64	341.24	339.74	339.08
26000	459.61	439.60	386.41	366.62	358.43	354.89	353.33	352.64
27000	477.29	456.51	401.27	380.72	372.21	368.54	366.92	366.21
28000	494.96	473.41	416.13	394.82	386.00	382.19	380.51	379.77
29000	512.64	490.32	430.99	408.92	399.78	395.84	394.10	393.33
30000	530.32	507.23	445.86	423.02	413.57	409.49	407.69	406.89
31000	547.99	524.14	460.72	437.12	427.35	423.13	421.28	420.46
32000	565.67	541.04	475.58	451.22	441.14	436.78	434.87	434.02
33000	583.35	557.95	490.44	465.32	454.92	450.43	448.46	447.58
34000	601.02	574.86	505.30	479.42	468.71	464.08	462.05	461.15
35000	618.70	591.77	520.16	493.52	482.49	477.73	475.64	474.71
40000	707.09	676.30	594.47	564.02	551.42	545.98	543.58	542.52
45000	795.47	760.84	668.78	634.53	620.35	614.23	611.53	610.34
50000	883.86	845.38	743.09	705.03	689.28	682.47	679.48	678.15
55000	972.24	929.91	817.40	775.53	758.20	750.72	747.43	745.97
60000	1060.63	1014.45	891.71	846.03	827.13	818.97	815.37	813.78
65000	1149.01	1098.99	966.01	916.53	896.06	887.21	883.32	881.60
70000	1237.40	1183.53	1040.32	987.04	964.98	955.46	951.27	949.41
75000	1325.78	1268.06	1114.63	1057.54	1033.91	1023.71	1019.22	1017.23
80000	1414.17	1352.60	1188.94	1128.04	1102.84	1091.95	1087.16	1085.04
85000	1502.55	1437.14	1263.25	1198.54	1171.77	1160.20	1155.11	1152.86
90000	1590.94	1521.67	1337.56	1269.05	1240.69	1228.45	1223.06	1220.67
95000	1679.33	1606.21	1411.86	1339.55	1309.62	1296.69	1291.01	1288.49
100000	1767.71	1690.75	1486.17	1410.05	1378.55	1364.94	1358.95	1356.30
105000	1856.10	1775.29	1560.48	1480.55	1447.47	1433.19	1426.90	1424.12
110000	1944.48	1859.82	1634.79	1551.06	1516.40	1501.43	1494.85	1491.93
115000	2032.87	1944.36	1709.10	1621.56	1585.33	1569.68	1562.80	1559.75
120000	2121.25	2028.90	1783.41	1692.06	1654.25	1637.93	1630.74	1627.56
125000	2209.64	2113.44	1857.72	1762.56	1723.18	1706.17	1698.69	1695.38
130000	2298.02	2197.97	1932.02	1833.06	1792.11	1774.42	1766.64	1763.19
135000	2386.41	2282.51	2006.33	1903.57	1861.04	1842.67	1834.59	1831.01
140000	2474.79	2367.05	2080.64	1974.07	1929.96	1910.91	1902.53	1898.82
145000	2563.18	2451.58	2154.95	2044.57	1998.89	1979.16	1970.48	1966.64
150000	2651.56	2536.12	2229.26	2115.07	2067.82	2047.41	2038.43	2034.45
155000	2739.95	2620.66	2303.57	2185.58	2136.74	2115.65	2106.38	2102.26
160000	2828.33	2705.20	2377.87	2256.08	2205.67	2183.90	2174.32	2170.08

AMOUNT OF LOAN	NUMBER OF YEARS IN TERM							
	1	2	3	4	5	6	7	8
$ 50	4.55	2.46	1.77	1.43	1.23	1.10	1.01	.94
100	9.10	4.92	3.54	2.86	2.46	2.19	2.01	1.88
200	18.19	9.83	7.07	5.71	4.91	4.38	4.02	3.75
300	27.28	14.75	10.61	8.56	7.36	6.57	6.03	5.63
400	36.37	19.66	14.14	11.42	9.81	8.76	8.04	7.50
500	45.46	24.58	17.68	14.27	12.26	10.95	10.04	9.38
600	54.55	29.49	21.21	17.12	14.72	13.14	12.05	11.25
700	63.64	34.40	24.74	19.98	17.17	15.33	14.06	13.13
800	72.73	39.32	28.28	22.83	19.62	17.52	16.07	15.00
900	81.82	44.23	31.81	25.68	22.07	19.71	18.07	16.88
1000	90.91	49.15	35.35	28.54	24.52	21.90	20.08	18.75
2000	181.82	98.29	70.69	57.07	49.04	43.80	40.16	37.50
3000	272.73	147.43	106.03	85.60	73.56	65.70	60.23	56.25
4000	363.64	196.57	141.37	114.14	98.08	87.60	80.31	75.00
5000	454.55	245.72	176.72	142.67	122.59	109.50	100.39	93.75
6000	545.46	294.86	212.06	171.20	147.11	131.40	120.46	112.50
7000	636.36	344.00	247.40	199.73	171.63	153.30	140.54	131.25
8000	727.27	393.14	282.74	228.27	196.15	175.20	160.61	150.00
9000	818.18	442.29	318.09	256.80	220.66	197.09	180.69	168.75
10000	909.09	491.43	353.43	285.33	245.18	218.99	200.77	187.50
11000	1000.00	540.57	388.77	313.86	269.70	240.89	220.84	206.25
12000	1090.91	589.71	424.11	342.40	294.22	262.79	240.92	225.00
13000	1181.81	638.86	459.46	370.93	318.74	284.69	261.00	243.75
14000	1272.72	688.00	494.80	399.46	343.25	306.59	281.07	262.50
15000	1363.63	737.14	530.14	428.00	367.77	328.49	301.15	281.25
16000	1454.54	786.28	565.48	456.53	392.29	350.39	321.22	300.00
17000	1545.45	835.43	600.83	485.06	416.81	372.29	341.30	318.75
18000	1636.36	884.57	636.17	513.59	441.32	394.18	361.38	337.50
19000	1727.26	933.71	671.51	542.13	465.84	416.08	381.45	356.25
20000	1818.17	982.85	706.85	570.66	490.36	437.98	401.53	375.00
21000	1909.08	1032.00	742.20	599.19	514.88	459.88	421.61	393.75
22000	1999.99	1081.14	777.54	627.72	539.40	481.78	441.68	412.50
23000	2090.90	1130.28	812.88	656.26	563.91	503.68	461.76	431.25
24000	2181.81	1179.42	848.22	684.79	588.43	525.58	481.83	450.00
25000	2272.72	1228.57	883.57	713.32	612.95	547.48	501.91	468.75
26000	2363.62	1277.71	918.91	741.86	637.47	569.37	521.99	487.50
27000	2454.53	1326.85	954.25	770.39	661.98	591.27	542.06	506.25
28000	2545.44	1375.99	989.59	798.92	686.50	613.17	562.14	525.00
29000	2636.35	1425.14	1024.94	827.45	711.02	635.07	582.22	543.75
30000	2727.26	1474.28	1060.28	855.99	735.54	656.97	602.29	562.50
31000	2818.17	1523.42	1095.62	884.52	760.06	678.87	622.37	581.25
32000	2909.07	1572.56	1130.96	913.05	784.57	700.77	642.44	600.00
33000	2999.98	1621.71	1166.31	941.58	809.09	722.67	662.52	618.75
34000	3090.89	1670.85	1201.65	970.12	833.61	744.57	682.60	637.50
35000	3181.80	1719.99	1236.99	998.65	858.13	766.46	702.67	656.25
40000	3636.34	1965.70	1413.70	1141.31	980.72	875.96	803.05	750.00
45000	4090.88	2211.42	1590.42	1283.98	1103.30	985.45	903.44	843.75
50000	4545.43	2457.13	1767.13	1426.64	1225.89	1094.95	1003.82	937.50
55000	4999.97	2702.84	1943.84	1569.30	1348.48	1204.44	1104.20	1031.25
60000	5454.51	2948.55	2120.55	1711.97	1471.07	1313.93	1204.58	1125.00
65000	5909.05	3194.27	2297.26	1854.63	1593.66	1423.43	1304.96	1218.75
70000	6363.59	3439.98	2473.98	1997.29	1716.25	1532.92	1405.34	1312.50
75000	6818.14	3685.69	2650.69	2139.96	1838.84	1642.42	1505.72	1406.25
80000	7272.68	3931.40	2827.40	2282.62	1961.43	1751.91	1606.10	1500.00
85000	7727.22	4177.12	3004.11	2425.28	2084.01	1861.41	1706.49	1593.75
90000	8181.76	4422.83	3180.83	2567.95	2206.60	1970.90	1806.87	1687.50
95000	8636.30	4668.54	3357.54	2710.61	2329.19	2080.39	1907.25	1781.25
100000	9090.85	4914.25	3534.25	2853.28	2451.78	2189.89	2007.63	1875.00
105000	9545.39	5159.97	3710.96	2995.94	2574.37	2299.38	2108.01	1968.75
110000	9999.93	5405.68	3887.67	3138.60	2696.96	2408.88	2208.39	2062.50
115000	10454.47	5651.39	4064.39	3281.27	2819.55	2518.37	2308.77	2156.25
120000	10909.01	5897.10	4241.10	3423.93	2942.14	2627.86	2409.15	2250.00
125000	11363.56	6142.81	4417.81	3566.59	3064.72	2737.36	2509.53	2343.75
130000	11818.10	6388.53	4594.52	3709.26	3187.31	2846.85	2609.92	2437.50
135000	12272.64	6634.24	4771.24	3851.92	3309.90	2956.35	2710.30	2531.25
140000	12727.18	6879.95	4947.95	3994.58	3432.49	3065.84	2810.68	2625.00
145000	13181.72	7125.66	5124.66	4137.25	3555.08	3175.34	2911.06	2718.75
150000	13636.27	7371.38	5301.37	4279.91	3677.67	3284.83	3011.44	2812.50
155000	14090.81	7617.09	5478.09	4422.57	3800.26	3394.32	3111.82	2906.25
160000	14545.35	7862.80	5654.80	4565.24	3922.85	3503.82	3212.20	3000.00

AMOUNT OF LOAN	9	10	15	20	25	30	35	40
	NUMBER OF YEARS IN TERM							
$ 50	.89	.85	.75	.71	.70	.69	.69	.69
100	1.78	1.70	1.50	1.42	1.39	1.38	1.37	1.37
200	3.56	3.40	2.99	2.84	2.78	2.76	2.74	2.74
300	5.33	5.10	4.49	4.26	4.17	4.13	4.11	4.10
400	7.11	6.80	5.98	5.68	5.56	5.51	5.48	5.47
500	8.88	8.50	7.48	7.10	6.95	6.88	6.85	6.84
600	10.66	10.20	8.97	8.52	8.34	8.26	8.22	8.20
700	12.43	11.90	10.47	9.94	9.72	9.63	9.59	9.57
800	14.21	13.59	11.96	11.36	11.11	11.01	10.96	10.94
900	15.98	15.29	13.46	12.78	12.50	12.38	12.33	12.30
1000	17.76	16.99	14.95	14.20	13.89	13.76	13.70	13.67
2000	35.51	33.98	29.90	28.39	27.77	27.51	27.39	27.34
3000	53.26	50.96	44.85	42.59	41.66	41.26	41.08	41.00
4000	71.02	67.95	59.80	56.78	55.54	55.01	54.77	54.67
5000	88.77	84.93	74.75	70.98	69.42	68.76	68.46	68.34
6000	106.52	101.92	89.70	85.17	83.31	82.51	82.16	82.00
7000	124.28	118.91	104.65	99.37	97.19	96.26	95.85	95.67
8000	142.03	135.89	119.60	113.56	111.08	110.01	109.54	109.34
9000	159.78	152.88	134.55	127.76	124.96	123.76	123.23	123.00
10000	177.54	169.86	149.50	141.95	138.84	137.51	136.92	136.67
11000	195.29	186.85	164.45	156.15	152.73	151.26	150.62	150.33
12000	213.04	203.83	179.40	170.34	166.61	165.01	164.31	164.00
13000	230.80	220.82	194.35	184.54	180.50	178.76	178.00	177.67
14000	248.55	237.81	209.30	198.73	194.38	192.51	191.69	191.33
15000	266.30	254.79	224.24	212.92	208.26	206.26	205.38	205.00
16000	284.06	271.78	239.19	227.12	222.15	220.01	219.08	218.67
17000	301.81	288.76	254.14	241.31	236.03	233.76	232.77	232.33
18000	319.56	305.75	269.09	255.51	249.91	247.51	246.46	246.00
19000	337.32	322.73	284.04	269.70	263.80	261.26	260.15	259.66
20000	355.07	339.72	298.99	283.90	277.68	275.01	273.84	273.33
21000	372.82	356.71	313.94	298.09	291.57	288.76	287.54	287.00
22000	390.58	373.69	328.89	312.29	305.45	302.51	301.23	300.66
23000	408.33	390.68	343.84	326.48	319.33	316.26	314.92	314.33
24000	426.08	407.66	358.79	340.68	333.22	330.01	328.61	328.00
25000	443.83	424.65	373.74	354.87	347.10	343.76	342.30	341.66
26000	461.59	441.63	388.69	369.07	360.99	357.51	356.00	355.33
27000	479.34	458.62	403.64	383.26	374.87	371.26	369.69	368.99
28000	497.09	475.61	418.59	397.46	388.75	385.02	383.38	382.66
29000	514.85	492.59	433.53	411.65	402.64	398.77	397.07	396.33
30000	532.60	509.58	448.48	425.84	416.52	412.52	410.76	409.99
31000	550.35	526.56	463.43	440.04	430.40	426.27	424.46	423.66
32000	568.11	543.55	478.38	454.23	444.29	440.02	438.15	437.33
33000	585.86	560.53	493.33	468.43	458.17	453.77	451.84	450.99
34000	603.61	577.52	508.28	482.62	472.06	467.52	465.53	464.66
35000	621.37	594.51	523.23	496.82	485.94	481.27	479.22	478.32
40000	710.13	679.44	597.98	567.79	555.36	550.02	547.68	546.66
45000	798.90	764.36	672.72	638.76	624.78	618.77	616.14	614.99
50000	887.66	849.29	747.47	709.74	694.20	687.52	684.60	683.32
55000	976.43	934.22	822.22	780.71	763.62	756.28	753.06	751.65
60000	1065.20	1019.15	896.96	851.68	833.04	825.03	821.52	819.98
65000	1153.96	1104.08	971.71	922.66	902.46	893.78	889.98	888.31
70000	1242.73	1189.01	1046.46	993.63	971.88	962.53	958.44	956.64
75000	1331.49	1273.94	1121.20	1064.60	1041.30	1031.28	1026.90	1024.97
80000	1420.26	1358.87	1195.95	1135.58	1110.71	1100.03	1095.36	1093.31
85000	1509.03	1443.79	1270.69	1206.55	1180.13	1168.79	1163..82	1161.64
90000	1597.79	1528.72	1345.44	1277.52	1249.55	1237.54	1232.28	1229.97
95000	1686.56	1613.65	1420.19	1348.50	1318.97	1306.29	1300.74	1298.30
100000	1775.32	1698.58	1494.93	1419.47	1388.39	1375.04	1369.20	1366.63
105000	1864.09	1783.51	1569.68	1490.44	1457.81	1443.79	1437.66	1434.96
110000	1952.86	1868.44	1644.43	1561.42	1527.23	1512.55	1506.12	1503.29
115000	2041.62	1953.37	1719.17	1632.39	1596.65	1581.30	1574.58	1571.63
120000	2130.39	2038.30	1793.92	1703.36	1666.07	1650.05	1643.04	1639.96
125000	2219.15	2123.22	1868.67	1774.34	1735.49	1718.80	1711.50	1708.29
130000	2307.92	2208.15	1943.41	1845.31	1804.91	1787.55	1779.96	1776.62
135000	2396.69	2293.08	2018.16	1916.28	1874.33	1856.30	1848.42	1844.95
140000	2485.45	2378.01	2092.91	1987.26	1943.75	1925.06	1916.88	1913.28
145000	2574.22	2462.94	2167.65	2058.23	2013.17	1993.81	1985.34	1981.61
150000	2662.98	2547.87	2242.40	2129.20	2082.59	2062.56	2053.80	2049.94
155000	2751.75	2632.80	2317.15	2200.18	2152.00	2131.31	2122.26	2118.28
160000	2840.52	2717.73	2391.89	2271.15	2221.42	2200.06	2190.72	2186.61

16½% MONTHLY AMORTIZING PAYMENTS

AMOUNT OF LOAN	NUMBER OF YEARS IN TERM							
	1	2	3	4	5	6	7	8
$ 50	4.55	2.47	1.78	1.43	1.23	1.10	1.01	.95
100	9.10	4.93	3.55	2.86	2.46	2.20	2.02	1.89
200	18.20	9.85	7.09	5.72	4.92	4.40	4.03	3.77
300	27.30	14.77	10.63	8.58	7.38	6.60	6.05	5.65
400	36.39	19.69	14.17	11.44	9.84	8.79	8.06	7.53
500	45.49	24.61	17.71	14.30	12.30	10.99	10.08	9.42
600	54.59	29.53	21.25	17.16	14.76	13.19	12.09	11.30
700	63.68	34.45	24.79	20.02	17.21	15.38	14.11	13.18
800	72.78	39.37	28.33	22.88	19.67	17.58	16.12	15.06
900	81.88	44.29	31.87	25.74	22.13	19.78	18.14	16.95
1000	90.97	49.21	35.41	28.60	24.59	21.97	20.15	18.83
2000	181.94	98.41	70.81	57.20	49.17	43.94	40.30	37.65
3000	272.91	147.61	106.22	85.80	73.76	65.91	60.45	56.48
4000	363.88	196.81	141.62	114.39	98.34	87.88	80.60	75.30
5000	454.84	246.02	177.03	142.99	122.93	109.85	100.74	94.12
6000	545.81	295.22	212.43	171.59	147.51	131.81	120.89	112.95
7000	636.78	344.42	247.84	200.18	172.10	153.78	141.04	131.77
8000	727.75	393.62	283.24	228.78	196.68	175.75	161.19	150.60
9000	818.71	442.83	318.64	257.38	221.27	197.72	181.34	169.42
10000	909.68	492.03	354.05	285.98	245.85	219.69	201.48	188.24
11000	1000.65	541.23	389.45	314.57	270.43	241.65	221.63	207.07
12000	1091.62	590.43	424.86	343.17	295.02	263.62	241.78	225.89
13000	1182.58	639.64	460.26	371.77	319.60	285.59	261.93	244.72
14000	1273.55	688.84	495.67	400.36	344.19	307.56	282.08	263.54
15000	1364.52	738.04	531.07	428.96	368.77	329.53	302.22	282.36
16000	1455.49	787.24	566.48	457.56	393.36	351.49	322.37	301.19
17000	1546.45	836.44	601.88	486.15	417.94	373.46	342.52	320.01
18000	1637.42	885.65	637.28	514.75	442.53	395.43	362.67	338.84
19000	1728.39	934.85	672.69	543.35	467.11	417.40	382.81	357.66
20000	1819.36	984.05	708.09	571.95	491.70	439.37	402.96	376.48
21000	1910.33	1033.25	743.50	600.54	516.28	461.33	423.11	395.31
22000	2001.29	1082.46	778.90	629.14	540.86	483.30	443.26	414.13
23000	2092.26	1131.66	814.31	657.74	565.45	505.27	463.41	432.96
24000	2183.23	1180.86	849.71	686.33	590.03	527.24	483.55	451.78
25000	2274.20	1230.06	885.11	714.93	614.62	549.21	503.70	470.60
26000	2365.16	1279.27	920.52	743.53	639.20	571.17	523.85	489.43
27000	2456.13	1328.47	955.92	772.12	663.79	593.14	544.00	508.25
28000	2547.10	1377.67	991.33	800.72	688.37	615.11	564.15	527.08
29000	2638.07	1426.87	1026.73	829.32	712.96	637.08	584.29	545.90
30000	2729.03	1476.08	1062.14	857.92	737.54	659.05	604.44	564.72
31000	2820.00	1525.28	1097.54	886.51	762.13	681.01	624.59	583.55
32000	2910.97	1574.48	1132.95	915.11	786.71	702.98	644.74	602.37
33000	3001.94	1623.68	1168.35	943.71	811.29	724.95	664.89	621.20
34000	3092.90	1672.88	1203.75	972.30	835.88	746.92	685.03	640.02
35000	3183.87	1722.09	1239.16	1000.90	860.46	768.89	705.18	658.84
40000	3638.71	1968.10	1416.18	1143.89	983.39	878.73	805.92	752.96
45000	4093.55	2214.11	1593.20	1286.87	1106.31	988.57	906.66	847.08
50000	4548.39	2460.12	1770.22	1429.86	1229.23	1098.41	1007.40	941.20
55000	5003.23	2706.13	1947.25	1572.84	1352.15	1208.25	1108.14	1035.32
60000	5458.06	2952.15	2124.27	1715.83	1475.08	1318.09	1208.88	1129.44
65000	5912.90	3198.16	2301.29	1858.81	1598.00	1427.93	1309.62	1223.56
70000	6367.74	3444.17	2478.31	2001.80	1720.92	1537.77	1410.36	1317.68
75000	6822.58	3690.18	2655.33	2144.78	1843.84	1647.61	1511.10	1411.80
80000	7277.42	3936.19	2832.36	2287.77	1966.77	1757.45	1611.84	1505.92
85000	7732.25	4182.20	3009.38	2430.75	2089.69	1867.29	1712.58	1600.04
90000	8187.09	4428.22	3186.40	2573.74	2212.61	1977.13	1813.32	1694.16
95000	8641.93	4674.23	3363.42	2716.72	2335.53	2086.97	1914.05	1788.28
100000	9096.77	4920.24	3540.44	2859.71	2458.46	2196.81	2014.79	1882.40
105000	9551.61	5166.25	3717.47	3002.69	2581.38	2306.65	2115.53	1976.52
110000	10006.45	5412.26	3894.49	3145.68	2704.30	2416.49	2216.27	2070.64
115000	10461.28	5658.28	4071.51	3288.66	2827.22	2526.33	2317.01	2164.76
120000	10916.12	5904.29	4248.53	3431.65	2950.15	2636.17	2417.75	2258.88
125000	11370.96	6150.30	4425.55	3574.63	3073.07	2746.01	2518.49	2353.00
130000	11825.80	6396.31	4602.57	3717.62	3195.99	2855.85	2619.23	2447.12
135000	12280.64	6642.32	4779.60	3860.60	3318.92	2965.69	2719.97	2541.24
140000	12735.47	6888.33	4956.62	4003.59	3441.84	3075.53	2820.71	2635.36
145000	13190.31	7134.35	5133.64	4146.57	3564.76	3185.37	2921.45	2729.48
150000	13645.15	7380.36	5310.66	4289.56	3687.68	3295.21	3022.19	2823.60
155000	14099.99	7626.37	5487.68	4432.54	3810.61	3405.05	3122.93	2917.72
160000	14554.83	7872.38	5664.71	4575.53	3933.53	3514.89	3223.67	3011.84

AMOUNT OF LOAN	NUMBER OF YEARS IN TERM							
	9	10	15	20	25	30	35	40
$ 50	.90	.86	.76	.72	.70	.70	.69	.69
100	1.79	1.71	1.51	1.43	1.40	1.39	1.38	1.38
200	3.57	3.42	3.01	2.86	2.80	2.78	2.76	2.76
300	5.35	5.12	4.52	4.29	4.20	4.16	4.14	4.14
400	7.14	6.83	6.02	5.72	5.60	5.55	5.52	5.51
500	8.92	8.54	7.52	7.15	7.00	6.93	6.90	6.89
600	10.70	10.24	9.03	8.58	8.39	8.32	8.28	8.27
700	12.49	11.95	10.53	10.01	9.79	9.70	9.66	9.64
800	14.27	13.66	12.03	11.44	11.19	11.09	11.04	11.02
900	16.05	15.36	13.54	12.87	12.59	12.47	12.42	12.40
1000	17.83	17.07	15.04	14.29	13.99	13.86	13.80	13.77
2000	35.66	34.13	30.08	28.58	27.97	27.71	27.59	27.54
3000	53.49	51.20	45.12	42.87	41.95	41.56	41.39	41.31
4000	71.32	68.26	60.15	57.16	55.93	55.41	55.18	55.08
5000	89.15	85.33	75.19	71.45	69.92	69.26	68.98	68.85
6000	106.98	102.39	90.23	85.74	83.90	83.11	82.77	82.62
7000	124.81	119.45	105.26	100.03	97.88	96.97	96.57	96.39
8000	142.64	136.52	120.30	114.32	111.86	110.82	110.36	110.16
9000	160.47	153.58	135.34	128.61	125.85	124.67	124.16	123.93
10000	178.30	170.65	150.38	142.90	139.83	138.52	137.95	137.70
11000	196.13	187.71	165.41	157.18	153.81	152.37	151.74	151.47
12000	213.96	204.78	180.45	171.47	167.79	166.22	165.54	165.24
13000	231.79	221.84	195.49	185.76	181.78	180.07	179.33	179.01
14000	249.62	238.90	210.52	200.05	195.76	193.93	193.13	192.78
15000	267.45	255.97	225.56	214.34	209.74	207.78	206.92	206.55
16000	285.28	273.03	240.60	228.63	223.72	221.63	220.72	220.32
17000	303.11	290.10	255.64	242.92	237.71	235.48	234.51	234.09
18000	320.94	307.16	270.67	257.21	251.69	249.33	248.31	247.86
19000	338.77	324.23	285.71	271.50	265.67	263.18	262.10	261.63
20000	356.59	341.29	300.75	285.79	279.65	277.03	275.90	275.40
21000	374.42	358.35	315.78	300.07	293.64	290.89	289.69	289.17
22000	392.25	375.42	330.82	314.36	307.62	304.74	303.48	302.94
23000	410.08	392.48	345.86	328.65	321.60	318.59	317.28	316.71
24000	427.91	409.55	360.90	342.94	335.58	332.44	331.07	330.48
25000	445.74	426.61	375.93	357.23	349.57	346.29	344.87	344.24
26000	463.57	443.67	390.97	371.52	363.55	360.14	358.66	358.01
27000	481.40	460.74	406.01	385.81	377.53	373.99	372.46	371.78
28000	499.23	477.80	421.04	400.10	391.51	387.85	386.25	385.55
29000	517.06	494.87	436.08	414.39	405.50	401.70	400.05	399.32
30000	534.89	511.93	451.12	428.68	419.48	415.55	413.84	413.09
31000	552.72	529.00	466.15	442.96	433.46	429.40	427.64	426.86
32000	570.55	546.06	481.19	457.25	447.44	443.25	441.43	440.63
33000	588.38	563.12	496.23	471.54	461.43	457.10	455.22	454.40
34000	606.21	580.19	511.27	485.83	475.41	470.96	469.02	468.17
35000	624.04	597.25	526.30	500.12	489.39	484.81	482.81	481.94
40000	713.18	682.57	601.49	571.57	559.30	554.06	551.79	550.79
45000	802.33	767.90	676.67	643.01	629.22	623.32	620.76	619.64
50000	891.48	853.22	751.86	714.46	699.13	692.58	689.73	688.48
55000	980.63	938.54	827.04	785.90	769.04	761.84	758.70	757.33
60000	1069.77	1023.86	902.23	857.35	838.95	831.09	827.68	826.18
65000	1158.92	1109.18	977.42	928.79	908.86	900.35	896.65	895.03
70000	1248.07	1194.50	1052.60	1000.24	978.78	969.61	965.62	963.88
75000	1337.22	1279.82	1127.79	1071.68	1048.69	1038.87	1034.60	1032.72
80000	1426.36	1365.14	1202.97	1143.13	1118.60	1108.12	1103.57	1101.57
85000	1515.51	1450.46	1278.16	1214.57	1188.51	1177.38	1172.54	1170.42
90000	1604.66	1535.79	1353.34	1286.02	1258.43	1246.64	1241.51	1239.27
95000	1693.81	1621.11	1428.53	1357.46	1328.34	1315.90	1310.49	1308.12
100000	1782.95	1706.43	1503.71	1428.91	1398.25	1385.15	1379.46	1376.96
105000	1872.10	1791.75	1578.90	1500.35	1468.16	1454.41	1448.43	1445.81
110000	1961.25	1877.07	1654.08	1571.80	1538.07	1523.67	1517.40	1514.66
115000	2050.40	1962.39	1729.27	1643.24	1607.99	1592.93	1586.38	1583.51
120000	2139.54	2047.71	1804.46	1714.69	1677.90	1662.18	1655.35	1652.36
125000	2228.69	2133.03	1879.64	1786.13	1747.81	1731.44	1724.32	1721.20
130000	2317.84	2218.35	1954.83	1857.58	1817.72	1800.70	1793.30	1790.05
135000	2406.99	2303.68	2030.01	1929.02	1887.64	1869.95	1862.27	1858.90
140000	2496.13	2389.00	2105.20	2000.47	1957.55	1939.21	1931.24	1927.75
145000	2585.28	2474.32	2180.38	2071.91	2027.46	2008.47	2000.21	1996.60
150000	2674.43	2559.64	2255.57	2143.36	2097.37	2077.73	2069.19	2065.44
155000	2763.57	2644.96	2330.75	2214.80	2167.28	2146.98	2138.16	2134.29
160000	2852.72	2730.28	2405.94	2286.25	2237.20	2216.24	2207.13	2203.14

MONTHLY AMORTIZING PAYMENTS

AMOUNT OF LOAN	NUMBER OF YEARS IN TERM 1	2	3	4	5	6	7	8
$ 50	4.56	2.47	1.78	1.44	1.24	1.11	1.02	.95
100	9.11	4.93	3.55	2.87	2.47	2.21	2.03	1.89
200	18.21	9.86	7.10	5.74	4.94	4.41	4.05	3.78
300	27.31	14.78	10.64	8.60	7.40	6.62	6.07	5.67
400	36.42	19.71	14.19	11.47	9.87	8.82	8.09	7.56
500	45.52	24.64	17.74	14.34	12.33	11.02	10.11	9.45
600	54.62	29.56	21.28	17.20	14.80	13.23	12.14	11.34
700	63.72	34.49	24.83	20.07	17.26	15.43	14.16	13.23
800	72.83	39.41	28.38	22.93	19.73	17.63	16.18	15.12
900	81.93	44.34	31.92	25.80	22.19	19.84	18.20	17.01
1000	91.03	49.27	35.47	28.67	24.66	22.04	20.22	18.90
2000	182.06	98.53	70.94	57.33	49.31	44.08	40.44	37.80
3000	273.09	147.79	106.40	85.99	73.96	66.12	60.66	56.70
4000	364.11	197.05	141.87	114.65	98.61	88.15	80.88	75.60
5000	455.14	246.32	177.34	143.31	123.26	110.19	101.10	94.50
6000	546.17	295.58	212.80	171.97	147.91	132.23	121.32	113.39
7000	637.19	344.84	248.27	200.63	172.56	154.27	141.54	132.29
8000	728.22	394.10	283.74	229.30	197.22	176.30	161.76	151.19
9000	819.25	443.37	319.20	257.96	221.87	198.34	181.98	170.09
10000	910.27	492.63	354.67	286.62	246.52	220.38	202.20	188.99
11000	1001.30	541.89	390.14	315.28	271.17	242.42	222.42	207.88
12000	1092.33	591.15	425.60	343.94	295.82	264.45	242.64	226.78
13000	1183.35	640.41	461.07	372.60	320.47	286.49	262.86	245.68
14000	1274.38	689.68	496.53	401.26	345.12	308.53	283.08	264.58
15000	1365.41	738.94	532.00	429.93	369.78	330.57	303.30	283.48
16000	1456.44	788.20	567.47	458.59	394.43	352.60	323.52	302.38
17000	1547.46	837.46	602.93	487.25	419.08	374.64	343.74	321.27
18000	1638.49	886.73	638.40	515.91	443.73	396.68	363.96	340.17
19000	1729.52	935.99	673.87	544.57	468.38	418.72	384.18	359.07
20000	1820.54	985.25	709.33	573.23	493.03	440.75	404.40	377.97
21000	1911.57	1034.51	744.80	601.89	517.68	462.79	424.62	396.87
22000	2002.60	1083.77	780.27	630.56	542.34	484.83	444.84	415.76
23000	2093.62	1133.04	815.73	659.22	566.99	506.87	465.06	434.66
24000	2184.65	1182.30	851.20	687.88	591.64	528.90	485.28	453.56
25000	2275.68	1231.56	886.66	716.54	616.29	550.94	505.50	472.46
26000	2366.70	1280.82	922.13	745.20	640.94	572.98	525.72	491.36
27000	2457.73	1330.09	957.60	773.86	665.59	595.01	545.94	510.25
28000	2548.76	1379.35	993.06	802.52	690.24	617.05	566.16	529.15
29000	2639.78	1428.61	1028.53	831.19	714.90	639.09	586.38	548.05
30000	2730.81	1477.87	1064.00	859.85	739.55	661.13	606.60	566.95
31000	2821.84	1527.14	1099.46	888.51	764.20	683.16	626.81	585.85
32000	2912.87	1576.40	1134.93	917.17	788.85	705.20	647.03	604.75
33000	3003.89	1625.66	1170.40	945.83	813.50	727.24	667.25	623.64
34000	3094.92	1674.92	1205.86	974.49	838.15	749.28	687.47	642.54
35000	3185.95	1724.18	1241.33	1003.15	862.80	771.31	707.69	661.44
40000	3641.08	1970.50	1418.66	1146.46	986.06	881.50	808.79	755.93
45000	4096.21	2216.81	1595.99	1289.77	1109.32	991.69	909.89	850.42
50000	4551.35	2463.12	1773.32	1433.07	1232.57	1101.88	1010.99	944.91
55000	5006.48	2709.43	1950.66	1576.38	1355.83	1212.06	1112.09	1039.40
60000	5461.62	2955.74	2127.99	1719.69	1479.09	1322.25	1213.19	1133.89
65000	5916.75	3202.05	2305.32	1863.00	1602.35	1432.44	1314.28	1228.38
70000	6371.89	3448.36	2482.65	2006.30	1725.60	1542.62	1415.38	1322.87
75000	6827.02	3694.67	2659.98	2149.61	1848.86	1652.81	1516.48	1417.36
80000	7282.16	3940.99	2837.32	2292.92	1972.12	1763.00	1617.58	1511.86
85000	7737.29	4187.30	3014.65	2436.22	2095.37	1873.18	1718.68	1606.35
90000	8192.42	4433.61	3191.98	2579.53	2218.63	1983.37	1819.78	1700.84
95000	8647.56	4679.92	3369.31	2722.84	2341.89	2093.56	1920.87	1795.33
100000	9102.69	4926.23	3546.64	2866.14	2465.14	2203.75	2021.97	1889.82
105000	9557.83	5172.54	3723.97	3009.45	2588.40	2313.93	2123.07	1984.31
110000	10012.96	5418.85	3901.31	3152.76	2711.66	2424.12	2224.17	2078.80
115000	10468.10	5665.17	4078.64	3296.07	2834.91	2534.31	2325.27	2173.29
120000	10923.23	5911.48	4255.97	3439.37	2958.17	2644.49	2426.37	2267.78
125000	11378.37	6157.79	4433.30	3582.68	3081.43	2754.68	2527.46	2362.27
130000	11833.50	6404.10	4610.63	3725.99	3204.69	2864.87	2628.56	2456.76
135000	12288.63	6650.41	4787.97	3869.29	3327.94	2975.05	2729.66	2551.25
140000	12743.77	6896.72	4965.30	4012.60	3451.20	3085.24	2830.76	2645.74
145000	13198.90	7143.03	5142.63	4155.91	3574.46	3195.43	2931.86	2740.23
150000	13654.04	7389.34	5319.96	4299.21	3697.71	3305.62	3032.96	2834.72
155000	14109.17	7635.66	5497.29	4442.52	3820.97	3415.80	3134.05	2929.21
160000	14564.31	7881.97	5674.63	4585.83	3944.23	3525.99	3235.15	3023.71

MONTHLY AMORTIZING PAYMENTS 16⅝%

AMOUNT OF LOAN	NUMBER OF YEARS IN TERM 9	10	15	20	25	30	35	40
$ 50	.90	.86	.76	.72	.71	.70	.70	.70
100	1.80	1.72	1.52	1.44	1.41	1.40	1.39	1.39
200	3.59	3.43	3.03	2.88	2.82	2.80	2.78	2.78
300	5.38	5.15	4.54	4.32	4.23	4.19	4.17	4.17
400	7.17	6.86	6.06	5.76	5.64	5.59	5.56	5.55
500	8.96	8.58	7.57	7.20	7.05	6.98	6.95	6.94
600	10.75	10.29	9.08	8.64	8.45	8.38	8.34	8.33
700	12.54	12.01	10.59	10.07	9.86	9.77	9.73	9.72
800	14.33	13.72	12.11	11.51	11.27	11.17	11.12	11.10
900	16.12	15.43	13.62	12.95	12.68	12.56	12.51	12.49
1000	17.91	17.15	15.13	14.39	14.09	13.96	13.90	13.88
2000	35.82	34.29	30.26	28.77	28.17	27.91	27.80	27.75
3000	53.72	51.43	45.38	43.16	42.25	41.86	41.70	41.62
4000	71.63	68.58	60.51	57.54	56.33	55.82	55.59	55.50
5000	89.53	85.72	75.63	71.92	70.41	69.77	69.49	69.37
6000	107.44	102.86	90.76	86.31	84.49	83.72	83.39	83.24
7000	125.35	120.01	105.88	100.69	98.57	97.67	97.28	97.12
8000	143.25	137.15	121.01	115.07	112.65	111.63	111.18	110.99
9000	161.16	154.29	136.13	129.46	126.74	125.58	125.08	124.86
10000	179.06	171.43	151.26	143.84	140.82	139.53	138.98	138.73
11000	196.97	188.58	166.38	158.22	154.90	153.48	152.87	152.61
12000	214.88	205.72	181.51	172.61	168.98	167.44	166.77	166.48
13000	232.78	222.86	196.63	186.99	183.06	181.39	180.67	180.35
14000	250.69	240.01	211.76	201.37	197.14	195.34	194.56	194.23
15000	268.59	257.15	226.88	215.76	211.22	209.30	208.46	208.10
16000	286.50	274.29	242.01	230.14	225.30	223.25	222.36	221.97
17000	304.41	291.43	257.13	244.52	239.38	237.20	236.26	235.85
18000	322.31	308.58	272.26	258.91	253.47	251.15	250.15	249.72
19000	340.22	325.72	287.38	273.29	267.55	265.11	264.05	263.59
20000	358.12	342.86	302.51	287.68	281.63	279.06	277.95	277.46
21000	376.03	360.01	317.63	302.06	295.71	293.01	291.84	291.34
22000	393.94	377.15	332.76	316.44	309.79	306.96	305.74	305.21
23000	411.84	394.29	347.88	330.83	323.87	320.92	319.64	319.08
24000	429.75	411.43	363.01	345.21	337.95	334.87	333.54	332.96
25000	447.65	428.58	378.13	359.59	352.03	348.82	347.43	346.83
26000	465.56	445.72	393.26	373.98	366.11	362.77	361.33	360.70
27000	483.47	462.86	408.38	388.36	380.20	376.73	375.23	374.57
28000	501.37	480.01	423.51	402.74	394.28	390.68	389.12	388.45
29000	519.28	497.15	438.63	417.13	408.36	404.63	403.02	402.32
30000	537.18	514.29	453.76	431.51	422.44	418.59	416.92	416.19
31000	555.09	531.43	468.88	445.89	436.52	432.54	430.82	430.07
32000	572.99	548.58	484.01	460.28	450.60	446.49	444.71	443.94
33000	590.90	565.72	499.13	474.66	464.68	460.44	458.61	457.81
34000	608.81	582.86	514.26	489.04	478.76	474.40	472.51	471.69
35000	626.71	600.01	529.38	503.43	492.85	488.35	486.40	485.56
40000	716.24	685.72	605.01	575.35	563.25	558.11	555.89	554.92
45000	805.77	771.43	680.63	647.26	633.66	627.88	625.38	624.29
50000	895.30	857.15	756.26	719.18	704.06	697.64	694.86	693.65
55000	984.83	942.86	831.88	791.10	774.47	767.40	764.35	763.02
60000	1074.36	1028.58	907.51	863.02	844.87	837.17	833.83	832.38
65000	1163.89	1114.29	983.13	934.93	915.28	906.93	903.32	901.75
70000	1253.42	1200.01	1058.76	1006.85	985.69	976.69	972.80	971.11
75000	1342.95	1285.72	1134.38	1078.77	1056.09	1046.46	1042.29	1040.48
80000	1432.48	1371.43	1210.01	1150.69	1126.50	1116.22	1111.78	1109.84
85000	1522.01	1457.15	1285.64	1222.60	1196.90	1185.98	1181.26	1179.21
90000	1611.54	1542.86	1361.26	1294.52	1267.31	1255.75	1250.75	1248.57
95000	1701.07	1628.58	1436.89	1366.44	1337.71	1325.51	1320.23	1317.94
100000	1790.60	1714.29	1512.51	1438.36	1408.12	1395.27	1389.72	1387.30
105000	1880.13	1800.01	1588.14	1510.27	1478.53	1465.04	1459.20	1456.67
110000	1969.66	1885.72	1663.76	1582.19	1548.93	1534.80	1528.69	1526.03
115000	2059.19	1971.44	1739.39	1654.11	1619.34	1604.56	1598.18	1595.40
120000	2148.72	2057.15	1815.01	1726.03	1689.74	1674.33	1667.66	1664.76
125000	2238.25	2142.86	1890.64	1797.95	1760.15	1744.09	1737.15	1734.12
130000	2327.78	2228.58	1966.26	1869.86	1830.55	1813.85	1806.63	1803.49
135000	2417.31	2314.29	2041.89	1941.78	1900.96	1883.62	1876.12	1872.85
140000	2506.83	2400.01	2117.51	2013.70	1971.37	1953.38	1945.60	1942.22
145000	2596.36	2485.72	2193.14	2085.62	2041.77	2023.14	2015.09	2011.58
150000	2685.89	2571.44	2268.76	2157.53	2112.18	2092.91	2084.58	2080.95
155000	2775.42	2657.15	2344.39	2229.45	2182.58	2162.67	2154.06	2150.31
160000	2864.95	2742.86	2420.01	2301.37	2252.99	2232.43	2223.55	2219.68

AMOUNT OF LOAN	NUMBER OF YEARS IN TERM							
	1	2	3	4	5	6	7	8
$ 50	4.56	2.47	1.78	1.44	1.24	1.11	1.02	.95
100	9.11	4.94	3.56	2.88	2.48	2.22	2.03	1.90
200	18.22	9.87	7.11	5.75	4.95	4.43	4.06	3.80
300	27.33	14.80	10.66	8.62	7.42	6.64	6.09	5.70
400	36.44	19.73	14.22	11.50	9.89	8.85	8.12	7.59
500	45.55	24.67	17.77	14.37	12.36	11.06	10.15	9.49
600	54.66	29.60	21.32	17.24	14.84	13.27	12.18	11.39
700	63.77	34.53	24.87	20.11	17.31	15.48	14.21	13.29
800	72.87	39.46	28.43	22.99	19.78	17.69	16.24	15.18
900	81.98	44.40	31.98	25.86	22.25	19.90	18.27	17.08
1000	91.09	49.33	35.53	28.73	24.72	22.11	20.30	18.98
2000	182.18	98.65	71.06	57.46	49.44	44.22	40.59	37.95
3000	273.26	147.97	106.59	86.18	74.16	66.33	60.88	56.92
4000	364.35	197.29	142.12	114.91	98.88	88.43	81.17	75.89
5000	455.44	246.62	177.65	143.63	123.60	110.54	101.46	94.87
6000	546.52	295.94	213.18	172.36	148.32	132.65	121.75	113.84
7000	637.61	345.26	248.70	201.09	173.03	154.75	142.05	132.81
8000	728.69	394.58	284.23	229.81	197.75	176.86	162.34	151.78
9000	819.78	443.91	319.76	258.54	222.47	198.97	182.63	170.76
10000	910.87	493.23	355.29	287.26	247.19	221.07	202.92	189.73
11000	1001.95	542.55	390.82	315.99	271.91	243.18	223.21	208.70
12000	1093.04	591.87	426.35	344.72	296.63	265.29	243.50	227.67
13000	1184.12	641.19	461.87	373.44	321.34	287.39	263.80	246.65
14000	1275.21	690.52	497.40	402.17	346.06	309.50	284.09	265.62
15000	1366.30	739.84	532.93	430.89	370.78	331.61	304.38	284.59
16000	1457.38	789.16	568.46	459.62	395.50	353.71	324.67	303.56
17000	1548.47	838.48	603.99	488.34	420.22	375.82	344.96	322.54
18000	1639.56	887.81	639.52	517.07	444.94	397.93	365.25	341.51
19000	1730.64	937.13	675.05	545.80	469.65	420.04	385.55	360.48
20000	1821.73	986.45	710.57	574.52	494.37	442.14	405.84	379.45
21000	1912.81	1035.77	746.10	603.25	519.09	464.25	426.13	398.43
22000	2003.90	1085.09	781.63	631.97	543.81	486.36	446.42	417.40
23000	2094.99	1134.42	817.16	660.70	568.53	508.46	466.71	436.37
24000	2186.07	1183.74	852.69	689.43	593.25	530.57	487.00	455.34
25000	2277.16	1233.06	888.22	718.15	617.96	552.68	507.29	474.32
26000	2368.24	1282.38	923.74	746.88	642.68	574.78	527.59	493.29
27000	2459.33	1331.71	959.27	775.60	667.40	596.89	547.88	512.26
28000	2550.42	1381.03	994.80	804.33	692.12	619.00	568.17	531.23
29000	2641.50	1430.35	1030.33	833.06	716.84	641.10	588.46	550.21
30000	2732.59	1479.67	1065.86	861.78	741.56	663.21	608.75	569.18
31000	2823.68	1528.99	1101.39	890.51	766.27	685.32	629.04	588.15
32000	2914.76	1578.32	1136.91	919.23	790.99	707.42	649.34	607.12
33000	3005.85	1627.64	1172.44	947.96	815.71	729.53	669.63	626.10
34000	3096.93	1676.96	1207.97	976.68	840.43	751.64	689.92	645.07
35000	3188.02	1726.28	1243.50	1005.41	865.15	773.75	710.21	664.04
40000	3643.45	1972.89	1421.14	1149.04	988.74	884.28	811.67	758.90
45000	4098.88	2219.51	1598.78	1292.67	1112.33	994.81	913.13	853.76
50000	4554.31	2466.12	1776.43	1436.30	1235.92	1105.35	1014.58	948.63
55000	5009.74	2712.73	1954.07	1579.93	1359.51	1215.88	1116.04	1043.49
60000	5465.17	2959.34	2131.71	1723.56	1483.11	1326.42	1217.50	1138.35
65000	5920.60	3205.95	2309.35	1867.19	1606.70	1436.95	1318.96	1233.21
70000	6376.04	3452.56	2487.00	2010.82	1730.29	1547.49	1420.42	1328.07
75000	6831.47	3699.17	2664.64	2154.44	1853.88	1658.02	1521.87	1422.94
80000	7286.90	3945.78	2842.28	2298.07	1977.47	1768.55	1623.33	1517.80
85000	7742.33	4192.39	3019.92	2441.70	2101.06	1879.09	1724.79	1612.66
90000	8197.76	4439.01	3197.56	2585.33	2224.66	1989.62	1826.25	1707.52
95000	8653.19	4685.62	3375.21	2728.96	2348.25	2100.16	1927.71	1802.39
100000	9108.62	4932.23	3552.85	2872.59	2471.84	2210.69	2029.16	1897.25
105000	9564.05	5178.84	3730.49	3016.22	2595.43	2321.23	2130.62	1992.11
110000	10019.48	5425.45	3908.13	3159.85	2719.02	2431.76	2232.08	2086.97
115000	10474.91	5672.06	4085.77	3303.48	2842.62	2542.29	2333.54	2181.83
120000	10930.34	5918.67	4263.42	3447.11	2966.21	2652.83	2435.00	2276.70
125000	11385.77	6165.28	4441.06	3590.74	3089.80	2763.36	2536.45	2371.56
130000	11841.20	6411.89	4618.70	3734.37	3213.39	2873.90	2637.91	2466.42
135000	12296.64	6658.51	4796.34	3878.00	3336.98	2984.43	2739.37	2561.28
140000	12752.07	6905.12	4973.99	4021.63	3460.57	3094.97	2840.83	2656.14
145000	13207.50	7151.73	5151.63	4165.26	3584.17	3205.50	2942.29	2751.01
150000	13662.93	7398.34	5329.27	4308.88	3707.76	3316.03	3043.74	2845.87
155000	14118.36	7644.95	5506.91	4452.51	3831.35	3426.57	3145.20	2940.73
160000	14573.79	7891.56	5684.55	4596.14	3954.94	3537.10	3246.66	3035.59

AMOUNT OF LOAN	NUMBER OF YEARS IN TERM							
	9	10	15	20	25	30	35	40
$ 50	.90	.87	.77	.73	.71	.71	.70	.70
100	1.80	1.73	1.53	1.45	1.42	1.41	1.40	1.40
200	3.60	3.45	3.05	2.90	2.84	2.82	2.80	2.80
300	5.40	5.17	4.57	4.35	4.26	4.22	4.20	4.20
400	7.20	6.89	6.09	5.80	5.68	5.63	5.60	5.60
500	9.00	8.62	7.61	7.24	7.09	7.03	7.00	6.99
600	10.79	10.34	9.13	8.69	8.51	8.44	8.40	8.39
700	12.59	12.06	10.65	10.14	9.93	9.84	9.80	9.79
800	14.39	13.78	12.18	11.59	11.35	11.25	11.20	11.19
900	16.19	15.50	13.70	13.04	12.77	12.65	12.60	12.58
1000	17.99	17.23	15.22	14.48	14.18	14.06	14.00	13.98
2000	35.97	34.45	30.43	28.96	28.36	28.11	28.00	27.96
3000	53.95	51.67	45.64	43.44	42.54	42.17	42.00	41.93
4000	71.94	68.89	60.86	57.92	56.72	56.22	56.00	55.91
5000	89.92	86.11	76.07	72.40	70.90	70.27	70.00	69.89
6000	107.90	103.34	91.28	86.87	85.08	84.33	84.00	83.86
7000	125.88	120.56	106.50	101.35	99.26	98.38	98.00	97.84
8000	143.87	137.78	121.71	115.83	113.44	112.44	112.00	111.82
9000	161.85	155.00	136.92	130.31	127.62	126.49	126.00	125.79
10000	179.83	172.22	152.14	144.79	141.80	140.54	140.00	139.77
11000	197.81	189.44	167.35	159.27	155.98	154.60	154.00	153.74
12000	215.80	206.67	182.56	173.74	170.16	168.65	168.00	167.72
13000	233.78	223.89	197.78	188.22	184.34	182.71	182.00	181.70
14000	251.76	241.11	212.99	202.70	198.52	196.76	196.00	195.67
15000	269.74	258.33	228.20	217.18	212.70	210.81	210.00	209.65
16000	287.73	275.55	243.42	231.66	226.88	224.87	224.00	223.63
17000	305.71	292.77	258.63	246.13	241.06	238.92	238.00	237.60
18000	323.69	310.00	273.84	260.61	255.24	252.98	252.00	251.58
19000	341.67	327.22	289.06	275.09	269.42	267.03	266.00	265.56
20000	359.66	344.44	304.27	289.57	283.60	281.08	280.00	279.53
21000	377.64	361.66	319.48	304.05	297.78	295.14	294.00	293.51
22000	395.62	378.88	334.70	318.53	311.96	309.19	308.00	307.48
23000	413.60	396.10	349.91	333.00	326.14	323.25	322.00	321.46
24000	431.59	413.33	365.12	347.48	340.32	337.30	336.00	335.44
25000	449.57	430.55	380.34	361.96	354.50	351.35	350.00	349.41
26000	467.55	447.77	395.55	376.44	368.68	365.41	364.00	363.39
27000	485.53	464.99	410.76	390.92	382.86	379.46	378.00	377.37
28000	503.52	482.21	425.97	405.39	397.04	393.52	392.00	391.34
29000	521.50	499.43	441.19	419.87	411.22	407.57	406.00	405.32
30000	539.48	516.66	456.40	434.35	425.40	421.62	420.00	419.30
31000	557.46	533.88	471.61	448.83	439.58	435.68	434.00	433.27
32000	575.45	551.10	486.83	463.31	453.76	449.73	448.00	447.25
33000	593.43	568.32	502.04	477.79	467.94	463.79	462.00	461.22
34000	611.41	585.54	517.25	492.26	482.12	477.84	476.00	475.20
35000	629.39	602.76	532.47	506.74	496.30	491.89	490.00	489.18
40000	719.31	688.87	608.53	579.13	567.20	562.16	560.00	559.06
45000	809.22	774.98	684.60	651.52	638.10	632.43	630.00	628.94
50000	899.13	861.09	760.67	723.91	709.00	702.70	699.99	698.82
55000	989.04	947.20	836.73	796.31	779.90	772.97	769.99	768.70
60000	1078.96	1033.31	912.80	868.70	850.80	843.24	839.99	838.59
65000	1168.87	1119.41	988.86	941.09	921.70	913.51	909.99	908.47
70000	1258.78	1205.52	1064.93	1013.48	992.60	983.78	979.99	978.35
75000	1348.69	1291.63	1141.00	1085.87	1063.50	1054.05	1049.99	1048.23
80000	1438.61	1377.74	1217.06	1158.26	1134.40	1124.32	1119.99	1118.11
85000	1528.52	1463.85	1293.13	1230.65	1205.30	1194.59	1189.99	1187.99
90000	1618.43	1549.96	1369.19	1303.04	1276.20	1264.86	1259.99	1257.88
95000	1708.35	1636.06	1445.26	1375.43	1347.10	1335.13	1329.99	1327.76
100000	1798.26	1722.17	1521.33	1447.82	1418.00	1405.40	1399.98	1397.64
105000	1888.17	1808.28	1597.39	1520.22	1488.90	1475.67	1469.98	1467.52
110000	1978.08	1894.39	1673.46	1592.61	1559.80	1545.94	1539.98	1537.40
115000	2068.00	1980.50	1749.52	1665.00	1630.70	1616.21	1609.98	1607.29
120000	2157.91	2066.61	1825.59	1737.39	1701.60	1686.48	1679.98	1677.17
125000	2247.82	2152.71	1901.66	1809.78	1772.50	1756.75	1749.98	1747.05
130000	2337.73	2238.82	1977.72	1882.17	1843.40	1827.02	1819.98	1816.93
135000	2427.65	2324.93	2053.79	1954.56	1914.30	1897.29	1889.98	1886.81
140000	2517.56	2411.04	2129.85	2026.95	1985.20	1967.56	1959.98	1956.69
145000	2607.47	2497.15	2205.92	2099.34	2056.10	2037.83	2029.98	2026.58
150000	2697.38	2583.26	2281.99	2171.73	2127.00	2108.10	2099.97	2096.46
155000	2787.30	2669.36	2358.05	2244.13	2197.90	2178.37	2169.97	2166.34
160000	2877.21	2755.47	2434.12	2316.52	2268.80	2248.64	2239.97	2236.22

17% MONTHLY AMORTIZING PAYMENTS

AMOUNT OF LOAN	NUMBER OF YEARS IN TERM 1	2	3	4	5	6	7	8
$ 50	4.57	2.48	1.79	1.45	1.25	1.12	1.03	.96
100	9.13	4.95	3.57	2.89	2.49	2.23	2.05	1.92
200	18.25	9.89	7.14	5.78	4.98	4.45	4.09	3.83
300	27.37	14.84	10.70	8.66	7.46	6.68	6.14	5.74
400	36.49	19.78	14.27	11.55	9.95	8.90	8.18	7.65
500	45.61	24.73	17.83	14.43	12.43	11.13	10.22	9.57
600	54.73	29.67	21.40	17.32	14.92	13.35	12.27	11.48
700	63.85	34.61	24.96	20.20	17.40	15.58	14.31	13.39
800	72.97	39.56	28.53	23.09	19.89	17.80	16.35	15.30
900	82.09	44.50	32.09	25.97	22.37	20.03	18.40	17.21
1000	91.21	49.45	35.66	28.86	24.86	22.25	20.44	19.13
2000	182.41	98.89	71.31	57.72	49.71	44.50	40.88	38.25
3000	273.62	148.33	106.96	86.57	74.56	66.74	61.31	57.37
4000	364.82	197.77	142.62	115.43	99.42	88.99	81.75	76.49
5000	456.03	247.22	178.27	144.28	124.27	111.24	102.18	95.61
6000	547.23	296.66	213.92	173.14	149.12	133.48	122.62	114.73
7000	638.44	346.10	249.57	201.99	173.97	155.73	143.06	133.86
8000	729.64	395.54	285.23	230.85	198.83	177.97	163.49	152.98
9000	820.85	444.99	320.88	259.70	223.68	200.22	183.93	172.10
10000	912.05	494.43	356.53	288.56	248.53	222.47	204.36	191.22
11000	1003.26	543.87	392.19	317.41	273.38	244.71	224.80	210.34
12000	1094.46	593.31	427.84	346.27	298.24	266.96	245.23	229.46
13000	1185.67	642.75	463.49	375.12	323.09	289.20	265.67	248.58
14000	1276.87	692.20	499.14	403.98	347.94	311.45	286.11	267.71
15000	1368.08	741.64	534.80	432.83	372.79	333.70	306.54	286.83
16000	1459.28	791.08	570.45	461.69	397.65	355.94	326.98	305.95
17000	1550.49	840.52	606.10	490.54	422.50	378.19	347.41	325.07
18000	1641.69	889.97	641.75	519.40	447.35	400.44	367.85	344.19
19000	1732.90	939.41	677.41	548.25	472.20	422.68	388.29	363.31
20000	1824.10	988.85	713.06	577.11	497.06	444.93	408.72	382.43
21000	1915.30	1038.29	748.71	605.96	521.91	467.17	429.16	401.56
22000	2006.51	1087.73	784.37	634.82	546.76	489.42	449.59	420.68
23000	2097.71	1137.18	820.02	663.67	571.61	511.67	470.03	439.80
24000	2188.92	1186.62	855.67	692.53	596.47	533.91	490.46	458.92
25000	2280.12	1236.06	891.32	721.38	621.32	556.16	510.90	478.04
26000	2371.33	1285.50	926.98	750.24	646.17	578.40	531.34	497.16
27000	2462.53	1334.95	962.63	779.09	671.02	600.65	551.77	516.28
28000	2553.74	1384.39	998.28	807.95	695.88	622.90	572.21	535.41
29000	2644.94	1433.83	1033.93	836.80	720.73	645.14	592.64	554.53
30000	2736.15	1483.27	1069.59	865.66	745.58	667.39	613.08	573.65
31000	2827.35	1532.72	1105.24	894.51	770.43	689.64	633.51	592.77
32000	2918.56	1582.16	1140.89	923.37	795.29	711.88	653.95	611.89
33000	3009.76	1631.60	1176.55	952.22	820.14	734.13	674.39	631.01
34000	3100.97	1681.04	1212.20	981.08	844.99	756.37	694.82	650.13
35000	3192.17	1730.48	1247.85	1009.93	869.85	778.62	715.26	669.26
40000	3648.20	1977.70	1426.11	1154.21	994.11	889.85	817.44	764.86
45000	4104.22	2224.91	1604.38	1298.48	1118.37	1001.08	919.62	860.47
50000	4560.24	2472.12	1782.64	1442.76	1242.63	1112.31	1021.80	956.08
55000	5016.27	2719.33	1960.91	1587.03	1366.90	1223.54	1123.97	1051.68
60000	5472.29	2966.54	2139.17	1731.31	1491.16	1334.77	1226.15	1147.29
65000	5928.31	3213.75	2317.43	1875.58	1615.42	1446.00	1328.33	1242.90
70000	6384.34	3460.96	2495.70	2019.86	1739.69	1557.23	1430.51	1338.51
75000	6840.36	3708.17	2673.96	2164.13	1863.95	1668.46	1532.69	1434.11
80000	7296.39	3955.39	2852.22	2308.41	1988.21	1779.70	1634.87	1529.72
85000	7752.41	4202.60	3030.49	2452.68	2112.47	1890.93	1737.05	1625.33
90000	8208.43	4449.81	3208.75	2596.96	2236.74	2002.16	1839.23	1720.94
95000	8664.46	4697.02	3387.01	2741.23	2361.00	2113.39	1941.41	1816.54
100000	9120.48	4944.23	3565.28	2885.51	2485.26	2224.62	2043.59	1912.15
105000	9576.50	5191.44	3743.54	3029.78	2609.53	2335.85	2145.76	2007.76
110000	10032.53	5438.65	3921.81	3174.06	2733.79	2447.08	2247.94	2103.36
115000	10488.55	5685.87	4100.07	3318.33	2858.05	2558.31	2350.12	2198.97
120000	10944.58	5933.08	4278.33	3462.61	2982.31	2669.54	2452.30	2294.58
125000	11400.60	6180.29	4456.60	3606.89	3106.58	2780.77	2554.48	2390.19
130000	11856.62	6427.50	4634.86	3751.16	3230.84	2892.00	2656.66	2485.79
135000	12312.65	6674.71	4813.12	3895.44	3355.10	3003.23	2758.84	2581.40
140000	12768.67	6921.92	4991.39	4039.71	3479.37	3114.46	2861.02	2677.01
145000	13224.69	7169.13	5169.65	4183.99	3603.63	3225.69	2963.20	2772.62
150000	13680.72	7416.34	5347.91	4328.26	3727.89	3336.92	3065.38	2868.22
155000	14136.74	7663.56	5526.18	4472.54	3852.15	3448.16	3167.55	2963.83
160000	14592.77	7910.77	5704.44	4616.81	3976.42	3559.39	3269.73	3059.44

AMOUNT OF LOAN	NUMBER OF YEARS IN TERM							
	9	10	15	20	25	30	35	40
$ 50	.91	.87	.77	.74	.72	.72	.72	.71
100	1.82	1.74	1.54	1.47	1.44	1.43	1.43	1.42
200	3.63	3.48	3.08	2.94	2.88	2.86	2.85	2.84
300	5.45	5.22	4.62	4.41	4.32	4.28	4.27	4.26
400	7.26	6.96	6.16	5.87	5.76	5.71	5.69	5.68
500	9.07	8.69	7.70	7.34	7.19	7.13	7.11	7.10
600	10.89	10.43	9.24	8.81	8.63	8.56	8.53	8.51
700	12.70	12.17	10.78	10.27	10.07	9.98	9.95	9.93
800	14.51	13.91	12.32	11.74	11.51	11.41	11.37	11.35
900	16.33	15.65	13.86	13.21	12.95	12.84	12.79	12.77
1000	18.14	17.38	15.40	14.67	14.38	14.26	14.21	14.19
2000	36.28	34.76	30.79	29.34	28.76	28.52	28.42	28.37
3000	54.41	52.14	46.18	44.01	43.14	42.78	42.62	42.55
4000	72.55	69.52	61.57	58.68	57.52	57.03	56.83	56.74
5000	90.69	86.90	76.96	73.35	71.89	71.29	71.03	70.92
6000	108.82	104.28	92.35	88.01	86.27	85.55	85.24	85.10
7000	126.96	121.66	107.74	102.68	100.65	99.80	99.44	99.29
8000	145.09	139.04	123.13	117.35	115.03	114.06	113.65	113.47
9000	163.23	156.42	138.52	132.02	129.41	128.32	127.85	127.65
10000	181.37	173.80	153.91	146.69	143.78	142.57	142.06	141.84
11000	199.50	191.18	169.30	161.35	158.16	156.83	156.26	156.02
12000	217.64	208.56	184.69	176.02	172.54	171.09	170.47	170.20
13000	235.78	225.94	200.08	190.69	186.92	185.34	184.67	184.39
14000	253.91	243.32	215.47	205.36	201.30	199.60	198.88	198.57
15000	272.05	260.70	230.86	220.03	215.67	213.86	213.08	212.75
16000	290.18	278.08	246.25	234.69	230.05	228.11	227.29	226.94
17000	308.32	295.46	261.64	249.36	244.43	242.37	241.49	241.12
18000	326.46	312.84	277.03	264.03	258.81	256.63	255.70	255.30
19000	344.59	330.22	292.42	278.70	273.19	270.88	269.90	269.49
20000	362.73	347.60	307.81	293.37	287.56	285.14	284.11	283.67
21000	380.86	364.98	323.20	308.03	301.94	299.40	298.32	297.85
22000	399.00	382.36	338.59	322.70	316.32	313.65	312.52	312.04
23000	417.14	399.74	353.98	337.37	330.70	327.91	326.73	326.22
24000	435.27	417.12	369.37	352.04	345.08	342.17	340.93	340.40
25000	453.41	434.50	384.76	366.71	359.45	356.42	355.14	354.59
26000	471.55	451.88	400.15	381.37	373.83	370.68	369.34	368.77
27000	489.68	469.26	415.54	396.04	388.21	384.94	383.55	382.95
28000	507.82	486.64	430.93	410.71	402.59	399.19	397.75	397.14
29000	525.95	504.02	446.32	425.38	416.97	413.45	411.96	411.32
30000	544.09	521.40	461.71	440.05	431.34	427.71	426.16	425.50
31000	562.23	538.78	477.10	454.71	445.72	441.96	440.37	439.69
32000	580.36	556.16	492.49	469.38	460.10	456.22	454.57	453.87
33000	598.50	573.54	507.88	484.05	474.48	470.48	468.78	468.05
34000	616.64	590.92	523.27	498.72	488.86	484.73	482.98	482.24
35000	634.77	608.30	538.66	513.39	503.23	498.99	497.19	496.42
40000	725.45	695.20	615.61	586.73	575.12	570.28	568.22	567.33
45000	816.13	782.09	692.56	660.07	647.01	641.56	639.24	638.25
50000	906.81	868.99	769.51	733.41	718.90	712.84	710.27	709.17
55000	997.50	955.89	846.46	806.75	790.79	784.13	781.29	780.08
60000	1088.18	1042.79	923.41	880.09	862.68	855.41	852.32	851.00
65000	1178.86	1129.69	1000.36	953.43	934.57	926.69	923.35	921.92
70000	1269.54	1216.59	1077.31	1026.77	1006.46	997.98	994.37	992.83
75000	1360.22	1303.49	1154.26	1100.11	1078.35	1069.26	1065.40	1063.75
80000	1450.90	1390.39	1231.21	1173.45	1150.24	1140.55	1136.43	1134.66
85000	1541.58	1477.29	1308.16	1246.79	1222.13	1211.83	1207.45	1205.58
90000	1632.26	1564.18	1385.11	1320.13	1294 02	1283.11	1278.48	1276.50
95000	1722.94	1651.08	1462.06	1393.47	1365.91	1354.40	1349.50	1347.41
100000	1813.62	1737.98	1539.01	1466.81	1437.80	1425.68	1420.53	1418.33
105000	1904.30	1824.88	1615.96	1540.15	1509.69	1496.96	1491.56	1489.24
110000	1994.99	1911.78	1692.91	1613.49	1581.58	1568.25	1562.58	1560.16
115000	2085.67	1998.68	1769.86	1686.83	1653.47	1639.53	1633.61	1631.08
120000	2176.35	2085.58	1846.81	1760.17	1725.36	1710.82	1704.64	1701.99
125000	2267.03	2172.48	1923.76	1833.51	1797.25	1782.10	1775.66	1772.91
130000	2357.71	2259.37	2000.71	1906.85	1869.14	1853.38	1846.69	1843.83
135000	2448.39	2346.27	2077.66	1980.19	1941.03	1924.67	1917.72	1914.74
140000	2539.07	2433.17	2154.61	2053.53	2012.92	1995.95	1988.74	1985.66
145000	2629.75	2520.07	2231.56	2126.87	2084.81	2067.23	2059.77	2056.57
150000	2720.43	2606.97	2308.51	2200.21	2156.70	2138.52	2130.79	2127.49
155000	2811.11	2693.87	2385.46	2273.55	2228.59	2209.80	2201.82	2198.41
160000	2901.80	2780.77	2462.41	2346.89	2300.48	2281.09	2272.85	2269.32

AMOUNT OF LOAN	NUMBER OF YEARS IN TERM 1	2	3	4	5	6	7	8
$ 50	4.57	2.48	1.79	1.45	1.25	1.12	1.03	.97
100	9.14	4.96	3.58	2.90	2.50	2.24	2.06	1.93
200	18.27	9.92	7.16	5.80	5.00	4.48	4.12	3.86
300	27.40	14.87	10.74	8.70	7.50	6.72	6.18	5.79
400	36.53	19.83	14.32	11.60	10.00	8.96	8.24	7.71
500	45.67	24.79	17.89	14.50	12.50	11.20	10.30	9.64
600	54.80	29.74	21.47	17.40	15.00	13.44	12.35	11.57
700	63.93	34.70	25.05	20.29	17.50	15.68	14.41	13.49
800	73.06	39.65	28.63	23.19	19.99	17.91	16.47	15.42
900	82.20	44.61	32.20	26.09	22.49	20.15	18.53	17.35
1000	91.33	49.57	35.78	28.99	24.99	22.39	20.59	19.28
2000	182.65	99.13	71.56	57.97	49.98	44.78	41.17	38.55
3000	273.98	148.69	107.34	86.96	74.97	67.16	61.75	57.82
4000	365.30	198.25	143.11	115.94	99.95	89.55	82.33	77.09
5000	456.62	247.82	178.89	144.93	124.94	111.93	102.91	96.36
6000	547.95	297.38	214.67	173.91	149.93	134.32	123.49	115.63
7000	639.27	346.94	250.45	202.90	174.92	156.71	144.07	134.90
8000	730.59	396.50	286.22	231.88	199.90	179.09	164.65	154.17
9000	821.92	446.07	322.00	260.87	224.89	201.48	185.23	173.44
10000	913.24	495.63	357.78	289.85	249.88	223.86	205.81	192.72
11000	1004.56	545.19	393.55	318.84	274.86	246.25	226.39	211.99
12000	1095.89	594.75	429.33	347.82	299.85	268.64	246.97	231.26
13000	1187.21	644.32	465.11	376.80	324.84	291.02	267.55	250.53
14000	1278.53	693.88	500.89	405.79	349.83	313.41	288.13	269.80
15000	1369.86	743.44	536.66	434.77	374.81	335.79	308.71	289.07
16000	1461.18	793.00	572.44	463.76	399.80	358.18	329.29	308.34
17000	1552.50	842.57	608.22	492.74	424.79	380.56	349.87	327.61
18000	1643.83	892.13	644.00	521.73	449.77	402.95	370.45	346.88
19000	1735.15	941.69	679.77	550.71	474.76	425.34	391.04	366.15
20000	1826.47	991.25	715.55	579.70	499.75	447.72	411.62	385.43
21000	1917.80	1040.82	751.33	608.68	524.74	470.11	432.20	404.70
22000	2009.12	1090.38	787.10	637.67	549.72	492.49	452.78	423.97
23000	2100.44	1139.94	822.88	666.65	574.71	514.88	473.36	443.24
24000	2191.77	1189.50	858.66	695.63	599.70	537.27	493.94	462.51
25000	2283.09	1239.07	894.44	724.62	624.68	559.65	514.52	481.78
26000	2374.41	1288.63	930.21	753.60	649.67	582.04	535.10	501.05
27000	2465.74	1338.19	965.99	782.59	674.66	604.42	555.68	520.32
28000	2557.06	1387.75	1001.77	811.57	699.65	626.81	576.26	539.59
29000	2648.38	1437.32	1037.55	840.56	724.63	649.19	596.84	558.87
30000	2739.71	1486.88	1073.32	869.54	749.62	671.58	617.42	578.14
31000	2831.03	1536.44	1109.10	898.53	774.61	693.97	638.00	597.41
32000	2922.35	1586.00	1144.88	927.51	799.60	716.35	658.58	616.68
33000	3013.68	1635.57	1180.65	956.50	824.58	738.74	679.16	635.95
34000	3105.00	1685.13	1216.43	985.48	849.57	761.12	699.74	655.22
35000	3196.33	1734.69	1252.21	1014.46	874.56	783.51	720.32	674.49
40000	3652.94	1982.50	1431.10	1159.39	999.49	895.44	823.23	770.85
45000	4109.56	2230.32	1609.98	1304.31	1124.43	1007.37	926.13	867.20
50000	4566.18	2478.13	1788.87	1449.23	1249.36	1119.30	1029.03	963.56
55000	5022.79	2725.94	1967.75	1594.16	1374.30	1231.23	1131.93	1059.91
60000	5479.41	2973.75	2146.64	1739.08	1499.24	1343.16	1234.84	1156.27
65000	5936.03	3221.57	2325.53	1884.00	1624.17	1455.09	1337.74	1252.62
70000	6392.65	3469.38	2504.41	2028.92	1749.11	1567.02	1440.64	1348.98
75000	6849.26	3717.19	2683.30	2173.85	1874.04	1678.94	1543.55	1445.33
80000	7305.88	3965.00	2862.19	2318.77	1998.98	1790.87	1646.45	1541.69
85000	7762.50	4212.82	3041.07	2463.69	2123.92	1902.80	1749.35	1638.04
90000	8219.11	4460.63	3219.96	2608.61	2248.85	2014.73	1852.25	1734.40
95000	8675.73	4708.44	3398.85	2753.54	2373.79	2126.66	1955.16	1830.75
100000	9132.35	4956.25	3577.73	2898.46	2498.72	2238.59	2058.06	1927.11
105000	9588.97	5204.06	3756.62	3043.38	2623.66	2350.52	2160.96	2023.47
110000	10045.58	5451.88	3935.50	3188.31	2748.60	2462.45	2263.86	2119.82
115000	10502.20	5699.69	4114.39	3333.23	2873.53	2574.38	2366.77	2216.18
120000	10958.82	5947.50	4293.28	3478.15	2998.47	2686.31	2469.67	2312.53
125000	11415.43	6195.31	4472.16	3623.07	3123.40	2798.24	2572.57	2408.89
130000	11872.05	6443.13	4651.05	3768.00	3248.34	2910.17	2675.48	2505.24
135000	12328.67	6690.94	4829.94	3912.92	3373.28	3022.10	2778.38	2601.60
140000	12785.29	6938.75	5008.82	4057.84	3498.21	3134.03	2881.28	2697.95
145000	13241.90	7186.56	5187.71	4202.76	3623.15	3245.95	2984.18	2794.31
150000	13698.52	7434.38	5366.60	4347.69	3748.08	3357.88	3087.09	2890.66
155000	14155.14	7682.19	5545.48	4492.61	3873.02	3469.81	3189.99	2987.02
160000	14611.75	7930.00	5724.37	4637.53	3997.96	3581.74	3292.89	3083.37

AMOUNT OF LOAN	NUMBER OF YEARS IN TERM							
	9	10	15	20	25	30	35	40
$ 50	.92	.88	.78	.75	.73	.73	.73	.72
100	1.83	1.76	1.56	1.49	1.46	1.45	1.45	1.44
200	3.66	3.51	3.12	2.98	2.92	2.90	2.89	2.88
300	5.49	5.27	4.68	4.46	4.38	4.34	4.33	4.32
400	7.32	7.02	6.23	5.95	5.84	5.79	5.77	5.76
500	9.15	8.77	7.79	7.43	7.29	7.23	7.21	7.20
600	10.98	10.53	9.35	8.92	8.75	8.68	8.65	8.64
700	12.81	12.28	10.90	10.41	10.21	10.13	10.09	10.08
800	14.64	14.04	12.46	11.89	11.67	11.57	11.53	11.52
900	16.47	15.79	14.02	13.38	13.12	13.02	12.97	12.96
1000	18.30	17.54	15.57	14.86	14.58	14.46	14.42	14.40
2000	36.59	35.08	31.14	29.72	29.16	28.92	28.83	28.79
3000	54.88	52.62	46.71	44.58	43.73	43.38	43.24	43.18
4000	73.17	70.16	62.28	59.44	58.31	57.84	57.65	57.57
5000	91.46	87.70	77.84	74.30	72.89	72.30	72.06	71.96
6000	109.75	105.24	93.41	89.16	87.46	86.76	86.47	86.35
7000	128.04	122.77	108.98	104.01	102.04	101.22	100.88	100.74
8000	146.33	140.31	124.55	118.87	116.62	115.68	115.29	115.13
9000	164.62	157.85	140.11	133.73	131.19	130.14	129.70	129.52
10000	182.91	175.39	155.68	148.59	145.77	144.60	144.11	143.91
11000	201.20	192.93	171.25	163.45	160.35	159.06	158.53	158.30
12000	219.49	210.47	186.82	178.31	174.92	173.52	172.94	172.69
13000	237.78	228.01	202.38	193.16	189.50	187.98	187.35	187.08
14000	256.07	245.54	217.95	208.02	204.07	202.44	201.76	201.47
15000	274.36	263.08	233.52	222.88	218.65	216.90	216.17	215.86
16000	292.65	280.62	249.09	237.74	233.23	231.36	230.58	230.25
17000	310.94	298.16	264.65	252.60	247.80	245.82	244.99	244.64
18000	329.23	315.70	280.22	267.46	262.38	260.28	259.40	259.03
19000	347.52	333.24	295.79	282.31	276.96	274.74	273.81	273.42
20000	365.81	350.78	311.36	297.17	291.53	289.20	288.22	287.81
21000	384.10	368.31	326.92	312.03	306.11	303.66	302.63	302.20
22000	402.40	385.85	342.49	326.89	320.69	318.12	317.05	316.59
23000	420.69	403.39	358.06	341.75	335.26	332.58	331.46	330.98
24000	438.98	420.93	373.63	356.61	349.84	347.04	345.87	345.37
25000	457.27	438.47	389.19	371.47	364.42	361.50	360.28	359.76
26000	475.56	456.01	404.76	386.32	378.99	375.96	374.69	374.15
27000	493.85	473.54	420.33	401.18	393.57	390.42	389.10	388.54
28000	512.14	491.08	435.90	416.04	408.14	404.88	403.51	402.93
29000	530.43	508.62	451.46	430.90	422.72	419.34	417.92	417.32
30000	548.72	526.16	467.03	445.76	437.30	433.80	432.33	431.71
31000	567.01	543.70	482.60	460.62	451.87	448.26	446.74	446.10
32000	585.30	561.24	498.17	475.47	466.45	462.72	461.15	460.49
33000	603.59	578.78	513.73	490.33	481.03	477.18	475.57	474.88
34000	621.88	596.31	529.30	505.19	495.60	491.64	489.98	489.27
35000	640.17	613.85	544.87	520.05	510.18	506.10	504.39	503.66
40000	731.62	701.55	622.71	594.34	583.06	578.40	576.44	575.61
45000	823.08	789.24	700.55	668.63	655.94	650.70	648.50	647.57
50000	914.53	876.93	778.38	742.93	728.83	723.00	720.55	719.52
55000	1005.98	964.62	856.22	817.22	801.71	795.30	792.61	791.47
60000	1097.43	1052.32	934.06	891.51	874.59	867.60	864.66	863.42
65000	1188.88	1140.01	1011.90	965.80	947.47	939.90	936.71	935.37
70000	1280.34	1227.70	1089.73	1040.09	1020.35	1012.20	1008.77	1007.32
75000	1371.79	1315.39	1167.57	1114.39	1093.24	1084.49	1080.82	1079.27
80000	1463.24	1403.09	1245.41	1188.68	1166.12	1156.79	1152.88	1151.22
85000	1554.69	1490.78	1323.25	1262.97	1239.00	1229.09	1224.93	1223.17
90000	1646.15	1578.47	1401.09	1337.26	1311.88	1301.39	1296.99	1295.13
95000	1737.60	1666.16	1478.92	1411.55	1384.76	1373.69	1369.04	1367.08
100000	1829.05	1753.86	1556.76	1485.85	1457.65	1445.99	1441.10	1439.03
105000	1920.50	1841.55	1634.60	1560.14	1530.53	1518.29	1513.15	1510.98
110000	2011.96	1929.24	1712.44	1634.43	1603.41	1590.59	1585.21	1582.93
115000	2103.41	2016.93	1790.28	1708.72	1676.29	1662.89	1657.26	1654.88
120000	2194.86	2104.63	1868.11	1783.02	1749.17	1735.19	1729.32	1726.83
125000	2286.31	2192.32	1945.95	1857.31	1822.06	1807.49	1801.37	1798.78
130000	2377.76	2280.01	2023.79	1931.60	1894.94	1879.79	1873.42	1870.74
135000	2469.22	2367.70	2101.63	2005.89	1967.82	1952.09	1945.48	1942.69
140000	2560.67	2455.40	2179.46	2080.18	2040.70	2024.39	2017.53	2014.64
145000	2652.12	2543.09	2257.30	2154.48	2113.59	2096.68	2089.59	2086.59
150000	2743.57	2630.78	2335.14	2228.77	2186.47	2168.98	2161.64	2158.54
155000	2835.03	2718.47	2412.98	2303.06	2259.35	2241.28	2233.70	2230.49
160000	2926.48	2806.17	2490.82	2377.35	2332.23	2313.58	2305.75	2302.44

MONTHLY AMORTIZING PAYMENTS

AMOUNT OF LOAN	NUMBER OF YEARS IN TERM 1	2	3	4	5	6	7	8
$ 50	4.58	2.49	1.80	1.46	1.26	1.13	1.04	.98
100	9.15	4.97	3.60	2.92	2.52	2.26	2.08	1.95
200	18.29	9.94	7.19	5.83	5.03	4.51	4.15	3.89
300	27.44	14.91	10.78	8.74	7.54	6.76	6.22	5.83
400	36.58	19.88	14.37	11.65	10.05	9.02	8.30	7.77
500	45.73	24.85	17.96	14.56	12.57	11.27	10.37	9.72
600	54.87	29.81	21.55	17.47	15.08	13.52	12.44	11.66
700	64.01	34.78	25.14	20.39	17.59	15.77	14.51	13.60
800	73.16	39.75	28.73	23.30	20.10	18.03	16.59	15.54
900	82.30	44.72	32.32	26.21	22.61	20.28	18.66	17.48
1000	91.45	49.69	35.91	29.12	25.13	22.53	20.73	19.43
2000	182.89	99.37	71.81	58.23	50.25	45.06	41.46	38.85
3000	274.33	149.05	107.71	87.35	75.37	67.58	62.18	58.27
4000	365.77	198.74	143.61	116.46	100.49	90.11	82.91	77.69
5000	457.22	248.42	179.52	145.58	125.62	112.64	103.63	97.11
6000	548.66	298.10	215.42	174.69	150.74	135.16	124.36	116.53
7000	640.10	347.78	251.32	203.81	175.86	157.69	145.09	135.95
8000	731.54	397.47	287.22	232.92	200.98	180.21	165.81	155.37
9000	822.98	447.15	323.12	262.03	226.10	202.74	186.54	174.80
10000	914.43	496.83	359.03	291.15	251.23	225.27	207.26	194.22
11000	1005.87	546.52	394.93	320.26	276.35	247.79	227.99	213.64
12000	1097.31	596.20	430.83	349.38	301.47	270.32	248.71	233.06
13000	1188.75	645.88	466.73	378.49	326.59	292.84	269.44	252.48
14000	1280.20	695.56	502.63	407.61	351.72	315.37	290.17	271.90
15000	1371.64	745.25	538.54	436.72	376.84	337.90	310.89	291.32
16000	1463.08	794.93	574.44	465.83	401.96	360.42	331.62	310.74
17000	1554.52	844.61	610.34	494.95	427.08	382.95	352.34	330.17
18000	1645.96	894.30	646.24	524.06	452.20	405.47	373.07	349.59
19000	1737.41	943.98	682.14	553.18	477.33	428.00	393.80	369.01
20000	1828.85	993.66	718.05	582.29	502.45	450.53	414.52	388.43
21000	1920.29	1043.34	753.95	611.41	527.57	473.05	435.25	407.85
22000	2011.73	1093.03	789.85	640.52	552.69	495.58	455.97	427.27
23000	2103.18	1142.71	825.75	669.64	577.82	518.10	476.70	446.69
24000	2194.62	1192.39	861.65	698.75	602.94	540.63	497.42	466.11
25000	2286.06	1242.08	897.56	727.86	628.06	563.16	518.15	485.54
26000	2377.50	1291.76	933.46	756.98	653.18	585.68	538.88	504.96
27000	2468.94	1341.44	969.36	786.09	678.30	608.21	559.60	524.38
28000	2560.39	1391.12	1005.26	815.21	703.43	630.73	580.33	543.80
29000	2651.83	1440.81	1041.16	844.32	728.55	653.26	601.05	563.22
30000	2743.27	1490.49	1077.07	873.44	753.67	675.79	621.78	582.64
31000	2834.71	1540.17	1112.97	902.55	778.79	698.31	642.50	602.06
32000	2926.16	1589.86	1148.87	931.66	803.92	720.84	663.23	621.48
33000	3017.60	1639.54	1184.77	960.78	829.04	743.36	683.96	640.90
34000	3109.04	1689.22	1220.68	989.89	854.16	765.89	704.68	660.33
35000	3200.48	1738.90	1256.58	1019.01	879.28	788.42	725.41	679.75
40000	3657.69	1987.32	1436.09	1164.58	1004.89	901.05	829.04	776.85
45000	4114.90	2235.73	1615.60	1310.15	1130.50	1013.68	932.67	873.96
50000	4572.12	2484.15	1795.11	1455.72	1256.12	1126.31	1036.29	971.07
55000	5029.33	2732.56	1974.62	1601.30	1381.73	1238.94	1139.92	1068.17
60000	5486.54	2980.98	2154.13	1746.87	1507.34	1351.57	1243.55	1165.28
65000	5943.75	3229.39	2333.64	1892.44	1632.95	1464.20	1347.18	1262.38
70000	6400.96	3477.80	2513.15	2038.01	1758.56	1576.83	1450.81	1359.49
75000	6858.17	3726.22	2692.66	2183.58	1884.17	1689.46	1554.44	1456.60
80000	7315.38	3974.63	2872.17	2329.15	2009.78	1802.09	1658.07	1553.70
85000	7772.59	4223.05	3051.68	2474.73	2135.39	1914.72	1761.70	1650.81
90000	8229.80	4471.46	3231.19	2620.30	2261.00	2027.35	1865.33	1747.91
95000	8687.01	4719.88	3410.70	2765.87	2386.62	2139.98	1968.96	1845.02
100000	9144.23	4968.29	3590.21	2911.44	2512.23	2252.61	2072.58	1942.13
105000	9601.44	5216.70	3769.72	3057.01	2637.84	2365.24	2176.21	2039.23
110000	10058.65	5465.12	3949.23	3202.59	2763.45	2477.87	2279.84	2136.34
115000	10515.86	5713.53	4128.74	3348.16	2889.06	2590.50	2383.47	2233.44
120000	10973.07	5961.95	4308.25	3493.73	3014.67	2703.13	2487.10	2330.55
125000	11430.28	6210.36	4487.76	3639.30	3140.28	2815.76	2590.73	2427.66
130000	11887.49	6458.78	4667.27	3784.87	3265.89	2928.39	2694.36	2524.76
135000	12344.70	6707.19	4846.78	3930.45	3391.50	3041.02	2797.99	2621.87
140000	12801.91	6955.60	5026.29	4076.02	3517.11	3153.65	2901.62	2718.97
145000	13259.12	7204.02	5205.80	4221.59	3642.73	3266.28	3005.25	2816.08
150000	13716.34	7452.43	5385.31	4367.16	3768.34	3378.91	3108.87	2913.19
155000	14173.55	7700.85	5564.83	4512.73	3893.95	3491.54	3212.50	3010.29
160000	14630.76	7949.26	5744.34	4658.30	4019.56	3604.17	3316.13	3107.40

AMOUNT OF LOAN	NUMBER OF YEARS IN TERM 9	10	15	20	25	30	35	40
$ 50	.93	.89	.79	.76	.74	.74	.74	.73
100	1.85	1.77	1.58	1.51	1.48	1.47	1.47	1.46
200	3.69	3.54	3.15	3.01	2.96	2.94	2.93	2.92
300	5.54	5.31	4.73	4.52	4.44	4.40	4.39	4.38
400	7.38	7.08	6.30	6.02	5.92	5.87	5.85	5.84
500	9.23	8.85	7.88	7.53	7.39	7.34	7.31	7.30
600	11.07	10.62	9.45	9.03	8.87	8.80	8.78	8.76
700	12.92	12.39	11.03	10.54	10.35	10.27	10.24	10.22
800	14.76	14.16	12.60	12.04	11.83	11.74	11.70	11.68
900	16.61	15.93	14.18	13.55	13.30	13.20	13.16	13.14
1000	18.45	17.70	15.75	15.05	14.78	14.67	14.62	14.60
2000	36.90	35.40	31.50	30.10	29.56	29.33	29.24	29.20
3000	55.34	53.10	47.24	45.15	44.33	43.99	43.86	43.80
4000	73.79	70.80	62.99	60.20	59.11	58.66	58.47	58.39
5000	92.23	88.49	78.73	75.25	73.88	73.32	73.09	72.99
6000	110.68	106.19	94.48	90.30	88.66	87.98	87.71	87.59
7000	129.12	123.89	110.23	105.35	103.43	102.65	102.32	102.19
8000	147.57	141.59	125.97	120.40	118.21	117.31	116.94	116.78
9000	166.01	159.29	141.72	135.45	132.98	131.97	131.56	131.38
10000	184.46	176.98	157.46	150.50	147.76	146.64	146.17	145.98
11000	202.90	194.68	173.21	165.55	162.53	161.30	160.79	160.58
12000	221.35	212.38	188.95	180.60	177.31	175.96	175.41	175.17
13000	239.79	230.08	204.70	195.65	192.08	190.63	190.02	189.77
14000	258.24	247.78	220.45	210.70	206.86	205.29	204.64	204.37
15000	276.69	265.47	236.19	225.75	221.63	219.95	219.26	218.97
16000	295.13	283.17	251.94	240.80	236.41	234.62	233.87	233.56
17000	313.58	300.87	267.68	255.85	251.19	249.28	248.49	248.16
18000	332.02	318.57	283.43	270.89	265.96	263.94	263.11	262.76
19000	350.47	336.26	299.17	285.94	280.74	278.61	277.72	277.35
20000	368.91	353.96	314.92	300.99	295.51	293.27	292.34	291.95
21000	387.36	371.66	330.67	316.04	310.29	307.93	306.96	306.55
22000	405.80	389.36	346.41	331.09	325.06	322.60	321.57	321.15
23000	424.25	407.06	362.16	346.14	339.84	337.26	336.19	335.74
24000	442.69	424.75	377.90	361.19	354.61	351.92	350.81	350.34
25000	461.14	442.45	393.65	376.24	369.39	366.59	365.42	364.94
26000	479.58	460.15	409.40	391.29	384.16	381.25	380.04	379.54
27000	498.03	477.85	425.14	406.34	398.94	395.91	394.66	394.13
28000	516.47	495.55	440.89	421.39	413.71	410.58	409.27	408.73
29000	534.92	513.24	456.63	436.44	428.49	425.24	423.89	423.33
30000	553.37	530.94	472.38	451.49	443.26	439.90	438.51	437.93
31000	571.81	548.64	488.12	466.54	458.04	454.57	453.12	452.52
32000	590.26	566.34	503.87	481.59	472.81	469.23	467.74	467.12
33000	608.70	584.03	519.62	496.64	487.59	483.89	482.36	481.72
34000	627.15	601.73	535.36	511.69	502.37	498.56	496.97	496.31
35000	645.59	619.43	551.11	526.73	517.14	513.22	511.59	510.91
40000	737.82	707.92	629.84	601.98	591.02	586.54	584.68	583.90
45000	830.05	796.41	708.57	677.23	664.89	659.85	657.76	656.89
50000	922.27	884.90	787.29	752.48	738.77	733.17	730.84	729.87
55000	1014.50	973.39	866.02	827.72	812.65	806.48	803.93	802.86
60000	1106.73	1061.88	944.75	902.97	886.52	879.80	877.01	875.85
65000	1198.95	1150.37	1023.48	978.22	960.40	953.12	950.09	948.83
70000	1291.18	1238.86	1102.21	1053.46	1034.28	1026.43	1023.18	1021.82
75000	1383.41	1327.35	1180.94	1128.71	1108.15	1099.75	1096.26	1094.81
80000	1475.63	1415.84	1259.67	1203.96	1182.03	1173.07	1169.35	1167.79
85000	1567.86	1504.32	1338.40	1279.21	1255.91	1246.38	1242.43	1240.78
90000	1660.09	1592.81	1417.13	1354.45	1329.78	1319.70	1315.51	1313.77
95000	1752.31	1681.30	1495.85	1429.70	1403.66	1393.01	1388.60	1386.75
100000	1844.54	1769.79	1574.58	1504.95	1477.53	1466.33	1461.68	1459.74
105000	1936.77	1858.28	1653.31	1580.19	1551.41	1539.65	1534.76	1532.73
110000	2028.99	1946.77	1732.04	1655.44	1625.29	1612.96	1607.85	1605.71
115000	2121.22	2035.26	1810.77	1730.69	1699.16	1686.28	1680.93	1678.70
120000	2213.45	2123.75	1889.50	1805.94	1773.04	1759.60	1754.02	1751.69
125000	2305.67	2212.24	1968.23	1881.18	1846.92	1832.91	1827.10	1824.67
130000	2397.90	2300.73	2046.96	1956.43	1920.79	1906.23	1900.18	1897.66
135000	2490.13	2389.22	2125.69	2031.68	1994.67	1979.54	1973.27	1970.65
140000	2582.35	2477.71	2204.41	2106.92	2068.55	2052.86	2046.35	2043.63
145000	2674.58	2566.20	2283.14	2182.17	2142.42	2126.18	2119.43	2116.62
150000	2766.81	2654.69	2361.87	2257.42	2216.30	2199.49	2192.52	2189.61
155000	2859.03	2743.18	2440.60	2332.66	2290.18	2272.81	2265.60	2262.59
160000	2951.26	2831.67	2519.33	2407.91	2364.05	2346.13	2338.69	2335.58

AMOUNT OF LOAN	NUMBER OF YEARS IN TERM							
	1	2	3	4	5	6	7	8
$ 50	4.58	2.50	1.81	1.47	1.27	1.14	1.05	.98
100	9.16	4.99	3.61	2.93	2.53	2.27	2.09	1.96
200	18.32	9.97	7.21	5.85	5.06	4.54	4.18	3.92
300	27.47	14.95	10.81	8.78	7.58	6.81	6.27	5.88
400	36.63	19.93	14.42	11.70	10.11	9.07	8.35	7.83
500	45.79	24.91	18.02	14.63	12.63	11.34	10.44	9.79
600	54.94	29.89	21.62	17.55	15.16	13.61	12.53	11.75
700	64.10	34.87	25.22	20.48	17.69	15.87	14.62	13.71
800	73.25	39.85	28.83	23.40	20.21	18.14	16.70	15.66
900	82.41	44.83	32.43	26.33	22.74	20.41	18.79	17.62
1000	91.57	49.81	36.03	29.25	25.26	22.67	20.88	19.58
2000	183.13	99.61	72.06	58.49	50.52	45.34	41.75	39.15
3000	274.69	149.42	108.09	87.74	75.78	68.01	62.62	58.72
4000	366.25	199.22	144.11	116.98	101.04	90.67	83.49	78.29
5000	457.81	249.02	180.14	146.23	126.29	113.34	104.36	97.86
6000	549.37	298.83	216.17	175.47	151.55	136.01	125.23	117.44
7000	640.93	348.63	252.19	204.72	176.81	158.67	146.11	137.01
8000	732.49	398.43	288.22	233.96	202.07	181.34	166.98	156.58
9000	824.05	448.24	324.25	263.21	227.32	204.01	187.85	176.15
10000	915.62	498.04	360.28	292.45	252.58	226.67	208.72	195.72
11000	1007.18	547.84	396.30	321.69	277.84	249.34	229.59	215.30
12000	1098.74	597.65	432.33	350.94	303.10	272.01	250.46	234.87
13000	1190.30	647.45	468.36	380.18	328.35	294.67	271.34	254.44
14000	1281.86	697.25	504.38	409.43	353.61	317.34	292.21	274.01
15000	1373.42	747.06	540.41	438.67	378.87	340.01	313.08	293.58
16000	1464.98	796.86	576.44	467.92	404.13	362.67	333.95	313.16
17000	1556.54	846.66	612.47	497.16	429.38	385.34	354.82	332.73
18000	1648.10	896.47	648.49	526.41	454.64	408.01	375.69	352.30
19000	1739.67	946.27	684.52	555.65	479.90	430.67	396.56	371.87
20000	1831.23	996.07	720.55	584.90	505.16	453.34	417.44	391.44
21000	1922.79	1045.88	756.57	614.14	530.42	476.01	438.31	411.02
22000	2014.35	1095.68	792.60	643.38	555.67	498.67	459.18	430.59
23000	2105.91	1145.48	828.63	672.63	580.93	521.34	480.05	450.16
24000	2197.47	1195.29	864.66	701.87	606.19	544.01	500.92	469.73
25000	2289.03	1245.09	900.68	731.12	631.45	566.67	521.79	489.30
26000	2380.59	1294.89	936.71	760.36	656.70	589.34	542.67	508.88
27000	2472.15	1344.70	972.74	789.61	681.96	612.01	563.54	528.45
28000	2563.71	1394.50	1008.76	818.85	707.22	634.67	584.41	548.02
29000	2655.28	1444.30	1044.79	848.10	732.48	657.34	605.28	567.59
30000	2746.84	1494.11	1080.82	877.34	757.73	680.01	626.15	587.16
31000	2838.40	1543.91	1116.85	906.59	782.99	702.67	647.02	606.73
32000	2929.96	1593.71	1152.87	935.83	808.25	725.34	667.89	626.31
33000	3021.52	1643.52	1188.90	965.07	833.51	748.01	688.77	645.88
34000	3113.08	1693.32	1224.93	994.32	858.76	770.67	709.64	665.45
35000	3204.64	1743.12	1260.95	1023.56	884.02	793.34	730.51	685.02
40000	3662.45	1992.14	1441.09	1169.79	1010.31	906.67	834.87	782.88
45000	4120.25	2241.16	1621.22	1316.01	1136.60	1020.01	939.23	880.74
50000	4578.06	2490.17	1801.36	1462.23	1262.89	1133.34	1043.58	978.60
55000	5035.86	2739.19	1981.50	1608.45	1389.17	1246.67	1147.94	1076.46
60000	5493.67	2988.21	2161.63	1754.68	1515.46	1360.01	1252.30	1174.32
65000	5951.47	3237.23	2341.77	1900.90	1641.75	1473.34	1356.66	1272.18
70000	6409.28	3486.24	2521.90	2047.12	1768.04	1586.67	1461.01	1370.04
75000	6867.08	3735.26	2702.04	2193.34	1894.33	1700.01	1565.37	1467.90
80000	7324.89	3984.28	2882.17	2339.57	2020.61	1813.34	1669.73	1565.76
85000	7782.69	4233.29	3062.31	2485.79	2146.90	1926.67	1774.09	1663.62
90000	8240.50	4482.31	3242.44	2632.01	2273.19	2040.01	1878.45	1761.48
95000	8698.31	4731.33	3422.58	2778.23	2399.48	2153.34	1982.80	1859.34
100000	9156.11	4980.34	3602.72	2924.46	2525.77	2266.67	2087.16	1957.20
105000	9613.92	5229.36	3782.85	3070.68	2652.06	2380.01	2191.52	2055.06
110000	10071.72	5478.38	3962.99	3216.90	2778.34	2493.34	2295.88	2152.92
115000	10529.53	5727.39	4143.12	3363.13	2904.63	2606.67	2400.23	2250.78
120000	10987.33	5976.41	4323.26	3509.35	3030.92	2720.01	2504.59	2348.64
125000	11445.14	6225.43	4503.39	3655.57	3157.21	2833.34	2608.95	2446.50
130000	11902.94	6474.45	4683.53	3801.79	3283.50	2946.67	2713.31	2544.36
135000	12360.75	6723.46	4863.66	3948.02	3409.78	3060.01	2817.67	2642.22
140000	12818.55	6972.48	5043.80	4094.24	3536.07	3173.34	2922.02	2740.08
145000	13276.36	7221.50	5223.94	4240.46	3662.36	3286.68	3026.38	2837.94
150000	13734.16	7470.51	5404.07	4386.68	3788.65	3400.01	3130.74	2935.79
155000	14191.97	7719.53	5584.21	4532.91	3914.94	3513.34	3235.10	3033.65
160000	14649.77	7968.55	5764.34	4679.13	4041.22	3626.68	3339.45	3131.51

AMOUNT OF LOAN	NUMBER OF YEARS IN TERM							
	9	10	15	20	25	30	35	40
$ 50	.94	.90	.80	.77	.75	.75	.75	.75
100	1.87	1.79	1.60	1.53	1.50	1.49	1.49	1.49
200	3.73	3.58	3.19	3.05	3.00	2.98	2.97	2.97
300	5.59	5.36	4.78	4.58	4.50	4.47	4.45	4.45
400	7.45	7.15	6.37	6.10	5.99	5.95	5.93	5.93
500	9.31	8.93	7.97	7.63	7.49	7.44	7.42	7.41
600	11.17	10.72	9.56	9.15	8.99	8.93	8.90	8.89
700	13.03	12.51	11.15	10.67	10.49	10.41	10.38	10.37
800	14.89	14.29	12.74	12.20	11.98	11.90	11.86	11.85
900	16.75	16.08	14.34	13.72	13.48	13.39	13.35	13.33
1000	18.61	17.86	15.93	15.25	14.98	14.87	14.83	14.81
2000	37.21	35.72	31.85	30.49	29.95	29.74	29.65	29.61
3000	55.81	53.58	47.78	45.73	44.93	44.61	44.47	44.42
4000	74.41	71.44	63.70	60.97	59.90	59.47	59.30	59.22
5000	93.01	89.29	79.63	76.21	74.88	74.34	74.12	74.03
6000	111.61	107.15	95.55	91.45	89.85	89.21	88.94	88.83
7000	130.21	125.01	111.48	106.69	104.83	104.07	103.76	103.64
8000	148.81	142.87	127.40	121.93	119.80	118.94	118.59	118.44
9000	167.41	160.73	143.33	137.17	134.78	133.81	133.41	133.25
10000	186.01	178.58	159.25	152.41	149.75	148.67	148.23	148.05
11000	204.61	196.44	175.18	167.66	164.73	163.54	163.06	162.85
12000	223.21	214.30	191.10	182.90	179.70	178.41	177.88	177.66
13000	241.82	232.16	207.03	198.14	194.67	193.27	192.70	192.46
14000	260.42	250.02	222.95	213.38	209.65	208.14	207.52	207.27
15000	279.02	267.87	238.87	228.62	224.62	223.01	222.35	222.07
16000	297.62	285.73	254.80	243.86	239.60	237.88	237.17	236.88
17000	316.22	303.59	270.72	259.10	254.57	252.74	251.99	251.68
18000	334.82	321.45	286.65	274.34	269.55	267.61	266.81	266.49
19000	353.42	339.30	302.57	289.58	284.52	282.48	281.64	281.29
20000	372.02	357.16	318.50	304.82	299.50	297.34	296.46	296.10
21000	390.62	375.02	334.42	320.07	314.47	312.21	311.28	310.90
22000	409.22	392.88	350.35	335.31	329.45	327.08	326.11	325.70
23000	427.82	410.74	366.27	350.55	344.42	341.94	340.93	340.51
24000	446.42	428.59	382.20	365.79	359.40	356.81	355.75	355.31
25000	465.03	446.45	398.12	381.03	374.37	371.68	370.57	370.12
26000	483.63	464.31	414.05	396.27	389.34	386.54	385.40	384.92
27000	502.23	482.17	429.97	411.51	404.32	401.41	400.22	399.73
28000	520.83	500.03	445.90	426.75	419.29	416.28	415.04	414.53
29000	539.43	517.88	461.82	441.99	434.27	431.15	429.86	429.34
30000	558.03	535.74	477.74	457.23	449.24	446.01	444.69	444.14
31000	576.63	553.60	493.67	472.48	464.22	460.88	459.51	458.95
32000	595.23	571.46	509.59	487.72	479.19	475.75	474.33	473.75
33000	613.83	589.32	525.52	502.96	494.17	490.61	489.16	488.55
34000	632.43	607.17	541.44	518.20	509.14	505.48	503.98	503.36
35000	651.03	625.03	557.37	533.44	524.12	520.35	518.80	518.16
40000	744.04	714.32	636.99	609.64	598.99	594.68	592.92	592.19
45000	837.04	803.61	716.61	685.85	673.86	669.02	667.03	666.21
50000	930.05	892.90	796.24	762.05	748.73	743.35	741.14	740.23
55000	1023.05	982.19	875.86	838.26	823.61	817.69	815.26	814.25
60000	1116.05	1071.48	955.48	914.46	898.48	892.02	889.37	888.28
65000	1209.06	1160.77	1035.11	990.67	973.35	966.35	963.48	962.30
70000	1302.06	1250.06	1114.73	1066.87	1048.23	1040.69	1037.60	1036.32
75000	1395.07	1339.35	1194.35	1143.08	1123.10	1115.02	1111.71	1110.35
80000	1488.07	1428.64	1273.98	1219.28	1197.97	1189.36	1185.83	1184.37
85000	1581.07	1517.93	1353.60	1295.49	1272.85	1263.69	1259.94	1258.39
90000	1674.08	1607.21	1433.22	1371.69	1347.72	1338.03	1334.05	1332.41
95000	1767.08	1696.50	1512.85	1447.90	1422.59	1412.36	1408.17	1406.44
100000	1860.09	1785.79	1592.47	1524.10	1497.46	1486.70	1482.28	1480.46
105000	1953.09	1875.08	1672.09	1600.31	1572.34	1561.03	1556.39	1554.48
110000	2046.09	1964.37	1751.72	1676.51	1647.21	1635.37	1630.51	1628.50
115000	2139.10	2053.66	1831.34	1752.72	1722.08	1709.70	1704.62	1702.53
120000	2232.10	2142.95	1910.96	1828.92	1796.96	1784.04	1778.74	1776.55
125000	2325.11	2232.24	1990.59	1905.13	1871.83	1858.37	1852.85	1850.57
130000	2418.11	2321.53	2070.21	1981.33	1946.70	1932.70	1926.96	1924.59
135000	2511.11	2410.82	2149.83	2057.54	2021.58	2007.04	2001.08	1998.62
140000	2604.12	2500.11	2229.46	2133.74	2096.45	2081.37	2075.19	2072.64
145000	2697.12	2589.40	2309.08	2209.95	2171.32	2155.71	2149.30	2146.66
150000	2790.13	2678.69	2388.70	2286.15	2246.19	2230.04	2223.42	2220.69
155000	2883.13	2767.98	2468.33	2362.36	2321.07	2304.38	2297.53	2294.71
160000	2976.13	2857.27	2547.95	2438.56	2395.94	2378.71	2371.65	2368.73

AMOUNT OF LOAN	NUMBER OF YEARS IN TERM 1	2	3	4	5	6	7	8
$ 50	4.59	2.50	1.81	1.47	1.27	1.15	1.06	.99
100	9.17	5.00	3.62	2.94	2.54	2.29	2.11	1.98
200	18.34	9.99	7.24	5.88	5.08	4.57	4.21	3.95
300	27.51	14.98	10.85	8.82	7.62	6.85	6.31	5.92
400	36.68	19.97	14.47	11.75	10.16	9.13	8.41	7.89
500	45.84	24.97	18.08	14.69	12.70	11.41	10.51	9.87
600	55.01	29.96	21.70	17.63	15.24	13.69	12.62	11.84
700	64.18	34.95	25.31	20.57	17.78	15.97	14.72	13.81
800	73.35	39.94	28.93	23.50	20.32	18.25	16.82	15.78
900	82.52	44.94	32.54	26.44	22.86	20.53	18.92	17.76
1000	91.68	49.93	36.16	29.38	25.40	22.81	21.02	19.73
2000	183.36	99.85	72.31	58.75	50.79	45.62	42.04	39.45
3000	275.04	149.78	108.46	88.13	76.19	68.43	63.06	59.17
4000	366.72	199.70	144.61	117.50	101.58	91.24	84.08	78.90
5000	458.40	249.63	180.77	146.88	126.97	114.04	105.09	98.62
6000	550.08	299.55	216.92	176.25	152.37	136.85	126.11	118.34
7000	641.76	349.47	253.07	205.63	177.76	159.66	147.13	138.07
8000	733.44	399.40	289.22	235.00	203.15	182.47	168.15	157.79
9000	825.12	449.32	325.38	264.38	228.55	205.28	189.17	177.51
10000	916.80	499.25	361.53	293.75	253.94	228.08	210.18	197.24
11000	1008.48	549.17	397.68	323.13	279.33	250.89	231.20	216.96
12000	1100.16	599.09	433.83	352.50	304.73	273.70	252.22	236.68
13000	1191.84	649.02	469.99	381.88	330.12	296.51	273.24	256.41
14000	1283.52	698.94	506.14	411.25	355.51	319.31	294.25	276.13
15000	1375.20	748.87	542.29	440.63	380.91	342.12	315.27	295.85
16000	1466.88	798.79	578.44	470.00	406.30	364.93	336.29	315.58
17000	1558.56	848.71	614.60	499.38	431.69	387.74	357.31	335.30
18000	1650.24	898.64	650.75	528.75	457.09	410.55	378.33	355.02
19000	1741.92	948.56	686.90	558.13	482.48	433.35	399.34	374.75
20000	1833.60	998.49	723.05	587.50	507.87	456.16	420.36	394.47
21000	1925.28	1048.41	759.21	616.88	533.27	478.97	441.38	414.19
22000	2016.96	1098.34	795.36	646.25	558.66	501.78	462.40	433.92
23000	2108.64	1148.26	831.51	675.63	584.05	524.58	483.42	453.64
24000	2200.32	1198.18	867.66	705.00	609.45	547.39	504.43	473.36
25000	2292.00	1248.11	903.81	734.38	634.84	570.20	525.45	493.09
26000	2383.68	1298.03	939.97	763.75	660.23	593.01	546.47	512.81
27000	2475.36	1347.96	976.12	793.13	685.63	615.82	567.49	532.53
28000	2567.04	1397.88	1012.27	822.50	711.02	638.62	588.50	552.25
29000	2658.72	1447.80	1048.42	851.88	736.41	661.43	609.52	571.98
30000	2750.40	1497.73	1084.58	881.25	761.81	684.24	630.54	591.70
31000	2842.08	1547.65	1120.73	910.63	787.20	707.05	651.56	611.42
32000	2933.76	1597.58	1156.88	940.00	812.59	729.85	672.58	631.15
33000	3025.44	1647.50	1193.03	969.38	837.99	752.66	693.59	650.87
34000	3117.12	1697.42	1229.19	998.75	863.38	775.47	714.61	670.59
35000	3208.80	1747.35	1265.34	1028.13	888.77	798.28	735.63	690.32
40000	3667.20	1996.97	1446.10	1175.00	1015.74	912.32	840.72	788.93
45000	4125.60	2246.59	1626.86	1321.88	1142.71	1026.36	945.81	887.55
50000	4584.00	2496.21	1807.62	1468.75	1269.68	1140.39	1050.90	986.17
55000	5042.40	2745.83	1988.39	1615.63	1396.64	1254.43	1155.99	1084.78
60000	5500.80	2995.45	2169.15	1762.50	1523.61	1368.47	1261.08	1183.40
65000	5959.20	3245.07	2349.91	1909.38	1650.58	1482.51	1366.16	1282.01
70000	6417.60	3494.69	2530.67	2056.25	1777.54	1596.55	1471.25	1380.63
75000	6876.00	3744.31	2711.43	2203.13	1904.51	1710.59	1576.34	1479.25
80000	7334.40	3993.93	2892.20	2350.00	2031.48	1824.63	1681.43	1577.86
85000	7792.80	4243.55	3072.96	2496.88	2158.45	1938.67	1786.52	1676.48
90000	8251.20	4493.17	3253.72	2643.75	2285.41	2052.71	1891.61	1775.09
95000	8709.60	4742.79	3434.48	2790.63	2412.38	2166.75	1996.70	1873.71
100000	9168.00	4992.42	3615.24	2937.50	2539.35	2280.78	2101.79	1972.33
105000	9626.40	5242.04	3796.01	3084.38	2666.31	2394.82	2206.88	2070.94
110000	10084.80	5491.66	3976.77	3231.25	2793.28	2508.86	2311.97	2169.56
115000	10543.20	5741.28	4157.53	3378.13	2920.25	2622.90	2417.06	2268.17
120000	11001.60	5990.90	4338.29	3525.00	3047.22	2736.94	2522.15	2366.79
125000	11460.00	6240.52	4519.05	3671.88	3174.18	2850.98	2627.23	2465.41
130000	11918.40	6490.14	4699.82	3818.75	3301.15	2965.02	2732.32	2564.02
135000	12376.80	6739.76	4880.58	3965.63	3428.12	3079.06	2837.41	2662.64
140000	12835.20	6989.38	5061.34	4112.50	3555.08	3193.10	2942.50	2761.25
145000	13293.60	7239.00	5242.10	4259.38	3682.05	3307.13	3047.59	2859.87
150000	13752.00	7488.62	5422.86	4406.25	3809.02	3421.17	3152.68	2958.49
155000	14210.40	7738.24	5603.63	4553.13	3935.99	3535.21	3257.77	3057.10
160000	14668.80	7987.86	5784.39	4700.00	4062.95	3649.25	3362.86	3155.72

AMOUNT OF LOAN	NUMBER OF YEARS IN TERM							
	9	10	15	20	25	30	35	40
$ 50	.94	.91	.81	.78	.76	.76	.76	.76
100	1.88	1.81	1.62	1.55	1.52	1.51	1.51	1.51
200	3.76	3.61	3.23	3.09	3.04	3.02	3.01	3.01
300	5.63	5.41	4.84	4.63	4.56	4.53	4.51	4.51
400	7.51	7.21	6.45	6.18	6.07	6.03	6.02	6.01
500	9.38	9.01	8.06	7.72	7.59	7.54	7.52	7.51
600	11.26	10.82	9.67	9.26	9.11	9.05	9.02	9.01
700	13.13	12.62	11.28	10.81	10.63	10.55	10.53	10.51
800	15.01	14.42	12.89	12.35	12.14	12.06	12.03	12.01
900	16.89	16.22	14.50	13.89	13.66	13.57	13.53	13.52
1000	18.76	18.02	16.11	15.44	15.18	15.08	15.03	15.02
2000	37.52	36.04	32.21	30.87	30.35	30.15	30.06	30.03
3000	56.28	54.06	48.32	46.30	45.53	45.22	45.09	45.04
4000	75.03	72.08	64.42	61.74	60.70	60.29	60.12	60.05
5000	93.79	90.10	80.53	77.17	75.88	75.36	75.15	75.06
6000	112.55	108.12	96.63	92.60	91.05	90.43	90.18	90.08
7000	131.30	126.13	112.73	108.04	106.23	105.50	105.21	105.09
8000	150.06	144.15	128.84	123.47	121.40	120.57	120.24	120.10
9000	168.82	162.17	144.94	138.90	136.57	135.64	135.27	135.11
10000	187.57	180.19	161.05	154.34	151.75	150.71	150.29	150.12
11000	206.33	198.21	177.15	169.77	166.92	165.78	165.32	165.14
12000	225.09	216.23	193.26	185.20	182.10	180.86	180.35	180.15
13000	243.84	234.25	209.36	200.64	197.27	195.93	195.38	195.16
14000	262.60	252.26	225.46	216.07	212.45	211.00	210.41	210.17
15000	281.36	270.28	241.57	231.50	227.62	226.07	225.44	225.18
16000	300.12	288.30	257.67	246.93	242.79	241.14	240.47	240.19
17000	318.87	306.32	273.78	262.37	257.97	256.21	255.50	255.21
18000	337.63	324.34	289.88	277.80	273.14	271.28	270.53	270.22
19000	356.39	342.36	305.98	293.23	288.32	286.35	285.55	285.23
20000	375.14	360.38	322.09	308.67	303.49	301.42	300.58	300.24
21000	393.90	378.39	338.19	324.10	318.67	316.49	315.61	315.25
22000	412.66	396.41	354.30	339.53	333.84	331.56	330.64	330.27
23000	431.41	414.43	370.40	354.97	349.01	346.63	345.67	345.28
24000	450.17	432.45	386.51	370.40	364.19	361.71	360.70	360.29
25000	468.93	450.47	402.61	385.83	379.36	376.78	375.73	375.30
26000	487.68	468.49	418.71	401.27	394.54	391.85	390.76	390.31
27000	506.44	486.51	434.82	416.70	409.71	406.92	405.79	405.32
28000	525.20	504.52	450.92	432.13	424.89	421.99	420.81	420.34
29000	543.95	522.54	467.03	447.57	440.06	437.06	435.84	435.35
30000	562.71	540.56	483.13	463.00	455.23	452.13	450.87	450.36
31000	581.47	558.58	499.24	478.43	470.41	467.20	465.90	465.37
32000	600.23	576.60	515.34	493.86	485.58	482.27	480.93	480.38
33000	618.98	594.62	531.44	509.30	500.76	497.34	495.96	495.40
34000	637.74	612.63	547.55	524.73	515.93	512.41	510.99	510.41
35000	656.50	630.65	563.65	540.16	531.11	527.48	526.02	525.42
40000	750.28	720.75	644.17	617.33	606.98	602.84	601.16	600.48
45000	844.06	810.84	724.69	694.50	682.85	678.19	676.31	675.54
50000	937.85	900.93	805.22	771.66	758.72	753.55	751.45	750.60
55000	1031.63	991.02	885.74	848.83	834.59	828.90	826.60	825.66
60000	1125.42	1081.12	966.26	925.99	910.46	904.26	901.74	900.71
65000	1219.20	1171.21	1046.78	1003.16	986.33	979.61	976.88	975.77
70000	1312.99	1261.30	1127.30	1080.32	1062.21	1054.96	1052.03	1050.83
75000	1406.77	1351.39	1207.82	1157.49	1138.08	1130.32	1127.17	1125.89
80000	1500.56	1441.49	1288.34	1234.65	1213.95	1205.67	1202.32	1200.95
85000	1594.34	1531.58	1368.86	1311.82	1289.82	1281.03	1277.46	1276.01
90000	1688.12	1621.67	1449.38	1388.99	1365.69	1356.38	1352.61	1351.07
95000	1781.91	1711.76	1529.90	1466.15	1441.56	1431.74	1427.75	1426.13
100000	1875.69	1801.86	1610.43	1543.32	1517.43	1507.09	1502.90	1501.19
105000	1969.48	1891.95	1690.95	1620.48	1593.31	1582.44	1578.04	1576.25
110000	2063.26	1982.04	1771.47	1697.65	1669.18	1657.80	1653.19	1651.31
115000	2157.05	2072.13	1851.99	1774.81	1745.05	1733.15	1728.33	1726.36
120000	2250.83	2162.23	1932.51	1851.98	1820.92	1808.51	1803.48	1801.42
125000	2344.62	2252.32	2013.03	1929.14	1896.79	1883.86	1878.62	1876.48
130000	2438.40	2342.41	2093.55	2006.31	1972.66	1959.22	1953.76	1951.54
135000	2532.18	2432.51	2174.07	2083.48	2048.54	2034.57	2028.91	2026.60
140000	2625.97	2522.60	2254.59	2160.64	2124.41	2109.92	2104.05	2101.66
145000	2719.75	2612.69	2335.12	2237.81	2200.28	2185.28	2179.20	2176.72
150000	2813.54	2702.78	2415.64	2314.97	2276.15	2260.63	2254.34	2251.78
155000	2907.32	2792.88	2496.16	2392.14	2352.02	2335.99	2329.49	2326.84
160000	3001.11	2882.97	2576.68	2469.30	2427.89	2411.34	2404.63	2401.90

MONTHLY PAYMENT NEEDED TO AMORTIZE A $1000 LOAN

YEARS	RATE							
	8.00%	8.10%	8.20%	8.30%	8.40%	8.50%	8.60%	8.70%
1	86.99	87.04	87.09	87.13	87.18	87.22	87.27	87.32
2	45.23	45.28	45.32	45.37	45.41	45.46	45.51	45.55
3	31.34	31.39	31.43	31.48	31.53	31.57	31.62	31.67
4	24.42	24.46	24.51	24.56	24.61	24.65	24.70	24.75
5	20.28	20.33	20.38	20.43	20.47	20.52	20.57	20.62
6	17.54	17.59	17.64	17.69	17.73	17.78	17.83	17.88
7	15.59	15.64	15.69	15.74	15.79	15.84	15.89	15.94
8	14.14	14.19	14.24	14.29	14.35	14.40	14.45	14.50
9	13.02	13.08	13.13	13.18	13.23	13.28	13.34	13.39
10	12.14	12.19	12.24	12.30	12.35	12.40	12.46	12.51
11	11.42	11.47	11.53	11.58	11.64	11.69	11.75	11.80
12	10.83	10.88	10.94	10.99	11.05	11.11	11.16	11.22
13	10.34	10.39	10.45	10.50	10.56	10.62	10.67	10.73
14	9.92	9.98	10.03	10.09	10.15	10.20	10.26	10.32
15	9.56	9.62	9.68	9.74	9.79	9.85	9.91	9.97
16	9.25	9.31	9.37	9.43	9.49	9.55	9.61	9.67
17	8.99	9.05	9.11	9.17	9.23	9.29	9.35	9.41
18	8.75	8.82	8.88	8.94	9.00	9.06	9.12	9.18
19	8.55	8.61	8.67	8.74	8.80	8.86	8.92	8.98
20	8.37	8.43	8.49	8.56	8.62	8.68	8.75	8.81
21	8.21	8.27	8.34	8.40	8.46	8.53	8.59	8.66
22	8.07	8.13	8.20	8.26	8.32	8.39	8.45	8.52
23	7.94	8.00	8.07	8.13	8.20	8.27	8.33	8.40
24	7.83	7.89	7.96	8.02	8.09	8.16	8.22	8.29
25	7.72	7.79	7.86	7.92	7.99	8.06	8.12	8.19
26	7.63	7.70	7.77	7.83	7.90	7.97	8.04	8.11
28	7.47	7.54	7.61	7.68	7.75	7.82	7.89	7.96
30	7.34	7.41	7.48	7.55	7.62	7.69	7.77	7.84
35	7.11	7.18	7.25	7.33	7.40	7.47	7.55	7.62
40	6.96	7.03	7.11	7.18	7.26	7.34	7.41	7.49

YEARS	RATE							
	8.80%	8.90%	9.00%	9.10%	9.20%	9.30%	9.40%	9.50%
1	87.36	87.41	87.46	87.50	87.55	87.60	87.64	87.69
2	45.60	45.64	45.69	45.74	45.78	45.83	45.87	45.92
3	31.71	31.76	31.80	31.85	31.90	31.94	31.99	32.04
4	24.80	24.84	24.89	24.94	24.99	25.03	25.08	25.13
5	20.67	20.71	20.76	20.81	20.86	20.91	20.96	21.01
6	17.93	17.98	18.03	18.08	18.13	18.18	18.23	18.28
7	15.99	16.04	16.09	16.14	16.20	16.25	16.30	16.35
8	14.55	14.60	14.66	14.71	14.76	14.81	14.86	14.92
9	13.44	13.49	13.55	13.60	13.65	13.71	13.76	13.81
10	12.56	12.62	12.67	12.73	12.78	12.84	12.89	12.94
11	11.86	11.91	11.97	12.02	12.08	12.13	12.19	12.24
12	11.27	11.33	11.39	11.44	11.50	11.55	11.61	11.67
13	10.79	10.84	10.90	10.96	11.02	11.07	11.13	11.19
14	10.38	10.44	10.49	10.55	10.61	10.67	10.73	10.79
15	10.03	10.09	10.15	10.21	10.27	10.33	10.39	10.45
16	9.73	9.79	9.85	9.91	9.97	10.03	10.09	10.15
17	9.47	9.53	9.59	9.65	9.72	9.78	9.84	9.90
18	9.24	9.31	9.37	9.43	9.49	9.56	9.62	9.68
19	9.05	9.11	9.17	9.24	9.30	9.37	9.43	9.49
20	8.87	8.94	9.00	9.07	9.13	9.20	9.26	9.33
21	8.72	8.79	8.85	8.92	8.98	9.05	9.11	9.18
22	8.59	8.65	8.72	8.78	8.85	8.92	8.98	9.05
23	8.46	8.53	8.60	8.66	8.73	8.80	8.87	8.93
24	8.36	8.42	8.49	8.56	8.63	8.70	8.76	8.83
25	8.26	8.33	8.40	8.47	8.53	8.60	8.67	8.74
26	8.17	8.24	8.31	8.38	8.45	8.52	8.59	8.66
28	8.03	8.10	8.17	8.24	8.31	8.38	8.45	8.52
30	7.91	7.98	8.05	8.12	8.20	8.27	8.34	8.41
35	7.70	7.77	7.84	7.92	7.99	8.07	8.15	8.22
40	7.56	7.64	7.72	7.80	7.87	7.95	8.03	8.11

MONTHLY PAYMENT NEEDED TO AMORTIZE A $1000 LOAN

YEARS	RATE 9.60%	9.70%	9.80%	9.90%	10.00%	10.10%	10.20%	10.30%
1	87.73	87.78	87.83	87.87	87.92	87.97	88.01	88.06
2	45.97	46.01	46.06	46.10	46.15	46.20	46.24	46.29
3	32.08	32.13	32.18	32.23	32.27	32.32	32.37	32.41
4	25.18	25.22	25.27	25.32	25.37	25.42	25.46	25.51
5	21.06	21.10	21.15	21.20	21.25	21.30	21.35	21.40
6	18.33	18.38	18.43	18.48	18.53	18.58	18.63	18.68
7	16.40	16.45	16.50	16.55	16.61	16.66	16.71	16.76
8	14.97	15.02	15.07	15.13	15.18	15.23	15.29	15.34
9	13.87	13.92	13.98	14.03	14.08	14.14	14.19	14.25
10	13.00	13.05	13.11	13.16	13.22	13.28	13.33	13.39
11	12.30	12.36	12.41	12.47	12.52	12.58	12.64	12.70
12	11.73	11.78	11.84	11.90	11.96	12.01	12.07	12.13
13	11.25	11.31	11.37	11.42	11.48	11.54	11.60	11.66
14	10.85	10.91	10.97	11.03	11.09	11.15	11.21	11.27
15	10.51	10.57	10.63	10.69	10.75	10.81	10.87	10.94
16	10.22	10.28	10.34	10.40	10.46	10.53	10.59	10.65
17	9.97	10.03	10.09	10.15	10.22	10.28	10.34	10.41
18	9.75	9.81	9.88	9.94	10.00	10.07	10.13	10.20
19	9.56	9.62	9.69	9.75	9.82	9.88	9.95	10.01
20	9.39	9.46	9.52	9.59	9.66	9.72	9.79	9.85
21	9.25	9.31	9.38	9.45	9.51	9.58	9.65	9.72
22	9.12	9.18	9.25	9.32	9.39	9.46	9.52	9.59
23	9.00	9.07	9.14	9.21	9.28	9.35	9.41	9.48
24	8.90	8.97	9.04	9.11	9.18	9.25	9.32	9.39
25	8.81	8.88	8.95	9.02	9.09	9.16	9.23	9.30
26	8.73	8.80	8.87	8.94	9.01	9.09	9.16	9.23
28	8.60	8.67	8.74	8.81	8.88	8.96	9.03	9.10
30	8.49	8.56	8.63	8.71	8.78	8.85	8.93	9.00
35	8.30	8.37	8.45	8.53	8.60	8.68	8.76	8.83
40	8.18	8.26	8.34	8.42	8.50	8.58	8.65	8.73

YEARS	RATE 10.40%	10.50%	10.60%	10.70%	10.80%	10.90%	11.00%	11.10%
1	88.11	88.15	88.20	88.25	88.29	88.34	88.39	88.43
2	46.33	46.38	46.43	46.47	46.52	46.57	46.61	46.66
3	32.46	32.51	32.55	32.60	32.65	32.70	32.74	32.79
4	25.56	25.61	25.66	25.71	25.75	25.80	25.85	25.90
5	21.45	21.50	21.55	21.60	21.65	21.70	21.75	21.80
6	18.73	18.78	18.83	18.89	18.94	18.99	19.04	19.09
7	16.81	16.87	16.92	16.97	17.02	17.07	17.13	17.18
8	15.39	15.45	15.50	15.55	15.61	15.66	15.71	15.77
9	14.30	14.36	14.41	14.47	14.52	14.58	14.63	14.69
10	13.44	13.50	13.55	13.61	13.67	13.72	13.78	13.84
11	12.75	12.81	12.87	12.92	12.98	13.04	13.10	13.16
12	12.19	12.25	12.30	12.36	12.42	12.48	12.54	12.60
13	11.72	11.78	11.84	11.90	11.96	12.02	12.08	12.14
14	11.33	11.39	11.45	11.51	11.57	11.63	11.70	11.76
15	11.00	11.06	11.12	11.18	11.25	11.31	11.37	11.43
16	10.71	10.78	10.84	10.90	10.97	11.03	11.10	11.16
17	10.47	10.54	10.60	10.66	10.73	10.79	10.86	10.92
18	10.26	10.33	10.39	10.46	10.52	10.59	10.66	10.72
19	10.08	10.15	10.21	10.28	10.35	10.41	10.48	10.55
20	9.92	9.99	10.06	10.12	10.19	10.26	10.33	10.40
21	9.78	9.85	9.92	9.99	10.06	10.12	10.19	10.26
22	9.66	9.73	9.80	9.87	9.94	10.01	10.08	10.15
23	9.55	9.62	9.69	9.76	9.83	9.90	9.98	10.05
24	9.46	9.53	9.60	9.67	9.74	9.81	9.89	9.96
25	9.38	9.45	9.52	9.59	9.66	9.73	9.81	9.88
26	9.30	9.37	9.45	9.52	9.59	9.66	9.74	9.81
28	9.18	9.25	9.32	9.40	9.47	9.55	9.62	9.69
30	9.08	9.15	9.23	9.30	9.38	9.45	9.53	9.60
35	8.91	8.99	9.06	9.14	9.22	9.30	9.37	9.45
40	8.81	8.89	8.97	9.05	9.13	9.21	9.29	9.37

MONTHLY PAYMENT NEEDED TO AMORTIZE A $1000 LOAN

YEARS	RATE 11.20%	11.30%	11.40%	11.50%	11.60%	11.70%	11.80%	11.90%
1	88.48	88.53	88.57	88.62	88.67	88.71	88.76	88.81
2	46.71	46.75	46.80	46.85	46.89	46.94	46.99	47.03
3	32.84	32.89	32.93	32.98	33.03	33.08	33.12	33.17
4	25.95	26.00	26.05	26.09	26.14	26.19	26.24	26.29
5	21.85	21.90	21.95	22.00	22.05	22.10	22.15	22.20
6	19.14	19.19	19.24	19.30	19.35	19.40	19.45	19.50
7	17.23	17.29	17.34	17.39	17.44	17.50	17.55	17.60
8	15.82	15.88	15.93	15.98	16.04	16.09	16.15	16.20
9	14.74	14.80	14.85	14.91	14.96	15.02	15.08	15.13
10	13.89	13.95	14.01	14.06	14.12	14.18	14.24	14.29
11	13.21	13.27	13.33	13.39	13.45	13.51	13.56	13.62
12	12.66	12.72	12.78	12.84	12.90	12.96	13.02	13.08
13	12.20	12.26	12.32	12.38	12.45	12.51	12.57	12.63
14	11.82	11.88	11.94	12.01	12.07	12.13	12.19	12.26
15	11.50	11.56	11.62	11.69	11.75	11.81	11.88	11.94
16	11.22	11.29	11.35	11.42	11.48	11.55	11.61	11.68
17	10.99	11.05	11.12	11.19	11.25	11.32	11.38	11.45
18	10.79	10.85	10.92	10.99	11.05	11.12	11.19	11.26
19	10.61	10.68	10.75	10.82	10.89	10.95	11.02	11.09
20	10.46	10.53	10.60	10.67	10.74	10.81	10.88	10.95
21	10.33	10.40	10.47	10.54	10.61	10.68	10.75	10.82
22	10.22	10.29	10.36	10.43	10.50	10.57	10.64	10.71
23	10.12	10.19	10.26	10.33	10.40	10.47	10.55	10.62
24	10.03	10.10	10.17	10.25	10.32	10.39	10.46	10.54
25	9.95	10.02	10.10	10.17	10.24	10.32	10.39	10.46
26	9.88	9.96	10.03	10.10	10.18	10.25	10.33	10.40
28	9.77	9.84	9.92	9.99	10.07	10.14	10.22	10.30
30	9.68	9.76	9.83	9.91	9.98	10.06	10.14	10.21
35	9.53	9.61	9.69	9.77	9.84	9.92	10.00	10.08
40	9.45	9.53	9.61	9.69	9.77	9.85	9.93	10.01

YEARS	RATE 12.00%	12.10%	12.20%	12.30%	12.40%	12.50%	12.60%	12.70%
1	88.85	88.90	88.95	88.99	89.04	89.09	89.13	89.18
2	47.08	47.13	47.17	47.22	47.27	47.31	47.36	47.41
3	33.22	33.27	33.31	33.36	33.41	33.46	33.51	33.55
4	26.34	26.39	26.44	26.49	26.54	26.58	26.63	26.68
5	22.25	22.30	22.35	22.40	22.45	22.50	22.55	22.60
6	19.56	19.61	19.66	19.71	19.76	19.82	19.87	19.92
7	17.66	17.71	17.76	17.82	17.87	17.93	17.98	18.03
8	16.26	16.31	16.37	16.42	16.48	16.53	16.59	16.64
9	15.19	15.25	15.30	15.36	15.42	15.47	15.53	15.59
10	14.35	14.41	14.47	14.53	14.58	14.64	14.70	14.76
11	13.68	13.74	13.80	13.86	13.92	13.98	14.04	14.10
12	13.14	13.20	13.26	13.32	13.38	13.44	13.50	13.57
13	12.69	12.75	12.82	12.88	12.94	13.00	13.07	13.13
14	12.32	12.38	12.45	12.51	12.57	12.64	12.70	12.76
15	12.01	12.07	12.14	12.20	12.27	12.33	12.40	12.46
16	11.74	11.81	11.87	11.94	12.01	12.07	12.14	12.20
17	11.52	11.58	11.65	11.72	11.78	11.85	11.92	11.99
18	11.32	11.39	11.46	11.53	11.60	11.67	11.73	11.80
19	11.16	11.23	11.30	11.37	11.44	11.50	11.57	11.64
20	11.02	11.09	11.16	11.23	11.30	11.37	11.44	11.51
21	10.89	10.96	11.03	11.10	11.18	11.25	11.32	11.39
22	10.78	10.86	10.93	11.00	11.07	11.14	11.22	11.29
23	10.69	10.76	10.84	10.91	10.98	11.05	11.13	11.20
24	10.61	10.68	10.76	10.83	10.90	10.98	11.05	11.12
25	10.54	10.61	10.69	10.76	10.83	10.91	10.98	11.06
26	10.47	10.55	10.62	10.70	10.77	10.85	10.92	11.00
28	10.37	10.45	10.52	10.60	10.68	10.75	10.83	10.91
30	10.29	10.37	10.45	10.52	10.60	10.68	10.76	10.83
35	10.16	10.24	10.32	10.40	10.48	10.56	10.64	10.72
40	10.09	10.17	10.25	10.33	10.41	10.49	10.58	10.66

MONTHLY PAYMENT NEEDED TO AMORTIZE A $1000 LOAN

YEARS	RATE 12.80%	12.90%	13.00%	13.10%	13.20%	13.30%	13.40%	13.50%
1	89.23	89.28	89.32	89.37	89.42	89.46	89.51	89.56
2	47.45	47.50	47.55	47.59	47.64	47.69	47.73	47.78
3	33.60	33.65	33.70	33.75	33.80	33.84	33.89	33.94
4	26.73	26.78	26.83	26.88	26.93	26.98	27.03	27.08
5	22.66	22.71	22.76	22.81	22.86	22.91	22.96	23.01
6	19.97	20.03	20.08	20.13	20.18	20.24	20.29	20.34
7	18.09	18.14	18.20	18.25	18.31	18.36	18.42	18.47
8	16.70	16.76	16.81	16.87	16.92	16.98	17.04	17.09
9	15.64	15.70	15.76	15.82	15.87	15.93	15.99	16.05
10	14.82	14.88	14.94	15.00	15.05	15.11	15.17	15.23
11	14.16	14.22	14.28	14.34	14.40	14.46	14.52	14.58
12	13.63	13.69	13.75	13.81	13.88	13.94	14.00	14.06
13	13.19	13.25	13.32	13.38	13.44	13.51	13.57	13.63
14	12.83	12.89	12.96	13.02	13.09	13.15	13.22	13.28
15	12.53	12.59	12.66	12.72	12.79	12.86	12.92	12.99
16	12.27	12.34	12.40	12.47	12.54	12.61	12.67	12.74
17	12.06	12.12	12.19	12.26	12.33	12.40	12.46	12.53
18	11.87	11.94	12.01	12.08	12.15	12.22	12.29	12.36
19	11.71	11.78	11.85	11.92	11.99	12.07	12.14	12.21
20	11.58	11.65	11.72	11.79	11.86	11.94	12.01	12.08
21	11.46	11.53	11.61	11.68	11.75	11.82	11.90	11.97
22	11.36	11.43	11.51	11.58	11.65	11.73	11.80	11.87
23	11.27	11.35	11.42	11.50	11.57	11.64	11.72	11.79
24	11.20	11.27	11.35	11.42	11.50	11.57	11.65	11.72
25	11.13	11.21	11.28	11.36	11.43	11.51	11.59	11.66
26	11.08	11.15	11.23	11.30	11.38	11.46	11.53	11.61
28	10.98	11.06	11.14	11.21	11.29	11.37	11.45	11.52
30	10.91	10.99	11.07	11.15	11.22	11.30	11.38	11.46
35	10.80	10.88	10.96	11.04	11.12	11.20	11.28	11.36
40	10.74	10.82	10.90	10.98	11.06	11.14	11.23	11.31

YEARS	RATE 13.60%	13.70%	13.80%	13.90%	14.00%	14.10%	14.20%	14.30%
1	89.60	89.65	89.70	89.75	89.79	89.84	89.89	89.93
2	47.83	47.88	47.92	47.97	48.02	48.07	48.11	48.16
3	33.99	34.04	34.09	34.13	34.18	34.23	34.28	34.33
4	27.13	27.18	27.23	27.28	27.33	27.38	27.43	27.48
5	23.07	23.12	23.17	23.22	23.27	23.33	23.38	23.43
6	20.40	20.45	20.50	20.56	20.61	20.66	20.72	20.77
7	18.52	18.58	18.63	18.69	18.75	18.80	18.86	18.91
8	17.15	17.21	17.26	17.32	17.38	17.43	17.49	17.55
9	16.11	16.16	16.22	16.28	16.34	16.40	16.46	16.51
10	15.29	15.35	15.41	15.47	15.53	15.59	15.65	15.71
11	14.65	14.71	14.77	14.83	14.89	14.95	15.02	15.08
12	14.12	14.19	14.25	14.31	14.38	14.44	14.50	14.57
13	13.70	13.76	13.83	13.89	13.96	14.02	14.09	14.15
14	13.35	13.41	13.48	13.54	13.61	13.68	13.74	13.81
15	13.05	13.12	13.19	13.26	13.32	13.39	13.46	13.52
16	12.81	12.88	12.95	13.01	13.08	13.15	13.22	13.29
17	12.60	12.67	12.74	12.81	12.88	12.95	13.02	13.09
18	12.43	12.50	12.57	12.64	12.71	12.78	12.85	12.92
19	12.28	12.35	12.42	12.49	12.56	12.64	12.71	12.78
20	12.15	12.22	12.30	12.37	12.44	12.51	12.59	12.66
21	12.04	12.11	12.19	12.26	12.33	12.41	12.48	12.56
22	11.95	12.02	12.10	12.17	12.24	12.32	12.39	12.47
23	11.87	11.94	12.02	12.09	12.17	12.24	12.32	12.39
24	11.80	11.87	11.95	12.02	12.10	12.18	12.25	12.33
25	11.74	11.81	11.89	11.97	12.04	12.12	12.20	12.27
26	11.69	11.76	11.84	11.92	11.99	12.07	12.15	12.22
28	11.60	11.68	11.76	11.84	11.91	11.99	12.07	12.15
30	11.54	11.62	11.70	11.77	11.85	11.93	12.01	12.09
35	11.44	11.52	11.60	11.68	11.76	11.84	11.92	12.00
40	11.39	11.47	11.55	11.63	11.72	11.80	11.88	11.96

QUARTERLY PAYMENT NEEDED TO AMORTIZE A $1000 LOAN

YEARS	RATE 8.00%	8.25%	8.50%	8.75%	9.00%	9.25%	9.50%	9.75%
1	262.63	263.03	263.43	263.82	264.22	264.62	265.02	265.42
2	136.51	136.88	137.25	137.62	137.99	138.36	138.73	139.10
3	94.56	94.93	95.29	95.66	96.02	96.39	96.76	97.12
4	73.66	74.02	74.39	74.75	75.12	75.49	75.86	76.23
5	61.16	61.53	61.90	62.27	62.65	63.02	63.40	63.77
6	52.88	53.25	53.63	54.01	54.39	54.77	55.15	55.53
7	46.99	47.38	47.76	48.14	48.53	48.92	49.31	49.70
8	42.62	43.00	43.39	43.79	44.18	44.57	44.97	45.37
9	39.24	39.63	40.03	40.43	40.83	41.23	41.64	42.05
10	36.56	36.96	37.37	37.77	38.18	38.59	39.01	39.42
11	34.39	34.80	35.21	35.63	36.04	36.46	36.88	37.31
12	32.61	33.02	33.44	33.86	34.29	34.71	35.14	35.58
13	31.11	31.54	31.96	32.39	32.82	33.26	33.70	34.14
14	29.85	30.28	30.71	31.15	31.59	32.03	32.48	32.93
15	28.77	29.21	29.65	30.09	30.54	30.99	31.44	31.90
16	27.84	28.29	28.73	29.19	29.64	30.10	30.56	31.02
17	27.04	27.49	27.94	28.40	28.86	29.32	29.79	30.26
18	26.33	26.79	27.25	27.71	28.18	28.65	29.13	29.61
19	25.71	26.18	26.64	27.11	27.59	28.07	28.55	29.04
20	25.17	25.64	26.11	26.59	27.07	27.55	28.04	28.54
21	24.68	25.16	25.64	26.12	26.61	27.10	27.60	28.10
22	24.25	24.73	25.22	25.71	26.20	26.70	27.20	27.71
23	23.86	24.35	24.84	25.34	25.84	26.34	26.85	27.36
24	23.52	24.01	24.51	25.01	25.52	26.03	26.54	27.06
25	23.21	23.71	24.21	24.72	25.23	25.75	26.27	26.79
26	22.93	23.43	23.94	24.46	24.97	25.49	26.02	26.55
28	22.45	22.96	23.48	24.01	24.53	25.07	25.60	26.14
30	22.05	22.58	23.11	23.64	24.18	24.72	25.27	25.81
35	21.34	21.89	22.44	22.99	23.55	24.11	24.68	25.25
40	20.88	21.45	22.02	22.59	23.16	23.74	24.32	24.91

YEARS	RATE 10.00%	10.25%	10.50%	10.75%	11.00%	11.25%	11.50%	11.75%
1	265.82	266.22	266.62	267.02	267.43	267.83	268.23	268.63
2	139.47	139.84	140.22	140.59	140.96	141.34	141.71	142.09
3	97.49	97.86	98.23	98.60	98.97	99.35	99.72	100.09
4	76.60	76.98	77.35	77.73	78.10	78.48	78.86	79.24
5	64.15	64.53	64.91	65.29	65.68	66.06	66.45	66.83
6	55.92	56.30	56.69	57.08	57.47	57.87	58.26	58.66
7	50.09	50.49	50.88	51.28	51.68	52.08	52.49	52.89
8	45.77	46.18	46.58	46.99	47.40	47.81	48.22	48.64
9	42.46	42.87	43.28	43.70	44.12	44.54	44.96	45.38
10	39.84	40.26	40.68	41.11	41.54	41.97	42.40	42.83
11	37.74	38.16	38.60	39.03	39.47	39.90	40.35	40.79
12	36.01	36.45	36.89	37.33	37.78	38.22	38.67	39.13
13	34.58	35.03	35.47	35.93	36.38	36.84	37.30	37.76
14	33.38	33.83	34.29	34.75	35.21	35.68	36.14	36.62
15	32.36	32.82	33.29	33.75	34.23	34.70	35.18	35.66
16	31.49	31.96	32.43	32.91	33.39	33.87	34.35	34.84
17	30.74	31.22	31.70	32.18	32.67	33.16	33.65	34.15
18	30.09	30.57	31.06	31.55	32.05	32.55	33.05	33.55
19	29.52	30.02	30.51	31.01	31.51	32.02	32.53	33.04
20	29.03	29.53	30.03	30.54	31.05	31.56	32.08	32.60
21	28.60	29.10	29.61	30.13	30.64	31.16	31.68	32.21
22	28.22	28.73	29.25	29.76	30.29	30.81	31.34	31.87
23	27.88	28.40	28.92	29.45	29.98	30.51	31.04	31.58
24	27.58	28.11	28.63	29.17	29.70	30.24	30.78	31.32
25	27.32	27.85	28.38	28.92	29.46	30.00	30.55	31.10
26	27.08	27.62	28.16	28.70	29.25	29.79	30.35	30.90
28	26.68	27.23	27.78	28.33	28.89	29.45	30.01	30.57
30	26.37	26.92	27.48	28.04	28.61	29.18	29.75	30.32
35	25.82	26.39	26.97	27.55	28.14	28.72	29.31	29.90
40	25.50	26.09	26.68	27.27	27.87	28.47	29.07	29.67

QUARTERLY PAYMENT NEEDED TO AMORTIZE A $1000 LOAN

YEARS	RATE 12.00%	12.25%	12.50%	12.75%	13.00%	13.25%	13.50%	13.75%
1	269.03	269.43	269.84	270.24	270.64	271.05	271.45	271.85
2	142.46	142.84	143.21	143.59	143.97	144.35	144.72	145.10
3	100.47	100.84	101.22	101.59	101.97	102.35	102.73	103.11
4	79.62	80.00	80.38	80.76	81.15	81.53	81.92	82.30
5	67.22	67.61	68.00	68.39	68.78	69.18	69.57	69.97
6	59.05	59.45	59.85	60.25	60.65	61.06	61.46	61.87
7	53.30	53.71	54.12	54.53	54.94	55.35	55.77	56.19
8	49.05	49.47	49.89	50.31	50.73	51.16	51.59	52.02
9	45.81	46.24	46.67	47.10	47.53	47.97	48.41	48.85
10	43.27	43.71	44.15	44.59	45.03	45.48	45.93	46.38
11	41.23	41.68	42.13	42.59	43.04	43.50	43.96	44.42
12	39.58	40.04	40.50	40.96	41.43	41.90	42.37	42.84
13	38.22	38.69	39.16	39.63	40.11	40.58	41.06	41.54
14	37.09	37.57	38.04	38.53	39.01	39.50	39.99	40.48
15	36.14	36.62	37.11	37.60	38.09	38.59	39.09	39.59
16	35.33	35.83	36.32	36.82	37.32	37.83	38.34	38.85
17	34.65	35.15	35.65	36.16	36.67	37.18	37.70	38.22
18	34.06	34.57	35.08	35.60	36.12	36.64	37.16	37.69
19	33.55	34.07	34.59	35.11	35.64	36.17	36.70	37.23
20	33.12	33.64	34.17	34.70	35.23	35.77	36.31	36.85
21	32.74	33.27	33.80	34.34	34.88	35.42	35.97	36.52
22	32.41	32.95	33.49	34.03	34.58	35.13	35.68	36.23
23	32.12	32.67	33.21	33.76	34.31	34.87	35.43	35.99
24	31.87	32.42	32.97	33.53	34.09	34.65	35.21	35.77
25	31.65	32.21	32.76	33.33	33.89	34.45	35.02	35.59
26	31.46	32.02	32.58	33.15	33.72	34.29	34.86	35.43
28	31.14	31.71	32.28	32.86	33.43	34.01	34.60	35.18
30	30.89	31.47	32.05	32.64	33.22	33.81	34.40	34.99
35	30.49	31.09	31.68	32.28	32.88	33.48	34.08	34.69
40	30.27	30.88	31.48	32.09	32.70	33.31	33.92	34.53

YEARS	RATE 14.00%	14.25%	14.50%	14.75%	15.00%	15.25%	15.50%	15.75%
1	272.26	272.66	273.06	273.47	273.87	274.28	274.68	275.09
2	145.48	145.86	146.24	146.62	147.00	147.39	147.77	148.15
3	103.49	103.87	104.25	104.63	105.02	105.40	105.79	106.17
4	82.69	83.08	83.47	83.86	84.25	84.64	85.04	85.43
5	70.37	70.76	71.16	71.57	71.97	72.37	72.77	73.18
6	62.28	62.69	63.10	63.51	63.92	64.34	64.76	65.17
7	56.61	57.03	57.45	57.87	58.30	58.73	59.16	59.59
8	52.45	52.88	53.31	53.75	54.19	54.63	55.07	55.51
9	49.29	49.73	50.18	50.63	51.08	51.53	51.98	52.44
10	46.83	47.29	47.74	48.20	48.66	49.13	49.59	50.06
11	44.88	45.35	45.82	46.29	46.76	47.23	47.71	48.19
12	43.31	43.79	44.27	44.75	45.23	45.72	46.20	46.69
13	42.03	42.52	43.01	43.50	43.99	44.49	44.98	45.48
14	40.97	41.47	41.97	42.47	42.97	43.48	43.99	44.50
15	40.09	40.60	41.11	41.62	42.13	42.65	43.16	43.68
16	39.36	39.87	40.39	40.91	41.43	41.96	42.48	43.01
17	38.74	39.26	39.79	40.32	40.85	41.38	41.91	42.45
18	38.21	38.75	39.28	39.82	40.35	40.89	41.44	41.98
19	37.77	38.31	38.85	39.39	39.94	40.49	41.04	41.59
20	37.39	37.94	38.48	39.03	39.59	40.14	40.70	41.26
21	37.07	37.62	38.17	38.73	39.29	39.85	40.41	40.98
22	36.79	37.35	37.91	38.47	39.03	39.60	40.17	40.74
23	36.55	37.11	37.68	38.25	38.82	39.39	39.96	40.54
24	36.34	36.91	37.48	38.06	38.63	39.21	39.79	40.37
25	36.16	36.74	37.32	37.89	38.47	39.06	39.64	40.23
26	36.01	36.59	37.17	37.75	38.34	38.92	39.51	40.10
28	35.76	36.35	36.94	37.53	38.12	38.72	39.31	39.91
30	35.58	36.17	36.77	37.36	37.96	38.56	39.16	39.77
35	35.29	35.90	36.50	37.11	37.72	38.33	38.95	39.56
40	35.15	35.76	36.38	36.99	37.61	38.23	38.84	39.46

SEMI-ANNUAL PAYMENT NEEDED TO AMORTIZE A $1000 LOAN

YEARS	RATE 8.00%	8.25%	8.50%	8.75%	9.00%	9.25%	9.50%	9.75%
1	530.20	531.15	532.10	533.05	534.00	534.95	535.91	536.86
2	275.50	276.31	277.12	277.93	278.75	279.56	280.38	281.20
3	190.77	191.54	192.32	193.10	193.88	194.67	195.45	196.24
4	148.53	149.30	150.07	150.84	151.61	152.39	153.17	153.95
5	123.30	124.06	124.84	125.61	126.38	127.16	127 94	128.72
6	106.56	107.33	108.11	108.89	109.67	110.46	111.25	112.04
7	94.67	95.46	96.24	97.03	97.83	98.62	99.42	100.22
8	85.82	86.62	87.42	88.22	89.02	89.83	90.64	91.46
9	79.00	79.80	80.61	81.42	82.24	83.06	83.89	84.72
10	73.59	74.40	75.22	76.05	76.88	77.72	78.56	79.40
11	69.20	70.03	70.87	71.71	72.55	73.40	74.25	75.11
12	65.59	66.43	67.28	68.13	68.99	69.86	70.72	71.60
13	62.57	63.43	64.29	65.15	66.03	66.90	67.79	68.68
14	60.02	60.89	61.76	62.64	63.53	64.42	65.32	66.22
15	57.84	58.72	59.60	60.50	61.40	62.30	63.21	64.13
16	55.95	56.85	57.75	58.65	59.57	60.49	61.41	62.35
17	54.32	55.23	56.14	57.06	57.99	58.92	59.86	60.81
18	52.89	53.81	54.74	55.67	56.61	57.56	58.51	59.47
19	51.64	52.57	53.51	54.45	55.41	56.37	57.33	58.31
20	50.53	51.47	52.42	53.38	54.35	55.32	56.30	57.29
21	49.55	50.50	51.46	52.44	53.41	54.40	55.39	56.39
22	48.67	49.64	50.61	51.60	52.59	53.58	54.59	55.60
23	47.89	48.87	49.85	50.85	51.85	52.86	53.88	54.90
24	47.19	48.18	49.17	50.18	51.19	52.22	53.24	54.28
25	46.56	47.56	48.57	49.58	50.61	51.64	52.68	53.73
26	45.99	47.00	48.02	49.05	50.08	51.13	52.18	53.23
28	45.01	46.04	47.08	48.13	49.19	50.25	51.32	52.40
30	44.21	45.26	46.32	47.38	48.46	49.54	50.63	51.73
35	42.75	43.84	44.94	46.05	47.17	48.29	49.42	50.56
40	41.82	42.95	44.08	45.23	46.38	47.53	48.69	49.86

YEARS	RATE 10.00%	10.25%	10.50%	10.75%	11.00%	11.25%	11.50%	11.75%
1	537.81	538.76	539.72	540.67	541.62	542.58	543.53	544.49
2	282.02	282.84	283.66	284.48	285.30	286.12	286.95	287.77
3	197.02	197.81	198.60	199.39	200.18	200.98	201.77	202.57
4	154.73	155.51	156.29	157.08	157.87	158.66	159.45	160.25
5	129.51	130.30	131.09	131.88	132.67	133.47	134.27	135.07
6	112.83	113.63	114.43	115.23	116.03	116.84	117.65	118.47
7	101.03	101.84	102.65	103.47	104.28	105.11	105.93	106.76
8	92.27	93.10	93.92	94.75	95.59	96.42	97.27	98.11
9	85.55	86.39	87.23	88.08	88.92	89.78	90.64	91.50
10	80.25	81.10	81.96	82.82	83.68	84.55	85.43	86.31
11	75.98	76.84	77.72	78.59	79.48	80.36	81.25	82.15
12	72.48	73.36	74.25	75.14	76.04	76.94	77.85	78.77
13	69.57	70.47	71.37	72.28	73.20	74.12	75.04	75.97
14	67.13	68.04	68.96	69.89	70.82	71.76	72.70	73.65
15	65.06	65.99	66.92	67.86	68.81	69.76	70.72	71.68
16	63.29	64.23	65.18	66.14	67.10	68.07	69.04	70.02
17	61.76	62.72	63.69	64.66	65.63	66.62	67.61	68.60
18	60.44	61.41	62.39	63.38	64.37	65.37	66.37	67.38
19	59.29	60.28	61.27	62.27	63.28	64.29	65.31	66.33
20	58.28	59.28	60.29	61.31	62.33	63.35	64.38	65.42
21	57.40	58.41	59.43	60.46	61.49	62.53	63.58	64.63
22	56.62	57.65	58.68	59.72	60.77	61.82	62.88	63.94
23	55.93	56.97	58.02	59.07	60.13	61.19	62.26	63.34
24	55.32	56.37	57.43	58.49	59.56	60.64	61.72	62.81
25	54.78	55.84	56.91	57.99	59.07	60.15	61.25	62.35
26	54.30	55.37	56.45	57.54	58.63	59.72	60.83	61.94
28	53.49	54.58	55.68	56.78	57.89	59.01	60.13	61.26
30	52.83	53.94	55.06	56.18	57.31	58.45	59.59	60.73
35	51.70	52.85	54.01	55.17	56.33	57.50	58.68	59.86
40	51.03	52.21	53.40	54.58	55.77	56.97	58.17	59.37

SEMI-ANNUAL PAYMENT NEEDED TO AMORTIZE A $1000 LOAN

YEARS	RATE 12.00%	12.25%	12.50%	12.75%	13.00%	13.25%	13.50%	13.75%
1	545.44	546.40	547.35	548.31	549.27	550.22	551.18	552.14
2	288.60	289.42	290.25	291.08	291.91	292.74	293.57	294.40
3	203.37	204.17	204.97	205.77	206.57	207.38	208.18	208.99
4	161.04	161.84	162.64	163.44	164.24	165.05	165.85	166.66
5	135.87	136.68	137.49	138.30	139.11	139.92	140.74	141.56
6	119.28	120.10	120.92	121.75	122.57	123.40	124.23	125.07
7	107.59	108.42	109.26	110.10	110.95	111.79	112.64	113.49
8	98.96	99.81	100.66	101.52	102.38	103.25	104.12	104.99
9	92.36	93.23	94.10	94.98	95.86	96.74	97.63	98.52
10	87.19	88.08	88.97	89.86	90.76	91.66	92.57	93.48
11	83.05	83.96	84.86	85.78	86.70	87.62	88.55	89.48
12	79.68	80.61	81.53	82.47	83.40	84.34	85.29	86.24
13	76.91	77.85	78.79	79.74	80.70	81.66	82.62	83.59
14	74.60	75.56	76.52	77.49	78.46	79.44	80.42	81.41
15	72.65	73.63	74.61	75.59	76.58	77.58	78.58	79.58
16	71.01	72.00	72.99	74.00	75.00	76.01	77.03	78.05
17	69.60	70.61	71.62	72.64	73.66	74.69	75.72	76.76
18	68.40	69.42	70.45	71.48	72.52	73.56	74.61	75.66
19	67.36	68.40	69.44	70.49	71.54	72.60	73.66	74.73
20	66.47	67.52	68.57	69.63	70.70	71.77	72.85	73.93
21	65.69	66.75	67.82	68.89	69.97	71.06	72.15	73.24
22	65.01	66.09	67.17	68.25	69.35	70.44	71.54	72.65
23	64.42	65.51	66.60	67.70	68.80	69.91	71.02	72.14
24	63.90	65.00	66.11	67.22	68.33	69.45	70.57	71.70
25	63.45	64.56	65.67	66.79	67.92	69.05	70.18	71.32
26	63.05	64.17	65.30	66.43	67.56	68.70	69.84	70.99
28	62.39	63.53	64.67	65.82	66.97	68.13	69.29	70.46
30	61.88	63.04	64.19	65.36	66.53	67.70	68.87	70.05
35	61.04	62.22	63.42	64.61	65.81	67.01	68.21	69.42
40	60.58	61.79	63.00	64.21	65.43	66.65	67.87	69.09

YEARS	RATE 14.00%	14.25%	14.50%	14.75%	15.00%	15.25%	15.50%	15.75%
1	553.10	554.06	555.01	555.97	556.93	557.89	558.85	559.81
2	295.23	296.07	296.90	297.74	298.57	299.41	300.25	301.09
3	209.80	210.61	211.42	212.24	213.05	213.87	214.68	215.50
4	167.47	168.28	169.10	169.91	170.73	171.55	172.37	173.20
5	142.38	143.21	144.03	144.86	145.69	146.52	147.36	148.20
6	125.91	126.75	127.59	128.43	129.28	130.13	130.99	131.84
7	114.35	115.21	116.07	116.93	117.80	118.67	119.55	120.42
8	105.86	106.74	107.62	108.51	109.40	110.29	111.18	112.08
9	99.42	100.32	101.22	102.12	103.03	103.95	104.86	105.78
10	94.40	95.32	96.24	97.17	98.10	99.03	99.97	100.91
11	90.41	91.35	92.29	93.24	94.19	95.15	96.11	97.07
12	87.19	88.15	89.12	90.08	91.06	92.03	93.01	93.99
13	84.57	85.54	86.53	87.51	88.50	89.50	90.50	91.50
14	82.40	83.39	84.39	85.40	86.41	87.42	88.44	89.47
15	80.59	81.61	82.62	83.65	84.68	85.71	86.75	87.79
16	79.08	80.11	81.15	82.19	83.23	84.28	85.33	86.39
17	77.80	78.85	79.90	80.96	82.02	83.09	84.16	85.23
18	76.72	77.78	78.85	79.92	81.00	82.08	83.17	84.26
19	75.80	76.88	77.96	79.05	80.14	81.23	82.33	83.44
20	75.01	76.11	77.20	78.30	79.41	80.51	81.63	82.74
21	74.34	75.44	76.55	77.67	78.78	79.90	81.03	82.16
22	73.76	74.88	76.00	77.12	78.25	79.38	80.52	81.66
23	73.26	74.39	75.52	76.66	77.80	78.94	80.09	81.24
24	72.84	73.97	75.11	76.26	77.41	78.56	79.72	80.88
25	72.46	73.61	74.76	75.92	77.08	78.24	79.41	80.58
26	72.14	73.30	74.46	75.62	76.79	77.96	79.14	80.31
28	71.63	72.80	73.97	75.15	76.33	77.52	78.71	79.90
30	71.23	72.42	73.61	74.80	76.00	77.19	78.39	79.60
35	70.62	71.84	73.05	74.26	75.48	76.70	77.92	79.15
40	70.32	71.55	72.77	74.00	75.24	76.47	77.70	78.94

ANNUAL PAYMENT NEEDED TO AMORTIZE A $1000 LOAN

YEARS	RATE 8.00%	8.25%	8.50%	8.75%	9.00%	9.25%	9.50%	9.75%
2	560.77	562.70	564.62	566.55	568.47	570.40	572.33	574.26
3	388.04	389.79	391.54	393.30	395.06	396.82	398.58	400.35
4	301.93	303.61	305.29	306.98	308.67	310.37	312.07	313.77
5	250.46	252.11	253.77	255.43	257.10	258.77	260.44	262.12
6	216.32	217.96	219.61	221.27	222.92	224.59	226.26	227.93
7	192.08	193.72	195.37	197.03	198.70	200.37	202.04	203.72
8	174.02	175.67	177.34	179.00	180.68	182.36	184.05	185.75
9	160.08	161.75	163.43	165.11	166.80	168.50	170.21	171.92
10	149.03	150.72	152.41	154.11	155.83	157.54	159.27	161.01
11	140.08	141.78	143.50	145.22	146.95	148.69	150.44	152.20
12	132.70	134.42	136.16	137.90	139.66	141.42	143.19	144.98
13	126.53	128.27	130.03	131.79	133.57	135.36	137.16	138.97
14	121.30	123.07	124.85	126.64	128.44	130.25	132.07	133.91
15	116.83	118.62	120.43	122.24	124.06	125.90	127.75	129.61
16	112.98	114.79	116.62	118.46	120.30	122.17	124.04	125.92
17	109.63	111.47	113.32	115.18	117.05	118.94	120.84	122.75
18	106.71	108.56	110.44	112.32	114.22	116.13	118.05	119.99
19	104.13	106.01	107.91	109.81	111.74	113.67	115.62	117.58
20	101.86	103.76	105.68	107.61	109.55	111.51	113.48	115.47
21	99.84	101.76	103.70	105.65	107.62	109.60	111.60	113.61
22	98.04	99.98	101.94	103.92	105.91	107.91	109.93	111.96
23	96.43	98.39	100.38	102.37	104.39	106.41	108.45	110.51
24	94.98	96.97	98.97	100.99	103.03	105.08	107.14	109.21
25	93.68	95.69	97.72	99.76	101.81	103.88	105.96	108.06
26	92.51	94.54	96.59	98.65	100.72	102.81	104.91	107.03
27	91.45	93.50	95.57	97.64	99.74	101.85	103.97	106.11
28	90.49	92.56	94.64	96.74	98.86	100.99	103.13	105.29
30	88.83	90.94	93.06	95.19	97.34	99.51	101.69	103.88
35	85.81	87.99	90.19	92.41	94.64	96.89	99.14	101.41
40	83.87	86.12	88.39	90.67	92.96	95.27	97.59	99.92

YEARS	RATE 10.00%	10.25%	10.50%	10.75%	11.00%	11.25%	11.50%	11.75%
2	576.20	578.13	580.06	582.00	583.94	585.88	587.82	589.76
3	402.12	403.89	405.66	407.44	409.22	411.00	412.78	414.57
4	315.48	317.18	318.90	320.61	322.33	324.05	325.78	327.51
5	263.80	265.49	267.18	268.88	270.58	272.28	273.99	275.70
6	229.61	231.30	232.99	234.68	236.38	238.09	239.80	241.51
7	205.41	207.10	208.80	210.51	212.22	213.94	215.66	217.39
8	187.45	189.16	190.87	192.60	194.33	196.06	197.80	199.55
9	173.65	175.37	177.11	178.86	180.61	182.37	184.13	185.90
10	162.75	164.50	166.26	168.03	169.81	171.59	173.38	175.18
11	153.97	155.74	157.53	159.32	161.13	162.94	164.76	166.58
12	146.77	148.57	150.38	152.20	154.03	155.87	157.72	159.58
13	140.78	142.61	144.45	146.30	148.16	150.02	151.90	153.79
14	135.75	137.61	139.47	141.35	143.23	145.13	147.04	148.95
15	131.48	133.36	135.25	137.16	139.07	140.99	142.93	144.87
16	127.82	129.73	131.65	133.58	135.52	137.47	139.44	141.41
17	124.67	126.60	128.55	130.51	132.48	134.46	136.45	138.45
18	121.94	123.90	125.87	127.85	129.85	131.85	133.87	135.90
19	119.55	121.54	123.54	125.55	127.57	129.60	131.65	133.70
20	117.46	119.48	121.50	123.53	125.58	127.64	129.71	131.79
21	115.63	117.66	119.71	121.77	123.84	125.93	128.02	130.13
22	114.01	116.07	118.14	120.22	122.32	124.43	126.54	128.67
23	112.58	114.66	116.75	118.86	120.98	123.11	125.25	127.40
24	111.30	113.41	115.52	117.65	119.79	121.94	124.11	126.28
25	110.17	112.30	114.43	116.58	118.75	120.92	123.10	125.30
26	109.16	111.31	113.47	115.64	117.82	120.01	122.22	124.43
27	108.26	110.43	112.60	114.79	116.99	119.21	121.43	123.66
28	107.46	109.64	111.83	114.04	116.26	118.49	120.73	122.99
30	106.08	108.30	110.53	112.78	115.03	117.29	119.57	121.85
35	103.69	105.99	108.29	110.61	112.93	115.27	117.61	119.96
40	102.26	104.62	106.98	109.35	111.72	114.11	116.50	118.90

ANNUAL PAYMENT NEEDED TO AMORTIZE A $1000 LOAN

YEARS	RATE 12.00%	12.25%	12.50%	12.75%	13.00%	13.25%	13.50%	13.75%
2	591.70	593.65	595.59	597.54	599.49	601.44	603.39	605.34
3	416.35	418.14	419.94	421.73	423.53	425.33	427.13	428.93
4	329.24	330.97	332.71	334.45	336.20	337.95	339.70	341.45
5	277.41	279.13	280.86	282.59	284.32	286.06	287.80	289.54
6	243.23	244.96	246.68	248.42	250.16	251.90	253.65	255.40
7	219.12	220.86	222.61	224.36	226.12	227.88	229.65	231.42
8	201.31	203.07	204.84	206.61	208.39	210.18	211.97	213.77
9	187.68	189.47	191.27	193.07	194.87	196.69	198.51	200.34
10	176.99	178.80	180.63	182.46	184.29	186.14	187.99	189.85
11	168.42	170.26	172.12	173.98	175.85	177.72	179.61	181.50
12	161.44	163.32	165.20	167.09	168.99	170.90	172.82	174.74
13	155.68	157.59	159.50	161.42	163.36	165.30	167.24	169.20
14	150.88	152.81	154.76	156.71	158.67	160.64	162.63	164.62
15	146.83	148.79	150.77	152.75	154.75	156.75	158.76	160.78
16	143.40	145.39	147.39	149.41	151.43	153.46	155.51	157.56
17	140.46	142.48	144.52	146.56	148.61	150.68	152.75	154.83
18	137.94	139.99	142.05	144.12	146.21	148.30	150.40	152.51
19	135.77	137.85	139.93	142.03	144.14	146.26	148.38	150.52
20	133.88	135.99	138.10	140.22	142.36	144.50	146.66	148.82
21	132.25	134.37	136.51	138.66	140.82	142.99	145.17	147.35
22	130.82	132.97	135.13	137.30	139.48	141.68	143.88	146.09
23	129.56	131.74	133.92	136.12	138.32	140.54	142.76	144.99
24	128.47	130.66	132.87	135.09	137.31	139.55	141.79	144.05
25	127.50	129.72	131.95	134.18	136.43	138.69	140.95	143.22
26	126.66	128.89	131.14	133.39	135.66	137.93	140.22	142.51
27	125.91	128.16	130.43	132.70	134.98	137.28	139.57	141.88
28	125.25	127.52	129.80	132.09	134.39	136.70	139.02	141.34
30	124.15	126.45	128.77	131.09	133.42	135.75	138.10	140.45
35	122.32	124.69	127.06	129.45	131.83	134.23	136.63	139.04
40	121.31	123.72	126.14	128.56	130.99	133.42	135.86	138.30

YEARS	RATE 14.00%	14.25%	14.50%	14.75%	15.00%	15.25%	15.50%	15.75%
2	607.29	609.25	611.21	613.16	615.12	617.08	619.04	621.00
3	430.74	432.54	434.35	436.17	437.98	439.80	441.62	443.44
4	343.21	344.97	346.73	348.50	350.27	352.04	353.82	355.60
5	291.29	293.04	294.80	296.56	298.32	300.09	301.86	303.64
6	257.16	258.93	260.69	262.47	264.24	266.02	267.81	269.60
7	233.20	234.98	236.77	238.57	240.37	242.17	243.98	245.80
8	215.58	217.39	219.20	221.03	222.86	224.69	226.53	228.38
9	202.17	204.01	205.86	207.72	209.58	211.45	213.32	215.20
10	191.72	193.59	195.47	197.36	199.26	201.16	203.07	204.98
11	183.40	185.31	187.22	189.14	191.07	193.01	194.96	196.91
12	176.67	178.62	180.56	182.52	184.49	186.46	188.44	190.43
13	171.17	173.14	175.13	177.12	179.12	181.12	183.14	185.16
14	166.61	168.62	170.64	172.66	174.69	176.73	178.78	180.84
15	162.81	164.85	166.90	168.96	171.02	173.10	175.18	177.27
16	159.62	161.69	163.77	165.86	167.95	170.06	172.17	174.29
17	156.92	159.02	161.13	163.25	165.37	167.51	169.65	171.80
18	154.63	156.75	158.89	161.04	163.19	165.35	167.52	169.70
19	152.67	154.82	156.99	159.16	161.34	163.53	165.73	167.93
20	150.99	153.17	155.36	157.56	159.77	161.98	164.20	166.43
21	149.55	151.76	153.97	156.19	158.42	160.66	162.91	165.16
22	148.31	150.54	152.77	155.02	157.27	159.53	161.80	164.08
23	147.24	149.49	151.74	154.01	156.28	158.56	160.85	163.15
24	146.31	148.58	150.86	153.14	155.43	157.74	160.04	162.36
25	145.50	147.79	150.09	152.39	154.70	157.02	159.35	161.68
26	144.81	147.11	149.43	151.75	154.07	156.41	158.75	161.10
27	144.20	146.52	148.85	151.19	153.53	155.88	158.24	160.60
28	143.67	146.01	148.35	150.70	153.06	155.43	157.80	160.17
30	142.81	145.17	147.54	149.92	152.31	154.69	157.09	159.49
35	141.45	143.86	146.28	148.71	151.14	153.57	156.01	158.45
40	140.75	143.20	145.65	148.11	150.57	153.03	155.49	157.96

LOAN PROGRESS CHART

Showing the dollar balance remaining per $1000 of loan

INT RATE	ORIG TERM	ELAPSED TERM IN YEARS 2	5	8	10	12	15	18	20	22	25
	10	859	600	269							
	15	926	789	615	473	307					
8⅛%	20	957	877	775	692	595	415	186			
	25	973	924	861	810	750	639	499	384	248	
	30	983	952	912	879	841	771	682	609	523	365
	10	860	601	271							
	15	927	791	617	476	308					
8¼%	20	957	878	777	695	597	418	188			
	25	974	925	863	813	753	643	502	387	251	
	30	983	953	914	882	844	774	685	613	527	368
	10	861	603	272							
	15	927	793	620	478	310					
8⅜%	20	958	880	780	697	600	420	189			
	25	974	927	865	815	756	646	505	390	253	
	30	984	954	915	884	847	778	689	616	530	372
	10	861	604	273							
	15	928	794	622	480	312					
8½%	20	958	881	782	700	603	423	191			
	25	975	928	867	818	759	649	508	392	255	
	30	984	955	917	886	849	781	693	620	534	375
	10	862	606	274							
	15	929	796	624	482	314					
8⅝%	20	959	883	784	703	606	426	192			
	25	975	929	869	820	762	653	512	395	257	
	30	985	956	919	888	852	784	696	624	538	378
	10	863	607	275							
	15	929	797	626	484	315					
8¾%	20	960	884	786	705	609	428	194			
	25	976	930	871	823	765	656	515	398	259	
	30	985	957	920	890	854	787	700	628	542	381
	10	864	609	276							
	15	930	799	628	486	317					
8⅞%	20	960	886	788	708	611	431	195			
	25	976	932	873	825	767	659	518	401	262	
	30	985	958	922	892	857	790	703	631	546	384
	10	865	610	277							
9%	15	931	801	630	489	319					
	20	961	887	791	710	614	433	197			
	25	977	933	875	827	770	662	522	404	264	
	30	986	959	924	894	859	793	707	635	549	388
	10	865	612	278							
9⅛%	15	931	802	633	491	321					
	20	961	888	793	713	617	436	198			
	25	977	934	877	830	773	666	525	407	266	
	30	986	960	925	896	862	796	711	639	553	391
	10	866	613	280							
	15	932	804	635	493	322					
9¼%	20	962	890	795	715	620	439	200			
	25	978	935	879	832	776	669	528	410	268	
	30	986	961	927	898	864	799	714	643	557	394
	10	867	615	281							
	15	933	805	637	495	324					
9⅜%	20	962	891	797	718	622	441	201			
	25	978	936	881	834	778	672	531	413	271	
	30	987	962	928	900	866	802	717	646	560	397

LOAN PROGRESS CHART

Showing the dollar balance remaining per $1000 of loan

INT RATE	ORIG TERM	ELAPSED TERM IN YEARS 2	5	8	10	12	15	18	20	22	25
9½%	10	868	616	282							
	15	934	807	639	497	326					
	20	963	893	799	720	625	444	203			
	25	978	937	883	837	781	675	535	416	273	
	30	987	962	930	902	869	805	721	650	564	400
9⅝%	10	869	618	283							
	15	934	809	641	499	328					
	20	964	894	801	723	628	446	205			
	25	979	938	885	839	784	678	538	419	275	
	30	987	963	931	904	871	808	724	653	568	404
9¾%	10	869	619	284							
	15	935	810	643	501	330					
	20	964	895	803	725	631	449	206			
	25	979	940	886	841	786	681	541	422	277	
	30	988	964	933	906	873	811	728	657	571	407
9⅞%	10	870	621	285							
	15	936	812	645	504	331					
	20	965	897	805	728	633	452	208			
	25	980	941	888	843	789	685	544	425	279	
	30	988	965	934	908	876	814	731	661	575	410
10%	10	871	622	286							
	15	936	813	647	506	333					
	20	965	898	807	730	636	454	209			
	25	980	942	890	846	792	688	547	428	282	
	30	988	966	935	909	878	817	734	664	578	413
10⅛%	10	872	623	288							
	15	937	815	649	508	335					
	20	966	899	810	733	639	457	211			
	25	980	943	892	848	794	691	551	431	284	
	30	989	967	937	911	880	819	738	668	582	416
10¼%	10	872	625	289							
	15	937	816	651	510	337					
	20	966	901	812	735	641	459	212			
	25	981	944	893	850	797	694	554	433	286	
	30	989	967	938	913	882	822	741	671	585	419
10⅜%	10	873	626	290							
	15	938	818	654	512	338					
	20	967	902	814	738	644	462	214			
	25	981	945	895	852	799	697	557	436	288	
	30	989	968	939	915	884	825	744	674	589	422
10½%	10	874	628	291							
	15	939	819	656	514	340					
	20	967	903	816	740	647	464	215			
	25	982	946	897	854	802	700	560	439	290	
	30	989	969	941	916	886	828	747	678	592	426
10⅝%	10	875	629	292							
	15	939	821	658	516	342					
	20	968	904	818	742	649	467	217			
	25	982	947	898	856	804	703	563	442	293	
	30	990	970	942	918	888	830	750	681	596	429
10¾%	10	875	631	293							
	15	940	822	660	519	344					
	20	968	906	820	745	652	470	218			
	25	982	948	900	858	807	706	566	445	295	
	30	990	970	943	919	890	833	754	685	599	432

LOAN PROGRESS CHART

Showing the dollar balance remaining per $1000 of loan

INT RATE	ORIG TERM	ELAPSED TERM IN YEARS 2	5	8	10	12	15	18	20	22	25
10⅞%	10	876	632	294							
	15	941	824	662	521	345					
	20	969	907	821	747	654	472	220			
	25	983	949	901	860	809	709	569	448	297	
	30	990	971	944	921	892	835	757	688	603	435
11%	10	877	634	296							
	15	941	825	664	523	347					
	20	969	908	823	749	657	475	221			
	25	983	950	903	862	812	712	572	451	299	
	30	990	972	945	923	894	838	760	691	606	438
11⅛%	10	878	635	297							
	15	942	827	666	525	349					
	20	970	909	825	752	660	477	223			
	25	983	950	905	864	814	714	575	454	302	
	30	991	972	947	924	896	840	763	695	610	441
11¼%	10	878	636	298							
	15	942	828	668	527	351					
	20	970	911	827	754	662	480	225			
	25	984	951	906	866	816	717	579	456	304	
	30	991	973	948	926	898	843	766	698	613	444
11⅜%	10	879	638	299							
	15	943	829	670	529	352					
	20	971	912	829	756	665	482	226			
	25	984	952	908	868	819	720	582	459	306	
	30	991	974	949	927	900	845	769	701	616	447
11½%	10	880	639	300							
	15	944	831	672	531	354					
	20	971	913	831	759	667	485	228			
	25	984	953	909	870	821	723	585	462	308	
	30	991	974	950	929	902	848	772	704	620	450
11⅝%	10	881	641	301							
	15	944	832	674	533	356					
	20	971	914	833	761	670	487	229			
	25	985	954	911	872	823	726	588	465	310	
	30	992	975	951	930	903	850	775	708	623	453
11¾%	10	881	642	302							
	15	945	834	676	535	358					
	20	972	915	835	763	672	490	231			
	25	985	955	912	874	826	729	591	468	313	
	30	992	975	952	931	905	852	777	711	626	456
11⅞%	10	882	644	304							
	15	945	835	678	537	360					
	20	972	916	837	765	675	492	232			
	25	985	956	913	876	828	731	594	471	315	
	30	992	976	953	933	907	855	780	714	630	459
12%	10	883	645	305							
	15	946	837	680	540	361					
	20	973	917	838	767	677	495	234			
	25	986	957	915	878	830	734	597	473	317	
	30	992	977	954	934	909	857	783	717	633	462
12⅛%	10	884	648	307							
	15	947	839	684	544	365					
	20	974	920	842	772	682	500	237			
	25	986	958	918	881	835	740	603	479	322	
	30	993	978	956	937	912	862	789	723	639	468

LOAN PROGRESS CHART

Showing the dollar balance remaining per $1000 of loan

INT RATE	ORIG TERM	ELAPSED TERM IN YEARS 2	5	8	10	12	15	18	20	22	25
12½%	10	886	651	309							
	15	948	842	688	548	368					
	20	974	922	845	776	687	505	240			
	25	987	960	920	885	839	745	608	485	326	
	30	993	979	958	939	915	866	794	729	646	474
12¾%	10	887	653	312							
	15	949	845	692	552	372					
	20	975	924	849	780	692	510	243			
	25	987	961	923	888	843	750	614	490	330	
	30	993	980	960	942	918	870	800	735	652	480
13%	10	888	656	314							
	15	950	847	695	556	376					
	20	976	926	852	785	697	515	246			
	25	988	963	926	891	847	755	620	496	335	
	30	994	981	962	944	922	874	805	741	658	486
13¼%	10	890	659	316							
	15	952	850	699	560	379					
	20	977	928	856	789	702	520	250			
	25	988	964	928	895	851	760	626	501	339	
	30	994	982	963	946	924	878	810	747	664	492
13½%	10	891	662	319							
	15	953	853	703	564	383					
	20	977	930	859	793	707	525	253			
	25	989	965	930	898	855	765	631	507	343	
	30	994	983	965	949	927	882	815	752	670	498
13¾%	10	892	665	321							
	15	954	855	707	568	386					
	20	978	932	862	797	711	530	256			
	25	989	967	933	901	859	770	637	512	348	
	30	995	983	967	951	930	886	820	758	676	504
14%	10	894	667	323							
	15	955	858	711	572	390					
	20	979	934	865	801	716	534	259			
	25	990	968	935	904	863	775	642	517	352	
	30	995	984	968	953	933	890	824	763	682	509
14¼%	10	895	670	326							
	15	956	860	714	576	393					
	20	980	936	868	805	720	539	262			
	25	990	969	937	907	867	780	648	523	357	
	30	995	985	970	955	935	893	829	768	688	515
14½%	10	896	673	328							
	15	957	863	718	580	397					
	20	980	937	871	809	725	544	265			
	25	991	970	939	910	870	785	653	528	361	
	30	996	986	971	957	938	897	834	774	694	520
14¾%	10	898	675	330							
	15	957	865	722	584	400					
	20	981	939	874	812	729	549	268			
	25	991	972	941	912	874	789	658	533	365	
	30	996	987	972	959	940	900	838	779	699	526
15%	10	899	678	333							
	15	958	868	725	588	404					
	20	981	941	877	816	734	554	272			
	25	991	973	943	915	877	794	664	538	369	
	30	996	987	973	960	942	903	842	784	705	532

INSTRUCTIONS FOR USE
POINTS DISCOUNT TABLES

These tables will illustrate the yield on a mortgage when the lender keeps points.

Example: A $10,000 loan written for 10% interest, the lender keeps 3 points and the term of the loan is 30 years. That means the borrower receives only $9,700 or 97%.

Locate the 10% section on page 207. Follow the 97 Net Price row until you reach the 30-year column. The answer is 10.37. That means the annual rate for disclosure is 10.37%.

LOAN PROGRESS CHARTS

The purpose of these tables is to show the balance remaining in principal on a loan at a given point during the term of the loan.

You will need to know the interest rate, the original term in years, the current age of the loan and the original loan amount.

Example: Take a $10,000 loan with a 20-year original term and an interest rate of 9⅛%. What is the principal balance remaining at the end of 10 years?

Turn to page 202 and locate the 9⅛% section. Follow the 20-year original term row until you reach the 10-year column. The number is 713. That's $713 balance remaining for each $1,000 of original loan amount.

For a $10,000 loan, the balance is $7,130.

POINTS DISCOUNT TABLE

The following table shows the yield to maturity on a mortgage when from 1 to 5 points discount are taken.

INT RATE	NET PRICE	TERM IN YEARS 5	10	15	20	25	30	35	40
9%	95	11.22	10.21	9.89	9.73	9.64	9.58	9.55	9.52
	96	10.76	9.96	9.70	9.58	9.51	9.46	9.43	9.42
	97	10.31	9.72	9.52	9.43	9.38	9.34	9.32	9.31
	98	9.87	9.48	9.35	9.28	9.25	9.23	9.21	9.20
	99	9.43	9.24	9.17	9.14	9.12	9.11	9.11	9.10
9⅛%	95	11.34	10.34	10.01	9.86	9.77	9.71	9.68	9.65
	96	10.89	10.09	9.83	9.71	9.63	9.59	9.56	9.54
	97	10.44	9.84	9.65	9.56	9.50	9.47	9.45	9.44
	98	9.99	9.60	9.47	9.41	9.38	9.35	9.34	9.33
	99	9.56	9.36	9.30	9.27	9.25	9.24	9.23	9.23
9¼%	95	11.47	10.47	10.14	9.99	9.90	9.84	9.81	9.78
	96	11.01	10.22	9.96	9.83	9.76	9.72	9.69	9.67
	97	10.56	9.97	9.78	9.68	9.63	9.60	9.58	9.56
	98	10.12	9.73	9.60	9.54	9.50	9.48	9.47	9.46
	99	9.68	9.49	9.42	9.39	9.38	9.36	9.36	9.35
9⅜%	95	11.60	10.60	10.27	10.11	10.03	9.97	9.94	9.91
	96	11.14	10.35	10.09	9.96	9.89	9.85	9.82	9.80
	97	10.69	10.10	9.90	9.81	9.76	9.73	9.71	9.69
	98	10.25	9.85	9.73	9.66	9.63	9.61	9.59	9.59
	99	9.81	9.61	9.55	9.52	9.50	9.49	9.48	9.48
9½%	95	11.73	10.73	10.40	10.24	10.16	10.10	10.07	10.05
	96	11.27	10.47	10.21	10.09	10.02	9.98	9.95	9.93
	97	10.82	10.22	10.03	9.94	9.89	9.85	9.83	9.82
	98	10.37	9.98	9.85	9.79	9.76	9.73	9.72	9.71
	99	9.93	9.74	9.67	9.64	9.63	9.62	9.61	9.61
9⅝%	95	11.86	10.85	10.53	10.37	10.28	10.23	10.20	10.18
	96	11.40	10.60	10.34	10.22	10.15	10.11	10.08	10.06
	97	10.94	10.35	10.16	10.07	10.01	9.98	9.96	9.95
	98	10.50	10.11	9.98	9.92	9.88	9.86	9.85	9.84
	99	10.06	9.86	9.80	9.77	9.75	9.74	9.74	9.73
9¾%	95	11.98	10.98	10.66	10.50	10.41	10.36	10.33	10.31
	96	11.52	10.73	10.47	10.35	10.28	10.23	10.21	10.19
	97	11.07	10.48	10.29	10.19	10.14	10.11	10.09	10.08
	98	10.62	10.23	10.10	10.04	10.01	9.99	9.97	9.97
	99	10.18	9.99	9.93	9.90	9.88	9.87	9.86	9.86
9⅞%	95	12.11	11.11	10.78	10.63	10.54	10.49	10.46	10.44
	96	11.65	10.86	10.60	10.47	10.40	10.36	10.34	10.32
	97	11.20	10.61	10.41	10.32	10.27	10.24	10.22	10.21
	98	10.75	10.36	10.23	10.17	10.14	10.11	10.10	10.09
	99	10.31	10.11	10.05	10.02	10.00	9.99	9.99	9.98
10%	95	12.24	11.24	10.91	10.76	10.67	10.62	10.59	10.57
	96	11.78	10.98	10.72	10.60	10.53	10.49	10.47	10.45
	97	11.32	10.73	10.54	10.45	10.40	10.37	10.35	10.33
	98	10.88	10.48	10.36	10.30	10.26	10.24	10.23	10.22
	99	10.43	10.24	10.18	10.15	10.13	10.12	10.11	10.11
10⅛%	95	12.37	11.37	11.04	10.89	10.80	10.75	10.72	10.70
	96	11.90	11.11	10.85	10.73	10.66	10.62	10.59	10.58
	97	11.45	10.86	10.67	10.57	10.52	10.49	10.47	10.46
	98	11.00	10.61	10.48	10.42	10.39	10.37	10.36	10.35
	99	10.56	10.37	10.30	10.27	10.26	10.25	10.24	10.24
10¼%	95	12.49	11.50	11.17	11.02	10.93	10.88	10.85	10.83
	96	12.03	11.24	10.98	10.86	10.79	10.75	10.72	10.71
	97	11.58	10.99	10.79	10.70	10.65	10.62	10.60	10.59
	98	11.13	10.74	10.61	10.55	10.52	10.50	10.48	10.47
	99	10.69	10.49	10.43	10.40	10.38	10.37	10.37	10.36

POINTS DISCOUNT TABLE

The following table shows the yield to maturity on a mortgage when from 1 to 5 points discount are taken.

INT RATE	NET PRICE	TERM IN YEARS 5	10	15	20	25	30	35	40
10⅜%	95	12.62	11.62	11.30	11.15	11.06	11.01	10.98	10.96
	96	12.16	11.37	11.11	10.99	10.92	10.88	10.85	10.84
	97	11.70	11.11	10.92	10.83	10.78	10.75	10.73	10.72
	98	11.25	10.86	10.74	10.68	10.64	10.62	10.61	10.60
	99	10.81	10.62	10.55	10.52	10.51	10.50	10.49	10.49
10½%	95	12.75	11.75	11.43	11.27	11.19	11.14	11.11	11.09
	96	12.29	11.49	11.24	11.11	11.05	11.01	10.98	10.97
	97	11.83	11.24	11.05	10.96	10.91	10.88	10.86	10.85
	98	11.38	10.99	10.86	10.80	10.77	10.75	10.74	10.73
	99	10.94	10.74	10.68	10.65	10.63	10.62	10.62	10.61
10⅝%	95	12.88	11.88	11.56	11.40	11.32	11.27	11.24	11.22
	96	12.41	11.62	11.36	11.24	11.18	11.14	11.11	11.10
	97	11.96	11.37	11.17	11.08	11.03	11.00	10.99	10.97
	98	11.51	11.12	10.99	10.93	10.90	10.88	10.86	10.86
	99	11.06	10.87	10.81	10.78	10.76	10.75	10.74	10.74
10¾%	95	13.01	12.01	11.68	11.53	11.45	11.40	11.37	11.35
	96	12.54	11.75	11.49	11.37	11.30	11.26	11.24	11.22
	97	12.08	11.49	11.30	11.21	11.16	11.13	11.11	11.10
	98	11.63	11.24	11.11	11.06	11.02	11.00	10.99	10.98
	99	11.19	10.99	10.93	10.90	10.88	10.88	10.87	10.87
10⅞%	95	13.13	12.14	11.81	11.66	11.58	11.53	11.50	11.48
	96	12.67	11.88	11.62	11.50	11.43	11.39	11.37	11.35
	97	12.21	11.62	11.43	11.34	11.29	11.26	11.24	11.23
	98	11.76	11.37	11.24	11.18	11.15	11.13	11.12	11.11
	99	11.31	11.12	11.06	11.03	11.01	11.00	11.00	10.99
11%	95	13.26	12.26	11.94	11.79	11.71	11.66	11.63	11.61
	96	12.80	12.00	11.75	11.63	11.56	11.52	11.50	11.48
	97	12.34	11.75	11.56	11.47	11.42	11.39	11.37	11.36
	98	11.88	11.49	11.37	11.31	11.28	11.26	11.24	11.24
	99	11.44	11.25	11.18	11.15	11.14	11.13	11.12	11.12
11⅛%	95	13.39	12.39	12.07	11.92	11.84	11.79	11.76	11.74
	96	12.92	12.13	11.88	11.76	11.69	11.65	11.63	11.61
	97	12.46	11.87	11.68	11.59	11.54	11.52	11.50	11.49
	98	12.01	11.62	11.49	11.43	11.40	11.38	11.37	11.36
	99	11.56	11.37	11.31	11.28	11.26	11.25	11.25	11.24
11¼%	95	13.52	12.52	12.20	12.05	11.97	11.92	11.89	11.87
	96	13.05	12.26	12.00	11.88	11.82	11.78	11.76	11.74
	97	12.59	12.00	11.81	11.72	11.67	11.64	11.63	11.62
	98	12.14	11.75	11.62	11.56	11.53	11.51	11.50	11.49
	99	11.69	11.50	11.43	11.40	11.39	11.38	11.37	11.37
11⅜%	95	13.64	12.65	12.33	12.18	12.10	12.05	12.02	12.00
	96	13.18	12.39	12.13	12.01	11.95	11.91	11.89	11.87
	97	12.72	12.13	11.94	11.85	11.80	11.77	11.75	11.74
	98	12.26	11.87	11.75	11.69	11.66	11.64	11.63	11.62
	99	11.82	11.62	11.56	11.53	11.51	11.50	11.50	11.50
11½%	95	13.77	12.78	12.46	12.31	12.23	12.18	12.15	12.13
	96	13.30	12.51	12.26	12.14	12.08	12.04	12.02	12.00
	97	12.84	12.25	12.06	11.98	11.93	11.90	11.88	11.87
	98	12.39	12.00	11.87	11.81	11.78	11.76	11.75	11.75
	99	11.94	11.75	11.69	11.66	11.64	11.63	11.63	11.62
11⅝%	95	13.90	12.90	12.58	12.44	12.36	12.31	12.28	12.26
	96	13.43	12.64	12.39	12.27	12.20	12.17	12.14	12.13
	97	12.97	12.38	12.19	12.10	12.06	12.03	12.01	12.00
	98	12.51	12.13	12.00	11.94	11.91	11.89	11.88	11.87
	99	12.07	11.87	11.81	11.78	11.77	11.76	11.75	11.75

POINTS DISCOUNT TABLE

The following table shows the yield to maturity on a mortgage when from 1 to 5 points discount are taken.

INT RATE	NET PRICE	TERM IN YEARS							
		5	10	15	20	25	30	35	40
11¾%	95	14.03	13.03	12.71	12.57	12.49	12.44	12.41	12.39
	96	13.56	12.77	12.51	12.40	12.33	12.30	12.27	12.26
	97	13.10	12.51	12.32	12.23	12.18	12.16	12.14	12.13
	98	12.64	12.25	12.13	12.07	12.04	12.02	12.01	12.00
	99	12.19	12.00	11.94	11.91	11.89	11.88	11.88	11.87
11⅞%	95	14.16	13.16	12.84	12.69	12.62	12.57	12.54	12.53
	96	13.69	12.90	12.64	12.52	12.46	12.43	12.40	12.39
	97	13.22	12.63	12.45	12.36	12.31	12.28	12.27	12.26
	98	12.77	12.38	12.25	12.19	12.16	12.15	12.13	12.13
	99	12.32	12.12	12.06	12.03	12.02	12.01	12.00	12.00
12%	95	14.28	13.29	12.97	12.82	12.74	12.70	12.67	12.66
	96	13.81	13.02	12.77	12.65	12.59	12.55	12.53	12.52
	97	13.35	12.76	12.57	12.49	12.44	12.41	12.40	12.39
	98	12.89	12.50	12.38	12.32	12.29	12.27	12.26	12.25
	99	12.44	12.25	12.19	12.16	12.14	12.13	12.13	12.13
12¼%	95	14.54	13.55	13.23	13.08	13.00	12.96	12.93	12.92
	96	14.07	13.28	13.03	12.91	12.85	12.81	12.79	12.78
	97	13.60	13.02	12.83	12.74	12.69	12.67	12.65	12.64
	98	13.15	12.76	12.63	12.57	12.54	12.53	12.52	12.51
	99	12.69	12.50	12.44	12.41	12.40	12.39	12.38	12.38
12½%	95	14.79	13.80	13.49	13.34	13.26	13.22	13.19	13.18
	96	14.32	13.53	13.28	13.17	13.11	13.07	13.05	13.04
	97	13.86	13.27	13.08	13.00	12.95	12.92	12.91	12.90
	98	13.40	13.01	12.88	12.83	12.80	12.78	12.77	12.76
	99	12.95	12.75	12.69	12.66	12.65	12.64	12.63	12.63
12¾%	95	15.05	14.06	13.74	13.60	13.52	13.48	13.46	13.44
	96	14.58	13.79	13.54	13.42	13.36	13.33	13.31	13.30
	97	14.11	13.52	13.34	13.25	13.21	13.18	13.17	13.16
	98	13.65	13.26	13.14	13.08	13.05	13.03	13.02	13.02
	99	13.20	13.00	12.94	12.91	12.90	12.89	12.89	12.88
13%	95	15.31	14.32	14.00	13.86	13.78	13.74	13.72	13.70
	96	14.83	14.04	13.79	13.68	13.62	13.59	13.57	13.56
	97	14.36	13.78	13.59	13.51	13.46	13.44	13.42	13.41
	98	13.90	13.51	13.39	13.33	13.30	13.29	13.28	13.27
	99	13.45	13.26	13.19	13.17	13.15	13.14	13.14	13.14
13⅛%	95	15.56	14.57	14.26	14.12	14.04	14.00	13.98	13.97
	96	15.09	14.30	14.05	13.94	13.88	13.85	13.83	13.82
	97	14.62	14.03	13.85	13.76	13.72	13.69	13.68	13.67
	98	14.15	13.77	13.64	13.59	13.56	13.54	13.53	13.53
	99	13.70	13.51	13.45	13.42	13.40	13.39	13.39	13.39
13½%	95	15.82	14.83	14.52	14.38	14.30	14.26	14.24	14.23
	96	15.34	14.55	14.31	14.19	14.14	14.10	14.09	14.08
	97	14.87	14.28	14.10	14.02	13.97	13.95	13.94	13.93
	98	14.41	14.02	13.90	13.84	13.81	13.80	13.79	13.78
	99	13.95	13.76	13.70	13.67	13.65	13.65	13.64	13.64
13¾%	95	16.07	15.09	14.77	14.63	14.56	14.52	14.50	14.49
	96	15.59	14.81	14.56	14.45	14.39	14.36	14.35	14.34
	97	15.12	14.54	14.35	14.27	14.23	14.21	14.19	14.18
	98	14.66	14.27	14.15	14.09	14.07	14.05	14.04	14.04
	99	14.20	14.01	13.95	13.92	13.91	13.90	13.89	13.89
14%	95	16.33	15.34	15.03	14.89	14.82	14.78	14.76	14.75
	96	15.85	15.07	14.82	14.71	14.65	14.62	14.60	14.60
	97	15.38	14.79	14.61	14.53	14.48	14.46	14.45	14.44
	98	14.91	14.52	14.40	14.35	14.32	14.30	14.30	14.29
	99	14.45	14.26	14.20	14.17	14.16	14.15	14.15	14.14

PRORATIONS FROM JAN. 1st TO PRORATION DATE

DATE	JAN Days Past	JAN % of 360	FEB Days Past	FEB % of 360	MAR Days Past	MAR % of 360	APR Days Past	APR % of 360	MAY Days Past	MAY % of 360	JUN Days Past	JUN % of 360	DATE
1	1	.28	31	8.61	61	16.94	91	25.28	121	33.61	151	41.94	1
2	2	.56	32	8.89	62	17.22	92	25.56	122	33.89	152	42.22	2
3	3	.83	33	9.17	63	17.50	93	25.83	123	34.17	153	42.50	3
4	4	1.11	34	9.44	64	17.78	94	26.11	124	34.44	154	42.78	4
5	5	1.39	35	9.72	65	18.06	95	26.39	125	34.72	155	43.06	5
6	6	1.67	36	10.00	66	18.33	96	26.67	126	35.00	156	43.33	6
7	7	1.94	37	10.28	67	18.61	97	26.94	127	35.28	157	43.61	7
8	8	2.22	38	10.56	68	18.89	98	27.22	128	35.56	158	43.89	8
9	9	2.50	39	10.83	69	19.17	99	27.50	129	35.83	159	44.17	9
10	10	2.78	40	11.11	70	19.44	100	27.78	130	36.11	160	44.44	10
11	11	3.06	41	11.39	71	19.72	101	28.06	131	36.39	161	44.72	11
12	12	3.33	42	11.67	72	20.00	102	28.33	132	36.67	162	45.00	12
13	13	3.61	43	11.94	73	20.28	103	28.61	133	36.94	163	45.28	13
14	14	3.89	44	12.22	74	20.56	104	28.89	134	37.22	164	45.56	14
15	15	4.17	45	12.50	75	20.83	105	29.17	135	37.50	165	45.83	15
16	16	4.44	46	12.78	76	21.11	106	29.44	136	37.78	166	46.11	16
17	17	4.72	47	13.06	77	21.39	107	29.72	137	38.06	167	46.39	17
18	18	5.00	48	13.33	78	21.67	108	30.00	138	38.33	168	46.67	18
19	19	5.28	49	13.61	79	21.94	109	30.28	139	38.61	169	46.94	19
20	20	5.56	50	13.89	80	22.22	110	30.56	140	38.89	170	47.22	20
21	21	5.83	51	14.17	81	22.50	111	30.83	141	39.17	171	47.50	21
22	22	6.11	52	14.44	82	22.78	112	31.11	142	39.44	172	47.78	22
23	23	6.39	53	14.72	83	23.06	113	31.39	143	39.72	173	48.06	23
24	24	6.67	54	15.00	84	23.33	114	31.67	144	40.00	174	48.33	24
25	25	6.94	55	15.28	85	23.61	115	31.94	145	40.28	175	48.61	25
26	26	7.22	56	15.56	86	23.89	116	32.22	146	40.56	176	48.89	26
27	27	7.50	57	15.83	87	24.17	117	32.50	147	40.83	177	49.17	27
28	28	7.78	58	16.11	88	24.44	118	32.78	148	41.11	178	49.44	28
29	29	8.06	59	16.39	89	24.72	119	33.06	149	41.39	179	49.72	29
30	30	8.33	60	16.67	90	25.00	120	33.33	150	41.67	180	50.00	30

PRORATIONS FROM PRORATION DATE TO DEC. 31st

DATE	JAN Days to Come	JAN % of 360	FEB Days to Come	FEB % of 360	MAR Days to Come	MAR % of 360	APR Days to Come	APR % of 360	MAY Days to Come	MAY % of 360	JUN Days to Come	JUN % of 360	DATE
1	360	100.00	330	91.67	300	83.33	270	75.00	240	66.67	210	58.33	1
2	359	99.72	329	91.39	299	83.06	269	74.72	239	66.39	209	58.06	2
3	358	99.44	328	91.11	298	82.78	268	74.44	238	66.11	208	57.78	3
4	357	99.17	327	90.83	297	82.50	267	74.17	237	65.83	207	57.50	4
5	356	98.89	326	90.56	296	82.22	266	73.89	236	65.56	206	57.22	5
6	355	98.61	325	90.28	295	81.94	265	73.61	235	65.28	205	56.94	6
7	354	98.33	324	90.00	294	81.67	264	73.33	234	65.00	204	56.67	7
8	353	98.06	323	89.72	293	81.39	263	73.06	233	64.72	203	56.39	8
9	352	97.78	322	89.44	292	81.11	262	72.78	232	64.44	202	56.11	9
10	351	97.50	321	89.17	291	80.83	261	72.50	231	64.17	201	55.83	10
11	350	97.22	320	88.89	290	80.56	260	72.22	230	63.89	200	55.56	11
12	349	96.94	319	88.61	289	80.28	259	71.94	229	63.61	199	55.28	12
13	348	96.67	318	88.33	288	80.00	258	71.67	228	63.33	198	55.00	13
14	347	96.39	317	88.06	287	79.72	257	71.39	227	63.06	197	54.72	14
15	346	96.11	316	87.78	286	79.44	256	71.11	226	62.78	196	54.44	15
16	345	95.83	315	87.50	285	79.17	255	70.83	225	62.50	195	54.17	16
17	344	95.56	314	87.22	284	78.89	254	70.56	224	62.22	194	53.89	17
18	343	95.28	313	86.94	283	78.61	253	70.28	223	61.94	193	53.61	18
19	342	95.00	312	86.67	282	78.33	252	70.00	222	61.67	192	53.33	19
20	341	94.72	311	86.39	281	78.06	251	69.72	221	61.39	191	53.06	20
21	340	94.44	310	86.11	280	77.78	250	69.44	220	61.11	190	52.78	21
22	339	94.17	309	85.83	279	77.50	249	69.17	219	60.83	189	52.50	22
23	338	93.89	308	85.56	278	77.22	248	68.89	218	60.56	188	52.22	23
24	337	93.61	307	85.28	277	76.94	247	68.61	217	60.28	187	51.94	24
25	336	93.33	306	85.00	276	76.67	246	68.33	216	60.00	186	51.67	25
26	335	93.06	305	84.72	275	76.39	245	68.06	215	59.72	185	51.39	26
27	334	92.78	304	84.44	274	76.11	244	67.78	214	59.44	184	51.11	27
28	333	92.50	303	84.17	273	75.83	243	67.50	213	59.17	183	50.83	28
29	332	92.22	302	83.89	272	75.56	242	67.22	212	58.89	182	50.56	29
30	331	91.94	301	83.61	271	75.28	241	66.94	211	58.61	181	50.28	30

PRORATIONS FROM JAN. 1st TO PRORATION DATE

	JUL		AUG		SEP		OCT		NOV		DEC		
DATE	Days Past	% of 360	Days Past	% of 360	Days Past	% of 360	Days Past	% of 360	Days Past	% of 360	Days Past	% of 360	DATE
1	181	50.28	211	58.61	241	66.94	271	75.28	301	83.61	331	91.94	1
2	182	50.56	212	58.89	242	67.22	272	75.56	302	83.89	332	92.22	2
3	183	50.83	213	59.17	243	67.50	273	75.83	303	84.17	333	92.50	3
4	184	51.11	214	59.44	244	67.78	274	76.11	304	84.44	334	92.78	4
5	185	51.39	215	59.72	245	68.06	275	76.39	305	84.72	335	93.06	5
6	186	51.67	216	60.00	246	68.33	276	76.67	306	85.00	336	93.33	6
7	187	51.94	217	60.28	247	68.61	277	76.94	307	85.28	337	93.61	7
8	188	52.22	218	60.56	248	68.89	278	77.22	308	85.56	338	93.89	8
9	189	52.50	219	60.83	249	69.17	279	77.50	309	85.83	339	94.17	9
10	190	52.78	220	61.11	250	69.44	280	77.78	310	86.11	340	94.44	10
11	191	53.06	221	61.39	251	69.72	281	78.06	311	86.39	341	94.72	11
12	192	53.33	222	61.67	252	70.00	282	78.33	312	86.67	342	95.00	12
13	193	53.61	223	61.94	253	70.28	283	78.61	313	86.94	343	95.28	13
14	194	53.89	224	62.22	254	70.56	284	78.89	314	87.22	344	95.56	14
15	195	54.17	225	62.50	255	70.83	285	79.17	315	87.50	345	95.83	15
16	196	54.44	226	62.78	256	71.11	286	79.44	316	87.78	346	96.11	16
17	197	54.72	227	63.06	257	71.39	287	79.72	317	88.06	347	96.39	17
18	198	55.00	228	63.33	258	71.67	288	80.00	318	88.33	348	96.67	18
19	199	55.28	229	63.61	259	71.94	289	80.28	319	88.61	349	96.94	19
20	200	55.56	230	63.89	260	72.22	290	80.56	320	88.89	350	97.22	20
21	201	55.83	231	64.17	261	72.50	291	80.83	321	89.17	351	97.50	21
22	202	56.11	232	64.44	262	72.78	292	81.11	322	89.44	352	97.78	22
23	203	56.39	233	64.72	263	73.06	293	81.39	323	89.72	353	98.06	23
24	204	56.67	234	65.00	264	73.33	294	81.67	324	90.00	354	98.33	24
25	205	56.94	235	65.28	265	73.61	295	81.94	325	90.28	355	98.61	25
26	206	57.22	236	65.56	266	73.89	296	82.22	326	90.56	356	98.89	26
27	207	57.50	237	65.83	267	74.17	297	82.50	327	90.83	357	99.17	27
28	208	57.78	238	66.11	268	74.44	298	82.78	328	91.11	358	99.44	28
29	209	58.06	239	66.39	269	74.72	299	83.06	329	91.39	359	99.72	29
30	210	58.33	240	66.67	270	75.00	300	83.33	330	91.67	360	100.00	30

PRORATIONS FROM PRORATION DATE TO DEC. 31st

	JUL		AUG		SEP		OCT		NOV		DEC		
DATE	Days to Come	% of 360	Days to Come	% of 360	Days to Come	% of 360	Days to Come	% of 360	Days to Come	% of 360	Days to Come	% of 360	DATE
1	180	50.00	150	41.67	120	33.33	90	25.00	60	16.67	30	8.33	1
2	179	49.72	149	41.39	119	33.06	89	24.72	59	16.39	29	8.06	2
3	178	49.44	148	41.11	118	32.78	88	24.44	58	16.11	28	7.78	3
4	177	49.17	147	40.83	117	32.50	87	24.17	57	15.83	27	7.50	4
5	176	48.89	146	40.56	116	32.22	86	23.89	56	15.56	26	7.22	5
6	175	48.61	145	40.28	115	31.94	85	23.61	55	15.28	25	6.94	6
7	174	48.33	144	40.00	114	31.67	84	23.33	54	15.00	24	6.67	7
8	173	48.06	143	39.72	113	31.39	83	23.06	53	14.72	23	6.39	8
9	172	47.78	142	39.44	112	31.11	82	22.78	52	14.44	22	6.11	9
10	171	47.50	141	39.17	111	30.83	81	22.50	51	14.17	21	5.83	10
11	170	47.22	140	38.89	110	30.56	80	22.22	50	13.89	20	5.56	11
12	169	46.94	139	38.61	109	30.28	79	21.94	49	13.61	19	5.28	12
13	168	46.67	138	38.33	108	30.00	78	21.67	48	13.33	18	5.00	13
14	167	46.39	137	38.06	107	29.72	77	21.39	47	13.06	17	4.72	14
15	166	46.11	136	37.78	106	29.44	76	21.11	46	12.78	16	4.44	15
16	165	45.83	135	37.50	105	29.17	75	20.83	45	12.50	15	4.17	16
17	164	45.56	134	37.22	104	28.89	74	20.56	44	12.22	14	3.89	17
18	163	45.28	133	36.94	103	28.61	73	20.28	43	11.94	13	3.61	18
19	162	45.00	132	36.67	102	28.33	72	20.00	42	11.67	12	3.33	19
20	161	44.72	131	36.39	101	28.06	71	19.72	41	11.39	11	3.06	20
21	160	44.44	130	36.11	100	27.78	70	19.44	40	11.11	10	2.78	21
22	159	44.17	129	35.83	99	27.50	69	19.17	39	10.83	9	2.50	22
23	158	43.89	128	35.56	98	27.22	68	18.89	38	10.56	8	2.22	23
24	157	43.61	127	35.28	97	26.94	67	18.61	37	10.28	7	1.94	24
25	156	43.33	126	35.00	96	26.67	66	18.33	36	10.00	6	1.67	25
26	155	43.06	125	34.72	95	26.39	65	18.06	35	9.72	5	1.39	26
27	154	42.78	124	34.44	94	26.11	64	17.78	34	9.44	4	1.11	27
28	153	42.50	123	34.17	93	25.83	63	17.50	33	9.17	3	.83	28
29	152	42.22	122	33.89	92	25.56	62	17.22	32	8.89	2	.56	29
30	151	41.94	121	33.61	91	25.28	61	16.94	31	8.61	1	.28	30

PRORATIONS FROM JAN. 1st TO PRORATION DATE

DATE	JAN Days Past	JAN % of 365	FEB Days Past	FEB % of 365	MAR Days Past	MAR % of 365	APR Days Past	APR % of 365	MAY Days Past	MAY % of 365	JUN Days Past	JUN % of 365	DATE
1	1	.27	32	8.77	60	16.44	91	24.93	121	33.15	152	41.64	1
2	2	.55	33	9.04	61	16.71	92	25.21	122	33.42	153	41.92	2
3	3	.82	34	9.32	62	16.99	93	25.48	123	33.70	154	42.19	3
4	4	1.10	35	9.59	63	17.26	94	25.75	124	33.97	155	42.47	4
5	5	1.37	36	9.86	64	17.53	95	26.03	125	34.25	156	42.74	5
6	6	1.64	37	10.14	65	17.81	96	26.30	126	34.52	157	43.01	6
7	7	1.92	38	10.41	66	18.08	97	26.58	127	34.79	158	43.29	7
8	8	2.19	39	10.68	67	18.36	98	26.85	128	35.07	159	43.56	8
9	9	2.47	40	10.96	68	18.63	99	27.12	129	35.34	160	43.84	9
10	10	2.74	41	11.23	69	18.90	100	27.40	130	35.62	161	44.11	10
11	11	3.01	42	11.51	70	19.18	101	27.67	131	35.89	162	44.38	11
12	12	3.29	43	11.78	71	19.45	102	27.95	132	36.16	163	44.66	12
13	13	3.56	44	12.05	72	19.73	103	28.22	133	36.44	164	44.93	13
14	14	3.84	45	12.33	73	20.00	104	28.49	134	36.71	165	45.21	14
15	15	4.11	46	12.60	74	20.27	105	28.77	135	36.99	166	45.48	15
16	16	4.38	47	12.88	75	20.55	106	29.04	136	37.26	167	45.75	16
17	17	4.66	48	13.15	76	20.82	107	29.32	137	37.53	168	46.03	17
18	18	4.93	49	13.42	77	21.10	108	29.59	138	37.81	169	46.30	18
19	19	5.21	50	13.70	78	21.37	109	29.86	139	38.08	170	46.58	19
20	20	5.48	51	13.97	79	21.64	110	30.14	140	38.36	171	46.85	20
21	21	5.75	52	14.25	80	21.92	111	30.41	141	38.63	172	47.12	21
22	22	6.03	53	14.52	81	22.19	112	30.68	142	38.90	173	47.40	22
23	23	6.30	54	14.79	82	22.47	113	30.96	143	39.18	174	47.67	23
24	24	6.58	55	15.07	83	22.74	114	31.23	144	39.45	175	47.95	24
25	25	6.85	56	15.34	84	23.01	115	31.51	145	39.73	176	48.22	25
26	26	7.12	57	15.62	85	23.29	116	31.78	146	40.00	177	48.49	26
27	27	7.40	58	15.89	86	23.56	117	32.05	147	40.27	178	48.77	27
28	28	7.67	59	16.16	87	23.84	118	32.33	148	40.55	179	49.04	28
29	29	7.95			88	24.11	119	32.60	149	40.82	180	49.32	29
30	30	8.22			89	24.38	120	32.88	150	41.10	181	49.59	30
31	31	8.49			90	24.66			151	41.37			31

PRORATIONS FROM PRORATION DATE TO DEC. 31st

DATE	JAN Days to Come	JAN % of 365	FEB Days to Come	FEB % of 365	MAR Days to Come	MAR % of 365	APR Days to Come	APR % of 365	MAY Days to Come	MAY % of 365	JUN Days to Come	JUN % of 365	DATE
1	365	100.00	334	91.51	306	83.84	275	75.34	245	67.12	214	58.63	1
2	364	99.73	333	91.23	305	83.56	274	75.07	244	66.85	213	58.36	2
3	363	99.45	332	90.96	304	83.29	273	74.79	243	66.58	212	58.08	3
4	362	99.18	331	90.68	303	83.01	272	74.52	242	66.30	211	57.81	4
5	361	98.90	330	90.41	302	82.74	271	74.25	241	66.03	210	57.53	5
6	360	98.63	329	90.14	301	82.47	270	73.97	240	65.75	209	57.26	6
7	359	98.36	328	89.86	300	82.19	269	73.70	239	65.48	208	56.99	7
8	358	98.08	327	89.59	299	81.92	268	73.42	238	65.21	207	56.71	8
9	357	97.81	326	89.32	298	81.64	267	73.15	237	64.93	206	56.44	9
10	356	97.53	325	89.04	297	81.37	266	72.88	236	64.66	205	56.16	10
11	355	97.26	324	88.77	296	81.10	265	72.60	235	64.38	204	55.89	11
12	354	96.99	323	88.49	295	80.82	264	72.33	234	64.11	203	55.62	12
13	353	96.71	322	88.22	294	80.55	263	72.05	233	63.84	202	55.34	13
14	352	96.44	321	87.95	293	80.27	262	71.78	232	63.56	201	55.07	14
15	351	96.16	320	87.67	292	80.00	261	71.51	231	63.29	200	54.79	15
16	350	95.89	319	87.40	291	79.73	260	71.23	230	63.01	199	54.52	16
17	349	95.62	318	87.12	290	79.45	259	70.96	229	62.74	198	54.25	17
18	348	95.34	317	86.85	289	79.18	258	70.68	228	62.47	197	53.97	18
19	347	95.07	316	86.58	288	78.90	257	70.41	227	62.19	196	53.70	19
20	346	94.79	315	86.30	287	78.63	256	70.14	226	61.92	195	53.42	20
21	345	94.52	314	86.03	286	78.36	255	69.86	225	61.64	194	53.15	21
22	344	94.25	313	85.75	285	78.08	254	69.59	224	61.37	193	52.88	22
23	343	93.97	312	85.48	284	77.81	253	69.32	223	61.10	192	52.60	23
24	342	93.70	311	85.21	283	77.53	252	69.04	222	60.82	191	52.33	24
25	341	93.42	310	84.93	282	77.26	251	68.77	221	60.55	190	52.05	25
26	340	93.15	309	84.66	281	76.99	250	68.49	220	60.27	189	51.78	26
27	339	92.88	308	84.38	280	76.71	249	68.22	219	60.00	188	51.51	27
28	338	92.60	307	84.11	279	76.44	248	67.95	218	59.73	187	51.23	28
29	337	92.33			278	76.16	247	67.67	217	59.45	186	50.96	29
30	336	92.05			277	75.89	246	67.40	216	59.18	185	50.68	30
31	335	91.78			276	75.62			215	58.90	184		

PRORATIONS FROM JAN. 1st TO PRORATION DATE

	JUL		AUG		SEP		OCT		NOV		DEC		
DATE	Days Past	% of 365	Days Past	% of 365	Days Past	% of 365	Days Past	% of 365	Days Past	% of 365	Days Past	% of 365	DATE
1	182	49.86	213	58.36	244	66.85	274	75.07	305	83.56	335	91.78	1
2	183	50.14	214	58.63	245	67.12	275	75.34	306	83.84	336	92.05	2
3	184	50.41	215	58.90	246	67.40	276	75.62	307	84.11	337	92.33	3
4	185	50.68	216	59.18	247	67.67	277	75.89	308	84.38	338	92.60	4
5	186	50.96	217	59.45	248	67.95	278	76.16	309	84.66	339	92.88	5
6	187	51.23	218	59.73	249	68.22	279	76.44	310	84.93	340	93.15	6
7	188	51.51	219	60.00	250	68.49	280	76.71	311	85.21	341	93.42	7
8	189	51.78	220	60.27	251	68.77	281	76.99	312	85.48	342	93.70	8
9	190	52.05	221	60.55	252	69.04	282	77.26	313	85.75	343	93.97	9
10	191	52.33	222	60.82	253	69.32	283	77.53	314	86.03	344	94.25	10
11	192	52.60	223	61.10	254	69.59	284	77.81	315	86.30	345	94.52	11
12	193	52.88	224	61.37	255	69.86	285	78.08	316	86.58	346	94.79	12
13	194	53.15	225	61.64	256	70.14	286	78.36	317	86.85	347	95.07	13
14	195	53.42	226	61.92	257	70.41	287	78.63	318	87.12	348	95.34	14
15	196	53.70	227	62.19	258	70.68	288	78.90	319	87.40	349	95.62	15
16	197	53.97	228	62.47	259	70.96	289	79.18	320	87.67	350	95.89	16
17	198	54.25	229	62.74	260	71.23	290	79.45	321	87.95	351	96.16	17
18	199	54.52	230	63.01	261	71.51	291	79.73	322	88.22	352	96.44	18
19	200	54.79	231	63.29	262	71.78	292	80.00	323	88.49	353	96.71	19
20	201	55.07	232	63.56	263	72.05	293	80.27	324	88.77	354	96.99	20
21	202	55.34	233	63.84	264	72.33	294	80.55	325	89.04	355	97.26	21
22	203	55.62	234	64.11	265	72.60	295	80.82	326	89.32	356	97.53	22
23	204	55.89	235	64.38	266	72.88	296	81.10	327	89.59	357	97.81	23
24	205	56.16	236	64.66	267	73.15	297	81.37	328	89.86	358	98.08	24
25	206	56.44	237	64.93	268	73.42	298	81.64	329	90.14	359	98.36	25
26	207	56.71	238	65.21	269	73.70	299	81.92	330	90.41	360	98.63	26
27	208	56.99	239	65.48	270	73.97	300	82.19	331	90.68	361	98.90	27
28	209	57.26	240	65.75	271	74.25	301	82.47	332	90.96	362	99.18	28
29	210	57.53	241	66.03	272	74.52	302	82.74	333	91.23	363	99.45	29
30	211	57.81	242	66.30	273	74.79	303	83.01	334	91.51	364	99.73	30
31	212	58.08	243	66.58			304	83.29			365	100.00	31

PRORATIONS FROM PRORATION DATE TO DEC. 31st

	JUL		AUG		SEP		OCT		NOV		DEC		
DATE	Days to Come	% of 365	Days to Come	% of 365	Days to Come	% of 365	Days to Come	% of 365	Days to Come	% of 365	Days to Come	% of 365	DATE
1	184	50.41	153	41.92	122	33.42	92	25.21	61	16.71	31	8.49	1
2	183	50.14	152	41.64	121	33.15	91	24.93	60	16.44	30	8.22	2
3	182	49.86	151	41.37	120	32.88	90	24.66	59	16.16	29	7.95	3
4	181	49.59	150	41.10	119	32.60	89	24.38	58	15.89	28	7.67	4
5	180	49.32	149	40.82	118	32.33	88	24.11	57	15.62	27	7.40	5
6	179	49.04	148	40.55	117	32.05	87	23.84	56	15.34	26	7.12	6
7	178	48.77	147	40.27	116	31.78	86	23.56	55	15.07	25	6.85	7
8	177	48.49	146	40.00	115	31.51	85	23.29	54	14.79	24	6.58	8
9	176	48.22	145	39.73	114	31.23	84	23.01	53	14.52	23	6.30	9
10	175	47.95	144	39.45	113	30.96	83	22.74	52	14.25	22	6.03	10
11	174	47.67	143	39.18	112	30.68	82	22.47	51	13.97	21	5.75	11
12	173	47.40	142	38.90	111	30.41	81	22.19	50	13.70	20	5.48	12
13	172	47.12	141	38.63	110	30.14	80	21.92	49	13.42	19	5.21	13
14	171	46.85	140	38.36	109	29.86	79	21.64	48	13.15	18	4.93	14
15	170	46.58	139	38.08	108	29.59	78	21.37	47	12.88	17	4.66	15
16	169	46.30	138	37.81	107	29.32	77	21.10	46	12.60	16	4.38	16
17	168	46.03	137	37.53	106	29.04	76	20.82	45	12.33	15	4.11	17
18	167	45.75	136	37.26	105	28.77	75	20.55	44	12.05	14	3.84	18
19	166	45.48	135	36.99	104	28.49	74	20.27	43	11.78	13	3.56	19
20	165	45.21	134	36.71	103	28.22	73	20.00	42	11.51	12	3.29	20
21	164	44.93	133	36.44	102	27.95	72	19.73	41	11.23	11	3.01	21
22	163	44.66	132	36.16	101	27.67	71	19.45	40	10.96	10	2.74	22
23	162	44.38	131	35.89	100	27.40	70	19.18	39	10.68	9	2.47	23
24	161	44.11	130	35.62	99	27.12	69	18.90	38	10.41	8	2.19	24
25	160	43.84	129	35.34	98	26.85	68	18.63	37	10.14	7	1.92	25
26	159	43.56	128	35.07	97	26.58	67	18.36	36	9.86	6	1.64	26
27	158	43.29	127	34.79	96	26.30	66	18.08	35	9.59	5	1.37	27
28	157	43.01	126	34.52	95	26.03	65	17.81	34	9.32	4	1.10	28
29	156	42.74	125	34.25	94	25.75	64	17.53	33	9.04	3	.82	29
30	155	42.47	124	33.97	93	25.48	63	17.26	32	8.77	2	.55	30
31	154	42.19	123	33.70			62	16.99			1	.27	31

CONSTANT ANNUAL PERCENT

The Annual Debt Service needed to Amortize a Loan Amount

YEARS	RATE 9.00%	9.25%	9.50%	9.75%	10.00%	10.25%	10.50%	10.75%
1	104.94	105.08	105.22	105.36	105.50	105.64	105.78	105.92
2	54.82	54.96	55.10	55.24	55.37	55.51	55.65	55.79
3	38.16	38.30	38.44	38.58	38.72	38.86	39.00	39.14
4	29.86	30.00	30.15	30.29	30.44	30.58	30.72	30.87
5	24.91	25.06	25.20	25.35	25.50	25.64	25.79	25.94
6	21.63	21.78	21.93	22.08	22.23	22.38	22.53	22.69
7	19.31	19.46	19.61	19.77	19.92	20.08	20.23	20.39
8	17.58	17.74	17.89	18.05	18.21	18.37	18.53	18.69
9	16.25	16.41	16.57	16.73	16.89	17.06	17.22	17.39
10	15.20	15.36	15.53	15.69	15.86	16.02	16.19	16.36
11	14.35	14.52	14.69	14.85	15.02	15.19	15.37	15.54
12	13.66	13.83	14.00	14.17	14.34	14.51	14.69	14.87
13	13.08	13.25	13.42	13.60	13.77	13.95	14.13	14.31
14	12.59	12.76	12.94	13.12	13.30	13.48	13.66	13.84
15	12.17	12.35	12.53	12.71	12.90	13.08	13.26	13.45
16	11.81	12.00	12.18	12.36	12.55	12.74	12.93	13.12
17	11.51	11.69	11.88	12.07	12.25	12.45	12.64	12.83
18	11.24	11.43	11.61	11.81	12.00	12.19	12.39	12.58
19	11.00	11.19	11.39	11.58	11.78	11.97	12.17	12.37
20	10.80	10.99	11.19	11.38	11.58	11.78	11.98	12.18
21	10.61	10.81	11.01	11.21	11.41	11.61	11.82	12.02
22	10.45	10.65	10.85	11.06	11.26	11.46	11.67	11.88
23	10.31	10.51	10.72	10.92	11.13	11.33	11.54	11.75
24	10.18	10.39	10.59	10.80	11.01	11.22	11.43	11.64
25	10.07	10.28	10.48	10.69	10.90	11.12	11.33	11.55
26	9.97	10.18	10.39	10.60	10.81	11.03	11.24	11.46
28	9.80	10.01	10.22	10.44	10.66	10.87	11.09	11.32
30	9.66	9.87	10.09	10.31	10.53	10.75	10.98	11.20
35	9.41	9.63	9.86	10.09	10.32	10.55	10.78	11.01
40	9.26	9.49	9.72	9.95	10.19	10.43	10.66	10.90

YEARS	RATE 11.00%	11.25%	11.50%	11.75%	12.00%	12.25%	12.50%	12.75%
1	106.06	106.20	106.34	106.48	106.62	106.76	106.90	107.04
2	55.93	56.07	56.21	56.35	56.49	56.63	56.77	56.91
3	39.29	39.43	39.57	39.71	39.86	40.00	40.14	40.29
4	31.01	31.16	31.31	31.45	31.60	31.75	31.90	32.04
5	26.09	26.24	26.39	26.54	26.69	26.85	27.00	27.15
6	22.84	22.99	23.15	23.30	23.46	23.62	23.77	23.93
7	20.55	20.71	20.86	21.02	21.18	21.34	21.51	21.67
8	18.85	19.01	19.18	19.34	19.50	19.67	19.83	20.00
9	17.55	17.72	17.88	18.05	18.22	18.39	18.56	18.73
10	16.53	16.70	16.87	17.04	17.22	17.39	17.57	17.74
11	15.71	15.89	16.06	16.24	16.41	16.59	16.77	16.95
12	15.04	15.22	15.40	15.58	15.76	15.94	16.13	16.31
13	14.49	14.67	14.86	15.04	15.22	15.41	15.60	15.79
14	14.03	14.21	14.40	14.59	14.78	14.97	15.16	15.35
15	13.64	13.83	14.02	14.21	14.40	14.60	14.79	14.99
16	13.31	13.50	13.69	13.89	14.08	14.28	14.48	14.68
17	13.02	13.22	13.42	13.62	13.81	14.02	14.22	14.42
18	12.78	12.98	13.18	13.38	13.58	13.79	13.99	14.20
19	12.57	12.77	12.97	13.18	13.38	13.59	13.80	14.01
20	12.39	12.59	12.80	13.00	13.21	13.42	13.63	13.85
21	12.23	12.43	12.64	12.85	13.06	13.28	13.49	13.71
22	12.09	12.30	12.51	12.72	12.94	13.15	13.37	13.58
23	11.96	12.18	12.39	12.61	12.82	13.04	13.26	13.48
24	11.86	12.07	12.29	12.51	12.72	12.94	13.17	13.39
25	11.76	11.98	12.20	12.42	12.64	12.86	13.08	13.31
26	11.68	11.90	12.12	12.34	12.56	12.79	13.01	13.24
28	11.54	11.76	11.99	12.21	12.44	12.67	12.90	13.13
30	11.43	11.66	11.88	12.11	12.34	12.57	12.81	13.04
35	11.24	11.48	11.71	11.95	12.19	12.42	12.66	12.90
40	11.14	11.38	11.62	11.86	12.10	12.34	12.59	12.83

CONSTANT ANNUAL PERCENT

The Annual Debt Service needed to Amortize a Loan Amount

YEARS	RATE							
	13.00%	13.25%	13.50%	13.75%	14.00%	14.25%	14.50%	14.75%
1	107.18	107.32	107.46	107.60	107.74	107.89	108.03	108.17
2	57.05	57.19	57.33	57.47	57.62	57.76	57.90	58.04
3	40.43	40.58	40.72	40.87	41.01	41.16	41.31	41.45
4	32.19	32.34	32.49	32.64	32.79	32.94	33.09	33.25
5	27.30	27.46	27.61	27.77	27.92	28.08	28.23	28.39
6	24.09	24.25	24.41	24.57	24.73	24.89	25.05	25.21
7	21.83	21.99	22.16	22.32	22.49	22.65	22.82	22.99
8	20.17	20.34	20.51	20.68	20.85	21.02	21.19	21.36
9	18.90	19.08	19.25	19.43	19.60	19.78	19.95	20.13
10	17.92	18.09	18.27	18.45	18.63	18.81	18.99	19.18
11	17.13	17.31	17.50	17.68	17.86	18.05	18.24	18.42
12	16.50	16.68	16.87	17.06	17.25	17.44	17.63	17.82
13	15.97	16.16	16.36	16.55	16.74	16.94	17.13	17.33
14	15.54	15.74	15.93	16.13	16.33	16.52	16.72	16.92
15	15.18	15.38	15.58	15.78	15.98	16.18	16.39	16.59
16	14.88	15.08	15.28	15.49	15.69	15.90	16.10	16.31
17	14.62	14.83	15.03	15.24	15.45	15.66	15.87	16.08
18	14.41	14.61	14.82	15.03	15.24	15.46	15.67	15.88
19	14.22	14.43	14.64	14.86	15.07	15.29	15.50	15.72
20	14.06	14.27	14.49	14.70	14.92	15.14	15.36	15.58
21	13.92	14.14	14.36	14.58	14.80	15.02	15.24	15.46
22	13.80	14.02	14.24	14.46	14.69	14.91	15.14	15.36
23	13.70	13.92	14.15	14.37	14.59	14.82	15.05	15.27
24	13.61	13.84	14.06	14.29	14.51	14.74	14.97	15.20
25	13.53	13.76	13.99	14.22	14.45	14.68	14.91	15.14
26	13.47	13.70	13.92	14.15	14.39	14.62	14.85	15.08
28	13.36	13.59	13.82	14.06	14.29	14.53	14.76	15.00
30	13.27	13.51	13.74	13.98	14.22	14.46	14.69	14.93
35	13.14	13.38	13.62	13.87	14.11	14.35	14.59	14.84
40	13.07	13.32	13.56	13.81	14.05	14.30	14.55	14.79

YEARS	RATE							
	15.00%	15.25%	15.50%	15.75%	16.00%	16.25%	16.50%	17.00%
1	108.31	108.45	108.59	108.74	108.88	109.02	109.16	109.45
2	58.18	58.33	58.47	58.61	58.76	58.90	59.04	59.33
3	41.60	41.75	41.89	42.04	42.19	42.34	42.49	42.78
4	33.40	33.55	33.70	33.85	34.01	34.16	34.32	34.63
5	28.55	28.71	28.86	29.02	29.18	29.34	29.50	29.82
6	25.37	25.54	25.70	25.87	26.03	26.20	26.36	26.70
7	23.16	23.32	23.49	23.66	23.83	24.01	24.18	24.52
8	21.53	21.71	21.88	22.06	22.23	22.41	22.59	22.95
9	20.31	20.49	20.67	20.85	21.03	21.21	21.40	21.76
10	19.36	19.54	19.73	19.92	20.10	20.29	20.48	20.86
11	18.61	18.80	18.99	19.18	19.37	19.56	19.76	20.15
12	18.01	18.20	18.40	18.59	18.79	18.99	19.18	19.58
13	17.52	17.72	17.92	18.12	18.32	18.52	18.72	19.13
14	17.12	17.33	17.53	17.73	17.94	18.14	18.35	18.77
15	16.80	17.00	17.21	17.42	17.62	17.83	18.04	18.47
16	16.52	16.73	16.94	17.15	17.37	17.58	17.79	18.22
17	16.29	16.51	16.72	16.93	17.15	17.37	17.58	18.02
18	16.10	16.32	16.53	16.75	16.97	17.19	17.41	17.86
19	15.94	16.16	16.38	16.60	16.82	17.04	17.27	17.72
20	15.80	16.02	16.25	16.47	16.70	16.92	17.15	17.60
21	15.69	15.91	16.14	16.36	16.59	16.82	17.05	17.51
22	15.59	15.81	16.04	16.27	16.50	16.73	16.96	17.42
23	15.50	15.73	15.96	16.19	16.42	16.66	16.89	17.36
24	15.43	15.66	15.89	16.13	16.36	16.59	16.83	17.30
25	15.37	15.60	15.84	16.07	16.31	16.54	16.78	17.25
26	15.32	15.55	15.79	16.02	16.26	16.50	16.74	17.21
28	15.23	15.47	15.71	15.95	16.19	16.43	16.67	17.15
30	15.17	15.41	15.65	15.90	16.14	16.38	16.62	17.11
35	15.08	15.33	15.57	15.82	16.06	16.31	16.55	17.05
40	15.04	15.29	15.53	15.78	16.03	16.28	16.52	17.02

LOAN TO VALUE RATIOS FOR FHA LOANS

APPROVED NEW CONSTRUCTION—APPROVED EXISTING CONSTRUCTION, LESS THAN ONE YEAR OLD—EXISTING CONSTRUCTION OVER ONE YEAR OLD

	MAXIMUM LOANS			MAXIMUM LOANS			MAXIMUM LOANS	
Appraised Value	REGULAR 203-B	VETERAN 203-B	Appraised Value	REGULAR 203-B	VETERAN 203-B	Appraised Value	REGULAR 203-B	VETERAN 203-B
15100	14647	14900	21100	20467	20900	27100	26140	26690
15200	14744	15000	21200	20564	21000	27200	26230	26780
15300	14841	15100	21300	20661	21100	27300	26320	26870
15400	14938	15200	21400	20758	21200	27400	26410	26960
15500	15035	15300	21500	20855	21300	27500	26500	27050
15600	15132	15400	21600	20952	21400	27600	26590	27140
15700	15229	15500	21700	21049	21500	27700	26680	27230
15800	15326	15600	21800	21146	21600	27800	26770	27320
15900	15423	15700	21900	21243	21700	27900	26860	27410
16000	15520	15800	22000	21340	21800	28000	26950	27500
16100	15617	15900	22100	21437	21900	28100	27040	27590
16200	15714	16000	22200	21534	22000	28200	27130	27680
16300	15811	16100	22300	21631	22100	28300	27220	27770
16400	15908	16200	22400	21728	22200	28400	27310	27860
16500	16005	16300	22500	21825	22300	28500	27400	27950
16600	16102	16400	22600	21922	22400	28600	27490	28040
16700	16199	16500	22700	22019	22500	28700	27580	28130
16800	16296	16600	22800	22116	22600	28800	27670	28220
16900	16393	16700	22900	22213	22700	28900	27760	28310
17000	16490	16800	23000	22310	22800	29000	27850	28400
17100	16587	16900	23100	22407	22900	29100	27940	28490
17200	16684	17000	23200	22504	23000	29200	28030	28580
17300	16781	17100	23300	22601	23100	29300	28120	28670
17400	16878	17200	23400	22698	23200	29400	28210	28760
17500	16975	17300	23500	22795	23300	29500	28300	28850
17600	17072	17400	23600	22892	23400	29600	28390	28940
17700	17169	17500	23700	22989	23500	29700	28480	29030
17800	17266	17600	23800	23086	23600	29800	28570	29120
17900	17363	17700	23900	23183	23700	29900	28660	29210
18000	17460	17800	24000	23280	23800	30000	28750	29300
18100	17557	17900	24100	23377	23900	30100	28840	29390
18200	17654	18000	24200	23474	24000	30200	28930	29480
18300	17751	18100	24300	23571	24100	30300	29020	29570
18400	17848	18200	24400	23668	24200	30400	29110	29660
18500	17945	18300	24500	23765	24300	30500	29200	29750
18600	18042	18400	24600	23862	24400	30600	29290	29840
18700	18139	18500	24700	23959	24500	30700	29380	29930
18800	18236	18600	24800	24056	24600	30800	29470	30020
18900	18333	18700	24900	24153	24700	30900	29560	30110
19000	18430	18800	25000	24250	24800	31000	29650	30200
19100	18527	18900	25100	24340	24890	31100	29740	30290
19200	18624	19000	25200	24430	24980	31200	29830	30380
19300	18721	19100	25300	24520	25070	31300	29920	30470
19400	18818	19200	25400	24610	25160	31400	30010	30560
19500	18915	19300	25500	24700	25250	31500	30100	30650
19600	19012	19400	25600	24790	25340	31600	30190	30740
19700	19109	19500	25700	24880	25430	31700	30280	30830
19800	19206	19600	25800	24970	25520	31800	30370	30920
19900	19303	19700	25900	25060	25610	31900	30460	31010
20000	19400	19800	26000	25150	25700	32000	30550	31100
20100	19497	19900	26100	25240	25790	32100	30640	31190
20200	19594	20000	26200	25330	25880	32200	30730	31280
20300	19691	20100	26300	25420	25970	32300	30820	31370
20400	19788	20200	26400	25510	26060	32400	30910	31460
20500	19885	20300	26500	25600	26150	32500	31000	31550
20600	19982	20400	26600	25690	26240	32600	31090	31640
20700	20079	20500	26700	25780	26330	32700	31180	31730
20800	20176	20600	26800	25870	26420	32800	31270	31820
20900	20273	20700	26900	25960	26510	32900	31360	31910
21000	20370	20800	27000	26050	26600	33000	31450	32000

LOAN TO VALUE RATIOS FOR FHA LOANS

APPROVED NEW CONSTRUCTION—APPROVED EXISTING CONSTRUCTION, LESS THAN ONE YEAR OLD—EXISTING CONSTRUCTION OVER ONE YEAR OLD

	MAXIMUM LOANS			MAXIMUM LOANS			MAXIMUM LOANS	
Appraised Value	REGULAR 203-B	VETERAN 203-B	Appraised Value	REGULAR 203-B	VETERAN 203-B	Appraised Value	REGULAR 203-B	VETERAN 203-B
33100	31540	32090	39100	36530	37285	50200	45410	46720
33200	31630	32180	39200	36610	37370	50400	45570	46890
33300	31720	32270	39300	36690	37455	50600	45730	47060
33400	31810	32360	39400	36770	37540	50800	45890	47230
33500	31900	32450	39500	36850	37625	51000	46050	47400
33600	31990	32540	39600	36930	37710	51200	46210	47570
33700	32080	32630	39700	37010	37795	51400	46370	47740
33800	32170	32720	39800	37090	37880	51600	46530	47910
33900	32260	32810	39900	37170	37965	51800	46690	48080
34000	32350	32900	40000	37250	38050	52000	46850	48250
34100	32440	32990	40200	37410	38220	52200	47010	48420
34200	32530	33080	40400	37570	38390	52400	47170	48590
34300	32620	33170	40600	37730	38560	52600	47330	48760
34400	32710	33260	40800	37890	38730	52800	47490	48930
34500	32800	33350	41000	38050	38900	53000	47650	49100
34600	32890	33440	41200	38210	39070	53200	47810	49270
34700	32980	33530	41400	38370	39240	53400	47970	49440
34800	33070	33620	41600	38530	39410	53600	48130	49610
34900	33160	33710	41800	38690	39580	53800	48290	49780
35000	33250	33800	42000	38850	39750	54000	48450	49950
35100	33330	33885	42200	39010	39920	54200	48610	50120
35200	33410	33970	42400	39170	40090	54400	48770	50290
35300	33490	34055	42600	39330	40260	54600	48930	50460
35400	33570	34140	42800	39490	40430	54800	49090	50630
35500	33650	34225	43000	39650	40600	55000	49250	50800
35600	33730	34310	43200	39810	40770	55200	49410	50970
35700	33810	34395	43400	39970	40940	55400	49570	51140
35800	33890	34480	43600	40130	41110	55600	49730	51310
35900	33970	34565	43800	40290	41280	55800	49890	51480
36000	34050	34650	44000	40450	41450	56000	50050	51650
36100	34130	34735	44200	40610	41620	56200	50210	51820
36200	34210	34820	44400	40770	41790	56400	50370	51990
36300	34290	34905	44600	40930	41960	56600	50530	52160
36400	34370	34990	44800	41090	42130	56800	50690	52330
36500	34450	35075	45000	41250	42300	57000	50850	52500
36600	34530	35160	45200	41410	42470	57200	51010	52670
36700	34610	35245	45400	41570	42640	57400	51170	52840
36800	34690	35330	45600	41730	42810	57600	51330	53010
36900	34770	35415	45800	41890	42980	57800	51490	53180
37000	34850	35500	46000	42050	43150	58000	51650	53350
37100	34930	35585	46200	42210	43320	58200	51810	53520
37200	35010	35670	46400	42370	43490	58400	51970	53690
37300	35090	35755	46600	42530	43660	58600	52130	53860
37400	35170	35840	46800	42690	43830	58800	52290	54030
37500	35250	35925	47000	42850	44000	59000	52450	54200
37600	35330	36010	47200	43010	44170	59200	52610	54370
37700	35410	36095	47400	43170	44340	59400	52770	54540
37800	35490	36180	47600	43330	44510	59600	52930	54710
37900	35570	36265	47800	43490	44680	59800	53090	54880
38000	35650	36350	48000	43650	44850	60000	53250	55050
38100	35730	36435	48200	43810	45020	60200	53410	55220
38200	35810	36520	48400	43970	45190	60400	53570	55390
38300	35890	36605	48600	44130	45360	60600	53730	55560
38400	35970	36690	48800	44290	45530	60800	53890	55730
38500	36050	36775	49000	44450	45700	61000	54050	55900
38600	36130	36860	49200	44610	45870	61200	54210	56070
38700	36210	36945	49400	44770	46040	61400	54370	56240
38800	36290	37030	49600	44930	46210	61600	54530	56410
38900	36370	37115	49800	45090	46380	61800	54690	56580
39000	36450	37200	50000	45250	46550	62000	54850	56750

MONTHLY PAYMENTS FOR 30-YR. FHA LOANS

INCLUDING FIRST YEAR ½% MORTGAGE INSURANCE PREMIUMS

AMOUNT	INTEREST						
	10.00%	10.25%	10.50%	10.75%	11.00%	11.25%	11.50%
50	0.46	0.47	0.48	0.49	0.50	0.51	0.52
100	0.92	0.94	0.96	0.97	0.99	1.01	1.03
250	2.30	2.34	2.39	2.44	2.48	2.53	2.58
500	4.60	4.70	4.79	4.88	4.98	5.07	5.17
10000	91.96	93.86	95.66	97.56	99.46	101.36	103.26
10100	92.88	94.80	96.62	98.53	100.45	102.37	104.29
10200	93.80	95.73	97.57	99.51	101.45	103.38	105.32
10300	94.71	96.67	98.53	100.48	102.44	104.40	106.35
10400	95.63	97.61	99.48	101.46	103.43	105.41	107.39
10500	96.55	98.55	100.45	102.44	104.44	106.43	108.43
10600	97.48	99.49	101.40	103.41	105.43	107.44	109.46
10700	98.40	100.43	102.36	104.39	106.42	108.45	110.49
10800	99.31	101.37	103.31	105.36	107.41	109.47	111.52
10900	100.23	102.30	104.27	106.34	108.41	110.48	112.55
11000	101.15	103.24	105.22	107.31	109.40	111.49	113.58
11100	102.07	104.18	106.18	108.29	110.40	112.51	114.62
11200	102.99	105.12	107.14	109.27	111.40	113.52	115.65
11300	103.91	106.06	108.10	110.24	112.39	114.54	116.68
11400	104.83	107.00	109.05	111.22	113.38	115.55	117.71
11500	105.75	107.94	110.01	112.19	114.38	116.56	118.75
11600	106.67	108.87	110.96	113.16	115.37	117.57	119.78
11700	107.59	109.81	111.92	114.14	116.36	118.59	120.82
11800	108.50	110.75	112.88	115.12	117.36	119.61	121.85
11900	109.43	111.69	113.84	116.10	118.36	120.62	122.88
12000	110.35	112.63	114.79	117.07	119.35	121.63	123.91
12100	111.27	113.57	115.75	118.04	120.34	122.64	124.94
12200	112.19	114.50	116.70	119.02	121.34	123.65	125.97
12300	113.10	115.44	117.66	119.99	122.33	124.67	127.01
12400	114.02	116.38	118.61	120.98	123.33	125.69	128.04
12500	114.95	117.33	119.58	121.95	124.33	126.70	129.08
12600	115.87	118.26	120.53	122.92	125.32	127.71	130.11
12700	116.79	119.20	121.49	123.90	126.31	128.72	131.14
12800	117.70	120.14	122.44	124.87	127.30	129.74	132.17
12900	118.62	121.07	123.40	125.85	128.30	130.75	133.21
13000	119.54	122.01	124.35	126.82	129.30	131.77	134.24
13100	120.46	122.96	125.32	127.80	130.29	132.78	135.27
13200	121.39	123.89	126.27	128.78	131.29	133.79	136.30
13300	122.30	124.83	127.23	129.75	132.28	134.81	137.33
13400	123.22	125.77	128.18	130.73	133.27	135.82	138.36
13500	124.14	126.71	129.14	131.70	134.27	136.83	139.40
13600	125.06	127.64	130.09	132.67	135.26	137.85	140.44
13700	125.98	128.58	131.06	133.66	136.26	138.86	141.47
13800	126.90	129.53	132.01	134.63	137.25	139.88	142.50
13900	127.82	130.46	132.97	135.61	138.25	140.89	143.53
14000	128.74	131.40	133.92	136.58	139.24	141.90	144.56
14100	129.66	132.34	134.88	137.55	140.23	142.91	145.59
14200	130.58	133.27	135.83	138.53	141.23	143.93	146.63
14300	131.49	134.21	136.79	139.51	142.23	144.95	147.66
14400	132.41	135.16	137.75	140.49	143.22	145.96	148.69
14500	133.34	136.10	138.71	141.46	144.22	146.97	149.73
14600	134.26	137.03	139.66	142.43	145.21	147.98	150.76
14700	135.18	137.97	140.62	143.41	146.20	148.99	151.79
14800	136.09	138.91	141.57	144.38	147.19	150.01	152.83
14900	137.01	139.84	142.53	145.36	148.20	151.03	153.86
15000	137.93	140.78	143.49	146.34	149.19	152.04	154.89
15100	138.86	141.73	144.45	147.31	150.18	153.05	155.92
15200	139.78	142.66	145.40	148.29	151.18	154.06	156.95
15300	140.69	143.60	146.36	149.26	152.17	155.08	157.98
15400	141.61	144.54	147.31	150.24	153.16	156.09	159.01
15500	142.53	145.48	148.27	151.21	154.17	157.11	160.06

MONTHLY PAYMENTS FOR 30-YR. FHA LOANS

INCLUDING FIRST YEAR ½% MORTGAGE INSURANCE PREMIUMS

AMOUNT	INTEREST						
	10.00%	10.25%	10.50%	10.75%	11.00%	11.25%	11.50%
15600	143.45	146.41	149.23	152.19	155.16	158.12	161.09
15700	144.38	147.36	150.19	153.17	156.15	159.13	162.12
15800	145.29	148.30	151.14	154.14	157.14	160.15	163.15
15900	146.21	149.23	152.10	155.12	158.14	161.16	164.18
16000	147.13	150.17	153.05	156.09	159.13	162.17	165.21
16100	148.05	151.11	154.01	157.06	160.12	163.19	166.25
16200	148.97	152.04	154.96	158.05	161.13	164.20	167.28
16300	149.88	152.99	155.93	159.02	162.12	165.22	168.31
16400	150.81	153.93	156.88	160.00	163.11	166.23	169.34
16500	151.73	154.87	157.84	160.97	164.11	167.24	170.38
16600	152.65	155.80	158.79	161.94	165.10	168.25	171.41
16700	153.57	156.74	159.75	162.92	166.09	169.26	172.45
16800	154.48	157.68	160.70	163.89	167.09	170.29	173.48
16900	155.40	158.61	161.67	164.88	168.09	171.30	174.51
17000	156.33	159.56	162.62	165.85	169.08	172.31	175.54
17100	157.25	160.50	163.58	166.82	170.07	173.32	176.57
17200	158.17	161.43	164.53	167.80	171.07	174.33	177.60
17300	159.08	162.37	165.49	168.77	172.06	175.35	178.63
17400	160.00	163.31	166.44	169.75	173.06	176.37	179.67
17500	160.92	164.25	167.41	170.73	174.06	177.38	180.71
17600	161.84	165.19	168.36	171.70	175.05	178.39	181.74
17700	162.77	166.13	169.32	172.68	176.04	179.40	182.77
17800	163.68	167.07	170.27	173.65	177.03	180.42	183.80
17900	164.60	168.00	171.23	174.63	178.03	181.43	184.83
18000	165.52	168.94	172.18	175.60	179.02	182.45	185.87
18100	166.44	169.88	173.14	176.58	180.02	183.46	186.90
18200	167.36	170.81	174.10	177.56	181.02	184.47	187.93
18300	168.28	171.76	175.06	178.53	182.01	185.49	188.96
18400	169.20	172.70	176.01	179.51	183.00	186.50	189.99
18500	170.12	173.64	176.97	180.48	184.00	187.51	191.03
18600	171.04	174.57	177.92	181.45	184.99	188.52	192.07
18700	171.96	175.51	178.88	182.43	185.99	189.54	193.10
18800	172.87	176.45	179.84	183.41	186.98	190.56	194.13
18900	173.80	177.39	180.80	184.39	187.98	191.57	195.16
19000	174.72	178.33	181.75	185.36	188.97	192.58	196.19
19100	175.64	179.27	182.71	186.33	189.96	193.59	197.22
19200	176.56	180.20	183.66	187.31	190.96	194.60	198.26
19300	177.47	181.14	184.62	188.28	191.96	195.63	199.29
19400	178.39	182.08	185.58	189.27	192.95	196.64	200.32
19500	179.31	183.03	186.54	190.24	193.95	197.65	201.36
19600	180.24	183.96	187.49	191.21	194.94	198.66	202.39
19700	181.16	184.90	188.45	192.19	195.93	199.67	203.42
19800	182.07	185.84	189.40	193.16	196.92	200.69	204.45
19900	182.99	186.77	190.36	194.14	197.92	201.71	205.49
20000	183.91	187.71	191.31	195.12	198.92	202.72	206.52
20100	184.83	188.65	192.28	196.09	199.91	203.73	207.55
20200	185.76	189.59	193.23	197.07	200.91	204.74	208.58
20300	186.67	190.53	194.19	198.04	201.90	205.76	209.61
20400	187.59	191.47	195.14	199.02	202.89	206.77	210.64
20500	188.51	192.41	196.10	199.99	203.89	207.78	211.69
20600	189.43	193.34	197.05	200.96	204.89	208.80	212.72
20700	190.35	194.28	198.02	201.95	205.88	209.81	213.75
20800	191.26	195.23	198.97	202.92	206.87	210.83	214.78
20900	192.19	196.16	199.93	203.90	207.87	211.84	215.81
21000	193.11	197.10	200.88	204.87	208.86	212.85	216.84
21100	194.03	198.04	201.84	205.84	209.85	213.86	217.88
21200	194.95	198.97	202.79	206.82	210.86	214.88	218.91
21300	195.86	199.91	203.75	207.80	211.85	215.90	219.94
21400	196.78	200.86	204.71	208.78	212.84	216.91	220.97
21500	197.71	201.80	205.67	209.75	213.84	217.92	222.01

MONTHLY PAYMENTS FOR 30-YR. FHA LOANS

INCLUDING FIRST YEAR ½% MORTGAGE INSURANCE PREMIUMS

AMOUNT	INTEREST						
	10.00%	10.25%	10.50%	10.75%	11.00%	11.25%	11.50%
21600	198.63	202.73	206.62	210.72	214.83	218.93	223.04
21700	199.55	203.67	207.58	211.70	215.82	219.94	224.07
21800	200.46	204.61	208.53	212.67	216.81	220.97	225.11
21900	201.38	205.54	209.49	213.66	217.82	221.98	226.14
22000	202.30	206.48	210.45	214.63	218.81	222.99	227.17
22100	203.23	207.43	211.41	215.60	219.80	224.00	228.20
22200	204.15	208.36	212.36	216.58	220.80	225.01	229.23
22300	205.06	209.30	213.32	217.55	221.79	226.03	230.26
22400	205.98	210.24	214.27	218.53	222.78	227.05	231.30
22500	206.90	211.18	215.23	219.50	223.79	228.06	232.34
22600	207.82	212.11	216.19	220.48	224.78	229.07	233.37
22700	208.74	213.06	217.15	221.46	225.77	230.08	234.40
22800	209.66	214.00	218.10	222.43	226.76	231.10	235.43
22900	210.58	214.93	219.06	223.41	227.76	232.11	236.46
23000	211.50	215.87	220.01	224.38	228.75	233.12	237.50
23100	212.42	216.81	220.97	225.35	229.75	234.14	238.53
23200	213.34	217.74	221.92	226.34	230.75	235.15	239.56
23300	214.25	218.68	222.89	227.31	231.74	236.17	240.59
23400	215.18	219.63	223.84	228.29	232.73	237.18	241.62
23500	216.10	220.57	224.80	229.26	233.73	238.19	242.66
23600	217.02	221.50	225.75	230.23	234.72	239.20	243.70
23700	217.94	222.44	226.71	231.21	235.71	240.22	244.73
23800	218.85	223.38	227.66	232.19	236.71	241.24	245.76
23900	219.77	224.31	228.63	233.17	237.71	242.25	246.79
24000	220.69	225.26	229.58	234.14	238.70	243.26	247.82
24100	221.62	226.20	230.54	235.11	239.69	244.27	248.85
24200	222.54	227.13	231.49	236.09	240.69	245.28	249.88
24300	223.45	228.07	232.45	237.06	241.68	246.31	250.92
24400	224.37	229.01	233.40	238.04	242.68	247.32	251.95
24500	225.29	229.95	234.37	239.02	243.68	248.33	252.99
24600	226.21	230.89	235.32	239.99	244.67	249.34	254.02
24700	227.14	231.83	236.28	240.97	245.66	250.35	255.05
24800	228.05	232.77	237.23	241.94	246.65	251.37	256.08
24900	228.97	233.70	238.19	242.92	247.65	252.38	257.12
25000	229.89	234.64	239.14	243.89	248.65	253.40	258.15
25100	230.81	235.58	240.10	244.87	249.64	254.41	259.18
25200	231.73	236.51	241.06	245.85	250.64	255.42	260.21
25300	232.65	237.46	242.02	246.82	251.63	256.44	261.24
25400	233.57	238.40	242.97	247.80	252.62	257.45	262.27
25500	234.49	239.34	243.93	248.77	253.62	258.46	263.32
25600	235.41	240.27	244.88	249.74	254.61	259.48	264.35
25700	236.33	241.21	245.84	250.73	255.61	260.49	265.38
25800	237.24	242.15	246.80	251.70	256.60	261.51	266.41
25900	238.16	243.09	247.76	252.68	257.60	262.52	267.44
26000	239.09	244.03	248.71	253.65	258.59	263.53	268.47
26100	240.01	244.97	249.67	254.62	259.58	264.54	269.50
26200	240.93	245.90	250.62	255.60	260.58	265.56	270.54
26300	241.84	246.84	251.58	256.57	261.58	266.58	271.57
26400	242.76	247.78	252.54	257.56	262.57	267.59	272.60
26500	243.68	248.72	253.50	258.53	263.57	268.60	273.64
26600	244.61	249.66	254.45	259.50	264.56	269.61	274.67
26700	245.53	250.60	255.41	260.48	265.55	270.62	275.70
26800	246.44	251.54	256.36	261.45	266.54	271.64	276.74
26900	247.36	252.47	257.32	262.43	267.55	272.66	277.77
27000	248.28	253.41	258.27	263.41	268.54	273.67	278.80
27100	249.20	254.35	259.24	264.38	269.53	274.68	279.83
27200	250.12	255.29	260.19	265.36	270.53	275.69	280.86
27300	251.04	256.23	261.15	266.33	271.52	276.71	281.89
27400	251.96	257.17	262.10	267.31	272.51	277.72	282.93
27500	252.88	258.11	263.06	268.28	273.51	278.74	283.97

MONTHLY PAYMENTS FOR 30-YR. FHA LOANS

INCLUDING FIRST YEAR ½% MORTGAGE INSURANCE PREMIUMS

AMOUNT	INTEREST						
	10.00%	10.25%	10.50%	10.75%	11.00%	11.25%	11.50%
27600	253.80	259.04	264.01	269.26	274.51	279.75	285.00
27700	254.72	259.98	264.98	270.24	275.50	280.76	286.03
27800	255.63	260.93	265.93	271.21	276.49	281.78	287.06
27900	256.56	261.86	266.89	272.19	277.49	282.79	288.09
28000	257.48	262.80	267.84	273.16	278.48	283.80	289.13
28100	258.40	263.74	268.80	274.13	279.47	284.82	290.16
28200	259.32	264.67	269.75	275.11	280.48	285.83	291.19
28300	260.23	265.61	270.71	276.09	281.47	286.85	292.22
28400	261.15	266.55	271.67	277.07	282.46	287.86	293.25
28500	262.08	267.50	272.63	278.04	283.46	288.87	294.29
28600	263.00	268.43	273.58	279.01	284.45	289.88	295.32
28700	263.92	269.37	274.54	279.99	285.44	290.89	296.36
28800	264.83	270.31	275.49	280.96	286.44	291.92	297.39
28900	265.75	271.24	276.45	281.95	287.44	292.93	298.42
29000	266.67	272.18	277.41	282.92	288.43	293.94	299.45
29100	267.59	273.13	278.37	283.89	289.42	294.95	300.48
29200	268.52	274.06	279.32	284.87	290.42	295.96	301.51
29300	269.43	275.00	280.28	285.84	291.41	296.98	302.55
29400	270.35	275.94	281.23	286.82	292.40	298.00	303.58
29500	271.27	276.88	282.19	287.80	293.41	299.01	304.62
29600	272.19	277.81	283.15	288.77	294.40	300.02	305.65
29700	273.11	278.75	284.11	289.75	295.39	301.03	306.68
29800	274.03	279.70	285.06	290.72	296.38	302.05	307.71
29900	274.95	280.63	286.02	291.70	297.38	303.06	308.75
30000	275.87	281.57	286.97	292.67	298.37	304.08	309.78
30100	276.79	282.51	287.93	293.64	299.37	305.09	310.81
30200	277.71	283.44	288.88	294.63	300.37	306.10	311.84
30300	278.62	284.38	289.85	295.60	301.36	307.12	312.87
30400	279.54	285.33	290.80	296.58	302.35	308.13	313.90
30500	280.47	286.27	291.76	297.55	303.35	309.14	314.94
30600	281.39	287.20	292.71	298.52	304.34	310.16	315.98
30700	282.31	288.14	293.67	299.50	305.34	311.17	317.01
30800	283.22	289.08	294.62	300.48	306.33	312.19	318.04
30900	284.14	290.01	295.59	301.46	307.33	313.20	319.07
31000	285.06	290.96	296.54	302.43	308.32	314.21	320.10
31100	285.99	291.90	297.50	303.40	309.31	315.22	321.13
31200	286.91	292.83	298.45	304.38	310.31	316.23	322.17
31300	287.82	293.77	299.41	305.35	311.30	317.26	323.20
31400	288.74	294.71	300.36	306.34	312.30	318.27	324.23
31500	289.66	295.65	301.33	307.31	313.30	319.28	325.27
31600	290.58	296.58	302.28	308.28	314.29	320.29	326.30
31700	291.50	297.53	303.24	309.26	315.28	321.30	327.33
31800	292.42	298.47	304.19	310.23	316.27	322.32	328.37
31900	293.34	299.40	305.15	311.21	317.27	323.34	329.40
32000	294.26	300.34	306.10	312.18	318.27	324.35	330.43
32100	295.18	301.28	307.06	313.16	319.26	325.36	331.46
32200	296.10	302.21	308.02	314.14	320.26	326.37	332.49
32300	297.01	303.16	308.98	315.11	321.25	327.39	333.52
32400	297.94	304.10	309.93	316.09	322.24	328.40	334.55
32500	298.86	305.04	310.89	317.06	323.24	329.42	335.60
32600	299.78	305.97	311.84	318.03	324.24	330.43	336.63
32700	300.70	306.91	312.80	319.02	325.23	331.44	337.66
32800	301.61	307.85	313.76	319.99	326.22	332.46	338.69
32900	302.53	308.79	314.72	320.97	327.22	333.47	339.72
33000	303.46	309.73	315.67	321.94	328.21	334.48	340.75
33100	304.38	310.67	316.63	322.91	329.20	335.49	341.79
33200	305.30	311.60	317.58	323.89	330.20	336.51	342.82
33300	306.21	312.54	318.54	324.86	331.20	337.53	343.85
33400	307.13	313.48	319.50	325.85	332.19	338.54	344.88
33500	308.05	314.42	320.46	326.82	333.19	339.55	345.92

MONTHLY PAYMENTS FOR 30-YR. FHA LOANS

INCLUDING FIRST YEAR ½% MORTGAGE INSURANCE PREMIUMS

AMOUNT	INTEREST						
	10.00%	10.25%	10.50%	10.75%	11.00%	11.25%	11.50%
33600	308.97	315.36	321.41	327.79	334.18	340.56	346.95
33700	309.90	316.30	322.37	328.77	335.17	341.57	347.99
33800	310.81	317.24	323.32	329.74	336.16	342.60	349.02
33900	311.73	318.17	324.28	330.72	337.17	343.61	350.05
34000	312.65	319.11	325.23	331.70	338.16	344.62	351.08
34100	313.57	320.05	326.20	332.67	339.15	345.63	352.11
34200	314.49	320.99	327.15	333.65	340.15	346.64	353.14
34300	315.41	321.93	328.11	334.62	341.14	347.66	354.18
34400	316.33	322.87	329.06	335.60	342.13	348.68	355.21
34500	317.25	323.81	330.02	336.57	343.14	349.69	356.25
34600	318.17	324.74	330.97	337.55	344.13	350.70	357.28
34700	319.09	325.68	331.94	338.53	345.12	351.71	358.31
34800	320.00	326.62	332.89	339.50	346.11	352.73	359.34
34900	320.92	327.56	333.85	340.48	347.11	353.74	360.37
35000	321.85	328.50	334.80	341.45	348.10	354.75	361.41
35100	322.77	329.44	335.76	342.42	349.09	355.77	362.44
35200	323.69	330.37	336.71	343.40	350.10	356.78	363.47
35300	324.60	331.31	337.68	344.38	351.09	357.80	364.50
35400	325.52	332.25	338.63	345.36	352.08	358.81	365.53
35500	326.44	333.20	339.59	346.33	353.08	359.82	366.57
35600	327.37	334.13	340.54	347.30	354.07	360.83	367.61
35700	328.29	335.07	341.50	348.28	355.06	361.85	368.64
35800	329.20	336.01	342.45	349.25	356.06	362.87	369.67
35900	330.12	336.94	343.41	350.24	357.06	363.88	370.70
36000	331.04	337.88	344.37	351.21	358.05	364.89	371.73
36100	331.96	338.83	345.33	352.18	359.04	365.90	372.76
36200	332.89	339.76	346.28	353.16	360.04	366.91	373.80
36300	333.80	340.70	347.24	354.13	361.03	367.94	374.83
36400	334.72	341.64	348.19	355.11	362.03	368.95	375.86
36500	335.64	342.58	349.15	356.09	363.03	369.96	376.90
36600	336.56	343.51	350.11	357.06	364.02	370.97	377.93
36700	337.48	344.45	351.07	358.04	365.01	371.98	378.96
36800	338.39	345.40	352.02	359.01	366.00	373.00	379.99
36900	339.32	346.33	352.98	359.99	367.00	374.01	381.03
37000	340.24	347.27	353.93	360.96	367.99	375.03	382.06
37100	341.16	348.21	354.89	361.93	368.99	376.04	383.09
37200	342.08	349.14	355.84	362.92	369.99	377.05	384.12
37300	342.99	350.08	356.81	363.89	370.98	378.07	385.15
37400	343.91	351.03	357.76	364.87	371.97	379.08	386.18
37500	344.84	351.97	358.72	365.84	372.97	380.09	387.23
37600	345.76	352.90	359.67	366.81	373.96	381.11	388.26
37700	346.68	353.84	360.63	367.79	374.96	382.12	389.29
37800	347.59	354.78	361.58	368.77	375.95	383.14	390.32
37900	348.51	355.71	362.55	369.75	376.95	384.15	391.35
38000	349.43	356.65	363.50	370.72	377.94	385.16	392.38
38100	350.35	357.60	364.46	371.69	378.93	386.17	393.42
38200	351.28	358.53	365.41	372.67	379.93	387.19	394.45
38300	352.19	359.47	366.37	373.64	380.93	388.21	395.48
38400	353.11	360.41	367.32	374.63	381.92	389.22	396.51
38500	354.03	361.35	368.29	375.60	382.92	390.23	397.55
38600	354.95	362.28	369.24	376.57	383.91	391.24	398.58
38700	355.87	363.23	370.20	377.55	384.90	392.25	399.62
38800	356.79	364.17	371.15	378.52	385.89	393.28	400.65
38900	357.71	365.10	372.11	379.50	386.89	394.29	401.68
39000	358.63	366.04	373.06	380.47	387.89	395.30	402.71
39100	359.55	366.98	374.02	381.45	388.88	396.31	403.74
39200	360.47	367.91	374.98	382.43	389.88	397.32	404.77
39300	361.38	368.86	375.94	383.40	390.87	398.34	405.80
39400	362.31	369.80	376.89	384.38	391.86	399.35	406.84
39500	363.23	370.74	377.85	385.35	392.86	400.37	407.88

MONTHLY PAYMENTS FOR 30-YR. FHA LOANS

INCLUDING FIRST YEAR ½% MORTGAGE INSURANCE PREMIUMS

AMOUNT	INTEREST						
	10.00%	10.25%	10.50%	10.75%	11.00%	11.25%	11.50%
39600	364.15	371.67	378.80	386.32	393.86	401.38	408.91
39700	365.07	372.61	379.76	387.31	394.85	402.39	409.94
39800	365.98	373.55	380.72	388.28	395.84	403.41	410.97
39900	366.90	374.48	381.68	389.26	396.84	404.42	412.00
40000	367.82	375.43	382.63	390.23	397.83	405.43	413.04
40100	368.75	376.37	383.59	391.20	398.82	406.45	414.07
40200	369.67	377.30	384.54	392.18	399.83	407.46	415.10
40300	370.58	378.24	385.50	393.16	400.82	408.48	416.13
40400	371.50	379.18	386.46	394.14	401.81	409.49	417.16
40500	372.42	380.12	387.42	395.11	402.81	410.50	418.20
40600	373.34	381.06	388.37	396.08	403.80	411.51	419.24
40700	374.27	382.00	389.33	397.06	404.79	412.53	420.27
40800	375.18	382.94	390.28	398.03	405.78	413.55	421.30
40900	376.10	383.87	391.24	399.01	406.79	414.56	422.33
41000	377.02	384.81	392.19	399.99	407.78	415.57	423.36
41100	377.94	385.75	393.16	400.96	408.77	416.58	424.39
41200	378.86	386.69	394.11	401.94	409.77	417.59	425.42
41300	379.77	387.63	395.07	402.91	410.76	418.61	426.46
41400	380.70	388.57	396.02	403.89	411.75	419.63	427.49
41500	381.62	389.51	396.98	404.86	412.76	420.64	428.53
41600	382.54	390.44	397.93	405.84	413.75	421.65	429.56
41700	383.46	391.38	398.90	406.82	414.74	422.66	430.59
41800	384.37	392.32	399.85	407.79	415.73	423.68	431.62
41900	385.29	393.26	400.81	408.77	416.73	424.69	432.66
42000	386.22	394.20	401.76	409.74	417.72	425.71	433.69
42100	387.14	395.14	402.72	410.71	418.72	426.72	434.72
42200	388.06	396.07	403.67	411.70	419.72	427.73	435.75
42300	388.97	397.01	404.64	412.67	420.71	428.75	436.78
42400	389.89	397.95	405.59	413.65	421.70	429.76	437.81
42500	390.81	398.90	406.55	414.62	422.70	430.77	438.86
42600	391.74	399.83	407.50	415.59	423.69	431.79	439.89
42700	392.66	400.77	408.46	416.57	424.69	432.80	440.92
42800	393.57	401.71	409.41	417.54	425.68	433.82	441.95
42900	394.49	402.64	410.37	418.53	426.68	434.83	442.98
43000	395.41	403.58	411.33	419.50	427.67	435.84	444.01
43200	397.25	405.46	413.24	421.45	429.66	437.86	446.08
43400	399.09	407.34	415.15	423.40	431.65	439.90	448.14
43600	400.93	409.21	417.07	425.35	433.64	441.92	450.21
43800	402.76	411.10	418.98	427.30	435.62	443.95	452.28
44000	404.61	412.97	420.89	429.25	437.62	445.98	454.34
44200	406.45	414.84	422.80	431.21	439.61	448.00	456.40
44400	408.28	416.73	424.72	433.16	441.59	450.03	458.47
44600	410.13	418.60	426.63	435.10	443.59	452.06	460.54
44800	411.96	420.48	428.54	437.06	445.57	454.09	462.60
45000	413.80	422.35	430.46	439.01	447.56	456.11	464.67
45200	415.65	424.23	432.37	440.96	449.55	458.14	466.73
45400	417.48	426.11	434.28	442.92	451.54	460.17	468.79
45600	419.32	427.98	436.20	444.86	453.53	462.19	470.86
45800	421.16	429.87	438.11	446.81	455.51	464.23	472.93
46000	423.00	431.74	440.02	448.77	457.51	466.25	474.99
46200	424.84	433.61	441.94	450.72	459.50	468.27	477.05
46400	426.67	435.50	443.85	452.67	461.48	470.31	479.12
46600	428.52	437.37	445.76	454.61	463.48	472.33	481.19
46800	430.35	439.25	447.68	456.57	465.46	474.36	483.25
47000	432.19	441.13	449.59	458.52	467.45	476.38	485.32
47200	434.04	443.00	451.50	460.47	469.45	478.41	487.38
47400	435.87	444.88	453.42	462.43	471.43	480.44	489.44
47600	437.71	446.76	455.33	464.37	473.42	482.46	491.52
47800	439.55	448.64	457.24	466.32	475.41	484.50	493.58
48000	441.39	450.51	459.15	468.28	477.40	486.52	495.64

MONTHLY PAYMENTS FOR 30-YR. FHA LOANS

INCLUDING FIRST YEAR ½% MORTGAGE INSURANCE PREMIUMS

AMOUNT	INTEREST						
	10.00%	10.25%	10.50%	10.75%	11.00%	11.25%	11.50%
48200	443.23	452.38	461.07	470.23	479.39	488.54	497.71
48400	445.07	454.27	462.98	472.18	481.38	490.58	499.77
48600	446.91	456.14	464.89	474.13	483.37	492.60	501.84
48800	448.74	458.02	466.81	476.08	485.35	494.63	503.91
49000	450.59	459.90	468.72	478.03	487.34	496.66	505.97
49200	452.43	461.77	470.63	479.99	489.34	498.68	508.03
49400	454.26	463.65	472.55	481.94	491.32	500.71	510.10
49600	456.10	465.53	474.46	483.88	493.31	502.74	512.17
49800	457.94	467.41	476.37	485.84	495.30	504.77	514.23
50000	459.78	469.28	478.29	487.79	497.29	506.79	516.29
50200	461.62	471.16	480.20	489.74	499.28	508.82	518.36
50400	463.46	473.04	482.11	491.69	501.27	510.85	520.42
50600	465.30	474.91	484.03	493.64	503.26	512.87	522.49
50800	467.13	476.80	485.94	495.59	505.24	514.91	524.56
51000	468.98	478.67	487.85	497.54	507.24	516.93	526.62
51200	470.82	480.54	489.77	499.50	509.23	518.95	528.68
51400	472.65	482.42	491.68	501.45	511.21	520.98	530.75
51600	474.50	484.30	493.59	503.39	513.21	523.01	532.82
51800	476.33	486.18	495.50	505.35	515.19	525.04	534.88
52000	478.17	488.05	497.42	507.30	517.18	527.06	536.95
52200	480.02	489.93	499.33	509.25	519.18	529.09	539.01
52400	481.85	491.81	501.24	511.21	521.16	531.12	541.07
52600	483.69	493.68	503.16	513.15	523.15	533.14	543.15
52800	485.52	495.57	505.07	515.10	525.13	535.18	545.21
53000	487.37	497.44	506.98	517.06	527.13	537.20	547.27
53200	489.21	499.31	508.90	519.01	529.12	539.22	549.34
53400	491.04	501.20	510.81	520.96	531.10	541.26	551.40
53600	492.89	503.07	512.72	522.91	533.10	543.28	553.47
53800	494.72	504.95	514.64	524.86	535.08	545.31	555.54
54000	496.56	506.83	516.55	526.81	537.07	547.34	557.60
54200	498.41	508.70	518.46	528.76	539.07	549.36	559.66
54400	500.24	510.58	520.38	530.72	541.05	551.39	561.72
54600	502.08	512.45	522.29	532.66	543.04	553.42	563.80
54800	503.92	514.34	524.20	534.61	545.03	555.45	565.86
55000	505.76	516.21	526.11	536.57	547.02	557.47	567.92
55200	507.60	518.08	528.03	538.52	549.01	559.49	569.99
55400	509.44	519.97	529.94	540.47	551.00	561.53	572.05
55600	511.28	521.84	531.85	542.42	552.99	563.55	574.12
55800	513.11	523.72	533.77	544.37	554.97	565.58	576.19
56000	514.95	525.60	535.68	546.32	556.97	567.61	578.25
56200	516.80	527.47	537.59	548.28	558.96	569.63	580.31
56400	518.63	529.35	539.51	550.23	560.94	571.66	582.38
56600	520.47	531.23	541.42	552.17	562.93	573.69	584.45
56800	522.31	533.11	543.33	554.13	564.92	575.72	586.51
57000	524.15	534.98	545.25	556.08	566.91	577.74	588.58
57200	525.99	536.86	547.16	558.03	568.90	579.77	590.64
57400	527.83	538.74	549.07	559.98	570.89	581.80	592.70
57600	529.67	540.61	550.99	561.93	572.88	583.82	594.78
57800	531.50	542.49	552.90	563.88	574.86	585.86	596.84
58000	533.35	544.37	554.81	565.83	576.86	587.88	598.90
58200	535.19	546.24	556.73	567.79	578.85	589.90	600.97
58400	537.02	548.12	558.64	569.74	580.83	591.94	603.03
58600	538.86	550.00	560.55	571.68	582.83	593.96	605.10
58800	540.70	551.88	562.46	573.64	584.81	595.99	607.16
59000	542.54	553.75	564.38	575.59	586.80	598.02	609.23
59200	544.38	555.63	566.29	577.54	588.80	600.04	611.29
59400	546.22	557.51	568.20	579.50	590.78	602.07	613.35
59600	548.06	559.38	570.12	581.44	592.77	604.09	615.43
59800	549.89	561.27	572.03	583.39	594.76	606.13	617.49
60000	551.74	563.14	573.94	585.35	596.75	608.15	619.55

MONTHLY PAYMENTS FOR 30-YR. FHA LOANS

INCLUDING FIRST YEAR ½% MORTGAGE INSURANCE PREMIUMS

AMOUNT	INTEREST						
	10.00%	10.25%	10.50%	10.75%	11.00%	11.25%	11.50%
60200	553.58	565.01	575.86	587.30	598.74	610.17	621.62
60400	555.41	566.90	577.77	589.25	600.72	612.21	623.68
60600	557.26	568.77	579.68	591.20	602.72	614.23	625.75
60800	559.09	570.65	581.60	593.15	604.70	616.26	627.82
61000	560.93	572.53	583.51	595.10	606.69	618.29	629.88
61200	562.78	574.40	585.42	597.05	608.69	620.31	631.94
61400	564.61	576.28	587.34	599.01	610.67	622.34	634.01
61600	566.45	578.15	589.25	600.95	612.66	624.37	636.08
61800	568.28	580.04	591.16	602.90	614.65	626.40	638.14
62000	570.13	581.91	593.07	604.86	616.64	628.42	640.21
62200	571.97	583.78	594.99	606.81	618.63	630.45	642.27
62400	573.80	585.67	596.90	608.76	620.62	632.48	644.33
62600	575.65	587.54	598.81	610.71	622.61	634.50	646.40
62800	577.48	589.42	600.73	612.66	624.59	636.54	648.47
63000	579.32	591.30	602.64	614.61	626.59	638.56	650.53
63200	581.17	593.17	604.55	616.57	628.58	640.58	652.59
63400	583.00	595.05	606.47	618.52	630.56	642.61	654.66
63600	584.84	596.93	608.38	620.46	632.56	644.64	656.73
63800	586.68	598.81	610.29	622.42	634.54	646.67	658.79
64000	588.52	600.68	612.21	624.37	636.53	648.69	660.86
64200	590.36	602.56	614.12	626.32	638.52	650.72	662.92
64400	592.20	604.44	616.03	628.28	640.51	652.75	664.98
64600	594.04	606.31	617.95	630.22	642.50	654.77	667.06
64800	595.87	608.19	619.86	632.17	644.48	656.81	669.12
65000	597.71	610.07	621.77	634.12	646.48	658.83	671.18
65200	599.56	611.94	623.69	636.08	648.47	660.85	673.25
65400	601.39	613.82	625.60	638.03	650.45	662.89	675.31
65600	603.23	615.70	627.51	639.97	652.45	664.91	677.38
65800	605.07	617.58	629.42	641.93	654.43	666.94	679.45
66000	606.91	619.45	631.34	643.88	656.42	668.97	681.51
66200	608.75	621.33	633.25	645.83	658.42	670.99	683.57
66400	610.59	623.21	635.16	647.79	660.40	673.02	685.64
66600	612.43	625.08	637.08	649.73	662.39	675.05	687.71
66800	614.26	626.97	638.99	651.68	664.38	677.08	689.77
67000	616.11	628.84	640.90	653.64	666.37	679.10	691.83
67200	617.95	630.71	642.82	655.59	668.36	681.13	693.90
67400	619.78	632.60	644.73	657.54	670.35	683.16	695.96
67600	621.63	634.47	646.64	659.49	672.34	685.18	698.03
67800	623.46	636.35	648.56	661.44	674.32	687.21	700.10
68000	625.30	638.22	650.47	663.39	676.31	689.24	702.16
68200	627.14	640.10	652.38	665.35	678.31	691.26	704.22
68400	628.98	641.98	654.30	667.30	680.29	693.29	706.29
68600	630.82	643.85	656.21	669.24	682.28	695.32	708.36
68800	632.65	645.74	658.12	671.19	684.27	697.35	710.42
69000	634.50	647.61	660.03	673.15	686.26	699.37	712.49
69200	636.34	649.48	661.95	675.10	688.25	701.40	714.55
69400	638.17	651.37	663.86	677.05	690.24	703.43	716.61
69600	640.02	653.24	665.77	679.00	692.23	705.45	718.69
69800	641.85	655.12	667.69	680.95	694.21	707.49	720.75
70000	643.69	657.00	669.60	682.90	696.21	709.51	722.81
70200	645.54	658.87	671.51	684.86	698.20	711.53	724.88
70400	647.37	660.75	673.43	686.81	700.18	713.57	726.94
70600	649.21	662.63	675.34	688.75	702.18	715.59	729.01
70800	651.05	664.51	677.25	690.71	704.16	717.62	731.08
71000	652.89	666.38	679.17	692.66	706.15	719.65	733.14
71200	654.73	668.25	681.08	694.61	708.15	721.67	735.20
71400	656.56	670.14	682.99	696.57	710.13	723.70	737.26
71600	658.41	672.01	684.91	698.51	712.12	725.72	739.34
71800	660.24	673.89	686.82	700.46	714.11	727.76	741.40
72000	662.08	675.77	688.73	702.42	716.10	729.78	743.46

MONTHLY PAYMENTS FOR 30-YR. FHA LOANS

INCLUDING FIRST YEAR ½% MORTGAGE INSURANCE PREMIUMS

AMOUNT	INTEREST						
	11.75%	12.00%	12.25%	12.50%	12.75%	13.00%	13.25%
50	0.53	0.53	0.54	0.55	0.56	0.57	0.58
100	1.05	1.07	1.09	1.11	1.13	1.15	1.17
250	2.63	2.67	2.72	2.77	2.82	2.87	2.92
500	5.26	5.36	5.45	5.55	5.65	5.75	5.84
10000	105.16	107.06	108.96	110.96	112.86	114.86	116.76
10100	106.21	108.13	110.05	112.07	113.99	116.01	117.93
10200	107.26	109.20	111.14	113.18	115.11	117.15	119.09
10300	108.31	110.27	112.23	114.29	116.25	118.31	120.27
10400	109.37	111.35	113.32	115.40	117.38	119.46	121.43
10500	110.42	112.42	114.41	116.51	118.51	120.61	122.60
10600	111.47	113.48	115.50	117.62	119.63	121.75	123.77
10700	112.52	114.55	116.59	118.73	120.76	122.90	124.93
10800	113.57	115.62	117.67	119.83	121.89	124.05	126.10
10900	114.62	116.69	118.76	120.94	123.02	125.20	127.27
11000	115.68	117.77	119.86	122.06	124.15	126.35	128.44
11100	116.73	118.84	120.95	123.17	125.28	127.50	129.61
11200	117.78	119.91	122.04	124.28	126.40	128.64	130.77
11300	118.83	120.98	123.12	125.38	127.53	129.79	131.94
11400	119.88	122.05	124.21	126.49	128.66	130.94	133.10
11500	120.93	123.12	125.30	127.60	129.79	132.10	134.28
11600	121.98	124.19	126.40	128.72	130.92	133.24	135.45
11700	123.04	125.26	127.49	129.83	132.05	134.39	136.61
11800	124.09	126.33	128.57	130.93	133.18	135.54	137.78
11900	125.14	127.40	129.66	132.04	134.30	136.68	138.94
12000	126.19	128.47	130.75	133.15	135.43	137.83	140.11
12100	127.24	129.54	131.84	134.26	136.56	138.98	141.29
12200	128.29	130.61	132.94	135.38	137.69	140.13	142.45
12300	129.35	131.69	134.02	136.48	138.82	141.28	143.62
12400	130.40	132.76	135.11	137.59	139.95	142.43	144.78
12500	131.45	133.83	136.20	138.70	141.08	143.58	145.95
12600	132.50	134.89	137.29	139.81	142.20	144.72	147.12
12700	133.55	135.96	138.38	140.92	143.33	145.87	148.29
12800	134.60	137.03	139.47	142.03	144.47	147.03	149.46
12900	135.66	138.11	140.56	143.14	145.59	148.17	150.62
13000	136.71	139.18	141.65	144.25	146.72	149.32	151.79
13100	137.76	140.25	142.74	145.36	147.85	150.47	152.96
13200	138.81	141.32	143.83	146.47	148.97	151.61	154.12
13300	139.86	142.39	144.91	147.57	150.10	152.76	155.29
13400	140.91	143.46	146.00	148.68	151.24	153.92	156.46
13500	141.97	144.54	147.10	149.80	152.37	155.07	157.63
13600	143.02	145.60	148.19	150.91	153.49	156.21	158.80
13700	144.07	146.67	149.28	152.02	154.62	157.36	159.96
13800	145.12	147.74	150.36	153.12	155.75	158.51	161.13
13900	146.17	148.81	151.45	154.23	156.87	159.65	162.29
14000	147.22	149.88	152.54	155.34	158.01	160.81	163.47
14100	148.27	150.96	153.64	156.46	159.14	161.96	164.64
14200	149.33	152.03	154.73	157.57	160.26	163.10	165.80
14300	150.38	153.10	155.81	158.67	161.39	164.25	166.97
14400	151.43	154.17	156.90	159.78	162.52	165.40	168.13
14500	152.48	155.24	157.99	160.89	163.65	166.55	169.30
14600	153.53	156.30	159.08	162.00	164.77	167.70	170.48
14700	154.58	157.37	160.18	163.12	165.91	168.85	171.64
14800	155.64	158.45	161.26	164.22	167.04	170.00	172.81
14900	156.69	159.52	162.35	165.33	168.16	171.14	173.97
15000	157.74	160.59	163.44	166.44	169.29	172.29	175.14
15100	158.79	161.66	164.53	167.55	170.42	173.44	176.31
15200	159.84	162.73	165.62	168.66	171.54	174.58	177.48
15300	160.89	163.80	166.71	169.77	172.68	175.74	178.65
15400	161.95	164.88	167.80	170.88	173.81	176.89	179.81
15500	163.00	165.95	168.89	171.99	174.94	178.04	180.98

MONTHLY PAYMENTS FOR 30-YR. FHA LOANS

INCLUDING FIRST YEAR ½% MORTGAGE INSURANCE PREMIUMS

AMOUNT	INTEREST						
	11.75%	12.00%	12.25%	12.50%	12.75%	13.00%	13.25%
15600	164.05	167.01	169.98	173.10	176.06	179.18	182.15
15700	165.10	168.08	171.07	174.21	177.19	180.33	183.31
15800	166.15	169.15	172.15	175.31	178.32	181.48	184.49
15900	167.20	170.22	173.24	176.43	179.45	182.63	185.65
16000	168.25	171.30	174.34	177.54	180.58	183.78	186.82
16100	169.31	172.37	175.43	178.65	181.71	184.93	187.99
16200	170.36	173.44	176.52	179.76	182.83	186.07	189.15
16300	171.41	174.51	177.60	180.86	183.96	187.22	190.32
16400	172.46	175.58	178.69	181.97	185.09	188.37	191.48
16500	173.51	176.65	179.78	183.08	186.23	189.53	192.66
16600	174.56	177.72	180.88	184.20	187.35	190.67	193.83
16700	175.62	178.79	181.97	185.31	188.48	191.82	194.99
16800	176.67	179.86	183.05	186.41	189.61	192.97	196.16
16900	177.72	180.93	184.14	187.52	190.73	194.11	197.32
17000	178.77	182.00	185.23	188.63	191.86	195.26	198.49
17100	179.82	183.07	186.32	189.74	193.00	196.42	199.67
17200	180.87	184.14	187.42	190.86	194.12	197.56	200.83
17300	181.93	185.22	188.50	191.96	195.25	198.71	202.00
17400	182.98	186.29	189.59	193.07	196.38	199.86	203.16
17500	184.03	187.36	190.68	194.18	197.51	201.01	204.33
17600	185.08	188.42	191.77	195.29	198.63	202.15	205.50
17700	186.13	189.49	192.86	196.40	199.76	203.31	206.67
17800	187.18	190.56	193.95	197.51	200.90	204.46	207.84
17900	188.24	191.64	195.04	198.62	202.02	205.60	209.00
18000	189.29	192.71	196.13	199.73	203.15	206.75	210.17
18100	190.34	193.78	197.22	200.84	204.28	207.90	211.34
18200	191.39	194.85	198.31	201.95	205.40	209.04	212.50
18300	192.44	195.92	199.39	203.05	206.53	210.19	213.68
18400	193.49	196.99	200.48	204.17	207.67	211.35	214.84
18500	194.54	198.07	201.58	205.28	208.80	212.50	216.01
18600	195.60	199.13	202.67	206.39	209.92	213.64	217.18
18700	196.65	200.20	203.76	207.50	211.05	214.79	218.34
18800	197.70	201.27	204.84	208.60	212.18	215.94	219.51
18900	198.75	202.34	205.93	209.71	213.30	217.08	220.68
19000	199.80	203.41	207.02	210.82	214.44	218.24	221.85
19100	200.85	204.49	208.12	211.94	215.57	219.39	223.02
19200	201.91	205.56	209.21	213.05	216.69	220.53	224.18
19300	202.96	206.63	210.29	214.15	217.82	221.68	225.35
19400	204.01	207.70	211.38	215.26	218.95	222.83	226.51
19500	205.06	208.77	212.47	216.37	220.08	223.98	227.68
19600	206.11	209.83	213.56	217.48	221.21	225.13	228.86
19700	207.16	210.90	214.66	218.60	222.34	226.28	230.02
19800	208.22	211.98	215.74	219.70	223.47	227.43	231.19
19900	209.27	213.05	216.83	220.81	224.59	228.57	232.35
20000	210.32	214.12	217.92	221.92	225.72	229.72	233.52
20100	211.37	215.19	219.01	223.03	226.85	230.87	234.69
20200	212.42	216.26	220.10	224.14	227.97	232.02	235.86
20300	213.47	217.33	221.19	225.25	229.11	233.17	237.03
20400	214.53	218.41	222.28	226.36	230.24	234.32	238.19
20500	215.58	219.48	223.37	227.47	231.37	235.47	239.36
20600	216.63	220.54	224.46	228.58	232.49	236.61	240.53
20700	217.68	221.61	225.55	229.69	233.62	237.76	241.69
20800	218.73	222.68	226.63	230.79	234.75	238.91	242.87
20900	219.78	223.75	227.72	231.91	235.88	240.06	244.03
21000	220.83	224.83	228.82	233.02	237.01	241.21	245.20
21100	221.89	225.90	229.91	234.13	238.14	242.36	246.37
21200	222.94	226.97	231.00	235.24	239.26	243.50	247.53
21300	223.99	228.04	232.08	236.34	240.39	244.65	248.70
21400	225.04	229.11	233.17	237.45	241.52	245.80	249.87
21500	226.09	230.18	234.26	238.56	242.66	246.96	251.04

MONTHLY PAYMENTS FOR 30-YR. FHA LOANS

INCLUDING FIRST YEAR ½% MORTGAGE INSURANCE PREMIUMS

AMOUNT	INTEREST						
	11.75%	12.00%	12.25%	12.50%	12.75%	13.00%	13.25%
21600	227.14	231.25	235.36	239.68	243.78	248.10	252.21
21700	228.20	232.32	236.45	240.79	244.91	249.25	253.37
21800	229.25	233.39	237.53	241.89	246.04	250.40	254.54
21900	230.30	234.46	238.62	243.00	247.16	251.54	255.70
22000	231.35	235.53	239.71	244.11	248.29	252.69	256.88
22100	232.40	236.60	240.80	245.22	249.43	253.85	258.05
22200	233.45	237.67	241.90	246.34	250.55	254.99	259.21
22300	234.51	238.75	242.98	247.44	251.68	256.14	260.38
22400	235.56	239.82	244.07	248.55	252.81	257.29	261.54
22500	236.61	240.89	245.16	249.66	253.94	258.44	262.71
22600	237.66	241.95	246.25	250.77	255.06	259.58	263.88
22700	238.71	243.02	247.34	251.88	256.20	260.74	265.05
22800	239.76	244.09	248.43	252.99	257.33	261.89	266.22
22900	240.81	245.17	249.52	254.10	258.45	263.03	267.38
23000	241.87	246.24	250.61	255.21	259.58	264.18	268.55
23100	242.92	247.31	251.70	256.32	260.71	265.33	269.72
23200	243.97	248.38	252.79	257.43	261.83	266.47	270.88
23300	245.02	249.45	253.87	258.53	262.96	267.63	272.06
23400	246.07	250.52	254.96	259.65	264.10	268.78	273.22
23500	247.12	251.60	256.06	260.76	265.23	269.93	274.39
23600	248.18	252.66	257.15	261.87	266.35	271.07	275.56
23700	249.23	253.73	258.24	262.98	267.48	272.22	276.72
23800	250.28	254.80	259.32	264.08	268.61	273.37	277.89
23900	251.33	255.87	260.41	265.19	269.73	274.51	279.06
24000	252.38	256.94	261.50	266.31	270.87	275.67	280.23
24100	253.43	258.02	262.60	267.42	272.00	276.82	281.40
24200	254.49	259.09	263.69	268.53	273.12	277.96	282.56
24300	255.54	260.16	264.77	269.63	274.25	279.11	283.73
24400	256.59	261.23	265.86	270.74	275.38	280.26	284.89
24500	257.64	262.30	266.95	271.85	276.51	281.41	286.07
24600	258.69	263.36	268.04	272.96	277.64	282.56	287.24
24700	259.74	264.43	269.14	274.08	278.77	283.71	288.40
24800	260.80	265.51	270.22	275.18	279.90	284.86	289.57
24900	261.85	266.58	271.31	276.29	281.02	286.00	290.73
25000	262.90	267.65	272.40	277.40	282.15	287.15	291.90
25100	263.95	268.72	273.49	278.51	283.28	288.30	293.08
25200	265.00	269.79	274.58	279.62	284.41	289.45	294.24
25300	266.05	270.86	275.67	280.73	285.54	290.60	295.41
25400	267.10	271.94	276.76	281.84	286.67	291.75	296.57
25500	268.16	273.01	277.85	282.95	287.80	292.90	297.74
25600	269.21	274.07	278.94	284.06	288.92	294.04	298.91
25700	270.26	275.14	280.03	285.17	290.05	295.19	300.07
25800	271.31	276.21	281.11	286.27	291.18	296.35	301.25
25900	272.36	277.28	282.20	287.39	292.31	297.49	302.41
26000	273.41	278.36	283.30	288.50	293.44	298.64	303.58
26100	274.47	279.43	284.39	289.61	294.57	299.79	304.75
26200	275.52	280.50	285.48	290.72	295.69	300.93	305.91
26300	276.57	281.57	286.56	291.82	296.82	302.08	307.08
26400	277.62	282.64	287.65	292.93	297.95	303.24	308.25
26500	278.67	283.71	288.74	294.05	299.09	304.39	309.42
26600	279.72	284.78	289.84	295.16	300.21	305.53	310.59
26700	280.78	285.85	290.93	296.27	301.34	306.68	311.75
26800	281.83	286.92	292.01	297.37	302.47	307.83	312.92
26900	282.88	287.99	293.10	298.48	303.59	308.97	314.08
27000	283.93	289.06	294.19	299.59	304.72	310.12	315.26
27100	284.98	290.13	295.28	300.70	305.86	311.28	316.43
27200	286.03	291.20	296.38	301.82	306.98	312.42	317.59
27300	287.09	292.28	297.46	302.92	308.11	313.57	318.76
27400	288.14	293.35	298.55	304.03	309.24	314.72	319.92
27500	289.19	294.42	299.64	305.14	310.37	315.87	321.09

MONTHLY PAYMENTS FOR 30-YR. FHA LOANS

INCLUDING FIRST YEAR ½% MORTGAGE INSURANCE PREMIUMS

AMOUNT	INTEREST						
	11.75%	12.00%	12.25%	12.50%	12.75%	13.00%	13.25%
27600	290.24	295.48	300.73	306.25	311.49	317.01	322.27
27700	291.29	296.55	301.82	307.36	312.63	318.17	323.43
27800	292.34	297.62	302.91	308.47	313.76	319.32	324.60
27900	293.39	298.70	304.00	309.58	314.88	320.46	325.76
28000	294.45	299.77	305.09	310.69	316.01	321.61	326.93
28100	295.50	300.84	306.18	311.80	317.14	322.76	328.10
28200	296.55	301.91	307.27	312.91	318.26	323.90	329.27
28300	297.60	302.98	308.35	314.01	319.40	325.06	330.44
28400	298.65	304.05	309.45	315.13	320.53	326.21	331.60
28500	299.70	305.13	310.54	316.24	321.66	327.36	332.77
28600	300.76	306.19	311.63	317.35	322.78	328.50	333.94
28700	301.81	307.26	312.72	318.46	323.91	329.65	335.10
28800	302.86	308.33	313.80	319.56	325.04	330.80	336.28
28900	303.91	309.40	314.89	320.67	326.16	331.95	337.44
29000	304.96	310.47	315.98	321.79	327.30	333.10	338.61
29100	306.01	311.54	317.08	322.90	328.43	334.25	339.78
29200	307.07	312.62	318.17	324.01	329.55	335.39	340.94
29300	308.12	313.69	319.25	325.11	330.68	336.54	342.11
29400	309.17	314.76	320.34	326.22	331.81	337.69	343.27
29500	310.22	315.83	321.43	327.33	332.94	338.85	344.45
29600	311.27	316.89	322.52	328.44	334.07	339.99	345.62
29700	312.32	317.96	323.62	329.56	335.20	341.14	346.78
29800	313.37	319.04	324.70	330.66	336.33	342.29	347.95
29900	314.43	320.11	325.79	331.77	337.45	343.43	349.11
30000	315.48	321.18	326.88	332.88	338.58	344.58	350.28
30100	316.53	322.25	327.97	333.99	339.71	345.73	351.46
30200	317.58	323.32	329.06	335.10	340.84	346.88	352.62
30300	318.63	324.39	330.15	336.21	341.97	348.03	353.79
30400	319.68	325.47	331.24	337.32	343.10	349.18	354.95
30500	320.74	326.54	332.33	338.43	344.23	350.33	356.12
30600	321.79	327.60	333.42	339.54	345.35	351.47	357.29
30700	322.84	328.67	334.51	340.65	346.48	352.62	358.46
30800	323.89	329.74	335.59	341.75	347.62	353.78	359.63
30900	324.94	330.81	336.69	342.87	348.74	354.92	360.79
31000	325.99	331.89	337.78	343.98	349.87	356.07	361.96
31100	327.05	332.96	338.87	345.09	351.00	357.22	363.13
31200	328.10	334.03	339.96	346.20	352.12	358.36	364.29
31300	329.15	335.10	341.04	347.30	353.25	359.51	365.47
31400	330.20	336.17	342.13	348.41	354.39	360.67	366.63
31500	331.25	337.24	343.22	349.53	355.52	361.82	367.80
31600	332.30	338.30	344.32	350.64	356.64	362.96	368.97
31700	333.36	339.38	345.41	351.75	357.77	364.11	370.13
31800	334.41	340.45	346.49	352.85	358.90	365.26	371.30
31900	335.46	341.52	347.58	353.96	360.02	366.40	372.47
32000	336.51	342.59	348.67	355.07	361.15	367.56	373.64
32100	337.56	343.66	349.76	356.18	362.29	368.71	374.81
32200	338.61	344.73	350.86	357.30	363.41	369.85	375.97
32300	339.66	5.81	351.94	358.40	364.54	371.00	377.14
32400	340.72	346.88	353.03	359.51	365.67	372.15	378.30
32500	341.77	347.95	354.12	360.62	366.80	373.30	379.47
32600	342.82	349.01	355.21	361.73	367.92	374.45	380.65
32700	343.87	350.08	356.30	362.84	369.06	375.60	381.81
32800	344.92	351.15	357.39	363.95	370.19	376.75	382.98
32900	345.97	352.23	358.48	365.06	371.31	377.89	384.14
33000	347.03	353.30	359.57	366.17	372.44	379.04	385.31
33100	348.08	354.37	360.66	367.28	373.57	380.19	386.48
33200	349.13	355.44	361.75	368.39	374.69	381.33	387.65
33300	350.18	356.51	362.83	369.49	375.83	382.49	388.82
33400	351.23	357.58	363.93	370.61	376.96	383.64	389.98
33500	352.28	358.66	365.02	371.72	378.09	384.79	391.15

MONTHLY PAYMENTS FOR 30-YR. FHA LOANS

INCLUDING FIRST YEAR ½% MORTGAGE INSURANCE PREMIUMS

AMOUNT	INTEREST						
	11.75%	12.00%	12.25%	12.50%	12.75%	13.00%	13.25%
33600	353.34	359.72	366.11	372.83	379.21	385.93	392.32
33700	354.39	360.79	367.20	373.94	380.34	387.08	393.48
33800	355.44	361.86	368.28	375.04	381.47	388.23	394.66
33900	356.49	362.93	369.37	376.15	382.60	389.38	395.82
34000	357.54	364.00	370.46	377.27	383.73	390.53	396.99
34100	358.59	365.07	371.56	378.38	384.86	391.68	398.16
34200	359.65	366.15	372.65	379.49	385.98	392.82	399.32
34300	360.70	367.22	373.73	380.59	387.11	393.97	400.49
34400	361.75	368.29	374.82	381.70	388.24	395.12	401.66
34500	362.80	369.36	375.91	382.81	389.37	396.28	402.83
34600	363.85	370.42	377.00	383.93	390.50	397.42	404.00
34700	364.90	371.49	378.10	385.04	391.63	398.57	405.16
34800	365.95	372.57	379.18	386.14	392.76	399.72	406.33
34900	367.01	373.64	380.27	387.25	393.88	400.86	407.49
35000	368.06	374.71	381.36	388.36	395.01	402.01	408.67
35100	369.11	375.78	382.45	389.47	396.14	403.17	409.84
35200	370.16	376.85	383.54	390.58	397.27	404.31	411.00
35300	371.21	377.92	384.63	391.69	398.40	405.46	412.17
35400	372.26	379.00	385.72	392.80	399.53	406.61	413.33
35500	373.32	380.07	386.81	393.91	400.66	407.76	414.50
35600	374.37	381.13	387.90	395.02	401.78	408.90	415.67
35700	375.42	382.20	388.99	396.13	402.91	410.05	416.84
35800	376.47	383.27	390.07	397.23	404.05	411.21	418.01
35900	377.52	384.34	391.17	398.35	405.17	412.35	419.17
36000	378.57	385.42	392.26	399.46	406.30	413.50	420.34
36100	379.63	386.49	393.35	400.57	407.43	414.65	421.51
36200	380.68	387.56	394.44	401.68	408.55	415.79	422.67
36300	381.73	388.63	395.52	402.78	409.68	416.94	423.85
36400	382.78	389.70	396.61	403.89	410.82	418.10	425.01
36500	383.83	390.77	397.70	405.01	411.95	419.25	426.18
36600	384.88	391.83	398.80	406.12	413.07	420.39	427.35
36700	385.93	392.91	399.89	407.23	414.20	421.54	428.51
36800	386.99	393.98	400.97	408.33	415.33	422.69	429.68
36900	388.04	395.05	402.06	409.44	416.45	423.83	430.85
37000	389.09	396.12	403.15	410.55	417.59	424.99	432.02
37100	390.14	397.19	404.24	411.67	418.72	426.14	433.19
37200	391.19	398.26	405.34	412.78	419.84	427.28	434.35
37300	392.24	399.34	406.42	413.88	420.97	428.43	435.52
37400	393.30	400.41	407.51	414.99	422.10	429.58	436.68
37500	394.35	401.48	408.60	416.10	423.23	430.73	437.86
37600	395.40	402.54	409.69	417.21	424.35	431.88	439.03
37700	396.45	403.61	410.78	418.32	425.49	433.03	440.19
37800	397.50	404.68	411.87	419.43	426.62	434.18	441.36
37900	398.55	405.76	412.96	420.54	427.74	435.32	442.52
38000	399.61	406.83	414.05	421.65	428.87	436.47	443.69
38100	400.66	407.90	415.14	422.76	430.00	437.62	444.87
38200	401.71	408.97	416.23	423.87	431.12	438.77	446.03
38300	402.76	410.04	417.31	424.97	432.26	439.92	447.20
38400	403.81	411.11	418.41	426.09	433.39	441.07	448.36
38500	404.86	412.19	419.50	427.20	434.52	442.22	449.53
38600	405.92	413.25	420.59	428.31	435.64	443.36	450.70
38700	406.97	414.32	421.68	429.42	436.77	444.51	451.86
38800	408.02	415.39	422.76	430.52	437.90	445.66	453.04
38900	409.07	416.46	423.85	431.63	439.03	446.81	454.20
39000	410.12	417.53	424.94	432.75	440.16	447.96	455.37
39100	411.17	418.60	426.04	433.86	441.29	449.11	456.54
39200	412.22	419.68	427.13	434.97	442.41	450.25	457.70
39300	413.28	420.75	428.21	436.07	443.54	451.40	458.87
39400	414.33	421.82	429.30	437.18	444.67	452.55	460.04
39500	415.38	422.89	430.39	438.29	445.81	453.71	461.21

MONTHLY PAYMENTS FOR 30-YR. FHA LOANS

INCLUDING FIRST YEAR ½% MORTGAGE INSURANCE PREMIUMS

AMOUNT	INTEREST						
	11.75%	12.00%	12.25%	12.50%	12.75%	13.00%	13.25%
39600	416.43	423.95	431.48	439.41	446.93	454.85	462.38
39700	417.48	425.02	432.58	440.52	448.06	456.00	463.54
39800	418.53	426.10	433.66	441.62	449.19	457.15	464.71
39900	419.59	427.17	434.75	442.73	450.31	458.29	465.87
40000	420.64	428.24	435.84	443.84	451.44	459.44	467.05
40100	421.69	429.31	436.93	444.95	452.57	460.60	468.22
40200	422.74	430.38	438.02	446.06	453.70	461.74	469.38
40300	423.79	431.45	439.11	447.17	454.83	462.89	470.55
40400	424.84	432.53	440.20	448.28	455.96	464.04	471.71
40500	425.90	433.60	441.29	449.39	457.09	465.19	472.88
40600	426.95	434.66	442.38	450.50	458.21	466.33	474.06
40700	428.00	435.73	443.47	451.61	459.34	467.49	475.22
40800	429.05	436.80	444.55	452.71	460.48	468.64	476.39
40900	430.10	437.87	445.65	453.83	461.60	469.78	477.55
41000	431.15	438.95	446.74	454.94	462.73	470.93	478.72
41100	432.20	440.02	447.83	456.05	463.86	472.08	479.89
41200	433.26	441.09	448.92	457.16	464.98	473.22	481.06
41300	434.31	442.16	450.00	458.26	466.11	474.38	482.23
41400	435.36	443.23	451.09	459.37	467.25	475.53	483.39
41500	436.41	444.30	452.18	460.49	468.38	476.68	484.56
41600	437.46	445.36	453.28	461.60	469.50	477.82	485.73
41700	438.51	446.44	454.37	462.71	470.63	478.97	486.89
41800	439.57	447.51	455.45	463.81	471.76	480.12	488.06
41900	440.62	448.58	456.54	464.92	472.88	481.26	489.23
42000	441.67	449.65	457.63	466.03	474.02	482.42	490.40
42100	442.72	450.72	458.72	467.15	475.15	483.57	491.57
42200	443.77	451.79	459.82	468.26	476.27	484.71	492.73
42300	444.82	452.87	460.90	469.36	477.40	485.86	493.90
42400	445.88	453.94	461.99	470.47	478.53	487.01	495.06
42500	446.93	455.01	463.08	471.58	479.66	488.16	496.24
42600	447.98	456.07	464.17	472.69	480.79	489.31	497.41
42700	449.03	457.14	465.26	473.80	481.92	490.46	498.57
42800	450.08	458.21	466.35	474.91	483.05	491.61	499.74
42900	451.13	459.29	467.44	476.02	484.17	492.75	500.90
43000	452.19	460.36	468.53	477.13	485.30	493.90	502.07
43200	454.29	462.50	470.71	479.35	487.55	496.20	504.41
43400	456.39	464.64	472.89	481.57	489.82	498.50	506.74
43600	458.49	466.78	475.07	483.79	492.07	500.79	509.08
43800	460.60	468.92	477.24	486.00	494.33	503.10	511.42
44000	462.70	471.06	479.42	488.23	496.59	505.39	513.75
44200	464.80	473.21	481.61	490.45	498.84	507.68	516.08
44400	466.91	475.35	483.78	492.66	501.10	509.99	518.42
44600	469.01	477.48	485.96	494.89	503.36	512.28	520.76
44800	471.11	479.63	488.14	497.10	505.62	514.58	523.09
45000	473.22	481.77	490.32	499.32	507.87	516.87	525.43
45200	475.32	483.91	492.50	501.55	510.13	519.17	527.76
45400	477.42	486.06	494.68	503.76	512.39	521.47	530.09
45600	479.53	488.19	496.86	505.98	514.64	523.76	532.44
45800	481.63	490.33	499.03	508.19	516.91	526.07	534.77
46000	483.73	492.48	501.22	510.42	519.16	528.36	537.10
46200	485.84	494.62	503.40	512.64	521.41	530.65	539.44
46400	487.94	496.76	505.57	514.85	523.68	532.96	541.77
46600	490.04	498.89	507.76	517.08	525.93	535.25	544.11
46800	492.15	501.04	509.93	519.29	528.19	537.55	546.45
47000	494.25	503.18	512.11	521.51	530.45	539.85	548.78
47200	496.35	505.32	514.30	523.74	532.70	542.14	551.11
47400	498.46	507.47	516.47	525.95	534.96	544.44	553.45
47600	500.56	509.60	518.65	528.17	537.22	546.74	555.79
47800	502.66	511.74	520.83	530.39	539.48	549.04	558.12
48000	504.76	513.89	523.01	532.61	541.73	551.33	560.46

MONTHLY PAYMENTS FOR 30-YR. FHA LOANS

INCLUDING FIRST YEAR ½% MORTGAGE INSURANCE PREMIUMS

AMOUNT	INTEREST						
	11.75%	12.00%	12.25%	12.50%	12.75%	13.00%	13.25%
48200	506.87	516.03	525.19	534.83	543.99	553.63	562.79
48400	508.97	518.17	527.37	537.05	546.25	555.93	565.12
48600	511.07	520.31	529.55	539.27	548.50	558.22	567.46
48800	513.18	522.45	531.72	541.48	550.76	560.53	569.80
49000	515.28	524.59	533.91	543.71	553.02	562.82	572.13
49200	517.38	526.74	536.09	545.93	555.27	565.11	574.46
49400	519.49	528.88	538.26	548.14	557.53	567.42	576.80
49600	521.59	531.01	540.44	550.37	559.79	569.71	579.14
49800	523.69	533.16	542.62	552.58	562.05	572.01	581.47
50000	525.80	535.30	544.80	554.80	564.30	574.31	583.81
50200	527.90	537.44	546.98	557.03	566.56	576.60	586.14
50400	530.00	539.59	549.16	559.24	568.82	578.90	588.47
50600	532.11	541.72	551.34	561.46	571.07	581.19	590.82
50800	534.21	543.86	553.51	563.67	573.34	583.50	593.15
51000	536.31	546.00	555.70	565.90	575.59	585.79	595.48
51200	538.42	548.15	557.88	568.12	577.84	588.08	597.82
51400	540.52	550.29	560.05	570.33	580.11	590.39	600.15
51600	542.62	552.42	562.24	572.56	582.36	592.68	602.49
51800	544.73	554.57	564.41	574.77	584.62	594.98	604.83
52000	546.83	556.71	566.59	576.99	586.88	597.28	607.16
52200	548.93	558.85	568.78	579.22	589.13	599.57	609.49
52400	551.04	561.00	570.95	581.43	591.39	601.87	611.83
52600	553.14	563.13	573.13	583.65	593.65	604.17	614.17
52800	555.24	565.27	575.31	585.87	595.91	606.47	616.50
53000	557.34	567.42	577.49	588.09	598.16	608.76	618.84
53200	559.45	569.56	579.67	590.31	600.42	611.06	621.17
53400	561.55	571.70	581.85	592.53	602.68	613.36	623.50
53600	563.65	573.84	584.03	594.75	604.93	615.65	625.85
53800	565.76	575.98	586.20	596.96	607.20	617.96	628.18
54000	567.86	578.12	588.39	599.19	609.45	620.25	630.51
54200	569.96	580.27	590.57	601.41	611.70	622.54	632.85
54400	572.07	582.41	592.74	603.62	613.97	624.85	635.18
54600	574.17	584.54	594.92	605.85	616.22	627.14	637.52
54800	576.27	586.69	597.10	608.06	618.48	629.44	639.85
55000	578.38	588.83	599.28	610.28	620.73	631.74	642.19
55200	580.48	590.97	601.46	612.51	622.99	634.03	644.52
55400	582.58	593.12	603.64	614.72	625.25	636.33	646.85
55600	584.69	595.25	605.82	616.94	627.50	638.63	649.20
55800	586.79	597.39	607.99	619.16	629.77	640.93	651.53
56000	588.89	599.53	610.18	621.38	632.02	643.22	653.86
56200	591.00	601.68	612.36	623.60	634.27	645.52	656.20
56400	593.10	603.82	614.53	625.81	636.54	647.82	658.53
56600	595.20	605.95	616.72	628.04	638.79	650.11	660.87
56800	597.31	608.10	618.89	630.25	641.05	652.41	663.21
57000	599.41	610.24	621.07	632.47	643.31	654.71	665.54
57200	601.51	612.38	623.26	634.70	645.56	657.00	667.87
57400	603.61	614.53	625.43	636.91	647.82	659.30	670.21
57600	605.72	616.66	627.61	639.13	650.08	661.60	672.55
57800	607.82	618.80	629.79	641.35	652.34	663.90	674.88
58000	609.92	620.95	631.97	643.57	654.59	666.19	677.22
58200	612.03	623.09	634.15	645.79	656.85	668.49	679.55
58400	614.13	625.23	636.33	648.01	659.11	670.79	681.88
58600	616.23	627.37	638.51	650.23	661.36	673.08	684.23
58800	618.34	629.51	640.68	652.44	663.63	675.39	686.56
59000	620.44	631.65	642.87	654.67	665.88	677.68	688.89
59200	622.54	633.80	645.05	656.89	668.13	679.97	691.23
59400	624.65	635.94	647.22	659.10	670.40	682.28	693.56
59600	626.75	638.07	649.40	661.33	672.65	684.57	695.90
59800	628.85	640.22	651.58	663.54	674.91	686.87	698.24
60000	630.96	642.36	653.76	665.76	677.17	689.17	700.57

MONTHLY PAYMENTS FOR 30-YR. FHA LOANS

INCLUDING FIRST YEAR ½% MORTGAGE INSURANCE PREMIUMS

AMOUNT	INTEREST						
	11.75%	12.00%	12.25%	12.50%	12.75%	13.00%	13.25%
60200	633.06	644.50	655.94	667.99	679.42	691.46	702.90
60400	635.16	646.65	658.12	670.20	681.68	693.76	705.24
60600	637.27	648.78	660.30	672.42	683.93	696.06	707.58
60800	639.37	650.92	662.47	674.64	686.20	698.36	709.91
61000	641.47	653.06	664.66	676.86	688.45	700.65	712.24
61200	643.58	655.21	666.84	679.08	690.70	702.95	714.58
61400	645.68	657.35	669.01	681.29	692.97	705.25	716.91
61600	647.78	659.48	671.20	683.52	695.22	707.54	719.25
61800	649.88	661.63	673.37	685.73	697.48	709.85	721.59
62000	651.99	663.77	675.55	687.95	699.74	712.14	723.92
62200	654.09	665.91	677.74	690.18	701.99	714.43	726.25
62400	656.19	668.06	679.91	692.39	704.25	716.73	728.59
62600	658.30	670.19	682.09	694.61	706.51	719.03	730.93
62800	660.40	672.33	684.27	696.83	708.77	721.33	733.26
63000	662.50	674.48	686.45	699.05	711.02	723.62	735.60
63200	664.61	676.62	688.63	701.27	713.28	725.92	737.93
63400	666.71	678.76	690.81	703.49	715.54	728.22	740.26
63600	668.81	680.90	692.99	705.71	717.79	730.51	742.61
63800	670.92	683.04	695.16	707.92	720.06	732.82	744.94
64000	673.02	685.18	697.35	710.15	722.31	735.11	747.27
64200	675.12	687.33	699.53	712.37	724.56	737.40	749.61
64400	677.23	689.47	701.70	714.58	726.83	739.71	751.94
64600	679.33	691.60	703.89	716.81	729.08	742.00	754.28
64800	681.43	693.75	706.06	719.02	731.34	744.30	756.62
65000	683.54	695.89	708.24	721.24	733.60	746.60	758.95
65200	685.64	698.03	710.42	723.47	735.85	748.89	761.28
65400	687.74	700.18	712.60	725.68	738.11	751.19	763.62
65600	689.85	702.31	714.78	727.90	740.37	753.49	765.96
65800	691.95	704.45	716.95	730.12	742.63	755.79	768.29
66000	694.05	706.59	719.14	732.34	744.88	758.08	770.63
66200	696.15	708.74	721.32	734.56	747.13	760.38	772.96
66400	698.26	710.88	723.49	736.78	749.40	762.68	775.29
66600	700.36	713.01	725.68	739.00	751.65	764.97	777.64
66800	702.46	715.16	727.85	741.21	753.91	767.28	779.97
67000	704.57	717.30	730.03	743.43	756.17	769.57	782.30
67200	706.67	719.44	732.22	745.66	758.42	771.86	784.64
67400	708.77	721.59	734.39	747.87	760.68	774.17	786.97
67600	710.88	723.72	736.57	750.09	762.94	776.46	789.31
67800	712.98	725.86	738.75	752.31	765.20	778.76	791.64
68000	715.08	728.01	740.93	754.53	767.45	781.06	793.98
68200	717.19	730.15	743.11	756.75	769.71	783.35	796.31
68400	719.29	732.29	745.29	758.97	771.97	785.65	798.64
68600	721.39	734.43	747.47	761.19	774.22	787.94	800.99
68800	723.50	736.57	749.64	763.40	776.49	790.25	803.32
69000	725.60	738.71	751.83	765.63	778.74	792.54	805.65
69200	727.70	740.86	754.01	767.85	780.99	794.83	807.99
69400	729.81	743.00	756.18	770.06	783.26	797.14	810.32
69600	731.91	745.13	758.37	772.29	785.51	799.43	812.66
69800	734.01	747.28	760.54	774.50	787.77	801.73	815.00
70000	736.12	749.42	762.72	776.72	790.03	804.03	817.33
70200	738.22	751.56	764.90	778.95	792.28	806.32	819.66
70400	740.32	753.70	767.08	781.16	794.54	808.62	822.00
70600	742.43	755.84	769.26	783.38	796.80	810.92	824.34
70800	744.53	757.98	771.43	785.60	799.06	813.22	826.67
71000	746.63	760.12	773.62	787.82	801.31	815.51	829.01
71200	748.73	762.27	775.80	790.04	803.57	817.81	831.34
71400	750.84	764.41	777.97	792.26	805.83	820.11	833.67
71600	752.94	766.54	780.16	794.48	808.08	822.40	836.02
71800	755.04	768.69	782.33	796.69	810.34	824.71	838.35
72000	757.15	770.83	784.51	798.92	812.60	827.00	840.68

MONTHLY PAYMENTS FOR 30-YR. FHA LOANS

INCLUDING FIRST YEAR ½% MORTGAGE INSURANCE PREMIUMS

AMOUNT	INTEREST						
	13.50%	13.75%	14.00%	14.25%	14.50%	14.75%	15.00%
50	0.59	0.60	0.61	0.62	0.63	0.64	0.65
100	1.19	1.21	1.23	1.25	1.27	1.29	1.31
250	2.97	3.02	3.06	3.11	3.16	3.21	3.26
500	5.94	6.04	6.14	6.24	6.34	6.44	6.54
10000	118.76	120.76	122.66	124.66	126.66	128.66	130.66
10100	119.95	121.97	123.89	125.91	127.93	129.95	131.97
10200	121.13	123.18	125.12	127.16	129.20	131.24	133.28
10300	122.33	124.39	126.35	128.41	130.47	132.53	134.59
10400	123.51	125.59	127.57	129.65	131.73	133.81	135.89
10500	124.70	126.80	128.80	130.90	133.00	135.10	137.20
10600	125.89	128.01	130.02	132.14	134.26	136.38	138.50
10700	127.07	129.21	131.25	133.39	135.53	137.67	139.81
10800	128.26	130.42	132.48	134.64	136.80	138.96	141.12
10900	129.45	131.63	133.71	135.89	138.07	140.25	142.43
11000	130.64	132.84	134.93	137.13	139.33	141.53	143.73
11100	131.83	134.05	136.16	138.38	140.60	142.82	145.04
11200	133.01	135.25	137.38	139.62	141.86	144.10	146.34
11300	134.20	136.46	138.61	140.87	143.13	145.39	147.65
11400	135.38	137.66	139.84	142.12	144.40	146.68	148.96
11500	136.58	138.88	141.07	143.37	145.67	147.97	150.27
11600	137.77	140.09	142.29	144.61	146.93	149.25	151.57
11700	138.95	141.29	143.52	145.86	148.20	150.54	152.88
11800	140.14	142.50	144.74	147.10	149.46	151.82	154.18
11900	141.32	143.70	145.97	148.35	150.73	153.11	155.49
12000	142.51	144.91	147.19	149.59	152.00	154.40	156.80
12100	143.71	146.13	148.43	150.85	153.27	155.69	158.11
12200	144.89	147.33	149.65	152.09	154.53	156.97	159.41
12300	146.08	148.54	150.88	153.34	155.80	158.26	160.72
12400	147.26	149.74	152.10	154.58	157.06	159.54	162.02
12500	148.45	150.95	153.33	155.83	158.33	160.83	163.33
12600	149.64	152.16	154.55	157.07	159.59	162.12	164.64
12700	150.83	153.37	155.79	158.33	160.87	163.41	165.95
12800	152.02	154.58	157.01	159.57	162.13	164.69	167.25
12900	153.20	155.78	158.24	160.82	163.40	165.98	168.56
13000	154.39	156.99	159.46	162.06	164.66	167.26	169.86
13100	155.58	158.20	160.69	163.31	165.93	168.55	171.17
13200	156.76	159.40	161.91	164.55	167.19	169.84	172.48
13300	157.96	160.62	163.15	165.81	168.47	171.13	173.79
13400	159.14	161.82	164.37	167.05	169.73	172.41	175.09
13500	160.33	163.03	165.60	168.30	171.00	173.70	176.40
13600	161.52	164.24	166.82	169.54	172.26	174.98	177.70
13700	162.70	165.44	168.05	170.79	173.53	176.27	179.01
13800	163.89	166.65	169.27	172.03	174.79	177.55	180.32
13900	165.07	167.86	170.51	173.29	176.07	178.85	181.63
14000	166.27	169.07	171.73	174.53	177.33	180.13	182.93
14100	167.46	170.28	172.96	175.78	178.60	181.42	184.24
14200	168.64	171.48	174.18	177.02	179.86	182.70	185.54
14300	169.83	172.69	175.41	178.27	181.13	183.99	186.85
14400	171.01	173.89	176.63	179.51	182.39	185.27	188.15
14500	172.20	175.10	177.87	180.77	183.67	186.57	189.47
14600	173.40	176.32	179.09	182.01	184.93	187.85	190.77
14700	174.58	177.52	180.32	183.26	186.20	189.14	192.08
14800	175.77	178.73	181.54	184.50	187.46	190.42	193.38
14900	176.95	179.93	182.77	185.75	188.73	191.71	194.69
15000	178.14	181.14	183.99	186.99	189.99	192.99	195.99
15100	179.33	182.35	185.23	188.25	191.27	194.29	197.31
15200	180.52	183.56	186.45	189.49	192.53	195.57	198.61
15300	181.71	184.77	187.68	190.74	193.80	196.86	199.92
15400	182.89	185.97	188.90	191.98	195.06	198.14	201.22
15500	184.08	187.18	190.13	193.23	196.33	199.43	202.53

MONTHLY PAYMENTS FOR 30-YR. FHA LOANS

INCLUDING FIRST YEAR ½% MORTGAGE INSURANCE PREMIUMS

AMOUNT	INTEREST						
	13.50%	13.75%	14.00%	14.25%	14.50%	14.75%	15.00%
15600	185.27	188.39	191.35	194.47	197.59	200.71	203.83
15700	186.45	189.59	192.58	195.73	198.87	202.01	205.15
15800	187.65	190.81	193.81	196.97	200.13	203.29	206.45
15900	188.83	192.01	195.04	198.22	201.40	204.58	207.76
16000	190.02	193.22	196.26	199.46	202.66	205.86	209.06
16100	191.21	194.43	197.49	200.71	203.93	207.15	210.37
16200	192.39	195.63	198.71	201.95	205.19	208.43	211.67
16300	193.58	196.84	199.94	203.20	206.47	209.73	212.99
16400	194.77	198.05	201.17	204.45	207.73	211.01	214.29
16500	195.96	199.26	202.40	205.70	209.00	212.30	215.60
16600	197.15	200.47	203.62	206.94	210.26	213.58	216.90
16700	198.33	201.67	204.85	208.19	211.53	214.87	218.21
16800	199.52	202.88	206.07	209.43	212.79	216.15	219.51
16900	200.70	204.08	207.30	210.68	214.06	217.45	220.83
17000	201.89	205.30	208.53	211.93	215.33	218.73	222.13
17100	203.09	206.51	209.76	213.18	216.60	220.02	223.44
17200	204.27	207.71	210.98	214.42	217.86	221.30	224.74
17300	205.46	208.92	212.21	215.67	219.13	222.59	226.05
17400	206.64	210.12	213.43	216.91	220.39	223.87	227.35
17500	207.83	211.33	214.66	218.16	221.66	225.17	228.67
17600	209.02	212.54	215.89	219.41	222.93	226.45	229.97
17700	210.21	213.75	217.12	220.66	224.20	227.74	231.28
17800	211.40	214.96	218.34	221.90	225.46	229.02	232.58
17900	212.58	216.16	219.57	223.15	226.73	230.31	233.89
18000	213.77	217.37	220.79	224.39	227.99	231.59	235.19
18100	214.96	218.58	222.02	225.64	229.26	232.88	236.51
18200	216.14	219.78	223.25	226.89	230.53	234.17	237.81
18300	217.34	221.00	224.48	228.14	231.80	235.46	239.12
18400	218.52	222.20	225.70	229.38	233.06	236.74	240.42
18500	219.71	223.41	226.93	230.63	234.33	238.03	241.73
18600	220.90	224.62	228.15	231.87	235.59	239.31	243.03
18700	222.08	225.82	229.38	233.12	236.86	240.60	244.34
18800	223.27	227.03	230.61	234.37	238.13	241.89	245.65
18900	224.46	228.24	231.84	235.62	239.40	243.18	246.96
19000	225.65	229.45	233.06	236.86	240.66	244.46	248.26
19100	226.84	230.66	234.29	238.11	241.93	245.75	249.57
19200	228.02	231.86	235.51	239.35	243.19	247.03	250.87
19300	229.21	233.07	236.74	240.60	244.46	248.32	252.18
19400	230.39	234.27	237.96	241.85	245.73	249.61	253.49
19500	231.59	235.49	239.20	243.10	247.00	250.90	254.80
19600	232.78	236.70	240.42	244.34	248.26	252.18	256.10
19700	233.96	237.90	241.65	245.59	249.53	253.47	257.41
19800	235.15	239.11	242.87	246.83	250.79	254.75	258.71
19900	236.33	240.31	244.10	248.08	252.06	256.04	260.02
20000	237.52	241.52	245.32	249.32	253.33	257.33	261.33
20100	238.71	242.74	246.56	250.58	254.60	258.62	262.64
20200	239.90	243.94	247.78	251.82	255.86	259.90	263.94
20300	241.09	245.15	249.01	253.07	257.13	261.19	265.25
20400	242.27	246.35	250.23	254.31	258.39	262.47	266.55
20500	243.46	247.56	251.46	255.56	259.66	263.76	267.86
20600	244.65	248.77	252.68	256.80	260.93	265.05	269.17
20700	245.83	249.98	253.92	258.06	262.20	266.34	270.48
20800	247.03	251.19	255.14	259.30	263.46	267.62	271.78
20900	248.21	252.39	256.37	260.55	264.73	268.91	273.09
21000	249.40	253.60	257.59	261.79	265.99	270.19	274.39
21100	250.59	254.81	258.82	263.04	267.26	271.48	275.70
21200	251.77	256.01	260.04	264.28	268.52	272.77	277.01
21300	252.96	257.22	261.28	265.54	269.80	274.06	278.32
21400	254.15	258.43	262.50	266.78	271.06	275.34	279.62
21500	255.34	259.64	263.73	268.03	272.33	276.63	280.93

MONTHLY PAYMENTS FOR 30-YR. FHA LOANS

INCLUDING FIRST YEAR ½% MORTGAGE INSURANCE PREMIUMS

AMOUNT	INTEREST						
	13.50%	13.75%	14.00%	14.25%	14.50%	14.75%	15.00%
21600	256.53	260.85	264.95	269.27	273.59	277.91	282.23
21700	257.71	262.05	266.18	270.52	274.86	279.20	283.54
21800	258.90	263.26	267.40	271.76	276.12	280.49	284.85
21900	260.08	264.46	268.64	273.02	277.40	281.78	286.16
22000	261.28	265.68	269.86	274.26	278.66	283.06	287.46
22100	262.47	266.89	271.09	275.51	279.93	284.35	288.77
22200	263.65	268.09	272.31	276.75	281.19	285.63	290.07
22300	264.84	269.30	273.54	278.00	282.46	286.92	291.38
22400	266.02	270.50	274.76	279.24	283.72	288.20	292.69
22500	267.21	271.71	276.00	280.50	285.00	289.50	294.00
22600	268.41	272.93	277.22	281.74	286.26	290.78	295.30
22700	269.59	274.13	278.45	282.99	287.53	292.07	296.61
22800	270.78	275.34	279.67	284.23	288.79	293.35	297.91
22900	271.96	276.54	280.90	285.48	290.06	294.64	299.22
23000	273.15	277.75	282.12	286.72	291.32	295.92	300.53
23100	274.34	278.96	283.35	287.98	292.60	297.22	301.84
23200	275.53	280.17	284.58	289.22	293.86	298.50	303.14
23300	276.72	281.38	285.81	290.47	295.13	299.79	304.45
23400	277.90	282.58	287.03	291.71	296.39	301.07	305.75
23500	279.09	283.79	288.26	292.96	297.66	302.36	307.06
23600	280.28	285.00	289.48	294.20	298.92	303.64	308.36
23700	281.46	286.20	290.71	295.46	300.20	304.94	309.68
23800	282.65	287.42	291.94	296.70	301.46	306.22	310.98
23900	283.84	288.62	293.17	297.95	302.73	307.51	312.29
24000	285.03	289.83	294.39	299.19	303.99	308.79	313.59
24100	286.22	291.04	295.62	300.44	305.26	310.08	314.90
24200	287.40	292.24	296.84	301.68	306.52	311.36	316.20
24300	288.59	293.45	298.07	302.93	307.80	312.66	317.52
24400	289.77	294.65	299.30	304.18	309.06	313.94	318.82
24500	290.97	295.87	300.53	305.43	310.33	315.23	320.13
24600	292.16	297.08	301.75	306.67	311.59	316.51	321.43
24700	293.34	298.28	302.98	307.92	312.86	317.80	322.74
24800	294.53	299.49	304.20	309.16	314.12	319.08	324.04
24900	295.71	300.69	305.43	310.41	315.40	320.38	325.36
25000	296.90	301.90	306.66	311.66	316.66	321.66	326.66
25100	298.10	303.12	307.89	312.91	317.93	322.95	327.97
25200	299.28	304.32	309.11	314.15	319.19	324.23	329.27
25300	300.47	305.53	310.34	315.40	320.46	325.52	330.58
25400	301.65	306.73	311.56	316.64	321.72	326.80	331.88
25500	302.84	307.94	312.79	317.89	322.99	328.10	333.20
25600	304.03	309.15	314.02	319.14	324.26	329.38	334.50
25700	305.22	310.36	315.25	320.39	325.53	330.67	335.81
25800	306.41	311.57	316.47	321.63	326.79	331.95	337.11
25900	307.59	312.77	317.70	322.88	328.06	333.24	338.42
26000	308.78	313.98	318.92	324.12	329.32	334.52	339.72
26100	309.97	315.19	320.15	325.37	330.59	335.82	341.04
26200	311.15	316.39	321.38	326.62	331.86	337.10	342.34
26300	312.35	317.61	322.61	327.87	333.13	338.39	343.65
26400	313.53	318.81	323.83	329.11	334.39	339.67	344.95
26500	314.72	320.02	325.06	330.36	335.66	340.96	346.26
26600	315.91	321.23	326.28	331.60	336.92	342.24	347.56
26700	317.09	322.43	327.51	332.85	338.19	343.53	348.88
26800	318.28	323.64	328.73	334.10	339.46	344.82	350.18
26900	319.46	324.85	329.97	335.35	340.73	346.11	351.49
27000	320.66	326.06	331.19	336.59	341.99	347.39	352.79
27100	321.85	327.27	332.42	337.84	343.26	348.68	354.10
27200	323.03	328.47	333.64	339.08	344.52	349.96	355.40
27300	324.22	329.68	334.87	340.33	345.79	351.25	356.72
27400	325.40	330.88	336.09	341.58	347.06	352.54	358.02
27500	326.59	332.10	337.33	342.83	348.33	353.83	359.33

MONTHLY PAYMENTS FOR 30-YR. FHA LOANS

INCLUDING FIRST YEAR ½% MORTGAGE INSURANCE PREMIUMS

AMOUNT	INTEREST						
	13.50%	13.75%	14.00%	14.25%	14.50%	14.75%	15.00%
27600	327.79	333.31	338.55	344.07	349.59	355.11	360.63
27700	328.97	334.51	339.78	345.32	350.86	356.40	361.94
27800	330.16	335.72	341.00	346.56	352.12	357.68	363.24
27900	331.34	336.92	342.23	347.81	353.39	358.97	364.55
28000	332.53	338.13	343.45	349.05	354.66	360.26	365.86
28100	333.72	339.34	344.69	350.31	355.93	361.55	367.17
28200	334.91	340.55	345.91	351.55	357.19	362.83	368.47
28300	336.10	341.76	347.14	352.80	358.46	364.12	369.78
28400	337.28	342.96	348.36	354.04	359.72	365.40	371.08
28500	338.47	344.17	349.59	355.29	360.99	366.69	372.39
28600	339.66	345.38	350.81	356.53	362.26	367.98	373.70
28700	340.84	346.58	352.05	357.79	363.53	369.27	375.01
28800	342.04	347.80	353.27	359.03	364.79	370.55	376.31
28900	343.22	349.00	354.50	360.28	366.06	371.84	377.62
29000	344.41	350.21	355.72	361.52	367.32	373.12	378.92
29100	345.60	351.42	356.95	362.77	368.59	374.41	380.23
29200	346.78	352.62	358.17	364.01	369.86	375.70	381.54
29300	347.97	353.83	359.41	365.27	371.13	376.99	382.85
29400	349.16	355.04	360.63	366.51	372.39	378.27	384.15
29500	350.35	356.25	361.86	367.76	373.66	379.56	385.46
29600	351.54	357.46	363.08	369.00	374.92	380.84	386.76
29700	352.72	358.66	364.31	370.25	376.19	382.13	388.07
29800	353.91	359.87	365.53	371.49	377.45	383.42	389.38
29900	355.09	361.07	366.77	372.75	378.73	384.71	390.69
30000	356.29	362.29	367.99	373.99	379.99	385.99	391.99
30100	357.48	363.50	369.22	375.24	381.26	387.28	393.30
30200	358.66	364.70	370.44	376.48	382.52	388.56	394.60
30300	359.85	365.91	371.67	377.73	383.79	389.85	395.91
30400	361.03	367.11	372.89	378.97	385.05	391.14	397.22
30500	362.22	368.32	374.12	380.23	386.33	392.43	398.53
30600	363.41	369.54	375.35	381.47	387.59	393.71	399.83
30700	364.60	370.74	376.58	382.72	388.86	395.00	401.14
30800	365.79	371.95	377.80	383.96	390.12	396.28	402.44
30900	366.97	373.15	379.03	385.21	391.39	397.57	403.75
31000	368.16	374.36	380.25	386.45	392.65	398.85	405.06
31100	369.35	375.57	381.48	387.71	393.93	400.15	406.37
31200	370.53	376.78	382.71	388.95	395.19	401.43	407.67
31300	371.73	377.99	383.94	390.20	396.46	402.72	408.98
31400	372.91	379.19	385.16	391.44	397.72	404.00	410.28
31500	374.10	380.40	386.39	392.69	398.99	405.29	411.59
31600	375.29	381.61	387.61	393.93	400.25	406.57	412.90
31700	376.47	382.81	388.84	395.19	401.53	407.87	414.21
31800	377.66	384.02	390.07	396.43	402.79	409.15	415.51
31900	378.85	385.23	391.30	397.68	404.06	410.44	416.82
32000	380.04	386.44	392.52	398.92	405.32	411.72	418.12
32100	381.23	387.65	393.75	400.17	406.59	413.01	419.43
32200	382.41	388.85	394.97	401.41	407.85	414.29	420.74
32300	383.60	390.06	396.20	402.66	409.13	415.59	422.05
32400	384.78	391.26	397.43	403.91	410.39	416.87	423.35
32500	385.98	392.48	398.66	405.16	411.66	418.16	424.66
32600	387.17	393.69	399.88	406.40	412.92	419.44	425.96
32700	388.35	394.89	401.11	407.65	414.19	420.73	427.27
32800	389.54	396.10	402.33	408.89	415.45	422.01	428.57
32900	390.72	397.30	403.56	410.14	416.73	423.31	429.89
33000	391.91	398.51	404.79	411.39	417.99	424.59	431.19
33100	393.11	399.73	406.02	412.64	419.26	425.88	432.50
33200	394.29	400.93	407.24	413.88	420.52	427.16	433.80
33300	395.48	402.14	408.47	415.13	421.79	428.45	435.11
33400	396.66	403.34	409.69	416.37	423.05	429.73	436.41
33500	397.85	404.55	410.92	417.62	424.32	431.03	437.73

MONTHLY PAYMENTS FOR 30-YR. FHA LOANS

INCLUDING FIRST YEAR ½% MORTGAGE INSURANCE PREMIUMS

AMOUNT	INTEREST						
	13.50%	13.75%	14.00%	14.25%	14.50%	14.75%	15.00%
33600	399.04	405.76	412.15	418.87	425.59	432.31	439.03
33700	400.22	406.97	413.38	420.12	426.86	433.60	440.34
33800	401.42	408.18	414.60	421.36	428.12	434.88	441.64
33900	402.60	409.38	415.83	422.61	429.39	436.17	442.95
34000	403.79	410.59	417.05	423.85	430.65	437.45	444.25
34100	404.98	411.80	418.28	425.10	431.92	438.75	445.57
34200	406.16	413.00	419.51	426.35	433.19	440.03	446.87
34300	407.35	414.22	420.74	427.60	434.46	441.32	448.18
34400	408.54	415.42	421.96	428.84	435.72	442.60	449.48
34500	409.73	416.63	423.19	430.09	436.99	443.89	450.79
34600	410.92	417.84	424.41	431.33	438.25	445.17	452.09
34700	412.10	419.04	425.64	432.58	439.52	446.47	453.41
34800	413.29	420.25	426.86	433.83	440.79	447.75	454.71
34900	414.47	421.45	428.10	435.08	442.06	449.04	456.02
35000	415.67	422.67	429.32	436.32	443.32	450.32	457.32
35100	416.86	423.88	430.55	437.57	444.59	451.61	458.63
35200	418.04	425.08	431.77	438.81	445.85	452.89	459.93
35300	419.23	426.29	433.00	440.06	447.12	454.18	461.25
35400	420.41	427.49	434.22	441.31	448.39	455.47	462.55
35500	421.60	428.70	435.46	442.56	449.66	456.76	463.86
35600	422.80	429.92	436.68	443.80	450.92	458.04	465.16
35700	423.98	431.12	437.91	445.05	452.19	459.33	466.47
35800	425.17	432.33	439.13	446.29	453.45	460.61	467.77
35900	426.35	433.53	440.36	447.54	454.72	461.90	469.09
36000	427.54	434.74	441.58	448.78	455.99	463.19	470.39
36100	428.73	435.95	442.82	450.04	457.26	464.48	471.70
36200	429.92	437.16	444.04	451.28	458.52	465.76	473.00
36300	431.11	438.37	445.27	452.53	459.79	467.05	474.31
36400	432.29	439.57	446.49	453.77	461.05	468.33	475.61
36500	433.48	440.78	447.72	455.02	462.32	469.62	476.93
36600	434.67	441.99	448.94	456.26	463.59	470.91	478.23
36700	435.85	443.19	450.18	457.52	464.86	472.20	479.54
36800	437.04	444.41	451.40	458.76	466.12	473.48	480.84
36900	438.23	445.61	452.63	460.01	467.39	474.77	482.15
37000	439.42	446.82	453.85	461.25	468.65	476.05	483.45
37100	440.61	448.03	455.08	462.50	469.92	477.34	484.77
37200	441.79	449.23	456.30	463.74	471.19	478.63	486.07
37300	442.98	450.44	457.54	465.00	472.46	479.92	487.38
37400	444.16	451.65	458.76	466.24	473.72	481.20	488.68
37500	445.36	452.86	459.99	467.49	474.99	482.49	489.99
37600	446.55	454.07	461.21	468.73	476.25	483.77	491.29
37700	447.73	455.27	462.44	469.98	477.52	485.06	492.60
37800	448.92	456.48	463.66	471.22	478.78	486.35	493.91
37900	450.10	457.68	464.90	472.48	480.06	487.64	495.22
38000	451.29	458.90	466.12	473.72	481.32	488.92	496.52
38100	452.49	460.11	467.35	474.97	482.59	490.21	497.83
38200	453.67	461.31	468.57	476.21	483.85	491.49	499.13
38300	454.86	462.52	469.80	477.46	485.12	492.78	500.44
38400	456.04	463.72	471.02	478.70	486.38	494.07	501.75
38500	457.23	464.93	472.25	479.96	487.66	495.36	503.06
38600	458.42	466.14	473.48	481.20	488.92	496.64	504.36
38700	459.61	467.35	474.71	482.45	490.19	497.93	505.67
38800	460.80	468.56	475.93	483.69	491.45	499.21	506.97
38900	461.98	469.76	477.16	484.94	492.72	500.50	508.28
39000	463.17	470.97	478.38	486.18	493.98	501.79	509.59
39100	464.36	472.18	479.61	487.44	495.26	503.08	510.90
39200	465.54	473.38	480.84	488.68	496.52	504.36	512.20
39300	466.74	474.60	482.07	489.93	497.79	505.65	513.51
39400	467.92	475.80	483.29	491.17	499.05	506.93	514.81
39500	469.11	477.01	484.52	492.42	500.32	508.22	516.12

MONTHLY PAYMENTS FOR 30-YR. FHA LOANS

INCLUDING FIRST YEAR ½% MORTGAGE INSURANCE PREMIUMS

AMOUNT	INTEREST						
	13.50%	13.75%	14.00%	14.25%	14.50%	14.75%	15.00%
39600	470.30	478.22	485.74	493.66	501.58	509.51	517.43
39700	471.48	479.42	486.97	494.92	502.86	510.80	518.74
39800	472.67	480.63	488.20	496.16	504.12	512.08	520.04
39900	473.86	481.84	489.43	497.41	505.39	513.37	521.35
40000	475.05	483.05	490.65	498.65	506.65	514.65	522.65
40100	476.24	484.26	491.88	499.90	507.92	515.94	523.96
40200	477.42	485.46	493.10	501.14	509.18	517.22	525.27
40300	478.61	486.67	494.33	502.39	510.46	518.52	526.58
40400	479.79	487.87	495.56	503.64	511.72	519.80	527.88
40500	480.98	489.09	496.79	504.89	512.99	521.09	529.19
40600	482.18	490.30	498.01	506.13	514.25	522.37	530.49
40700	483.36	491.50	499.24	507.38	515.52	523.66	531.80
40800	484.55	492.71	500.46	508.62	516.78	524.94	533.11
40900	485.73	493.91	501.69	509.87	518.06	526.24	534.42
41000	486.92	495.12	502.92	511.12	519.32	527.52	535.72
41100	488.11	496.34	504.15	512.37	520.59	528.81	537.03
41200	489.30	497.54	505.37	513.61	521.85	530.09	538.33
41300	490.49	498.75	506.60	514.86	523.12	531.38	539.64
41400	491.67	499.95	507.82	516.10	524.38	532.66	540.95
41500	492.86	501.16	509.05	517.35	525.66	533.96	542.26
41600	494.05	502.37	510.28	518.60	526.92	535.24	543.56
41700	495.23	503.57	511.51	519.85	528.19	536.53	544.87
41800	496.43	504.79	512.73	521.09	529.45	537.81	546.17
41900	497.61	505.99	513.96	522.34	530.72	539.10	547.48
42000	498.80	507.20	515.18	523.58	531.98	540.38	548.78
42100	499.99	508.41	516.41	524.83	533.25	541.68	550.10
42200	501.17	509.61	517.63	526.08	534.52	542.96	551.40
42300	502.36	510.82	518.87	527.33	535.79	544.25	552.71
42400	503.55	512.03	520.09	528.57	537.05	545.53	554.01
42500	504.74	513.24	521.32	529.82	538.32	546.82	555.32
42600	505.93	514.45	522.54	531.06	539.58	548.10	556.62
42700	507.11	515.65	523.77	532.31	540.85	549.40	557.94
42800	508.30	516.86	524.99	533.56	542.12	550.68	559.24
42900	509.48	518.06	526.23	534.81	543.39	551.97	560.55
43000	510.68	519.28	527.45	536.05	544.65	553.25	561.85
43200	513.05	521.69	529.90	538.54	547.18	555.82	564.46
43400	515.42	524.10	532.35	541.04	549.72	558.40	567.08
43600	517.80	526.53	534.81	543.53	552.25	560.97	569.69
43800	520.18	528.94	537.26	546.02	554.78	563.54	572.30
44000	522.55	531.35	539.71	548.51	557.32	566.12	574.92
44200	524.92	533.77	542.17	551.01	559.85	568.69	577.53
44400	527.30	536.18	544.62	553.50	562.38	571.26	580.14
44600	529.68	538.60	547.07	555.99	564.92	573.84	582.76
44800	532.05	541.02	549.53	558.49	567.45	576.41	585.37
45000	534.43	543.43	551.98	560.98	569.98	578.98	587.98
45200	536.80	545.84	554.43	563.47	572.52	581.56	590.60
45400	539.17	548.25	556.89	565.97	575.05	584.13	593.21
45600	541.56	550.68	559.34	568.46	577.58	586.70	595.82
45800	543.93	553.09	561.79	570.95	580.12	589.28	598.44
46000	546.30	555.50	564.25	573.45	582.65	591.85	601.05
46200	548.68	557.92	566.70	575.94	585.18	594.42	603.66
46400	551.05	560.33	569.15	578.43	587.71	597.00	606.28
46600	553.43	562.75	571.61	580.93	590.25	599.57	608.89
46800	555.81	565.17	574.06	583.42	592.78	602.14	611.50
47000	558.18	567.58	576.51	585.91	595.31	604.72	614.12
47200	560.55	569.99	578.97	588.41	597.85	607.29	616.73
47400	562.93	572.41	581.42	590.90	600.38	609.86	619.34
47600	565.31	574.83	583.87	593.39	602.91	612.44	621.96
47800	567.68	577.24	586.33	595.89	605.45	615.01	624.57
48000	570.06	579.66	588.78	598.38	607.98	617.58	627.18

MONTHLY PAYMENTS FOR 30-YR. FHA LOANS

INCLUDING FIRST YEAR ½% MORTGAGE INSURANCE PREMIUMS

AMOUNT	INTEREST						
	13.50%	13.75%	14.00%	14.25%	14.50%	14.75%	15.00%
48200	572.43	582.07	591.23	600.87	610.51	620.16	629.80
48400	574.80	584.48	593.69	603.37	613.05	622.73	632.41
48600	577.19	586.91	596.14	605.86	615.58	625.30	635.02
48800	579.56	589.32	598.59	608.35	618.11	627.87	637.64
49000	581.93	591.73	601.05	610.85	620.65	630.45	640.25
49200	584.31	594.15	603.50	613.34	623.18	633.02	642.86
49400	586.68	596.56	605.95	615.83	625.71	635.59	645.48
49600	589.06	598.98	608.40	618.33	628.25	638.17	648.09
49800	591.44	601.40	610.86	620.82	630.78	640.74	650.70
50000	593.81	603.81	613.31	623.31	633.31	643.31	653.32
50200	596.18	606.22	615.76	625.81	635.85	645.89	655.93
50400	598.55	608.64	618.22	628.30	638.38	648.46	658.54
50600	600.94	611.06	620.67	630.79	640.91	651.03	661.16
50800	603.31	613.47	623.12	633.29	643.45	653.61	663.77
51000	605.68	615.89	625.58	635.78	645.98	656.18	666.38
51200	608.06	618.30	628.03	638.27	648.51	658.75	668.99
51400	610.43	620.71	630.48	640.77	651.05	661.33	671.61
51600	612.81	623.14	632.94	643.26	653.58	663.90	674.22
51800	615.19	625.55	635.39	645.75	656.11	666.47	676.83
52000	617.56	627.96	637.84	648.24	658.65	669.05	679.45
52200	619.93	630.37	640.30	650.74	661.18	671.62	682.06
52400	622.31	632.79	642.75	653.23	663.71	674.19	684.67
52600	624.69	635.21	645.20	655.72	666.25	676.77	687.29
52800	627.06	637.62	647.66	658.22	668.78	679.34	689.90
53000	629.44	640.04	650.11	660.71	671.31	681.91	692.51
53200	631.81	642.45	652.56	663.20	673.85	684.49	695.13
53400	634.18	644.86	655.02	665.70	676.38	687.06	697.74
53600	636.57	647.29	657.47	668.19	678.91	689.63	700.35
53800	638.94	649.70	659.92	670.68	681.45	692.21	702.97
54000	641.31	652.11	662.38	673.18	683.98	694.78	705.58
54200	643.69	654.53	664.83	675.67	686.51	697.35	708.19
54400	646.06	656.94	667.28	678.16	689.05	699.93	710.81
54600	648.44	659.36	669.74	680.66	691.58	702.50	713.42
54800	650.82	661.78	672.19	683.15	694.11	705.07	716.03
55000	653.19	664.19	674.64	685.64	696.64	707.65	718.65
55200	655.56	666.60	677.10	688.14	699.18	710.22	721.26
55400	657.94	669.02	679.55	690.63	701.71	712.79	723.87
55600	660.32	671.44	682.00	693.12	704.24	715.37	726.49
55800	662.69	673.85	684.46	695.62	706.78	717.94	729.10
56000	665.07	676.27	686.91	698.11	709.31	720.51	731.71
56200	667.44	678.68	689.36	700.60	711.84	723.09	734.33
56400	669.81	681.09	691.82	703.10	714.38	725.66	736.94
56600	672.20	683.52	694.27	705.59	716.91	728.23	739.55
56800	674.57	685.93	696.72	708.08	719.44	730.81	742.17
57000	676.94	688.34	699.18	710.58	721.98	733.38	744.78
57200	679.31	690.76	701.63	713.07	724.51	735.95	747.39
57400	681.69	693.17	704.08	715.56	727.04	738.52	750.01
57600	684.07	695.59	706.53	718.06	729.58	741.10	752.62
57800	686.44	698.01	708.99	720.55	732.11	743.67	755.23
58000	688.82	700.42	711.44	723.04	734.64	746.24	757.85
58200	691.19	702.83	713.89	725.54	737.18	748.82	760.46
58400	693.56	705.25	716.35	728.03	739.71	751.39	763.07
58600	695.95	707.67	718.80	730.52	742.24	753.96	765.69
58800	698.32	710.08	721.25	733.02	744.78	756.54	768.30
59000	700.69	712.49	723.71	735.51	747.31	759.11	770.91
59200	703.07	714.91	726.16	738.00	749.84	761.68	773.53
59400	705.44	717.32	728.61	740.50	752.38	764.26	776.14
59600	707.82	719.74	731.07	742.99	754.91	766.83	778.75
59800	710.20	722.16	733.52	745.48	757.44	769.40	781.37
60000	712.57	724.57	735.97	747.97	759.98	771.98	783.98

MONTHLY PAYMENTS FOR 30-YR. FHA LOANS

INCLUDING FIRST YEAR ½% MORTGAGE INSURANCE PREMIUMS

AMOUNT	INTEREST						
	13.50%	13.75%	14.00%	14.25%	14.50%	14.75%	15.00%
60200	714.94	726.98	738.43	750.47	762.51	774.55	786.59
60400	717.32	729.40	740.88	752.96	765.04	777.12	789.21
60600	719.70	731.82	743.33	755.45	767.58	779.70	791.82
60800	722.07	734.23	745.79	757.95	770.11	782.27	794.43
61000	724.45	736.65	748.24	760.44	772.64	784.84	797.04
61200	726.82	739.06	750.69	762.93	775.18	787.42	799.66
61400	729.19	741.47	753.15	765.43	777.71	789.99	802.27
61600	731.58	743.90	755.60	767.92	780.24	792.56	804.88
61800	733.95	746.31	758.05	770.41	782.78	795.14	807.50
62000	736.32	748.72	760.51	772.91	785.31	797.71	810.11
62200	738.70	751.14	762.96	775.40	787.84	800.28	812.72
62400	741.07	753.55	765.41	777.89	790.38	802.86	815.34
62600	743.45	755.97	767.87	780.39	792.91	805.43	817.95
62800	745.83	758.39	770.32	782.88	795.44	808.00	820.56
63000	748.20	760.80	772.77	785.37	797.97	810.58	823.18
63200	750.57	763.21	775.23	787.87	800.51	813.15	825.79
63400	752.94	765.63	777.68	790.36	803.04	815.72	828.40
63600	755.33	768.05	780.13	792.85	805.57	818.30	831.02
63800	757.70	770.46	782.59	795.35	808.11	820.87	833.63
64000	760.07	772.88	785.04	797.84	810.64	823.44	836.24
64200	762.45	775.29	787.49	800.33	813.17	826.02	838.86
64400	764.82	777.70	789.95	802.83	815.71	828.59	841.47
64600	767.20	780.13	792.40	805.32	818.24	831.16	844.08
64800	769.58	782.54	794.85	807.81	820.77	833.74	846.70
65000	771.95	784.95	797.30	810.31	823.31	836.31	849.31
65200	774.32	787.37	799.76	812.80	825.84	838.88	851.92
65400	776.70	789.78	802.21	815.29	828.37	841.46	854.54
65600	779.08	792.20	804.66	817.79	830.91	844.03	857.15
65800	781.45	794.62	807.12	820.28	833.44	846.60	859.76
66000	783.83	797.03	809.57	822.77	835.97	849.18	862.38
66200	786.20	799.44	812.02	825.27	838.51	851.75	864.99
66400	788.57	801.85	814.48	827.76	841.04	854.32	867.60
66600	790.96	804.28	816.93	830.25	843.57	856.89	870.22
66800	793.33	806.69	819.38	832.75	846.11	859.47	872.83
67000	795.70	809.10	821.84	835.24	848.64	862.04	875.44
67200	798.08	811.52	824.29	837.73	851.17	864.61	878.06
67400	800.45	813.93	826.74	840.23	853.71	867.19	880.67
67600	802.83	816.35	829.20	842.72	856.24	869.76	883.28
67800	805.21	818.77	831.65	845.21	858.77	872.33	885.90
68000	807.58	821.18	834.10	847.70	861.31	874.91	888.51
68200	809.95	823.59	836.56	850.20	863.84	877.48	891.12
68400	812.33	826.01	839.01	852.69	866.37	880.05	893.74
68600	814.71	828.43	841.46	855.18	868.91	882.63	896.35
68800	817.08	830.84	843.92	857.68	871.44	885.20	898.96
69000	819.46	833.26	846.37	860.17	873.97	887.77	901.58
69200	821.83	835.67	848.82	862.66	876.51	890.35	904.19
69400	824.20	838.08	851.28	865.16	879.04	892.92	906.80
69600	826.59	840.51	853.73	867.65	881.57	895.49	909.42
69800	828.96	842.92	856.18	870.14	884.11	898.07	912.03
70000	831.33	845.33	858.64	872.64	886.64	900.64	914.64
70200	833.70	847.75	861.09	875.13	889.17	903.21	917.25
70400	836.08	850.16	863.54	877.62	891.71	905.79	919.87
70600	838.46	852.58	866.00	880.12	894.24	908.36	922.48
70800	840.83	855.00	868.45	882.61	896.77	910.93	925.09
71000	843.21	857.41	870.90	885.10	899.31	913.51	927.71
71200	845.58	859.82	873.36	887.60	901.84	916.08	930.32
71400	847.95	862.24	875.81	890.09	904.37	918.65	932.93
71600	850.34	864.66	878.26	892.58	906.90	921.23	935.55
71800	852.71	867.07	880.72	895.08	909.44	923.80	938.16
72000	855.08	869.49	883.17	897.57	911.97	926.37	940.77

MONTHLY PAYMENTS FOR 30-YR. FHA LOANS

INCLUDING FIRST YEAR ½% MORTGAGE INSURANCE PREMIUMS

AMOUNT	INTEREST						
	15.25%	15.50%	15.75%	16.00%	16.25%	16.50%	16.75%
50	0.66	0.67	0.68	0.69	0.70	0.71	0.72
100	1.33	1.35	1.37	1.39	1.41	1.43	1.45
250	3.31	3.36	3.41	3.46	3.51	3.57	3.62
500	6.64	6.74	6.84	6.94	7.04	7.14	7.24
10000	132.66	134 66	136.66	138.66	140.66	142.76	144.76
10100	133.99	136.02	138.04	140.06	142.08	144.20	146.22
10200	135.32	137.36	139.40	141.44	143.48	145.62	147.66
10300	136.65	138.71	140.77	142.83	144.89	147.05	149.11
10400	137.97	140.05	142.13	144.21	146.29	148.47	150:55
10500	139.30	141.40	143.50	145.60	147.70	149.90	152.00
10600	140.62	142.74	144.86	146.98	149.10	151.33	153.45
10700	141.95	144.09	146.24	148.38	150.52	152.76	154.90
10800	143.28	145.44	147.60	149.76	151.92	154.19	156.35
10900	144.61	146.79	148.97	151.15	153.33	155.61	157.79
11000	145.93	148.13	150.33	152.53	154.73	157.04	159.24
11100	147.26	149.48	151.70	153.92	156.14	158.47	160.69
11200	148.58	150.82	153.06	155.30	157.54	159.89	162.13
11300	149.91	152.17	154.43	156.70	158.96	161.33	163.59
11400	151.24	153.52	155.80	158.08	160.36	162.75	165.03
11500	152.57	154.87	157.17	159.47	161.77	164.18	166.48
11600	153.89	156.21	158.53	160.85	163.17	165.61	167.93
11700	155.22	157.56	159.90	162.24	164.58	167.03	169.37
11800	156.54	158.90	161.26	163.62	165.98	168.46	170.82
11900	157.87	160.25	162.63	165.01	167.40	169.89	172.27
12000	159.20	161.60	164.00	166.40	168.80	171.32	173.72
12100	160.53	162.95	165.37	167.79	170.21	172.75	175.17
12200	161.85	164.29	166.73	169.17	171.61	174.17	176.61
12300	163.18	165.64	168.10	170.56	173.02	175.60	178.06
12400	164.50	166.98	169.46	171.94	174.42	177.02	179.50
12500	165.83	168.33	170.83	173.33	175.84	178.46	180.96
12600	167.16	169.68	172.20	174.72	177.24	179.89	182.41
12700	168.49	171.03	173.57	176.11	178.65	181.31	183.85
12800	169.81	172.37	174.93	177.49	180.05	182.74	185.30
12900	171.14	173.72	176.30	178.88	181.46	184.16	186.74
13000	172.46	175.06	177.66	180.26	182.86	185.59	188.19
13100	173.79	176.41	179.03	181.65	184.27	187.02	189.65
13200	175.12	177.76	180.40	183.04	185.68	188.45	191.09
13300	176.45	179.11	181.77	184.43	187.09	189.88	192.54
13400	177.77	180.45	183.13	185.81	188.49	191.30	193.98
13500	179.10	181.80	184.50	187.20	189.90	192.73	195.43
13600	180.42	183.14	185.86	188.58	191.30	194.16	196.88
13700	181.75	184.49	187.23	189.97	192.71	195.58	198.32
13800	183.08	185.84	188.60	191.36	194.12	197.02	199.78
13900	184.41	187.19	189.97	192.75	195.53	198.44	201.22
14000	185.73	188.53	191.33	194.13	196.93	199.87	202.67
14100	187.06	189.88	192.70	195.52	198.34	201.30	204.12
14200	188.38	191.22	194.06	196.90	199.74	202.72	205.56
14300	189.71	192.57	195.43	198.29	201.15	204.15	207.01
14400	191.04	193.92	196.80	199.68	202.56	205.58	208.46
14500	192.37	195.27	198.17	201.07	203.97	207.01	209.91
14600	193.69	196.61	199.53	202.45	205.37	208.44	211.36
14700	195.02	197.96	200.90	203.84	206.78	209.86	212.80
14800	196.34	199.30	202.26	205.22	208.18	211.29	214.25
14900	197.67	200.65	203.63	206.61	209.59	212.71	215.69
15000	198.99	202.00	205.00	208.00	211.00	214.15	217.15
15100	200.33	203.35	206.37	209.39	212.41	215.58	218.60
15200	201.65	204.69	207.73	210.77	213.81	217.00	220.04
15300	202.98	206.04	209.10	212.16	215.22	218.43	221.49
15400	204.30	207.38	210.46	213.54	216.62	219.85	222.93
15500	205.63	208.73	211.83	214.93	218.03	221.28	224.38

MONTHLY PAYMENTS FOR 30-YR. FHA LOANS

INCLUDING FIRST YEAR ½% MORTGAGE INSURANCE PREMIUMS

AMOUNT	INTEREST						
	15.25%	15.50%	15.75%	16.00%	16.25%	16.50%	16.75%
15600	206.95	210.08	213.20	216.32	219.44	222.72	225.84
15700	208.29	211.43	214.57	217.71	220.85	224.14	227.28
15800	209.61	212.77	215.93	219.09	222.25	225.57	228.73
15900	210.94	214.12	217.30	220.48	223.66	226.99	230.17
16000	212.26	215.46	218.66	221.86	225.06	228.42	231.62
16100	213.59	216.81	220.03	223.25	226.47	229.85	233.07
16200	214.91	218.15	221.40	224.64	227.88	231.28	234.52
16300	216.25	219.51	222.77	226.03	229.29	232.71	235.97
16400	217.57	220.85	224.13	227.41	230.69	234.13	237.41
16500	218.90	222.20	225.50	228.80	232.10	235.56	238.86
16600	220.22	223.54	226.86	230.18	233.50	236.99	240.31
16700	221.55	224.89	228.23	231.57	234.91	238.41	241.75
16800	222.87	226.23	229.59	232.96	236.32	239.85	243.21
16900	224.21	227.59	230.97	234.35	237.73	241.27	244.65
17000	225.53	228.93	232.33	235.73	239.13	242.70	246.10
17100	226.86	230.28	233.70	237.12	240.54	244.13	247.55
17200	228.18	231.62	235.06	238.50	241.94	245.55	248.99
17300	229.51	232.97	236.43	239.89	243.35	246.98	250.44
17400	230.83	234.31	237.79	241.28	244.76	248.41	251.89
17500	232.17	235.67	239.17	242.67	246.17	249.84	253.34
17600	233.49	237.01	240.53	244.05	247.57	251.27	254.79
17700	234.82	238.36	241.90	245.44	248.98	252.69	256.23
17800	236.14	239.70	243.26	246.82	250.38	254.12	257.68
17900	237.47	241.05	244.63	248.21	251.79	255.54	259.12
18000	238.79	242.39	245.99	249.59	253.20	256.98	260.58
18100	240.13	243.75	247.37	250.99	254.61	258.41	262.03
18200	241.45	245.09	248.73	252.37	256.01	259.83	263.47
18300	242.78	246.44	250.10	253.76	257.42	261.26	264.92
18400	244.10	247.78	251.46	255.14	258.82	262.68	266.36
18500	245.43	249.13	252.83	256.53	260.23	264.11	267.81
18600	246.75	250.47	254.19	257.91	261.64	265.55	269.27
18700	248.09	251.83	255.57	259.31	263.05	266.97	270.71
18800	249.41	253.17	256.93	260.69	264.45	268.40	272.16
18900	250.74	254.52	258.30	262.08	265.86	269.82	273.60
19000	252.06	255.86	259.66	263.46	267.26	271.25	275.05
19100	253.39	257.21	261.03	264.85	268.67	272.68	276.50
19200	254.71	258.55	262.39	266.23	270.08	274.10	277.95
19300	256.05	259.91	263.77	267.63	271.49	275.54	279.40
19400	257.37	261.25	265.13	269.01	272.89	276.96	280.84
19500	258.70	262.60	266.50	270.40	274.30	278.39	282.29
19600	260.02	263.94	267.86	271.78	275.70	279.82	283.74
19700	261.35	265.29	269.23	273.17	277.11	281.24	285.18
19800	262.67	266.63	270.59	274.55	278.51	282.67	286.64
19900	264.00	267.99	271.97	275.95	279.93	284.10	288.08
20000	265.33	269.33	273.33	277.33	281.33	285.53	289.53
20100	266.66	270.68	274.70	278.72	282.74	286.96	290.98
20200	267.98	272.02	276.06	280.10	284.14	288.38	292.42
20300	269.31	273.37	277.43	281.49	285.55	289.81	293.87
20400	270.63	274.71	278.79	282.87	286.95	291.23	295.32
20500	271.96	276.07	280.17	284.27	288.37	292.67	296.77
20600	273.29	277.41	281.53	285.65	289.77	294.10	298.22
20700	274.62	278.76	282.90	287.04	291.18	295.52	299.66
20800	275.94	280.10	284.26	288.42	292.58	296.95	301.11
20900	277.27	281.45	285.63	289.81	293.99	298.37	302.55
21000	278.59	282.79	286.99	291.19	295.39	299.80	304.00
21100	279.92	284.14	288.37	292.59	296.81	301.24	305.46
21200	281.25	285.49	289.73	293.97	298.21	302.66	306.90
21300	282.58	286.84	291.10	295.36	299.62	304.09	308.35
21400	283.90	288.18	292.46	296.74	301.02	305.51	309.79
21500	285.23	289.53	293.83	298.13	302.43	306.94	311.24

MONTHLY PAYMENTS FOR 30-YR. FHA LOANS

INCLUDING FIRST YEAR ½% MORTGAGE INSURANCE PREMIUMS

AMOUNT	INTEREST						
	15.25%	15.50%	15.75%	16.00%	16.25%	16.50%	16.75%
21600	286.55	290.87	295.19	299.51	303.83	308.37	312.69
21700	287.88	292.22	296.57	300.91	305.25	309.80	314.14
21800	289.21	293.57	297.93	302.29	306.65	311.23	315.59
21900	290.54	294.92	299.30	303.68	308.06	312.65	317.03
22000	291.86	296.26	300.66	305.06	309.46	314.08	318.48
22100	293.19	297.61	302.03	306.45	310.87	315.51	319.93
22200	294.51	298.95	303.39	307.83	312.27	316.93	321.37
22300	295.84	300.30	304.76	309.23	313.69	318.37	322.83
22400	297.17	301.65	306.13	310.61	315.09	319.79	324.27
22500	298.50	303.00	307.50	312.00	316.50	321.22	325.72
22600	299.82	304.34	308.86	313.38	317.90	322.65	327.17
22700	301.15	305.69	310.23	314.77	319.31	324.07	328.61
22800	302.47	307.03	311.59	316.15	320.71	325.50	330.06
22900	303.80	308.38	312.96	317.55	322.13	326.93	331.51
23000	305.13	309.73	314.33	318.93	323.53	328.36	332.96
23100	306.46	311.08	315.70	320.32	324.94	329.79	334.41
23200	307.78	312.42	317.06	321.70	326.34	331.21	335.85
23300	309.11	313.77	318.43	323.09	327.75	332.64	337.30
23400	310.43	315.11	319.79	324.47	329.15	334.06	338.74
23500	311.76	316.46	321.16	325.87	330.57	335.50	340.20
23600	313.09	317.81	322.53	327.25	331.97	336.93	341.65
23700	314.42	319.16	323.90	328.64	333.38	338.35	343.09
23800	315.74	320.50	325.26	330.02	334.78	339.78	344.54
23900	317.07	321.85	326.63	331.41	336.19	341.20	345.98
24000	318.39	323.19	327.99	332.79	337.59	342.63	347.43
24100	319.72	324.54	329.36	334.18	339.01	344.07	348.89
24200	321.05	325.89	330.73	335.57	340.41	345.49	350.33
24300	322.38	327.24	332.10	336.96	341.82	346.92	351.78
24400	323.70	328.58	333.46	338.34	343.22	348.34	353.22
24500	325.03	329.93	334.83	339.73	344.63	349.77	354.67
24600	326.35	331.27	336.19	341.11	346.03	351.20	356.12
24700	327.68	332.62	337.56	342.50	347.45	352.63	357.57
24800	329.00	333.97	338.93	343.89	348.85	354.06	359.02
24900	330.34	335.32	340.30	345.28	350.26	355.48	360.46
25000	331.66	336.66	341.66	346.66	351.66	356.91	361.91
25100	332.99	338.01	343.03	348.05	353.07	358.34	363.36
25200	334.31	339.35	344.39	349.43	354.47	359.76	364.80
25300	335.64	340.70	345.76	350.82	355.89	361.19	366.26
25400	336.96	342.05	347.13	352.21	357.29	362.62	367.70
25500	338.30	343.40	348.50	353.60	358.70	364.05	369.15
25600	339.62	344.74	349.86	354.98	360.10	365.48	370.60
25700	340.95	346.09	351.23	356.37	361.51	366.90	372.04
25800	342.27	347.43	352.59	357.75	362.91	368.33	373.49
25900	343.60	348.78	353.96	359.14	364.32	369.75	374.94
26000	344.92	350.13	355.33	360.53	365.73	371.19	376.39
26100	346.26	351.48	356.70	361.92	367.14	372.62	377.84
26200	347.58	352.82	358.06	363.30	368.54	374.04	379.28
26300	348.91	354.17	359.43	364.69	369.95	375.47	380.73
26400	350.23	355.51	360.79	366.07	371.35	376.89	382.17
26500	351.56	356.86	362.16	367.46	372.76	378.32	383.63
26600	352.88	358.20	363.53	368.85	374.17	379.76	385.08
26700	354.22	359.56	364.90	370.24	375.58	381.18	386.52
26800	355.54	360.90	366.26	371.62	376.98	382.61	387.97
26900	356.87	362.25	367.63	373.01	378.39	384.03	389.41
27000	358.19	363.59	368.99	374.39	379.79	385.46	390.86
27100	359.52	364.94	370.36	375.78	381.20	386.89	392.32
27200	360.84	366.28	371.73	377.17	382.61	388.32	393.76
27300	362.18	367.64	373.10	378.56	384.02	389.75	395.21
27400	363.50	368.98	374.46	379.94	385.42	391.17	396.65
27500	364.83	370.33	375.83	381.33	386.83	392.60	398.10

MONTHLY PAYMENTS FOR 30-YR. FHA LOANS

INCLUDING FIRST YEAR ½% MORTGAGE INSURANCE PREMIUMS

AMOUNT	INTEREST						
	15.25%	15.50%	15.75%	16.00%	16.25%	16.50%	16.75%
27600	366.15	371.67	377.19	382.71	388.23	394.03	399.55
27700	367.48	373.02	378.56	384.10	389.64	395.45	400.99
27800	368.80	374.36	379.93	385.49	391.05	396.89	402.45
27900	370.14	375.72	381.30	386.88	392.46	398.31	403.89
28000	371.46	377.06	382.66	388.26	393.86	399.74	405.34
28100	372.79	378.41	384.03	389.65	395.27	401.17	406.79
28200	374.11	379.75	385.39	391.03	396.67	402.59	408.23
28300	375.44	381.10	386.76	392.42	398.08	404.02	409.68
28400	376.76	382.44	388.12	393.81	399.49	405.45	411.13
28500	378.10	383.80	389.50	395.20	400.90	406.88	412.58
28600	379.42	385.14	390.86	396.58	402.30	408.31	414.03
28700	380.75	386.49	392.23	397.97	403.71	409.73	415.47
28800	382.07	387.83	393.59	399.35	405.11	411.16	416.92
28900	383.40	389.18	394.96	400.74	406.52	412.58	418.36
29000	384.72	390.52	396.32	402.13	407.93	414.02	419.82
29100	386.06	391.88	397.70	403.52	409.34	415.45	421.27
29200	387.38	393.22	399.06	404.90	410.74	416.87	422.71
29300	388.71	394.57	400.43	406.29	412.15	418.30	424.16
29400	390.03	395.91	401.79	407.67	413.55	419.72	425.60
29500	391.36	397.26	403.16	409.06	414.96	421.15	427.05
29600	392.68	398.60	404.52	410.45	416.37	422.59	428.51
29700	394.01	399.96	405.90	411.84	417.78	424.01	429.95
29800	395.34	401.30	407.26	413.22	419.18	425.44	431.40
29900	396.67	402.65	408.63	414.61	420.59	426.86	432.84
30000	397.99	403.99	409.99	415.99	421.99	428.29	434.29
30100	399.32	405.34	411.36	417.38	423.40	429.72	435.74
30200	400.64	406.68	412.72	418.76	424.81	431.15	437.19
30300	401.97	408.04	414.10	420.16	426.22	432.58	438.64
30400	403.30	409.38	415.46	421.54	427.62	434.00	440.08
30500	404.63	410.73	416.83	422.93	429.03	435.43	441.53
30600	405.95	412.07	418.19	424.31	430.43	436.86	442.98
30700	407.28	413.42	419.56	425.70	431.84	438.28	444.42
30800	408.60	414.76	420.92	427.08	433.25	439.72	445.88
30900	409.93	416.12	422.30	428.48	434.66	441.14	447.32
31000	411.26	417.46	423.66	429.86	436.06	442.57	448.77
31100	412.59	418.81	425.03	431.25	437.47	444.00	450.22
31200	413.91	420.15	426.39	432.63	438.87	445.42	451.66
31300	415.24	421.50	427.76	434.02	440.28	446.85	453.11
31400	416.56	422.84	429.12	435.40	441.69	448.28	454.56
31500	417.89	424.19	430.50	436.80	443.10	449.71	456.01
31600	419.22	425.54	431.86	438.18	444.50	451.14	457.46
31700	420.55	426.89	433.23	439.57	445.91	452.56	458.90
31800	421.87	428.23	434.59	440.95	447.31	453.99	460.35
31900	423.20	429.58	435.96	442.34	448.72	455.41	461.79
32000	424.52	430.92	437.32	443.72	450.13	456.84	463.25
32100	425.85	432.27	438.70	445.12	451.54	458.28	464.70
32200	427.18	433.62	440.06	446.50	452.94	459.70	466.14
32300	428.51	434.97	441.43	447.89	454.35	461.13	467.59
32400	429.83	436.31	442.79	449.27	455.75	462.55	469.03
32500	431.16	437.66	444.16	450.66	457.16	463.98	470.48
32600	432.48	439.00	445.52	452.04	458.56	465.41	471.94
32700	433.81	440.35	446.90	453.44	459.98	466.84	473.38
32800	435.14	441.70	448.26	454.82	461.38	468.27	474.83
32900	436.47	443.05	449.63	456.21	462.79	469.69	476.27
33000	437.79	444.39	450.99	457.59	464.19	471.12	477.72
33100	439.12	445.74	452.36	458.98	465.60	472.55	479.17
33200	440.44	447.08	453.72	460.36	467.00	473.97	480.62
33300	441.77	448.43	455.10	461.76	468.42	475.41	482.07
33400	443.10	449.78	456.46	463.14	469.82	476.83	483.51
33500	444.43	451.13	457.83	464.53	471.23	478.26	484.96

MONTHLY PAYMENTS FOR 30-YR. FHA LOANS

INCLUDING FIRST YEAR ½% MORTGAGE INSURANCE PREMIUMS

AMOUNT	INTEREST						
	15.25%	15.50%	15.75%	16.00%	16.25%	16.50%	16.75%
33600	445.75	452.47	459.19	465.91	472.63	479.69	486.41
33700	447.08	453.82	460.56	467.30	474.04	481.11	487.85
33800	448.40	455.16	461.92	468.68	475.44	482.54	489.31
33900	449.73	456.51	463.29	470.08	476.86	483.97	490.75
34000	451.06	457.86	464.66	471.46	478.26	485.40	492.20
34100	452.39	459.21	466.03	472.85	479.67	486.83	493.65
34200	453.71	460.55	467.39	474.23	481.07	488.25	495.09
34300	455.04	461.90	468.76	475.62	482.48	489.68	496.54
34400	456.36	463.24	470.12	477.00	483.88	491.10	497.98
34500	457.69	464.59	471.49	478.40	485.30	492.54	499.44
34600	459.01	465.94	472.86	479.78	486.70	493.97	500.89
34700	460.35	467.29	474.23	481.17	488.11	495.39	502.33
34800	461.67	468.63	475.59	482.55	489.51	496.82	503.78
34900	463.00	469.98	476.96	483.94	490.92	498.24	505.22
35000	464.32	471.32	478.32	485.32	492.32	499.67	506.67
35100	465.65	472.67	479.69	486.72	493.74	501.11	508.13
35200	466.97	474.02	481.06	488.10	495.14	502.53	509.57
35300	468.31	475.37	482.43	489.49	496.55	503.96	511.02
35400	469.63	476.71	483.79	490.87	497.95	505.38	512.46
35500	470.96	478.06	485.16	492.26	499.36	506.81	513.91
35600	472.28	479.40	486.52	493.64	500.76	508.24	515.36
35700	473.61	480.75	487.89	495.04	502.18	509.67	516.81
35800	474.93	482.10	489.26	496.42	503.58	511.10	518.26
35900	476.27	483.45	490.63	497.81	504.99	512.52	519.70
36000	477.59	484.79	491.99	499.19	506.39	513.95	521.15
36100	478.92	486.14	493.36	500.58	507.80	515.38	522.60
36200	480.24	487.48	494.72	501.96	509.20	516.80	524.04
36300	481.57	488.83	496.09	503.35	510.62	518.24	525.50
36400	482.89	490.18	497.46	504.74	512.02	519.66	526.94
36500	484.23	491.53	498.83	506.13	513.43	521.09	528.39
36600	485.55	492.87	500.19	507.51	514.83	522.52	529.84
36700	486.88	494.22	501.56	508.90	516.24	523.94	531.28
36800	488.20	495.56	502.92	510.28	517.64	525.37	532.73
36900	489.53	496.91	504.29	511.67	519.06	526.80	534.18
37000	490.85	498.25	505.66	513.06	520.46	528.23	535.63
37100	492.19	499.61	507.03	514.45	521.87	529.66	537.08
37200	493.51	500.95	508.39	515.83	523.27	531.08	538.52
37300	494.84	502.30	509.76	517.22	524.68	532.51	539.97
37400	496.16	503.64	511.12	518.60	526.08	533.93	541.41
37500	497.49	504.99	512.49	519.99	527.50	535.37	542.87
37600	498.81	506.33	513.86	521.38	528.90	536.80	544.32
37700	500.15	507.69	515.23	522.77	530.31	538.22	545.76
37800	501.47	509.03	516.59	524.15	531.71	539.65	547.21
37900	502.80	510.38	517.96	525.54	533.12	541.07	548.65
38000	504.12	511.72	519.32	526.92	534.52	542.50	550.10
38100	505.45	513.07	520.69	528.31	535.94	543.93	551.56
38200	506.77	514.41	522.06	529.70	537.34	545.36	553.00
38300	508.11	515.77	523.43	531.09	538.75	546.79	554.45
38400	509.43	517.11	524.79	532.47	540.15	548.21	555.89
38500	510.76	518.46	526.16	533.86	541.56	549.64	557.34
38600	512.08	519.80	527.52	535.24	542.96	551.07	558.79
38700	513.41	521.15	528.89	536.63	544.37	552.49	560.24
38800	514.73	522.49	530.26	538.02	545.78	553.93	561.69
38900	516.07	523.85	531.63	539.41	547.19	555.35	563.13
39000	517.39	525.19	532.99	540.79	548.59	556.78	564.58
39100	518.72	526.54	534.36	542.18	550.00	558.21	566.03
39200	520.04	527.88	535.72	543.56	551.40	559.63	567.47
39300	521.37	529.23	537.09	544.95	552.81	561.06	568.93
39400	522.69	530.57	538.45	546.34	554.22	562.49	570.37
39500	524.02	531.93	539.83	547.73	555.63	563.92	571.82

MONTHLY PAYMENTS FOR 30-YR. FHA LOANS

INCLUDING FIRST YEAR ½% MORTGAGE INSURANCE PREMIUMS

AMOUNT	INTEREST						
	15.25%	15.50%	15.75%	16.00%	16.25%	16.50%	16.75%
39600	525.35	533.27	541.19	549.11	557.03	565.35	573.27
39700	526.68	534.62	542.56	550.50	558.44	566.77	574.71
39800	528.00	535.96	543.92	551.88	559.84	568.20	576.16
39900	529.33	537.31	545.29	553.27	561.25	569.62	577.61
40000	530.65	538.65	546.65	554.66	562.66	571.06	579.06
40100	531.98	540.01	548.03	556.05	564.07	572.49	580.51
40200	533.31	541.35	549.39	557.43	565.47	573.91	581.95
40300	534.64	542.70	550.76	558.82	566.88	575.34	583.40
40400	535.96	544.04	552.12	560.20	568.28	576.76	584.84
40500	537.29	545.39	553.49	561.59	569.69	578.19	586.30
40600	538.61	546.73	554.85	562.98	571.10	579.63	587.75
40700	539.94	548.09	556.23	564.37	572.51	581.05	589.19
40800	541.27	549.43	557.59	565.75	573.91	582.48	590.64
40900	542.60	550.78	558.96	567.14	575.32	583.90	592.08
41000	543.92	552.12	560.32	568.52	576.72	585.33	593.53
41100	545.25	553.47	561.69	569.91	578.13	586.76	594.98
41200	546.57	554.81	563.05	571.30	579.54	588.19	596.43
41300	547.90	556.17	564.43	572.69	580.95	589.62	597.88
41400	549.23	557.51	565.79	574.07	582.35	591.04	599.32
41500	550.56	558.86	567.16	575.46	583.76	592.47	600.77
41600	551.88	560.20	568.52	576.84	585.16	593.90	602.22
41700	553.21	561.55	569.89	578.23	586.57	595.32	603.66
41800	554.53	562.89	571.25	579.61	587.98	596.76	605.12
41900	555.86	564.24	572.63	581.01	589.39	598.18	606.56
42000	557.19	565.59	573.99	582.39	590.79	599.61	608.01
42100	558.52	566.94	575.36	583.78	592.20	601.04	609.46
42200	559.84	568.28	576.72	585.16	593.60	602.46	610.90
42300	561.17	569.63	578.09	586.55	595.01	603.89	612.35
42400	562.49	570.97	579.45	587.93	596.42	605.32	613.80
42500	563.82	572.32	580.83	589.33	597.83	606.75	615.25
42600	565.15	573.67	582.19	590.71	599.23	608.18	616.70
42700	566.48	575.02	583.56	592.10	600.64	609.60	618.14
42800	567.80	576.36	584.92	593.48	602.04	611.03	619.59
42900	569.13	577.71	586.29	594.87	603.45	612.45	621.03
43000	570.45	579.05	587.65	596.25	604.86	613.89	622.49
43200	573.11	581.75	590.39	599.03	607.67	616.74	625.38
43400	575.76	584.44	593.12	601.80	610.48	619.59	628.27
43600	578.41	587.13	595.85	604.57	613.30	622.46	631.18
43800	581.07	589.83	598.59	607.35	616.11	625.31	634.07
44000	583.72	592.52	601.32	610.12	618.92	628.16	636.96
44200	586.37	595.21	604.05	612.89	621.74	631.02	639.86
44400	589.02	597.91	606.79	615.67	624.55	633.87	642.75
44600	591.68	600.60	609.52	618.44	627.36	636.73	645.65
44800	594.33	603.29	612.25	621.21	630.18	639.58	648.55
45000	596.98	605.99	614.99	623.99	632.99	642.44	651.44
45200	599.64	608.68	617.72	626.76	635.80	645.29	654.33
45400	602.29	611.37	620.45	629.53	638.61	648.14	657.23
45600	604.94	614.07	623.19	632.31	641.43	651.01	660.13
45800	607.60	616.76	625.92	635.08	644.24	653.86	663.02
46000	610.25	619.45	628.65	637.85	647.05	656.71	665.92
46200	612.90	622.15	631.39	640.63	649.87	659.57	668.81
46400	615.56	624.84	634.12	643.40	652.68	662.42	671.70
46600	618.21	627.53	636.85	646.17	655.49	665.28	674.61
46800	620.86	630.23	639.59	648.95	658.31	668.14	677.50
47000	623.52	632.92	642.32	651.72	661.12	670.99	680.39
47200	626.17	635.61	645.05	654.49	663.93	673.84	683.29
47400	628.82	638.30	647.79	657.27	666.75	676.70	686.18
47600	631.48	641.00	650.52	660.04	669.56	679.56	689.08
47800	634.13	643.69	653.25	662.81	672.37	682.41	691.97
48000	636.78	646.38	655.99	665.59	675.19	685.27	694.87

MONTHLY PAYMENTS FOR 30-YR. FHA LOANS

INCLUDING FIRST YEAR ½% MORTGAGE INSURANCE PREMIUMS

AMOUNT	INTEREST						
	15.25%	15.50%	15.75%	16.00%	16.25%	16.50%	16.75%
48200	639.44	649.08	658.72	668.36	678.00	688.12	697.76
48400	642.09	651.77	661.45	671.13	680.81	690.97	700.65
48600	644.74	654.46	664.19	673.91	683.63	693.84	703.56
48800	647.40	657.16	666.92	676.68	686.44	696.69	706.45
49000	650.05	659.85	669.65	679.45	689.25	699.54	709.34
49200	652.70	662.54	672.39	682.23	692.07	702.40	712.24
49400	655.36	665.24	675.12	685.00	694.88	705.25	715.13
49600	658.01	667.93	677.85	687.77	697.69	708.11	718.03
49800	660.66	670.62	680.59	690.55	700.51	710.97	720.93
50000	663.32	673.32	683.32	693.32	703.32	713.82	723.82
50200	665.97	676.01	686.05	696.09	706.13	716.67	726.71
50400	668.62	678.70	688.78	698.87	708.95	719.53	729.61
50600	671.28	681.40	691.52	701.64	711.76	722.39	732.51
50800	673.93	684.09	694.25	704.41	714.57	725.24	735.40
51000	676.58	686.78	696.98	707.19	717.39	728.10	738.30
51200	679.24	689.48	699.72	709.96	720.20	730.95	741.19
51400	681.89	692.17	702.45	712.73	723.01	733.80	744.08
51600	684.54	694.86	705.18	715.51	725.83	736.67	746.99
51800	687.20	697.56	707.92	718.28	728.64	739.52	749.88
52000	689.85	700.25	710.65	721.05	731.45	742.37	752.77
52200	692.50	702.94	713.38	723.83	734.27	745.23	755.67
52400	695.16	705.64	716.12	726.60	737.08	748.08	758.56
52600	697.81	708.33	718.85	729.37	739.89	750.94	761.46
52800	700.46	711.02	721.58	732.15	742.71	753.80	764.36
53000	703.12	713.72	724.32	734.92	745.52	756.65	767.25
53200	705.77	716.41	727.05	737.69	748.33	759.50	770.14
53400	708.42	719.10	729.78	740.47	751.15	762.36	773.04
53600	711.08	721.80	732.52	743.24	753.96	765.22	775.94
53800	713.73	724.49	735.25	746.01	756.77	768.07	778.83
54000	716.38	727.18	737.98	748.78	759.59	770.93	781.73
54200	719.03	729.88	740.72	751.56	762.40	773.78	784.62
54400	721.69	732.57	743.45	754.33	765.21	776.63	787.51
54600	724.34	735.26	746.18	757.10	768.03	779.50	790.42
54800	726.99	737.96	748.92	759.88	770.84	782.35	793.31
55000	729.65	740.65	751.65	762.65	773.65	785.20	796.20
55200	732.30	743.34	754.38	765.42	776.47	788.06	799.10
55400	734.95	746.04	757.12	768.20	779.28	790.91	801.99
55600	737.61	748.73	759.85	770.97	782.09	793.77	804.89
55800	740.26	751.42	762.58	773.74	784.91	796.63	807.79
56000	742.91	754.12	765.32	776.52	787.72	799.48	810.68
56200	745.57	756.81	768.05	779.29	790.53	802.33	813.57
56400	748.22	759.50	770.78	782.06	793.35	805.19	816.47
56600	750.87	762.20	773.52	784.84	796.16	808.05	819.37
56800	753.53	764.89	776.25	787.61	798.97	810.90	822.26
57000	756.18	767.58	778.98	790.38	801.79	813.75	825.16
57200	758.83	770.28	781.72	793.16	804.60	816.61	828.05
57400	761.49	772.97	784.45	795.93	807.41	819.46	830.94
57600	764.14	775.66	787.18	798.70	810.23	822.32	833.85
57800	766.79	778.35	789.92	801.48	813.04	825.18	836.74
58000	769.45	781.05	792.65	804.25	815.85	828.03	839.63
58200	772.10	783.74	795.38	807.02	818.66	830.88	842.53
58400	774.75	786.43	798.12	809.80	821.48	833.74	845.42
58600	777.41	789.13	800.85	812.57	824.29	836.60	848.32
58800	780.06	791.82	803.58	815.34	827.10	839.45	851.22
59000	782.71	794.51	806.32	818.12	829.92	842.31	854.11
59200	785.37	797.21	809.05	820.89	832.73	845.16	857.00
59400	788.02	799.90	811.78	823.66	835.54	848.01	859.90
59600	790.67	802.59	814.52	826.44	838.36	850.88	862.80
59800	793.33	805.29	817.25	829.21	841.17	853.73	865.69
60000	795.98	807.98	819.98	831.98	843.98	856.58	868.59

MONTHLY PAYMENTS FOR 30-YR. FHA LOANS

INCLUDING FIRST YEAR ½% MORTGAGE INSURANCE PREMIUMS

AMOUNT	INTEREST						
	15.25%	15.50%	15.75%	16.00%	16.25%	16.50%	16.75%
60200	798.63	810.67	822.72	834.76	846.80	859.44	871.48
60400	801.29	813.37	825.45	837.53	849.61	862.29	874.37
60600	803.94	816.06	828.18	840.30	852.42	865.15	877.28
60800	806.59	818.75	830.92	843.08	855.24	868.01	880.17
61000	809.25	821.45	833.65	845.85	858.05	870.86	883.06
61200	811.90	824.14	836.38	848.62	860.86	873.71	885.96
61400	814.55	826.83	839.11	851.40	863.68	876.57	888.85
61600	817.21	829.53	841.85	854.17	866.49	879.43	891.75
61800	819.86	832.22	844.58	856.94	869.30	882.28	894.64
62000	822.51	834.91	847.31	859.72	872.12	885.14	897.54
62200	825.17	837.61	850.05	862.49	874.93	887.99	900.43
62400	827.82	840.30	852.78	865.26	877.74	890.84	903.32
62600	830.47	842.99	855.51	868.04	880.56	893.71	906.23
62800	833.13	845.69	858.25	870.81	883.37	896.56	909.12
63000	835.78	848.38	860.98	873.58	886.18	899.41	912.01
63200	838.43	851.07	863.71	876.36	889.00	902.27	914.91
63400	841.09	853.77	866.45	879.13	891.81	905.12	917.80
63600	843.74	856.46	869.18	881.90	894.62	907.98	920.70
63800	846.39	859.15	871.91	884.68	897.44	910.84	923.60
64000	849.04	861.85	874.65	887.45	900.25	913.69	926.49
64200	851.70	864.54	877.38	890.22	903.06	916.54	929.38
64400	854.35	867.23	880.11	893.00	905.88	919.40	932.28
64600	857.00	869.93	882.85	895.77	908.69	922.26	935.18
64800	859.66	872.62	885.58	898.54	911.50	925.11	938.07
65000	862.31	875.31	888.31	901.32	914.32	927.97	940.97
65200	864.96	878.01	891.05	904.09	917.13	930.82	943.86
65400	867.62	880.70	893.78	906.86	919.94	933.67	946.75
65600	870.27	883.39	896.51	909.63	922.76	936.54	949.66
65800	872.92	886.09	899.25	912.41	925.57	939.39	952.55
66000	875.58	888.78	901.98	915.18	928.38	942.24	955.44
66200	878.23	891.47	904.71	917.95	931.20	945.10	958.34
66400	880.88	894.17	907.45	920.73	934.01	947.95	961.23
66600	883.54	896.86	910.18	923.50	936.82	950.81	964.13
66800	886.19	899.55	912.91	926.27	939.64	953.67	967.03
67000	888.84	902.25	915.65	929.05	942.45	956.52	969.92
67200	891.50	904.94	918.38	931.82	945.26	959.37	972.81
67400	894.15	907.63	921.11	934.59	948.08	962.23	975.71
67600	896.80	910.33	923.85	937.37	950.89	965.09	978.61
67800	899.46	913.02	926.58	940.14	953.70	967.94	981.50
68000	902.11	915.71	929.31	942.91	956.52	970.80	984.40
68200	904.76	918.40	932.05	945.69	959.33	973.65	987.29
68400	907.42	921.10	934.78	948.46	962.14	976.50	990.18
68600	910.07	923.79	937.51	951.23	964.96	979.37	993.09
68800	912.72	926.48	940.25	954.01	967.77	982.22	995.98
69000	915.38	929.18	942.98	956.78	970.58	985.07	998.87
69200	918.03	931.87	945.71	959.55	973.40	987.93	1001.77
69400	920.68	934.56	948.45	962.33	976.21	990.78	1004.66
69600	923.34	937.26	951.18	965.10	979.02	993.64	1007.56
69800	925.99	939.95	953.91	967.87	981.84	996.49	1010.46
70000	928.64	942.64	956.65	970.65	984.65	999.35	1013.35
70200	931.30	945.34	959.38	973.42	987.46	1002.20	1016.24
70400	933.95	948.03	962.11	976.19	990.28	1005.05	1019.14
70600	936.60	950.72	964.85	978.97	993.09	1007.92	1022.04
70800	939.26	953.42	967.58	981.74	995.90	1010.77	1024.93
71000	941.91	956.11	970.31	984.51	998.71	1013.62	1027.83
71200	944.56	958.80	973.05	987.29	1001.53	1016.48	1030.72
71400	947.22	961.50	975.78	990.06	1004.34	1019.33	1033.61
71600	949.87	964.19	978.51	992.83	1007.15	1022.19	1036.52
71800	952.52	966.88	981.25	995.61	1009.97	1025.05	1039.41
72000	955.18	969.58	983.98	998.38	1012.78	1027.90	1042.30